Gender and Number Agreement in Arabic

Studies in Semitic Languages and Linguistics

VOLUME 109

The titles published in this series are listed at *brill.com/ssl*

Gender and Number Agreement in Arabic

By

Simone Bettega and Luca D'Anna

BRILL

LEIDEN | BOSTON

Cover illustration: Bobo the Lizard, a male specimen of *Pseudotrapelus Sinaitus*, poses on a rock in the archeological site of Bat (Oman). Photo by Simone Bettega.

Library of Congress Cataloging-in-Publication Data

Names: Bettega, Simone, author. | D'Anna, Luca, 1985- author.
Title: Gender and number agreement in Arabic / by Simone Bettega, Luca D'Anna.
Description: Leiden ; Boston : Brill, [2023] | Series: Studies in Semitic languages and linguistics, 0081-8461 ; volume 109 | Includes bibliographical references and index.
Identifiers: LCCN 2022048690 (print) | LCCN 2022048691 (ebook) | ISBN 9789004527232 (hardback) | ISBN 9789004527249 (ebook)
Subjects: LCSH: Arabic language–Agreement. | Arabic language–Gender. | Arabic language–Number.
Classification: LCC PJ6395 .B48 2023 (print) | LCC PJ6395 (ebook) | DDC 492.75/5–dc23/eng/20221018
LC record available at https://lccn.loc.gov/2022048690
LC ebook record available at https://lccn.loc.gov/2022048691

Typeface for the Latin, Greek, and Cyrillic scripts: “Brill”. See and download: brill.com/brill-typeface.

ISSN 0081-8461
ISBN 978-90-04-52723-2 (hardback)
ISBN 978-90-04-52724-9 (e-book)

La menzogna non è nel discorso, è nelle cose.

CALVINO

•••

كل الناس خايفة من بكرا
ويجي بكرا ولسه خايفين
(كايروكى)

•:

Contents

Acknowledgments IX
List of Tables and Figures X
Note on Terminology and Transcriptions XIII
Introductory Note XVII

1 **Previous Studies on Agreement in Arabic** 1
1.1 Agreement through Time: Arabic Old and New 1
1.2 Written Arabic 10
1.3 Spoken Arabic 16

2 **Describing the Systems** 28
2.1 Agreement from a Typological Perspective 29
2.2 Morphological Markers of Gender and Number in Arabic 33
2.2.1 *Written Arabic* 33
2.2.2 *Gender-Distinguishing Varieties of Spoken Arabic* 39
2.2.3 *Non-distinguishing Varieties of Spoken Arabic* 41
2.2.4 *Divergent Inventories* 43
2.3 The Spoken Dialects 48
2.3.1 *Singular Agreement* 49
2.3.2 *Plural Agreement in Gender-Distinguishing Dialects: Sources* 54
2.3.2.1 Morocco and Algeria 57
2.3.2.2 Tunisia 58
2.3.2.3 Libya 59
2.3.2.4 Egypt 60
2.3.2.5 Chad, Cameroon and Nigeria 62
2.3.2.6 Sudan 63
2.3.2.7 Palestine and Israel 65
2.3.2.8 Syria, Lebanon and Turkey 68
2.3.2.9 Jordan 69
2.3.2.10 Iraq 71
2.3.2.11 Saudi Arabia 72
2.3.2.12 Gulf States 73
2.3.2.13 Yemen 74
2.3.2.14 Oman 74
2.3.2.15 Iran 76

2.3.2.16 Uzbekistan 77
2.3.2.17 Summary 78
2.3.3 *Plural Agreement in Gender-Distinguishing Dialects: A Corpus-Based Analysis* 80
2.3.3.1 Our Corpus of Najdi Texts 81
2.3.3.2 Agreement with Human Controllers 84
2.3.3.3 Agreement with Nonhuman Controllers: Collective Controllers 87
2.3.3.4 Agreement with Nonhuman Controllers: Plural Controllers 90
2.3.4 *Plural Agreement in Gender-Distinguishing Dialects: Description* 110
2.3.4.1 Apophonic Plurals 117
2.3.4.2 F.SG Agreement with Plural Controllers 122
2.3.5 *Plural Agreement in Non-distinguishing Dialects: The Question of Complexity* 123
2.3.6 *Plural Agreement in Non-distinguishing Dialects: Sources* 127
2.3.7 *Plural Agreement in Non-distinguishing Dialects: Description* 133
2.3.8 *Divergent Systems* 138
2.3.8.1 F.PL Adjectival Agreement in Non-distinguishing Dialects 139
2.3.8.2 Agreement in Ḥassāniyya 141
2.3.8.3 Agreement in Darfur Arabic 143
2.3.8.4 Dialects with Exceptional Morphosyntactic Behavior 145
2.3.9 *The Effects of Word Order: Target-Controller Agreement* 145
2.4 Pre-Classical Arabic: Pre-Islamic Poetry and the Quran 152
2.5 The Odd Ones Out: Classical and Modern Standard Arabic 166
2.6 Summary 171

3 A Diachronic Account of Agreement: Formal and Written Arabic 178
3.1 An Overview of Agreement in Central Semitic 178
3.2 Methodological Issues in the Selection of the Corpora 193
3.3 A Change in Progress? Resemanticization in Pre-Islamic Poetry 197
3.4 Down the Agreement Hierarchy (and a Few Pragmatic Detours): Evidence from the Quran 205
3.4.1 *Collectives in the Quran: Two Possibilities of Semantic Agreement* 217

3.5 Post-7th Century Poetry 222
3.6 The Dawn of Arabic Prose: Translated Syntax in *Kalīla wa-Dimna* 234
3.7 From [-Individuated] to [-Human]: The Reanalysis of Semantic Features in Classical Arabic 244
3.8 After the 10th Century: What Escaped Standardization 254
3.9 Nabaṭī Poetry: Poetic Register or Survival of the Old System? 262
3.10 Summary 271

4 The Approach of Traditional Grammar: An Attempt at Reconstruction 277
4.1 Scope of the Chapter 277
4.2 Early Arabic Grammarians: From Sībawayh to al-Mubarrad 280
4.3 From 10th Century Grammars to Didactic Manuals: Further Developments 298
4.4 Between Tradition and Standardization: Arabic Grammar during the *Nahḍa* 307
4.5 Summary 321

5 A Diachronic Account of Agreement: Spoken Arabic 325
5.1 Feminine Singular Agreement with Plural Controllers: Modern Innovation or Ancient Retention? 325
5.2 The Loss of Feminine Plural Agreement 331
5.2.1 *Internally Motivated Change: Phonological Erosion* 333
5.2.2 *Externally Motivated Change: Language Contact and the Question of Polygenesis* 337
5.2.3 *A Critical Reading of al-Sharkawi (2014): The Timescale of Loss* 345
5.2.4 *Agreement and the City: Urbanization as a Driver of Syntactic Change* 351
5.2.5 *After the Fall: Reorganizing the System* 364
5.3 Summary 370

Bibliography 377
Index of Languages, Dialects, Tribes and Places 400
General Index 404

Acknowledgments

This book has been a long time in the making. This is probably unsurprising, since its subject is vast and complex, and since it has been written during somewhat troubled times. Luckily, we had help along the way—both with the subject and with the troubles—so that acknowledgements are certainly in order at this point.

Simone Bettega would like to thank all the numerous members of his family for the constant support they have offered over the years: without them, not only this book, but many other things would probably never have come into being. Thanks are also due to a long list of friends, the special people who have always been there when it mattered most: Ale, Benni, Cami, Fra, Guido, Ila, Ire, Julia, Malvina, Mino, Mattia, Olfa, Pre, Presi, Scozzi, the whole Crota Team and two wonderful colleagues, Bobo and Elis. Not all that were with us at the beginning still are today, because life runs its course, for good and for bad. They are still remembered, though, and this book is dedicated to them as well.

Luca D'Anna would like to thank the members of his family. Alessandro, for the magic he brings to every single day; Samuele, whose smile lit up the darkest of nights; Giovanna, for sticking with me; my father, for carrying an impossible burden with love; my mother, for being there nonetheless; my brother and sister who, like me, are trying their best; my grandparents, for all their love. My thanks also go to my friends Leo, Massimo, Nino and Salvatore for never giving up on me. To all my students, for their curiosity, patience and support. Finally, to Gaetano, for showing me a way out.

A great number of colleagues, whom we have the privilege of calling friends, have helped us in various ways during the writing process: they have shared their knowledge with us, read draft versions of this or that chapter, and helped locating otherwise difficult-to-access bibliographical resources. Although we remain solely responsible for any error, imprecision or faulty idea that appear in the following pages, we would like to express our utmost gratitude to Adam Benkato, Carmen Berlinches Ramos, Giovanni Canova, Riccardo Contini, Fabio Gasparini, Ana Iriarte Diez, Maciej Klimiuk, Bettina Leitner, Stefano Manfredi, Giuliano Mion, Roberta Morano, Mara Nicosia, Simona Olivieri, Stephan Procházka, Esther Ravier, Valentina Serreli, Antonella Torzullo and Marijn van Putten. We are also thankful to the two anonymous reviewers who offered insightful comments on many aspects of this work.

Tables and Figures

Tables

1.1 Agreement patterns with plural and collective controllers in Reckendorf (1895, 89–90) 11
2.1 S-stem and P-stem in written Arabic (*kataba* 'to write') 34
2.2 Free and bound pronouns in written Arabic 34
2.3 The inflection of nominals in written Arabic 35
2.4 Apophonic Plural patterns in written Arabic 36
2.5 Relative pronouns in written Arabic 38
2.6 Demonstratives in written Arabic 38
2.7 The inflection of *ḏū* 38
2.8 S-stem and P-stem in Najdi Arabic (*kitab* 'to write') 40
2.9 Independent and bound pronouns in Najdi Arabic 40
2.10 The inflection of nominals in Najdi Arabic 41
2.11 Demonstratives in Najdi Arabic 41
2.12 S-stem and P-stem in Damascus Arabic (*katab* 'to write') 42
2.13 Independent and bound pronouns in Damascus Arabic 42
2.14 The inflection of nominals in Damascus Arabic 43
2.15 Demonstratives in Damascus Arabic 43
2.16 Effects of CT distance on agreement 106
2.17 Agreement with plural controllers in gender-distinguishing varieties 111
2.18 Agreement with all controller types in gender-distinguishing varieties 111
2.19 Agreement classes in gender-distinguishing varieties of Arabic 112
2.20 Agreement in gender-distinguishing varieties of Arabic (Type A) 123
2.21 Agreement in non-distinguishing varieties of Arabic (Type B) 134
2.22 Agreement in non-distinguishing varieties of Arabic (Type C) 135
2.23 Adjectival/participial agreement in *Ḥassāniyya* (Type D) 144
2.24 The authors of the seven canonical *Muʕallaqāt* (Johnson 1893) 154
2.25 Agreement patterns with post-controller targets in the seven *Muʕallaqāt* (nonhuman animate and inanimate controllers) 156
2.26 Percentages of feminine singular + broken plural agreement in adjectives 158
2.27 Agreement in pre-Classical Arabic (Type E) 162
2.28 Agreement patterns of pre-controller verbal targets in Najdi *Nabaṭī* poetry 164
2.29 Agreement patterns with human controllers in the *Muʕallaqāt* and in Najdi *Nabaṭī* poetry 165
2.30 Agreement in Classical and Modern Standard Arabic (type F) 167

3.1 Percentages of feminine singular + broken plural agreement in adjectives vs feminine singular in pronouns (data from the *Muʕallaqāt*) 188
3.2 Agreement possibilities with singular and plural controllers in Classical and Modern Standard Arabic 202
3.3 Percentage of feminine singular agreement with plural nonhuman controllers in the pre-Islamic data and Corbett's agreement hierarchy 203
3.4 Feminine singular agreement in nonhuman post-controller targets: pre-Islamic poetry vs Quran 207
3.5 Incidence of feminine singular agreement in inanimate, animal and human controllers: *Muʕallaqāt* vs Quran 208
3.6 Agreement patterns with morphologically feminine singular human collectives 220
3.7 Agreement patterns in Ibn al-Muqaffaʕ's *Tale of the owls and the crows*, from *Kalīla wa-Dimna* (post-controller targets) 237
3.8 Percentages of feminine singular vs feminine plural agreement with post-controller targets in the *Muʕallaqāt* and *Kalīla wa-Dimna* (average) 238
3.9 Agreement system with post-controller targets in gender-distinguishing varieties of Arabic (pre-Islamic Arabic and contemporary dialects) 238
3.10 Agreement system with post-controller targets in Classical and Modern Standard Arabic 239
3.11 Agreement system with post-controller targets in *Kalīla wa-Dimna* 239
3.12 Verbal agreement with plural controllers in *Kalīla wa-Dimna* and in Persian 242
3.13 Agreement system with post-controller targets in Classical and Modern Standard Arabic 248
3.14 Incidence of feminine singular agreement in the Quran 250
3.15 Agreement patterns with post-nonhuman controller targets by target type in ad-Dindān's poetry 267
3.16 Agreement patterns with post-nonhuman controllers by target type in the seven *Muʕallaqāt* 267
3.17 Percentages of feminine singular + broken plural agreement in adjectives compared to feminine singular agreement in pronouns (*Muʕallaqāt*) 268
3.18 Percentages of feminine singular + broken plural agreement in adjectives compared to feminine singular agreement in pronouns (Quran) 268
3.19 Percentages of feminine singular + broken plural agreement in adjectives compared to feminine singular agreement in pronouns (*Nabaṭī* poetry) 268
3.20 Agreement patterns with post-nonhuman controller targets in Najdi *Nabaṭī* poetry and plain spoken Najdi 270
4.1 Relevant thresholds on the animacy hierarchy for Persian vs Arabic and Sībawayh's *Kitāb* 289

Figures

2.1 Visual representation of agreement classes in gender-distinguishing varieties of Arabic 113
2.2 Two possible representations of the agreement system of CA/MSA 170
3.1 Hetzron's classification models with modifications (Huehnergard and Rubin 2011, 263) 181
3.2 Semitic languages prevalently featuring internal plurals (left) and Semitic languages featuring partially semantically motivated agreement systems (right) 192
3.3 Spread of feminine singular agreement in the Agreement Hierarchy: *Muʕallaqāt* vs Quran 208
3.4 Spread of feminine singular agreement in the Animacy Hierarchy: *Muʕallaqāt* vs Quran 209
3.5 Diachrony of agreement in Arabic 253
3.6 Agreement hierarchy in pre-Islamic Arabic and the modern dialects 263
3.7 West Semitic according to Hetzron's classification models (with modifications) (Huehnergard and Rubin 2011, 263) 272

Note on Terminology and Transcriptions

What follows is a list of all the abbreviations used in the glosses, and of the symbols used for transcription. In compiling this book, we have quoted examples from a great number of different studies. In order to maintain the internal coherence of our work, these have been mostly adapted to our transcription and glossing style. Note in particular that, for the sake of consistency, we have systematically transcribed ض as *ḍ* also in quotes from Classical and pre-Classical texts, even though in the period in which those texts were composed this sound was probably realized as a faringalized voiced lateral fricative.

In the transcriptions and glosses of examples, clitic boundaries are marked with the symbol = (equals). Boundaries of non-clitic (i.e. inflectional) morphemes are only marked where relevant to the discussion, with the symbol - (hyphen). Non-relevant boundaries are not marked in transcription, and in the corresponding gloss they are marked with the symbol : (colon), as per the Leipzig Glossing Rules, section 4c. In order to avoid excessively lengthy glosses, we have not segmented nor glossed the case markers of formal/written varieties of Arabic (these are, at any rate, irrelevant to the topics treated here).

Note that these conventions only apply to the glosses and examples proper, and not to the Latinized versions of the names of Arabic authors, titles of Arabic works, or transcribed excerpts of said works; in all these cases, clitic boundaries are marked with a hyphen, and non-clitic boundaries are not marked at all, according to the common practice for the transcription of Arabic in Latin characters.

Glosses

ACC	accusative
ACT	active
APOC	apocopate
C.PL	common plural
COLL	collective
COMP	complementizer
DEF	definite
DEM	demonstrative
DUAL	dual
F	feminine
IMP	imperative

INDEF	indefinite
INT	interrogative
IPFV	imperfective
IRR	irrealis
M	masculine
NEG	negative
PASS	passive
PFV	perfective
PL	plural
PTCP	participle
SBJV	subjunctive
SG	Singular
SGLTV	Singulative

Symbols Used for Transcription

b	[b] voiced bilabial stop
p	[p] voiceless bilabial stop
m	[m] voiced bilabial nasal
ṃ	[mˤ] emphatic voiced bilabial nasal
w	[w] voiced labiovelar approximant
f	[f] voiceless labiodental fricative
v	[v] voiced labiodental fricative
ṯ	[θ] voiceless interdental fricative
ḏ	[ð] voiced interdental fricative
ḏ̣	[ðˤ] emphatic voiced interdental fricative
t	[t] voiceless alveolar stop
ṭ	[tˤ] emphatic voiceless alveolar stop
d	[d] voiced alveolar stop
ḍ	[dˤ] emphatic voiced alveolar stop
n	[n] voiced alveolar nasal
s	[s] voiceless alveolar fricative
ṣ	[sˤ] emphatic voiceless alveolar fricative
z	[z] voiced alveolar fricative
ẓ	[zˤ] voiced emphatic alveolar fricative
ǵ	[ʣ] voiced alveolar affricate
ć	[ts] voiceless alveolar affricate
ž	[ʒ] voiced palato-alveolar fricative
š	[ʃ] voiceless palato-alveolar fricative

ǧ [ʤ] voiced palato-alveolar affricate
č [tʃ] voiceless palato-alveolar affricate
l [l] alveolar lateral approximant
ḷ [lˤ] emphatic alveolar lateral approximant
r [r] voiced alveolar trill
ṛ [rˤ] emphatic voiced alveolar trill
y [j] voiced palatal approximant
k [k] voiceless velar stop
g [g] voiced velar stop
x [x] voiceless velar fricative
ġ [ɣ] voiced velar fricative
q [q] voiceless uvular stop
ḥ [ħ] voiceless pharyngeal fricative
ʕ [ʕ] voiced pharyngeal fricative
ʔ [ʔ] voiceless glottal stop
h [h] voiceless glottal fricative

Other Abbreviations

CA and MSA will be used to refer to Classical Arabic and Modern Standard Arabic respectively. These two labels are not entirely uncontroversial, and their exact definition will be discussed in the relevant passages of the book.

We will not make use of the labels OA (Old Arabic) and NA (Neo-Arabic), except when discussing works of other scholars in which they are employed. In this case as well, definitions will be discussed in the relevant sections.

Terminological Issues

Given the subject of this study, throughout the book we have found ourselves in continuous need of referring to the difference that exists between the forms of Arabic that have preserved the feminine plural forms of adjectives, verbs and pronouns, and those that have lost them. We have therefore decided to employ the shorthand labels "gender-distinguishing varieties" for the former and "non-distinguishing varieties" for the latter. It is obvious that the reference here is to gender distinction *in the plural*, since no variety of Arabic exists that has entirely lost the possibility of distinguishing gender in the singular (discounting pidginized/creolized forms of Arabic).

Transcription of Quranic Samples

A final note concerns the employment and transcription of Quranic samples. The reading tradition used for this book is that of Ḥafṣ ʿan ʿĀṣim. Moreover, in Quranic recitation, the bound pronouns *-hū* "3.M.SG" and *-hī* "3.F.SG" are used after light vowels, while *-hu* and *-hi* after heavy syllables (see Van Putten 2022: 20–23), even though the long vowel does not appear in today's printed texts and is not reported in our transcription. Most of the Quranic verses quoted in this book, moreover, present alternative readings, for which the reader is likewise referred to Van Putten (2022).

Introductory Note

As is the case with every research work, this one, too, was born out of questions. The specific questions that originally informed the idea of this book have haunted us for a long time, and their origins can be traced a long way back in time, to when both authors of this study were still in the early phases of their careers as students and scholars of Arabic, marveling at certain complexity of the language(s) they were just starting to get acquainted with.

Two aspects of Arabic syntax, in particular, perplexed us, that apparently resided at the opposite ends of the Arabic sociolinguistic spectrum, but that had nonetheless something in common. On the one side, in the solemn and formal Standard version of the language, the well-known rule that dictates mandatory feminine singular agreement with plural nonhuman subjects left us puzzled. Little did we know, at that time, about linguistic typology, or about languages other than the ones we had grown up speaking and studying, and this sounded to us like a linguistic oddity, one that deserved a thorough investigation (as it later turned out, we were both wrong and correct at the same time).

At the other end of the continuum resided certain lesser-known and somehow "peripheral" spoken dialects, which had at first no doubt caught our interest also due to their geographical and typological remoteness, and with which we first became familiar during the early years of our researches, while working on their documentation. These dialects all had an important characteristic in common, namely the retention of feminine plural forms in the paradigms of adjectives, verbs and pronouns. In particular, it struck us as odd that, in these varieties, along with nouns referring to human females, all nonhuman subjects triggered feminine plural agreement. This wasn't, *per se*, a particular remarkable finding: most existing grammars of gender-distinguishing dialects (though by no means all) briefly referred to this phenomenon in some way or another. What no author clearly spelled out, however, was that—among these nonhuman nouns that triggered feminine plural agreement when plural—many were masculine in the singular. These nouns, in other words, changed gender when switching from singular to plural. In this case as well, this is not a particularly unusual trait: such gender-shifting nouns can be encountered in several languages of the world, including "familiar" ones such as Italian of French. The striking characteristic of these varieties of Arabic, however, was the sheer size of the phenomenon. What we were looking at was not a restricted subgroup consisting of a handful of irregular lexical elements: it was a sizeable portion of the language's vocabulary, consisting of thousands, perhaps tens of thousands, of nouns. To us, it was clear that the topic warranted further investigation. And yet, no matter how carefully we looked, we couldn't find a single reference to this typological oddity in the literature. How was it possible that such a macroscopic phenomenon had gone unnoticed for hundreds of years?

We say "hundreds of years" because, as it soon started to become clear, this peculiar syntactical behavior was not restricted to the modern spoken varieties of Arabic. Coming full circle, and going back to the written version of the language, we realized that he same agreement patterns could be found in the oldest existing Arabic texts, including the pre-Islamic poetic corpus and the Quran itself. Here as well, however, the strangeness of this behavior had not attracted but a few sparse and inconclusive remarks. In the case of written Arabic, the picture was further complicated by the aforementioned oddity: somehow, in the passage from the pre-Classical to the Classical and then contemporary formulation of the language, a weird shift had happened, because of which the old patterns were lost and now all nonhuman plural subjects mandatorily required feminine singular agreement. In this case as well, little was known about how, when and why had this change happened, and no studies existed on the subject.

Contrary to the other topics just mentioned, that of feminine singular agreement with plural nouns was a rather well-studied phenomenon, at least as far as spoken Arabic was concerned. Starting with the last decade of the 20th century, a number of studies had begun to appear that dealt with the question in a rather exhaustive manner, explaining the rules that governed the apparently arbitrary variation between plural and feminine singular agreement in several dialects of Arabic. All these studies, however, focused on dialects that had lost gender distinction in the plural. One could reasonably wonder whether or not a system with two options for plural agreement (feminine singular and common plural) worked in the same way as one with three different options (feminine singular, masculine plural and feminine plural). None of the aforementioned studies, moreover, provided a satisfactory explanation as to why feminine singular became an agreement option for plural controllers in the first place.

Predictably enough, by staring too deep into the problem, we soon found ourselves tumbling down the proverbial rabbit hole. Questions engendered questions that engendered even more questions. Why did varieties with no gender distinction in the plural existed in the first place? And when did this process of morphosyntactic reduction first happened, historically? Why did feminine plural adjectives occasionally resurface in dialects that had otherwise lost gender distinction in the plural? And what about those varieties where even feminine singular agreement with plural subjects was no longer an option—thus leaving a single, common possibility for plural agreement? And so on, and so on.

Confronted with all these questions, we turned to the two disciplines that offered the most promising tools to tackle the problem: historical linguistics and linguistic typology. We felt that a reconciliation between the latter and the field of Arabic studies, in particular, was long overdue. The Arabic languages, in all their incredibly varied manifestations that span thousands of years in time and thousands of kilometers in space, host a treasure trove of linguistic diversity that for too long has fallen outside the attention of language typologists. One of the ambitions of the present work is to build yet another bridge over this gap, showing that a dialogue between the two fields of inquiry is not only possible, but also necessary and fruitful.

At this point, it is worth noting that, of the four agreement features that exist in Arabic (gender, number, definiteness and person), only the former two are dealt with in this book (as we have made clear from the very title). We felt that definiteness and person agreement, fascinating topics as they may be, depended on factors entirely different from the ones described in this study, and as such they were better addressed separately.

As far as gender and number are concerned, the reader will find the first chapter to consist, fundamentally, in a "history of ideas" about agreement in Arabic. Here we list all the works dedicated to agreement that have appeared in the field of Arabic studies prior to the publication of the present volume, summarizing their findings and conclusions, highlighting their merits and possible shortcomings. More in general, we discuss how and why the topics of gender and agreement in Arabic came to be conceptualized in a certain way, and in so doing, we take issue with some of the categories that have traditionally been employed to classify and subdivide the various "types" of Arabic, explaining why these labels are only partially relevant when considering agreement-related phenomena. In general, Chapter 1 will probably appeal more to the scholar of Arabic than to the general linguist, who will find some of the themes treated therein somewhat unfamiliar.

Chapter 2, conversely, is probably where the language typologists will find themselves most at home. Here we present an attempt at a description that can account for every single existing variety of Arabic, ancient or modern, spoken or written, from the shores of Morocco to the mountains of Oman. After introducing the topic of agreement from the perspective of general linguistics (§ 2.1), we present the basic morphemes that Arabic varieties have at their disposal to express the categories of gender and number (§ 2.2). Readers already acquainted with Arabic won't probably find much new information in this latter section, although we made an effort to at least mention even the typologically most unusual varieties—as dialects of Arabic go. Sections from § 2.3 on are entirely devoted to description, starting with the spoken dialects that have preserved gender distinction in the plural, and then moving on to the ones that have lost this morphological option, before further proceeding to the written forms of the language, from the pre-classical to the modern. The descriptions that appear in each one of these sections are based on extensive bibliographical research, to make sure that data from all different varieties are brought to bear, no matter how peripheral or remote. The end result of this substantial research effort is the subdivision of all Arabic languages into six different Types, as far as agreement is concerned, each labelled with a different letter of the Latin alphabet: five fundamental ones (A, B, C, E and F) and a possible outlier (D).

Chapter 3 investigates the evolution of agreement in Arabic from a diachronic perspective, with particular emphasis on the appearance of feminine singular agreement as an agreement option for plural controllers. When the first epigraphic or literary attestations of Arabic appear, the change is clearly in progress, so that its origins and ultimate causes have to be searched for in previous stages of the language. In § 3.1, thus, the reader will find a reconstruction of the evolution of agreement in (mostly written) Arabic from a Semitic perspective, in which we advance the hypothesis that the spread of broken plurals was primarily responsible for the appearance of feminine singular agreement with plural controllers. Subsequent sections concern stages of written Arabic for which data are plentiful, which allowed the authors to work on representative corpora and to draw more certain conclusions. Sections 3.2 to 3.7 follow the evolution of the innovative agreement pattern and its spread through different domains, applying the tools of linguistic typology to the available data. In particular, § 3.7 focuses on the dramatic change that the agreement patterns of written Arabic underwent starting from the 10th century. § 3.9, finally, compares the data collected from pre-Islamic poetry with a contemporary corpus of Najdi Nabati poetry, in order to gauge the degree of consistency between the two systems, separated by a time gap of over 15 centuries.

The research questions that inspired this book were also an object of reflection for the Arab grammarians, starting from al-Xalīl and Sībawayh (8th century CE). Chapter 4 reconstructs the conceptualization of agreement in Arabic in the works of the most influent scholars of the language, in a time period spanning from the 8th to the 19th century. In particular, the chapter tries to answer two fundamental questions: 1) How did Arabic grammarians describe the agreement system of the language, before and after its standardization? 2) When was the rule dictating mandatory feminine singular agreement with plural nonhuman controllers first explicitly spelled out? The reader will realize that Arab grammarians produced very fine descriptions of the rules governing agreement, reaching conclusions which are similar to the ones of the authors of this book. The mandatory rule of feminine singular agreement, however, was only formalized at a very late stage, well within the 19th century, although the standardization of the language that originated it had occurred several centuries before. Arab grammarians, thus, continued to describe an agreement system that had since long ceased to exist, while conforming to the new standard in their writing practice.

Finally, in Chapter 5 we come back to the spoken varieties of Arabic, this time focusing on their diachronic evolution. Two main questions are addressed in this chapter, namely: 1) whether should feminine singular agreement in spoken Arabic be considered as a modern innovation—at least in some dialects—or as an ancient common retention. 2) When, where and how was the possibility of feminine plural agreement first lost, and how did this loss affect the agreement system overall. While the answer to the first question appears relatively straightforward to us—feminine singular agreement represents an extremely old ancient retention, and the actual innovation is represented by those varieties that have lost this syntactical option—the second problem proves more complex to solve. It is our opinion that loss of feminine plural morphology in Arabic was not an internally motivated change, but it was brought about by extra-linguistic factors, in particular urbanization, at different times in the history of Arabic languages, and in several different places independently. Loss of feminine plural agreement would represent, in other words, a textbook example of multiple parallel linguistic innovations.

As a final remark, we specify that Chapters 1, 2 and 5 of this book have been written by Simone Bettega, with the exception of sections § 1.2 and § 2.4, while Luca D'Anna authored Chapters 3 and 4, along with sections § 1.2 and § 2.4.[1]

Salalah and Terrasini
29 January 2022

1 To be fair, Luca D'Anna is also responsible for the concluding lines of Chapter 5, and the quote from Labīd that appears therein, because no matter the years that have passed, deep down he remains a poet at heart. Simone Bettega, conversely, has chosen the quote by Italo Calvino that opens the book, probably because he sometimes still doubts the reality of things, or forgets about it.

CHAPTER 1

Previous Studies on Agreement in Arabic

This chapter offers a critical survey of the studies on agreement in Arabic that exist to date. The definition "studies on agreement in Arabic" is purposely vague, since it encompasses a rather heterogeneous set of elements. While some of the works that will be discussed in this chapter are indeed exclusively focused on grammatical agreement, others are more general treatises dealing with various aspects of the Arabic language(s), more or less tangentially also concerned with the topic of agreement.

In order to address the question in an orderly fashion, this chapter is divided into three sections. The first one deals with studies that approach the broad field of Arabic linguistics from a very general perspective (often discussing both the written and oral varieties of the language, and offering comparative remarks about the two groups). The second and the third section are narrower in scope, focusing only on studies about Classical and Modern Standard Arabic (§ 1.2) and the spoken dialects (§ 1.3).[1]

1.1 Agreement through Time: Arabic Old and New

References to the topic of agreement, albeit sometimes marginal, can be found in most of the general works on Arabic published between the second half of the 20th century and beginning of the 21st. Although often very different in scope, all these studies share a number of common theoretical tenets, the most important of which is the distinction between two different linguistic types of Arabic, labelled respectively Old Arabic (OA) and Neo Arabic (NA).

As their names suggest, the relation between OA and NA is diachronic in nature, the latter being the putative descendant of the former. These labels are far from being theoretically unproblematic, to the point that even providing a straightforward and consistent definition for the two poses significant challenges.[2] That of the OA/NA distinction is a long-standing question in the field of

1 Neither whole grammars of specific spoken varieties nor the treatises of the early Arab grammarians will be discussed here. For a detailed overview of the treatment of agreement in several grammars of spoken Arabic dialects, see § 2.3.2 and § 2.3.6. For a discussion of how agreement was conceived by the Arabic grammatical tradition, see Chapter 4.

2 NA should encompass all contemporary varieties of spoken Arabic. However, dialects of the

 | DOI:10.1163/9789004527249_002

Arabic linguistics, and one whose remarkable complexity cannot be addressed here in full. For the sake of our analysis, we will only focus on how well the OA/NA hypothesis fares if tested against the evidence provided by agreement patterns.

Grammatical agreement is one of the features most often cited in lists of traits that (supposedly) set NA apart from OA. As a matter of fact, when it comes to syntax, agreement is often the *only* feature mentioned, such lists normally relying more heavily on phonological and morphological structures.

A good example of this tendency is offered by Fischer's and Jastrow's *Handbuch der Arabischen Dialekte*. After discussing in detail several phono-morphological peculiarities of NA, the two authors lament a lack of studies in the area of syntax, so severe that the only topic that can be securely addressed is agreement in verb-subject structures. On this topic, they write that:

> Auf dem Gebiet der Syntax fällt vor allem die Vereinfachung der Kongruenzverhältnisse ins Gewicht. Zwar kann auch im Neuarabischen das verbale Prädikat unter Umständen vor dem Subjekt stehen, doch kongruiert es dann nach Genus und Numerus mit dem Subjekt, sodaß der für das Altarabische Typische Unterschied zwischen verbal- und nominal- bzw. Kopulativsatz entfällt[3]
>
> FISCHER AND JASTROW 1980: 47

NA type have probably existed since before the time of the Islamic conquests (or, to put it differently, features that are now commonly associated to NA-type dialects have been known to exist for more than 1,500 years). The question could be neutralized by saying that it is NA everything that has evolved from an earlier OA stage through the various means of linguistic change (it does not really matter when this change began). This, however, leaves us in need of a definition for OA. OA could simply A) coincide with Classical Arabic as codified by the first Arab grammarians, or as it appears in the pre- and early-Islamic texts. Or it could mean B) the type of Arabic that was spoken in the Arabian Peninsula at the time of the prophet Muhammad, or before that (a type of Arabic about which, for obvious reasons, we know remarkably little: in particular, it is not clear to what extent did it coincide with the definition in A). Recently, several scholars have argued that the label OA should be reserved for, or at least include, C) the language of the oldest epigraphic texts that can be securely identified as Arabic (needless to say, opinions on the subject vary considerably: see for instance Macdonald 2000 and Al-Jallad 2018). In general, in the present section, we will use the term OA as defined in A: this is not because we necessarily commit to this definition, but because it appears to be the one adopted in the works under scrutiny.

3 "In the area of syntax, the simplification of agreement conditions is particularly important. Although the verbal predicate can occur before the subject in Neo-Arabic as well, it will then agree with the subject in gender and number, so that the distinction between verbal and nominal or copulative sentence—typical of Old Arabic—is lost" (our translation).

Similar views are expressed in a number of other important studies. These include Ferguson's well-known article *Grammatical Agreement in Classical Arabic and the Modern Dialects: a Response to Versteegh's Pidginization Hypothesis* ("The modern dialects have moved toward elimination of the differences between verb-initial and verb-second patterns and toward increased use of strict agreement", Ferguson 1989: 14);[4] Clive Holes's *Modern Arabic: Structures, Functions and Varieties* ("Unlike MSA, agreement between V[erb] and S[ubject] in the modern dialects is not dependent on word order [...]. Relative position per se of V and S does not seem to affect agreement", Holes 2004: 264); and Kees Versteegh's *The Arabic Language* ("The sentence structure of Classical Arabic has changed drastically in the modern dialects [...]. But even in those cases in which the verb precedes the subject, there is full number agreement between them", Versteegh 2014: 136).

As will be shown in § 2.3.9, these claims need to be reconsidered when counterchecked in the light of new data. Word order (or *precedence*) is a powerful and typologically common condition affecting agreement (so common, in fact, that it even informs one of Greenberg's universal principles).[5] Spoken dialects of Arabic represent no exception, and in every variety for which statistical data are available, singular agreement in pre-controller position is systematically more common than in post-controller position.

Admittedly, the role of word order seems to be stronger in certain dialects, and less evident in others. In addition, while in NA this appears to be a matter of statistical tendency, singular agreement in pre-controller position is almost systematic in the earliest OA texts (the pre-Islamic poetic corpus and the Quran).[6] However, the distinction here appears not to be a typological one, but rather the kind of difference one would expect between a variety that has gone through a process of standardization and regularization, and one that has not. Furthermore, even if we were to believe that systematic singular agreement in pre-controller position constituted an absolute condition in the ancestor(s) of

4 Ferguson (1989: 15) also adds that the few occurrences still found in the spoken dialects of singular agreement in a verb coming before a plural subject are to be regarded as "a last residue of a pattern which has been slowly disappearing from the spoken language". For a discussion of the term "strict agreement", employed here by Ferguson, see below.

5 "When number agreement between the noun and verb is suspended and the rule is based on order, the case is always one in which the verb precedes and the verb is in the singular" (universal 33). The effects of precedence can be observed in several Indo-European languages which are probably familiar to the readers of this book, including English, Spanish, Italian and Russian.

6 See, however, Corriente (1976: 95), who writes that "natural" agreement (i.e. a plural verb preceding a plural controller) was common "in all types of OA".

the modern dialects before any formal codification,[7] the fact remains that word order *does have* an influence on agreement in NA, contrary to what many scholars have claimed.

Besides the question of pre-controller agreement, another oft-cited characteristic of OA is the distinctive agreement rule that dictates F.SG agreement with plural nonhuman controllers. It is perhaps ironic that two works such as Versteegh (1984) and Ferguson (1989), intended the latter as the confutation of the former, end up expressing remarkably similar views on the topic of agreement.

Versteegh (1984: 103) correctly points out that, while the (allegedly) old rule of F.SG agreement with nonhuman plurals is no longer compulsory in any spoken dialect, it is still found as an alternative to plural agreement in several modern varieties. However, he describes the latter pattern as an innovation, and seems to ascribe the presence of F.SG agreement to the influence of Classical Arabic. In chapters 3 and 4, we will show how the opposite is probably true, in that the dialects preserved the old pattern of oscillation between plural and F.SG agreement, while CA/MSA innovated by making F.SG agreement obligatory.

Versteegh also writes that "in the modern dialects there is a tendency towards complete agreement between substantive and adjective, regardless of the (in)animateness of the substantive". This statement is more problematic, because the formula "complete agreement" is intrinsically vague. If one is to understand, by "complete agreement", a type of agreement where all the information about the gender and number of the controller is also present on the target, then this definition does not apply to any existing dialect. It is a well-known fact that many dialects of Arabic have lost gender distinction in the

7 Ideas about what "correct" or "good" Arabic is must have existed since long before the grammarians of the Islamic tradition started to write them down, so that the systematic use of pre-controller singular agreement that the authors of the pre-Islamic odes made in their poetic writings is no proof of the fact that they actually used it in their everyday speech. Theoretically, the well-known case of the sentence *ʔakalū-ni l-barāǧīṯu* (found in the works of Sībawayh and other grammarians) could be adduced as counterevidence to this claim. After all, reporting the use of plural pre-controller agreement as a linguistic peculiarity would have been pointless unless a larger group of speakers existed who, by contrast, systematically employed singular agreement in the same context. Levin (1989), however, has convincingly shown that agreement was not what the early grammarians were interested in when analyzing this construction, and that they have never condemned it as an example of "bad" Arabic (apparently, the first to do so has been Al-Ḥarīrī, in the 12th century; see however Guillaume 2011: 283–284 and 288–289). Examples of plural agreement in pre-controller verbs, reported by Sībawayh, occurred as well in the speech of those who *did not* say *ʔakalū-ni l-barāǧīṯu* (Levin 1989: 51). Furthermore, in the *Kitāb*, the *ʔakalū-ni l-barāǧīṯu* syndrome is not associated with any specific tribe or location, so that it could well have represented widespread idiolectal variation (for more details see Guillaume 2011: 279).

plural forms of the adjective, verb and pronoun, and "complete agreement" in these dialects is consequently impossible, since they lack the morphological means to produce such an agreement. Conversely, as will be discussed in detail in sections from § 2.3.2 to § 2.3.4, dialects that still retain gender distinction in the plural often employ F.PL agreement with plural controllers that are masculine in the singular. In both cases, agreement can be said to be "complete" only with respect to the feature of number, but things become more complicated when gender is taken into account. This lack of attention to the question of gender agreement in studies of Arabic linguistics, far from being a secondary or negligible flaw, is precisely what hindered an accurate description of the Arabic agreement system(s). This will be one of the main theses discussed in this book, in particular in Chapter 2.

Unlike Versteegh, Ferguson points out the fact that plural agreement with nonhuman controllers has always been an option in Arabic, even in the oldest texts available to us.[8] As we have seen, he is entirely correct in this respect, the two patterns (plural and F.SG agreement) having apparently coexisted for a very long time. As a matter of fact, this could be adduced as an instance of remarkable similarity between the vast majority of the modern dialects[9] and OA (to the point that one wonders if it makes any sense to refer to a "typological" NA/OA distinction in this respect).

Ferguson (1989: 11), however, also maintains that "the use of plural agreement with plural [nonhuman] nouns began to spread as an alternative to the more common feminine singular agreement of OA". Ferguson believed that F.SG agreement was once associated with nonhuman and broken plurals; in the dialects, however, plural agreement came "to be used with a distributive or enumerative value as opposed to the simple plurality of more-than-one". While he is absolutely correct in the latter part of this statement (as plenty of subsequent studies have shown, see § 1.3), this is not a peculiar feature of NA; on the contrary, these semantic constraints were already in place in (at least some varieties of) Arabic in the 7th century, and possibly before that. The sharp "human vs nonhuman" distinction was established much later, and became part of the received set of rules of what is today MSA.[10]

---

8 Holes (2004: 202–203) as well acknowledges this. In particular, he is one of the few to specify that *feminine* plural agreement did sometimes occur in these contexts. As we will see, this remark is of the utmost importance.

9 A number of modern dialects exist where F.SG agreement with plural controllers is very rare, to the point that the few occurrences that one still encounters can be considered fossilized relics of a now extinct system. For more details, see § 2.3.6 and § 2.3.7.

10 Here as well, the remarks of Holes (2004: 203) are particularly accurate: "This agreement

This common confusion between the modern, partially artificial *rule* (based on humanness) and the old *preferred pattern* (based on the distributive/collective opposition, or, in the terms that we will use in this book, on *individuation* or *salience*) is probably another reason that contributed to blur the picture of the Arabic agreement systems. These themes will be addressed in detail in the following chapters.

It is also worth pointing out that Ferguson's claim of F.SG being more common than plural agreement in OA[11] is questionable in itself. While this is probably true on a very general level, agreement actually depends on what type of targets one takes into consideration, their relative position with respect to the controller, and whether or not one considers apophonic "broken" agreement as proper plural agreement (and also on the corpus under scrutiny: percentages of F.SG agreement vary significantly from the pre-Islamic poetry to the Quran, for instance). Ferguson himself was perfectly aware of these complications, and wrote: "In various collocation types (of locus, word order, and kind of plural) both strict and deflected agreement were grammatical but in each case there was a strong preference (the "unmarked" choice) for one or the other [...]. Unfortunately, no thoroughgoing investigation of actual preferences over large bodies of text has been carried out" (Ferguson 1989: 11; on the use of the terms "strict" and "deflected", see below). All these questions will be discussed in more detail in the second and third chapter of this book.

In general, while Ferguson's 1989 article was remarkably insightful in many respects (especially in light of the scarcity of data on the topic that existed at the time), and in spite of the fact that it laid the foundations for many subsequent studies on agreement (as we will see in § 1.3), it did contain a few oversimplifications. We strongly disagree, for instance, with his view of the evolution of the Arabic agreement systems over time as a "progression from the complex agreement patterns of OA to the simpler, stricter ones of NA" (Ferguson 1989: 14; on this point, see § 2.3.5 and § 2.6). More importantly, some comments are due on the labels "strict" and "deflected" agreement that he employs in the paper.

---

system, nowadays the norm in [MSA], is a simplification of the CLA (roughly pre-tenth century) one, which is thought was a reflection of the situation in the Old Arabic dialects". On this point, see Chapters 3 and 4.

11 The idea that OA and NA differ in terms of how frequent a use they make of F.SG agreement is echoed in another distinction traditionally made by scholars of Arabic, that between "Bedouin" and "sedentary" dialects. According to some authors, F.SG agreement would be more common in the more conservative Bedouin varieties, which remain closer to the OA model, and rare in the innovative sedentary varieties. These ideas will be discussed in § 2.3.

Ferguson (1989: 9) defines "strict" agreement as a type of agreement in which "some category that is overtly or inherently present in the 'controller' (subject or head-noun) is copied in the 'target' (verb, noun-modifier)". We have "deflected" agreement, on the other hand, when "a plural controller is associated with a feminine singular target".

Ferguson's definition of strict agreement works very well for the analysis of dialects in which gender distinction in the plural has collapsed, because in such dialects a plural controller can only attract two types of agreement (i.e. common plural or feminine singular, that is, strict or deflected[12]). It is no coincidence, in this sense, that Ferguson first introduced the two terms in his textbook of Damascene Arabic (Ferguson and Ani, 1961). When it comes to non-distinguishing dialects, however, the use of the label "strict" only tells us that the agreement is plural, without providing any information with respect to gender.[13]

This is the same problem we have highlighted when commenting Versteegh's definition of "complete" agreement, the main difference between the two terminologies being that Ferguson's ended up being adopted in a vast portion of the studies on agreement that followed. Probably, the fact that the two labels "strict" and "deflected" had been conceived for the description of a dialect which had no gender distinction in the plural should have dissuaded scholars to apply them indiscriminately to any variety of Arabic. This was not the case, however, and the term "strict" ended up being equated to "plural" throughout all subsequent literature, thus giving rise to a series of misunderstandings concerning the nature of agreement in Arabic.

In particular, the problem with the adoption of this terminology is that it automatically renders any type of variation other than the singular/plural opposition irrelevant, because it makes analysis "blind", so to speak, to the potential meaningfulness of gender variation in plural agreement. As we have seen, F.PL agreement with allegedly "masculine" nonhuman controllers is a common feature of both early Arabic texts and modern gender-distinguishing dialects: the importance of this phenomenon is lost when looked at through the

12 Of course, this is without taking into consideration the possibility of M.SG agreement in the case of a verb preceding its plural subject, which Ferguson (1989: 13) termed "equivocal" agreement. We have already discussed this topic in the first part of this section, and we will return on it in § 2.3.9.

13 Though Ferguson—to the best of our knowledge—never made any specific claim as to this point, Kirk Belnap, who worked under his supervision as a PhD student, made clear that "strict agreement […] means plural form targets occurring with plural controllers, however, grammatical gender of target and controller may or may not be the same" (Belnap and Shabaneh 1992: 247).

lenses of Ferguson's terminology. As already said, we will return on the importance of gender distinction in plural agreement in § 2.3.

One last work that deserves a short mention here is Corriente 2008, a relatively recent and concise study on the evolution of OA into NA. Corriente's article analyzes a number of features that are thought to differentiate the two linguistic types (his list of traits is based on Fischer and Jastrow, 1980). As can be expected, agreement is the only syntactic feature mentioned in the paper. Corriente provides a relatively detailed description of the agreement system of OA, and he, as well, mentions the possibility of F.PL agreement with plural nonhuman controllers. Unlike the other works analyzed so far, Corriente shows extreme care in sieving the available information about agreement in several modern dialects, and provides a wealth of notions on the subject (albeit confined to a long footnote, see Corriente 2008: 20–21). Despite this effort, he still laments "the lack of a detailed comparative survey of this matter taking into consideration every dialect or at least a large enough sample of them".

His conclusions on the subject, however cautious, seem to echo those of the other authors analyzed until now. According to him, in NA "it could be said that natural [i.e. plural] agreement is the rule, with frequent exceptions due to survival or the interference of the old or high registers, in a wide range from zero [...] up to nearly optional agreement in feminine singular of irrational plurals". It is not clear why Corriente feels the need to refer to this phenomenon as "a rule", given the high number of exceptions that he himself openly acknowledges. Furthermore, OA showed the same variation between singular and plural agreement (as pointed out, once more, by Corriente himself), so that speaking of an evolution (rather than a continuity) in this context appears questionable.

Summing up what has been said up to this moment, we have focused our attention on a number of studies that include agreement among the features that could help setting apart a hypothetical OA linguistic type from an NA one. The two traits more often mentioned in this respect are singular agreement with plural controllers in verbs occurring before their subjects and F.SG agreement with plural nonhuman controllers. These two features are commonly encountered in a wide variety of modern dialects of Arabic, so that neither one can be safely identified as a major discriminating factor between an OA and a NA type. Admittedly, some differences exist in the distribution of singular pre-controller agreement in NA and OA texts. The latter, however, pertain to a formally codified register of the language, so that the extent to which they can be thought of as representative of actual linguistic usage remains open to debate. In the following chapters we will also offer plenty of evidence that Ferguson's claim, according to which F.SG agreement in OA marked a human vs nonhuman distinction, which later evolved in a distributive/non-distributive one, is to be rejected (in a sense, the opposite is actually true).

There is a third trait that we have mentioned in our overview, and that only sporadically appears in the studies we reviewed, namely the OA pattern of F.PL agreement with nonhuman plural controllers. It is our opinion that the importance of gender distinction in plural agreement has been widely underestimated in studies on the subject, also because of the terminology they employed, that focused on the singular/plural opposition rather than on the masculine/feminine one. We will continue discussing this issue in § 1.3.

In conclusion, general studies on Arabic linguistics have devoted a variable amount of attention to the topic of agreement, and even the ones that have focused on this subject have reached conclusions that we do not find entirely satisfying. In this respect, one cannot but be reminded of Pat-El's (2017: 19) warning that "although dialects are normally mined for their innovative and divergent features, they can also be conservative, while the standard may be counter-conservative, that is: not innovative, but puristic, ideological and disdainful of unfamiliar features regardless of their origin". In the case of agreement, this seems precisely to be the case. In particular, some confusion appears to have arisen in attributing to OA certain agreement behaviors that are instead typical of today's MSA. The common assumption that today's standard version of the language is fundamentally one with the language of the earliest Arabic texts—allowing for some obvious stylistic differences—does not apply to the realm of syntactic agreement, where sharp differences exist between the two.

All these topics will be the object of our survey of the existing studies about agreement in written Arabic, to which we shall presently turn.[14]

---

14 Right before this book was sent for review, an important article by Jonathan Owens appeared, dealing with the historical development of agreement in Arabic, with a specific focus on the topic of singular agreement with plural subjects. The theses that Owens (2021) puts forward are relevant to the topics treated in this book, and would deserve to be extensively discussed here. Unfortunately, when the article reached us, it was too late for implementing major alterations to our work. While the discussion of Owens' study must unfortunately remain the topic for a future publication, the contents of the present book will make it clear to our readers that we disagree with some of the conclusions reached by Owens. In particular, we take issue with the idea that the agreement system of dialects such as Cairene or Damascene could be assimilated to that of Modern Standard Arabic (in fact, in the following chapters we propose very different evolutionary paths for the current situation in both the spoken dialects and in written Arabic), and we see no argument because of which pre-controller F.SG agreement should have, in time, transitioned to M.SG agreement. The presence of non-agreeing pre-controller targets in Arabic is easily explained in typological terms, it being an extremely common phenomenon crosslinguis-

1.2 Written Arabic

In 1968, Carolyn G. Killean opened an interesting article on agreement with the following statement:

> Open any textbook or descriptive grammar of modern literary Arabic and you will find statements such as the following: Literary Arabic has two genders, masculine and feminine and three numbers, singular dual and plural. These statements are not only dull; they are misleading.
>
> KILLEAN 1968, 40

In her paper, Killean also advanced the hypothesis that F.SG agreement with plural controllers actually represents a kind of neuter agreement.[15]

While some descriptive grammars of Arabic actually offer some account of the variation that will be described in this book, all of them stick to the two genders—three numbers description mentioned by Killean. As a matter of fact, agreement is an understudied topic in the field of Arabic syntax, even more so if the scope is restricted to agreement in Classical Arabic. No full-sized monograph has been devoted to the study of its variation and rules of distribution, and descriptive grammars usually devote to agreement no more than a few pages. Since 1968, the dearth of studies lamented by Killean has been partially filled, yet most works tend to focus on agreement in spoken Arabic, using written varieties only as a term of comparison.

Taking a step back to analyze the comprehensive descriptions of Classical Arabic published in the 19th and 20th century, Reckendorf (1895) and Wright (1896a) (translated from Caspari's German original, with additions and corrections) are among the few who devote some space to agreement. Reckendorf (1895, 89–90) lists all the possible agreement patterns, including plural and collective controllers:

---

tically (as discussed in § 2.3.9), and does not require the extra logical step of the development of F.SG agreement with plural controllers, which is, in our view, an entirely unrelated phenomenon.

15 Féghali and Cuny (1924, 83) reached the same conclusions, suggesting that, in the transition from the prehistorical stage to common Afroasiatic, an ancient neuter / inanimate gender was lost. The domains of the old neuter, then, were mostly occupied by feminine nouns. Kuryłowicz (1973, 137–139) also advanced the hypothesis that Arabic had "three genders", although in a very different way from the hypothesis presented in this book.

TABLE 1.1 Agreement patterns with plural and collective controllers in Reckendorf (1895, 89–90)

Type of controller	Allowed agreement patterns
Sound masculine plural (human)	Plural
Sound masculine plural (nonhuman)	Feminine singular; Plural
Sound feminine plural (human)	Plural; Feminine singular (rare)
Sound feminine plural (nonhuman)	Feminine singular; Plural (rare)
Sound feminine plural (biologically masculine nonhuman)	Plural
Broken plural (animate nonhuman)	Plural; Feminine singular (rare)
Broken plural (nonhuman)	Feminine singular; Plural (rare)
Collective (animate nonhuman)	Plural; Singular (rare)
Collective (nonhuman)	Feminine singular; Masculine singular; Feminine plural
Name of tribe	Feminine singular; Plural

Wright's grammar includes a relatively long section named *Concord in Gender and Number between the Parts of a Sentence* (Wright 1896a, 2:288–299). Wright describes in good detail agreement patterns in Classical Arabic, and his description accounts for the variation emerging from the ancient texts. In particular, he mentions both the possibility of F.PL agreement with nonhuman plural controllers, provided that their number does not exceed ten (Wright 1896a, 2:293), and the possibility of F.SG agreement with broken plurals, independently of the nature of the controller (Wright 1896a, 2:296).[16]

After Killean's (1968) paper, a small number of studies contributed to draw attention to agreement in Classical and pre-Classical Arabic. Beeston (1975, 65–66), describing different features of Modern Standard Arabic, pointed out that the agreement patterns emerging from the ancient texts denote a change in progress: "The use of the feminine singular concord with 'irrational' substantives is a neologism in Arabic which only gradually won its way to becoming the norm." The analysis of the process that culminated in the generalization

16 Some of Wright's considerations on agreement are more debatable. For instance, he writes that "In general, when once [sic!] the subject has been mentioned, any following verb must agree with it strictly in gender and number (Wright 1896a, 2:292)." As evident from statistics and samples presented in § 2.4, this type of agreement represents the prevalent pattern in such cases, not the only one.

of F.SG agreement with nonhuman plural controllers (i.e. with “irrational substantives”) is the specific topic of chapters 3 and 4 of this book. In any case, it is clear that such an evolution resulted in a mandatory agreement pattern that is peculiar to Classical and (even more so) Modern Standard Arabic, but absent from both pre- and early Classical Arabic and the dialects. The consistency of agreement patterns between the pre-Classical texts in our possession (i.e. pre-Islamic poetry and the Quran) and the modern dialects was among the traits employed in Ferguson (1989) to confute Versteegh’s (1984) theory of pidginization, as discussed in § 1.1. Following Ferguson (1989), Kirk Belnap, whose first interest lied in the description of agreement in Cairene, started analyzing the development of the agreement system of Arabic from a diachronic perspective (K.R. Belnap and Shabaneh 1992; K.R. Belnap and Gee 1994; R.K. Belnap 1999). In particular, Belnap’s studies analyze the transition from the variable agreement system observed in pre- and early Classical Arabic to the mandatory agreement patterns prescribed in late Classical and Modern Standard Arabic, taking into consideration the role of non-native speakers of Arabic and of diamesic variation between spoken and written Arabic. In Belnap and Gee (1994), theoretical tools drawn from SLA (Second Language Acquisition) studies are successfully employed to explain the transition toward mandatory agreement patterns at the hands of non-native speakers who started writing in their newly-acquired language. Belnap (1999), finally, integrates the diachronic study of agreement into a typological perspective, analyzing factors such as animacy, morphology and distance between controller and target.

Written at the same time when Belnap started working on agreement, Roman (1991) discusses different aspects of agreement in Arabic, including the role of F.SG agreement with plural controllers. According to Roman, this type of agreement is used to signal the *res générale* or, in the case of human controllers, unanimity, and was only gradually reinterpreted as a mark of nonhumanness.

Descriptive works on Arabic published in the late 20th century and at the beginning of the 21st provide (more or less) comprehensive accounts of agreement. Cantarino (1975, 2:53–60), similarly to Reckendorf, provides a full list of possible agreement patterns in Modern Arabic prose, with a rich exemplification of authentic samples. Holes (2004, 201–204) includes a brief but very illustrative overview of agreement patterns in Old Arabic, Classical Arabic and the modern dialects, also discussing the influence of word order (Holes 2004, 262–264), while Ryding’s (2005) grammar does not deal with agreement in detail. Badawi, Carter and Gully (2004, 102–103) discuss the possible exceptions to the mandatory F.SG pattern with nonhuman nouns but, once again, without much detail, which is to be expected in a grammar focusing on Modern Standard Arabic. Syntactic descriptions of Arabic grounded in a generativist perspective seem to focus less on agreement patterns and more on the influence of word order, as in Fassi Fehri (1988), Benmamoun (2000) and Aoun, Benmamoun and Choueiri (2010, 5). Fassi Fehri (2012, 317–318), on the other hand, offers an extremely interesting description of possible agreement patterns with human collectives.[17]

Despite the absence of monographic works on agreement in written Arabic, a few more papers, published in the first two decades of the 21st century, have contributed to further our understanding of variation in pre- and early-Islamic Arabic. Ferrando (2006) analyzes the plural of paucity in Arabic, with interesting remarks concerning its agreement patterns. Guillaume (2011) studies in detail the so-called *ʔakalū-nī l-barāġīṯu* syndrome and its actual scope within the framework of Arabic traditional grammar. Dror (2013) deals with adjectival agreement in the Quran, showing the full range of variation of possible agreement patterns, while Dror (2016b) focuses on collective agreement. Even though a historical dimension is absent from Dror (2016b), collective agreement in modern journalistic Arabic is analyzed in a different paper (Dror 2016a), which gives the reader the possibility to grasp the evolution of agreement patterns with specific reference to collective controllers. Dror (2016b) has been particularly useful to the authors of this book, since it analyzes in detail all the possible factors that influence the occurrence of the different agreement options attested in the Quran.[18]

Not many other studies on agreement in written Arabic are available to the reader. Agreement in mixed varieties, such as Middle Arabic, is briefly dealt with in Hopkins (1984, 92, 94–97, 144), while Educated Spoken Arabic is the object of Sallam (1979).

If we move a step further from agreement *stricto sensu*, there is another related topic that attracted the interest of both Semistists and Arabists, i.e. the study of broken (or internal) plurals. As discussed in § 3.1, the spread of broken plurals in Arabic is considered to be one of the major factors in the evolution of its agreement system. Ratcliffe (1992; 1998) represent, so far, the most detailed and up-to-date morphological studies on broken or internal plurals in Arabic and Afroasiatic, even though some of the author's conclusions are questionable.[19] Ratcliffe (1998, 120–130), in particular, provides an exhausting

17 Given that this book is grounded in a historical and typological approach, only the major contributions offered by generative linguists have been mentioned.

18 In her paper, however, Dror tends to focus on number, partially neglecting gender. For a critical analysis of Dror (2016b) and a reassessment of agreement patterns with collective controllers in the Quran, see D'Anna (2020a).

19 For a critical, but well balanced review of Ratcliffe (1998), and a survey of scholarship on

survey of the major theories concerning the origin of broken plurals in Arabic and Semitic, which are then weighed against the data emerging from the analysis of the broken plural system of Arabic (as well of other Semitic languages). Such theories include Barth (1894), Brockelmann (1908), Kuryłowicz (1962; 1973), Murtonen (1964) and Corriente (1971).

Barth (1894) builds his theory on the fundamentally untenable hypothesis that all nouns derive from verbs, from which he derives the idea that plural forms were originally deverbal abstract nouns. This theory is only justified by the formal resemblance between some broken plurals and some deverbal nouns, but fails to account for the large majority of them, so that it can be safely discarded (Ratcliffe 1998, 123–124). Brockelmann (1908) postulated the existence, within Proto-Semitic, of a single category that included abstract, collective and plural nouns, from which internal and external plurals would have been gradually distinguished. This theory, however appealing, is also based on a very restricted number of broken plural forms, but cannot explain the more common and productive ones, so that it must also be rejected (Ratcliffe 1998, 121). Kuryłowicz's two main studies (1962; 1973) ultimately stem from Barth's theory, which the author tries to bring within commonly accepted linguistic theory. Kuryłowicz, however, seems to believe that apophony was originally restricted to the verb, which is untenable, and that "the original relationship between singulars and broken plurals is one between a verbal adjective or participle and the infinitive or abstract noun from the same verb" (Ratcliffe 1998, 126). Murtonen (1964) bases the change that brought about the existence of broken plurals on a complex series of accentual shifts occurred at different stages of the evolution from Proto-Semitic to Arabic. The main problem with Murtonen's theories is that no independent evidence on the occurrence of such changes is provided, except the fact that they resulted in the formation of broken plurals (Ratcliffe 1998, 128). The argument is, thus, largely circular. Corriente (1971) offers the most original attempt at explaining the rise and spread of broken plurals in Semitic, even though he admits the possibility that Brockelmann was right in hypothesizing that the quantitative distinction between singular and plural did not yet exist in Proto-Semitic. Corriente's innovative hypothesis is that Proto-Semitic originally possessed a rich system of noun classes, from which the broken plurals ultimately derived.[20] However

the broken plurals in Semitic, see Villa (2010). Also, Ratcliffe's idea that the Semitic root is only an abstraction devised by grammarians seems to be confuted by psycholinguistic studies such as Boudelaa (2013).

20 Even though he rejects Corriente's hypothesis, Ratcliffe admits something that is of ex-

original, this hypothesis is not confirmed by independent Semitic (or Hamito-Semitic) evidence, so that it must as well be rejected (Ratcliffe 1998, 132–133).

The reader who is interested in a detailed review of such theories will find Ratcliffe's chapter to be quite exhaustive. All the above-mentioned authors attempted a morphological or semantic reconstruction of the origin of broken plurals. The idea that broken plurals derive from deverbal abstract nouns or collectives (Brockelmann) or that they are the vestiges of an ancient system of noun classes (Corriente) does not hold up to Ratcliffe's scrutiny. In general, all the reconstructions work only for a limited set of broken plurals, but are unable to account for the others.[21] Ratcliffe's theory itself, based on the prosodic analysis of pluralization strategies, is not fully convincing (Gianto 2000; Villa 2010). His analysis of the different chronological layers of broken plurals, on the other hand, offers a sound basis for the reconstruction of the development of broken plurals in Semitic (Ratcliffe 1998, 211). Despite never being confuted, this part of Ratcliffe's work has probably not received the attention it deserves from scholars who later focused on the analysis of broken plurals in Semitic.

This book, however, is not concerned with the morphological or semantic origin of the nominal templates that form the system of broken plurals in Arabic and other languages of the Central Semitic group. Our interest lies only in their syntactic behavior, and specifically in their agreement patterns. As will become evident in Chapter 4, Brockelmann was not alone in linking broken plurals to collectives. Quite to the contrary, the opinion was very widespread among Arabic grammarians, probably due to the similarities in the agreement patterns of the two categories of nouns.

Given the dearth of studies focusing on agreement in written varieties of Arabic from both a typological and historical perspective, chapters 3 and 4 of this book aim at filling this lacuna, at least partially. § 3 provides a thor-

---

treme importance to the argument pursued in this book, i.e. that at least some Semitic languages had semantic distinctions within the category of the plural:

> There is some support for Corriente's view that semantic subdivisions may exist or have existed within the category 'plural'. According to the Arab grammarians, Arabic has, for example, a distinction between plurals of paucity and multiplicity, distinctions in syntactic agreement between rational and non-rational plurals, a collective-singulative distinction, multiple plurals with different senses for polysemous nouns, and a dual category. The first two distinctions are not found in NW and E Semitic (Ratcliffe 1998, 132–133).

21 This argument, of course, is based on the non-demonstrated premise that a monogenetic explanation exists which is capable to account for the existence of all broken plurals.

ough description of the evolution of the agreement system of written Arabic from the pre-Islamic stage to the complete standardization of the language, while § 4 offers a survey of the way in which this evolution reflects in the Arabic grammatical tradition.

1.3 Spoken Arabic

In § 1.1, we have seen how studies aimed at comparing OA and NA often made improper generalizations concerning the topic of agreement. This happened either because A) they conflated the agreement rules of what they called OA with those of MSA (as we discussed in § 1.1 and § 1.2, the two systems differ significantly), or because B) existing descriptions of dialectal agreement systems were too few/not accurate enough. In fact, only a small number of studies dealing specifically with the topic of agreement in spoken Arabic were published before the beginning of the 21st century. We will begin this section by examining them in turn.

The first important contribution on the subject is Blanc 1970.[22] Admittedly, the main focus of Blanc's article are the categories of duals and pseudo-duals in spoken Arabic. However, in his treatment of the topic, Blanc inevitably devotes ample space to agreement patterns. Blanc (1970: 49–53) was the first, and one of the few, to look at agreement in a cross-dialectal perspective, providing a wealth of comparative data from several different varieties. He was also among the first to point out two fundamental facts, often overlooked in later works on the subject.

The first one of these facts is that, in most dialects, plural and F.SG agreement are both available as agreement options for nonhuman plural controllers (so that no well-defined tendency exists for NA as "a type", contrary to what many scholars later claimed).

The second fact is that, in some dialects, when a nonhuman referent triggers plural agreement, this is normally *feminine* plural agreement. This latter consideration was, unfortunately, confined to a brief footnote (n. 30, p. 50) and dismissed by Blanc himself as "irrelevant for this discussion" (that is, his

22 Admittedly, a much earlier work on the topic exists, namely Boris' (1945–1948) study on the use of F.PL forms in the dialect of the Marāzīg of southern Tunisia. Despite its very limited size (a mere three pages), Boris' article is thought-provoking, and points out a number of important facts that have been mostly neglected by later scholarship. It foreshadowed several of the research questions that will be addressed in more detail in this book.

discussion on the kind of agreement duals and pseudo-duals tend to attract). Furthermore, Blanc apparently considered this a "generalization" of F.PL agreement (at the expense, one imagines, of other types of agreement, though which ones, Blanc does not specify: we will return on this issue in § 2.3.2).

Blanc goes on by illustrating the rules that, according to him, govern oscillation between plural and F.SG agreement with nonhuman referents. He notes that plural agreement is particularly frequent in what he dubs "enumerative constructions" (i.e. "Expressions involving a numeral or some other enumerating or quantifying device", Blanc 1970: 52). These obviously include constructions where the controller is a dual noun. These observations by Blanc were to prove fundamental for later scholarship, in that they paved the ground for some of the most insightful studies on agreement in Arabic that exist to date (specifically that of Ferguson, already discussed in § 1.1, and those of Belnap and Brustad, to be discussed below).

Two more works on the topic of agreement in spoken Arabic were published in the 70s, although very different from Blanc's article in both scope and underlying theoretical background. Unlike all the other studies that will be discussed in this section, Mitchell's (1973) and Sallam's (1979) articles focus heavily on the type of agreement that is triggered by *singular* controllers, and in particular the type of agreement that occurs in adjectival targets. Since agreement with singular controllers will be the topic of § 2.3.1, here we will limit ourselves to evaluating the conclusions of these two studies. The reader is referred to chapter 2 for a more in-depth analysis of Mitchell's and Sallam's insights concerning the agreement behavior of singular nouns.

Mitchell and Sallam both agree on the fact that, in Cairene Arabic as well as other (mostly Levantine) varieties, certain adjectival classes exist which apparently defy normal rules of concord. These include mostly *nisba*-adjectives (i.e. adjectives ending in *-i*), adjectives related to "biological aspects of female development and childbearing", and a few others. Both authors also remark how plural nouns can often trigger F.SG agreement, a fact that—however—does not make these nouns *inherently* feminine (in the same way as it does not make them singular in the plural, which would be nonsensical).

In light of these considerations, Mitchell (1973: 38, 40) comes to the conclusion that "It would be erroneous to claim that nouns control adjectival form in the C[airene] A[rabic] noun phrase", and that "it would be unnecessary as well as mistaken to talk of masculine and feminine nouns" in this variety. These considerations are brought even further by the author, who maintains that describing gender as a "linguistic classification of nouns into arbitrary groups for syntactic purposes" has "led to serious distortion in accounting for CA facts" (Mitchell 1973: 36), and that, in conclusion, gender as a linguistic category should not be thought of as an inherent characteristic of the noun. Sallam's work (which is openly indebted to that of Mitchell) shares most of these views.[23]

Although Mitchell's and Sallam's analysis is insightful in many respects, it seems to us that their conclusions cannot be accepted in their entirety. In the first place, the fact that a number of adjectives are morphologically defective, in that they cannot, or tend not to, inflect for gender, does not mine the tenability of gender as a general linguistic category, as it does not prove that nouns in Cairene Arabic cannot be divided into classes depending on the type of agreement they trigger.[24] Mitchell's and Sallam's studies are limited to the analysis of agreement within the noun phrase: however, the examination of any verb or pronoun following the NP would show that, even in the case of such "defective" adjectives, the inherent gender of the noun can easily be retrieved by looking at other types of agreeing target.[25]

The question of F.SG agreement with plural nouns is a more complex one, and it will be discussed at length throughout this book. In general, our view on the subject is that F.SG agreement in all varieties of Arabic except MSA constitutes a tool for marking the referent's low level of individuation. This marking is in complementary distribution with gender marking, in that the two cannot

23 Fassi Fehri (2018: ix), in his detailed treatment of the functions and meanings associated with feminine morphological markers, expounds views that are very similar to those of Mitchell and Sallam ("Gender cannot be 'inherent' or confined morpho-syntactically to nouns"). Although we do not agree with this position, and in spite of the fact that Fassi Fehri's work is rooted in a tradition (that of generativism) which is quite removed from the approach we adopt in this book, we believe it to be an extremely valuable contribution to the study of Arabic morphosyntax. Note that, while in Fassi Fehri's volume ample space is devoted to the values of the morphemes themselves (e.g. the ability of a F.SG ending to codify the singulative, the plurative, etc.), our book is solely concerned with the topic of agreement.

24 This is also in line with the guidelines proposed by Corbett (1991: 147–148) to establish the number of agreement classes in a given language (see § 2.1). One of the rules require that the same lexical item is used as an agreement target in all tests run to determine the number of classes. Using irregular/defective targets for the study of the general properties of an agreement system is methodologically questionable.

25 Another problem with Mitchell's and Sallam's studies is that, while they recognize the possibility of different types of agreement with the same controller (one option being normally much more common than the others), they say nothing of the reasons that prompt speakers to opt for one or the other solution. Saying that one possibility is statistically more common does not exempt the researcher from trying to explain why is it that the less common option exists as well. In other words, while Mitchell's and Sallam's analyses do highlight the existence of complex agreement phenomena, they possess very little predictive or explanatory power.

co-occur (at least not in the same target, although chains of targets showing mixed agreement are relatively common). The lack of gender agreement in a F.SG target, however, does not imply that the noun lacks an inherent gender. Given the right context, *any* noun in Arabic is capable of triggering plural agreement (and therefore its gender can always be retrieved). Admittedly, this consideration is only significant when referred to gender-distinguishing varieties of Arabic. In the case of non-distinguishing ones, the problem of the gender of a given noun in the plural does not arise, so that this whole discussion becomes less relevant.

Going back to our survey of the studies on agreement in spoken Arabic, it is perhaps curious that the next study to appear that focused on the topic of agreement in an Arabic dialect entirely contradicted the hypotheses put forward by Blanc's some twenty years prior. Owens' and Bani-Yasin's 1987 article analyzed the lexical basis of variation in a rural dialect on northern Jordan. This is a remarkable paper, in that it has been the first one to focus exclusively on a dialect that retains gender distinction in the plural. Upon analysis of the materials they collected, Owens and Bani-Yasin (1987: 708) conclude that "the sets of words triggering one agreement pattern or the other are lexically distinct: f. sg. is by and large associated with nouns of S[tandard] A[arabic] provenance, f. pl. with Col[loquial Arabic]". In other words, variation between singular and plural agreement is not governed by a distinction between enumerative and simple plurality, as Blanc maintained. Rather, the distinction is sociolinguistic in nature, and pertains to the various registers of the language.

Although their analysis appears solid on a general level, the two authors themselves admit that some inconsistencies appear within their data. This is most prominently the case with morphologically "broken" (apophonic) plural forms (especially colloquial ones), which appear to optionally trigger F.SG or F.PL agreement (Owens and Bani-Yasin, 1987: 712, 719, 725). Sound plurals, on the contrary, tend to behave more regularly: standard ones almost systematically trigger F.SG agreement, while colloquial ones are almost systematically associated with F.PL agreement. Exceptions, however, exist for this category as well (Owens and Bani-Yasin, 1987: 712, 718–719, 721, 735 fn. 18).[26] The two authors

26 Overall, Owens' and Bani-Yasin's classification of the various lexical items in their corpus as having a standard or colloquial origin seems to be questionable. The two authors admit that a number of borderline items exists, that is, items whose classification is doubtful. It would seem that, to an extent, the annexation of these items to one category or the other depended on whether or not this endorsed the authors' conclusions (Owens and Bani-Yasin, 1987: 726). Furthermore, their classification appears to be circular at times (that is, an item is assigned to the standard or colloquial set depending on which kind of agree-

offer no explanation as to the possible motivation behind such discrepancies and, although noting a similar variation for some broken *human* controllers in their corpus, they refrain from addressing the issue (Owens and Bani-Yasin, 1987: 733 fn. 7).

Possibly also because of these inconsistencies, Owens' and Bani-Yasin's theory has rarely been mentioned in subsequent studies, and most authors instead reverted to Blanc's hypothesis, expanding on it. In light of what is today know to us about agreement in Arabic, the claim expressed by Owens and Bani-Yasin (1987: 731) that "were these [i.e. Standard] nouns suddenly removed from the language it is most likely that the SA agreement rule itself would disappear" seems hardly tenable.[27] In particular, the definition "SA agreement rule" is inappropriate: F.SG agreement with nonhuman plural controllers appears to be an inherent feature of the grammar of almost all colloquial varieties as well as of the standard one, the difference between the two being that in the latter the rule is (allegedly) categorical, while in the former it is not. This is not to say, however, that MSA plays no role at all in shaping the agreement patterns of the modern dialects. This point will be discussed in more depth in § 5.1. Furthermore, Owens' and Bani-Yasin's paper is important in that it has been the first to ever discuss agreement patterns in a gender-distinguishing variety.[28] After the publication of this study, the importance of F.PL agreement in this type of dialects became evident.

Two years after the appearance of Owens' and Bani-Yasin's article, Ferguson's study on the evolution of agreement in Arabic was published. We have already

---

ment it triggers: Owens and Bani-Yasin, 1987: 724–725). In addition, no convincing explanation is provided as to why many colloquial broken plurals triggering F.SG agreement have not been included in the figures presented in Tables 8 and 9 (Owens and Bani-Yasin, 1987: 725).

27 Note for instance how Owens and Bani-Yasin (1987: 735 n. 18) report seven occurrences of the word *šaġlāt* 'things', appearing in their corpus and triggering F.SG agreement. This is in spite of the fact that "the word has a highly Col[loquial] 'feel' to it, [...] and that it has the *-āt* suffix". The authors comment that this is probably "a case of a Col[loquial] item being influenced by an SA agreement rule". As an alternative explanation, we suggest that the word might have had non-specific reference in the original contexts (although these are not given, so it is impossible to check for the validity of such a hypothesis). This, however, is exactly the kind of lexical item with a rather generic, non-individuated meaning that one would expect to attract F.SG agreement.

28 Owen's and Bani-Yasin's study was followed, a few years later, by Cadora's (1992) study on the effects of contact between urban and rural Palestinian varieties. Despite not being specifically focused on agreement, this topic features prominently in the fourth chapter of Cadora's book, where the author reaches conclusions that closely resemble those of Owens and Bani-Yasin.

discussed the impact that Ferguson (1989) has had on subsequent scholarship in § 1.1. The year 1989, however, saw the publication of another important study on gender and agreement in spoken Arabic, namely Caubet, Simeone-Senelle, Vanhove (1989). This article consists in an overview of the feature of gender in a number of Arabic dialects. The article has the great merit of bringing together for comparative purposes data and examples from a variety of different areas. Obviously, it is not possible to discuss linguistic gender without examining agreement as well, and the authors devote an entire section to the topic. However, the considerations they offer on the subject present problems that are similar to those already referred to in § 1.1, with reference to Versteegh's notion of "complete" agreement, and Ferguson's labels "strict" and "deflected".

Caubet, Simeone-Senelle, Vanhove (1989: 60) write that "dans les dialects qui possèdent des formes verbales différenciées en genre au pluriel, l'accord se fait automatiquement: si le sujet est féminin pluriel, le verbe est au féminin pluriel, ni la place du sujet par rapport au verbe, ni la nature du sujet (animé ou inanimé) n'interviennent". This is an oversimplified account of how agreement actually works in these dialects (whose agreement patterns will be the object of sections from 2.3.2 to 2.3.4), and the idea that agreement is "automatic" is problematic for several reasons. First of all, we have seen that the position of the verb (preceding or following its subject) *does* have an impact on agreement choices. The rule is not a strict one, but a strong statistical tendency exists for pre-controller verbs to manifest singular agreement. Secondly, the nature of the subject *does* influence agreement, to an extent at least. Controllers denoting inanimate entities have a markedly higher statistical tendency to attract F.SG agreement. Here as well, we are not looking at a mandatory rule (such as the one that exists in MSA), but the trend is nonetheless clear, and is part of the larger set of phenomena rubricated under the label "individuation" (more on this topic below).

Most importantly, the statement "feminine plural subjects attract feminine plural agreement" is a mere tautology. Such statements offer no help in disentangling the complex puzzle of Arabic agreement, in that they eschew the most basic questions. How we decide what a "feminine plural subject" is? On the basis of its morphological form, the biological sex of its referent in the real world, or on the basis of the agreement it triggers? If we opt for one of the first two options, then we are met with the problem that—as already said—many controllers that trigger M.SG agreement in the singular often trigger F.PL agreement in the plural. These controllers can refer to inanimate and animate (but nonhuman) beings, and, in the case of the latter, these can be biologically *masculine* animates. In addition, none of these controllers is explicitly marked for feminine, so that they defy both the morphological and the "biological sex" criteria (they are not morphologically feminine, they are not biologically feminine, and yet they trigger feminine agreement in the plural).

If we opt for the latter option, then our reasoning becomes entirely circular. A noun triggers feminine agreement if it is feminine, and it is feminine if it triggers feminine agreement. Such a definition is evidently unacceptable. Furthermore, besides representing a logical loop, it still cannot account for those controllers that trigger M.SG agreement when singular but F.PL when plural. What gender class do they belong to? This question has already been raised when commenting on Versteegh's definition of "complete agreement" (see § 1.1 above), and will be tackled in detail in § 2.3.

The last decade of the 20th century represented a turning point in the study of agreement in Arabic. In 1991, Kirk Belnap defended his (yet unpublished) doctoral dissertation at the University of Pennsylvania. This work was titled *Grammatical Agreement Variation in Cairene Arabic*, and its content were later summarized in the short article Belnap (1993). Although the figures presented in the latter work appear to have been updated a little, the treatment of the subject is necessarily not as detailed as in the original (due to space constraints), so that we will here refer to the former only.

Belnap (1991) was the first study ever published on Arabic agreement to include statistical data. Completed only two years after the publication of Ferguson's 1989 article, Belnap's dissertation relied heavily on the terminology and methodology introduced in the former.[29] It remains, to this day, one of the most thorough analyses ever produced of agreement patterns in an Arabic dialect, and its sound methodological approach has been later adopted, with varying degrees of accuracy, in a number of other studies. Belnap worked on a remarkably large corpus of data, drawn from oral interviews with native speakers of Cairene Arabic conducted by other native speakers. His dataset, in its final version, included 873 agreement targets depending on 520 controllers. A number of potential variables were examined that Belnap deemed likely to affect agreement behavior. These included the morphological status of the controller, its semantics (i.e. its referring to a human, animate nonhuman or inanimate entity), its being quantified or not, abstract or concrete, and specific or generic. Factors related to the target were examined as well: distance between target

29 Which is not surprising, if one considers that Belnap was one of Ferguson's students. As a matter of fact, one could read certain passages of Ferguson's work as programmatical statements of what Belnap's thesis was later to become. Consider for instance Ferguson (1989: 11): "Unfortunately, no thoroughgoing investigation of actual preferences [in agreement variation] over large bodies of text has been carried out, an exercise whose results could be presented, for example, as a variable rule with quantified conditioning factors".

and controller (in terms of intervening words), relative position of target and controller (i.e. CT vs TC), and target type (i.e. verb, adjective or pronoun).

The results emerging from Belnap's analysis will be more thoroughly discussed in sections 2.3.5 and 2.3.6. At present, it is important to focus on one of the aforementioned categories, namely specificity. As already said, Belnap's work heavily influenced subsequent studies about agreement, most prominently Brustad 2000.

In her comparative study *The Syntax of Spoken Arabic*, Brustad devotes a long chapter to agreement and the factors influencing it. Her list strongly resembles that of Belnap, with minor modifications. Brustad saw most of these factors as part of an overarching macro-category she called *individuation*. Though Brustad was the first to explicitly use the term individuation with reference to agreement in Arabic, this idea was clearly foreshadowed in Belnap's work.[30]

Both Belnap and Brustad agreed on the idea that speakers can use agreement pragmatically to signal their perception of the referent. Belnap (1991: 74), in particular, remarked that "for languages whose inflectional morphology marks a singular/plural distinction, agreement may function to further indicate the classification or perception of referents as a group or collection, or as individuated entities". This opposition of grouped vs individuated is indeed very similar to the enumerative vs non-enumerative one proposed by Blanc and later adopted by Ferguson.[31] Since individuation will be a key concept in the remaining chapters of this book, it is worth briefly expanding on it here.

The term individuation (or salience) has been in use for quite some time among typologists,[32] in an attempt to explain a variety of phenomena. Comrie (1989: 199), in particular, while discussing animacy as a conceptual category that interacts importantly with language structure, focuses on the relation between animacy and salience/individuation:

30 Belnap uses the adjective "individuated" at least twice in his dissertation (see Belnap 1991: 74, 76).

31 As a matter of fact, this opposition goes back as far as 1964, when Cowell first proposed it in his grammar of Damascus Arabic. This one quote from Cowell has been so influential as to appear in all the works of Blanc, Ferguson, Belnap and Brustad discussed so far, and in Hanitsch's paper discussed below. It is only fair to credit Cowell for at least part of this insight. The quote goes as follows: "Most inanimate plurals, and some animate plurals and collectives, have feminine agreement in the predicate when collectivity or generality is emphasized, rather than heterogeneity or particularity" (Cowell 1964: 423).

32 The same is true of the concept of "specificity". Hoyt (2000: 116) provides a good synthesis of the use that has been done of this term by linguists, along with a list of references on the topic.

> Salience relates to the way in which certain actants present in a situation are seized on by humans as foci of attention, only subsequently attention being paid to less salient, less individuated objects […]. Salience is not treated as a primitive in itself, but rather as the result of the interaction of a number of factors, such as animacy in the strict sense, definiteness, singularity, concreteness, assignability of a proper name.

The first to apply the concept to the field of Semitic linguistics was Khan (1984: 469–470), which has been later extensively cited by Brustad. In addition to the factors we have already seen listed by Comrie, he remarks how nominals which refer to specific entities are more individuated than generic nominals referring to a whole class of entities, and also how the perceptual salience of a referent affects its level of individuation (several factors may be responsible for perceptual saliency: animacy, or the quality of being more "ego-like"—that is, human-like—is one of those factors. Another is textual salience, i.e. whether or not the referent has a prominent role within the text).

As can be seen, individuation appears to be a somewhat loose umbrella term, referring to a series of interrelated and interdependent factors. As Comrie himself remarked, "the overall pattern is of a complex intertwining rather than of a single, linear hierarchy". Individuation, in other words, has to be thought of as a complex, recursive phenomenon, rather than a linear one.[33] What matters to our present discussion, at any rate, is that individuation has proven effective in explaining agreement behavior in several studies on Arabic dialects.

To conclude, there is no doubt that Belnap's and Brustad's works have been fundamental in paving the way for all the following literature on the topic of agreement in Arabic. In particular, Brustad's book aimed at comparing the realization of a number of syntactic structures in four different dialects of Arabic (Urban Moroccan, Cairene, Damascene and Kuwaiti). In this respect, her study has been groundbreaking and, as of today, unparalleled. It has to be noted, however, that both Belnap and Brustad adopted the terms "strict" and "deflected" coined by Ferguson. Although this posed no particular problem to their analysis (both their studies being focused on dialects with no gender differentiation in the plural), this further reinforced the perception that variation in number, rather than gender, was the main relevant feature to be investigated in studies on agreement in Arabic.

---

33 To make but an obvious example, both animacy and concreteness are often cited as factors influencing individuation levels. However, abstract controllers are, by definition, also inanimate (while the opposite is not true). In other words, it is not possible to analyze the effects that concreteness has on agreement behavior without implicitly also taking animacy into account.

A scholar who did not employ Ferguson's terminology is Melanie Hanitsch. In her work on agreement variation in Damascus Arabic, Hanitsch (2011) recognizes the fact that in CA agreement with nonhuman plural controllers could vary between F.SG and plural, just as it does in the dialects today (though the question of the gender of said plural is only addressed to a limited extent). Hanitsch as well reaches conclusions similar to those of the authors who preceded her, although developing her own original terminology and list of factors influencing agreement. Taking into account nonhuman controllers only, Hanitsch maintains that the main division between them is that between abstract and concrete nouns. While the former almost systematically attract F.SG agreement, in the case of the latter agreement behavior is largely dependent on three subfactors, namely their being mobile, tridimensional and solid objects ("[+ mobil], [+ dreidimensional], [+ Festkörper]", Hanitsch 2011: 142). Controllers characterized by these three qualities are referred to as "prototypical concrete controllers"; those that are not, conversely, are referred to as "non-prototypical", and, according to Hanitsch, almost systematically attract F.SG agreement (in other words, agreement variation is a phenomenon mostly restricted to prototypical concrete nouns, and thus a largely semantic-based).

Hanitsch also recognizes the importance of other factors, namely specificity and quantification (this is in agreement with Belnap 1991). Quantification, in particular, seems to have a remarkably strong influence on individuation levels, since it is only quantified non-prototypical concrete controllers that can trigger sound plural agreement (non-quantified ones, on the other hand, can only trigger *apophonic* plural agreement).[34]

Starting with Hanitsch, the second decade of the 21st century has seen a sudden renewal of interest in the topic of agreement in spoken Arabic. In 2013, an article by Herin and Al-Wer was published that dealt, among other issues, with agreement in the Jordanian dialect of Salt. Twenty-six years after the publication of Owen's and Bani-Yasin's paper, a second study appeared that focused on a gender-distinguishing dialect. Herin and Al-Wer (2013) come to conclusions similar to those of Owens and Bani-Yasin, with the difference that they suggest the dialect of the capital Amman (instead of Standard Arabic) as the source of the "innovative" rule which associates items scoring low on the individuation scale with F.SG agreement. In other words, Herin and Al-Wer maintain, in the same way as Owens and Bani-Yasin did, that F.PL agreement with nonhuman plural controllers is the "original" dialectal rule. The association of

34 Hanitsch 2011: 146. On the semantic values associated with suffixal (or sound) and apophonic (or broken) plurals, see § 2.3.4.1.

non-individuated plural nouns with F.SG agreement is an innovation caused by contact with prestigious urban varieties in which this pattern is attested. Herin's and Al-Wer's hypothesis will be discussed in more depth in § 2.3.2 and § 5.1.

Shortly after Herin's and Al Wer's study, another article was to appear that focused on a variety that distinguishes gender in the plural: Ritt-Benmimoun's paper on agreement patterns in the Bedouin dialects of the Nifzāwa region, in southern Tunisia. This article has the great merit of being the first to apply the methodologies developed by Belnap and Brustad to such a dialect[35] (though it does not provide statistical data). The results presented by Ritt-Benmimoun (2017) clearly show that 1) it is only masculine human plural controllers that trigger M.PL agreement, otherwise 2) all other types of plural controllers (human feminine, animal and inanimate) attract F.PL agreement; however, 3) controllers of both type (1) and (2) can trigger F.SG agreement if they score low on the individuation scale. This last point can hardly be considered an innovation caused by contact with a neighboring urban variety, since in the local prestigious variety, the dialect of Tunis, F.SG agreement with plural human controllers appears to be rarer.[36] This is demonstrated in Procházka and Gabsi 2017, a paper that appears in the same volume as Ritt-Benmimoun's, and intended as complementary to it, focused on the urban varieties of northern Tunisia instead of those of the rural south.

Besides the two works on agreement in Tunisian Arabic just mentioned, another important piece of research dealing with agreement appeared in the same year. Although at the beginning of this chapter we have pointed out that individual grammars of specific dialects will be commented upon in chapter 2, it would be unfair not to mention in our survey Holes' grammar of Bahraini. In the book, almost 30 pages are devoted to a detailed description of agreement patterns in this dialect, and the treatment is accompanied by a wealth of examples.

In general, the three works just mentioned all adapt Belnap's and Brustad's theories to different case studies, and in each case they provide further evidence to support them. They also employ the deflected vs strict terminology

35 These works were not mentioned in Herin and al-Wer (2013). However, reference to Brustad's work can be found in Herin's dissertation on the dialect of Salt (see Herin 2010: 289).

36 Though the influence of Tunis Arabic in the southern dialects investigated by Ritt-Benmimoun is manifest in another agreement-related phenomenon, i.e. the increasingly common substitution of F.PL forms with the corresponding masculine ones. Far from being restricted to Bedouin Tunisian varieties, this process of morphological erosion has been reported for virtually all gender-distinguishing dialects. We will return on this topic in Chapter 5.

introduced by Ferguson and discussed above. We will analyze the data presented in these studies in more detail in § 2.3.

What has just been said about Holes', Ritt-Benmimoun's and Procházka's and Gabsi's works also holds true for a number of articles recently published by the authors of the present book, all dealing with different varieties of Arabic (all of them with gender distinction in the plural). These are D'Anna (2017) on Libyan Fezzani Arabic, Bettega (2017) and (2019b) on Omani Arabic, and Bettega and Leitner (2019) on Khuzestani Arabic.[37] These will be dealt with in § 2.3 as well.

Finally, Bettega (2019a), moving from an analysis of agreement patterns in Najdi Arabic, proposes a radical re-discussion of the nature of gender in Arabic. Sections 2.3.3 and 2.3.4 of this book represent an expanded and more detailed version of that paper and, because of this, it will not be discussed here.[38]

37 Note that in Bettega and Leitner (2019) Ferguson's labels "strict" and "deflected" are finally abandoned.

38 The survey we have presented in this section does not include studies that adopt a generative theoretical framework. As already said (§ 1.2), generative studies on agreement in Arabic are mostly focused on the effects of word order on verb-subject agreement, which represents only a tiny portion of all the agreement contexts and phenomena we will analyze in this book. Some of these studies are based on extremely limited data sets, and focus on an extremely narrow set of structures (basically a single sentence in the case of Hallman 2000). Others are focused on very specific theoretical problems within generativism, and therefore of limited interest for us here (e.g. Mohammad 2000). Contrary to these trends, Hoyt (2002) includes a wealth of original examples at least partially derived from spontaneous speech, and an insightful discussion of many of them. This work will be more thoroughly discussed in Chapter 2.

CHAPTER 2

Describing the Systems

Let us briefly consider this quote by Gensler (2011: 291–292) about gender in Semitic:

> Gender is defined in terms of agreement patterns, and this does not present any difficulty in Semitic. There are two genders, masculine and feminine. Generally a noun's gender is reflected formally on modifiers and on the verb: a masculine noun will take masculine modifiers, will be referred to with a masculine pronoun, and will trigger masculine gender on the verb of which it is the subject, and thus also for feminine. The form of the noun itself is not a reliable guide to its gender.

The first part of this statement ("gender is defined in terms of agreement patterns") poses no problem at all. In fact, this is the position that we will adopt in § 2.1, where we discuss the definitions given by modern linguistic theory of the categories of gender and agreement.

From this first consideration stems a second, namely that, in Gensler's own words, "the form of the noun itself is not a reliable guide to its gender". This is another fundamental remark, and one whose importance will be stressed several times in the course of this chapter.

The remaining parts of the passage reported above are more problematic. While Gensler's considerations may adequately describe the situation of the other Semitic languages, we contend that things are not so straightforward in the case of Arabic.

Our considerations, in particular, arise from the fact that—as we have seen in the first chapter of the book—semantically and/or formally masculine plural nouns often take F.PL agreement in those varieties of Arabic that possess gender distinction in the plural (this also includes written pre- and early-Islamic Arabic). This phenomenon (that is confined to the semantic field of nonhuman referents, animate or inanimate) poses a problem for the description of Arabic as a language with a simple binary gender system. In a way, we are confronted here with the same problem we faced in the previous chapter when discussing the claim by Caubet, Simeone-Senelle, Vanhove (1989) that agreement in the dialects is "automatic" (i.e. feminine subjects automatically attract feminine agreement, see § 1.3).

Words whose gender varies depending on the number they stand in exist in several languages of the world, but are normally very rare, and should be

 | DOI:10.1163/9789004527249_003

considered as exceptional lexical items. In certain contexts, they are analyzed together as members of an "inquorate" gender, that is, a gender-like subgroup of nouns that only contains a handful of elements (see Corbett 1991: 170–175 for some examples and a discussion). As we will argue in the rest of this chapter (see in particular § 2.3.4), this is not the case with Arabic, where these nouns number in the thousands and are to be regarded as a separate agreement class.

As anticipated, in § 2.1 we will discuss how linguistic facts such as gender and agreement are conceptualized by modern linguistics, while in § 2.2, we will present a list of all the morphological options that the different varieties of Arabic have at their disposal for the expression of gender and number.

§ 2.3 is concerned with agreement in the contemporary spoken dialects of Arabic. § 2.3.1, in particular, will deal with the topic of singular agreement, while all the following subsections will be devoted to the analysis of agreement with plural controllers, first in gender-distinguishing varieties of Arabic (§ 2.3.2–§ 2.3.4) and then in non-distinguishing ones (§ 2.3.5–§ 2.3.7). In § 2.3.8 we will analyze the small and heterogeneous group of dialects that cannot be classified according to the distinguishing/non-distinguishing opposition. § 2.3.9, finally, will be dedicated to an important agreement condition that is operative in all dialectal types: precedence.

After concluding our survey of agreement in spoken varieties of Arabic, we will focus on the written ones. § 2.4 deals with the forms of Arabic that appear in the oldest (non-epigraphic) written documents that have been passed down to us: the pre-Islamic poetic corpus and the Quran. § 2.5, conversely, will describe agreement pattern in the formalized and standardized versions of the language that began to appear after the Islamic conquests: Classical Arabic and Modern Standard Arabic.

2.1 Agreement from a Typological Perspective

One of the world's foremost linguists once wrote, perhaps ironically, that agreement represents "information in the wrong place" (Corbett 2006: 2). This consideration was inspired by Moravcsik's definition of agreement as "displaced" grammatical meaning (Moravcsik 1988: 90).

Many linguists have indeed struggled with the task of finding an adequate definition for the complex phenomenon of agreement. The two quotes reported above, however, already tell us two important things about agreement, namely that 1) agreement has to do with information and 2) agreement constitutes an asymmetrical relationship. In other words, there is a certain amount of information, that stems from an element X, that is (also) present on another element Y.[1] If we were to change the nature of X, then the information shown on Y would change as well. Crucially, *the opposite is not true*. Agreement is a matter of systematic covariance (Steele 1978: 610), but this covariance is asymmetrical.

In this book, we follow the current linguistic practice of referring to element X (which is normally a noun) as the *controller*, and to element Y as the *target*. The information that is found on the target, but whose source is actually the controller, can be of many types. It can refer to number, gender, person, and other categories as well. These are what we will call *agreement features*. The present volume is specifically concerned with the two features of number and gender.

Gender, in particular, plays a special role when it comes to agreement, so we will briefly expand on the topic here. The difference between gender and other features such as number or definiteness is that gender is inherent to the noun, while number and definiteness are not. Nouns are, in the vast majority of cases, assigned to a single value of the gender feature, while they have access to several values of the number feature (in the case of Arabic, for instance, to the three values singular, dual and plural). This characteristic of gender has sometimes been labelled "unique value accessibility". We will return on the topic in § 2.3.5.

Gender represents, so to speak, a function of agreement. In other words, linguistic gender can only exist in languages that show agreement (see Corbett 1991: 146). This is a point worth stressing: contrary to what common sense might suggest, linguistic gender is not necessarily connected to the biological sex of real-world referents, and it is not necessarily connected to the morphological forms of the nouns. It *can* be connected to these aspects, but not necessarily so. In many languages (like Arabic) it is, but several exceptions exist. In particular, if the gender of a noun can be predicted on the basis of its morphological properties, then we say that gender is *overt*. In the opposite case, we speak of *covert* gender. We will discuss the degree of overtness of gender in Arabic in the following sections. It is also important to remark that linguistic gender is often assigned to inanimate entities that possess no inherent biological gender. If,

1 Note that the information may or may not be overtly marked on element X (see Audring, 2014: 6: "gender appears overwhelmingly elsewhere—in fact, many languages do not mark it on the noun at all"). This is of relative importance. What is important is that all the relevant information about X can be retrieved by examining the agreeing Ys. It is possible that some exceptional Y exists which also shows no overt marking: this is the case, for instance, of a number of adjectives in several varieties of Arabic, that tend not to inflect for gender and number. These will be discussed in § 2.3.1. In general, however, the majority of Ys will show agreement. If no Y exists that is able to display agreement, then the language in question does not possess an agreement system.

then, linguistic gender is not (only) an expression of the sex of real-world referents, and if it is not (only) dependent on nominal morphology, how do we define it?

Linguistic gender is fundamentally a classificatory system. Nouns are grouped into different classes, and these classes are distinguished by their agreement properties. So, for instance, we see that nouns that belong to class A behave in certain way, while those that belong to class B behave in a different way, and those belonging to class C in yet another. Theoretically there is no limit to the number of agreement classes that can exist in a language, but in practice the number of languages with five or more genders is very limited, and the crosslinguistically most common system only features two separate classes (see Corbett 2013a for an overview).

To the external observer, the assignment of nouns to the different agreement classes may appear arbitrary. To an extent, it often is. It is important to note, however, that this does not prevent us from securely identify these classes. One might wonder, for instance, why is it that the Italian words *ragazza/-e* 'girl/-s', *sedia/-e* 'chair/-s' and *lepre/-i* 'hare/-s' all belong to the same agreement class. The first refers to a biologically feminine human referent, the second to an inanimate one, and the third to an animate but nonhuman referent whose morphological form, however, does not vary depending on the sex of the animal (i.e. the word *lepre* is used to refer to both a male and a female hare).[2] From a semantic point of view, then, this collection of nouns is remarkably heterogeneous. At the morphological level, also, there is no uniformity: the singular of the first two nouns ends with an *-a* suffix, replaced by *-e* in the plural. The third, on the contrary, opposes a singular in *-e* to a plural in *-i*. Despite all these differences, the three nouns can be securely identified as members of the same agreement class (conventionally labeled "feminine" in grammars of Standard Italian) by observing their agreement behavior. All articles, pronouns and regular adjectives referred to these nouns will assume the same form, thus allowing us to infer their linguistic gender.

It is then possible to further investigate *why* this happens, what processes have shaped the gender system of Standard Italian precisely in this way, and whether or not this underlies some cognitive or logical universal. While these are all fascinating questions worth exploring, they do not alter the synchronic description that we make of the system.

---

2 In Standard Italian, in other words, a mismatch exists between *genders* and *inflectional classes* (to adopt the terminology employed by—among others—Loporcaro 2015). In this book our focus on the morphological properties of the controllers (nouns) themselves will be limited, so that we will not make use of the latter term. For more insights on this topic, the reader is refererred to Loporcaro's study.

Note that, until this moment, we have used the two labels "(linguistic) gender" and "agreement class" somewhat interchangeably. To an extent, this use is justifiable. However, in certain contexts they need to be kept distinct. Corbett (1991: 147), in particular, provides a set of rules to determine the number of agreement classes that a language possess. We say that two or more nouns belong to the same agreement class if, whenever they stand in the same morphosyntactic form (e.g. accusative singular, plural, and so on), occur in the same domain, and have the same lexical item as a target, then their targets have the same morphological realization. Crosslinguistically, it is not always the case that the number of genders in a given language corresponds to that of its agreement classes. In the following sections, where relevant, we will point the reader's attention to the importance of this distinction (see in particular § 2.3.4).[3]

One last definition that we need is that of *agreement condition*. A condition is a factor that has an effect on agreement but is not directly reflected by it, in the same way as features are. Corbett (2006: 176) notes that "conditions can have an absolute effect, making one agreement outcome obligatory or impossible. Frequently, however, they are relative, just favouring a particular outcome, and so conditions are often linked to agreement choices". As we will see, while in spoken varieties of Arabic it is possible to find a number of relative agreement conditions, absolute ones are a prerogative of the written language.

Conditions can sometimes interact with one another, potentially giving rise to complex agreement phenomena that pose significant descriptive challenges. Conditions are also non-canonical with respect to agreement, "in that it is more canonical to have no conditions. They often apply to non-canonical situations" Corbett (2006: 183). One fundamental agreement condition in Arabic, whose importance has already been partially discussed in § 1.1, is word order. We will return on the topic in more detail in § 2.3.9.[4]

We will now move forward to analyze the various means that the Arabic languages have at their disposal to mark gender and number. The readers interested in a more extensive treatment of agreement from the point of view of modern linguistic theory are referred to Moravcsik (1978), Corbett (2006) and Aikhenvald (2016).

3 Yet another definition is "noun class". Linguists have often distinguished between languages with genders and languages with noun classes. Corbett (1991: 146) has argued against the necessity of such a distinction. We will not make use of this label in this book.

4 For a discussion of agreement *domains*, see the appropriate subsection in § 2.3.3.4. Note that we follow Corbett (2006: 21–22) in treating antecedent-anaphor relations as normal instances of agreement. In other words, our analysis here is not restricted to local domains, and anaphoric pronouns will be treated together with all other target types.

2.2 Morphological Markers of Gender and Number in Arabic

In the previous section, we have seen how gender can fundamentally be described as a syntactical system for the classification of nouns. The building blocks of such a system, however, are morphological in nature: through the combination of these morphological markers agreement classes are created.

In some languages, markers of gender and number are kept distinct. In fusional languages such as Arabic, a single morpheme tends to be used to express both gender *and* number, so that the two features interact in important ways.

Obviously, it is not possible to describe a language's agreement system without a solid knowledge of its morphological inventory. Therefore, we will now analyze the morphological means available to users of several varieties of Arabic to express the aforementioned features.

2.2.1 *Written Arabic*

We will start by looking at written Arabic. Although we have repeatedly noted that remarkable differences exist between the earliest Arabic documents and contemporary MSA in terms of agreement behavior, this distinction only exists at the syntactical level. From the point of view of morphological categories, all varieties of written Arabic are identical,[5] and can therefore be analyzed together.

All varieties of Arabic possess two finite forms of the verb (commonly referred to as "suffix stem" and "prefix stem"[6]) and two sets of pronouns (free and bound). Their fully inflected paradigms are given in Tables 2.1 and 2.2:

5 With the obvious exception of Middle Arabic texts. We are also not concerned here with pre-Islamic epigraphic materials. As an anonymous reviewer pointed out, more allomorphs existed in Classical and pre-Classical Arabic texts than the ones we list in the following tables (especially in the realm of pronouns, Table 2.2, and demonstratives, Tables 2.6 and 2.7). Since it is mostly the number of morphological categories we are interested in, rather than the morphemes actually used to expressed them, we have decided—for the sake of brevity—not to provide an exhaustive list of each and every one of these morphemes.

6 The forms of the prefix stem are given in the indicative mood (*al-marfūʕ* المرفوع) in the following tables. The labels "suffix" and "prefix" stems are preferable to the traditional "perfective" and "imperfective" ones because of the ongoing debate on the nature of the Arabic finite verbs as encoding primarily aspect or time referece (on the topic, see among others Eisele, 2006 and Horesh, 2009). The suffix and prefix stems have been glossed as PFV and IPFV respectively in this book, according to what is common practice in studies of Arabic linguistics, without this implying our supporting one or the other theoretical position.

TABLE 2.1 S-stem and P-stem in written Arabic (*kataba* 'to write')

	Suffix stem		Prefix stem	
1 SG	*katab-**tu***	كتبتُ	*ʔa-ktubu*	أكتب
2 M.SG	*katab-**ta***	كتبتَ	***ta**-ktubu*	تكتب
2 F.SG	*katab-**ti***	كتبتِ	***ta**-ktub-**īna***	تكتبين
3 M.SG	*katab-**a***	كتبَ	*ya-ktubu*	يكتب
3 F.SG	*katab-**at***	كتبتْ	***ta**-ktubu*	تكتب
2 DUAL	*katab-**tumā***	كتبتما	***ta**-ktub-**āni***	تكتبان
3 M.DUAL	*katab-**ā***	كتبا	*ya-ktub-**āni***	يكتبان
3 F.DUAL	*katab-**atā***	كتبتا	***ta**-ktub-**āni***	تكتبان
1 PL	*katab-**nā***	كتبْنا	***na**-ktubu*	نكتب
2 M.PL	*katab-**tum***	كتبتم	***ta**-ktub-**ūna***	تكتبون
2 F.PL	*katab-**tunna***	كتبتنّ	***ta**-ktub-**na***	تكتبن
3 M.PL	*katab-**ū***	كتبوا	*ya-ktub-**ūna***	يكتبون
3 F.PL	*katab-**na***	كتبن	*ya-ktub-**na***	يكتبن

TABLE 2.2 Free and bound pronouns in written Arabic

	Free pronouns		Bound pronouns	
1 SG	*ʔana*	أنا	*-ī / -ya/ -nī*	ـي / ـني
2 M.SG	*ʔanta*	أنتَ	*-ka*	ـكَ
2 F.SG	*ʔanti*	أنتِ	*-ki*	ـكِ
3 M.SG	*huwa*	هو	*-hu*	ـه
3 F.SG	*hiya*	هي	*-hā*	ـها
2 DUAL	*antumā*	أنتما	*-kumā*	ـكما
3 DUAL	*humā*	هما	*-humā*	ـهما
1 PL	*naḥnu*	نحن	*-nā*	ـنا
2 M.PL	*ʔantum*	أنتم	*-kum*	ـكم
2 F.PL	*ʔantunna*	أنتنّ	*-kunna*	ـكنّ
3 M.PL	*hum*	هم	*-hum*	ـهم
3 F.PL	*hunna*	هنّ	*-hunna*	ـهنّ

TABLE 2.3 The inflection of nominals in written Arabic[a]

M.SG	*muslim-un*	مسلم
F.SG	*muslim-a(t)-un*	مسلمة
M.DUAL	*muslim-āni*	مسلمان
F.DUAL	*muslim-at-āni*	مسلمتان
M.PL	*muslim-ūna*	مسلمون
F.PL	*muslim-āt-un*	مسلمات

a Only the nominative forms of the dual and masculine plural are shown in the table. Two more F.SG suffixes exist in the language, namely *-ā* and *-āʔ*: since these are only adopted by a closed set of nominal elements, they are not listed in the table.

As can be seen, written Arabic distinguishes three numbers, namely singular, dual and plural. It also possess two morphological genders, conventionally labelled masculine and feminine, that are kept distinct in all persons except for the first ones and the second (or second and third in the case of pronouns) person dual.[7]

The inflection of nominals (noun and adjectives) presents the same distinctions as verbs in terms of gender and number, so that a total of six combinations are possible, as shown in Table 2.3. There is no difference between the inflection of nouns and that of adjectives, so that the example word given here (*muslim*) can fulfil both roles, depending on context. Note that the masculine singular is unmarked.

This apparently straightforward system is complicated by the presence of another type of nominal pluralization, namely the apophonic alteration of the vocalic structure of the singular. The tradition of Semitic studies has normally referred to these two pluralization strategies as "sound" or "external" (i.e. suffixal) vs "broken" or "internal" (i.e. apophonic). While most nouns can only form the plural through one of these strategies, a limited number of lexical items exist that possess both a sound and a broken plural. Apophonic plurals are not always formed following the same pattern: on the contrary, several different plural "templates" exist. Since the formal differences between the various

7 Note the syncretism between the 2nd M.SG and 3rd F.SG persons and between the 2nd DUAL and 3rd DUAL.F persons, all in the prefix stem. Note also the two forms of the 1st person singular suffix pronoun in Table 2.2: the latter is used when the pronoun appears as the object of a transitive verb (as well as in a limited number of other contexts), the former when it is used in a possessive construction and with most prepositions.

TABLE 2.4 Apophonic Plural patterns in written Arabic

Singular		Plural		Translation
كِتَابٌ	*kitab-un*	كُتُبٌ	*kutub-un*	Book(s)
كَلْبٌ	*kalb-un*	كِلَابٌ	*kilāb-un*	Dog(s)
سِرٌّ	*sirr-un*	أَسْرَارٌ	*ʔasrār-un*	Secret(s)
رَأْسٌ	*raʔs-un*	رُؤُوسٌ	*ruʔūs-un*	Head(s)

types of broken plural are of limited interest for us here, we will not provide an exhaustive list of all possible patterns.[8] A limited number of examples are presented in Table 2.4. The interested reader is referred to Ratcliffe 1998.

One of the most striking features of apophonic plurals is that they are not overtly marked for gender. Theoretically, the gender of the plural form could be derived from its singular; however, as we will see in § 2.3.4, the gender of a noun in the singular is only partially relevant to determine the gender of its broken plural.[9] In the case of adjectives, the question becomes even more complicated,

8 As will be discussed in more detail in Chapter 4, the ancient grammarians maintained that certain types of broken plural patterns were associated to specific semantic nuances, mainly related to the conceptual fields of quantification and paucity/abundance. It is possible that this had an effect on the syntactic behavior of such plurals, in terms of agreement patterns. Unfortunately, to verify this hypothesis by using statistical tools, a much larger corpus of data would be needed than those currently at our disposal. On this topic see also Ferrando (2006).

9 More precisely, if a noun that takes masculine agreement in the singular has a broken plural, then this plural can take either M.PL or F.PL agreement. This cannot be predicted on the basis of morphology alone, but has to do with the semantics of the noun. On the contrary, the broken plural of a noun which takes feminine agreement in the singular will take F.PL agreement. These considerations, obviously, are only valid in the case of gender-distinguishing varieties of Arabic (and they do not hold in the case of MSA, which has developed a different system of agreement, see § 2.5). In the case of non-distinguishing ones, the question of the gender of broken plurals is irrelevant. Owens (1993: 28) points out that some broken plurals can be said to be implicitly masculine, because they contrast with a sound feminine plural. Owens notes this for Nigerian Arabic, but this consideration is valid for almost all gender-distinguishing varieties of Arabic, including all forms of written Arabic. As an example, consider the word عم (*ʕamm*) 'paternal uncle', and its feminine counterpart, عمة (*ʕamma*) 'paternal aunt'. The respective plurals are عموم or أعمام (*ʕumūm* or *ʔaʕmām*, both broken and implicitly masculine) and عمات (*ʕammāt*, sound feminine).

since adjectives have no inherent gender but derive it from the noun they are attributed to or predicated of.

If, thus, we are confronted with a plural controller whose only target is a broken adjective, we have no instruments at our disposal to determine the agreement class to which that controller belongs.[10] Obviously, any accompanying verb or pronoun depending on that same controller will solve the problem immediately. However, the fact that some adjectival targets in Arabic can, because of their morphological nature, agree in *number* but not in *gender*, probably contributed to reinforce the tendency of many scholars (already discussed in §1.1 and §1.3) to focus on the study of number rather than gender agreement.

The question of what number apophonic plurals express may seem more straightforward: a plural is, by definition, plural in number. And yet, the concept of plurality can have different nuances of meaning. Several scholars have noted how broken plurals tend to be semantically distinct from their suffixal counterparts. Wright (1896b, 1:233), for instance, noted how sound plurals "denote several *distinct* individuals of a genus", while broken ones "a number of individuals viewed *collectively*".[11] Sallam (1979: 24), although writing about agreement in Educated Spoken Arabic, expresses similar views. He reports that some collective nouns have two different forms of plural: for instance, from *ward* 'roses' and *baṣal* 'onions' both a suffixal plural (*wardāt*/*baṣalāt*) and an apophonic plural (*wurūd*/*ʔabṣāl*) can be derived. The first plural type Sallam calls "little plural" or "paucal", and notes how it "occurs most commonly in association with a numeral form from 3 to 10." The second one he calls "big plural", and translates the examples provided as '(kinds of) roses' and '(kinds of) onions'.

The problem of how to semantically categorize apophonic plurals (especially in the case of the analysis of large corpora of data) will be more thoroughly discussed in §2.3.4.1. On apophonic plurals, see also §1.2 and §3.1.

Finally, gender and number are also marked on relative pronouns and demonstratives in written Arabic. These are shown in Tables 2.5 and 2.6 respectively:

10 More precisely, as we will see in §2.3.4, if the noun in question is overtly marked by a masculine plural suffix, then it belongs to what we refer to as agreement class I. Conversely, we have no means to determine its agreement properties.

11 See also Brustad (2008: 3), who speaks of this as a "general principle" in Arabic: "plurals formed by suffixation tend to be marked for individuation".

TABLE 2.5 Relative pronouns in written Arabic

M.SG	*allaḏī*	الذي
F.SG	*allatī*	التي
M.DUAL	*allaḏāni*	اللذان
F.DUAL	*allatāni*	اللتان
M.PL	*allaḏīna*	الذين
F.PL	*allawātī*[a]	اللواتي

a The variants اللاتي (*allātī*) and اللائي (*allāʔī*) exist for the F.PL pronoun.

TABLE 2.6 Demonstratives in written Arabic[a]

	Proximal		**Distal**	
M.SG	*hāḏā*	هذا	*ḏālika*	ذلك
F.SG	*hāḏihi*	هذه	*tilka*	تلك
M.DUAL	*hāḏāni*	هذان	*ḏānika*	ذانك
F.DUAL	*hātāni*	هتان	*tānika*	تانك
PL	*hāʔulāʔi*	هؤلاء	*ʔūlāʔika*	أولئك

a Only the nominative form of the dual demonstratives is given here. Variant forms exist for some of these elements.

TABLE 2.7 The inflection of *ḏū*

M.SG	*ḏū*	ذو
F.SG	*ḏāt*	ذات
M.DUAL	*ḏawā*	ذوا
F.DUAL	*ḏātā*	ذاتا
M.PL	*ḏawū*	ذوو
F.PL	*ḏawāt*	ذوات

Note that demonstratives, unlike all other elements seen so far, do not distinguish gender in the plural. An ancient element *ḏū* however exists, clearly related to demonstratives, which shows gender distinction (see Table 2.7). In CA/MSA it is used to express possession of a quality or thing, and normally translates as 'the one with/of'.

2.2.2 *Gender-Distinguishing Varieties of Spoken Arabic*

When it comes to spoken Arabic, the description of the morphological markers used to express gender and number becomes more complicated, because of the high degree of variation that exists among the dialects.

We will, therefore, divide the spoken dialects into two main subgroups, namely those that still retain gender distinction in the plural forms of the adjective, verb and pronouns, and those that do not.[12] Let us first consider the inflectional inventory of the former group.

In gender-distinguishing varieties of spoken Arabic, the verbal, pronominal and adjectival paradigms are similar to those of written Arabic already discussed (here as well, note the unmarked forms of the masculine singular, the syncretism between the 2nd person M.SG and the 3rd F.SG in the verbal paradigm, and the split form of the 1st person suffix pronoun). The main difference is that all dual forms are no longer present, so that—even if most dialects retain the possibility of inflecting a noun for dual number—dual agreement is no longer available in any spoken variety, and dual nouns normally attract plural agreement.

Tables 2.8, 2.9, 2.10 and 2.11 (adapted from Ingham 1994 and Ingham 2008) summarize the inflectional inventory of Najdi Arabic, a well-described dialect that belongs to the gender-distinguishing group. Najdi Arabic has here been chosen as representative of the whole group, but in general—though surface realizations may vary[13]—the vast majority of gender-distinguishing dialects present the same morphemic distribution. Dialects with an inventory that diverges from the one illustrated here will be discussed in § 2.2.4.

As was the case for written Arabic, many nominals in Najdi can function as both nouns and adjectives, depending on the context. Unlike their standard counterparts, however, their paradigms differ, since—as we have seen—it is only nouns (and not adjectives) that can take dual endings.

---

12 The question could be posed of which ones are the dialects that retain gender distinction in the plural, and where/by whom are they spoken (or, conversely, which ones are those that do *not* retain this distinction). Although providing an exhaustive list of every gender-distinguishing dialect of Arabic is probably impossible, we will discuss the topic in more depth in § 2.3.2.

13 For instance, in sedentary Omani dialects the 3M.PL marker in the suffix stem is *-u*, not *-ūn* (Holes 2008). In the Jordanian dialect of Salt the 2M.PL suffix pronoun is *-ku*, not *-kum*, and the 2F.PL one is *-čin*, not *-ćin* (Herin and Al-Wer 2013). In most gender-distinguishing dialects, the latter has the form *-kin* (see for instance Watson 2009 for Sanaa). In Sanaa the 2F.PL independent pronoun is *antayn*, not *antin*. The list could go on forever: such formal differences, however, are not relevant to the theses discussed in this book.

TABLE 2.8 S-stem and P-stem in Najdi Arabic (*kitab* 'to write')

	Suffix stem	**Prefix stem**
1 SG	*kitab*-***t***	***a***-*ktib*
2 M.SG	*kitab*-***ta***	***ta***-*ktib*
2 F.SG	*kitab*-***ti***	***ta***-*ktib*-***īn***
3 M.SG	*kitab*	***ya***-*ktib*
3 F.SG	*ktib*-***at***	***ta***-*ktib*
1 PL	*kitab*-***na***	***na***-*ktib*
2 M.PL	*kitab*-***tu***	***ta***-*ktib*-***ūn***
2 F.PL	*kitab*-***tin***	***ta***-*ktib*-***in***
3 M.PL	*ktib*-***aw***	***ya***-*ktib*-***ūn***
3 F.PL	*ktib*-***an***	***ya***-*ktib*-***in***

TABLE 2.9 Independent and bound pronouns in Najdi Arabic[a]

	Independent pronouns	**Bound pronouns**
1 SG	*ana*	*-i* / *-ni*
2 M.SG	*ant(a)*	*-ik*
2 F.SG	*anti*	*-ić*
3 M.SG	*hu*	*-ih*
3 F.SG	*hi*	*-ha*
1 PL	*ḥinna*	*-na*
2 M.PL	*antum*	*-kum*
2 F.PL	*antin*	*-ćin*
3 M.PL	*hum*	*-hum*
3 F.PL	*hin*	*-hin*

a Bound pronouns are given in their post-consonantic realization.

Note that, in Table 2.9, a lexical element has been selected that possesses a "sound" suffixal plural. As was the case with written Arabic, however, the majority of nouns (and several adjectives) in gender-distinguishing dialects can also form their plural by means of apophonic alteration. The same considerations made in § 2.2.1 are valid in this case.

An important difference between written Arabic and virtually all spoken dialects is that relative pronouns cannot be inflected for number or gender, i.e.

TABLE 2.10 The inflection of nominals in Najdi Arabic

M.SG	*muslim*
F.SG	*muslim-**ah*** (*-**at***)
M.DUAL (nouns only)	*muslim-**ēn***
F.DUAL (nouns only)	*muslim-**at-ēn***
M.PL	*muslim-**īn***
F.PL	*muslim-**āt***

TABLE 2.11 Demonstratives in Najdi Arabic

	Proximal	Distal
M.SG	*(hā)ḏa*	*(ha)ḏāk*
F.SG	*(hā)ḏi*	*(ha)ḏīć*
M.PL	*(ha)ḏōl(a)*	*(ha)ḏōlāk*
F.PL	*(ha)ḏōli*	*(ha)ḏōlīć*

they exist in a single invariable form. This form can vary from dialect to dialect (and sometimes competing forms exist within a single dialect), but they all lack the possibility of showing grammatical agreement.

On the contrary, Najdi Arabic has more gender distinctions than written Arabic when it comes to demonstratives, in that they also distinguish gender in the plural (see Table 2.11 above). Note that, however, dual demonstratives do not exist in Najdi Arabic, as in any other spoken variety (as we have said, dual agreement is *de facto* impossible in all modern dialects). It has also to be remarked that not all gender-distinguishing dialects possess separate forms for masculine and feminine plural demonstratives.

2.2.3 *Non distinguishing Varieties of Spoken Arabic*

We will now turn our attention to those dialects of Arabic that have lost gender distinction in the plural. This has been the fate of almost all dialects spoken in large urban centers, especially outside of Arabia. Typical exponents of this group of dialects are, for example, the urban varieties of the Levant (i.e. Damascus, Beirut, Jerusalem) and Egypt (Cairo, Alexandria), and virtually all dialects of the western Maghreb.

The Tables from 2.12 to 2.15 show the inflected paradigms of verbs, pronouns, nominals and demonstratives in the dialect of Damascus (as given in

TABLE 2.12 S-stem and P-stem in Damascus Arabic (*katab* 'to write')

	Suffix stem	Prefix stem
1 SG	*katab-t*	*ʔə-ktob*
2 M.SG	*katab-t*	*tə-ktob*
2 F.SG	*katab-ti*	*tə-kətb-i*
3 M.SG	*katab*	*yə-ktob*
3 F.SG	*katb-et*	*tə-ktob*
1 PL	*katab-na*	*nə-ktob*
2 PL	*katab-tu*	*tə-kətb-u*
3 PL	*katab-u*	*yə-kətb-u*

TABLE 2.13 Independent and bound pronouns in Damascus Arabic[a]

	Independent pronouns	Bound pronouns
1 SG	*ʔana*	*-i / -ni*
2 M.SG	*ʔənte*	*-ak*
2 F.SG	*ʔənti*	*-ek*
3 M.SG	*huwwe*	*-o*
3 F.SG	*hiyye*	*-(h)a*
1 PL	*nəḥna*	*-na*
2 PL	*ʔəntu*	*-kon*
3 PL	*hənne(n)*	*-hon*

a Bound pronouns are given in their post-consonantal realization.

Lentin 2006).[14] The majority of the other non-distinguishing varieties present the same morphemic distribution (but see § 2.2.4 for important exceptions).

As was the case with Najdi Arabic, here as well we can see that dual agreement is no longer an option, no matter what part of speech one considers. It is only nouns that retain the possibility of being inflected for dual number.

14 Along with the syncretism between the 2nd person M.SG and the 3rd F.SG in the prefix stem, already noted for written Arabic and Najdi Arabic, in Damascus Arabic and several other dialects the 1st and 2nd M singular persons of the suffix stem are formally identical.

TABLE 2.14 The inflection of nominals in Damascus Arabic

M.SG	*məsləm*
F.SG	*məsəlm-e(t)*
M.DUAL (nouns only)	*məsəlm-ēn*
F.DUAL (nouns only)	*məsləm-t-ēn*
PL	*məsəlm-īn*

TABLE 2.15 Demonstratives in Damascus Arabic[a]

	Proximal	Distal
M.SG	*hāda*	*hadāk*
F.SG	*hādi / hay*	*hadīk*
PL	*hadōl*	*hadolīk / hadənk*

a When used as adjectives, proximal demonstratives are often shortened to *ha(l)-* and prefixed to the noun they refer to, so that agreement in that context is not possible.

Like every other variety examined so far, non-distinguishing dialects form the plural of nouns and adjectives by means of two different pluralization strategies (suffixation and/or apophony). It is worth noting that the status of apophonic plurals—in terms of their involvement in agreement procedures—is slightly different in non-distinguishing varieties of Arabic. Here, all plurals have lost gender distinction, so that "sound" suffixal plurals are now entirely equivalent to broken ones in their capacity of agreeing with a given controller (i.e. they agree in number but not in gender). Therefore, although still differentiated at the semantic level (see § 2.2.1), apophonic plurals in non-distinguishing varieties have lost the somehow "special" status they enjoyed in gender-distinguishing ones.

2.2.4 *Divergent Inventories*

What has been presented in § 2.2.2 and § 2.2.3 is a somewhat idealized representation of the morphological inventories available to speakers of, respectively, gender-distinguishing and non-distinguishing varieties of Arabic. Although it is true that, in several dialects, these schematizations represent the actual state of affairs, many other dialects exist that deviate from such patterns, to a lesser or greater degree. We will now briefly examine these divergent morphological inventories, keeping in mind that the amount of variation encountered across the Arabic-speaking world is huge, and that our list could probably be expanded to include even more "exceptional" cases.

The most important deviation from the paradigms presented above is found in the western Maghreb. Across Morocco, Algeria and Tunisia, a number of non-distinguishing dialects have lost gender distinction also in the second person singular of the pronominal and/or verbal paradigm.[15]

In particular, there is no gender distinction in the 2nd person singular of the suffix stem in what Caubet (2008: 273) terms the "Moroccan koine", spoken in most urban areas of Morocco. In this variety, the historically feminine form has taken over as the only morpheme marking the 2nd person singular (Caubet 1993: 31). Harrell (1962: 40, 46) notes how in the dialects he describes (the urban dialects of north-western Morocco, in particular those of Fes, Rabat and Casablanca), gender distinction is commonly lost also in the 2nd person singular of the prefix stem.

In several Algerian dialects this process of morphological erosion appears to be even more advanced: Grand'Henry (2006: 54) notes how so called "pre-Hilali" dialects have lost gender distinction in the 2nd person singular of the verb and pronoun, in all paradigms (see also Cantineau 1937: 7). In the case of dialects spoken in rural/mountainous areas, this loss is systematic, while in the case of urban dialects, the distinction is lost in eastern and western varieties, but retained in the dialects of central Algeria (such as those of Cherchell and Algiers itself: see respectively Grand'Henry, 1972: 46, 130, and Boucherit 2006: 63).[16] According to Cantineau (1938: 7), in some dialects it is the masculine form that has taken over (at least in the suffix stem: Jijel, Taherl and El Milia; see also Marçais, 1902: 61, 120, for Tlemcen). In other dialects, it is the originally feminine form the one that survived (Collo and the neighboring eastern provinces). In Oran the masculine is retained in the verbal paradigms, but the feminine form has taken over in the set of independent pronouns (Cantineau 1940: 223).

As far as Tunisia is concerned, the urban koine that has developed in Tunis is characterized by the same dichotomy observed for Oran: complete loss of gen-

---

15 A few rare cases exist of Arabic dialects that have lost all kinds of gender distinction. Writing about Darfur Arabic, for instance, Roset (2018: 259) comments that "we can state that there is no synchronic gender system". Dialects of this type have not been taken into account in the analysis that will be presented in the rest of this section (see however § 2.3.8.3 for more information about Darfur Arabic).

16 Note however that Boucherit (2002: 60) gives a single form for the 2nd person singular suffix pronoun.

der distinction in the 2nd persons, with the originally feminine forms taking over in the pronominal paradigms and the originally masculine ones surviving in the verbal conjugation (Gibson 2009: 565–568).

Lastly, gender distinction in the 2nd person singular is completely lost in Maltese as well. As in Tunisia, the originally masculine forms are now the only ones left in the verbal paradigm, while the originally feminine independent pronouns are the ones in use (Borg and Azzopardi-Alexander 1997: 195, 244; Mifsud 2008). Gender agreement in the second persons is typologically uncommon in the languages of the world (Gensler 2011: 290; Siewierska 2013). It is perhaps not surprising, then, that several dialects that have lost this distinction in the plural are now in the process of levelling it in the singular as well (on this point, see also Chapter 5).

In general, gender distinction in the plural appears to be rather unstable in Arabic dialects. Many varieties have lost it, but even in those that retain it, exceptions abound. It is not uncommon to hear a masculine plural form where a feminine one would be expected instead. In some dialects, this phenomenon is so widespread that it probably foreshadows the collapse of the entire plural gender system.

In the majority of cases, the substitution of a F.PL form with a M.PL one occurs in a mostly random fashion, and can involve any part of speech (see for instance the Bedouin dialects of southern Tunisia documented by Ritt-Benmimoun 2017). In a few cases, however, the presence (or lack) of gender distinction is localized in a specific area of morphology. This is for instance the case of Ḥassāniyya, which seems to be unique among all dialects of Arabic in that it shows gender distinction in plural free pronouns, but not in bound ones or in verbs (Taine-Cheikh 2007: 242–243; Cohen 1963: 87, 147, 150).[17]

Even among gender-distinguishing dialects, it is not always the case that gender distinction is marked on plural demonstratives. As we have seen, this is the case for instance with Najdi Arabic, but several other dialects behave dif-

17 The peculiar form of the 2nd and 3rd F.PL pronouns in Ḥassāniyya (*əntūmāti* and *hūmāti*, respectively) makes it likely that, rather than a retention, these represent a backformation based on the masculine pronouns (*antūmä* and *hūmä*; on this point, see Taine-Cheikh 1993: 99–100, and Procházka 2014: 135). If this is correct, it would mean that Ḥassāniyya developed innovative forms for the 3rd F.PL independent pronouns after losing them at a certain point in the past (this loss might have happened in Ḥassāniyya proper or in one of its ancestors, perhaps long before it reached its current geographical distribution). Admittedly, Ḥassāniyya is not the only dialect in which gender-distinguishing plural pronouns seem to have been first lost and then re-developed: Procházka (2014: 134) also mentions the Syrian villages of Ḥafar (where the m/f 3rd person plural independent pronouns appear as *huwwin* and *hiyyin* respectively) and Ṭayyibt əl-ʔImām (*hinhan* and *hinhin*).

ferently. Omani Arabic, for instance, has a single invariable form for both the proximal and distal plural demonstrative (Holes 2008: 483). The same is true of Sanaani Arabic (Watson 2009: 110) and some of the Bedouin dialects of Sinai (though not all, De Jong 2009).

In general, these defective inventories appear to be intermediate stages in a process that, through the centuries, has brought many varieties of Arabic to completely abandon gender distinction in the plural. Even in non-distinguishing dialects, however, relics of the old system can still be seen, in particular in the realm of adjectives, where F.PL agreement can occasionally resurface (this is probably due to the fact that adjectives are morphologically akin to nouns, so that nominal F.PL morphology is never entirely lost). Hanitsch (2011) writes that adjectival F.PL agreement still occurs, occasionally, in the dialects of Damascus and Tetouan. The uncommon (though possible) occurrence of F.PL agreement in adjectives in Damascene Arabic is confirmed by Cowell (1964: 425) and, indirectly, also by Sallam. In his article, Sallam (1979: 47–49) reports a wealth of examples that show how this type of agreement almost never appears in Educated Egyptian Arabic, while it is more common in Educated Levantine Arabic.[18] For a more extensive treatment of F.PL adjectival agreement in non-distinguishing dialects, see § 2.3.7.

Yemen is well-known among scholars of Arabic for hosting a number of typologically unusual varieties. This is true also with respect to gender and agreement. A small number of northern Yemeni varieties exist that display a reduced number of gender contrasts in the pronominal paradigm. Unlike other dialects, however—where the contrast is reduced in the 2nd person singular and /or in the plural—the dialects of Bani Abādil, Bani Minabbih (Behnstedt 1987: 65–66) and im-Maṯṯah (Behnstedt 1987: 65–66; Caubet, Simeone-Senelle, Vanhove, 1989: 43) have lost gender distinction in the 3rd person singular of the free pronoun. This trait is all the more striking when considering that the distinction is retained in the suffix pronouns as well as in all plural forms.[19]

18 In the case of F.PL adjectives, the influence of MSA can never be entirely dismissed. It has to be noted, however, that F.PL morphology in verbs and pronouns is never restored. This proves that it is the persistence of F.PL forms in the morphology of the dialectal noun what makes these markers, so to speak, occasionally available for adjectives as well. Two additional facts prove that this is an actual dialectal trend: first, the fact that F.PL adjectives tend to occur in some dialects, but not in others; second, the fact that F.PL morphology is normally associated to certain classes of dialectal adjectives, but not others.

19 See Behnstedt 1987: 66 for a possible diachronic explanation of this merger. It is worth noting that an apparently minor trait such as this one could have huge repercussions on agreement behavior. A lack of gender distinction in the 3rd person singular makes F.SG agreement impossible, at least in the case of free pronouns, so that it is not clear how

Other Yemeni varieties have moved in the opposite direction, increasing the number of contrasts in the pronominal paradigms. This is true of the dialects spoken in the areas of Yāfiʕ, Ḏālaʕ and Lahej (Vanhove 2009: 755), and in general of western Yemen (Behnstedt 1985: 71). Here, gender distinction has been extended to the first person singular (not plural), so that all singular pronouns are now divided into two forms, M and F.[20]

Finally, at least one dialect in the Asir area has been shown to possess a relative pronoun that can inflect for number and gender in the singular (Watson 2011: 905). At present, this is the only known case of an inflectable relative pronoun in spoken Arabic.

One last issue needs to be discussed in this section, namely the case of those dialects where agreement can be expressed by other parts of speech apart from adjectives, verbs, pronouns and deictics.[21]

It is a well-known fact that, in almost every variety of spoken Arabic, certain particles exist that are used to express various types of linguistic possession. These particles have received different labels from different scholars:[22] here we will follow the lead of Holes (2008) in referring to them as "genitive markers". What is relevant to our present discussion is that, in several dialects, these elements can inflect for gender and number.[23]

In the case of dialects that have lost gender distinction in the plural, these particles can show gender opposition in the singular only (it is the case of Cairene *bitāʕ*, F.SG *bitāʕit* or *bitāʕt*, C.PL *bitūʕ*, Belnap 1991: 27). Even in gender-distinguishing varieties, however, it is not always the case that these elements possess distinct forms for feminine and masculine in the plural: see for instance Coastal Dhofari Arabic, where both *ḥaqq* (F.SG *ḥaqqat* or *ḥaqt*, C.PL *ḥaqqōt*)

---

non-individuated plural controllers behave in this dialect. Is F.SG agreement still available in verbs, adjectives and bound pronouns? Or is it disappearing from the language? Standing our present knowledge of these dialects, it is impossible to answer these questions.

20 According to Behnstedt (1985: 78), though most dialects that distinguish gender in the 1st person singular of the free pronoun also have this distinction in bound ones, this is not always the case.

21 The term "deictics" obviously include all types of demonstratives, but is not necessarily limited to them. Consider for instance the deictic presentatives that exist in Kordofanian Baggara Arabic (Manfredi 2014: 39 ff.), which can also be inflected for gender and number.

22 Belnap (1991), for instance, refers to them as *possessive adjectives*. Ingham (1994) calls them *possessive particles*, Brustad (2000) *genitive exponents*, and Davey (2016) *genitive linkers*.

23 For a discussion of typologically unusual agreement targets, see Corbett (2006: 44–53).

and *māl* (F.SG *mālat* or *mālt*, C.PL *malūt*) only possess a common plural form (Davey 2016: 229). We will return on this point in Chapter 5.

These particles always inflect like nominals. They have unmarked M.SG, a -(*V*)*t* suffix for F.SG, and a plural which is either apophonic (e.g. Cairo) or suffixal (e.g. Dhofar). This is unsurprising if one considers that all these elements derive from the grammaticalization of different nouns. This incipient grammaticalization process is also manifest in the fact that, apparently, some of the dialects whose possessive markers are able to inflect for gender are slowly losing this possibility (i.e. the two forms, inflected and non-inflected, appear now in free variation: it is for instance the case of Gulf Arabic, see Johnstone 1967: 69, 90–91).

2.3 The Spoken Dialects

Having described in detail the morphological inventories that the different varieties of Arabic have at their disposal for marking gender and number, the time has now come to analyze the way in which these elements combine syntactically to produce agreement.

The present section is dedicated to the contemporary spoken dialects of Arabic.[24] It is ideally divided into three parts: singular agreement, post-controller plural agreement, and pre-controller plural agreement.

§ 2.3.1 deals with the topic of agreement with singular controllers. This type of agreement, although not entirely devoid of irregularities, is relatively straightforward in Arabic, especially when compared to agreement with plural controllers. In fact, one of the main tenets of this book is that plural agreement is precisely what defines the actual level of complexity and typological nature of the agreement system(s) of Arabic. This is why, for the most part, our analysis will focus on plural agreement, which will be the object of sections from § 2.3.2 to § 2.3.8.

In particular, sections from § 2.3.2 to § 2.3.4 are devoted to the analysis of plural agreement patterns in gender-distinguishing varieties of Arabic. Sections § 2.3.5 and § 2.3.7, conversely, are dedicated to non-distinguishing ones (the topic of linguistic complexity is addressed specifically in § 2.3.5). § 2.3.8 deals with a small group of dialects which cannot be safely classified as either distinguishing or non-distinguishing.

---

24 We will also consider data from Andalusi Arabic, a now extinct variety.

While all the aforementioned sections focus on the types of agreement that can occur in post-controller targets, we argue that pre-controller agreement is an entirely different topic, that deserves separate treatment. Target-controller structures are therefore the object of § 2.3.9.

Both gender-distinguishing and non-distinguishing varieties are treated in the same way. First, we offer a comprehensive survey of the bibliographical sources available about the two dialect groups, extracting the relevant data from existing descriptions, and then we attempt generalizations. In the case of gender-distinguishing varieties, the statistical analysis of a corpus of texts is also presented to the reader (§ 2.3.4), so that specific examples can be examined and discussed in context.

2.3.1 *Singular Agreement*

In this section we will examine the general tendencies of agreement with singular controllers in spoken Arabic, and the main exceptions that exist to these trends. It has to be pointed out that these exceptions, in the vast majority of cases, only concern the realm of adjectival agreement. As we have seen (§ 1.3), the exceptional behavior of some adjectives in several Arabic dialects has led scholars such as Mitchell and Sallam to radically de-construct the concepts of gender and agreement in Arabic (Mitchell 1973, Sallam 1979). Although we do not share their views on the topic, the works of these two authors offer remarkable insight on a number of phenomena that are worth examining here as well.

As a very general rule, it is possible to state the following: in all varieties of spoken Arabic, singular nouns that are morphologically marked for feminine trigger F.SG agreement, whereas nouns that show no such marking trigger M.SG agreement. A small number of nouns exist in every variety of Arabic that, although not explicitly marked as feminine, still trigger F.SG agreement. The size of this group can vary, and the same lexical item may or may not belong to it depending on the dialect. However, a few general trends can be identified:

- Nouns denoting biologically feminine animate entities are treated as feminine no matter their morphological form (e.g. *ʔumm* 'mother', *ʕarūs* 'bride', *bint* 'girl/daughter', etc.).
- Certain parts of the body (especially those that come in pairs) tend to be treated as feminine in almost every known dialect of Arabic: among these, the equivalents of 'eye' (*ʕayn*), 'ear' (*ʔuḏun*), 'hand' (*yad*) and 'foot' (*riǧl*; other terms are in use as well). However, most body parts (paired or not) are masculine in contemporary dialects.[25]

25 Hasselbach (2014a: 44) notes how the fact that paired body parts are often treated as fem-

- Several words referring to the basic constituents of the physical world are feminine: among these, the most common are the equivalents of ‘earth’ (*ʔarḍ*), ‘sun’ (*šams*) and ‘fire’ (*nār*). The words for ‘sky’ (*samāʔ*), ‘wind’ (*rīḥ*) and ‘rain/winter’ (*maṭar*/*šitāʔ*) are often feminine as well. It is interesting to note how concepts that tend to be conceived of as inherently feminine in Arabic retain their gender even in those dialects where they are referred to by means of a different lexical element. This is for instance the case of the F.SG noun *ḥarrāy* ‘sun’ in Kordofanian Baggara Arabic (Manfredi 2010: 73).
- Several words related to urbanization/anthropization are treated as feminine in many dialects, though usage varies: in particular, *balad* ‘village’ or ‘country’, *ṭarīq* ‘road’ and *dār*, which can have several different meanings, from ‘country’ (Nigerian Arabic, Owens 1993: 48) to ‘nomad’s homestead’ (Kordofanian Baggara Arabic, Manfredi 2010: 73), ‘room’ (Libya) or ‘house’ (most of the Maghreb).

Most of the facts presented in the list above are drawn from Procházka’s (2004) very informative article on unmarked feminine nouns in Arabic dialects. The original paper treats the topic with a level of detail that is beyond the scope of our present discussion, so the interested reader is referred to it for a more comprehensive survey of the phenomenon.

At the opposite end of the spectrum from unmarked feminine nouns are those nouns that are formally marked as feminine while behaving as syntactically masculine. In this case as well, the list can vary from dialect to dialect, but this group is always extremely limited in size. In Bedouin Negev Arabic, for instance, we find two such nouns: *zalamah* ‘man’, and *sāmʕih* ‘man appointed by the parties to witness the trial by fire’ (Shawarbah 2012: 129). The word *xalīfa* ‘caliph’, constitutes another example, along with the whole class of nouns that adopt the intensive pattern *CaCCāCa* (*ʕallāma*, ‘most knowledgeable’, *raḥḥāla* ‘traveller’, etc.).

Deviations from the expected agreement outcomes do not depend exclusively on nouns and their form. Mitchell (1973) and Sallam (1979) note how certain classes of adjectives exist that tend not to show agreement in some contexts.[26]

---

inine in Semitic languages “has nothing to do with semantics but with the fact that the dual marker *-ā* reflects an older FEM PL ending that was replaced by *-āt* and relegated to a more restricted function”.

26 The two authors base their analysis on Cairene Arabic, but similar remarks can be found in the description of several varieties of spoken Arabic (see for instance Brustad 2000: 62–63, who compares agreement patterns in Cairene, Damascene, Kuwaiti and Urban Moroccan; many of the grammars that will be analyzed in the next sections also make

Mitchell (1973: 36) refers to this class of non-agreeing adjectives as "adjectives of origin", and gives the examples *siggāda ʕarīḍa* 'a wide carpet' and *siggāda ʕagami* 'a Persian carpet', where the same controller triggers F.SG agreement in the first adjective but M.SG agreement in the second one. Sallam (1979: 28) goes into greater detail, explaining that so-called "adjectives of origin" may display no agreement when following a nonhuman controller (singular or plural). This rule however is not adamant, since exceptions exist in both cases: it is possible to have a feminine human controller not triggering F.SG agreement (e.g. *sitt baladi* 'a vulgar woman') and it is also possible to have a nonhuman, morphologically feminine noun triggering F.SG agreement (e.g. *warda maṣriyya* 'an Egyptian rose'). Sallam (1979: 29) also notes that the definition "adjectives of origin" is confusing, since many of the elements that fall into this class do not specify any type of geographical or material "origin" (e.g. *wardi* 'pink', *ʕilmi* 'scientific'): he therefore proposes the definition "relational adjectives". It can be seen how all adjectives listed so far belong to the class, familiar to scholars of Arabic, of the "*nisba* adjectives", i.e. adjectives that—in spoken Arabic—end with an *-i* sound, and that are more or less equivalent to English relative adjectives. Therefore, it can be concluded that a sub-group of adjectives exists whose agreement properties differ from those of the majority of adjectives: in particular, their agreement options seem to be reduced in several contexts.[27]

While the agreement behavior of this specific subset is certainly of interest, it seems to us there is no case for Sallam's claim that noun-controlled gender as a syntactic category does not exist in Arabic vernaculars. Such conclusion cannot be reached on the basis of a few irregular items belonging to a much larger group of elements that behave according to expectations. Furthermore, adjectives represent only a portion of the possible agreement domains (Sallam does not consider verbal or pronominal targets in his study). In addition to this, as Brustad notes, the vacillation between agreement and non-agreement with singular controllers seems to follow the same logic as plural agreement: as partially anticipated in §1.3, and as will be discussed at length in the next sections, agreement with plural controllers in spoken Arabic is heavily dependent

similar reports). Another study on the lack of agreement displayed by certain adjectives in Cairene Arabic is Wilmsen (1999).

27 Watson (1993: 211–212) reports very similar tendencies for *-i* ending adjectives in the Arabic of Sanaa. See also Owens (1993: 50), who gives a short list of Nigerian Arabic adjectives which are invariable for gender and number. Although he does not comment on this, most of them would seem to be lexical loans.

on the referent's level of individuation. The same appears to be true of singular agreement. In Brustad's own words:

> Individuation [...] seems to affect the neutralized agreement patterns of certain adjectives. Most of Sallam's examples consist of words for nationality, educational classes, such as class or course curriculum, and the like; in other words, they provide classificatory description (membership in a class) rather than the identification of a specific or particular item [...]. Classificatory adjectives are more likely to show neutralized agreement. Sallam's data [...] center on indefinite nouns, and thus do not provide adequate samplings covering the entire individuation continuum
>
> BRUSTAD 2000: 63

Admittedly, a second group of non-agreeing adjectives exists, morphologically independent from the *nisba*-class discussed above. In the case of these elements, however, the origin of their irregular behavior is easily determined. This group is identified on a semantic basis, and includes adjectives that refer to different aspects of female biology (human or animal). These include *ḥāmil* 'pregnant', *ḥalūb* 'that gives milk',[28] *ḥāʔiḍ* 'menstruating', and so on (see Sallam 1979: 30–32 for a more comprehensive treatment). Although some of these adjectives, in certain contexts, can indeed be marked by the F.SG *-a* ending, in most cases they appear in a single invariable form (which is formally M.SG, in spite of the fact that they are always referred to feminine controllers).

The obvious consequence of what has been said so far is that, in certain rare cases, a F.SG noun not explicitly marked for feminine (such as *ʕarūs* 'bride' or *sitt* 'woman') can be accompanied by a formally masculine adjective (such as *ḥāmil* 'pregnant', or *baladi* 'vulgar'; obviously the lexical elements involved, their combination and their realization can vary from dialect to dialect). These occurrences, although admittedly exceptional, constitute no reason to reject the validity of the category of gender as a descriptive tool. By simply comparing other examples, where *ʕarūs* and *sitt* are accompanied by pronominal, verbal, or regular adjectival targets, the inherent gender of these nouns would be easily determined.

The last exceptional situation that needs to be discussed here concerns an entirely different agreement condition, namely word order. As already said, in our analysis we will keep controller-target structures separated from target-

28 *CaCūC* adjectives in general tend not to show gender agreement, in both written Arabic and several varieties of spoken Arabic.

controller ones, since agreement seems to operate differently in these two contexts. This topic will be dealt with in § 2.3.9, where we will discuss plural agreement in pre-controller targets. Singular agreement, however, can also be affected by word order, in that (mostly verbal) targets preceding a feminine controller can sometimes show M.SG agreement. Although most of the studies on the effect of precedence on agreement tend to focus on agreement with plural targets, and on the meaning of the variation between SG and PL agreement in this context, neutralization of gender agreement in pre-controller position is also possible.

Hoyt (2002) offers several examples of this phenomenon in Rural Palestinian Arabic, and links oscillation between "impersonal" (i.e. M.SG) and "full" agreement to semantic and pragmatic factors. While the two types of agreement often imply a change in the overall meaning of the sentence when the opposition is between SG and PL agreement, M.SG agreement with feminine singular controllers does not radically alter meaning. However, although both types of agreement are usually acceptable, Hoyt (2002: 113) notes that speakers often show "a predilection" for one or the other, depending on context. For example, he writes, "indefinites with 'rich descriptive content' (such as adjectives or relative clauses) can favor full agreement. In particular, the more referentially specific the modification, the more likely there is to be a preference for full agreement". He provides the following examples: *bāḳi /bāḳye hanāk ḥayye bidd-ha tōčil ifrāx ṭēr* 'There was a snake there that was going to eat a bird's chicks', and *bāḳi /bāḳye hanāk ḥayye bidd-ha tōčil ifrāx iṭ-ṭēr* 'There was a snake there that was going to eat the bird's chicks'. While in the first sentence the two possible agreement options (M.SG or F.SG) appear to be entirely interchangeable, in the second one, where the relative clause is of higher referential specificity, F.SG agreement (*bāḳye*) is the preferred option.

In the following sections we will return on these topics in more detail, when analyzing agreement with plural controllers. For the sake of expository clarity, we have decided to treat singular and plural agreement in separate sections: however, the real nature of agreement in Arabic (as probably any other language) can only be grasped by looking at the system in its entirety. Saying that masculine singular controllers attract M.SG agreement while feminine singular one trigger F.SG agreement is not particularly meaningful, if one does not take into account the behavior of these same controllers in their plural form. The interdependency between SG and PL agreement will be one of the topics that we will focus on in the rest of this chapter, and its consequences will be explored in particular in § 2.3.4.

2.3.2 *Plural Agreement in Gender-Distinguishing Dialects: Sources*

As already mentioned, the types of agreement triggered by plural controllers constitute the real crux of the problem. Plural agreement is where most of the complexity of the various systems analyzed in this book is concentrated, and this is true of virtually all varieties of Arabic, written or spoken, ancient or modern.[29] As will be shown in the next sections and chapters, however, remarkable differences exist between the syntactical behavior of these varieties. In particular, a fundamental divide appears to be represented by the retention (or loss) of gender distinction in the plural. While this consideration could appear obvious, its consequences are not. For this reason, in the next pages we will treat gender-distinguishing dialects separately from non-distinguishing ones, starting in the present section with the former group.

When it comes to the distinction between these two types of dialects, one cannot but notice an imbalance in the sources. Today, the amount of descriptive materials available to scholars of Arabic dialectology is huge. However, and quite predictably, not every variety is equally well-documented. In particular, the dialects of large urban centers are generally better known than those spoken in remote rural areas.

As will be discussed in more detail in Chapter 5, if one analyzes the morphological inventories of all the dialects spoken across the Arab world, a clear trend emerges: it is the dialects spoken outside of urban areas that more commonly retain F.PL marking on adjectives, verbs and pronouns. Urban dialects, conversely, have almost systematically lost this distinction.

The obvious consequence of this trend is that information about gender-distinguishing varieties is not as abundant as that about non-distinguishing ones. Furthermore, even among the available materials, qualitative and quantitative differences exist. Several sources are now outdated, and some of the texts are hard to access. In a few lucky cases, a study specifically dedicated to the topic of agreement exists (these have all been mentioned in § 1.3). More commonly, however, either a descriptive grammar is available, or the dialect is known only through a number of short articles—sometimes only one. As a general trend, descriptive works about Arabic dialects are heavily focused on phonology and morphology, offering only sketchy descriptions of syntactical structures (if any at all). Even when syntax is discussed, it is not always the case that agreement figures among the topics in focus. Information on the subject, if present, has to be pieced together by browsing through different sections, so

29 The only exception is constituted by a small number of dialects that have (almost?) entirely abandoned the possibility of F.SG agreement with plural controllers (see sections 2.3.6 and 2.3.7).

that the resulting picture is often far-from-complete, and data about certain key aspects of agreement may still be lacking. In particular, even when discussing agreement explicitly, the vast majority of authors tend to focus on adjectival agreement. Verbal and pronominal agreement are commonly left aside. As we will see in the next sections, adjectives are probably the least canonical target type in Arabic, because of the language's inherent morphological idiosyncrasies. As a result, the available data about agreement are *de facto* incomplete for several dialects.

Despite these difficulties, in the following pages we have tried to offer the reader a coverage as complete as possible of agreement patterns in gender-distinguishing dialects across the Arabic-speaking world. We have analyzed dialects moving from country to country, sieving through all the materials available for each specific region. Our presentation starts with the western Maghreb and moves roughly eastwards, allowing for occasional detours. There is obviously a certain degree of arbitrariness in this system, since it is not always the case that dialects which coexist within the borders of the same country are closely related to each other (or, conversely, dialectal continua sometimes exist that cut across political borders). As a result, in the list that follows, some countries have been grouped together, while others include reference to several distinct varieties. This method, however, represents a convenient way for the authors to organize the existing bibliography, and for the reader to easily navigate through the data presented.

We would like to point out that, in compiling our list, we have exclusively made use of descriptive materials, without taking into account collections of texts that were not accompanied by a syntactical description. While valuable information about agreement could have been extracted from such texts, this process would have been excessively time-consuming. Even so, we believe our survey to be fairly comprehensive. In particular, we have tried not to discriminate between those traditionally considered as "core" Arabic dialects and "peripheral" ones (so that, for instance, we made sure to include plenty of data about countries where Arabic is spoken as a minority language).

Before we begin our examination of each single variety, reference has to be made to certain conceptual categories that have traditionally been employed by Arabic dialectologists. Scholars in this field tend to identify two distinct typological groups of dialects, namely "Bedouin" and "sedentary" ones. Gender distinction in the plural is one of the traits typically associated with the former group, so that one might think that, for it to be complete, an analysis of gender-distinguishing dialects needs only to focus on the so-called Bedouin varieties.

In fact, things are more complicated than that, and this is for three main reasons: I) "Bedouin" and "sedentary" can be misleading labels, since they can be (and, in fact, have often been) used to refer to both the lifestyle of a group of speakers (or that of their ancestors), and to the actual linguistic features that characterize their dialect. This is problematic as well as confusing, because the two do not always coincide. This bring us to point II): in certain areas of the Arabic-speaking world—in particular within the borders of the Arabian Peninsula, but not only—the Bedouin/sedentary distinction is of very limited typological efficacy. Several dialects are found, spoken by historically sedentary populations, that abound with traits normally associated to Bedouin varieties. The opposite is also true, and even more common, to the point that III) several historically Bedouin dialects exist that have lost many of the features that used to characterize them. This might have happened for different reasons (mainly contact with typologically different dialects and ecological factors such as sedentarization and urbanization, see Chapter 5). The result, at any rate, is that it is not clear whether or not these dialects should be classified as Bedouin. On the one hand, they preserve certain traits which are typical of this group, and are spoken by people of Bedouin ancestry. On the other, they have lost some of these traits, and today they have come to represent the main speech type of large urban centers.[30]

The question could be tentatively neutralized by stating the following: there is a very high probability that, in the speech of those groups which a) inhabit rural areas and b) still practice nomadic pastoralism (or have done so until recently),[31] one will encounter the traits typically associated with Bedouin dialects, and in particular gender distinction in the plural. This, while often (but by no means universally) true, still fails to account for all those dialects that retain gender distinction in the plural but whose speakers do not meet the criteria (a) and/or (b).

Because of all the above, in this book we will not use the labels "Bedouin" and "sedentary" in a typological sense, except in quotes from other authors. In the following pages, these adjectives will be used sparingly, and only with reference to the actual lifestyle of a given social group (or of their ancestors). As repeatedly stressed, our main typological distinction will oppose gender-distinguishing dialects to non-distinguishing ones.

---

30 Note that one of the traits which appears to be more subject to disappearance in sedentarized Bedouin varieties is indeed gender distinction in the plural, so that the use of this label becomes even more problematic for the purpose of this book.

31 The number of people who still engage in this type of traditional activity has obviously plummeted during the 20th century.

One of the most important works to focus on the alleged Bedouin/sedentary divide is Rosenhouse's study of the general characteristics of Bedouin dialects throughout the Arab world. Since several of the dialects she analyzes retain feminine plural morphology, Rosenhouse's (1984: 46–47) remarks about agreement represent a valid starting point for our discussion. The section devoted to agreement in her study is very short, but two main points emerge:

1) Bedouin dialects tend to retain gender distinction in the plural. When this happens, feminine plural agreement is often associated with animal controllers (this last part is actually a quote from Johnstone 1967: 165–166).
2) F.SG agreement with plural controllers is common, in particular with *human* plural controllers.[32] In addition, Rosenhouse comments that "Pl. concord [...] is the common form of concord in sedentary dialects", so that "we may [...] see in the f.sg. concord in Bedouin dialects a typical old feature".

We have already seen (§1.1) how F.SG agreement with plural controllers has often been considered by scholars of Arabic as one of the features that set apart the "Old" type of Arabic from a "New" one (i.e. the spoken dialects). Rosenhouse's remarks on the topic follow the same line of thought, since she considers "Bedouin" varieties as representative of an older stage of the language, more closely related to its Classical manifestation. We will check the tenability of this hypothesis in sections 2.3.6 and 2.3.7, when we will try to determine how common F.SG agreement actually is in non-distinguishing (i.e. mostly "sedentary") dialects. At present, we are interested in knowing if the traits (1) and (2) are mentioned in the descriptions of the various gender-distinguishing dialects analyzed here. Let us now examine each variety individually.

2.3.2.1 Morocco and Algeria

As far as the western Maghreb is concerned, it is a well-known fact that gender distinction in the plural is only rarely encountered in the area. Consider for instance this quote from Marçais' (1908: 76–77) description of the Algerian dialect of the Ūlad Brāhim Bedouins: "Au pluriel [...] la distinction de genres, fréquente dans tous les dialectes bédouins d'Orient aux 2e et 3e pers. est inconnue à Saïda. Je ne la connais au Maghrib que dans le dialecte du Souf".[33] After almost one century, Heath (2002: 271) has very little to add on this sub-

32 This is also stressed in Rosenhouse (2006: 268): "When the subject denotes an animate group of people (whether morphologically singular or plural), there is a strong tendency for the verb or adjectival predicate to take the feminine singular".

33 Boris (1945–1948: 21) confirms this, stating that plural gender distinction is "conservée en Algérie dans le seul parler de l'Oued Souf".

ject: "Maghrebi survivals of MaPl versus FePl oppositions in pronominal affixes, e.g. perfective subject suffixes, seem to be confined to southern Tunisia and a small part of Algeria". Apart from this brief remark, Heath's treatise on the Arabic dialects of Morocco makes no mention of gender distinction in the plural, except for Ḥassāniyya. Ḥassāniyya, however, only distinguishes gender in the adjective/participle[34] and in the free plural pronouns, and in the latter case this distinction is likely an innovation, and not a retention (as seen in § 2.2.4). For this reason, we have not grouped Ḥassāniyya together with all other gender-distinguishing varieties, and it will be discussed separately in § 2.3.8.2.

It is not clear whether or not gender-distinguishing varieties of Arabic still exist today in the modern states of Morocco and Algeria. If they do, they are—to the best of our knowledge—entirely undocumented.

2.3.2.2 Tunisia

Feminine plural forms are retained in certain dialects of the south. Ritt-Benmimoun's (2017) article about agreement in the Bedouin dialects of the Nifzāwa region is extremely detailed and informative. Here the author notes that F.PL agreement is possible with feminine plural human subjects, but not masculine ones or mixed groups. As for nonhuman controllers, they all have access to this type of agreement.[35] Among the examples the author offers, we find: *ʕind=i žmāl hiyyāž xāyif yfikk=**hin** min=ni il=lēl yḏīʕ-**in** ʕalay=y* 'I had rutting camels and was afraid that the night would take **them** from me, that they **would get lost**' (with a broken plural adjective, and F.PL verb and pronoun) and *yaḷˀṣg-**an** il=xubzāt **hāḏēkin** ʕalā=ha*, '**Those** flat loaves of bread **stick** to it' (with a F.PL pre-controller verb and a F.PL post-controller demonstrative).

F.SG agreement with plural controllers is also present. Ritt-Benmimoun (2017) maintains that oscillation between plural and F.SG agreement is related to the controller's level of individuation. This is context-dependent: for instance, it is increased by the presence of a numerical quantifier (including the dual suffix), while non-numerical quantifiers such as *kull* 'all', have the opposite effect, lowering the referent's level of individuation. Individuation is enhanced if the reference is to a specific, well-delimited group of entities, and diminished

34 Taine-Cheikh (2017: 34) reports that gender distinction in the plural of participles is also retained in the Algerian dialects of the ʔArbaʕ.

35 Ritt-Benmimoun repeatedly stresses that, especially in the speech of the younger generations, F.PL forms are more and more commonly being replaced by M.PL ones. On this point, see Chapter 5. Note that all of Ritt-Benmimoun's findings confirm the (much shorter, but earlier) work of Boris (1945–1948).

if the reference is non-specific and if the group is viewed collectively rather than as the sum of several, separated individuals.

Ritt-Benmimoun does not report any particular difference between (feminine) human, animal or inanimate controllers in terms of frequency of co-occurrence with F.PL agreement, though certain classes of nouns have a strong preference either toward F.SG or F.PL agreement. Body parts, for instance, seem to be always perceived as highly individuated, while landscape elements and abstract nouns have a strong tendency to attract F.SG agreement. This is also the case with nouns with an inherently generic meaning, such as *ḥāžāt* 'things', and *umūr* 'issues', and with collectives such as *flūs* 'money' (Ritt-Benmimoun 2017: 279). The general topic of the text can also be of importance: for instance, the individuation level of referents tends to decrease when the speaker is relating of past habits. Loans from MSA, when denoting inanimate entities, also have a strong tendency to attract F.SG agreement: this probably represents an interference of the standard agreement system with the dialectal one.

In the concluding section of her paper, Ritt-Benmimoun (2017: 282) summarizes her findings as follows: "The factors that decide between deflected feminine singular and strict plural agreement are generality, collectivity, and abstractness on the one hand and specificity, individuality, and concreteness on the other hand. Thus, humanness or non-humanness is *not* a deciding factor" (emphasis in the original). Among the examples of F.SG agreement with plural controllers we find: *il=ḥīšān* ***biʕīda*** *ʕala baʕəḏ=****ha*** 'The houses used to be **far** from **each other**', and *nihāṛ badw il=ʕirəs iṣ=ṣubəḥ naʕṭu l=iṛ=ṛažžāla t=tāy w=il=qahwa,* ***ta****-šṛab. ət-bārik ir=ržāl* ... 'At the day of the beginning of the wedding, in the morning, we give the men tea and coffee, and **they** drink. The men **congratulate** ...'. Note that in the last example the broken plural of *ṛāžil* 'man', appears in two different forms: both, however, trigger F.SG agreement in the verb, because they appear in the description of a habitual event, and the reference is to 'men' in a very generic sense.

2.3.2.3 Libya

As far as we know, all Libyan dialects except for that of Tripoli retain gender distinction in the plural. Unfortunately, information about agreement in these varieties is hard to come by, with the exception of D'Anna's (2017) study of agreement patterns in Fezzani Arabic. This study is based on texts gathered by Philippe Marçais in the central decades of the 20th century, and the author provides a quantitative analysis of the data, which consists of a corpus of 158 controllers (including proper plurals, collectives, and chains of conjoined singulars) and 373 targets. As was the case with Ritt-Benmimoun's material, masculine human controllers systematically trigger M.PL agreement, as do mixed groups. Feminine plural ones, on the contrary, have a preference for F.PL agreement, but they also trigger M.PL agreement in a minority of cases (around 35%). Again, this is similar to what Ritt-Benmimoun reported for southern Tunisia, where F.PL forms are gradually being replaced by M.PL ones. The situation is pretty much the same with animal controllers, which show a preference for F.PL agreement, although M.PL is found as well. Inanimate controllers behave somewhat differently, in that they, as well, can occasionally trigger M.PL agreement, but much more rarely than animal or human feminine controllers (the percentage here is around 17% of cases). It would seem that the expansion of M.PL agreement, at the expenses of F.PL, proceeds faster in the realm of animate controllers (and human ones in particular: this had already been observed by Ritt-Benmimoun, 2017: 283, and Ingham, 1994: 64). Examples of F.PL agreement with nonhuman controllers include: *īḏa ʕand=ak žedyān ṣġāṛ txāf ʕalē=**hen** mn en=now* 'If you have young goats and you fear about **them** because of the heat …', with a F.PL resumptive pronoun, and *l=ḥawāiž gṛomfəl šuššwarᵉd* (…) *bēš l=maṛa tuḏfoṛ bī=**hen** šaʕar=ha* 'The things—cloves, rose water (…) for the woman to plait her hair with (**them**)', where again the pronoun is in the F.PL.

In D'Anna's data, F.SG agreement seems to be restricted to collective controllers, human and nonhuman, with very few exceptions (a single instance of F.SG agreement is found triggered by a non-collective human controller, and three triggered by inanimate ones). D'Anna's corpus is somewhat limited in size, so it is possible that the analysis of a larger amount of data would yield more occurrences of this type of agreement, but in general, F.SG agreement seems to be less frequent in Fezzani than in other varieties. Here as well, however, animacy and humanness seem not to play a decisive role, the main factor being apparently countability/individuation vs. collectiveness.

2.3.2.4 Egypt

Maṭar (1981) is a study of the Bedouin dialects spoken in the northern coastal area between Alexandria and the Libyan border (referred to as *ʔiqlīm sāḥil maryūṭ*). Matar (1981: 226) writes that nonhuman collectives attract F.SG agreement, and provides some examples of this. In the same section, he also claims that nonhuman plurals attract F.SG agreement: the one example sentence that he provides, however, features another collective controller (*bill* 'camels'). This is somewhat confusing, given that in the preceding and following pages it is possible to find numerous examples of F.PL agreement co-occurring with nonhuman referents (see for instance Matar 1981: 220, 226 and 228).

Dialects of Bedouin descent also exist in Egypt in the east, in the Sinai Peninsula, and these have been thoroughly documented by De Jong (2011). Data about agreement are limited, but a strong correlation is found to exist between F.PL agreement and "limited or countable numbers of things" and "plurals of animals" (this is apparently true of all varieties investigated in the book, see De Jong 2011: 116 and 192). Examples include: *fīh amākin igṣūr in=nās imsawwyīn=**hin** zamān fa bi=ytaxazzan fī=**hin*** 'there are places for storage that people made (**them**) in the old days, so they store (goods) in **them**', with two F.PL pronouns referred to "places", and *al=ġizlān ḏillah mā bi=yṭīḥ-**in** fi l=wāṭiy* 'these gazelles don't **come down** in low areas' (note that here the verb is in the F.PL while the demonstrative only possesses a common plural form).

Since De Jong notes that it is only these specific types of controllers that tend to be referred to in the F.PL, one imagines that a different type of agreement (i.e. F.SG) is possible with other types of controllers. This, however, is not discussed in the book, and no examples are provided.[36]

An important note appears in De Jong (2009: 250), where the author writes that "limited or countable numbers of objects, and even male persons [...] tend to be referred to in the feminine plural". He gives the following example: *w=ixwān xamsit=**hin** iwlād ḥamdān* 'and the brothers, the five of **them** are sons of Ḥamdān', where the anaphoric pronoun is actually in the F.PL.

Sinai dialects, then, seem to represent a unique exception throughout the Arabic-speaking world, in that the otherwise absolute predominance of M.PL forms in the agreement triggered by human masculine plural controllers is here challenged by the intrusion of F.PL morphology. It is possible that speakers of these varieties have ended up over-extending the use of F.PL agreement as a marker of individuation, to the point that these forms are now in use with all controller types, not only nonhuman or feminine ones.[37] This must remain for

36 Note, however, how F.SG agreement with plural controllers is mentioned in the descriptions of several closely related dialects, such as the Bedouin dialects of Jordan and the Negev. On the relations between Sinai dialects and other Bedouin varieties, see Palva (2008).

37 D'Anna (2017: 107) reports some unusual occurrences of F.PL agreement with the collective *nās* 'people', in Fezzani Arabic. Adam Benkato (p.c.) has informed us that F.PL agreement does sometimes co-occurr with masculine human controllers in Libyan poetry. While these occurrences are too scattered and anecdotical for a systematic analysis, we would like to put forward a hypothesis, to be tested in future studies. Several languages exist in which the gender that normally encompasses human beings, or masculine human beings, is reserved to the member of one's own social group. Foreigners and outsiders are systematically referred to using another gender (that may be the same as women, or animals, or certain nonhuman entities). This is the case for instance in Lokono (Arawakan) and Setswana (Bantu); see Aikhenvald (2016; 104, 192). Could it be that the dialects just mentioned, in which F.PL agreement is sometimes assigned to masculine human controllers, employ a similar strategy, and that all these controllers are actually referred to "outsiders", from the speaker's relative point of view? On a somehow related topic, see also footnote 50 on the dialect of Sanaa.

now in the realm of speculation, since more data would be needed to substantiate such a hypothesis (also because De Jong does not discuss the possibility of F.SG agreement with plural or collective controllers, so that we do not know what type of balance exists between these competing forms in Bedouin Sinai Arabic).

Finally, some remarks on agreement can be found in Woidich's (2006a) short description of Bʕēri Arabic, a variety spoken in southern Egypt, near Luxor. Woidich (2006a: 308) reports that "Plural nouns of animals and objects can agree with the 3rd pers. pl. fem", and gives the examples *il=ʕanzāt wullid-**an*** 'the goats **gave** birth', and *faddanēn ʔarḍ, yaʕni law zaraḥt=**hin** ḥašīš* … 'two feddans of land, if I were to sow **them** with grass …'.

2.3.2.5 Chad, Cameroon and Nigeria

Although Arabic is one of the languages spoken in Cameroon, virtually no information is available about the dialects that exist in the country.

As far as Chad is concerned, it would seem that F.PL forms have entirely disappeared from the dialect of N'Djamena (Jullien de Pommerol, 1999), and that they are also very rarely encountered in the northern part of the country (the area formerly known as Borkou-Ennedi-Tibesti, whose largest city is Faya). Abu Absi (1995: 13) reports the existence of F.PL pronouns (but not verbs) in the local dialect, noting however that "the occurrence of *hinna* is quite rare, both as independent pronoun and as pronominal suffix". Curiously enough, F.PL demonstratives are listed in the grammar (Abu Absi 1995: 14), though no information is provided as to agreement patterns.

Apparently, F.PL morphology only resists in full vigor in the Lake Chad area, at least in the dialect of the Ulād Eli investigated by Zeltner and Tourneux (1986: 42–43). The two authors note that F.PL agreement is used with reference to human and animal females, collectives denoting groups of large animals, and in general with all nouns that possess an apophonic plural (except those referred to human males). Examples include: *ʔal=kilāb ʔakal-**an** al=lehem* 'the dogs **ate** the meat' (where the controller is an animal plural), *kasāwi sumh-**āt*** 'nice clothes' (where the controller is an inanimate apophonic plural), and *ʔal=xēl b=igallib-**an*** 'the horses **gallop**' (where the controller is an animal collective).

The use of F.SG agreement is apparently very restricted in this dialect. Human collectives always trigger M.PL agreement, and only collectives denoting animals and ending with *-a(t)* can attract F.SG agreement (as in *ʔal=ʔarḍa akal-**at** al=kitāb* 'the termites **ate** the book'). However, nouns denoting certain species of birds can also be accompanied by F.SG targets (*ʔal=hibtir **tu**-ʔūm ʔejala* 'teals **swim** fast').

Owens (1993) is a description of the dialect of Maiduguri in north-eastern Nigeria. While human referents attract M or F agreement depending on their biological gender (mixed groups always trigger M.PL agreement), nonhuman plural controllers tend to attract F.PL agreement. It would seem that quantification tends to favor plural agreement, while non-numerical quantifiers have the opposite effect. Owens 1993: 264, in particular, states that: "Dual nouns take the agreement of plural nouns. Generally plural nouns are feminine [...] and so a dual noun will take feminine agreement even if it is built on a stem which is masculine in the singular", and offers the following example: *at=tōrēn b=injamm-**an*** 'the two bulls rest', where the verb is F.PL. Owens (1993: 50) also remarks that "grammatically most broken plurals—nearly all except those which refer to masculine objects [...]—are feminine in their agreement rules". Consider the following example: *ad=durūb dēla talfān-**āt*** 'these roads are **bad**', where an apophonic plural attracts F.PL agreement in the adjective.

Owens makes no mention of the possibility of F.SG agreement with plural controllers, which—however—appears in the description of other related dialects of the area (see below).

2.3.2.6 Sudan

Several Sudanese dialects preserve gender distinction in the plural.

Dickins (2007: 561), speaking of the dialect of Khartoum, lists F.PL forms for the verbal and pronominal paradigms, stating however that they "are considered a rural feature". Interestingly, he also notes that "where a sound plural is used, there seems to be an increasing tendency for feminine plural human nouns to take masculine plural adjectives". Reichmuth (1983: 201) confirms this, and claims that in Khartoum and Omdurman the loss of F.PL form is almost complete (see also below).

Trimingham (1946), writing around forty years before Reichmuth, lists F.PL forms in his grammar of the dialect of Omdurman. However, he advises students of this dialect "not to waste their time learning the feminine plural forms of the verb since the men usually use the masculine plural when speaking of women. It is, however, always used by the women themselves" (Trimingham 1939: 65; no similar comment is found concerning F.PL pronouns). This comment is remarkable because it contradicts what several other authors have noted for other dialects, that is, the tendency of F.PL forms to disappear more rapidly in the speech of women. As a general agreement rule, Trimingham (1946: 27) notes how "irrational plural nouns may be accompanied by fem. sing adjectives". However, in a footnote on p. 23 he notes how countable items accompanied by a numeral between 3 and 10 take F.PL agreement.

Hillelson (1935) is a collection of texts from Sudan. Unfortunately, the exact locations in which the texts have been collected is not specified, so that it is impossible to know of which variety each text is representative.[38] In the introduction, Hillelson (1935: XX) writes that "the feminine [plural] exists in full vigour. Idiomatically it is used of animals, even when males are spoken of", and provides several examples, including the following: *at=tērān ǧā-**n*** 'the bulls **came**'. By examining the texts, however, it can be seen that also inanimate controllers can trigger F.PL agreement, at least when they are numbered (e.g. *qinṭarēn masāmīr* […] *al=fār akal-**an** kulle=**hin*** 'two *kantars* of nails […] they had all (of **them**) being **eaten** by mice'; note that here both the pronoun referring to the *kantars* and the verb referred to 'mice' appear in the F.PL). Hillelson says nothing about F.SG agreement in Khartoum/Sudani Arabic, but this type of agreement appears in the texts he presents, at least with inanimate controllers (e.g. *īyām ketīr-**a*** '**many** days').

Manfredi (2010) is an (as of yet unpublished) study of the type of Arabic spoken by the *Baggara* ('cattle herders') of Kordofan. Similar dialects are spoken along the so-called "Baggara Belt", an area that runs from western Sudan all the way through Chad and into northern Cameroon and eastern Nigeria. Manfredi (2010: 227) states that "Plural nouns of animals, for their part, have feminine plural agreement […]. Agreement of adjectives to inanimate plural heads nouns varies between plural and feminine singular".[39] Among the example sentences we find: *al=kulāb al=jaxrān-**āt** b=isaww-**an*** 'The **rabid** dogs **do** …', where both the verb and the adjective appear in the F.PL.

Manfredi also mentions the possibility of F.SG agreement for inanimate referents, and provides the example *al=buyūt al=kabīr-**e*** 'the **big** houses'.

Reichmuth (1983) focuses on the dialect of the Šukriyya in eastern Sudan, describing agreement in detail. According to Reichmuth (1983: 200), agreement in the plural is M.PL for masculine human controllers and F.PL for all others if the reference is to a group of countable and distinguishable individuals (this he calls *Zählkongruenz*). If, on the other hand, the group is seen as a non-differentiated mass, then we have *Mengenkongruenz*, and agreement is in the F.SG, irrespective of the gender of the referent. Reichmuth writes that plural agreement is mandatory in the case of numbered controllers, and gives

38 Hillelson (1935: 10) remarks that the texts were "written down […] by pupils of the Gordon College at Khartoum". This is however no guarantee that they are actual examples of Khartoum Arabic, though some probably are.

39 He also notes that "The majority of KBA speakers still retain the productivity of PL.F as morphological category. Only urban speakers tend to generalize the masculine plural for marking also feminine plural" (Manfredi 2010: 126).

the example *sabʕa byūt samḥ-**āt*** 'seven **nice** houses', with a F.PL adjective. He also shows the opposition between the two types of agreement he describes by giving two examples with the same controller attracting two different types of agreement: *šaf al=ġarāyir katīr-**a*** 'he saw **many** sacks', and *ligu al=ġarāyir al fī=**hin** al=ʕēš* 'they found the sacks with the rice in **them**'. In the first sentence the inanimate controller triggers F.SG agreement in the non-numerical quantifier *katīr* 'a lot', while in the second the anaphoric pronoun referred to the same noun is in the F.PL, because the controller is here clearly qualified and hence more individuated.

Reichmuth (1983: 200–201) also makes two important remarks that are worth reporting here. The first one concerns the fact that speakers are able to manipulate agreement in order to heighten the saliency of the individuals or entities they are referring to. This is yet another endorsement of the general claims about agreement in Arabic dialects that appeared—almost two decades later—in Brustad's (2000) book about the syntax of spoken Arabic.

The second fact Reichmuth notes is that F.PL agreement is sometimes replaced by M.PL agreement in the speech of women, when referring to themselves or groups of other women. Reichmuth points out how this had already been reported by Blau for Palestine and Reinhardt for Oman (see below), and correctly wonders "ob hierin nicht der Ausgangspunkt für die Aufgabe der Pl.f.-Formen liegt".[40] Thus, not only does Reichmuth acknowledge the existence of a tendency we have already observed in other dialects (the substitution of F.PL forms with M.PL ones, especially in the case of human controllers); he also remarks how this phenomenon is normally more common in the speech of women. This is consistent with the typological literature about linguistic change, which indicates that innovations tend to spread first among female speakers.[41] However, see Chapter 5 for a more in-depth discussion of this point.

2.3.2.7 Palestine and Israel

Several dialects are spoken in Palestine and Israel that retain F.PL forms,[42] and only some of these belong to the group traditionally identified as "Bedouin". Among these we find the dialect of the ʕAzāzmih tribe in the Negev. Shawar-

40 "Whether this is the starting point of the process of loss of the F.PL forms".

41 This tendency was even present in Classical Arabic, according to Brockelmann, who gives the example *wa-naḥnu mustaḥwišūna* 'since we were afraid', uttered by two women (Brockelmann 1913: 97, cited in Hasselbach 2014a: 56).

42 Specifically for the area of Galilee, one can consult the detailed atlas by Behnstedt and Geva-Kleinberger (2019). Given the nature of the study, however, no information about syntax or agreement is provided.

bah (2012: 148) remarks that "syntactically [...] the concord is not always complete", and notes how—dual agreement being impossible—dual subjects tend to attract plural agreement, but targets "that refer to dual nominal headwords denoting *non*-human beings usually appear in the feminine plural" (emphasis in the original). The same is true of nonhuman plurals. All types of plural controllers can also trigger F.SG agreement. A wealth of examples follow, including *finǧalēn mgaṭṭam-**āt*** 'two **broken** demitasses' (where the adjective is in the F.PL), *aḏ=ḏiyābih yintš-**in** min ġanaṃ=ah* 'the jackals **would devour** some of his sheep' (where the verb is in the F.PL), and *an=nās gḷayyl-**ih** middit=**ah** muš kiṯīr-**ih*** 'In those days, the Bedouin were **small** in (**their**) number and not **many**' (where the three agreement targets in the F.SG are actually referred to a collective controller).

The already mentioned work by Rosenhouse (1984), besides offering a survey of all traits commonly encountered in Bedouin varieties throughout the Arabic-speaking world, also presents a more in-depth analysis of the Bedouin dialects spoken in northern Israel. Concerning these dialects, we find that the same considerations made for "Bedouin" varieties in general remain valid in this case: plural controllers (even human ones) can attract F.SG agreement if the referents are considered as a group rather than separate individuals, as in the following example: *čān-**at** al=fellāḥīn **ti**-mši kul=**ha*** 'the farmers **would go**, all of **them**' (Rosenhouse 1984: 115). Here we see both the verb preceding its controller and the verb following it attracting F.SG agreement, together with the anaphoric pronoun. Nonhuman plural nouns can trigger both F.SG and F.PL agreement, according to the same distinction (grouped/individuated), but the F.PL option seems to be restricted almost exclusively to animal controllers. Examples include: *ʔint lāzem čint tisakkā=l=na čam ʕanz kalā=l=ak w=əḥna nidfaʕ=l=ak ḥagg=**hen*** 'You should have complained with us about how many goats it had eaten from you and we would have paid you **their** price', where the pronoun referring to the goats appears in the F.PL.

As far as the sedentary dialects of Palestine and Israel are concerned, several gender-distinguishing varieties exist in the area (Jastrow 2009: 267) whose agreement systems have not, however, been described in detail. The only information we have on the subject come from Blau's treatise on the dialect of Bir Zeit and Cadora's comparative analysis of the urban and rural varieties of the area of Ramallah.[43] Blau (1960: 180) writes that non-human controllers very

43 Bauer (1913: 105) also offers some remarks on agreement in the dialects of Palestine. In his book, however, he treats the urban dialect of Jerusalem together with the varieties spoken in the rural areas around the city, so that it is not always clear whether his remarks on a given topic apply to both groups or not. Bauer mentions the possibility of adjectival

rarely trigger M.PL agreement, and that when they do so, it is normally with pronominal targets.[44]

According to Blau, the most common type of agreement with nonhuman controllers is F.PL agreement, which can appear in adjectives, verbs and pronouns alike, both with collectives and real plurals.[45] Examples include: *wi=l=ʕaṣāfīr b=ikul-**in*** 'And the birds will **say** …', *māḍ-**en** yōmēn palāpe* 'two or three days **passed**'. F.SG agreement is also possible, also with human controllers, at least collective ones: *čill il=ʕarab bāky-**e** **ti**-kḍi ʕind=e* 'all the Bedouin **continued** to **treat** him right'.

As was the case for other dialects we have analyzed in this chapter, Blau (1960: 181) notes that women often use M.PL agreement, rather than F.PL, when referring to themselves.

In the work of Cadora (1992: 128–131) one reads that in the Bedouin and rural dialects spoken around the city of Ramallah nonhuman plurals can trigger F.SG, F.PL or apophonic agreement, the latter two being apparently more common than the first, which is more frequently employed in the neighboring urban varieties. Among the examples he gives, we find *wēn il=lērāt il=bāky-**āt*** 'Where is the **remaining** money', *čill il=ġanam fakas-**in*** 'All the goats **ran away**', *dur-**in** li=ḥǧār* 'The stones **moved**' and *l=wasāyd baku yiḥuttu fī=**hin** tibin* 'The cushions, they used to stuff **them** with straw'. In all these examples we see non-

F.SG agreement only in connection with collectives (which can also trigger M.SG or broken plural agreement, see for instance *tīn mistuwi* 'ripe figs', where agreement is M.SG, and *xēl mlīḥ-**a**/mlāḥ* '**good** horses', with F.SG/broken agreement). On the following page, however, one finds the example *marrāt ktīr-**e*** '**several** times', with F.SG agreement. He reports the possibility of F.PL adjectival agreement with inanimate plurals, but only if a broken plural is not available (*qanādīl šalabīž-**āt*** '**nice** lamps'). Bauer also gives two agreement options for feminine human controllers (namely M.PL and F.PL, as in *banāt šāṭr-**īn**/šāṭr-**āt*** '**clever** girls'), and this probably reflects the different usage of the urban (non-distinguishing) and rural (distinguishing) dialects.

44 As we have seen, in virtually every gender-distinguishing variety F.PL agreement is sometimes replaced by M.PL agreement, a fact that we ascribe to an incipient process of morphological loss that will eventually bring about the total disappearance of F.PL forms. Non-distinguishing varieties have probably gone through this same process a long time ago, and the agreement system that is now in place in these dialects is the final result of this process. The fact that such a change should start in the realm of pronominal targets, gradually expanding to verbs and then adjectives, moving leftwards along the *agreement hierarchy*, is consistent with the typological literature on the subject. This topic will be discussed in dept in Chapters 3 and 5.

45 Blau weirdly remarks that this type of agreement has emerged in the dialect of Bir Zeit as the result of a "contamination" between F.SG and M.PL agreement. It seems to us that this hypothesis is entirely *ad hoc* and not supported by any type of evidence, so that it can be safely discarded.

human controllers triggering F.PL agreement in adjectival, verbal and pronominal targets (note the particularly interesting case of the pre-controller verb in the third sentence, which takes F.PL agreement despite preceding its subject).

2.3.2.8 Syria, Lebanon and Turkey

Several recent studies have highlighted the persistence of F.PL forms in numerous Lebanese varieties. Among these we note the Sunni Bedouin dialects (as Younes and Bensaria, 2017: 132, define them) spoken by the Abu ʕīd and ʕīdīn tribes in the villages of Hōš an-Nibi and aǧ-Ǧirāhiyyä respectively, in the Beqaa valley. No information about agreement patterns, however, is provided in the paper (with the exception of a single example on page 135 featuring feminine human plural controllers predictably attracting F.PL agreement). Younes and Herin (2013) also report the presence of F.PL verbs, pronouns and demonstratives in the dialect of the ʕatīǧ tribe, who live in Wādī Xālid (northeastern Lebanon). In this case as well, no information about agreement appears in the paper, but in the text presented at the end of the article one can see at least one nonhuman plural controller accompanied by two F.SG targets (*ʔaʕṛās mašhūṛ-**a** ʔaẉẉaḷ šaġlä b=ačəl=**hä*** 'weddings are **famous** first of all for **their** food').

Ana Iriarte Diez of the University of Vienna, who has recently conducted extensive fieldwork among several Bedouin tribes of Lebanon, has informed us that F.PL agreement with nonhuman plural controllers is found in the dialects of all these tribes (including the ʕaramša, the Gleyṭāt, the Hrūk, the Lwāys, the Nʕēm, the Zreyqāt and the aforementioned Abu ʕīd), and she has shared with us he following examples from her own notes: *mḥammad kala tlāt ʕaǧwāt bas ma čān-**an** ṭayb-**āt** ma ʕaǧab-**ann**=o ma ḥabb=**hən*** 'Mhammad ate three dates but they **were** not **good**. They **weren't** of his taste. He did not like **them**' (ʕaramša dialect from Dhayra in Southern lebanon, with the controller preceding F.PL adjectives, verbs and pronuns); and ***haḏanna** əč=člāb nāym-**āt** w=**haḏannāka** č=člāb ʕa=yʕaw-**an*** 'These dogs are sleeping and those dogs are barking' (Zreyqāt dialect from ʕarab Xalde in central Lebanon, with both controllers being preceded by F.PL demonstratives and followed by a F.PL participle and a F.PL verb in the p-stem). She further commented that "the young generation from the tribes closer to Beirut seemed to be more flexible and also accepted demonstratives like *hādōl* and *hādōlīk* in place of their F.PL counterparts, but they never made an attempt to change the conjugation of the verbs [from F.PL to M.PL]" (Iriarte Diez, personal communication).

Several Syrian dialects still preserve F.PL forms, including the central dialect of Mharde. Yoseph (2012: 195) remarks that "collectives and feminine plural nouns" can sometimes trigger F.SG agreement (as in *ṭabbūqat … tāxod šəhra hāy fī=**ha*** 'The straw plates … [the bride] will sometimes become famous for **them**').

As far as F.PL agreement with nonhuman controllers is concerned, Yoseph makes no mention of it, but it nonetheless appears in one of the examples he provides (*makīntayn qadīm-**āt*** 'two **old** cars', which he lists as a possible alternative to the F.SG *makīntayn qadīm-i*). As far as southern Syria is concerned, F.PL is found in several dialects in the Horan (about which see also the section on Jordan below). Cantineau (1946: 346–348) does not offer much information about agreement in these dialects, except for a passing comment in which he notes that several collectives and plural nouns are feminine (in particular, he later states that all broken plurals are feminine; it is not clear what he means by that that, i.e. if they trigger *singular* or *plural* feminine agreement, or both).

The Bedouin dialects spoken in the Syrian desert also preserve F.PL morphology, and they are typologically one with the *Šāwi* dialects spoken in southern Turkey (Procházka 2003). Unfortunately, very little information is available about agreement in these varieties. Cantineau's (1936–1937) extensive work on the dialects of the nomadic people of the Levant only focuses on phonology and morphology, so that the only source we have is represented by Cantineau's (1934) study on the dialect of Palmyra. Here the author notes that adjectives referred to human controllers can take either masculine, feminine, or broken plural agreement. Nonhuman controllers, on the other hand, tend to attract F.SG agreement in adjectives, which is "beaucoup plus frequent" than plural agreement, unless the adjective has broken plural (in this case, that is the preferred option; Cantineau 1934: 234). Conversely, in the case of verbs, it seems that F.SG agreement is infrequent (or at least, Cantineau 1934: 236 writes that this is "his impression"). Oddly enough, Cantineau does not discuss the possibility of F.PL agreement with nonhuman controllers, although at least one of the examples he provides clearly features it: *wu=l=ḥaz sār-**en** ṭāḥūntēn nār … bo=ṭḥan-**en** kṯir* 'now **there are** two motorized mills … they **mill** a lot', where both verbs are in the F.PL.

2.3.2.9 Jordan

Some notes on the dialect of the Bdūl Bedouins, spoken in Petra, are found in Owens and Bani-Yasin (1984). According to Owens and Bani-Yasin (1984: 222–223), in the Bdūl dialect "plural nouns of whatever referent almost always take plural agreement. Plural non-human nouns generally have feminine plural agreement". They give the following example: *ha=l=wiḥdāt iḥna mn an=nās alli muš rāḏy-**īn** fī=**hin*** 'As for these housing units, we are among the people who do not **want them**'. In this sentence, the human collective *nās* takes M.PL agreement in the verb, while the nonhuman plural *wiḥdāt* triggers F.PL agreement in the resumptive pronoun. The two authors remark how F.SG agreement with plural controllers is rare, and they provide a single example sentence of this pattern, where a F.SG resumptive pronoun appears: *al=mināṭig alli fī=**ha** al=aṯāṛ* 'the areas that (have) ruins in **them**'.

Agreement in the sedentary dialects of Jordan has been described in detail in a number of works, namely Owens and Bani-Yasin (1987), Herin (2010) and Herin and Al-Wer (2013). Since the contents of Owens' and Bani-Yasin's (1987) study have been discussed in detail in § 1.3, here we will focus only on the other two.[46]

Both Herin's unpublished PhD dissertation and Herin's and Al-Wer's 2013 article are focused on the dialect of Salt, a medium-sized urban center located in the proximity of Jordan's capital Amman. This dialect belongs to a group of closely interrelated varieties spoken all over the Horan Plateau. The Horan is home to "one of the oldest settlements of agrarian communities in the Levant" (Herin and Al-Wer 2013: 56),[47] and it is today divided between southern Syria and northern Jordan.

Herin (2010: 277–291) represents an invaluable contribution to the study of agreement in spoken Arabic because of the large amount of examples it contains. In general, it is possible to see that plural controllers of all types have access to both singular and plural agreement, although the latter appears to be more common. Human controllers, in particular, tend to attract plural agreement (masculine or feminine, depending on their biological sex) except in the case of collectives and nouns that refer to geographical origin and/or ethnic belonging. See for instance *ağ-**at** əl=inglīz u=ḥaṭṭ-**at** īd=**ha** ʕa ha=lə=blād* 'the English **came** and **put their** hands on this country', where the two verbs and the possessive pronoun are in the F.SG.

In the case of nonhuman plural controllers, these tend to attract plural agreement when they are quantified or when they are constituted by a chain of conjoined singular nouns. Herin notes how nonhuman controllers tend to trigger F.PL agreement, although M.PL agreement does sometimes occur (apparently, more often with inanimate controller than animal ones). Herin compares his data with those of Owens and Bani-Yasin (1987), where M.PL agreement was apparently absent. This could represent yet another piece of evidence of the fact that urbanization tends to affect the gender system of Arabic dialects, causing the gradual disappearance of F.PL forms (Salt is today a medium-sized metropolis; unlike Herin, Owens and Bani-Yasin gathered their data in smaller villages in the Jordan Horan). All of the above is basically confirmed by Herin

46 The interested reader, however, could usefully consult the original article, since in it the authors provide several interesting examples of agreement structures.

47 Palva (2008: 53) also agrees that the retention of gender distinction in the plural in Salti is to be regarded as a conservative sedentary trait.

and Al-Wer (2013), who, however, put forward the hypothesis, already discussed in §1.3, that the use of F.SG agreement with plural controllers is actually an innovation induced by contact with the neighboring and more prestigious dialect of Amman. We will not discuss this point here, since we will return on it at the end of the present section. Note, however, that some of the examples presented in Herin (2010) do not seem to support such an interpretation, most notably the case of the noun *šaġlāt* 'things', that is described as systematically attracting F.SG agreement in the speech of all informants. In this case, we are prone to think that the cause of such uniformity is the controller's intrinsically low level of individuation. If the only factors favoring F.SG agreement were sociolinguistic in nature, one would expect variation—or lack thereof—to be speaker or context dependent, rather than lexically conditioned (at least in the case of an element such as *šaġlāt*, which clearly belongs to the "core" vocabulary of the dialect).

2.3.2.10 Iraq

Data about agreement in gender-distinguishing dialects of Iraq are regrettably scarce. Salonen's (1980) description of the dialect of Širqāṭ is but a sketch of phonology and morphology. The collection of texts from southern Iraq by Denz and Edzard (1966) contains no grammatical description. Denz (1971), on the contrary, very accurately describes the temporal, modal and aspectual functions of the verb in the dialect of the Kwayriš, but provides no information about agreement. Mahdi (1985) gives no information about agreement in the dialect of Basra.

It is only in Meißner's short anthology of Iraqi Folktales that we find a short grammatical description of the rural dialect of Kwayriš. According to the author (Meißner 1903: xxvii), in this variety adjectives that refer to human controllers (broken or sound plurals, or collectives), take either broken or M.PL agreement. Adjectives that refer to any other type of plural controller take F.SG, or F.PL, or broken agreement. The same seems to be true for verbs (Meißner 1903: xxxviii), though there are exceptions with morphologically singular nouns denoting groups (half of, all of, etc.). Examples of F.PL agreement include: *naxlāt ṭawīl-**āt*** 'tall palm trees', *ṯirān meʕammam-**āt*** 'bulls **wearing** a turbant', *inlāx-**an** hudūm=ha* 'her clothes **were spotted**'. Examples of F.SG agreement include: *ašǧār ketīr-**e*** '**many** trees', ***ti**-tlawwax hudūm=i* 'my clothes **get dirty**'.

McCarthy's and Raffouli's manual of Baghdadi Arabic is also worth mentioning. The two authors remark that, although not part of the dialect of the city itself, F.PL forms are sometimes used "due to tribal influence" (this passage is unclear: the authors probably mean that these forms are in use among certain Bedouin speakers outside of Baghdad). Be that as it may, McCarthy and Raffouli's (1965: 177–178) note that nouns of nonhuman reference, when plural, can take either F.SG or F.PL adjectives. According to them, the latter form is only allowed in the case of nouns whose singular is morphologically feminine, but as they themselves admit, the topic is in need of more accurate research.

Leitner, German and Procházka (2021: 47–48) are apparently in agreement: they write that F.PL agreement is possible with nonhuman referents, although "viel seltener" ("much more rarely") than M.PL, broken or F.SG agreement. In particular, they note that its use is more common "wenn das Subjekt [...] näher bezeichnet wird" ("when the subject [...] is more specifically described"), though F.SG agreement is always a possible alternative (with abstract nouns in particular, it seems to be almost mandatory). Among the examples they offer we find: *šūf* ***hadanni*** *il=bizāzīn il=ḥilw-****āt*** / *šūf* ***hay*** *il=bizāzīn il=ḥilw-****a*** 'look at **these nice** cats!'. In the first version of the sentence, the demonstrative is in the C.PL and the adjective is F.PL. In the alternative version, both elements stand in the F.SG.

2.3.2.11 Saudi Arabia

Saudi Arabia is a vast country that encompasses several different dialectal areas. In the west we find the urban dialects of Hijaz, that have lost gender distinction in the plural. Gender-distinguishing varieties exist in this area as well, but they remain undocumented to this day.

The dialects spoken along the eastern shore, in the province of al-Ḥasa, are akin to those spoken in the rest of Gulf, and so they will be treated in the next section.

As far as central Arabia is concerned, the dialects of the Najdi plateau are rather well-known: they have been the object of several detailed studies, most of which authored by Bruce Ingham, whose thorough grammar stands out as exemplar in the field. In spite of all the attention they have received, however, their agreement system remains in need of a more accurate description.

Ingham (1994: 61–62) notes that "the most general rule is that [...] the plural of a noun with a non-human referent takes feminine singular concord"; however, he adds that such controllers can also attract feminine plural agreement, and provides several examples of this (Ingham 1994: 64–65). In general, he remarks that "the picture with regard to this system is not at all clear".

In § 2.3.3 we will try to further our knowledge of the Najdi agreement system, by providing a statistical analysis of all the agreement occurrences appearing in a corpus of Najdi texts. For the sake of our present discussion, it is sufficient to say that these varieties show all the typical traits described by Rosenhouse as representative of "Bedouin" dialects, i.e. F.PL agreement with nonhuman plural controllers and F.SG agreement with all types of plural controllers, including human ones.

Interestingly, although the inner Peninsula remains one of the main strongholds of resistance for F.PL forms across the Arabic-speaking World, the beginning of a process of morphological loss can be seen here as well. Ingham (1994: 66) notes how, in the material he gathered in Riyadh, the F.PL "was more often present in the speech of members of the older generation and with the speech of those who were more 'traditional'". According to Prochazka (1988: 24), F.PL verbs and pronouns are not present at all in Riyadh Arabic.[48]

2.3.2.12 Gulf States

The dialects spoken along the western shore of the Persian Gulf, from southern Iraq in the north to the United Arab Emirates in the south, are all structurally very similar, to the point that they are normally referred to as a homogeneous entity in the literature. Most of them have lost gender distinction in the plural, though a few exceptions reportedly exist, on which we will focus in the present section.

According to Johnstone (1967: 165), certain Qatari speakers still employ F.PL forms. In these cases, "feminine plurals of adjectives and verbs [...] are often applied to animals, particularly to camels". Johnstone (1967: 166) also notes that "the plural of a noun denoting an inanimate object has a feminine singular verb". As far as pronouns are concerned, he remarks that F.PL forms are commonly replaced by M.PL ones, and that inanimate objects can trigger plural agreement "especially where the noun and the pronoun are not in immediate contiguity".[49] In general, however, F.SG forms are more common in this context as well.

The same considerations made for Qatari Arabic are apparently valid for the dialects of Buraimi and Abu Dhabi (but not Dubai, where F.PL forms have been lost). However, even in these Emirati dialects Johnstone (1967: 170) reports that M.PL forms are often interchangeable with F.PL ones.

48 Even certain prototypically "Bedouin" dialects from the area appear to have lost F.PL morphology, such as the dialect of the Āl Murra (see § 2.3.6). Consider also footnote 58 in § 2.3.3.1 about the dialect of the Dawāsir. It might be worth mentioning that a generative study on agreement in Najdi Arabic exists, namely Kramer and Winchester (2018). In this article, however, the two authors oddly lump Najdi Arabic together with the (non-distinguishing) dialects of urban Hijaz, and F.PL agreement is never mentioned in the paper. The study is, therefore, of little interest for our current survey.

49 Johnstone is one of the few authors to refer to the influence that distance between target and controller has on agreement outcomes. We will discuss this topic in depth in § 2.3.3.4.

Holes (1990: 155–157) focuses on the same area as Johnstone. He devotes a lengthy section to agreement in the Gulf dialects, noting in particular how "the gender of plural nouns is a more complex issue [than the gender of singular nouns], and is subject to much individual and communal variation". This is not surprising since, as we have seen, some varieties in the area have lost F.PL forms while others still retain them, but seem to be progressively reducing their contexts of use. In general, Holes claims that it is only in the southern Gulf that one still encounters F.PL agreement (i.e. in the UAE and northern Oman), and that in these cases this is restricted to human feminine or nonhuman controllers. The latter, however, can also variably attract F.SG agreement.

2.3.2.13 Yemen

Yemen is renowned among scholars of Arabic dialectology for hosting a remarkable amount of linguistic diversity. However, although materials about Yemeni varieties are relatively abundant, not much has been written concerning their syntax, and very little in particular on the topic of agreement.

The only data on the subject are to be found in Watson's description of the dialect of the Yemeni capital, Sanaa. Watson (1993: 101, 213–214) writes that, in the case of nonhuman controllers, adjectives can take either F.PL or F.SG (or broken) agreement. This is also true of anaphoric pronouns (Watson 1993: 385). In particular, she specifies that F.SG agreement "is generally used when the subject referents are viewed as a collectivity". Among the examples of F.PL adjectives, we find *al=jibāl ʕāliy-**āt*** 'the mountains are **high**' and *basātīn wāsiʕ-**āt*** '**wide** gardens'. Among the examples of F.SG agreement, we have *al=ayyām gadīm-**ih*** 'the days are **old**', and *biyūt ʕāliy-**ih*** '**tall** houses'.[50] Watson does not comment on verbal agreement, but the examples that appear on page 115 show that in this case as well both F.SG and F.PL agreement with nonhuman controllers are possible.

2.3.2.14 Oman

Oman is idiosyncratic among all the countries where Arabic is spoken as a majority language in that all its dialects still retain gender distinction in the plural. Although most Omani varieties remain gravely under-researched, data about agreement are fairly abundant.

50 Watson (1993: 102–103) makes another interesting remark about agreement in Sanaani, namely the fact that M.PL agreement can be used as a mark of respect with reference to individuals at least one generation older than the speaker. Elderly speakers and people of relatively higher rank can even use plural forms with reference to themselves (as in ***ʔaḥna*** *bixayr-**īn*** 'I am well', literally '**we** are **well**').

In his grammar of the dialect of the Bani Xarūṣ, Reinhardt (1894: 265) observes that broken plurals always attract F.PL agreement unless they denote human males. Examples include both animate and inanimate controllers: *mištān-**āt** lo=xyūl min ḍarb l=medfaʕ* 'the horses **were scared** by gunfire', *mitšakl-**āt** ḏylāk l=kerāsi* 'those chairs are **similar**'. Sometimes, however, agreement can be F.SG, especially if the quantifier *kill* 'all, every' is present: *henāk šġār aʕaraf=ši sum=**he*** 'there are trees there, the names of **which** I do not know', *l=umwāl kill=**he** maḥdūr-**a*** 'the properties are all (of **them**) **fenced**'. It would seem that here, as well, a distinction between individuated and grouped perception of the referents is at work. This finds further confirmation in Reinhardt's (1894: 266) remarks about collective controllers. Both collectives that possess a singulative and those that do not can attract either plural or singular agreement "je nach der Auffassung des Sprechenden".[51] In particular, collectives denoting animals will always trigger feminine agreement (be that plural or singular), while collectives denoting human males or mixed groups attract masculine agreement in the plural. Examples include: *l=ġanem yišter=l=**hin** ḏne=**hin** yōm yiḥamr-**an*** 'small cattle, **their** ears are cut (to **them**) when they **go into heat**'.

Reinhardt does not mention the possibility of F.SG agreement with human plurals or collectives, but several examples of this appear in Bettega (2017: 158, 165): *əl=awādəm illi məttaxxar-**a** ʕalā d=dwām* 'The people who **are late** for work', *n=nās **t**-zīd* 'people become more numerous'. Bettega presents a statistical analysis of a small corpus of 180 plural controllers with 269 corresponding targets, based on materials drawn from Omani TV shows. In this study, the author notes how nonhuman plural controllers can either attract F.SG agreement (64,5% of cases) or F.PL agreement (35,5%). Examples of F.SG agreement include: *ʕyūn=hum muġlān-**a*** 'their eyes are reddened', *ayyām=ak ṣār-**at** maʕdūd-**a*** 'your days **are numbered**'. Among the examples of F.PL agreement we find: *s=suwārāt illi štarētī=**hən** min-ni* 'the bracelets you bought (**them**) from me' and *ašyā hāḏēla muxtarb-**āt*** 'these things are **broken**'. Bettega investigates several factors that may induce this type of oscillation between singular and plural agreement, including concreteness, quantification, target type and so on. These topics will be addressed in more detail in § 2.3.3.

It is perhaps worth noting that the percentages of F.SG agreement in Bettega's corpus are higher than those observed in other gender-distinguishing dialects, but this might be due to the nature of the data employed, where an influence from the standard language is to be expected. The sociolinguistic and

51 "Depending on the speaker's perception".

diachronic motivations behind the variation found in the data are addressed in Bettega (2019b), and will be discussed in more depth in Chapter 5. Bettega (2019b: 156) also reports a very few examples of M.PL agreement where F.PL would be expected instead. The author suggests that the influence of the neighboring and more prestigious Gulf dialects is responsible for this shift. This tendency was already noted by Jayakar (1889: 664–665) more than one century earlier. Interestingly, in the materials on which Morano's (2019) PhD dissertation is based, gathered in the northern district of Al Awabi, all cases of substitution of F.PL with M.PL agreement concern feminine human controllers (Roberta Morano, personal communication with the authors).

Southern Oman is partially covered by Davey's detailed grammar of Coastal Dhofari Arabic (CDA). Davey (2016: 77) reports that "Non-human plural nominal forms in cda, along with most body parts that occur in pairs, are also considered to be underlying feminine forms, regardless of their lexical referents". Davey (2016: 88) also comments on the possibility of F.SG agreement with non-human controllers, saying that this almost never occurs with adjectives, but it is more common in verbs, demonstratives and pronouns. The possibility of F.SG agreement with human referents is not discussed.

2.3.2.15 Iran

Arabic is spoken as a minority language by several communities residing in Iran, most notably along the coast of the Persian Gulf, and in the provinces of Khuzestan and Khorasan.

Agreement patterns in Khuzestani Arabic have been carefully analyzed by Bettega and Leitner in an article that features statistical analysis of a corpus consisting of 270 plural or collective controllers with 521 corresponding targets. The data presented by Bettega and Leitner (2019) seem to confirm the existence of an "animacy hierarchy" (first postulated by Belnap for Cairene Arabic), in that their data show a monotonic increase of the use of F.SG agreement with plural controllers, starting low with human controllers (1.9%) and then getting progressively higher with nonhuman animates (14.8%) and inanimates (30.9%). They analyze collective controllers separately from proper plurals, showing that F.SG agreement is normally more common with the former group. In addition, the animacy hierarchy is not entirely respected in the case of collectives, because F.SG agreement appears to be more common with animal controllers than inanimate ones. F.SG agreement, at any rate, can occur with any controller type. Examples of collective human controllers triggering F.SG agreement include *gabul memš-**a** l=wādim ət-rūḥ l=əl=ḥaǧǧ* 'In former times, people (used to) **walk** when they **went** on *ḥaǧǧ*'. F.SG agreement with non-collective human controllers, though rarer, is also possible: *hāy lə=frūx kəll=**ha***

'These children, all of **them** ...'. Among the examples of nonhuman controllers attracting F.SG agreement we find: *ləga əl=ġanam kəll=**ha** mkəssar-**a*** 'He found the sheep, all of **them broken footed**', *ət-taʕaddā=l=ha taġrīban šahrēn* 'More or less two months **passed**' (note that here the subject is marked for dual: nonetheless, the preceding verb agrees in the F.SG).

Bettega and Leitner also note that, in the case of nonhuman controllers, agreement, when plural, is always feminine. M.PL agreement is reserved for human males and, in some rare cases, higher animates. Some examples of F.PL agreement with nonhuman controllers are: *madārəs=kum ntum hna lli tšūfū=**hən*** 'These schools of yours, which you see (**them**)', ***hadanni*** *məṣṭala-ḥāt maḥalliyy-**āt** ṭabʕan maḥḥad yəfham=**hən*** '**These** are **local** expressions, of course no one understands **them**'.

As was the case for Bettega's (2017) paper about agreement in Omani dialects, Bettega and Leitner also investigate the causes that induce variation between singular and plural agreement in Khuzestani Arabic, which will be more thoroughly discussed in § 2.3.3.

As far as the Iranian dialects of the coast or those of Khorasan are concerned, at present not enough data are available to analyze their agreement patterns in detail. We know, however, that the dialects of Khorasan preserve gender distinction in the plural in the same way as those of Uzbekistan and Afghanistan do (Seeger 2013), and they are considered to be an offshoot of the latter (Ingham 2006: 28). It is therefore to be expected that they show a certain amount of similarity also in agreement behavior, so the reader is referred to the next section. In the short text presented at the end of Seeger 2013, examples abound of animal plurals triggering F.PL agreement in verbs and pronouns.

2.3.2.16 Uzbekistan

Very little is known about agreement in the few dialects of Arabic still spoken in Uzbekistan. Most of the descriptions that exist of these varieties are written in Russian, and some of these are hard to access. The ones that we were able to consult contain no information about the agreement behavior of the different controller types. All that we know on the subject comes from this observation by Blanc (1970: 50): "In Bukhara, Cereteli's texts and Vinnikov's examples show an overwhelming preponderance of PC, but FSC does occur occasionally in both adjectives and verbs". Blanc gives a single example of the latter phenomenon, namely *ijra=y halk-**a*** 'My legs are **tired**'. It can be of some interest the observation, made by Fischer (1961: 243), that Uzbekistan Arabic seems to have generalized suffixation as the standard pluralization strategy for nouns, at the expenses of the apophony. The ending *-īn*, in particular, is reserved to human males, while all other plurals (human females and nonhuman entities) form their plural by the addition of *-āt*. It stands to reason, then, that this latter group of nouns will also trigger F.PL agreement.

2.3.2.17 Summary

Having presented all the available information on the topic of agreement in gender-distinguishing dialects, we can now move on to discuss the implications of the data.

From what we have seen so far, and with reference to Rosenhouse's traits (1) and (2) discussed at the beginning of this section, the following can be concluded: as far as F.PL agreement with nonhuman plural controllers is concerned (trait number 1), the results of our survey are strikingly uniform. There is not a single dialect, among those analyzed, in which this type of agreement does not occur. This feature cuts across even the traditional Bedouin/sedentary distinction, in that certain historically sedentary dialects employ F.PL forms as well (Salt in Jordan, Bir Zeit in Palestine, the Bani Xarūṣ of northern Oman and Coastal Dhofari Arabic in southern Oman, Sanaa in Yemen). With respect to this specific point, then, this classification appears to be of only limited typological significance.

This uniformity in syntactical behavior is a particularly remarkable finding. In §1.3 we mentioned the fact that Blanc was one of the first scholars to note how F.PL agreement with nonhuman controllers is widespread in Arabic dialects. Let us now consider the original quote in its entirety:

> It is irrelevant, for this discussion [about variation between singular and plural agreement with plural controllers], that some dialects (Palestine, Najd, Bukhara, much of Mesopotamia etc.) have generalized the feminine plural forms for concord with nouns of non-personal reference, while others have only a single form (the historical masculine plural) for plural concord
>
> BLANC 1970: 50

We can now demonstrate that it is not "some dialects" that use F.PL agreement in this context. It is actually all dialects that retain gender distinction in the plural. Also, this can hardly be considered a "generalization" of what was once a more restricted pattern. If that was the case, we would expect exceptions to exist (why would all dialects have evolved in exactly the same way, from Tunisia to Uzbekistan?). If we insist in considering the use of F.PL agreement with nonhuman plurals a generalization, the only possible explanation is that this generalization happened at a very early (Proto-Arabic?) stage, long before the various dialects reached their current geographical distribution. We will not insist on this point here, since the diachronic evolution of agreement in Arabic will be treated in more depth in Chapters 3 and 5.

In the case of F.SG agreement with plural controllers (trait number 2), our results also appear remarkably uniform. In the vast majority of cases, this type of agreement appears to be possible. A few descriptions exist that make no mention of the phenomenon, but, as we have seen, in two cases (the Arabic of Maiduguri and that of Sinai Bedouins) F.SG agreement is shown to be present in closely related varieties. In another (Bʕēri Arabic), the little information we have comes from a short entry in the Encyclopedia of Arabic language and linguistics, where the topic is only summarily sketched. None of the aforementioned studies makes any explicit statement about the impossibility of this type of agreement, and the topic is simply left unaddressed. If F.SG agreement were actually impossible, one would expect the authors to comment on the subject (as regularly happens in grammars of non-distinguishing varieties where this phenomenon does not occur, see § 2.3.6).

Standing these considerations, we believe it is safe to conclude that F.SG agreement with plural controllers is actually in use in all gender-distinguishing varieties, although with varying degrees of frequency. In particular, it appears to be very rare in Fezzani Arabic, in the dialect of the Ulād Eli of Chad, in the dialect of the Bdūl of Jordan, and in the dialect of Bukhara.

The same considerations we made for F.PL agreement are thus valid for F.SG agreement: firstly, this feature cuts across the traditional Bedouin/sedentary distinction (as will become clear in § 2.3.6, it even cuts across the distinguishing/non-distinguishing distinction). Secondly, this type of agreement is, in all likelihood, a very old shared retention.

In § 1.3, we have seen how Herin and Al-Wer considered F.SG agreement with plural nonhuman controllers an innovation in the Jordanian dialect of Salt, caused by contact with urban varieties:

> Plural feminine agreement represents the old, native pattern and the appearance of the singular feminine singular is an innovation […]. In the case of Salti, the source of the variation attested in our data is likely to be the dialect of Amman which […] lacks the plural feminine as an inflectional category
>
> HERIN AND AL-WER, 2013: 71

If the use of F.SG agreement with plural controller was indeed an innovation, then one would expect at least some dialects to lack it (especially dialects that have not been in contact with other varieties of Arabic for a very long time, such as most of the dialects of Iran and Uzbekistan and those spoken in Sub Saharan Africa).[52] This is not, however, the case. It seems reasonable to think, then, that, far from being an innovation, this type of agreement represents a very old shared retention. With this, we do not intend to rule out the possibility that contact with other varieties (either standard or dialectal ones) can actually induce an increase in the frequency of use of F.SG agreement. On the contrary, as we will see, our data seem to confirm this. It is probably the case, however, that F.SG forms have always constituted a part—albeit possibly minor—of the agreement systems of all varieties of Arabic.

The diachronic dimension of our research will be discussed in more depth in Chapters 3 and 5. Let us now continue our analysis of the nature of gender and agreement in gender-distinguishing dialects of Arabic.

2.3.3 *Plural Agreement in Gender-Distinguishing Dialects: A Corpus-Based Analysis*

As anticipated in § 1.3, the present section and the next one represent an expanded version of Bettega's (2019a) paper on the nature of agreement in gender-distinguishing varieties of Arabic. Although the theses put forward in that paper will be re-proposed unaltered here, the discussion of the theoretical points underpinning them has been greatly expanded.

A practical way to investigate the remarkable complexity of agreement phenomena in any given language is represented by the analysis of statistically relevant corpora of data, which can help in the identification of tendencies and recurring patterns. Several corpus-based studies of agreement in Arabic dialects exist to this day, which have contributed to increase our knowledge of this aspect of syntax.

In the present section we will try to summarize what is currently known about agreement in spoken Arabic, comparing the results presented in the aforementioned studies and adding new data of our own, before attempting a wider synthesis in § 2.3.4. Note that, since variation between F.SG and plural agreement is governed by similar principles in both distinguishing and non-distinguishing varieties of Arabic, our discussion will also include reference to works dealing with the latter, where relevant.

In the following pages, we will first introduce the nature of our corpus of data, and then move on to investigate the different agreement phenomena that

52 Note that these varieties have not been in contact with Standard Arabic, either, so that Owens' and Bani-Yasin's hypothesis, discussed in § 1.3, cannot be accepted in its entirety (though it is probably true that, in other varieties, loans from the standard language tend to bring their idiosyncratic agreement system with them; on this point, see also Chapter 5).

occur within it and the factors that affect them. In particular, we will briefly discuss the topic of agreement with human controllers, before moving on to a more in-depth analysis of agreement patterns with nonhuman ones. As far as the latter are concerned, our analysis will focus on the following factors, in the given order:

I) Factors related to the controller (collectiveness, quantification and coordination, animacy and concreteness, specificity, definiteness and qualification)
II) Factors related to the target (distance between target and controller, agreement domains and target type).[53]

2.3.3.1 Our Corpus of Najdi Texts

As we have seen in § 2.3.2, the dialects of Arabic that still retain gender distinction in the plural are fairly numerous. Not all of them, though, are equally well known, and stark differences also exist between them in terms of number of speakers, geographical diffusion, and perceived sociolinguistic prestige. Najdi Arabic undisputedly represents one of the most important members of this group, and probably the best documented.

The name "Najd" refers to the plateau that rises at the center of the Arabian Peninsula, and identifies a geographical region roughly delimited by the mountains of Hijaz and Yemen in the west and south-west, the Empty Quarter desert in the south, the Dahana dunes in the east, and the Nafud desert and the Euphrates valley in the north. This vast area is inhabited by what Ingham (1994: 4) refers to as a "geographically far-flung but culturally relatively homogenous" population, who speaks "a group of dialects which are also fairly homogenous and which we can term the Najdi dialects".

Ingham (1994: 5) divides Najdi Arabic into four main subgroups.[54] Despite their presenting a number of superficial differences, Ingham repeatedly insists on the fundamental homogeneity of these dialects at the syntactical level.[55] Therefore, in creating our corpus of data, we have drawn linguistic material from texts in different varieties of Najdi Arabic.[56] This was also done in light

53 A third target-related factor, namely its relative position with respect to the controller (i.e. word order), will be discussed separately in § 2.3.9.

54 Namely Central Najdi (spoken by the tribes of ʕanizah, ʕutaibah, Subaiʕ, Suhūl, Bugūm, Dawāsir, Ḥarb, Muṭair, ʕawāzim and Rašāyidah), Northern Najdi (Šammar), mixed Northern-Central Najdi (Qaṣīm, Ḍhafīr) and Southern Najdi ("The dialect of Najrān and the Għaṭān tribe of the south and of the Āl Murrah and ʕĀjmān tribes of the east").

55 "The main difference between the three types, Northern, Southern and Central is morphological, while they agree broadly in the phonological inventory and distribution and even more so in the syntax and grammar" (Ingham 1994: xi).

56 In order to double-check Ingham's claims, we independently tried to determine if some

of the fact that none of the works consulted, taken singularly, provided a large enough sample of agreement occurrences.

In particular, the following works have been employed as primary sources:

1) Ten short Central Najdi texts: two contained in Ingham (1979), one in Ingham (1980), three in Ingham (1982a),[57] two in Ingham (1994), and two in Kurpershoek (1993).[58]

---

observable difference existed between Northern and Central Najdi in terms of syntactic behavior. This was done by analyzing each sub-corpora separately before merging them together. No discrepancy worth mentioning emerged from our analysis, however, except maybe for a slight predilection for F.PL agreement in the Northern Najdi material. Given the limited size of the sub-corpora, however, we deem these minor fluctuations to be statistically irrelevant. It seems to us that our analysis confirms Ingham's intuition about the syntactic homogeneity of these dialects, and the figures presented in the following pages are therefore derived from calculations based on all the materials included in the corpus.

57 Namely texts 3 to 5. The first text presented in the book did not contain any nonhuman plural or collective controller, and the second two (2a and 2b) are the same texts as those contained in Ingham 1979.

58 In our original intentions, the corpus should have been expanded by including all the prose texts contained in the fourth volume of Kurpershoek's monumental work on the oral traditions of the Dawāsir. However, a careful examination of these materials revealed a surprising fact. No variation in agreement with nonhuman plural controllers appears in the texts of Kurpershoek (2002): agreement patterns are remarkably uniform, with nonhuman plurals consistently attracting F.SG agreement throughout the corpus (even with dual and quantified controllers). F.PL agreement only occurs in conjunction with the (extremely rare) feminine human plural subjects (e.g. *wsēm al=ʕāmiriyya hi w=iyya uxt=ha mšarrif-***āt***=in li=***hin** *fi rās ğibal* […] *yiṭalb-***in** 'Wsēm al-ʕāmiriyya and her sister **were watching** [the battle] from a lookout on a mountain […] **they sent up** fervent prayers', pp. 240–241). While the absence of F.PL agreement with nonhuman controllers is systematic in prose texts, it does occasionally appear in poetry. In this case as well, however, the preponderance of F.SG agreement is overwhelming, the ratio of F.SG and F.PL targets being in the order of several hundreds to one (for an example of this, see p. 272: … *w=farš=in ygallat fōg=***hinn** *dlāl-ha* '… and carpets upon **which** they serve their coffee pots'). This peculiarity remains in need of an adequate explanation, but the influence of the normative MSA rule that dictates F.SG agreement with nonhuman controllers seems the most obvious one. It is possible that Kurpershoek's informants were to an extent influenced by it, but it appears more likely that agreement variation was expunged from the texts during the transcription sessions, which were carried out with the help of younger informants with a higher level of education (Kurpershoek's describes this activity in detail, see pp. 100–105). Of course, the possibility cannot be ruled out that the agreement system found in these texts represents the actual state of affairs in the dialect of the Dawāsir. In light of all the comparative evidence presented in § 2.3.2, however, this seems highly unlikely to us, since it would represent a *unicum* in the whole Arabic-speaking world, exceptional even with respect to the "divergent" agreement systems discussed in § 2.3.8. Further independent research would be needed to confirm this point.

2) One short Northern Najdi text (text 6 from Ingham 1982a), plus the long narrative contained in Sowayan's (1992) monograph on the oral traditions of the Šammar.
3) Two short Ḍhafīri (mixed Northern-Central) texts, contained in Ingham (1982b) and Ingham (1986a).

As can been seen, our corpus does not include any Southern Najdi Material. This is because the only available text representative of this variety (an ʕağmāni text included in Ingham 1982a) does not contain any target depending on a nonhuman plural controller. Āl Murrah texts have not been included, as well, since in this dialect feminine plural morphological markers have been lost (Ingham 1994: 66). As far as the other two subgroupings are concerned, our corpus is fairly balanced, since it includes 53 nonhuman agreement controllers taken from Central Najdi texts and 58 from Northern Najdi texts, plus 17 controllers taken from mixed Northern-Central Najdi texts. It can be noted that, overall, the corpus is relatively limited in size. This is regrettable but, unfortunately, unavoidable: when it comes to gender-distinguishing dialects of Arabic, finding large corpora of data on which to base statistical analyses is virtually impossible. All the corpus-based quantitative studies that exist to date concerning gender-distinguishing dialects have been carried out by the two authors of this book (D'Anna 2017, Bettega 2017, Bettega 2019a, Bettega and Leitner 2019), and all suffer from the same scarcity of data (the largest of these corpora is the one constituted by Leitner's Khuzestani dataset, which amounts to a total of 270 plural/collective controllers: that is, roughly twice the number of controllers that appear in our Najdi corpus, but still an extremely limited sample). The obvious consequence of this is that the figures presented in next pages, as well as the conclusions that are derived from said figures, must be approached with some caution, and always keeping in mind that in most cases they represent moderate statistical tendencies. On the other hand, the reader will appreciate the fact that these tendencies, moderate as they may be, appear to be always consistent cross-dialectally (and this remains true even if we consider distinguishing and non-distinguishing dialects together, and—as we will see—seems also to apply to the very ancient, pre-Classical written materials). In other words, while certain agreement tendencies may be more marked in some varieties, and less evident in others, the *direction* of these tendencies remains constant diatopically and diachronically, with few to none counterexamples. This makes us confident as to the general validity of our description.

The vast majority of the texts on which our Najdi corpus is based consist of oral narratives dealing with the topic of Bedouin life in the pre-oil era, though a few dialogues appear among Ingham's own data. Only agreement occurrences found in prose texts have been considered for the sake of our analysis, while the poetic material contained in some of the works has not been included in the corpus (see § 3.9 for a discussion of agreement in modern *nabaṭī* poetry).

Note that the following sections will only focus on agreement with plural and collective controllers. The topic of singular agreement has been discussed in § 2.3.1.

2.3.3.2 Agreement with Human Controllers

Human controllers in the corpus have not been made the object of statistical analysis, since this would have been of little significance. These controllers number in the thousands, and the overwhelming majority refer to human males and attract M.PL agreement, as in examples (1) and (2):[59]

(1) *ar=rǧāl al=awwil-**īn***
DEF=men DEF =first-M.PL
'The ancients' (Sowayan 1992: 138)

(2) *gām-**aw** ḥatta xwān=ih yi-xz-**ūn** ʕalē=h*
start-3.PFV.M.PL even brothers=his 3.IPFV-revile-M.PL on=him
'Even his brothers started to revile him' (Ingham 1982a: 113)

Human controllers referring to groups consisting exclusively of women are very rare in the texts, but when they appear, they predictably trigger feminine plural agreement, as in (3) and (4):

(3) *l=ḥarīm [...] **hin** mxallṣ-**āt**=in zihbuwwāt=ihum*
the=women [...] they. F.PL prepare.PTCP-F.PL=INDEF provisions:F.PL=their
'The women [...] prepared the provisions (for the men)' (Sowayan 1992: 150)

(4) *ṯalaṯ banāt ǧa-**nn** [...] y-ʕāyid-**inn** ubū=**hin***
three girl.PL come-3.PFV.F.PL [...] 3.IPFV-visit-F.PL father=their.F.PL
'Three daughters came [...] to visit their father' (Ingham 1980)

59 The transcriptions of the examples have been adapted, while the original translations have been maintained. All the examples are presented with a reference to the original source, and with a partially glossed and more literal translation. Relevant morphological elements marking gender and number have been highlighted in bold.

Mixed groups of people containing both men and women (or groups of individuals whose gender is unspecified) always attracted masculine plural agreement, as in (5), (6) and (7):

(5) *nād-i* *l=ʕyāl* *u=xallī=**hum*** *yi-stiʕidd-**ūn***
call-IMP.F.SG DEF=child.PL and=let=them.M.PL 3.IPFV-prepare-M.PL
'Call the children and let them get ready' (Ingham 1994: 151)

(6) *al=misilm-īn* *mā=**hum*** *bi=y-gaṣṣir-**ū***
DEF=muslim-M.PL NEG=they.M.PL IRR=3.IPFV-forsake-M.PL
'The Muslims, they do not forsake (their friends)' (Ingham 1982a: 113)

(7) *al=atrāk* […] *ʕind=**hum***
DEF=turk.PL […] with=them.M.PL
'The Turks […] they had …' (Ingham 1982a: 103)

The co-occurrence of plural agreement with human controllers, however, is not an absolute rule. In § 2.3.2 we have seen how the majority of gender-distinguishing dialects contemplate the possibility of F.SG agreement with human subjects, and Najdi Arabic represents no exception. Ingham (1994: 63) notes that it is possible for plural or collective nouns denoting human beings to take F.SG agreement.

In the materials we examined, plural agreement was by far the most common type of agreement with human controllers: however, several dozen targets appeared in the corpus depending on human controllers and showing F.SG agreement. As Ingham remarks, this is particularly common with collectives. The most typical representative of this category is *nās* 'people', which we see in example (8) attracting F.SG agreement in three verbal targets:

(8) *nās* ***ti-ḏbaḥ*** *nās* ***ti-ṭbax*** *nās*
people 3.IPFV.F.SG-slaightering people 3.IPFV.F.SG-cooking people
ti-nɟax
3.IPFV.F.SG-pounding
'Some people were slaughtering [sheep], and others cooking, and others pounding [coffee beans]' (Ingham 1982a: 142–143).

In example (9), *nās* attracts F.SG agreement in the verb that precedes it, but M.PL agreement in the one that follows. The effects of word order on agreement will be more thoroughly discussed in § 2.3.9, but we can already see how these examples of "mixed" agreement are far from uncommon:

(9) *w=***ta***-fraḥ* *an-nās* *w=ya-rčib-***ūn** *miʕ=uh*
and=3.IPFV.F.SG-rejoyce DEF=people and=3.IPFV-ride-M.PL with=him
'The men were overjoyed and rode with him' (Sowayan 1992: 92)

In example (10) we can see another very common factor having an effect on agreement, namely distance between controller and target. The word *ʕarab* attracts F.SG agreement in the first two verbs, but when another subject is mentioned, the verb that follows—which refers back to *ʕarab*—shows M.PL agreement instead:

(10) *wa=l=ʕarab* **t***-banni* *byūt=***ah** *wi=***t***-ḥafr*
and=DEF=people 3.IPFV.F.SG-build house.PL =her and=3.IPFV.F.SG-dig
al=ma *bēṭ* *mindif=in* *w=ya-ḥafr-***ūn***=uh*
DEF=water Bēṭ buried.PTCP=INDEF and=3.IPFV-dig-M.PL=it
'The people were setting up their tents and clearing the water wells. Bēṭ had been buried and they were digging it clear' (Sowayan 1992: 102)

In examples (11) and (12) two morphologically M.SG controllers (*gōm* 'crowd, people, tribe' and *ʕālam* 'world', but also 'people, crowd, multitude') attract F.SG agreement:

(11) *tifassar-***t** *gōm=uh*
dwindle-3.PFV.F.SG people=his
'The troops dwindled' (Sowayan 1992: 150)

(12) *ʕālam=in* *ma* **ti***-ḥṣa*
people=INDEF NEG 3.IPFV.F.SG-be.counted
'Multitudes that could not be counted' (Sowayan 1992: 160)

With reference to the following example, Ingham notes that F.SG agreement is common with nouns denoting tribal units:

(13) *ṣār-***at** *āḷ* *ḏufīr* *hu* *šēx=***ah** *ḥamdān*
became-3.PFV.F.SG tribe Ḍhafīr he shaikh=her Ḥamdān
*u=gām-***at** **t***-āxiḏ* *ray=u*
and=begin-3.PFV.F.SG 3.IPFV.F.SG-take opinion=his
'Ḥamdān became shaikh of the Ḍhafīr and they began to follow his leadership' (Ingham 1982b: 253)

Note how the plural of the word 'tribe' (*gubāyil*) triggers F.SG agreement in the following example:

(14) *al=gubāyil* *ta-mši* *maʕ* *aṭ=ṭumaʕ*
DEF=tribes.PL 3.IPFV.F.SG-walk with DEF=greed
'These tribes were driven by the desire for gain' (Ingham 1986a: 51)

Finally, in example (15), we see a proper plural denoting human beings triggering F.SG agreement. Here the factor that influences agreement is obviously the very low individuation of the controller, and the genericness of the statement:

(15) *ar=rǧāl* *ti-ḍīm* *ar=rǧāl*
DEF=men 3.IPFV.F.SG-subdue DEF=men
'Men subdue men' (Sowayan 1992: 138)

2.3.3.3 Agreement with Nonhuman Controllers: Collective Controllers

The corpus of Najdi text we analyzed contained 206 agreement targets depending on 128 nonhuman plural or collective controllers. Of these 206 targets, 8 (3,9 %) showed M.SG agreement, 15 (7,3 %) showed M.PL agreement, 116 (56,3 %) showed F.SG agreement, and 63 (30,6 %) showed F.PL agreement. The remaining 4 targets were adjectives with apophonic plural forms which possess no inherent gender (on the topic of apophonic agreement, see § 2.3.4.1).

At first sight, these percentages would seem to confirm Ingham's statement (seen in § 2.3.2) that nonhuman plurals are normally associated with F.SG agreement, with F.PL agreement representing a relatively common alternative. However, these figures have, *per se*, little meaning, and must be analyzed in light of the different types of controllers and agreement conditions we are considering. Furthermore, minor percentages of masculine agreement (both singular and plural) have to be accounted for.

Let us first consider the various types of controller that appear in the corpus. 47 of the 128 controllers in our texts are actually collectives. 79 targets depend on these controllers. Of these, 4 (5,1 %) show M.SG agreement, 8 (10,1 %) M.PL agreement, 54 (68,4 %) F.SG agreement, and 11 (13,9 %) F.PL agreement. The remaining 2 targets are adjectives with apophonic plural forms.

It is possible to see how singular agreement appears to be strongly connected with collective nouns (73,8 % of the total targets depending on these controllers show singular agreement). In particular, half of the targets in the corpus that show masculine singular agreement depend on a collective controller (4 out of 8).[60] These controllers, however, attract F.SG agreement in the

60 The remaining four are occurrences of almost grammaticalized elements which tend to

vast majority of cases. The rare occurrences of M.SG agreement are probably a consequence of the morphological similarity that exists between collectives and M.SG nouns (i.e. both classes show no outward sign of feminine or plural inflection). It might also be the case that M.SG agreement represents an even lower level of the individuation hierarchy, as postulated for instance by Herin and Al-Wer with the respect to the collective *nās* in Salti Arabic.[61] Occurrences of M.SG agreement with collective controllers, however, are relatively rare, so that a much larger database would be needed in order to accurately verify this hypothesis.

The word *bill* or *ibil* 'camels' represents a good example of a collective controller. *bill* almost systematically attracts F.SG agreement (15 out of 17 targets), as in example (16), but it appears once triggering M.SG agreement instead (example 17):

(16)	*al=bill*	[...]	*ahal=**ha***	*xallū=**ha***	***ta**-srah̩*
	DEF=camel.COLL	[...]	family=her	let:3.PFV.M.SG=her	3.IPFV.F.SG-graze

'The camels [...] their owners let them graze' (Kurpershoek 1993: 54)

(17)	*min*	*hu=l=u*	*ha=l=bill*	***hāḏa***
	who	he=to=him	DEM=DEF=camel.COLL	DEM.M.SG

'Whose are these camels?' (Ingham 1986a: 64)

With regard to M.PL agreement occurring with nonhuman collectives, this is normally triggered by these nouns being used metaphorically to refer to human beings. This appears to be particularly frequent in the case of the word *xēl* 'horses', which is normally employed to refer to the actual mounts,

no longer show any type of agreement, namely the participles *bāgi* 'remaining, left' and *wāǧid* 'many, a lot' (lit. 'present, existing'). Apart from these exceptional elements, M.SG agreement is never an option with proper plural controllers.

61 "Examples [where *nās* triggers M.SG agreement] seem to suggest that in Salti there is an even lower category on the individuation scale and this category triggers masculine singular agreement: MS < FS < PL" (Herin and Al-Wer, 2013: 67). The data in Bettega and Leitner (2019: 18) seem to confirm this. Brustad (2000: 67–68) also notes that controllers referred to time periods often trigger M.SG agreement, possibly because of their inherently low individuation. Interestingly, it is not just collectives that can trigger M.SG agreement, but also nouns accompanied by a numeral higher than ten, which always appear in their singular form. Mitchell (1973: 39–40) maintains that, in Cairo Arabic, M.SG is the most common agreement type in such contexts, though plural agreement does sometimes occur. The similarity that Quranic Arabic shows with contemporary dialects in this respect is remarkable: see § 3.4.1 for a discussion.

but can sometimes refer to the men who ride them (and is therefore better translated as 'cavalry'). Compare for instance example (18), where *xēl* attracts F.SG agreement (as it commonly does, with 20 targets out of 37), with (19) below:

(18) *xēl=i* *glayyl-**ah*** *w=šāḥḥ=in* *fī=**ha***
horse.COLL=my few-F.SG spare.PTCP=INDEF in=her
'I only have a few horses and have to be sparing with them' (Kurpershoek 1993: 49)

(19) *wu=hum* *yirdūn* *yōm* *wrid-**aw*** *al=xēl*
and=they 3.IPFV:ride:M.PL when ride-3.PFV.M.PL DEF=horse.COLL
gāl
say.3.IPFV.M.SG
'And so they marched. As the horsemen rode, he said …' (Kurpershoek 1993: 57)

Even when clearly denoting human beings, however, *xēl* can still attract F.SG agreement, thus showing once more the high degree of dependency that exists between this type of agreement and collectiveness (be it human or nonhuman).

All in all, as we have seen, targets depending on nonhuman collectives are largely the preserve of F.SG agreement. F.PL agreement, however, is also possible, although rarer. As was the case with human collectives, an increase in distance between controller and target can sometimes prompt a variation in the agreement patterns of collective nouns. Consider for instance the behavior of *bill* in (20), where only the fourth and most distant pronoun shows F.PL agreement instead of F.SG:

(20) *w=yāxḏ* *al=bill* *xaḏ=**ah*** *ma* *hu*
and=3.IPFV.M.SG:take DEF=camel.COLL take.3.PFV.M.SG=her NEG he
mn *ul=mu* *xaḏ=**ah*** *mn* *al=falāyh,* *ma* *maʕ=**ah***
from DEF=water take.3.PFV.M.SG=her from DEF=desert NEG with=it
ullu *r=rlʕyān.* *w=yiğī=k*
but DEF=herdsman.PL and=3.IPFV.M.SG:come=you
minćf=in *bi=**hin***
return.PTCP=INDEF with=them.F.PL
'He took the camels. He took them not from the wells, he took them from the desert pasture where they were attended only by the herdsmen. He drove them back home' (Sowayan 1992: 130)

Quantification is another element that strongly favors plural agreement. Collectives are, by definition, uncountable, but in certain rare cases they can appear alongside a numeral. Consider for instance the behavior of the word *xēl* in the following sentence:[62]

(21) *xēl-ih* *ma* *ġār* *ṯintēn* *w=allah* *ma=ni*
horse.COLL =his NEG but two by=God NEG=I
b=āxḏ=in *min=**hin*** *šī=n*
with=take.PTCP=INDEF from=them.F.PL thing=INDEF
'The two of them are the only horses he has. By God, I am not going to take anything from him' (Kurpershoek 1993: 50)

From a typological perspective, the erratic agreement patterns associated with collective controllers are well documented. Collective nouns are known to trigger variable agreement in several different languages. Among these, Moravcsik (1978: 346) cites Latin (*populus*), French (*la plupart*), English (*crowd, police*), along with Finnish, Akkadian and Coptic. In certain cases, this only applies to targets preceding the collective, or to certain specific target types; in other languages, all targets depending on a collective can attract either singular or plural agreement, depending on the circumstances. As we have seen, Arabic dialects appear to be particularly permissive with respect to the agreement types that collectives can trigger: their targets can show F.SG or plural agreement (mostly C.PL or F.PL in the case of nonhuman collectives), and even M.SG agreement, although more rarely.

2.3.3.4 Agreement with Nonhuman Controllers: Plural Controllers

If we now turn to the remaining 81 nonhuman, non-collective controllers, we see that among the 127 related targets 4 attract M.SG agreement (3,2 %, these have already been discussed in footnote 60), 7 attract M.PL agreement (5,5 %), 62 attract F.SG agreement (48,8 %) and 52 F.PL agreement (40,9 %). The remaining 2 targets are adjectives with apophonic plural forms.

These figures show that proper plurals tend to favor F.PL agreement more than collectives, and that F.SG agreement is less common with this type of controllers. All in all, if we dismiss the few instances of M.PL agreement as the result of a metaphorical use of some nonhuman plural,[63] we see that there are only

62 An interesting parallel can be drawn with example (23) in D'Anna (2017: 122), and the relative discussion.

63 As was the case with nonhuman collectives. See how, for example, the word *byūt* 'tents' is used in this sentence to refer to the actual inhabitants of the encampment, always attract-

two possible agreement options for this type of controllers: F.PL or F.SG. This type of variation is nonrandom, and in the following sections we will analyze all the factors that can affect speakers' choice in this respect.[64] We will first analyze the factors that are related to the agreement controller (namely: quantification, chains of conjoined controllers, animacy, concreteness, definiteness, specificity, qualification), and then move on to discuss those related to the agreement target (distance between target and controller, target type, agreement domain).

As far as factors related to the controller are concerned, we have already mentioned several of them when we introduced the concept of "salience" or "individuation" in § 1.3. In particular, we have quoted Comrie's statement according to which "salience is not treated as a primitive in itself, but rather as the result of the interaction of a number of factors". These factors include humanness and collectiveness, which we have already discussed, and humanness in turn is but an aspect of animacy. The reader is therefore once more reminded that, while these neat subdivisions undoubtedly help the exposition, they are to an extent arbitrary, individuation constituting a complex and recursive phenomenon.

2.3.3.4.1 *Quantification, Dual Nouns and Chains of Conjoined Controllers*

While discussing the types of agreement normally associated with collective and quantified controllers, Cerruti (2014: 54) notes the existence of a "generale preferenza del parlato per una modalità di strutturazione a base semantica

---

ing M.PL agreement: *w=yalga* [...] *sabʕ byūt šararāh w=yāxiḏ=***hum***, kill ḥalāl=***hum***. yōm xaḏā=***hum***, w=yiǧī-k minćif*, lit. 'and he found [...] seven tents of the aš-šararāt and he plundered **them**, all **their** livestock. Once he had plundered **them**, he came back from the raid' (Sowayan 1992: 92). Admittedly, a very few occurrences of M.PL agreement with nonhuman controllers appear in the texts for which no explanation seems to be at hand. As repeatedly noted in the previous sections, and as will be further discussed in the next ones, no gender-distinguishing variety of Spoken Arabic seems to be unaffected by this type of variation, which is probably to be regarded as an incipient process of morphological loss. An alternative explanation is also possible, namely that M.PL agreement is sometimes used in connection with nonhuman or nonfeminine controllers to enhance their perceived saliency (in the same way as M.SG agreement might sometimes be used to lower it, see footnote 61 above). In this case as well, however, occurrences of this peculiar agreement pattern are too few to draw reliable conclusions.

64 With the exception of word order, which will be treated separately in § 2.3.9. Even a cursory glance at the data, however, is enough to show the effects of word order on agreement. In our corpus, 28 of the 127 targets depending on nonhuman plural subjects precede their controller. Of these, 19 show F.SG agreement, and only 7 F.PL agreement. Conversely, among the targets which follow their controller, singular and plural feminine agreement are more or less evenly distributed (43 and 45 occurrences each, respectively).

piuttosto che sintattica".[65] We have seen several examples of this tendency in the previous section, and we will now see how these considerations remain valid in the case of different types of quantified controllers.

The literature on agreement in spoken Arabic abounds with references to the effects that quantification has on syntactic behavior. Several authors (most notably Brustad 2000: 23–25) have suggested that a correlation might exist between particularly high percentages of plural agreement and the presence of numerical quantifiers lower than 10. However, factual evidence in support of this claim is scarce, and, sieving through the existing sources, one gets the impression that numerical quantifiers in general (higher or lower than ten) all tend to favor plural agreement.[66] This is stated very clearly by Belnap (1991: 69–70) for Cairene Arabic. Belnap, in particular, notes how it is only the three quantifiers "ten", "twenty" and "one hundred" that appear to actually favor F.SG agreement, in opposition to all other numerical quantifiers. According to Belnap, a possible explanation for this behavior is that these specific elements are commonly used with reference to sums of money (i.e. single coins or bills).

This hypothesis would seem to be corroborated by our Najdi data. If we compare examples (22) and (23) below, we see how the five riyals in the first sentence trigger F.PL agreement, contrary to the one hundred riyals in the second example (though the different word orders of the two sentences might be another factor at play):

(22) *ixḏi* *ha=l=xams* [*riyālāt*] ***hāḏōli***
take:IMP.F.SG DEM=DEF=five [riyal] DEM.PL
*u=xallī=**hin*** *maʕ=ič*
and=keep:IMP.F.SG=them.F.PL with=you.F
'Take these five [riyals] and keep them with you' (Ingham 1994: 153)

65 "General preference of the spoken language for a semantic, rather than syntactic, structuring".

66 That is, they tend to favor plural agreement more than non-quantified nouns do. It is of course possible that this tendency is stronger with low numerals (in particular, it seems that plural agreement is mandatory with plural of unit nouns accompanied by a numeral lower than ten, see Cowell 1964: 503). The extent of this preference, however, remains to be determined. On the topic of agreement with numbered controllers see Blanc (1970: 52); Mitchell (1973: 40) on Cairene; Holes (2016: 346) on Bahraini; Procházka and Gabsi (2017: 245) on Tunis Arabic; Ritt-Benmimoun (2017: 280, 282) on the Bedouin dialects of Southern Tunisia; D'Anna (2017: 116–117) on Fezzani Arabic. The data presented in Bettega (2017: 163) on Omani Arabic and Bettega and Leitner (2019: 25–26) on Khuzestani Arabic are ultimately inconclusive as to the different effects that numerals higher or lower than ten might have on agreement.

(23) ***hāḏi*** *miyat* *riyāl*
DEM.F.SG hundred riyal
'Here is one hundred riyāls' (Ingham 1994: 156)

Apart from expressions related to money, numerals tend to favor F.PL agreement, no matter the number of referents involved:

(24) *xamsīn* *waḏḥa* *wi=slaʕ=***hin**
fifty white.camel and= *slaʕ*=their.F.PL
'Fifty white camels and their *slaʕ*' (Sowayan 1992: 142)

In commenting example (21) above, we have seen that the effects of numerical quantification are so strong that even collectives can sometimes be accompanied by a plural target. In that specific case the entities being referred to were just two, and the connection between dual number and plural agreement seems indeed to be a particularly strong one.

Plural agreement with dual controllers is often presented as an absolute rule in works on Arabic dialects. Haim Blanc, in his insightful study on duals and pseudo-duals in spoken Arabic, acknowledges the rare possibility of F.SG agreement with dual nouns, though he remarks how this pattern is "the exception rather than the norm" (Blanc 1970: 50).[67] Our data and the literature seem to confirm this: although it is possible to find scattered examples of F.SG agreement with dual controllers, in the vast majority of cases plural agreement appears to dominate. The few dual controllers that appear in our corpus of Najdi Arabic all attract plural agreement, as in the following example:

(25) *āmar* *ʕala* *āl* *ḏufīr* [...] *yʕagil=l=u*
order.3.PFV.M.SG on tribe Ḏafīr [...] 3.IPFV.M.SG:leave=for=him
ḥāyl-ēn *ʕind* *guṣīr=u* ***hāḏōli*** *l=ağil* *as=sināʕ*
she.camel-DUAL for neighbor=his DEM.PL for=sake DEF=good.will

67 See also pp. 51–52. Sallam 1973: 46–47 reports plural agreement with dual nouns as mandatory in Cairene. Hanitsch (2011: 147) notes how, in Damascus Arabic, F.SG adjectival agreement is possible, albeit marginal. She links this type of agreement, in particular, to *nisba*-adjectives. Corriente (2008: 108) notes that F.SG agreement with dual controllers was possible in Andalusi Arabic. Bettega and Leitner (2019: 25–26) have one example of a F.SG verb preceding a dual controller in Khuzestani Arabic. Bettega also reports, from his personal experience with Omani Arabic, the phrase *hāḏi r-riyālēn* 'these two riyāls'. Here as well, the F.SG target precedes the controller. The last two examples attest the importance of word order as an agreement condition, one whose effects are so strong as to subvert an otherwise nearly absolute rule. On the effects of precedence on agreement, see § 2.3.9.

'He ordered the Āl Ḍafīr […] to leave for his neighbor two young unfoaled she-camels. These were for good will' (Ingham 1986a: 53–54)

A type of controller which bears a strong similarity with dual and enumerated controllers is represented by chains of conjoined nouns. All sources agree on the fact that these controllers are treated as if they were enumerated, and as such systematically trigger plural agreement,[68] as long as all the names in the chain are singular. Belnap (1991: 81) specifies that in Cairene "heads containing one or more singular count noun categorically occur with plural agreement […]. However, heads which consist only of plural forms show no such tendencies: they behave, instead, like heads consisting of a single plural noun" (on this point see also Ferguson 1989: 88).

The few chains consisting exclusively of singular nouns found in our Najdi dataset do indeed trigger plural agreement, as in (26), where two specific horses are referred to using their proper names (here the two controllers are also highly specific):

(26) *taxayyar* *fi* *krūš* *w=rabda* *ʕan=**hin***
2.IPFV.M.SG:choose between Krūš and=Rabda on=them.F.PL
'I offer you either Krūš or Rabda, there they are' (Kurpershoek 1993: 50)

However, the possibility exists for a chain of controllers to consist not just of singular and/or plural nouns, but also collective ones. No reference is found in the literature concerning this specific phenomenon, with the exception of D'Anna (2017: 110, 113). The question is worth exploring because collective nouns are morphologically singular, though referring to a semantic plurality. In this case as well, semantics seems to play a greater role in determining agreement choices, because these chains either attract singular agreement only (as in D'Anna's data) or variable F.SG/F.PL agreement. In this respect, they are opposed to chains consisting exclusively of proper singular nouns, where F.SG agreement would not be allowed.

In our corpus, five chains of collective controllers appear. While F.SG agreement seems indeed to be the preferred option (4 cases out of 5, see example 27), F.PL agreement does occur once (example 28). This behavior is similar to that displayed by single collectives referred to animals, that generally attract F.SG agreement but can occasionally trigger F.PL:

68 Blanc (1970: 52); Ritt-Benmimoun (2017: 281); Bettega (2017: 166–167). See also Owens (1993: 261) for Nigerian Arabic.

(27) *al=bill* *wa=l=ġanam* *ma* *ḏāg-**t**=ih*
DEF=camel.COLL and=DEF=goat.COLL NEG taste-3.PFV.F.SG=it
'The camels and the goats didn't taste it' (Kurpershoek 1993: 54)

(28) *aǵim* *yi-stiriḥ-**in*** *xēl=ikum* *w=zammālat=ikum*
repose.IMP 3.IPFV-rest-F.PL horse.COLL =your and=camels.COLL=your
'Repose here and let your horses and camels rest' (Sowayan 1992: 154)

One last type of quantifier still needs to be discussed, namely non-numerical quantifiers. These might be of different types.

Commenting on the role of the quantifier *kull* 'all', in the dialects of Tunisia, both Ritt-Benmimoun (2017: 272, 283) and Procházka and Gabsi (2017: 245) agree that it strongly favors the occurrence of F.SG agreement, though plural agreement is also occasionally possible. The same is true for Damascus Arabic (Berlinches Ramos, 2021) and apparently Khuzestani Arabic (although Bettega and Leitner, 2019: 26, only have two instances of *kull* in their data). Bettega (2017: 163) finds that also in Omani Arabic controllers quantified by *kull* show a predilection for F.SG agreement, though apparently not as strong as in Tunisian or Syrian varieties.[69] In our Najdi data, all but one occurrences of *kull*/*kill* are accompanied by singular agreement, be it M.SG—in the case of collective controllers—or F.SG (see example (36) below).

The only exception is shown in (29). Here the narrator is relating of three young warriors, each of whom was brave and valiant, and rode a purebred horse. In this case the agreement is F.PL because a) the controller is understood as quantified by a low numeral, although in this context it does not explicitly appear; b) here *kill* is used in the sense of 'each, each and every one of them', rather than 'all'; c) the horses in question are female, and are actually referred to as "*banāt ḥṣān*", literally 'daughters of a thoroughbred stallion' (Sowayan 1992: 250). All these factors combined induce plural agreement, despite *kill* normally requiring F.SG:

(29) *w=taḥta=hum* *mhār=in* *kill=**ihin*** *banāt*
and=under=them.M.PL steed.PL=INDEF all=them.F.PL daughter.PL
ḥṣān
thoroughbred
'They had under them noble steeds' (Sowayan 1992: 150)

69 Holes (2016: 340) is the only author who describes *kull* as an "individuating element". The only example he provides is, however, ultimately unconvincing, because it features a morphologically singular noun that triggers mixed agreement (first F.SG and then C.PL).

Unlike *kull*, the quantifier *kam* 'some, a few', seems to favor plural agreement (Blanc 1970: 52). The same is apparently true for the semantically similar *šiwayya* 'a few, a little', at least in Cairo (Belnap 1991: 72).[70] The only occurrence of *kam* in our data does indeed appear alongside a F.PL target:

(30) *in kān miʕ=ič kam garš tsallfīn=iyyā=**hin***
if with=you.F.SG few money 2.IPFV:lend:F.SG=COMP=them.F.PL
'If you have a little money, I would like you to lend me it' (Ingham 1994: 164)

Finally, the situation concerning quantifiers meaning "many, a lot" is not clear. Procházka and Gabsi (2017: 246) report that Tunisian *barša* fosters F.SG agreement, although if the referent is further specified plural agreement is also possible (p. 243). In her corpus of Damascus Arabic, Berlinches Ramos (2021) finds several occurrences of *ktīr* triggering C.PL agreement, though she comments that all of them are further specified by other elements. All the occurrences of *wāǧid* in our Najdi material are indeed singular (M.SG or F.SG), but these are somehow problematic, in that in all these cases *wāǧid* represents at the same time the quantifier *and* the target, so that it is not possible to discern the effects that one has on the other. In addition to this, several of these elements, in various dialects of Arabic, are undergoing a process of grammaticalization because of which they tend not to inflect for number and gender anymore.

In general, information about non-numerical quantifiers is scarcer in the literature on agreement in spoken Arabic, probably because the overall frequency of these quantifiers is rather low. The corpora that Arabic dialectologists normally have at their disposal tend to be relatively small, so that statistical analyses run on said corpora risk not to yield enough occurrences for the data to be significant. This undoubtedly remains a topic worthy of further investigation.

2.3.3.4.2 *Animacy and Concreteness*

In the introduction of the present section, we said that a controller's level of individuation may depend on several intrinsic qualities such as humanness and/or animacy. As we have seen in the last sections, human controllers do

70 Although the Egyptian example in Brustad (2000: 58) seems to describe a more complex picture. Note also that Bettega and Leitner (2019: 26), in their corpus of Khuzestani Arabic, find one controller quantified by *čam* (i.e. *kam*) and three controllers quantified by *ġalīl* (a few, a little), all attracting F.SG agreement.

indeed show a markedly different behavior from nonhuman ones, in Najdi Arabic as well as in almost every other dialect of Arabic.

As far as animacy is concerned, it would also seem that animal controllers have a higher chance than inanimate ones to trigger plural agreement. In order to verify this, however, we need to set collective controllers apart from non-collective ones, because, as said, collectiveness often correlates with F.SG agreement, and collectives are particularly common in the realm of animal controllers.[71]

Bettega and Leitner (2019: 17ff.) show that there is a monotonic increase in the percentages of F.SG agreement with non-collective controllers, starting low with human ones and then progressively rising with animal and inanimate ones. This suggests that an animacy hierarchy actually exists in Arabic dialects, similarly to what happens in several languages of the world.[72] Belnap (1991: 62ff.) was the first to theorize this, but his Cairene corpus contained only a handful of animal controllers.

Our Najdi data are consistent with that of Bettega and Leitner and offer further support to this hypothesis: while 57,5% of all targets depending on a non-collective inanimate controller show singular agreement (42 out of 73), only 47% of those depending on a non-collective animal controller do (24 out of 51).[73] In particular, non-collective animal controllers tend to trigger F.SG agreement only in contexts where other factors contribute to make this agreement outcome more likely (the presence of *kull*, a verb-subject construction, and so on). Apart from these cases, it is very rare to find these controllers spontaneously attracting F.SG agreement. We provide an example of this in (31), while in (32) we see a controller of the same type triggering F.PL agreement instead.

71 This is one of those cases in which several of the factors that make up the "individuation hierarchy" overlap, affecting one another, to the point that it is not easy to tell them apart. Asking whether it is animacy or collectiveness that takes precedence in determining the type of agreement that a given controller will trigger does not always make sense, because the two concepts are often entwined and inextricably connected to the nature of the real-world referent. It is true that collectives systematically correlate with very high percentages of F.SG agreement: but it is also true that animal pluralities tend to be linguistically codified as collectives because of their tendency to come in herds, packs, flocks and so on.

72 Among others, Russian, Turkish, Inari Sami (Uralic) and Miya (West Chadic), see Corbett (2006: 177–178, 184–185 and 190–191).

73 Bettega's and Leitner's Khuzestani data were more significant in this respect, because the difference in that case was around 20 percentage points, while in the case of our Najdi corpus it is only around 10. While it is true that these tendencies are moderate, it is also true that no counterexamples have yet been found (i.e. dialects in which animate non-collective controllers attract more F.SG agreement than inanimate ones).

Note that (31) appears in a narrative context, while (32) is taken from direct speech. As we will see below, this is another factor that can have an influence on agreement:

(31) *aṭ-ṭarš* *ma* *ǧa* *wa=r=rḥāl*
DEF=herd.COLL NEG come.3.PFV.M.SG and=DEF=pack.camel.PL
*maxūḏ-**ih***
take.PTCP-F.SG
'The herds had not come back from pasture and the pack camels had been taken' (Sowayan 1992: 104)[74]

(32) *ibāʕir=na* [...] *tiǧi*
camel.PL=our [...] 2.IPFV.M.SG:come
*w=tanhab=**hin***
and=2.IPFV.M.SG:plunder=them.F.PL
'Our camels [...] you come and take them!' (Sowayan 1992: 144)

The data presented in Procházka and Gabsi (2017: 249–252), Ritt-Benmimoun (2017: 273–281) and D'Anna (2017: 110–114) seem to confirm our conclusions on the subject. Though these authors all insist on the fact that the mass/count distinction takes precedence on animacy, it is also clear that, with non-collective animal controllers, plural agreement is much more common than with inanimate ones. In particular, F.PL agreement with non-collective controllers appears to be almost categorical in Fezzani Arabic, to the point that only three such controllers in D'Anna's dataset take F.SG agreement. It is no coincidence, however, that these three controllers are inanimate ones. The situation is more nuanced in Tunisia (both northern and southern), where F.SG agreement is possible with both animate and inanimate nonhuman controllers, depending on their perceived level of specificity. Procházka and Gabsi make the interesting remark that size is an important variable in the case of animals, in that pluralities of small animals, such as mice, tend to systematically attract F.SG agreement.

If we now focus on inanimate controllers alone, we see that even within this group it is possible to operate further subdivisions. The most important opposition appears to be that between concrete and abstract controllers. This has been noted by virtually all the authors who worked on the subject, starting with Belnap (1991: 80–81) and Brustad (2000). Hanitsch (2011: 146) goes into

74 Here it is also possible to see a collective controller attracting M.SG verbal agreement.

greater detail, stating that, even within the class of concrete controllers, some can be singled out as "non-prototypical" (nicht-prototypische Konkreta). These are nouns that lack one or more of the following traits: [+mobile] [+tridimensional] [+solid], and include landscape elements, clouds, lines, roads and so on. Hanitsch finds that in Damascus Arabic these controllers show a strong predilection for F.SG agreement.[75] In our corpus, we find an interesting example of landscape elements triggering F.PL agreement:

(33) *šaṭṭ-ēn* *w=nağd* *giṭaʕt=**ihin***
river.bank-DUAL and=Najd cross:1.PFV.SG=them.F.PL
'Two river banks and Najd I have crossed' (Sowayan 1992: 160)

Although these are elements that would normally attract F.SG agreement, here two factors intervene to raise the referents' level of individuation: the first is quantification, that we have discussed in the previous section (the controller is actually a chain of controllers, and one of the two stands in the dual number). The second factor, that we will analyze in the next section, is specificity. The speaker didn't just cross any desert, or any river banks. He is referring specifically to entities that are well-known to him and his interlocutors, namely the Najdi desert and the two banks of the Euphrates. Whenever proper names are mentioned, it is very rare for anything but plural agreement to occur.

Procházka and Gabsi (2017: 252–254) and Ritt-Benmimoun (2017: 277–280) comment extensively on the concrete/abstract opposition in Tunisian dialects. The former, in particular, note how "abstract nouns usually exhibit deflected agreement even if highly salient and prominently marked by a following genitive or pronominal suffix". This seems not to be necessarily the case in the Bedouin dialects of Southern Tunisia, where Ritt-Benmimoun observes that even a very generic abstract term such as *ayyām* 'days', can take F.PL agreement if quantified by a numeral.

In our corpus, we find 14 abstract nouns controlling 24 targets, all but two showing singular agreement (mostly F.SG, but two are the grammaticalized

75 Yet another sub-group of concrete controllers seems to be represented by body parts. These appear to behave somehow unpredictably: they almost systematically trigger F.PL agreement in Bedouin Tunisian dialects (Ritt-Benmimoun 2017: 277), while they seem to be consistently associated with F.SG agreement in Bahraini Arabic (Holes 2016: 349, though Holes comments that other effects connected to specificity are probably at play as well). Here Blanc's (1970) original article on duals and pseudo-duals is certainly of relevance.

participles discussed in footnote 60 above, which always appear in the M.SG). Examples from (34) to (36) show some of these nouns:

(34) ***hāḏi*** [...] *umūr* *riyāliyy-**ah*** *u=ma* *l=ku* *fī=**ha***
DEM.F.SG [...] matter.PL manly-F.SG and=NEG for=you.PL in=her
ʕalāqah
relation
'These [...] are manly matters and you have no connection with them' (Ingham 1994: 162)

(35) *as=suwālif* *ṭwīl-**it**=in* *ʕarīḍ-**ih***
DEF=story.PL long-F.SG=INDEF wide-F.SG
'Narratives are long and wide' (Sowayan 1992: 86)

(36) *kill* *hā=l=afkār* [...] *wa=la* *darēna* *ʕan=**ha***
all DEM=DEF=thought.PL [...] and=NEG know:1.PFV.PL about=her
'All these thoughts [...] and we didn't know about them' (Ingham1994: 170)

Of the two exceptions, one is shown in example (37), and the other will be discussed in the next section. In the following example, it is once again possible to see how quantification (in this case represented by the dual marking) tends to correlate with plural agreement, even when the controller is an abstract one:

(37) *hu* [...] *yṣalli* *arbaʕ* *rakʕāyh* *arbaʕ*
he [...] 3.IPFV.M.SG:pray four prostration.PL four
rakʕāt=in *wāgif*
prostration:F.PL=INDEF stand.PTCP
w=rakʕ-at-ēn=in *ṣallā=**hin***
and=prostration-F.SG-DUAL=INDEF pray.3.PFV.M.SG=them.F.PL
ġāʕid
sit.PTCP
'He [...] knelt four times in prayer, four times while standing up and two times while sitting down' (Sowayan 1992: 144)

Summing up, it would seem that animacy and concreteness are relevant agreement conditions in almost every Arabic dialect (exceptions to this rule are represented by those few dialects where variation between F.SG and plural agreement has entirely disappeared, see § 2.3.6 and § 2.3.7). We have already reported Corbett's definition of agreement conditions in § 2.1. In particular, it is extremely relevant that the animacy hierarchy that we have just discussed for several Arabic dialects perfectly matches the general description of this universal linguistic tendency as described by Corbett (2006: 185):

Human > Other animate > Concrete inanimate > Abstract inanimate

2.3.3.4.3 *Specificity*

In the previous sections, we have already stressed how several factors can contribute in determining a referent's overall level of individuation, so that it is not always easy to keep these factors distinct.

Sometimes, however, the only thing inducing plural agreement is specificity, that is, the extent to which the speaker has a specific referent in mind. The analysis of this pragmatic notion is, of course, more complex, since it cannot always be defined in absolute terms (in the same way quantification can, for instance). Nonetheless, references to specificity abound in the literature on agreement: this is true of general typological works (see for instance Moravcsik, 1978: 345: "noun phrases which refer to kinds of things rather than to specific objects are deviant or unstable in their number and in their number agreement requirements"), and also of studies dealing specifically with Arabic varieties. This is the case with virtually all works on agreement in Arabic that we have mentioned so far, but consider in particular this quote from Hoyt (2002: 113): "indefinites with 'rich descriptive content' (such as adjectives or relative clauses) can favor full agreement. In particular, the more referentially specific the modification, the more likely there is to be a preference for full agreement". In his article on the relation between specificity and agreement in Rural Palestinian Arabic, Hoyt offers several revealing examples of how agreement can be used by speakers to semantically disambiguate between two possible interpretations of the same sentence. For example, the sentence *čill yōm* ***biği/biğu*** *la=l=ṣaff ulād* translates to 'every day, there are boys (not necessarily the same ones each day) who come to class' if agreement is M.SG, but it is understood to mean 'every day, there are boys (a particular set of boys) who come to class' if agreement is M.PL.

Even in our small corpus of Najdi data, it is possible to find examples of the effects of specificity on agreement. In example (15) above, we have seen how the complete lack of specificity induces F.SG agreement with a non-collective human controller. In examples (22) and (26), specificity might be another factor favoring plural agreement, together with quantification (in both cases the referents, five riyals and two horses, are physically present to the speaker at the moment of utterance; in addition, the horses are referred to using their proper names).

One of the best examples of the effects of specificity that we have found in our corpus is shown in (38). In the previous section we have seen how abstract controllers systematically trigger singular agreement, with only two exceptions. The second one of these exceptions is shown below: in the example, we see two abstract controllers attracting F.PL pronominal agreement. Here the speaker is referring to two hypothetical activities, and the controllers' level of abstractness is therefore very high. However, these two activities are described in detail, and are also familiar and habitual for both the speaker and the hearer. As a result, the type of agreement that obtains is that reserved for specific controllers:

(38)

*ayyi=**hin***	*aḥsan*	*aḥsan*	*ṭalʕat=k*	*la=l=barr*	*walla*
which=them.F.PL	best	best	going=your	to=DEF=desert	or

ǧayyat=k	*hnayya*
coming=your	here

'Which of them is best? Is it best to go out to the desert or to come here?' (Ingham 1982: 118)

One last thing that needs to be considered is that text type can affect agreement to an extent. When categories such as specificity are taken into consideration, it is obvious that a dialogue between two speakers talking about a number of objects which are presently visible to them will contain more perceptually salient controllers than a monological narrative about the deeds of long-dead Bedouin riders in the pre-oil era (example 38 above, for instance, is taken from a dialogical text).

Holes (2016: 334), commenting on the agreement patterns of Bahraini Arabic (a non-distinguishing variety), makes a similar remark: "The likelihood of strict [i.e. plural] agreement is higher where the verb […] describes an actual event, lower when it […] describes habits or in unspecific terms what generally happens/used to happen". In other words, the topic of the text, and therefore the type of text one considers, does have an impact on the overall chances of plural agreement to occur. The same seems to be true for Ritt-Benmimoun's (2017: 275) Tunisian texts, as emerges for these two examples: *kān hāk iḏ-ḏyōba alla* ***tugtil*** *l-^{ə}ʕbād* 'there used to be those jackals that killed people', and *gāl il-hum wṣilt il-blāṣa il-fulānīya lamkinti rāḥu baʕd-in* **k^{i}lū**-*ni ḏ-ḏyōba il-yōm xāf min-**hin** r^{i}žaʕ* 'He said to them: "I reached the place so-and-so today, but only after the jackals had (almost) eaten me". He was afraid of them and turned back'. In the first sentence the speaker is talking about the past habits of jackals in general, while in the second one the jackals being referred to are a specific pack that the protagonist of the story encountered earlier that day. As a consequence, we find F.SG verbal agreement in the first case and plural agreement in the second[76]

The vast majority of the Najdi material we have analyzed for the present study was monological and narrative in nature. It is possible that the analysis of a corpus of texts of a different kind would yield even higher percentages of F.PL agreement.

2.3.3.4.4 *Definiteness and Qualification*

Two more factors related to the controller need to be briefly discussed, namely definiteness and qualification. Some authors (most notably Brustad 2000) have suggested a connection between these factors and agreement outcomes. As a general trend, definite and qualified controllers should be more likely to trigger plural agreement than their indefinite and non-qualified counterparts, in that they are more likely to be perceived as individuated. Note that in this section we will adopt a purely formal definition of definiteness, that is, a noun is considered definite if it is preceded by the definite article, or if it constitutes the first (possessed) element of an *ʔiḍāfa* (synthetic genitive construction).

While the idea that definite nouns are inherently more individuated does certainly stand to reason, the data often go in a different direction. In the Omani corpus analyzed in Bettega (2017: 161), definite controllers show only a very slight preference for plural agreement (72% of all nonhuman controllers attracting singular agreement in at least one of their targets were definite, against 80% of all controllers attracting plural agreement, i.e. a difference of 8 percentage points). The controllers in our Najdi dataset contradict expectations even more strongly: 82,2% of all controllers attracting singular agreement in at least one target are definite (37 out of 45), while only 64,1% of all those that attract plural agreement in at least one target are (25 out of 39).

A remark by Brustad (2000: 22–23) herself could help explain this apparently counterintuitive behavior. She notes that "since abstract nouns in Arabic normally take the definite article, concreteness appears to have less central a role than specification and qualification in the syntactic marking of nouns". It

76 In particular, we have M.PL agreement in the verb appearing before the controller, while we find F.PL agreement in the pronoun following it. Mismatches of this kind are common in the Bedouin dialect of southern Tunisian, were F.PL paradigms are apparently deteriorating fast.

seems that the reasoning could be reversed, stating that, since concreteness obviously plays a major role in determining agreement, definiteness is necessarily subordinated to it, and therefore less relevant. In addition to this, it should be noted that generic nouns in Arabic are often marked by the definite article (as is the case with English, e.g. "The elephant is a big animal"), so that also specifity seems to have a stronger impact on agreement than formal definiteness. This is well illustrated by the following Damascene examples (taken from Cowell 1964: 424): *l=kətᵊb mā b=**ihemmū*** 'The books don't **interest (C.PL)** him', and *l=kətᵊb mā b=ᵊ**thəmm**=o* 'Books don't **interest (F.SG)** him'. Although both controllers are definite on a formal level, it is only the former that can be described as specific. This is a very good example of how variation between F.SG and plural agreement can be used by speakers of Arabic to disambiguate meaning, but it also shows how the use that Arabic makes of definite articles is rather different from that of languages more familiar to the western reader. In conclusion, examples of this type being very common, it would seem that the role played by formal definiteness in determining agreement is rather limited.[77]

As far as qualification is concerned, the data once again contradict expectations. Bettega (2017: 161), for instance, has shown how, in his corpus of Omani Arabic, qualified controllers have higher chances to attract F.SG than plural agreement (54,9% vs. 40%). The explanation for this resides in the fact that, more often than not, qualified controllers are accompanied by adjectives, and all quantitative studies dealing with agreement in spoken Arabic confirm that adjectives represent the target type more likely to attract F.SG agreement. In other words, it would seem that target type (a target-related factor) takes precedence over qualification (a controller-related factor) in determining the kind of agreement that will occur. At the present state of research, it is debatable whether or not qualification alone plays any role in determining agreement outcomes.

77 Though this does not mean that it plays no role at all: see for instance Herin and Al-Wer (2013: 67), who maintain that in Salti the collective *nās* can trigger M.SG agreement only when indefinite. In light of everything that has been said so far, it could also be argued that not all *formally* definite controllers in Arabic are indeed to be considered definite. This, while undoubtedly true, represents a complex topic that we cannot address here in depth (the reader is referred to Lyons, 1999, for a basic introduction). A study of the relation that may or may not exist in Arabic between agreement variation and definiteness—defined on semantic/pragmatic grounds—remains a desideratum.

2.3.3.4.5 *Distance between Controller and Target, Agreement Domains and Target Type*

While analyzing agreement patterns in in his corpus of Cairene Arabic texts, Belnap (1991: 86–87) found distance between controller and target (CT distance) to be the second most relevant factor affecting agreement after animacy. He linked this phenomenon to the notion of recoverability of information, stating that:

> It would appear there may be a functional basis to the distance factor [...]. The nearer an agreement locus is to its head the more immediate is the association between the two: deflected [i.e. F.SG] or neutralized [i.e. M.SG] agreement are far less likely to interfere with the interlocutor's perceiving the grammatical relationship between the head and locus.

All subsequent studies that have applied Belnap's methodology to the analysis of corpora of different varieties have come to the same conclusions. This apparently universal trend could be formalized as follows: the likelihood of a target depending on a plural controller to show plural agreement increases as increases the distance between that target and its controller (distance is here understood as expressed in terms of phonological words).

Unfortunately, our Najdi dataset is too small to offer statistically significant evidence of this for each possible increase of lexical distance. However, it is possible to glimpse this trend by comparing the two groups of targets occurring after their controller at shorter distances (1 to 3 words) versus those occurring at longer distances (4 to 8 words).[78] In the first group, 31 targets show F.SG agreement and 27 show F.PL agreement. In the second group, conversely, 12 targets show F.PL agreement and only 3 show F.SG agreement (in particular, no target at a distance of 6 or more words from its controller shows F.SG agreement).

Other quantitative studies on agreement in spoken Arabic, using larger corpora, have been able to provide more fine-grained analyses. We report the findings of these studies in Table 2.16. The sources are Belnap (1991: 87) for Cairene, Bettega (2017: 169) for Omani, Bettega and Leitner (2019: 27) for Khuzestani Arabic.

78 6 targets appeared in the context of the few dialogical interactions contained in the corpus which depended on a controller previously mentioned by a different speaker. These targets were not considered here, since it was impossible to determine the distance between the target and its original controller.

TABLE 2.16 Effects of CT distance on agreement

Cairene Arabic		Omani Arabic		Khuzestani Arabic	
Distance	**% of singular targets**	**Distance**	**% of singular targets**	**Distance**	**% of singular targets**
1	79%	1	88.1%	1	48.6%
2	64%	2	53.1%	2	31%
3–5	57%	3–4	52%	3–4	25.6%
6–8	53%	5–7	27.8%	5–6	18.1%
9+	9%	8+	20%	7+	17.1%

Table 2.16 very effectively demonstrates how, in spite of the fact that the overall frequency of singular agreement varies from dialect to dialect, the effects of CT distance are consistent cross-dialectally. The probabilities of singular agreement to occur decrease monotonically with every increase of lexical distance.

Even studies that do not provide quantitative data indirectly confirm this trend: both Holes (2016: 334–337, 353) for Bahrain and Ritt-Benmimoun (2017: 267–268) for Southern Tunisia observe that, in the case of controllers that trigger mixed agreement, singular targets always precede plural ones.[79] Counterexamples (i.e. a controller attracting first plural and *then* singular agreement) are virtually unheard of. We have seen two examples of a collective controller (respectively human and nonhuman) triggering mixed agreement in (10) and (20) above.

From what has been said up to this moment, the relation between agreement and CT distance might appear a fairly straightforward question. However, the picture is made more complex by the interaction (and partial overlap) of CT distance with two other factors, namely agreement domain and target type.

In § 2.1 we had left agreement domains out of our terminological discussion, because they require a more critical analysis. A consensus seems to exist in the literature that agreement is affected by its occurring at phrase level, clause level, sentence level, or beyond sentence level. Moravcsik (1978: 344), for instance, offers several examples of how agreement with conjoined and/or numerated controllers tends to vary depending on its being NP-internal or external. Corbett (2006: 21) states that "smaller" domains are more canonical, and rephrases

79 See also a passing reference to the topic in Procházka and Gabsi (2017: 258).

the concept as follows: "the smaller the structural distance between controller and target, the more canonical is the instance of agreement". The use of the term "distance" in this sentence is revealing of how the two questions of CT distance and agreement domains are hard to keep distinct.

Corbett (1979) has famously addressed the question of agreement variation across domains by formulating the existence of an "agreement hierarchy". The agreement hierarchy predicts that, in languages where agreement variation occurs, the agreement option with the greater degree of semantic justification will become more and more frequent as we move from left to right along the hierarchy. The hierarchy itself is thus organized:

Attribute > Predicate > Relative pronoun > Personal pronoun

Corbett (1979: 216) poses the question of whether the hierarchy represents a primitive in itself or if it can be derived from some more general principle, and he finds the latter option to be impossible. In other words, CT distance would be subordinated to the hierarchy, and not the other way around. This is because in certain languages, certain agreement options are only possible within certain domains (and thus it is only in the context of those domains that the effects of CT distance become observable).[80]

This is not, however, the case of Arabic dialects, where variation between F.SG and plural agreement is possible with all targets in all domains. It is true that not all target types, and not all domains, are equally likely to show F.SG agreement. But an analysis of the probabilities of F.SG agreement based on these criteria would yield as a result the same type of monotonic decrease seen in Table 2.16, only less fine-grained. Furthermore, the use of agreement domains and target types as variables for the analysis of agreement patterns in spoken Arabic present additional problems.

Let us first consider the question of domains. As we have seen, Corbett claims that smaller domains are more canonical. This is obviously problematic when referred to Arabic dialects, since, as we have seen, F.SG agreement tends to cluster near the controller in all varieties. This would be tantamount to saying that F.SG agreement is the more canonical option in spoken Arabic for

80 See (Corbett 1979: 220): "The predictions that can be made on the basis of […] real distance are at corpus level: given sets of sentences which are equivalent as far as the agreement hierarchy is concerned (i.e. the same position is represented in each) any effect of greater syntactic distance in terms of […] real distance will be to favour (absolutely or relatively) semantic agreement".

plural controllers, which is counterintuitive. It is only by looking at the type of agreement that a given controller triggers in a plural target that we can establish the gender of that controller, while F.SG targets always appear in the same form no matter the controller.[81] In other words, we maintain that individuated agreement is more canonical than non-individuated agreement, because subject to less conditions.[82]

Another way to frame this is to focus on the definition of "semantic" agreement itself. Corbett's hierarchy had been primarily developed to address this long-standing linguistic problem. Semantic agreement is defined as the type of agreement that "cannot be justified solely by syntactic features" (Corbett 1979: 203–204). Perhaps the most iconic example of this phenomenon is represented by nouns that behave as the English word "committee", which can trigger both singular and plural agreement, depending on context. In this case, it has been demonstrated that higher percentages of semantic agreement are systematically found at the rightmost end of the hierarchy (i.e. away from the controller). However, what exactly constitutes semantic agreement in the case of spoken Arabic is a question open to debate. The more intuitive answer would probably be F.SG agreement. However, as already said, F.SG targets in Arabic dialects are more common in the leftmost positions of the hierarchy. In his insightful dissertation on agreement in Cairene, Belnap (1991: 88–89) already showed awareness of the problem when he wrote:

81 Obviously, this consideration is only relevant in the case of gender-distinguishing dialects. We will return on this point in the next section, when discussing the nature of the gender and agreement system of these varieties.

82 This argument cannot be invalidated by reversing the reasoning. It is not possible to say that F.SG agreement is the prototypical agreement for all plural controllers in spoken Arabic, and that conditions such as animacy, quantification and so on cause the emergence of a non-canonical agreement in the form of M.PL or F.PL agreement (in distinguishing varieties) or C.PL agreement (in non-distinguishing ones). First of all, because this would require an explanation for the fact that, in gender-distinguishing varieties, non-canonical agreement in the plural shows gender distinction while canonical agreement does not. Secondly, because F.SG agreement is more commonly associated with collectives than any other type of controller, and collectives are themselves non-canonical controllers. Thirdly, because plural agreement is overwhelmingly more common than F.SG agreement with human controllers (and also with other controller types in certain dialects, though here the question becomes more complex, and one needs to refer to the description of that specific dialect: F.SG agreement could perhaps be described as the canonical type of agreement for nonhuman nouns in Cairene Arabic, but it is highly debatable whether or not this consideration could be extended to any other variety; on this point, see § 2.3.6 and § 2.3.7).

> Whether or not Corbett's agreement hierarchy can be applied without modification to these data is contingent, of course, on whether deflected [i.e. F.SG] agreement can be interpreted as grammatical agreement and plural agreement can be interpreted as semantic agreement: it is not clear that this is the case.

The question of the relation between spoken Arabic and the agreement hierarchy has been left largely unaddressed in subsequent works on the subject. To this day, this remains an important avenue for further research in the fields of Arabic dialectology and linguistic typology alike. In particular, a conceptual reconciliation of the hierarchy with the uncanny behavior of F.SG (semantic?) agreement is needed. It is even possible that the hierarchy cannot be applied at all to the question of F.SG agreement, and that its use should be confined to the investigation of M.SG/plural agreement variation that, we have seen, sometimes occurs with collective controllers.[83] After all, the majority of the studies that have investigated the question of the agreement hierarchy have focused only on specific sub-sets of controllers (collective controllers, or chains of collective controllers, or quantified controllers). In most varieties of Arabic, however, *any* non-singular controller is theoretically able to trigger different types of agreement.

In addition to this, more corpus-based analyses would be needed to establish whether target-related factors outweigh controller-related ones, or vice versa. In other words, we could ask ourselves if the conditions that we have explored in the previous sections (collectiveness, animacy, concreteness, etc.) exert more powerful an effect on agreement than the constrains imposed by CT distance. Corbett (2006: 206) maintains that these types of constraints normally take priority over conditions. There is no guarantee that Arabic dialects would confirm this trend, however. Belnap found controller type to have a stronger effect than CT distance in Cairene Arabic. Further studies, based on corpora large enough to allow for statistically meaningful analysis of each distance tier, could confirm or disprove his findings. It seems to us hardly likely that some effect can

83 See § 2.3.3.3, and also § 2.3.9 below. The problems connected to applying the hiearachy to the F.SG/PL agreement variation in Arabic becomes even more apparent when one considers the agreement patterns that emerge from the analysis of pre- and early-Islamic materials. In these texts, the exact opposite of what we have seen in the case of spoken Arabic happens, that is, F.SG agreement becomes more and more commont the further away one moves from the controller (i.e. pronominal targets show the highest amount of F.SG agreement, and adjectival targets the lowest amount). This will be discussed in depth in § 2.4 and in the concluding section of this chapter.

be found which is stronger than the tendency of certain controllers to systematically co-occur with certain types of agreement (be that F.SG or plural). This, however, needs to be confirmed by more empirical evidence.

Finally, we can turn to another possibility for the investigation of the role of targets in influencing agreement, namely the subdivision of targets into different target types. This methodology has indeed been applied in a number of studies.[84] The problem with this approach is that certain types of agreement targets in Arabic show an irregular behavior that complicates analysis. This is specifically the case of adjectives, that, as we have seen in § 2.2, can adopt two different pluralization strategies (i.e. suffixal or apophonic). Most studies on agreement in Arabic have equated apophonic plurals to "normal" ones, lumping them together with other plural targets. However, it is not entirely clear if adjectives in Arabic can be analyzed in this way. The considerations made by Wright and Sallam, which we have reported in § 2.2.1, seem to suggest that they cannot. We will pursue the question further in § 2.3.4.1, where we will discuss the nature of "broken" adjectives in depth, as well as in § 2.4, where we will bring data from early Arabic sources to bear.

2.3.4 *Plural Agreement in Gender-Distinguishing Dialects: Description*

In § 2.3.2 we have seen how, in gender-distinguishing varieties of Arabic, whenever plural agreement co-occurs with a nonhuman plural or collective controller, it is always *feminine* plural agreement, and not masculine. This is a point worth stressing: as far as we know, no variety of Arabic has ever been described in which gender distinction in the plural is retained and in which nonhuman plural controllers preferentially attract masculine plural agreement. In all likelihood, such a variety never existed.

§ 2.3.3 has provided further evidence of this, and examined in more dept the factors that induce variation between plural and F.SG agreement.

In light of everything that has been discussed so far, we will now move on to consider the implications these phenomena have on the way we describe and conceptualize gender and agreement in Arabic.

84 These are the same as those on which Table 2.16 is based. On a general level, they all show F.SG agreement to be most common among attributive adjectives. The relative position of predicative adjectives and verbs seems to vary. Anaphoric pronouns are almost systematically the least likely target type for F.SG to occur. Human collective controllers in Belnap's Cairene corpus and demonstrative targets in Bettega's and Leitner's Khuzestani data are characterized by highly irregular behavior.

TABLE 2.17 Agreement with plural controllers in gender-distinguishing varieties

Type of controller	Agreement
Masculine human	M.PL
Others	F.PL

TABLE 2.18 Agreement with all controller types in gender-distinguishing varieties

Type of controller	Agreement
Masculine singular	Masculine singular
Feminine singular	Feminine singular
Masculine human plural	Masculine plural
Others	Feminine plural

If we set aside for a moment the possibility of F.SG agreement with non-singular controllers, and focus only on plural agreement, we can schematize the agreement behavior of gender-distinguishing dialects as shown in Table 2.17.[85]

An important fact emerges from Table 2.17, namely that both humanness and biological sex are relevant in determining the kind of agreement that a given plural controller will trigger. If we now add singular controllers to the picture, we obtain the representation shown in Table 2.18.

As can be seen, Table 2.18 is characterized by a strong asymmetry: humanness is a relevant factor in determining agreement in the case of plural controllers, but it plays no role in determining the type of agreement triggered by singular controllers. This asymmetry is the result, so to speak, of an optical illusion, in turn derived by the traditional classification of Arabic as a language with a binary gender system.

85 The table does not take into account the occasional substitution, relatively common in certain dialects and virtually absent in others, of F.PL with M.PL forms. This is a diachronic phenomenon related to the progressive disappearance of F.PL morphology in Arabic dialects. This topic has been partially addressed in § 2.3.2, and will be further discussed in Chapter 5.

TABLE 2.19 Agreement classes in gender-distinguishing varieties of Arabic[a]

Class	Agreement in the singular	Agreement in the plural	Semantic fields
I	Masculine singular	Masculine plural	Biologically masculine human beings
II	Feminine singular	Feminine plural	Biologically feminine human beings, Nonhuman animates, Inanimates,
III	Masculine singular	Feminine plural	Nonhuman animates, Inanimates

a The term "biologically" in Table 2.19 is to be understood as opposed to "morphologically". As we have seen, certain nouns in Arabic can refer to masculine animate beings and still be marked with morphemes that have traditionally been labelled as "feminine" (or vice-versa). The morphology that the noun itself displays is not relevant to us here, and agreement classes are to be established only on the basis of syntactic behavior. We are aware of the fact that the whole concept of "biological gender" can, in some cases, be perceived as controversial. For a treatment of the linguistic use of these terms that transcends the merely linguistic aspects of the question see Aikhenvald (2016).

This classification does actually stand to reason if one considers the morphological means that Arabic has at its disposal for marking gender, which we have explored in § 2.2. Nominal and verbal paradigms in Arabic are actually split into two sets of forms, conventionally labelled masculine and feminine, and the same is true for personal pronouns and demonstratives.

However, even if the array of morphological markers seems to actually reflect a binary gender division, the syntactical distribution of the morphemes does not. On the basis of the type of agreement they attract, and irrespectively of what type of morphology they themselves display, nouns in gender-distinguishing varieties of Spoken Arabic can be grouped into three agreement classes.[86] This is illustrated in Table 2.19, and can be alternatively schematized as follows:[87]

86 The methodology for determining the number of agreement classes in a language has been discussed in § 2.1.

87 The schematization that appears in Figure 2.1 is based on the illustrations found in Corbett (1991: 151ff.). In the Figure we have used as examples the inflectional morphemes of a regular adjective that forms its plural by suffixation instead of apophony. These could be replaced with verbal inflectional morphemes or with pronouns, with identical results.

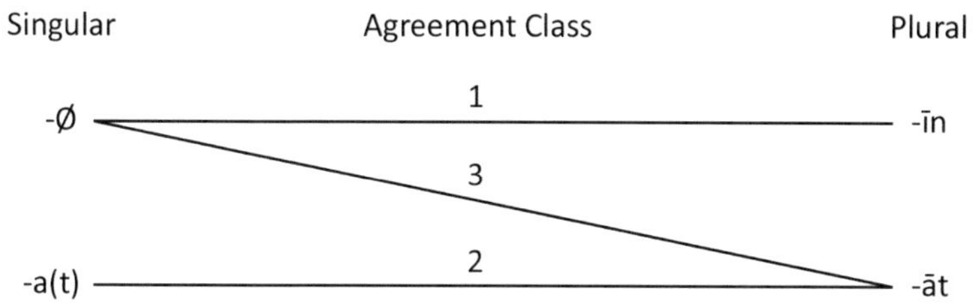

FIGURE 2.1 Visual representation of agreement classes in gender-distinguishing varieties of Arabic

We will now provide some examples for each class. All the examples are taken by the Najdi texts analyzed in the previous sections, but similar ones could be found in any gender-distinguishing variety.

A typical example of a Class I noun is *rağğāl* 'man'. Compare for instance examples (39) and (40) (example (40) is the same as (1) above; it has been repeated here for the sake of clarity):

(39) *rağğāl=in* *habb* *l=**uh*** *saʕad*
man=INDEF blow.3.PFV.M.SG to=him wind.of.luck
'A man in whose direction the wind of luck blew' (Sowayan 1992: 86)

(40) *ar=rğāl* *al=awwil-**īn***
DEF=men DEF=first-M.PL
'The ancients' (Sowayan 1992: 138)

In (39) we see *rağğāl* triggering masculine singular agreement in the anaphoric pronoun, while in (40) the apophonic plural *rğāl* 'men' triggers masculine plural agreement in the adjective which accompanies it.

Typical examples of Class II nouns are *ḥurma* 'woman' and *bint* 'girl', the plurals of which we have seen triggering F.PL agreement in examples (3) and (4) above. These are repeated here as (42) and (44). Compare them with (41) and (43), respectively:

(41) *al=ḥurm-ah* *wagf-**ah***
DEF=woman-F.SG stand.PTCP-F.SG
'The woman had raised herself' (Kupershoek 1993: 59)

(42) *l=ḥarīm* [...] ***hin*** *mxallṣ-**āt**=in*
the=women [...] they.F.PL prepared.PTCP-F.PL=INDEF
zihbuwwāt=ihum
provisions:F.PL=their
'The women [...] prepared the provisions (for the men)' (Sowayan 1992: 150)

(43) *bint=ill=u mā māt-**at** illa grayyb*
girl=to=him NEG die-3.PFV.F.SG but recently
'His daughter who only died recently' (Ingham 1986a: 82)

(44) *ṯalaṯ banāt ǧa-**nn*** [...] *y-ʕāyid-**inn** ubū=**hin***
three girl.PL came-3.PFV.F.PL [...] 3.IPFV-visit-F.PL father=their.F.PL
'Three daughters came [...] to visit their father' (Ingham 1980)

Consider also examples (45) and (46), where *nāga(t)* 'she-camel' and its (apophonic) plural *nyāg* attract feminine singular and feminine plural agreement respectively. These are exponents of the nonhuman members of Class II:

(45) *an=nāg-t alli **ti-**ǧūz l=ak*
DEF=camel-F.SG that 3.IPFV.F.SG-appeal to=you
'The camel that strikes your fancy' (Sowayan 1992: 88)

(46) *kill nyāg=ik* [...] *ma agbal=**hin***
all camel.PL [...] NEG accept=them.F.PL
'All your camels [...] I would not accept them' (Sowayan 1992: 88)

Finally, nouns such as *biʕīr* 'male camel' (pl. *ibāʕir*) and *bēt* 'tent, house' (pl. *byūt*) are typical exponents of Class III. Compare (47) and (48), which are taken from Ingham's own examples, and where the singular nouns attract masculine singular agreement, with (49) and (50), which come from our corpus of Najdi texts. Here the plural forms of these same nouns trigger feminine plural agreement:

(47) *biʕīr=in **ʕōd**=in*
camel=INDEF big.M.SG=INDEF
'A large male camel' (Ingham 1994: 50)

(48) *bēt=ih* ***kibīr***
house=his big.M.SG
'His house is large' (Ingham 1994: 37)

(49) *ibāʕir=na* [...] *w=tanhab=****hin***
camel.PL =our [...] and=2.IPFV.M.SG:plunder=them.F.PL
'Our camels [...] you take them' (Sowayan 1992: 144)

(50) *al=byūt* *mafrūš-****āt***
DEF=tent.PL carpeted-F.PL
'The tents were cleared of all grudges' (Ingham 1982b: 253)

The complex agreement behavior we have just observed is not unique to gender-distinguishing varieties of Arabic. Several languages exist (or have existed) that show similar, if not identical, agreement patterns. Representative examples from the Indo-European family include Tocharian (Fellner 2014: 15ff.), several dialects of central and southern Italy (Loporcaro and Paciaroni, 2011; Loporcaro 2015) and, most notably, Romanian.[88]

Corbett (1991: 150–153) solves the long-standing problem of the number of genders in Romanian by introducing a distinction between *controller gender* and *target gender*. Since three distinct agreement classes can be identified for Romanian, he claims, then three separate genders have to be recognized. However, it is not possible to say that Romanian has three genders in the same way that, for instance, German or Tamil have three genders (where three distinct set of morphological markers exist for marking each one). Rather, it is possible to say that Romanian has three controller genders (that is, its nouns are divided into three different agreement classes) but only two target genders (since there is no independent set of morphemes for marking class III).[89] The same, we maintain, holds true for all gender-distinguishing varieties of Arabic.[90]

88 Telugu (Dravidian) and Lak (North-East Caucasian) are two other languages where a mismatch exists between the number of controller genders and that of target genders. Their agreement systems, however, differ from that of Romanian, Tocharian and gender-distinguishing varieties of Arabic in several important ways (see Corbett 1991: 153–154).

89 It should now be clear why it is terminologically better to keep the labels "(linguistic) gender" and "agreement class" distinct from each other. See § 2.1.

90 Attempts at describing the so-called Romanian neuters as nouns which have masculine gender when singular and feminine gender when plural had already been dismissed by Jakobson (1971: 188). Loporcaro, Faraoni and Gardani (2014) have dealt another serious blow to other, alternative descriptions of the Romanian system (note how, in this article, the three authors argue that a tripartite gender system needs to be recognized for Old Ital-

Some typological considerations arise from the analysis we have proposed here. The first one is that the gender system of gender-distinguishing varieties of Arabic is not a "purely" formal one, but a mixed formal-semantic one. Purely formal gender systems are believed not to exist in natural languages (by purely formal it is meant a system in which nouns are divided into two or more agreement classes on a phonological and/or morphological basis, with no connection whatsoever with their semantics; Corbett 1991: 33 ff.). Languages such as Italian or French, however, go a long way in the direction of pure formality, since in these languages every noun is assigned to one of two genders and, with the exception of human referents and some animal ones, this happens on a non-semantic basis.

This is not the case for gender-distinguishing varieties of Arabic, where members of Class I are identified on purely semantic grounds (biologically masculine human entities[91]), and members of Classes II and III are identified on mixed formal/semantic grounds (nouns belonging to Class II can refer to biologically feminine human entities or nonhuman ones; nouns belonging to Class III are exclusively nonhuman[92]).

---

ian as well). It is also worth pointing out that, besides the structural similarities, the Romanian and Arabic agreement systems share apparently similar semantic bases. According to Jakobson (1971: 188–189): "In the singular, Rumanian nouns oppose a delimited category of feminine to the non-feminine, while in the plural, they oppose a delimited category of masculine to the non-masculine [...]. Each of these three genders carries its own semantic information: only the masculine gender can be applied for designating males, and only the feminine for designating females; neuter cannot be applied to sexed beings and is used only for inanimate, collective, and abstract units". This description could very well be applied to gender-distinguishing varieties of Arabic, the only difference being that the Arabic "neuter" can also be applied to nonhuman sexed beings (i.e. it is not restricted to inanimate entities, but encompasses several nouns referring to animals).

91 Occasional exceptions can occur. In Najdi Arabic, for example, the word for "horses" can take masculine plural agreement when it is used to refer figuratively to the men who mount them. It would also seem that personified animals in the context of fairytales, and large domestic animals in general, can sometimes attract masculine plural agreement. On this point see Bettega and Leitner (2019: 21, fn. 17), and in particular the following Khuzestani example: *u-təlga čaləb u-ṯōr marbūṭ-**īn*** 'And you will find a dog and a bull tied up' (with a M.PL participle). Crosslinguistically, it is rather common for large and/or domestic animals to enjoy a special (often human-like) agreement status (see for instance Corbett 1991: 10 on Kannada). Having an agreement class dedicated exclusively to masculine human referents is also not uncommon: this happens in several Dravidian languages, such as Tamil, Telugu and Kolami (Corbett 1991: 202–203; see also p. 168). The latter, in particular, features an opposition "human masculine VS everything else" similar to that expressed by M.PL/F.PL markers in Arabic.

92 It might be an interesting object of inquiry to analyze the semantics of nonhuman nouns belonging to Classes II and III in various dialects, in order to ascertain whether or not

This brings us to a second consideration, namely how do speakers know to which agreement class each noun belongs? We can say that controller gender is only partially overt in the dialects in question, since all nouns ending in *-a*(*t*) in the singular belong to Class II, but the remaining ones are distributed between classes I and III on mostly semantic grounds (plural nouns ending in *-īn* belong to Class I with very few exceptions; however, there is no formal way of determining if an apophonic plural will fall into Class I or III). In other words, the morphology of a noun is not, by itself, sufficient to determine to which agreement class it belongs.[93]

So far, the description of the agreement system of gender-distinguishing dialects appears to be relatively straightforward: however, for this description to be complete, three important aspects still need to be discussed, namely: (1) apophonic plurals; (2) F.SG agreement with plural controllers; (3) word order. The latter will be the object of § 2.3.9. The following two subsections are dedicated to (1) and (2), respectively.

2.3.4.1 Apophonic Plurals

The question of Apophonic plurals (also called "internal" or "broken" plurals) has already been introduced in § 2.2.1. As we have seen, these plurals do not display the morphological elements that have traditionally been associated with masculine and feminine gender in Arabic (the *-īn* and *-āt* plural suffixes, respectively). In other words, apophonic plurals can be said to have covert gender.[94] This does not represent a problem, since their agreement class can be easily determined by the type of agreement they attract (as is the case for any noun with covert gender in any language of the world).

What is most peculiar about Arabic apophonic plurals, however, is that a good number of adjectives exist which form their plural in the same way (perhaps due to the high degree of permeability that exists between the two classes

some kind of rationale underlies this subdivision. Note that, obviously, the labels "Class I, II and III" are conventional, and could be replaced by, for instance, "Masculine, Feminine and Neuter". Since a good deal of semantic overlapping exists between Classes II and III, however, we prefer to stick to a more neutral terminology.

93 Exceptions can be found even for Class II, as we have seen in § 2.3.1. An extremely small number of nouns exist which show an *-a*(*t*) ending in the singular and that, nonetheless, require masculine agreement both in the plural and in the singular. These belong to Class I. More numerous (though still not abundant) are those nouns which belong to Class II in spite of the fact that they do not show the "feminine" ending *-a*(*t*).

94 See Corbett 1991: 62–63, for a definition of the labels *covert* and *overt gender*. Note that, according to the description given above, nouns showing the *-āt* plural morpheme cannot be said to have overt gender, too, since they can fall in either Class II or III.

of nouns and adjectives in Arabic). Therefore, in Arabic it is sometimes possible to have covert gender on targets, and not only on controllers.[95] This has not been factored in the description of the agreement system shown in the previous section because, even when a controller of the "broken" type triggers apophonic agreement, the underlying gender can still be derived by analyzing different types of co-occurring targets (such as verbs or pronouns). What if all other targets depending on that controller are in the F.SG, however?

This scenario could represent a borderline case. If a class of plural controllers were to be identified that systematically trigger apophonic agreement in adjectives and F.SG agreement in all other targets, then these controllers would not fall in any of the three agreement classes described above. Some authors have indeed noted that apophonic adjectival agreement tends to co-occur with F.SG agreement (see for instance Hanistsch 2011: 146).

In light of the evidence derived from the analysis of our and other corpora, and from all the existing works that deal with the topic of agreement in Arabic, it is our opinion that such a class of names does not exist. Even the controllers that are inherently more prone to trigger F.SG agreement (such as abstract and non-prototypical concrete nouns) do sometimes trigger plural agreement.

A typical exponent of this category is *ayyām* 'days' (sg. *yōm*), which has repeatedly been described has having a strong tendency to attract singular agreement, even in dialects where percentages of plural agreement with non-human controllers are particularly high (we have seen several examples of this in § 2.3.2; see also Owens and Bani-Yasin 1987: 712 and Bettega 2017: 163, 165; see also Brustad 2000: 66–67 on a non-distinguishing dialect). Even in the case of *ayyām*, however, Ritt-Benmimoun (2017: 277) reports that quantification positively affects the level of individuation of the referent, causing it to trigger plural agreement, and gives the following example for Bedouin Tunisian: ***tʕaddan*** *ʕalay=y tisʕ ayyām* 'Nine days went by' (lit. 'went-F.PL over=me nine day.PL'). Examples such as this one show that *yōm*/*ayyām* is yet another member of Agreement Class III, despite its tendency to attract F.SG agreement in virtue of its intrinsically low level of individuation.

The second question that concerns adjectives with apophonic plural forms is what type of agreement they should be considered to express, i.e. individ-

95 Most likely, this is yet another element which caused studies on agreement in Arabic to focus more on the feature of number than on that of gender. When it comes to apophonic adjectives, it is easy to determine whether they are in the singular or in the plural, but their gender is not so easily assessed. It may be noted here that in several gender-distinguishing varieties of Arabic (including written Arabic), plural demonstratives are also underspecified for gender.

uated or non-individuated. In other words, does their agreement type aligns with that of plural targets or F.SG targets?

Over the course of the years, a huge amount of literature has been dedicated to the question of apophony in Arabic and Semitic languages, but this specific problem has rarely been tackled. In § 2.2.1 we have seen that Wright, Sallam and Brustad, although referring to different varieties of Arabic, all agree on the fact that suffixal plurals tend to denote several distinct individuals, while apophonic ones a group of individuals viewed collectively.[96] We are thus inclined to believe that, in ancient varieties of Arabic at least, a semantic distinction actually existed between the two plural forms, and that nouns with competing plural forms (i.e. a suffixal and an apophonic one) were more common than they are today. This will be discussed more thoroughly in the third chapter of this book.

What remains to be understood is whether or not this distinction is still operative in contemporary dialects, where nouns—and especially adjectives—with more than one plural form are rare. Sallam's observations seem to suggest that the broken/sound opposition remains valid in the case of certain nouns, in some dialects at least. As far as adjectives are concerned, Sallam (1979: 48) also remarks that the factors which motivate speakers to choose between broken and other types of agreement "are quite obscure".

In order to gain more insight into this issue, we would need to compare adjectival behavior in a relevant number of examples. Unfortunately, the overall frequency of broken plural adjectives appears to be rather low at corpus level.

Our corpus of Najdi texts includes 206 agreement targets. Of these, 28 are adjectives, and only 4 are apophonic plurals. Bettega and Leitner (2019: 16–18) worked on a larger corpus (521 targets), but even in their Khuzestani dataset broken adjectives were rare (10 occurrences out of 72 adjectives). Bettega's (2017) Omani corpus consisted of 269 agreement targets, and no apophonic plural appeared among them (out of 65 adjectival targets).

These figures, although based on a restricted sample, seem to suggest that broken adjectives are relatively uncommon. Readers who are familiar with spo-

96 Clearly, the question remains open of how to classify nouns that possess all three possible forms: a collective, a sound plural and a broken plural. What is the difference in meaning, in this case, between the apophonic plural and the collective? We have reported some examples of those in § 2.2.1, when commenting on Sallam's notion of "big" and "little" plural. In Sallam's examples, the distinction here appear to be an opposition between "collective X" and "types of X" (as in *ward* 'roses' in a collective sense, and *wurūd* 'types of roses'). More research, however, would be needed to ascertain wether or not this distinction applies to all triads of this kind.

ken Arabic may find this counterintuitive, since it is a well-known fact that, in most dialects, several high-frequency adjectives form their plural by means of apophony (e.g. color adjectives, the words for "big", "small", "long", "new", etc.). This, however, is no guarantee that a high number of these elements is to be found in any randomly selected set of data. As a consequence, in order to glimpse any significant statistical trend hidden in the behavior of apophonic adjectives, we should work with corpora that are at least several thousand targets strong. As of yet, no study about agreement in Arabic has been carried out on a corpus of this size.

An additional problem that we face when analyzing adjectival targets is that several studies lump broken and sound plurals together, so that separate examination of the two groups becomes impossible. We know, for instance, that 231 out of 873 total targets in Belnap's (1991: 57) corpus of Cairene Arabic were adjectives. Belnap gives no information, however, as to how many among these where apophonic plurals, his attention being focused exclusively on the F.SG/plural distinction.

Similarly, Holes' (2016: 341) corpus of Bahraini Arabic appears to be characterized by a remarkably high incidence of plural targets (as opposed to F.SG ones). The majority of the examples he gives, however, feature an adjective in the broken plural, so that it would be interesting to know how much of this plural agreement is actually apophonic agreement.

Holes and Belnap focus on non-distinguishing dialects. The question becomes even more complicated in the case of distinguishing ones, because—even if we were to consider apophonic plurals as expressing an individuated type of plurality—the fact remains that we wouldn't know if they are to be assimilated to *masculine* or *feminine* plurals (or neither of the two). Herin (2010: 279) seems to be aware of the problem when, after suggesting that apophonic plurals in the dialect of Salt could perhaps be considered as instances of M.PL agreement, notes that "Il est cependant impossible de statuer sur le genre des deux adjectifs *zġār*, pluriel de *zġīr* 'petit', et *kbār*, pluriel de *kbīr* 'grand'".

One important observation that could help to better assess the status of apophonic plurals comes from several works that have focused on agreement in spoken Arabic. It has often been remarked that, whenever an adjective that possess an apophonic plural agrees with a plural controller, then the apophonic plural will be the agreement form selected irrespectively of semantics or context. In other words, if speakers of Arabic are normally able to control agreement in order to obtain various nuances of meaning, this would not seem to be true in the case of broken adjectives. These elements tend to possess a single invariable plural form that is used independently of pragmatic/semantic considerations.

Consider for instance the following quote from Procházka and Gabsi (2017: 256) for Tunis Arabic:

> A very obvious tendency found throughout the corpora is that adjectives denoting colours (e.g. *zruq* 'blue', *ḥmuṛ* 'red', and *kḥul* 'black') mostly show plural agreement whether the controller is animate or inanimate. Numerous examples in unmonitored speech convey the impression that internal plural forms of frequent adjectives such as *kbāṛ* 'big', *ṣġāṛ* 'small', *ždud* 'new' are more often found in strict agreement patterns than adjectives which are less frequent and/or have external plural formation.

Watson (1993: 213) for Sanaani Arabic, Erwin (2004: 274–275) for Baghdadi Arabic and Holes (2016: 327) for Bahraini Arabic seem to point in the same direction.

It might be, then, that adjectives that possess a plural of the apophonic type are in the process of losing their ability to participate in agreement variation, more and more commonly adopting what is becoming their only plural form. From the point of view of the individuated/non-individuated opposition (as well as that of the F.PL/M.PL opposition in distinguishing dialects), their agreement type should be then considered neutral.

At present, it is impossible to say whether this phenomenon is a recent development, or if dates back centuries or millennia. It is also not clear if this hypothesis can be applied to all Arabic dialects, or only a part of them. From what we know of agreement in Cairene, for instance, it would seem that the situation in this variety is more nuanced (Mitchell 1973, Sallam 1979, Belnap 1991). Other dialects exist where the variation between F.SG and plural forms has disappeared entirely (§ 2.3.6 and § 2.3.7), so that, in this case, the question of the status of apophonic agreement is no longer relevant.

What emerges from the discussion above is that, in studies that intend to tackle the problem of agreement in Arabic by means of statistical analysis of corpora of data, instances of apophonic adjectival agreement should probably not be factored, since their partial or total inability to show any other type of agreement would muddle the results. At the same time, more research would be needed on the role and status of apophonic agreement, in order to understand A) whether or not it is true that apophonic adjectives show an absolute/strong preference towards this type of agreement, and B) if, in the cases in which variation is still found, this variation is to be considered meaningful, i.e. if the behavior of apophonic targets aligns with that of F.SG targets or other plural targets.[97]

---

97 As already said, this would require larger corpora than those on which scholars have been

2.3.4.2 Feminine Singular Agreement with Plural Controllers

In § 2.3.4 (Table 2.19) we have provided a schematized description of the agreement system of gender-distinguishing varieties of Arabic. That description was obviously a simplified one because, as we are well aware by now, no description of agreement in Arabic can be said to be complete if it does not address the question of F.SG agreement with plural controllers.

In the previous sections we have repeatedly discussed this phenomenon, analyzing it in detail. We have seen how this type of agreement occurs in all gender-distinguishing varieties of Arabic, though with varying frequency of use. We have also noted that it constitutes a tool for marking low individuation. This marking is in complementary distribution with gender marking, in that the two cannot co-occur in the same target. In light of this, we can say that F.SG agreement does not represent a separate agreement class—in the way Classes I, II and III do. Rather, it represents an alternative agreement option for plural controllers, available to nouns belonging to all three classes that are perceived by the speaker as non-individuated.

Several works have discussed this same topic in the past. Procházka and Gabsi (2017: 241), for instance, write that agreement is "sensitive to non-syntactic discourse information" and thus is "in part controlled by the speakers, who can choose between several options to vary what we can call perceptual salience and textual prominence". In the previous sections we have tried to summarize the findings of these works, and isolate the factors that have the most impact on agreement outcomes. We have seen that these appear to be humanness and animacy, collectiveness vs. individuality, quantification, abstractness vs. concreteness, specificity and distance between target and controller.

The time has now come to integrate F.SG/plural variation in our schematization of the agreement system of gender-distinguishing varieties of Arabic. This is done in Table 2.20, a partial modification of Table 2.19. We will label this agreement system "Type A", to distinguish it from other systems that will be described in the following sections.

---

working so far. From a methodological point of view, however, the process of analysis could be relatively easy. It would be sufficient to compare the percentages of F.SG agreement in non-adjectival targets with the combined total of the percentages of F.SG and broken agreement in adjectival targets. This is what has been done in the present study for the analysis of pre- and early-Islamic materials (see § 2.4). If the two figures were roughly overlapping, it would then mean that a relation still exists between apophonic plural adjectives and lack of individuation.

TABLE 2.20 Agreement in gender-distinguishing varieties of Arabic (Type A)[a]

Class	Agreement in the singular	Agreement in the plural		Semantic fields
		Individuated nouns	**Non-individuated nouns**	
I	Masculine singular	Masculine plural		Biologically masculine human beings
II	Feminine singular	Feminine plural	Feminine singular	Biologically feminine human beings, Nonhuman animates, Inanimates
III	Masculine singular	Feminine plural		Nonhuman animates, Inanimates

a The table does not feature a separate column for the type of agreement that obtains with dual controllers because this is assimilated to plural agreement (the only difference being that dual controllers are normally perceived as highly individuated because of their being inherently quantified, so that they rarely attract F.SG agreement; see § 2.3.3.4 for a discussion). Also, the possibility of apophonic adjectival agreement is not factored in the table: on this point, see § 2.3.4.1.

We believe Table 2.20 to be a good approximation of the actual functioning of these agreement systems. This, of course, is not to say that our schematization does not involve a certain degree of simplification. One important shortcoming of this representation, for instance, is that it does not factor the relative likelihood of the various agreement outcomes. We know that F.SG agreement is inherently rarer with members of Class I, and more common with members of Class III, but this complexity is flattened, as it were, in the table, since all the options are presented as equivalent and equally probable.

Including this further level of analysis in our scheme would make it so complex as to ultimately defeat its original purpose. Table 2.20 constitutes an idealized representation of the basic structure of the agreement systems in gender-distinguishing varieties of Arabic. Further elements of complexity are better tackled discursively, and for this the reader is referred to § 2.3.3 and § 2.3.5.

2.3.5 *Plural Agreement in Non-distinguishing Dialects: The Question of Complexity*

This section and the next two are dedicated to those dialects of spoken Arabic that have lost gender distinction in the plural forms of the verb, adjective and pronoun. Specific agreement-related phenomena (such as the influence on agreement of factors such as animacy, quantification, target type, etc.) have been thoroughly discussed in § 2.3.3, with abundant references to the literature on non-distinguishing dialects. Therefore, these topics will not be addressed again here if not passingly, and the reader is referred to the previous sections for a more detailed examination.

As we have seen, the main difficulty in describing the agreement system of gender-distinguishing dialects is represented by the interaction of singular and plural agreement. One might think, then, that the agreement system of non-distinguishing varieties is inherently less complex: since these dialects only possess a single form for plural agreement, they allow for less possible combinations.

From a certain perspective, this line of reasoning is sound: the number of formal distinctions that exist within a given system is actually one of the principles on which the analysis of linguistic complexity is based. This is known among typologists as the *principle of fewer distinction*, or *principle of economy* (Miestamo 2008, Audring 2016). Linguistic complexity, however, cannot be measured on the basis of morphology alone, and several other factors have to be taken into account, among which syntactic behavior.

The question of linguistic complexity is a long standing (and partially unresolved) problem in the field of linguistics, and one that we do not intend to address here in detail. It is sufficient to remind the reader that, while the measurement of the overall level of complexity of an entire language (*global complexity*) is considered by some a theoretical impossibility (Miestamo 2008), measuring the complexity of specific subsystems within a language (*local complexity*) is a feasible task, provided the right tools are employed.

Both Audring (2016) and Di Garbo (2016), for instance, propose a set of criteria to measure and compare the relative level of complexity of gender systems across different languages. The two authors note how, besides the number of distinctions that appear in a given grammatical domain, the independence of that domain from semantic and functional properties of other grammatical domains also has to be taken into account. This is what they call *principle of independence*. For instance, an interaction between the feature of gender and that of number increases the level of complexity of a language's gender system. If such an interaction allows the same noun to access different gender values, depending on the number it stands in, we then have a violation of the principle that Di Garbo and Agbetsoamedo (2016) call *unique value accessibility*. Canonically, gender is an inherent property of the noun, and each noun in a language should only have access to a single gender value. In certain cases, however, the gender of a noun can vary because of the context. Corbett (2013b) calls this process "recategorization", while Di Garbo and Agbetsoamedo (2016) use the expression "manipulable gender assignment". In their own words, "canonical gender should [...] not [be] manipulable for semantic or pragmatic purposes".

As we have seen, however, this is exactly what happens in spoken Arabic, where agreement with plural nouns can vary from plural to F.SG depending on a number of factors (among which quantification). In addition, it seems that speakers have a certain degree of liberty when choosing between the different agreement options, and that they are able to manipulate gender to obtain certain pragmatic or semantic effects. The gender system of spoken Arabic would then appear to be non-canonical.

Another element of non-canonicity in these systems is the presence of conditions (we have seen how, according to Corbett 2006: 183, "it is more canonical to have no conditions"). One of the most relevant conditions we have seen up to this moment is animacy (§ 2.3.3.4), that can induce an oscillation between plural and F.SG agreement.

What matters to us here is that this non-canonicity cuts across the distinction between distinguishing and non-distinguishing dialects, in that almost all of them include both agreement options. So, while it is undisputable that gender-distinguishing varieties are more complex from the point of view of morphology, it has also to be noted that non-distinguishing varieties also retain certain traits characteristic of highly complex gender systems.[98]

This observation entails two questions. The first one is theoretical in nature, and goes as follows: when we talk about nouns that have access to more than one gender value, can feminine singular be actually considered *a different gender value*? In other words, whenever a plural noun attracts F.SG agreement, should we think of that as an actual occurrence of the feminine singular? Or is it an entirely different phenomenon, which only bears a random formal coincidence with F.SG morphology? Is it, in other words, a mere case of homophony?

Several authors have addressed the question before. Mitchell (1973: 37) is categorical as to the answer. Given the fact that the type of agreement triggered by plural nouns is indeed identical to that of F.SG nouns in the realms of adjectives, verbs and pronouns, he concludes that "there can be no doubt from overwhelming evidence elsewhere in the language that the adjectival form *is*

98 Another one of such traits is the number of word classes that are able to show inflection, which is one of the parameters for the measurement of gender complexity employed by Di Garbo (2016: 53), and referred to as *complexity of formal marking*. As we have seen, Arabic has a rather pervasive system of gender marking. Certain dialects, both gender-distinguishing and not, can even mark agreement on possessive particles, another typologically uncommon trait (see § 2.2.4). We are not concerned, here, with the *domains* of agreement, because these are the same in all Arabic dialects, and so there is no complexity variation in this respect.

one and the same" (emphasis in the original). If we accept Mitchell's argument, we are then led to think that lack of individuation is, in Arabic, somehow connected to the concept of femininity.

The notion is well established in the literature that, in Semitic languages in general, feminine markers tend to carry semantic values that go well beyond the expression of biological sex. Caubet, Simeone-Senelle and Vanhove (1989: 39), for instance, offer a summary of all these functions. They remark how, in Semitic nouns,[99] the F.SG suffix can: a) express the opposition between a non-human *singulative* and a collective; b) express the opposition between a human *group* and an individual; c) express the opposition between a *specialized* meaning and a generic one; d) give rise to an *abstract* noun. The list of functions of the -*a*(*t*) marker in Arabic dialects that the authors provide on page 48 includes even more elements (note that these are more or less the same functions listed by Fassi Fehri, 2018, in his very detailed treatment of F.SG markers in Arabic). They remark, after Cohen, how in Semitic "ce n'est que plus tardivement, et par raccroc, que ce suffix sera amené à marquer l'opposition masculin-*feminin*".

This is obviously not the place to discuss the role and function of the -(*a*)*t* ending in Semitic. As far as Arabic in particular is concerned, we limit ourselves to observe that what we are dealing with here is possibly a problem of *definitions* and *descriptions*, rather than one intrinsic to the language. If Mitchell was lamenting the "illogicity" of asserting that a given noun is masculine singular in the singular and feminine singular in the plural, maybe the problem is in the definition that we give of the -(*a*)*t* ending itself.

If it sounds indeed odd to say that "the feminine singular marker also marks abstractness, collectiveness and lack of individuation in groups", the same statement could perhaps result more acceptable if we used a more neutral terminology. No linguist would probably show any surprise in learning that, in language X, the morpheme Y can be used to mark the opposition of abstractness, vs. concreteness, the opposition of genericness vs. specificity, and, in the case of human beings and some higher animates, the opposition between feminine and masculine gender.[100]

99 As will be discussed in more detail in § 3.1, it is mostly in Arabic that the "special status" of the F.SG markers has extended beyond the realm of nouns, giving rise to the peculiar F.SG agreement patterns discussed here. Sporadic uses of this pattern are, however, attested in other Semitic languages, such as Hebrew and Ancient South Arabian (see Hasselbach 2014a: 53–54).

100 It might be worth stressing that the semantic groupings and associations that each one of us perceives as "natural" and "logical" are not necessarily the same, and that this largely depends on one's cultural and linguistic background. The Aboriginal Australian language

The fact that, in Arabic, this role of the "feminine" ending has been extended beyond the realm of nouns, to include adjectives, verbs and even demonstratives, is probably a later and accidental development, which resulted from paradigmatic pressure (as discussed in more detail in § 3.1). We will not, at any rate, insist further on this specific terminological question, and throughout the book we will continue to employ the received terminology of Arabic and Semitic studies.

The second question that arises from our reflections on the topic of complexity is more pragmatic. Is it really the case that all varieties of spoken Arabic feature the possibility of F.SG agreement with plural controllers? We have shown this to be the case for gender-distinguishing dialects, but what about non-distinguishing ones?

In order to answer this question, we will now proceed to a survey of the available descriptions of agreement systems in non-distinguishing dialects.

2.3.6 *Plural Agreement in Non-distinguishing Dialects: Sources*

In § 2.3.2, we have seen how the materials available for the study of agreement in gender-distinguishing varieties of Arabic are often not as exhaustive as one could hope for. As far as non-distinguishing varieties are concerned, the situation is slightly better, because the main urban dialects of the Arab World are normally well-studied and documented. Even in this case, however, a general tendency exists for grammars to focus more on phonology and morphology, at the expenses of syntax. As a result, information about agreement, when present, is often confined to a short section, and many aspects of the phenomenon (such as variation, or agreement with non-adjectival targets) are not investigated in depth. In addition, not every non-distinguishing dialect is spoken in a large urban center. Many are found in remote areas, sometimes in isolated *Sprachinseln* at the very periphery of the Arabic-speaking continuum. In these cases, too, documentation is sometimes lacking.

Despite these difficulties, in the following pages we have done our best to present an overview as exhaustive as possible of the descriptions of agreement phenomena in non-distinguishing varieties. In this case, even more than with distinguishing dialects, the sheer amount of existing literature is huge. We can-

---

Dyirbal, when compared to Arabic or any major European language, represents a good example of how languages set their semantic boundaries at very different, and very arbitrary, intervals. The semantic subdivisions that underlie Dyirbal's four-gender system are: (I) animateness and human masculinity; (II) human femininity and everything connected to fighting, fire and water; (III) non-flesh foodstuff; (IV) everything else (Dixon 2010: 29).

not claim, therefore, that our list is utterly comprehensive. However, having consulted more than fifty different studies dealing with dialects from all over the Arabic-speaking world (including geographically and sociolinguistically "peripheral" areas), we believe the resulting picture to be fairly representative.

The trends emerging from our bibliographical survey are rather clear: the majority of non-distinguishing dialects retain the possibility of F.SG agreement with plural controllers (as was the case for distinguishing ones). A few, however, do not. Admittedly, these constitute a small minority, and many of them still exhibit traces of the old agreement system. Still, their presence cannot be ignored.

A second fact that emerges from the data is that, even among the dialects that do retain F.SG agreement, syntactic behavior is not uniform. Frequency of use appears to vary wildly, so that while some of them seem to be on their way to ultimately lose this type of agreement, others appear to have overextended it, making F.SG agreement the almost default option with certain controller types.

It would seem, then, that it is not possible to neatly divide non-distinguishing varieties into two groups (those that allow F.SG agreement with plural controllers and those that do not). Rather, they appear to be organized along a continuum, with dialects with exactly 0 occurrences of F.SG agreement at one end, and dialects where F.SG agreement has become increasingly more common at the other. Let us now examine the details of this picture in more depth.

If we start our survey with the dialects of the major urban centers of the Arabic-speaking world, we see that the majority of them retain the possibility of F.SG agreement in the plural. These are all well-known varieties, whose agreement systems are fairly well described. The reader can consult Tapiéro (1971: 42) for the dialect of Algiers,[101] Procházka & Gabsi (2017) for the dialect of Tunis,[102] Belnap (1991), Belnap (1993) and Woidich (2006b) for that of Cairo, Rosenhouse (2007: 491) for Jerusalem, Cowell (1964: 420–427, 501–504), Hanitsch (2011) and Berlinches Ramos (2021) for Damascus, Feghali (1928: 143–145) for Beirut, McCarthy and Raffouli (1965: 177–178) and Erwin (2004: 273–275) for Muslim Baghdad, Abu-Haidar (1991: 101) for Christian Baghdad, Sieny (1978:

101 See also Marçais (1956: 343) on the dialect of Jijel: his grammar offers almost no remark about syntactic structures, but he notes how F.SG agreement is very rarely associated with collective nouns (M.SG and C.PL being more common in this context).

102 For Tunisia, see also Talmoudi's (1980: 83) on the dialect of Sousse, who notes how F.SG agreement is possible in verbs with all nonhuman and human collective controllers, and that it is mandatory with plurals of small animals.

197) and Kramer and Winchester (2018) for the Urban Hijaz (Jedda, Mecca and Medina), and Holes (2016: 326–353) for Bahrain and more in general the urban dialects of the Gulf Coast.[103] F.SG agreement with plural controllers was also present in the now extinct dialects of Andalusia (Corriente 2008: 108 notes that even dual controllers could sometimes trigger it).[104]

The systems described in these works are all remarkably similar: F.SG agreement with plural controllers is a possibility in almost all urban varieties of spoken Arabic (this includes human collectives and, at least in the cases of Cairo and Damascus,[105] proper human plurals). Variation between F.SG and plural agreement is mainly governed by the referent's level of individuation/specificity, thus once more confirming the findings of Brustad 2000.

The main exception to this general trend seems to be represented by the urban dialects of the western Maghreb. Working on the dialects of Fes, Rabat and Casablanca, Harrell (1962: 158) notes that "there are a few rare cases of inanimate plural nouns taking feminine singular agreement with pronouns, adjectives and verbs [...]. Only isolated idioms and stereotyped phrases require this type of agreement". The two examples he provides both feature a verb in pre-controller position, a context that tends to favor singular agreement (see § 2.3.9): *dazet ši=iyyamat* 'a few days passed' and *mnin ka=tebqa saʕtayn l=le=fžer* 'when two hours are left until dawn'. Both the study of Caubet, Simeone-Senelle and Vanhove (1989: 60) and that of Brustad (2000: 59) show that, in Moroccan Arabic, F.SG agreement mostly occurs in relation with loans from Standard Arabic (though they both provide at least one example of F.SG agreement with the collective *nās* 'people'). These observations seem to corroborate Harrell's claim that F.SG agreement is not typically part of the Moroccan system.

However, the following remarks by Buret (1944: 80–81, cited in Corriente 2008: 20), seem to suggest that F.SG agreement might have been more common until a few decades ago: "Vous trouverez souvent, dans les texts, des verbes,

103 Holes discusses both urban and rural dialects in his study. On Gulf Arabic, see also Holes 1990, and for Baghdadi see also the appropriate subsection in § 2.3.2. We have not included Tripoli in our list because Pereira's (2010) otherwise excellent grammar of Muslim Tripoli Arabic does not discuss agreement phenomena. Cesaro (1939) makes no mention of F.SG agreement in the dialect, but it sometimes appears in D'Anna's own texts. D'Anna also notes how, in Tripoli Arabic, F.PL adjectival targets are still occasionally found, in particular when associated to controllers that display regular F.PL morphology.

104 On agreement in Andalusi, see also Marugán (1994).

105 On F.SG agreement with human plurals, see Belnap (1991) for Cairene and Brustad (2000: 60) and Cowell (1964: 423–424) for Damascus.

ou des adjectives, au feminine singulier se rapportant à des noms au pluriels. Dans certains cas cela était obligatoire en arabe classique. Aujourd'hui, dans certaines expressions, on emploie volontier le feminine singulier, mais il n'est pas incorrect d'employer le pluriel". If urban Moroccan is actually on its way to lose F.SG agreement altogether, then this change may be a relatively recent development.

Caubet, Simeone-Senelle and Vanhove (1989: 60–61) also comment on the situation in Malta. They note that F.SG agreement with plural controllers never occurs in their texts, although it can be found in poetry and in certain idiomatic expressions. In this respect, then, the Maltese situation seems to be very similar to the Moroccan one. In this case as well, traces of F.SG agreement can be found in older descriptions of the dialect. Blanc (1970: 50) writes that "In Malta, verbs and pronouns have PC exclusively, but some adjectives and participles have FS forms that are fully equivalent to P forms, viz. occur both with nouns of personal reference and with those of non-personal reference". All the examples Blanc provides are drawn from previous studies (Aquilina 1965; Stumme 1904; Vella 1831), and include: *irjiel tayba* 'good men' and *karti tayba* 'good cards'; in both cases, the adjective is in the F.SG. Aquilina (1973: 327–328), in particular, notes how collectives are "treated as a sing. fem. unit". Among the examples he gives, which include the common collective *nies* (i.e. *nās* 'people'), a non-collective plural appears: *it=tfāl* [...] *imqārb-**a** u ma **t**-hobb=š **t**-istūdya* 'the children [...] are naughty and do not like to study'.[106] Here 'children' attracts F.SG agreement in both verbs and the adjective. Aquilina also notes that, "less idiomatically", collectives can alternatively attract plural agreement.

One last urban dialect that appears to entirely lack F.SG agreement with plural controllers is Tripoli Jewish Arabic. Yoda (2005: 285) is categorical: "pl. nouns (whether indicating human beings or inanimate objects) always agree with the pl. form [...] and not with the f.sg form. In other dialects, the plural of an inanimate object may agree with the singular feminine, but such an agreement is not attested in TJ". As we have seen, F.SG. agreement would also seem to be rare in the Muslim dialects of Tripoli. D'Anna however advises caution, since F.SG agreement is present, albeit rarely, in his texts from Jewish Benghazi (and since interference from Hebrew might be at play for informants living in Israel). It would seem that, in general, Libyan dialects make little use of this syntactic option (this is also true of gender-distinguishing Libyan varieties, see § 1.3 and the relevant subsection in § 2.3.2).

106 As was the case for most of the works cited, we have adapted Aquilina's original transcription to the system employed in this book. Oddly enough, Aquilina does not use Maltese ortography in his study.

If we now move outside the main urban centers of the Arab world, we see that non-distinguishing varieties are found here as well.[107] Among these, F.SG agreement with plural controllers is also commonly encountered. The remarks that Marçais (1977: 158) offers about the Maghreb as a whole seem to confirm what we have seen so far: "la tendence dialectale générale consiste à faire l'accord au pluriel des verbes (adjectives et pronoms) qui se rapportent à des noms comportant l'idée manifeste de pluralité [...]. Il est cependant courant, surtout dans les parlers bédouins et dans les parlers de l'Est maghrébin, de relever l'accord au feminine des verbes (adjectives et pronoms) se rapportant à des pluriels et collectifs". In other words, F.SG agreement is less common in the west, and more in the east, especially in rural areas where so-called "Bedouin" dialects are spoken. This would seem to be the case in the Mzāb region of the Algerian Sahara, investigated by Grand'Henry (1976: 64, 80). Here human collectives are normally treated as F.SG, and the same is true for animal ones. Even proper plurals can sometimes trigger F.SG agreement. D'Anna (2018: 53) notes how F.SG agreement is possible, even with human controllers, in the coastal Tunisian dialect of Chebba, giving the following example: *mā=ixallū=š ṣġār=həm* ***tə****-lʕab mʕā ṣġār=nā* 'They don't let their children play with our children', where the verb is in the F.SG.

About the Arabic spoken in the Egyptian oasis of el-Bahariya, Drop and Woidich (2007: 106) write that nonhuman plural controllers can "also" take plural agreement, as is the case in Cairo (thus implying that another nonplural type of agreement is possible, namely F.SG). This, however, only happens when the plural refers to a small and well-defined number of objects. In particular, C.PL agreement is more or less mandatory when the noun stands in the dual, or is accompanied by a quantifier.

As far as sub-Saharan dialects are concerned, an interesting remark is found in Jullien de Pommerol (1999: 189) about the Arabic of N'Djamena: "L'usage apprendra qu'il y a des noms pluriels qui provoquent un accord de leur qualificatif au féminin singulier, apportant une nuance d'austeritè ou de souffrance devant une situation pénible". The author gives the examples *al=sinīn al=murr-****a*** *al fāt-****at*** 'The bitter years that have gone by', where both the adjective and the verb stand in the F.SG, and *al=ayyām al=tawīl-****a*** *fi wakit al-žuʔ* "the long days at the time of the famine", again with a F.SG adjective. It would seem that in this Chadian variety F.SG agreement has become more restricted in use than it

107 Among these, we find the Arabic dialect spoken by the Maronite community of Cyprus. Unfortunately, Borg (1985) offers no description of this variety's agreement patterns.

is in other dialects, and that this reduction in frequency has brought about a semantic specialization not observed anywhere else.

Moving now to the Mashreq, we find that F.SG agreement is even more commonly encountered here than it is in North Africa.

According to Abu-Haidar (1979: 124), in the Lebanese village of Baskinta adjectival agreement with nonhuman controllers is always F.SG when the controller is an abstract one, while it is usually plural with concrete controllers. In the Syrian dialect of Sukhne, Behnstedt (1994: 171–173) observes that adjectives depending on plural controllers take plural agreement, only rarely appearing in the F.SG. According to him, the two forms *šabībīč mkarkaʕ-**āt**/mkarkʕ-**a*** 'broken (F.PL/F.SG) windows', are equally acceptable (note that the dialect retains F.PL forms of adjectives and participles, even if it has lost them in the verbal and pronominal paradigms; on this point, see § 2.3.8). Verbs also tend to agree in the plural, but they can appear in the F.SG if the subject is a collective (human or not) or an animal one: *əl=ʔawādim/əč=člīb bi=**t**-mūt* 'the people/the dogs die (F.SG)'.

An interesting example of a non-urban Peninsular dialect lacking F.PL pronouns and verbs is that of the Āl Murra. According to Ingham (1986b), this variety appears to be very conservative in many respects, the absence of F.PL morphology thus being all the more striking. Although Ingham does not comment on the topic, examples of F.SG agreement with plural and collective controllers can be found in the texts at the end of the article (see, for instance, Ingham 1986b: 284, *fi=s=snīn is=sābig-**ah*** 'in years gone by', and *al=bil māxūḏ-**ah*** 'the camels had been taken').

The only eastern exception to the omnipresence of F.SG agreement with plural controllers seems to be represented by the dialects of Turkey. For the Cilician region, Procházka (2002: 154–157) notes how, in the dialects of the Çukurova, adjectives referred to plural controllers always agree in the plural (sound or broken[108]) and never in the feminine singular. This is true even in the case of nonhuman controllers. F.SG agreement is only found occasionally in verbs preceding their subjects, as shown by the following examples: *rāḥ-**it** ᵊṣbāya l=ᵊbnāt la=ʕand imm=u* 'The young women hit the road to his mother', and *ma=**t**-fūt il=īyēm* 'the days are passing by'.

Commenting on Anatolian dialects, Blanc (1970: 50) offers the following remark: "in Anatolia, Jastrow assures me there is no FSC in adjectives; in the three hours of tape he graciously sent me, the one example I found (*ḥawēwīn*

108 Despite the dialect having lost F.PL verbal and pronominal morphology, F.PL agreement in adjectives and participles is still widespread. This is an important point that will be discussed further in § 2.3.8.

waḥšīye, 'wild animals') he considers an ordinary plural form, viz. one applying to nouns of personal reference as well. For verbal concord the picture is similar, with a single instance on the aforesaid tapes".

This overview of agreement patterns in non-urban dialects concludes our survey of the behavior of non-distinguishing varieties across the Arabic-speaking world. In the next section, we will discuss the implications of the data presented.

2.3.7 *Plural Agreement in Non-distinguishing Dialects: Description*

As we have seen, our analysis of the available materials suggests that non-distinguishing dialects can be broadly divided into two subgroups, i.e. those that have retained F.SG agreement with plural controllers, and those that have not.

The latter group is much smaller than the former, and it includes Maltese, the urban dialects of Morocco, the Jewish dialect of Tripoli, and the dialects of the Çukurova (Cilicia) and Anatolia in Turkey. In these varieties, the few examples of F.SG agreement that can still be found appear to be mostly fossilized remnants of a once more widespread systems, that today only survives in proverbs and idioms, or very specific syntactic contexts.

The second group of dialects includes all the other non-distinguishing varieties. Among these, frequency of use of the F.SG varies, to the point that it is not clear whether it is possible to speak of neatly divided groups, or if all non-distinguishing varieties are better conceptualized as organized along a continuum.

For the sake of practical analysis, let us for a moment accept the two-groups model as true. Such a subdivision obviously implies the existence of two different agreement systems, one more complex than the other (based on the definition of complexity given in § 2.3.5). We will label these two systems, respectively Type B and Type C.

System B is the more complex of the two, although simpler than the one that we have seen in the case of gender-distinguishing dialects (that is, Type A; see § 2.3.4, Table 2.20). Compared to that system, its description requires less subdivisions at the morphosyntactic and semantic levels. In other words, we only have two agreement classes left, which can be considered as fully fledged genders, and not "controller genders", because each has morphological forms uniquely associated with it (see § 2.3.4). If we compare Table 2.21 below with Table 2.20, we see that biologically masculine human beings no longer occupy their own slot, but have merged with a group of nonhuman controllers. This is because, at the syntactic level, they no longer possess a dedicated type of plural agreement (i.e. M.PL agreement). On the contrary, a single type of plu-

TABLE 2.21 Agreement in non-distinguishing varieties of Arabic (Type B)

Gender	Agreement in the singular	Agreement in the plural		Semantic fields
		Individuated nouns	Non-individuated nouns	
I	Masculine singular	Common plural	Feminine singular	Biologically masculine human beings, some non-humans
II	Feminine singular			Biologically feminine human beings, some nonhumans

ral agreement now exists, accessible to all individuated plural controllers. One important consequence of this change is that the system of gender assignment has shifted from partially to completely overt, since it does not rely on mixed formal-semantic criteria anymore, but it is now only based on formal (i.e. morphological) ones.[109] The situation for non-individuated controllers, on the other hand, has remained exactly the same, in that they all attract F.SG agreement.[110]

System C, as said, is much simpler, in that the division between individuated and non-individuated controllers is no longer relevant. In other words, the prototypical *unique value accessibility* has been restored to the system (§ 2.3.5), which is no longer characterized by *manipulable gender assignment*. A bipartite gender distinction is all that is left, one that only operates in the singular.[111]

109 With the obvious exception of the few nouns, already discussed, that are morphologically M.SG but take F.SG agreement and vice versa.

110 The rules that govern variation between F.SG and PL agreement in non-distinguishing varieties are the same that we have described for distinguishing dialects, so we will not return on this point here. Note that table 2.21 is similar to table 2.20 in 2.3.4 in that here, too, dual controllers are assimilated to individuated plural ones (though F.SG agreement with dual controllers, in the dialects where dual inflection of nouns is still productive, can sporadically occur). In addition, the possibility of apophonic plural agreement is not factored in the description. For a treatment of all these topics, the reader is referred to § 2.3.3.4 and § 2.3.4.1.

111 Note that in some of the dialects that display this particular agreement system, gender distinction has been lost in the second person singular of verbs and/or pronouns as well (see § 2.2.4). This makes these systems the typologically simplest of all.

TABLE 2.22 Agreement in non-distinguishing varieties of Arabic (Type C)

Gender	Agreement in the singular	Agreement in the plural	Semantic fields
I	Masculine singular	Common plural	Biologically masculine human beings, some nonhuman
II	Feminine singular		Biologically feminine human beings, some nonhuman

As we have already stressed, these descriptions represent somewhat idealized simplifications of a more complex reality. They constitute a good approximation of the real state of affairs, but a number of caveats are to be kept in mind.

The first one is that, as we have seen, F.SG agreement, although extremely rare, has not disappeared completely from Type C dialects. This is not factored in Table 2.22. Since this type of agreement appears to be confined to idioms and fixed expressions, its role could be deemed negligible, because it does not affect the overall behavior of the system. Some of the examples discussed in § 2.3.5, however, may lead one to suspect that in some dialects (Urban Moroccan, Maltese), a minor degree of variation still exists (with certain controller types at least, such as *nās* 'people').[112]

The second element of complexity is that, in Type B dialects, frequency of use of F.SG agreement may vary dramatically. While in some cases it has become so rare that the agreement system now approximates a type C one (and, in these cases, it is not clear where the dividing line should be drawn), in others it has expanded. This is most notably the case in Cairo Arabic, where the unusually high frequency of F.SG forms has been reported independently by several different authors.

Sallam (1979: 49), analyzing the results of several interviews he conducted with native speakers from Egypt and various Levantine countries, concludes that it is only the Egyptian informants who judge F.SG agreement with human plurals acceptable (in sentences such as *ʔaṭfāl miṭṭaʕam-**a*** 'vaccinated children', or *banāt mitʕallim-**a*** 'educated girls').

Belnap (1991: 63–64) claims that "Cairenes tend to use deflected [feminine] agreement more than speakers of other dialects". He, as well, provides several

112 We are not concerned, here, with the occurrences of F.SG agreement that may appear in these dialects as a consequence of lexical and syntactic borrowing from MSA.

examples of F.SG agreement with human plural controllers, and notes how, with nonhuman controllers, this type of agreement becomes the almost default option. In his texts, the percentages of F.SG targets depending on a nonhuman plural controller are much higher than those observed in any other dialect for which we have documentation (between 96% and 97%).

Brustad (2000: 62), commenting on this, hypothesizes a connection between this idiosyncrasy of Cairene Arabic and other morphosyntactic peculiarities of the dialect: "This Cairene tendency to accord less syntactic attention to the individuation of nouns is mirrored as well in the absence in Egyptian of certain specifying articles and demonstrative forms found in other dialects".

The case of Cairo Arabic admittedly poses a problem for the schematization of Type B agreement system, displayed in Table 2.21. On the one hand, although the description presented here is technically still valid, the fact that the "non-individuated" option has become the widely preferred one cannot be ignored. On the other hand, the simple association of nonhuman controllers with F.SG agreement would again be an oversimplification. Despite its having become pervasive with this type of controllers, percentages of F.SG agreement still plummet in certain syntactic contexts (for instance, whenever the nonhuman controller is accompanied by a numeral, see Belnap 1991: 69 and § 2.3.3.4). This means, in other words, that the little variation that is left is nonrandom.

It is not easy to fully account for an agreement system such as that of Cairo Arabic. It would appear that agreement in Cairene is currently in a state of flux, possibly evolving in the direction of a yet unseen system (as Arabic varieties go). The idea that F.SG agreement could eventually be overextended as the default agreement option for all nonhuman plural controllers, giving rise to an MSA-like agreement system,[113] is a fascinating one. Given the generally slow pace of this kind of linguistic change, however, it is unlikely that we will be able to check this hypothesis during the course of our lifetimes.

To conclude our examination of agreement patterns in non-distinguishing varieties, we would like to offer two last considerations.

The first one is that the high degree of variation encountered in the frequency of F.SG agreement in these dialects is yet another characteristic that sets non-distinguishing varieties apart from distinguishing ones. The dialects that still retain F.PL verbal and pronominal forms know no such extremes, with no documented dialect having entirely abandoned F.SG agreement, or overex-

113 The two systems, however, would still be different, in that MSA still retains separate agreement patterns for M.PL and F.PL human controllers. See § 2.5.

tended it as the quasi-default agreement type for nonhuman controllers. This, in turn, brings us back to the traditional conception of F.SG agreement with plural controllers as a typical characteristic of Old Arabic (§ 1.1), one often encountered in so-called "Bedouin" dialects but rare in "sedentary" (and thus mostly non-distinguishing) varieties (§ 2.3.2).

As should be clear by now, this picture represents, at best, an oversimplification. While it is true that it is only among non-distinguishing dialects that we find those that have entirely dismissed F.SG agreement, it is also true that this only happens in a handful of cases. In some varieties, F.SG agreement appears to be rare (but this can also be said of several distinguishing dialects), while in others it has become more common than in any "Bedouin" variety. Finally, it has to be remarked that many historically Bedouin dialects exist where gender distinction in the plural is no longer an option (this is true in large parts of the Maghreb, but also in several peninsular dialects, such as that of the Āl Murra or the dialects of the Gulf Coast). In § 2.3.2 we have seen how, on the contrary, several historically sedentary varieties preserve this distinction: this poses yet another problem for the idea that a correspondence exists between Bedouin/sedentary varieties, on one side, and distinguishing/non-distinguishing dialects, on the other. All things considered, this alleged rule knows so many exceptions that it holds very little explanatory or classificatory power, and is thus probably better abandoned.[114]

The second consideration brings us back to the idea of a "continuum" of non-distinguishing dialects, to which we have repeatedly alluded in this section and the previous one. It must be clear that this, as well, represents a convenient theoretical abstraction. In practice, it would be very hard (if not altogether impos-

114 Our critique of the Bedouin/sedentary divide is informed by the evidence coming from gender markers and agreement patterns, and it is therefore limited to these specific areas of the language. Several scholars have however examined the question more thoroughly, and raised similar concerns. See e.g. Palva (2006: 605): "In a classification exclusively based on linguistic contrasts, scarcely any single criterion besides the reflexes of *q distinguishing between the Bedouin-type and sedentary type dialects can be found", or Watson (2011: 869): "The Bedouin sedentary split has [...] been shown to be both an oversimplification and of diminishing sociological appropriacy. [...]. While the nomadic sedentary lifestyle difference may be reflected in a set of certain linguistic features in certain regions, in others it is not". Magidow (2016: 93), acutely observes how, if we insist on conceiving two groups of dialects distinguished by a set of linguistic variables, and call one of these groups more "conservative" (Bedouin dialects) and the other more "innovative" (sedentary dialects), then it follows that "it is sedentary dialects that have all changed in specific ways with respect to these variables. Bedouin dialects, in contrast, are similar only in that they have not changed, so only sedentary dialects can potentially be said to form a cohesive group".

sible) to hierarchically rank dialects on the basis of how frequent F.SG agreement with plural controllers is. Such a task would require statistical analyses to be run on huge corpora, one for every dialect, each thousands of controllers strong, and each containing a wealth of different text-types (monologues, dialogues, narrative and argumentative texts, and so on; as we have seen, the topic and type of a given text can have a strong influence on agreement outcomes).

That such a study is probably impossible is regrettable, because being able to rank dialects according to the use they make of F.SG agreement would help answer a number of diachronic questions. In particular, if we accept the idea that the loss of F.PL forms happened independently in several different occasions throughout the history of the Arabic languages (see Chapter 5), then it would be interesting to know whether dialects that lost these forms only recently are more prone to use F.SG agreement than dialects that lost them in the distant past, or the other way around. It is beyond doubt that the disappearance of F.PL morphology brought about a restructuring of the whole agreement system in the dialects where it occurred. The precise effects of this change, however, are less clear.

These questions will be more thoroughly discussed in the last chapter of the book, where the diachronic dimension of agreement in spoken Arabic will be explored. We will now move on to analyze a last set of agreement systems, that apparently deviate from what we have seen so far in the case of both gender-distinguishing and non-distinguishing varieties.

2.3.8 *Divergent Systems*

To conclude our survey of the functioning of agreement in the spoken varieties of Arabic, one last and heterogeneous group of dialects needs to be examined. Up until this moment, we have conveniently separated dialects into two discrete groups, which we have labelled, respectively, "gender-distinguishing" and "non-distinguishing". However, as is the case with most classificatory systems of natural phenomena, our proposed taxonomy remains, to an extent, an artificial oversimplification.

In reality, some dialects, or certain phenomena that are attested across a number of dialects, appear to defy the definitions that we have employed so far. In this paragraph we will focus on four main points: F.PL adjectival agreement in non-distinguishing varieties, agreement in Ḥassāniyya, agreement in Darfur Arabic, and agreement in those dialects that display exceptional morphosyntactic behavior.

2.3.8.1 F.PL Adjectival Agreement in Non-distinguishing Dialects

In § 2.2.4 we have hinted at the fact that adjectival F.PL agreement can occasionally occur with plural controllers in non-distinguishing dialects. We have already noted how the morphological affinity of nouns and adjectives in Arabic is probably responsible for the survival of these forms in dialects that have otherwise lost all traces of F.PL morphology in verbs and pronouns.

Incidentally, this is yet another reason because of which adjectives in Arabic dialects are very poor indicators of how the gender/agreement system is structured. Besides possessing two alternative pluralization strategies (suffixation and apophony), adjectives in non-distinguishing varieties can sometimes also display relics of the old morphological inventory, rendering the general picture extremely fuzzy. In this respect, post-controller verbal and pronominal targets are far more regular, and represent a more reliable source of information. Unfortunately, as we have seen, even in those dialectological studies that do devote some attention to agreement, the description is normally based on adjectival behavior. The risk in these cases is that of focusing on a narrow set of very specific, exceptional or particularly complex agreement phenomena, losing sight of the general picture.

Caubet, Simeone-Senelle and Vanhove (1989: 58–59) identify three contexts in which the occurrence of F.PL adjectives in non-distinguishing dialects appears to be particularly common. The first of these contexts is their co-occurrence with a controller marked by the regular suffix for the F.PL. They call this tendency "un phénomène d'assonance", and note how it is particularly common in Moroccan dialects. Harrell (2004: 157) seems to agree with this, and writes that "the feminine plural adjective, ending in *-at*, is almost never used except in conjunction with a feminine plural noun also ending in -*at*", and gives the examples *ši=ḥkayat maġribiy-**at*** 'some Moroccan stories', and *le=ʕyalat l=meʕruḍ-**at*** 'the invited women'.

The second context is the co-occurrence of the adjective with the plural form of a singulative, in turn derived from a collective. In this case, the F.PL adjective "et utilisé avec les numéraux, ou pour désigner un petit nombre d'éléments". In other words, this would seem to be connected to the referent's level of individuation. The example they provide, *banadorayāt māwiyy-**āt*** 'a few juicy tomatoes', is taken from Damascus Arabic, and appears to be in line with Cowell's (1964) observations on the subject (note however that this example also features a plural noun ending in *-āt*).

Lastly, adjectives in the F.PL appear to be particularly common when they indicate "appartenance à un groupe social" (e.g. *nəswān məsəlm-**āt*** 'muslim women').

It has to be kept in mind that, in all these cases, the alternative M.PL (C.PL) option is always possible, and normally preferred. A single exception apparently exists, and it is noted by Caubet, Simeone-Senelle and Vanhove in a very interesting example they provide. The authors note how F.PL adjectives are sometimes associated with feminine domestic animals of large size. In Takrouna, in particular, the adjective *zəbbād* can be used with reference to animals that produce large quantities of milk, or plants that—when eaten by the animals—help them produce large quantities of milk. In the latter case, when the controller is inanimate, the adjective regularly appears in the M.PL/C.PL form (*zəbbādīn*). In the former, when the controller is nonhuman, but animate, the adjective must occur in the F.PL form (*zəbbādāt*). It would seem that what we are dealing with here are the last fossilized remnants of a bygone agreement system, in which the occurrence of F.PL agreement with nonhuman nouns was meant to indicate a higher level of individuation (based, in this case, on the animacy hierarchy).

Participles appear to be another common target type in which F.PL agreement occurs. Erwin (2004: 274) remarks how, in Baghdadi, F.PL agreement is common in participles "that indicate physical position of motion, such as *gāʕid* 'sitting' and *rāyiḥ* 'going'".[115] Contrary to Baghdadi Arabic, the Bedouin dialects of southern Tunisia investigated by Ritt-Benmimoun are still of the gender-distinguishing type. They are, however, going through a process of loss of F.PL morphology, which is being replaced by the corresponding masculine forms. Ritt-Benmimoun (2017: 274, 276, 284) repeatedly stresses how participles appear to be particularly resistant to this process of erosion. In particular, she notes how "participles often show the externally inflected form with *-āt* even when all other concordants show masculine plural agreement". The same appears to be true in Fezzani Arabic (D'Anna 2017: 111).[116]

115 Note that both Erwin and Abu Haidar (2006: 230) seem to agree on the fact that F.PL adjectival agreement with feminine human controllers is rather frequent in Baghdadi, where it might even represent the preferred option. The only example that Abu Haidar gives, however, involves yet another controller marked by the suffix *-āt*: *ʕammāt ḥanūn-āt* 'loving paternal aunts'.

116 Some authors have reported the opposite tendency in other dialects. Procházka (2002: 154), for instance, notes that F.PL agreement is rarer in participles than it is in adjectives in the dialects of the Çukurova, and Procházka and Gabsi (2017: 249) write that "Participles of derived stems and passive participles of Form I verbs are particularly prone to deflected agreement". The distinction between active and passive participles here might be of importance: active participles are often used with verbal force in spoken Arabic, and this implies that the controller they refer to has a higher degree of agency. This, in turn, makes it more likely that the subject is perceived as individuated. In Tunis Arabic there is no morphological distinction between active and passive participles of derived stems, so that it is not possible to know if this statement by Procházka and Gabsi is valid for both types, or if percentages of F.SG agreement are higher in one of the two cases but lower in the other.

If we look at the general picture, we see that, in this case as well, non-distinguishing varieties appear to be organized along a continuum. At one extreme are those dialects where adjectival F.PL agreement is utterly impossible (this would seem to be the case of Cairene, for instance: see Sallam 1979: 49). In between are dialects where F.PL adjectives occasionally occur, though the corresponding M.PL/C.PL forms are far more common (e.g. Damascus). At the other end of the continuum, we have dialects where F.PL adjectives appear to be the preferred, or only, option.

This happens in the dialects of the Çukurova, where, according to Procházka (2002: 154), occurrences such as *bnāt il=kayys-**īn*** 'beautiful (M.PL) girls', are rarer than the corresponding *bnāt il=kayys-**āt*** (where the adjective is in the F.PL). In these Cilician varieties it is not only human females, but all types of non-human controllers, that trigger F.PL adjectival agreement (e.g. *ḥkāyāt ᵊktīr-**āt*** 'many tales', *qnēni milyān-**āt*** 'full bottles'). The same holds true in the rural Syrian dialect of Sukhne, where, according to Behnstedt (1994: 172–173), adjectives and participles depending on feminine human or nonhuman plural controllers systematically show F.PL agreement (e.g. *bnayyāt niyym-**āt*** 'sleeping girls', and *čṛaṛa ćifl-**āt*** 'shy donkeys'). Note that also genitive exponents appear to follow the same agreement rules as adjectives: *li=hwāš hadōl gayy-**āt**=na* 'these houses belong to us', where the possessive *gayy* is inflected for F.PL.

The case of these dialects appears to be unique in the Arabic-speaking world, and, from a diachronic perspective, seems to represent the "missing link" between Type A and Type B agreement systems. The dialect of Sukhne and, to an extent, those of the Çukurova, cannot be fully described as neither distinguishing nor non-distinguishing: in the realm of adjectival agreement, they still follow the "old" system, with M.PL forms being restricted to masculine human plurals (this is apparently true of genitive exponents as well). In the case of verbs, pronouns and demonstratives, however, the "new" agreement type has taken over completely, and F.PL agreement is no longer possible. See Chapter 5 for a discussion of the implications.

2.3.8.2 Agreement in Ḥassāniyya

Some observations on the Ḥassāniyya dialect spoken mostly in Mauritania (but also Southern Morocco and Mali) have already appeared in §2.2.4 and §2.3.2. We have decided to treat Ḥassāniyya separately from all other dialects because of its unique characteristics.

As we have seen, Ḥassāniyya shows gender distinction in free plural pronouns and plural adjectives (Heath 2002: 259 and Taine-Cheikh 1993 provide several examples of this). The dialect, however, cannot be grouped together with other gender-distinguishing varieties because it shows a single plural form in the verbal paradigms and in bound pronouns. Furthermore, the feminine plural pronouns in Ḥassāniyya are clearly not retentions of older forms, but rather innovations (as discussed in § 2.2.4).

Information about agreement in Ḥassāniyya is not abundant, but the little data we have is intriguing. Taine-Cheikh (1993) focuses on the question of the feminine gender in Ḥassāniyya, offering many examples of F.PL agreement in adjectives and participles. It is clear that, at least with this type of targets, human plural controllers agree in the feminine if feminine, and in the masculine if masculine (see for instance the pair *hūme rāgd-**īn*** / *hūmāti rāgd-**āt*** 'they (m/f) are sleeping', Taine-Cheikh 1993: 95). This is similar to what happens in gender-distinguishing dialects (while in non-distinguishing ones both would normally agree in the common plural).

The situation becomes more complex when it comes to nonhuman controllers. Taine-Cheikh 1993: 105 claims that "en règle générale, l'accord avec le substantif féminin pluriel (ou duel) se fait au féminine pluriel", and the same appears to be true for the plural masculine. As we have seen, if referred to one of the gender-distinguishing dialects discussed in section from § 2.3.2 to § 2.3.4, this sentence would have little meaning (since in these dialects, all nonhuman nouns trigger feminine agreement in the plural, irrespectively of the type of agreement they trigger in the singular). Judging by the few examples that Taine-Cheikh provides, however, it seems that in Ḥassāniyya all plural nouns tend to trigger the same type of agreement that they trigger in the singular. Said examples include *l=kīsān əz=zyn-**īn** əṯ=ṯemin-**īn** tdegᵊdg-**u*** 'the beautiful expensive glasses broke' (where the two adjectives stand in the M.PL and the verb in the C.PL), and *qaṣāyəd zeyn-**āt*** 'some nice *qasidas*' (where the adjective is, conversely, F.PL; note that the noun *qaṣīda* 'ode', is marked for feminine in the singular).

We used Heath's (2004) dictionary of Ḥassāniyya Arabic to countercheck all the lexical items whose plural forms appear in § 3.2.3 and § 3.2.4 of Taine-Cheikh's article, and that refer to nonhuman entities. We found that all nouns that attract F.PL agreement when plural are morphologically marked for feminine in the singular (with one exception, namely *dṛuṣ* 'teeth', whose singular, *daṛṣ*, is morphologically masculine). Vice-versa, and more significantly, nouns that trigger M.PL agreement in the plural are not marked for feminine in the singular. If confirmed, this would be remarkable, since in gender-distinguishing dialects nonhuman nouns can never attract M.PL agreement. It would seem that Ḥassāniyya has moved (or is moving) towards a type of agreement which is unique, as far as Arabic dialects go, in that a) it possesses F.PL agreement, at least in the case of adjective/participles and free pronouns, and b) all nouns trigger in the plural the same type of agreement they trigger in the singular.

Of course, a number of caveats are in order: first of all, the number of actual examples on which this analysis is based is extremely limited (a total of 10 lexical items). Secondly, even within this restricted sample, one exception occurred (the case of *ḍruṣ* discussed above). Lastly, and more important, no examples of pronominal agreement occurred in Taine-Cheikh's paper. Obviously, since it is only free plural pronouns that inflect for gender, occurrences of such an agreement must be extremely rare, especially with nonhuman controllers. Still, it would be interesting to see what type of agreement nonhuman nouns trigger when referred to by means of anaphora. Such a study would require a very large corpus of texts, which is currently lacking.[117] Standing our present knowledge, it seems possible that Ḥassāniyya is the only dialect of Arabic with (partial) gender distinction in the plural where the morphology of a given controller in the singular is sufficient to determine the type of agreement it will trigger in the plural (standing a few exceptional items that, however, are also present in most varieties of Arabic). In other words, gender assignment in Ḥassāniyya would seem to be entirely overt.

Adjectival/participial (and possibly pronominal?) agreement in Ḥassāniyya can tentatively be schematized as shown in Table 2.23.

Agreement in the realm of verbs and bound pronouns, on the other hand, works as it does in the majority of other non-distinguishing varieties (see Table 2.21), where all plural controllers attract the same type of agreement (that is, C.PL). As far as F.SG agreement is concerned, it appears to be relatively rare with proper plurals, being often confined to poetry or loans from the standard language (see however the following example, taken from a text in prose: *t=tlāmīd kāml-e* 'all the students', with a F.SG adjective). It is, on the contrary, relatively common with collective controllers (see Taine-Cheikh 1993: 87 and 106–109).

2.3.8.3 Agreement in Darfur Arabic

Darfur Arabic needs to be briefly mentioned here because of the most unique development that the feature of gender has undergone in this dialect. What we see in this variety are the last stages of a complete collapse of the agreement system, one that has occurred as a consequence of intense contact with other non-Semitic languages.

117 We have briefly surveyed Heath's (2003) collection of texts, but we were unable to locate examples of pronominal agreement in the 3rd person plural with nonhuman plural controllers. The few adjectives that we found referred to this type of controllers, though, seem to confirm the analysis presented above.

TABLE 2.23 Adjectival/participial agreement in *Ḥassāniyya* (Type D)

<table>
<tr><th rowspan="2">Gender</th><th rowspan="2">Agreement in the singular</th><th colspan="2">Agreement in the plural</th><th rowspan="2">Semantic Fields</th></tr>
<tr><th>Individuated nouns</th><th>Non-individuated nouns</th></tr>
<tr><td>I</td><td>Masculine singular</td><td>Masculine plural</td><td rowspan="2">Feminine Singular (uncommon)</td><td>Biologically masculine human beings, some nonhuman</td></tr>
<tr><td>II</td><td>Feminine singular</td><td>Feminine plural</td><td>Biologically feminine human beings, some nonhuman</td></tr>
</table>

Roset (2018: 178) notes how the verbal paradigm still preserves two distinct forms (originally M.SG and F.SG) in the 2nd and 3rd person singular of the suffix conjugation and in the 2nd person singular of the prefix conjugation (while these distinctions are lost in the plural and in the 3rd person singular of the prefix conjugation). However, in Roset's own words:

> Those historically feminine forms, like their historically masculine equivalents, only agree at random with the gender of their subject […]. Historically feminine and masculine verb forms have thus only remained as interchangeable forms that distinguish person, but not gender. So in spite of the presence of historical gender-distinguishing forms, there are no gender distinctions in the verb in Darfur Arabic from a synchronic point of view since both are used indiscriminately, just like there is no gender distinction in the Nilo-Saharan substrates of the area.

The same appears to be true of adjectives and pronouns. Roset (2018: 259) also notes that, although it is not possible to predict whether a given noun will agree or not, a clear preference exists for the historically masculine forms. The M.SG *hu* pronoun, for instance, appears 67 times in Roset's corpus, while its feminine counterpart *hi* only four (and reflexes of the historical F.SG bound pronoun are completely absent). The author observes that "a process of gender neutralization" seems to be in progress. However, this process of reduction of the morphosyntactic options available in the language seems not to be confined to the realm of gender: number agreement is also not always realized on targets depending on plural controllers.

Roset (2018: 261–263) notes how, despite the fact that F.SG agreement with plural controllers is no longer an option in the dialect, plural agreement appears to be more stable in the realm of animate controllers (human and animal), while inanimate controllers almost regularly trigger singular agreement in demonstratives and pronouns. It is possible that these peculiar patterns constitute the last vestiges of a system once based on individuation, similar to that of most contemporary dialects.

In conclusion, it would seem that a schematic description of Darfur's Arabic agreement system is impossible. In fact, it is doubtful whether or not is it possible to say that a system still exists. Interestingly, as Roset repeatedly remarks, several parallelisms with the situation of Darfur Arabic are to be found in the Chadian dialect of Abéché, although in this case the erosion of the agreement system appears to be in a less advanced stage of development (see Roth 1979: 69, 131 and 183–184).

2.3.8.4 Dialects with Exceptional Morphosyntactic Behavior

Some dialects that we have already commented on deserve to be briefly mentioned here, before we conclude our survey of divergent agreement systems.

In § 2.2.4 we have seen how certain Yemeni varieties have lost gender distinction in the 3rd person singular independent pronoun. This means that it is only bound pronouns that can produce F.SG anaphoric agreement, and not free ones. We also know (§ 2.3.2) that in some Bedouin dialects of Sinai (and Libya?) masculine plural human controllers can sometimes trigger F.PL agreement. In footnote 17 we have mentioned the fact that, in some gender-distinguishing dialects of Syria (Ḥafar and Ṭayyibt əl-ʔImām), gender distinction in 3rd person plural pronouns was first lost and then re-developed by means of morphologically innovative forms.

Standing our present knowledge of Arabic dialects, these morphosyntactic peculiarities are unique. Data about agreement in these dialects are almost non-existent, so that we do not know how these factors affect the system. It might be that agreement in these varieties works more or less in the same way as it does in all other gender-distinguishing dialects, albeit with some minor differences, or it might be that their systems radically differ from those that we have described so far. We have, at present, no way to know, and this must remain the topic for further research.

2.3.9 *The Effects of Word Order: Target-Controller Agreement*

In § 2.1, we saw how Corbett (2006: 176) remarked that "agreement may be determined in part by factors which are not themselves realized directly in agreement". Corbett labels such factors "conditions" (see pp. 181–183 for a detailed treatment). Several agreement conditions that are operative in Arabic have been analyzed in detail in the preceding paragraphs (see in particular § 2.3.3.4). The last agreement condition that needs to be discussed here is called precedence. Corbett (2006: 180) notes how "precedence is a clear example of a condition, since there is no agreement form for precedence". As anticipated, precedence is treated last, and separately from all other agreement-related phenomena.

Up until this moment, in sections from § 2.3.2 to § 2.3.8, we have discussed all types of agreement possibilities that occur with targets located after their controllers. However, agreement targets in Arabic, as in many other languages, can also appear *before* their controllers. Although this is the statistically less common option, pre-controller targets are still fairly common in all varieties of spoken Arabic. Obviously, not all target types are equally likely to appear as part of a target-controller (TC) structure. While it is virtually impossible for an adjective to precede its controller, and anaphoric pronouns in the same position are extremely rare too, verbs and demonstratives are often found in such contexts.

The reason why TC structures were not included in the analysis presented in the previous sections is that we wanted to single out the effects that factors such as animacy or abstractness have on agreement. In this respect, post-controller targets can be considered as more prototypical, or more canonical. Separating pre-controller targets from post-controller ones is important because, as we have seen, a neat discrimination between agreement conditions such as animacy, specificity, concreteness, etc. is not possible. The dividing lines between them are fuzzy, and they all interact and overlap in complex ways. This has been discussed in § 2.3.3. By contrast, the distinction between word order and other factors influencing agreement is a well-defined one. Since it is always possible to set TC structures apart from CT ones, it is always possible to determine if, all other factors being equal, word order is having an effect on agreement or not.[118]

118 With one partial exception: distance between target and controller is obviously more likely to have an effect on targets that follow their controller, rather than those which precede it. This is a consequence of the fact that, while it is relatively common to find targets appearing at a great distance from their controllers in CT structures, this almost never happens in TC ones. As a consequence, CT structures have much higher chances of being influenced by distance than TC ones, and therefore it is not entirely possible to set apart distance and precedence as two entirely independent agreement conditions. In addition, it is not clear if distance in TC structures has any effect on agreement at all.

As already said (§ 2.1), the fact that word order (i.e. precedence) can affect TC structures, but not CT ones, makes the former less canonical (in that "it is more canonical to have no conditions").

Precedence is a well described phenomenon in typological literature (see for instance Moravcsik 1978: 340–341), and it has powerful effects on agreement, which manifest themselves consistently across languages. This is not to say that precedence is a relevant agreement condition in all languages: however, when it is, it consistently induces agreement mismatches, specifically lack of gender and number agreement (singular agreement with plural controllers is a particularly common outcome).[119]

Precedence can affect all controllers, or just specific sub-sets. For instance, discussing chains of conjoined nouns, Corbett (2000: 201) compares the effects of precedence in Medieval Spanish, German, Russian and Serbo-Croatian, showing that singular agreement is more common with this type of controllers in TC structures than it is in CT ones. The same holds true for Palestinian Arabic, according to Mohammad (2000: 111 ff.).[120] It can also be the case that precedence only affects certain sub-sets of targets: Salvi (2010: 577), for instance, notes how, in ancient written Italian, unaccusative and passive verbs preceding their subjects often show no agreement.

It has also to be kept in mind, as Corbett (2006: 176) remarks, that "conditions can have an absolute effect, making one agreement outcome obligatory or impossible. Frequently, however, they are relative, just favouring a particular outcome". Arabic offers good examples of both tendencies. As already pointed out (§ 1.1), in all varieties of written Arabic (be it pre- or early Islamic, Classical or Modern Standard), verbs preceding their subjects obligatorily demand singular agreement.[121] It is unlikely that we will ever know if this state of affairs once reflected the actual linguistic reality of some spoken variety, or if the absolute effect of precedence in written Arabic has always been due exclusively to the more formal nature of the medium[122] (in other words, if a common pat-

119 See Greenberg's universal 33: "When number agreement between the noun and verb is suspended and the rule is based on order, the case is always one in which the verb precedes and the verb is in the singular".

120 Regrettably, Mohammad does not specify what he actually refers to with the expression "Palestinian Arabic". By looking at the examples he gives in the book, it is clear that the author is not dealing with any of the major urban dialects of Palestine.

121 See footnote 146 in § 2.4 for possible exceptions to this rule found in the Quran.

122 Concerning this topic, it might be worth citing Fleischer's, Rieken's and Wiedmer's caveat that "Scholars dealing with the history of agreement systems, and the history of language in general, need to be aware of prescriptive tendencies and of the selective perception of elites producing the prescriptive norms in question" (Fleischer, Rieken and Wiedmer, 2015: 5).

tern of the informal register of the language has artificially been transformed in an absolute rule in the formal register; on this point, see also § 2.4). What we know for sure is that, in today's colloquials, plural agreement is almost always possible, even in pre-controller position.

Generally speaking, the effects of precedence on agreement are a well-known and much discussed phenomenon in the literature on Arabic languages. Unsurprisingly, this discussion has often gone hand in hand with another hotly debated theme, namely the status of the modern dialects as VSO or SVO languages. The theoretical details of the question are not of immediate relevance for us here, and we will not pursue the topic further (the interested reader is referred to Brustad 2000: 316 ff.). What matters to us now is to determine to what extent precedence can determine agreement outcomes in spoken Arabic (and therefore to explain why we have decided to analyze TC-structures separately in this chapter).

Overall, we mostly agree with Brustad's (2000: 67) claim that "In VS sentences [...] verb-subject agreement may be neutralized in most (if not all) forms of Arabic". The literature on Arabic dialects abounds with references to this phenomenon, and it appears to cut across the distinction between gender-distinguishing and non-distinguishing varieties.

In Tunisia, for example, in both the dialects of the urban north (Procházka and Gabsi, 2017: 246, 258) and those of the Bedouin south (Ritt-Benmimoun, 2017: 270, 283), F.SG agreement with plural controllers is more common in TC structures than in CT ones. The same appears to be true in all varieties of Bahraini Arabic (all non-distinguishing dialects, though some of Bedouin descent; Holes 2016: 334–336, 353). Both Holes' and Procházka's and Gabsi's studies provide several examples of sentences where a single subject is preceded by a F.SG verb and then followed by a C.PL one. The authors all seem to agree on the fact that, in these cases, the first sentence tends to introduce a new topic, providing some general information about it, while the second one builds on the first by providing more details and thus further specifying the nature of the subject. It seems likely that, in these cases as well, individuation plays a role in determining agreement. In addition, a general cognitive process appears to be at work, because of which the still unmentioned subjects are perceived as scarcely specific, thus triggering non-individuated agreement. Brustad (2000: 68) supports this hypothesis when she writes that subjects, in these cases, "represent new topics; as such, they carry the pragmatic focus of the sentence. The verb, on the other hand, is thematic. Perhaps the neutralization of thematic sentence elements, such as sentence- or clause-initial verbs, lends greater prominence to the new topic".

One of the most detailed studies investigating the effects of precedence in spoken Arabic is Hoyt's (2002) article on Rural Palestinian Arabic. The study deals with what its author labels "impersonal" agreement in TC existential constructions. In particular, Hoyt focuses on the occurrence of M.SG agreement with non-M.SG (that is, F.SG or plural) indefinite subjects. Hoyt notes how definite subjects, or indefinite ones that are followed by a predicative complement, tend to trigger "full" agreement. Non-modified indefinites, however, have a preference for M.SG agreement. This connection between indefiniteness and agreement neutralization in TC structures has been highlighted in several other studies, most notably Cowell (1964: 421–422) and Brustad (2000: 67 ff.).

Despite adopting a theoretical framework that is rather distant from that of all the studies on agreement analyzed so far, Hoyt comes to conclusions that are remarkably similar to those already discussed. Agreement variation in pre-controller targets correlates with variation in the referent's level of specificity, and semantic and pragmatic factors affect the type of agreement which obtains. Richness of descriptive content and quantification, in particular, both tend to favor "full" agreement (Hoyt, 2002: 113–114).

In support of his claims Hoyt offers several examples, including the following pair:

a) *čill yowm b=**īži** la=l=ṣaff ulād* 'Every day, boys (some or another) come (M.SG) to class'
b) *čill yowm b=**īž-u** la=l=ṣaff ulād* 'Every day, (some particular) boys come (M.PL) to class'

Here it is possible to see how speakers are able to manipulate agreement in order to control meaning. In the first case, the low degree of individuation of the subject induces M.SG agreement in the preceding verb. In the second, the same subject attracts plural agreement, because here the speaker is referring to a specific group of boys.

The fact that a study developed within a generative framework aligns with the results presented here is remarkable, because it provides further and independent confirmation to the hypotheses on which our theory of agreement in Arabic is based. In addition, Hoyt's study demonstrates and important fact, namely that variation in pre-controller agreement is influenced by the same factors that affect post-controller agreement.[123]

123 The only difference being that, while in CT structures this variation is mostly limited to an opposition between plural and F.SG agreement, in the case of TC ones we often find variation involving a M.SG vs plural opposition, or even M.SG vs F.SG when the subject is singular. Note that Kramer and Winchester (2018) is another study rooted in the generative tradition that confirms how individuation is actually responsible for the oscillation between F.SG and plural agreement (in this case, in urban Hijazi Arabic).

Admittedly, Hoyt does not distinguish between occurrences of M.SG agreement before a F.SG subject or before a plural one, since both are treated as occurrences of "impersonal" agreement. Also, his study tells us nothing about the differences that exist between F.SG and plural agreement in TC constructions that feature a plural or collective subject (in § 2.3.3.3 we have seen, for instance, how a controller such as *nās* "people", can trigger three different types of agreement: M.SG, F.SG and plural: this is also the case with targets that precede *nās*). However, Hoyt's findings suggest that in TC structures the same "individuation hierarchy" applies, namely M.SG < F.SG < plural. This seems to be confirmed by Brustad's work on the topic (see in particular Brustad 2000: 68).

Another important remark to be found in Hoyt's study concerns target type, and how this factor can influence agreement. Hoyt (2002: 121–122) notes how, in Rural Palestinian Arabic, M.SG agreement only occurs with unaccusative verbs (i.e. verbs whose subjects share syntactic properties with the objects of transitive verbs). Impersonal agreement, he writes, "is marginal or unacceptable with verbs like *wašwaš* 'whisper,' *nām* 'sleep,' or *rakaḏ* 'run' [...]. This suggests that the ability to show variable agreement with an indefinite, post-verbal subject is a diagnostic for unaccusativity in RPA". As we have seen, similar observations have also been made for other languages.

If we now move on to analyze works about agreement in Arabic that include statistical data, we see that they all confirm the general trend according to which pre-controller targets are more likely to show singular agreement than post controller ones.[124]

In Belnap's (1991: 89) corpus of Cairene Arabic, 92 % of all verbs preceding an inanimate controller show F.SG agreement, while only 80 % of the verbs that follow their subject do so. The difference is even more pronounced in the case of broken human controllers: in TC structures the frequency of F.SG agreement is 60 %, while it drops to 10 % in CT ones. In his corpus of Omani Arabic, Bettega (2017: 158, 171) finds that 60 % of all pre-controller targets take singular agreement, against 47,6 % of post-controller ones (this is normally F.SG agreement,

124 D'Anna's (2017) article about Libyan Fezzani Arabic constitutes the only partial exception. In D'Anna's corpus of data, there seems to be little statistical correlation between TC structures and singular agreement with plural controllers. In general, D'Anna's material contain very few occurrences of F.SG agreement, as already discussed in § 2.3.2. TC structures involving a feminine plural human subject, however, do occasionally show M.PL agreement where F.PL would be expected (D'Anna 2017: 106–107). The same type of mismatch occurs once with the collective *nās* 'people', that attracts F.SG agreement in the verb following it, but M.SG in the preceding one (see example 17 on p. 109).

but a few instances of M.SG agreement occur as well). The same appears to be true in Khuzestani Arabic. Bettega and Leitner (2019: 30–31) show how 43 % of all targets appearing in TC structures are singular, while only 31,4 % of those appearing in CT ones are.

The corpus of Najdi texts that we introduced in § 2.3.3 provides further evidence of this trend. Among the 36 targets that appear in TC structures, 26 (72,2 %) show singular agreement (two M.SG, twenty-four F.SG). Of the 158 targets that occur after their controller, only 96 do (60, 8 %).[125]

Berlinches Ramos (2021) runs an analysis of the agreement patterns triggered by the two human collectives *ʕālam* and *nās* in the dialect of Damascus, and notes that word order only slightly affects the behavior of verbal targets (pre-controller personal pronouns and demonstratives are rare in her texts, and the few that do occur systematically show plural agreement[126]).

Berlinches Ramos reports that 34,8 % (8 out of 23) of all verbal targets occurring in pre-controller position in her texts show singular agreement, and concludes that precedence is not a key factor in determining agreement. This percentage is admittedly rather low, and in general agreement variation seems not as common in these texts as it was in the aforementioned corpora. Berlinches Ramos, however, does not say what the percentage of singular targets is among the 243 verbs that appear in CT structures, so that an actual comparison is impossible.

By looking at her collection of texts (published in Berlinches Ramos 2016), our impression is that plural agreement in post-controller verbal targets is rather systematic. Although not common, some examples of M.SG verbs preceding their subjects are to be found in Berlinches Ramos data (these are mostly occurrences of the two verbs *kān* 'to be' and *ṣār* 'to happen, become', e.g. *b=**ikūn** fiyy=a ʔuwaḍ ən=nōm u=ʔūdet el=ʔabb wə=l=ʔəmm* 'there were in it bedrooms and the parent's bedroom').

In order for our survey to be as complete as possible, we also analyzed a small corpus of texts in Moroccan Arabic, a representative of Type C agreement systems (see § 2.3.7). The corpus is based on Rahmouni's (2015) collection of texts from Chefchaouen. In particular, we have analyzed all the texts contained in

125 These calculations are based on all targets depending on nonhuman controllers, both plurals and collectives, with the exception of those targets that show apophonic agreement. An example of the effects of precedence in Najdi Arabic can be found in § 2.3.3.2, example 9 (although the controller in this case is a human collective).

126 In Damascene Arabic, pre-posed demonstratives can appear in the shortened prefixal form *ha-*. Since this form has no agreement properties, demonstratives in this dialect are poor indicators of agreement behavior in TC structures.

the second half of the corpus.[127] As expected, the Moroccan texts are those in which the least variation is found. However, even here singular agreement in TC structures can sometimes be encountered when the controller is a collective noun. Examples include: *lā=**yikūn** l=ḥāšārāt kull=**em*** [...] *lā=yġawwṯ-**u*** 'all the insects, all of them are [...] crying out' (p. 276); ***bda** l=flūs ṭāyḥ-**īn*** 'the money started to fall down' (pp. 303–304); *ʕarṭ-**at** n=nās* 'the people chewed' (p. 287).[128] Note how, in the first two examples, the verb preceding the subject is M.SG but the verbs and pronouns following it are actually in the C.PL.

On the topic of TC agreement in Moroccan, several interesting remarks are found in Brustad (2000: 88ff.). Brustad agrees on the fact that "Moroccan does not seem to show the same degree of agreement neutralization as do other dialects", but also gives a meaningful example worth reporting. Compare: *māt-**u**=l=ha rəbʕa d l=wlād* 'died-C.PL four of her kids' with ***māt**=l=ha rəbʕa d l=wlād* 'died-F.SG four of her kids'. While the first sentence actually translates as 'Four of her kids died', an accurate rendition of the second one would be 'She had four kids die'. Brustad thus comments: "In the [first example], the children who died are more individuated, and hence plural agreement is used. By contrast, in the [second example] the children have lower textual prominence, and hence less individuation".

Summing up, we have seen how precedence plays a role in all the dialects we have examined. This partially contradicts the common belief according to which word order would not be a relevant agreement condition in spoken Arabic. While it is true that, among the conditions we have discussed in this chapter, precedence is probably not the one with the strongest effect, it is also true that its effects are virtually omnipresent and extremely consistent (though they are felt more powerfully in certain dialects, and more marginally in others).

2.4 Pre-Classical Arabic: Pre-Islamic Poetry and the Quran

In § 2.3, we offered a detailed description of the agreement systems obtaining in spoken varieties of Arabic. We will now turn our attention to the written

127 Those narrated by his female informant, which, according to Rahmouni, are the ones least influenced by the rural dialects of the area, and more similar to the urban koine of northern Morocco.

128 *nās* is consistently followed by plural targets, with a single exception: *n=nās lā=č-čūf* 'the people F.SG-see' (p. 291; the form *č-čūf* results from ***t**-čūf* via assimilation). Rahmouni's very accurate transcription has been slightly simplified in the examples reported.

forms of the language, starting with pre-Classical Arabic and then moving on to the Classical and Modern Standard versions of the language (§ 2.5). When we say "pre-Classical" Arabic we refer to the (non-epigraphic) written sources that predate, or are coeval with, the beginning of the Islamic conquests. These include the Quranic text and pre-Islamic poetry.[129]

One of the factors that originally sparked interest in the study of agreement was the claim made by Ferguson (1989), according to which agreement patterns in Arabic display a great degree of consistency over a time-span ranging from pre-Islamic Arabic to the contemporary spoken dialects.[130]

Following Ferguson's lead, Belnap (1991) provided the first in-depth study of agreement in a specific dialect, i.e. Cairene. Belnap and Shabaneh (1992), then, started an investigation of the diachronic change that took place in the period spanning from the 6th century to modern times, expanded in Belnap and Gee (1994) and Belnap (1999). The details of the diachronic change that accompanied the process of standardization of Arabic are presented in Chapter 3. By Belnap and Shabaneh's (1992, 260) own admission, however, one of the desiderata in the study of agreement was an expansion of the data set on which their analysis was based.[131]

This section aims at filling this lacuna, by providing a survey of agreement patterns in pre-Islamic Arabic based on a more representative corpus. Our analysis enlarges Belnap's dataset to include the full anthology of the seven canonical *Muʕallaqāt*:[132]

---

129 Although epigraphic attestations of varieties such as Safaitic are not included in our definition, available descriptions of said varieties have also been consulted, and will be referred to when relevant in the next chapters. It can already be anticipated that, from what can be glimpsed of its agreement system, Safaitic appears to show strinking similarities with gender-distinguishing varieties of Arabic.

130 Ferguson employed this argument as counterevidence to Versteegh's (1984) provocative hypothesis that extra-peninsular dialects of Arabic underwent a process of pidginization and creolization (and subsequent depidginization and decreolization).

131 Belnap and Shabaneh (1992) bases the survey of pre-Islamic Arabic on the analysis of Imruʔ al-Qays' (6th century) famous *Muʕallaqa*, while Belnap and Gee (1994) and Belnap (1999) enlarge the corpus to include also poems by Ṭarafa (6th century), ʕAntara (6th century) and al-Xansāʔ (7th century).

132 Due to the meaning of the verb *ʕallaqa* 'to suspend', of which *Muʕallaqāt* is a F.PL passive participle, the word has been usually translated as *The suspended* (*odes*). The story behind this denomination, according to which these odes were 'suspended' from the walls of the *Kaʕba* in pre-Islamic times, however, is considered by Bauer (1998, 532) as a later fabrication. Bauer suggests, as a tentative translation, 'esteemed precious'.

TABLE 2.24 The authors of the seven canonical *Muʕallaqāt*

Poet	Length of the *qaṣīda*
Imruʔ al-Qays (500–535 CE)	82 lines
Ṭarafa ibn al-ʕAbd (543–568 CE)	103 lines
Zuhayr ibn Abī Sulmā (520–609 CE)	59 lines
ʕAntara ibn Šaddād (525–615 CE)	79 lines
ʕAmr ibn Kulṯūm (6th–7th century CE)	94 lines
al-Ḥāriṯ ibn Ḥilliza (d. ca. 570 CE)	84 lines
Labīd ibn Rabīʕa (560–661 CE)	88 lines

JOHNSON 1893

As evident from the following samples, and as noted by previous scholars (Beeston 1975; Belnap and Shabaneh 1992; Ferguson 1989), the system displays a variability comparable to that observed in contemporary dialects:

(51) *wa=ʔayyāmin la=nā ġurrin ṭiwālin ʕaṣaynā l=malka*
and=day.PL to=us illustrious.PL long.PL rebel:1.PFV.PL DEF=king
fī=hā ʔan nadīnā
in=her COMP 1.IPFV.PL:obey:SBJV
'And our illustrious, long days in which we rebelled against the king, unwilling to obey him'[133] (ʕAmr, 29).[134]

(52) *bi=hā l=ʕīnu wa=l=ʔarʔāmu yamšīna*
in=it DEF=wild.cow.PL and=DEF=white.antelope.PL 3.IPFV:go:F.PL
xilfatan wa=aṭlāʔu=hā yanhaḍna min kulli
in.succession and=young.PL=her 3.IPFV:rise:F.PL from every
maǧṯami
resting.place

133 Translations are drawn, unless specifically mentioned, from Johnson (1893).

134 Ferrando (2006, 53) gives a different interpretation of the 'mismatch' in this sentence, considering the two broken plurals as plurals of paucity and the F.SG (in the pronoun) as a plural of abundance. In our interpretation, on the contrary, both the two adjectives in the broken plural and the pronoun in the F.SG denote non-individuated plural reference (in traditional grammatical terms, a plural of abundance).

'The wild cows and the white deer are wandering about there, one herd behind the other, while their young spring up from every lying-down place' (Zuhayr, 3).

(53) *wa=**l=xaylu*** ***taqtaḥimu*** *l=xabāra* ***ʕawābisan***
and=DEF=horse.COLL 3.IPFV.F.SG:charge DEF=soil frowning.PL
'And the horses were charging over the soft soil, frowning' (ʕAntara, 88).

(54) *fa=waqaftu* *ʔasʔalu=**hā*** *wa=kayfa suʔālu=nā* ***ṣumman***
and=stop:1.PFV.SG 1.IPFV.SG:ask=her and=how question=our deaf.PL
xawālida *mā yabīnu* *kalāmu=**hā***
eternal.PL NEG 3.IPFV.M:be.clear.SG speech=her
'Then I stood questioning them, and of what avail is questioning rocks lying in their place for ever, whose speech is not clear?' (Labīd, 10).

Samples 51–54 show that animal and inanimate plural controllers variably trigger agreement in the F.SG, F.PL and in the broken plural (for adjectives), thus displaying the same degree of variation observed in the spoken dialects. The employment of poetry as a source of syntactic information might raise some doubts, due to the possible influence of meter and rhyme, yet other sources (e.g. the epigraphic materials) generally lack the degree of complexity (in terms of sentence and phrasal structure) that is necessary to observe agreement patterns in detail. In addition to that, it is highly unlikely that poets renowned for the stylistic perfection of their language would consistently choose ungrammatical agreement patterns only in order to fill a metric (or rhyme) template (see also § 3.2). If agreement patterns depended on, or were heavily influenced by, metrical necessities, one would expect a somewhat random distribution. The data gathered from the seven *Muʕallaqāt*, quite to the contrary, point to a definite direction, which is even more surprising when considering that numbers are relatively small and cannot ensure statistic regularities. Table 2.25 reports agreement patterns with nonhuman animate (animal) controllers and with inanimate ones.

The data presented in Table 2.25 require a detailed explanation. It is a well-known fact that, in Classical and Modern Standard Arabic, F.SG agreement is associated to nonhuman plural controllers. Concerning F.SG agreement as a whole (independently of its association with nonhuman plural controllers), Beeston (1975, 65–66) first argued that a) F.SG agreement with plural controller was an innovative pattern and b) that it made its first appearance in the domain of pronouns. His insights are all the more remarkable given that they predated Corbett's (1991; 2006) typological works on agreement and are solely based on the observation of raw data.

TABLE 2.25 Agreement patterns with post-controller targets in the seven *Muʕallaqāt* (nonhuman animate and inanimate controllers)

Animate	Total targets	M. Sg.	F. Sg.	Br. Pl.	F. Pl.
Attr. adj.	10	-	1 (10%)	8 (80%)	1 (10%)
Verbs	18	-	4 (22.2%)	-	14 (77.7%)
Pronouns	21	-	19 (90.5%)	-	2 (7.5%)
Inanimate	**Total targets**	**M. Sg.**	**F. Sg.**	**Br. Pl.**	**F. Pl.**
Attr. adj.	11	-	3 (27.3%)	6 (54.5%)	2 (18.2%)
Verbs	32	2 (6.3%)	17 (53.1%)	-	13 (40.6%)
Pronouns	47	-	38 (80.9%)	-	9 (19.1%)

Corbett's agreement hierarchy, based on a typological survey of distant and unrelated languages, predicts the following:

> attributive > predicate > relative pronoun > personal pronoun
> [...]
> For any controller that permits alternative agreements, as we move rightwards along the Agreement Hierarchy, the likelihood of agreement with greater semantic justification will increase monotonically (that is, with no intervening decrease).
>
> G.G. CORBETT 2006, 207

Unlike Beeston, Belnap was aware of Corbett's works and checked his data against the agreement hierarchy, with positive results (R.K. Belnap 1999, 184). On the basis of Bailey (1973), pronouns (more specifically, demonstrative pronouns) were identified as the locus of innovation, i.e. of the spread of F.SG agreement with plural controllers (K.R. Belnap and Shabaneh 1992, 256–258).

Table 2.25 presents a simplified version of the agreement hierarchy, featuring attributive adjectives, verbal predicates and pronouns (including anaphoric pronouns). If we only consider the two extremes, i.e. adjectives and pronouns, the data perfectly align along Corbett's agreement hierarchy.[135] With both non-

135 As already discussed in § 2.3.3.4, this is true as long as we consider F.SG agreement as the type of agreement with "the greater degree of semantic justification". If we accept

human animate and inanimate controllers, adjectives feature the lowest percentage of F.SG agreement, while pronouns feature the highest. Things are more complicated if we consider plural agreement and if we include verbal predicates. As far as the plural is concerned, Table 2.25 splits the data according to the two possibilities of plural agreement for adjectives (with nonhuman controllers), i.e. broken and sound feminine plural. If the two categories are merged, then adjectives consistently display the highest percentage of 'plural' agreement. If, on the other hand, we consider only F.PL agreement, then verbs do not conform to expectations, showing higher percentages of F.PL agreement than adjectives. We will return to that shortly. Before that, let us examine the behavior of adjectives vs pronouns in some more depth. As discussed in § 2.2 and 2.3.4.1, we argue that both the broken plural and the F.SG serve to mark a form of [-individuated] agreement, so that broken plurals should not be considered as part of the same category as sound ones (this is why the relative data were kept distinct in Table 2.25). If we look at the percentages of F.PL agreement in adjectives and pronouns, we find that they are surprisingly stable (10 % vs 7.5 % for animate controllers, 18.2 % vs 19.1 % for inanimate ones), given that the two categories stand at the opposite extremes of Corbett's agreement hierarchy. The difference, however, is striking if we look at the percentages of F.SG agreement (10 % vs 90.5 % for animate controllers, 27.3 % vs 80.9 % for inanimate ones). Even with the limited numbers at our disposal, it is evident that the percentage of F.SG in pronouns almost exactly equates the sum of F.SG + broken plural agreement in adjectives.[136]

This fact is not a happy coincidence. The same distribution, in fact, emerges even from the small corpus discussed in Belnap and Gee (1994, 132) and seems to be linked to a peculiar behavior of adjectives that has been observed in

this definition as true, however, we are confronted with the problem that the Agreement Hierarchy cannot be valid for both pre-Classical written Arabic and the contemporary dialects. This is because, in the former, F.SG agreement tends to cluster away from the controller (i.e. it is mostly found in pronominal targets), while in contemporary spoken Arabic it is mostly found in adjectives (that is, near the controller). This possibly speaks of an interesting diachronic development that the Arabic languages have undergone in the course of several centuries (see the concluding section of the present chapter for a discussion of this point), but also brings us back to the major theoretical problem, already explored, that concerns the applicability of the hierarchy to a language such as Arabic (and in particular spoken Arabic), which possesses an agreement form specifically dedicated to non-individuated agreement. The reader is referred to the previous section for a more in-depth examination of this issue.

136 This fact has, in our opinion, important repercussions at the diachronic level, which will be the object of detailed discussion in § 3.3.

TABLE 2.26 Percentages of feminine singular + broken plural agreement in adjectives

Animate	**Tot.**	**F. Sg. + Br. Pl.**
Attr. adj.	10	9 (90%)
		F. Sg.
Pronouns	21	19 (90.5%)
Inanimate	**Tot.**	**F. Sg. + Br. Pl.**
Attr. adj.	11	9 (81.8%)
		F. Sg.
Pronouns	47	38 (80.9%)

different Arabic dialects. When adjectives agree with nonhuman controllers, they usually do so in the broken plural, provided they possess a broken plural form. If they do not, however, F.SG agreement is usually selected instead of the expected F.PL (or C.PL for those dialects that lost gender distinction in the plural). This phenomenon has been observed, for instance, in Sanaani Arabic (Watson 1993, 213) and Urban Tunisian (Prochàzka and Gabsi 2017, 256–257). The same pattern seems to be described in Marugán (1994, 393) with reference to the Andalusi Arabic emerging from Ibn Quzmān's (1078–1160 CE) poem (*ʔazǧāl*): "e.g. 114/11/12 /*šufayfát riqáq*/ 'delicate lips' (in a high register *zajal*) and 134/6/1 /*sufayfátak ḥumár*/ 'your lips are red', or 133/3/4 /*ḍuraysát manẓúma*/ 'beautiful teeth'". Even though Marugán does not tackle the issue from this perspective, we observe two similar controllers modified by the broken plurals *riqāq* 'delicate.PL' < *raqīq* and *ḥumar* 'red.PL' < *ʔaḥmar*, but triggering F.SG agreement in the adjective *manḏ̣ūma* 'beautiful:F.SG' (the adjective actually means 'ordered', here referring to the beloved's teeth). The same happens with verbs and pronouns, which do not have any form of broken plural. When a controller triggers broken plural agreement in the adjectival target, subsequent verbal and pronominal targets tend to agree in the F.SG (Ritt-Benmimoun 2017, 271). Once again, Andalusi Arabic seems to confirm this trend, even though Marugán considers the occurrence as a mismatch: "In other instances, the author is so hesitant that he mixes both types of concord in the same *zajal*, e.g.: 9/41/2 /*ḏa ı-azjál kama taráha ḥisán*/ 'These *azjal* as you see are good'". On the whole, these phenomena seem to indicate that broken plural is semantically more akin to F.SG than to masculine / feminine plural.

It is now time to return to the partial exception represented by verbs, which in Table 2.25 display unexpectedly high percentages of F.PL agreement (i.e. much higher than adjectives) with both animate and inanimate controllers. In sections 2.3.2–2.3.4, we argued that the agreement system obtaining in gender-distinguishing varieties of Arabic is governed by individuation, which is not conceivable univocally, but rather as a complex set of subfactors, "such as animacy in the strict sense, definiteness, singularity, concreteness, assignability of a proper name (Comrie 1989, 199)", "perceptual salience" and the quality of being "ego-like" (Khan 1984, 469–470). The quality of being ego-like described by Khan is not, in its turn, a primitive, but consists of different categories. Among this categories, the role of agenthood[137] and volition in verbal predicated has been convincingly illustrated by De Vos (2015, 131) with reference to Southern Dutch.

Southern Dutch is switching from an exclusively syntactic system to a (partially) semantically motivated one and verbal semantics, with specific reference to volition and agenthood, significantly increases the likelihood of syntactic agreement. The same tendency was observed in Quranic Arabic, where "All the occurrences of syntactic agreement [with verbal targets], in fact, were action verbs where the subject possessed some degree of volition (D'Anna 2020b)."[138] Given a sufficient degree of volition and agenthood, thus, also inanimate controllers in the broken plural can trigger F.PL agreement:

(55)	… *wa=saxxarnā*	***l=ǧibāla***	*maʕa*	*Dāwūda*
	and=subject:1.PFV.PL	DEF=mountain.PL	with	David
	yusabbiḥna *…*			
	3.IPFV:praise:F.PL			

'And with David We subjected the mountains to give glory'[139] (XXI, 79).

137 Agenthood is not a primitive either, but can be further investigated. Prototypical agenthood is described as follows by Lyons (1977, 2:483): "We may think of the paradigm instance as being one in which an animate entity, X, intentionally and responsibly uses its own force, or energy, to bring about an event or to initiate a process; and the paradigm instance of an event or a process in which agency is most obviously involved will be one that results in a change in the physical condition or location of X or of some other entity, Y".

138 The opposite however, does not obtain, i.e. agenthood is not a sufficient factor to guarantee the occurrence of syntactic agreement.

139 Unless differently specified, the translation of Quranic verses is drawn from Arberry (1964). It might be of some interest to note that the same controller as in (55), *ǧibāl* 'mountains', triggers 2nd person F.SG agreement in a vocative construction in Quran XXXIV, 10.

Most traits defining individuation (i.e. humanness, quantification, assignability of a proper name etc.) lie with the controller. Agenthood, on the other hand, can be considered as an individuating trait dislocated to the (verbal) target, independently of the status of its controller. A verbal target, thus, can occur in the F.PL even when all the other targets occur in the F.SG.[140] In sample 55, for instance, a clearly inanimate controller, formally in the broken plural, is figuratively assigned volition and agenthood through its association with the verb *sabbaḥa* 'to praise', which occurs in the F.PL. The same occurs in sample 52 above, here reported again:

(56) *bi=hā* ***l=ʕīnu*** *wa=l=ʔarʔāmu* ***yamšīna***
in=it DEF=wild.cow.PL and=DEF=white.antelope.PL 3.IPFV:go:F.PL
xilfatan *wa=aṭlāʔu=**hā*** *yanhaḍna* *min* *kulli*
in.succession and=young.PL=her 3.IPFV:rise:F.PL from every
mağṯami
resting.place
'The wild cows and the white deer are wandering about there, one herd behind the other, while their young spring up from every lying-down place' (Zuhayr, 3).

The first controller consists of a chain of two [-individuated] broken plurals, triggering F.SG agreement in the possessive pronoun *–hā* 'her'. The verb *yamšīna* '3.IPFV:go:F.PL', on the other hand, clearly implies volition and agenthood, and consequently occurs in the F.PL.

While semantic factors play a great role in determining agreement choices, the formal characteristics of the controller should not be underestimated. The corpus of inanimate controllers, for instance, features only 4 sound F.PL controllers, from which 6 post-controller targets depend, of which 5 occur in the plural.[141] Even though numbers are too small to allow for generalizations, the

140 The same can be said of the attributive adjective, yet for different reasons. Attributive adjectives stand at the extreme left of the agreement hierarchy, preserving syntactic agreement much more often than other categories. Verbs, on the other hand, stand at the center of the agreement hierarchy, so that the occurrence of F.PL is linked to the factors discussed above and not to their intrinsic conservativeness.

141 Among the five plural targets, three occur in the F.PL, while the two predicative adjectives are adjectives of color (*bīḍ* 'white.PL' and *ḥumr* 'red.PL'), which only have a common plural. It is also worth noting that the only target that does not feature plural agreement is a M.SG verb in the passive. As noted by D'Anna (2020b) with reference to Quranic Arabic, passive verbs trigger syntactic agreement much more rarely than active ones, due to the

fact is worth noting, especially because none of the plural targets (2 predicative adjectives, 2 verbs and 2 pronouns) is an attributive adjective, the most conservative category.

As we have seen in § 2.3, several varieties of spoken Arabic admit the possibility of F.SG agreement with human plural controllers. It should be emphasized that this is not a dialectal innovation. F.SG agreement with human broken plurals also occurs in pre-Islamic poetry and the Quran, as the following examples illustrate:

(57) ***ġulbun*** ***tašaddaru***[142] *bi=d=duḥūli*
thick.necked.man.PL 3.IPFV.F.SG:threaten with=DEF=revenge
*kaʔanna=**hā** ǧinnu l=Badiyyi rawāsiyan*
as.if=her jinn.COLL DEF=Badiyy firm.PL
ʔaqdāmu=hā
foot.PL=her
'Bold men threatening each other with blood revenge, as if they were the *jinn* of al-Badiyy, whose feet are firm' (Labīd, 71).[143]

(58) *yudahdūna r=ruʔūsa ka=mā* ***tudahdī*** ***ḥazāwiratun***
3.IPFV:roll:M.PL DEF=head.PL as 3.IPFV.F.SG:roll strong.boy.PL
*bi=abṭāḥi=**hā** l=kurīna*[144]
in=playground.PL-her DEF=ball:M.PL
'They cause the heads to roll on the ground, as strong boys roll balls in their playgrounds' (ʕAmr, 97).

complete lack of agenthood of the grammatical subject, which in passive constructions is semantically a patient.

142 Syncopated form for *tatašaddaru*.

143 It is worth mentioning that also the collective *ǧinn* 'jinn.COLL', referring to supernatural beings, triggers agreement in the F.SG (in the possessive pronoun –*hā* 'her'). Controllers referring to supernatural beings are usually treated as human ones, so that the occurrence of F.SG agreement is comparable.

144 ʕAmr employs here a sound masculine plural for the word *kura* 'ball', whose usual plural is *kurāt* or *kuran*. The form did not survive in dictionaries of Classical Arabic, and seems to be indicative of a period in which plural patterns were more flexible. It is worth noting that this is not an isolated example. When describing the semantic difference between sound and broken plurals, for instance, Wright writes: "For example, *ʕabdūn* are *slaves* (*servi*), i.e. several individuals who are slaves, *ʕabīd slaves* collectively (*servitium* or *servitus*) (Wright 1896b, 1:233)." The plural *ʕabdūn*, similarly to *kurīna*, did not make it into dictionaries of Classical Arabic and is not considered as a productive plural of the word *ʕabd* 'slave, servant'.

TABLE 2.27 Agreement in pre-Classical Arabic (Type E)

Class	Agreement in the singular	Agreement in the dual	Agreement in the plural		Semantic fields
			Individuated nouns	Non-individuated nouns	
I	Masculine singular	Masculine dual	Masculine plural	Feminine singular (or apophonic adjectival agreement)	Biologically masculine human beings
II	Feminine singular	Feminine dual	Feminine plural		Biologically feminine human beings, Nonhuman animates, Inanimates
III	Masculine singular	Masculine dual	Feminine plural		Nonhuman animates, Inanimates

(59) ***tilka*** ***r=rusulu*** *faḍḍalnā* *baʕḍa=hum* *ʕalā* *baʕḍin*
that.F DEF=messenger.PL prefer:1.PFV.PL some=them.M over some
min=hum ...
of-them.M
'And those Messengers, some We have preferred above others;' (II, 253).

In the light of the examples and the numbers presented in this section, it is clear that F.SG agreement functions as a mark of [-individuated] agreement, available to all types of controllers, also in pre-Islamic Arabic. All things considered, then, pre-Classical Arabic would seem to be yet another exponent of the Type A agreement category (§ 2.3.4), with the only difference that, in this variety, dual agreement is still possible. Therefore, by partial modification of Table 2.20, we obtain the agreement system outlined in Table 2.27.

This confirms Ferguson's intuition concerning the consistency of agreement patterns in Arabic (excluding Classical and Modern Standard Arabic) over a very long period. Fifteen centuries, however, did not elapse leaving the system completely unchanged. On the contrary, a few recognizable differences tell apart the agreement system of pre-Classical Arabic, at least as it emerges from our poetic sources, from that of contemporary dialects.[145]

145 In order to obviate the objective discrepancy between the literary sources from which pre-Classical data are drawn and the non-literary ones employed for contemporary dialects

The first, as we said, concerns the disappearance of dual agreement in adjectives, verbs and pronouns in contemporary dialects. The dialects of Arabic retain dual morphology on nouns to different extents, yet they have lost dual agreement. With dual nouns, dual agreement was already in free variation with plural and even F.SG agreement in the papyri analyzed by Hopkins (1984, 37:94–97), dating before 912 CE. The construction 'numeral 2 + plural' to express the dual, however, also occurs in an early Islamic poet, al-Naḏḏār ibn Hāšim:

(60) *ʔaw ka=l=mudāriyyi wa=sufʕin duhmin wa=kunna*
or like=DEF=horn.PL and=brown.PL black.PL and=be:3.PFV.F.PL
*ʔudman wa=**dawādī** **iṯnāni***
grey.PL and=see.saw.PL two
'Or (pegs looking) like horns, and brownish, dark-coloured (hearthstones),
Which were formerly grey, and two see-saws' (Ḥusain 1938, 101).

The early occurrence of both plural agreement with dual nouns and the construction "numeral two + plural noun" (in this case, "plural noun + numeral two") to express dual number morphologically testifies that the category of the dual became unstable at a very early stage.

The second trait that sets apart the system of pre-Islamic Arabic from that of contemporary dialects is the status of word order as an absolute or relative condition. We already commented on this fact in § 1.1 and § 2.3.9. In pre-Islamic Arabic, varieties where pre-controller verbal targets systematically occur in the singular (while gender agreement displays more complex patterns) coexisted with the so-called *luġat ʔakalū-nī l-barāġīṯu*. This stock example has been used to describe the occurrence of number agreement between a pre-verbal target and its controller in pre-Islamic varieties of Arabic. The phenomenon described is usually thought of as circumscribed to a set of (unfortunately unspecified) dialects (Versteegh 2014, 51–52), even though an early commentator of the Quran, ʔAbū ʕUbayda (d. 207/822 CE), rather considers it as a trait of informal registers (Guillaume 2011, 283–284). The phenomenon, however, never occurs in the *Muʕallaqāt*, where word order is an absolute condition and pre-controller verbal targets always occur in the singular.[146]

(mostly dialectal interviews, spontaneous speech and collections of ethnographic texts), section 3.8 provides a comparison between pre-Islamic poetry and its closest offspring, Najdi Nabaṭī poetry.

146 In the Quran, number agreement in pre-controller verbal targets does not occur either. The two possible exceptions are verses XXI, 3 and V, 71, yet they can hardly be considered

TABLE 2.28 Agreement patterns of pre-controller verbal targets in Najdi *Nabaṭī* poetry

	Total	M. Sg.	M. Pl.	F. Sg.	F. Pl
Human	12	1 (8.3%)	8 (66.7%)	3 (25%)	-
Animate	9	2 (22.2%)	-	7 (77.8%)	-
Inanimate	44	6 (13.6%)	-	33 (75%)	5 (11.4%)

In contemporary dialects, where pre-controller verbal targets usually display higher percentages of singular agreement than post-controller ones, this is only a relative condition, i.e. it is not a systematic rule, and intra-dialectal variation does occur. Table 2.28, for instance, reports the percentage of singular and plural agreement with pre-controller verbal targets in a corpus of contemporary Najdi Nabaṭī poetry, whose detailed analysis will be the object of section § 3.9.[147]

The final trait is less clear-cut, and has to do with the process of resemanticization and spread of F.SG agreement that will be dealt with in detail in Chapter 3. Let us consider the following data, concerning agreement patterns with human controllers in the *Muʕallaqāt* and in contemporary Najdi Nabaṭī poetry:

as prototypical examples of agreement. In XXI, 3, the possible exception is represented by the expression ***wa-ʔasarrū** n-naǧwā **lladīna** ḍalamū* 'The evildoers whisper one to another'. The controller is here a relative pronoun without antecedent, not a noun, and the verb *ʔasarrū* 'keep.secret:3.PFV.M.PL' follows six targets in the masculine plural, so that we are probably dealing here with an instance of attraction (G.G. Corbett 2006, 62–63, 279). In V, 71, we read the following: *wa-ḥasibū ʔallā takūna fitnatun fa-ʕamaw wa-ṣammū ṯumma tāba Llāhu ʕalay-him ṯumma **ʕamaw wa-ṣammū kaṯīrun min-hum*** 'And they supposed there should be no trial; but blind they were, and deaf. Then God turned towards them; then again blind they were, many of them, and deaf.' Also in this case, however, the controller is not a plural noun, but the noun phrase *kaṯīrun min-hum* 'many of them'. As already observed in XXI, 3, moreover, the two plural pre-controller verbal targets follow four plural targets, two of them being occurrences of the very same verbs, so that attraction seems, once again, the more suitable explanation. Generally speaking, the occurrence of only two possible (but very debatable) exceptions is not enough to deny that word order is an absolute condition in the Quran as well. See also Guillaume (2011).

147 Once again, the employment of a poetic corpus is due to the necessity to ensure a minimum degree of homogeneity, in terms of literary genre, between the two data sets. More data concerning agreement patterns with pre-controller targets in the spoken dialects can be found in § 2.3.9.

TABLE 2.29 Agreement patterns with human controllers in the *Muʕallaqāt* and in Najdi *Nabaṭī* poetry

	Total	F.sg.	Plural
***Muʕallaqāt* (including collectives)**	134	18 (13.4%)	116 (86.6%)
***Muʕallaqāt* (without collectives)**	78	4 (5.1%)	74 (94.9%)
Najdi poetry (including collectives)	108	39 (36.1%)	69 (63.9%)
Najdi poetry (without collectives)	63	23 (36.5%)	40 (51.3%)

The picture emerging from the data shows a considerable increase of F.SG agreement with human controllers: data drawn from Najdi poetry are three times as high as data from the *Muʕallaqāt* if we count collective controllers in, seven times if collectives are excluded. It must be made clear that the comparison is here between agreement patterns occurring in the poetic tradition of a circumscribed area, i.e. the central part of the Arabian Peninsula. For contemporary Najdi, the data in our possession (see § 2.3.3) show that, although the system of agreement of poetry and ordinary speech features the same categories, their percentages vary, as is probably to be expected for any given language. The same variation might be projected back onto the pre-Islamic stage, imagining a similar situation between poetry and ordinary speech. For that period, however, only poetic data are available, since epigraphic materials (which, at any rate, hardly represent everyday speech more than poetry does) do not usually provide enough occurrences (see § 3.2). Even with these caveats, the difference between pre-Islamic and contemporary Najdi poetry is so considerable that it needs to be accounted for. The same can be said of the other two main differences discussed above, i.e. the loss of dual agreement and the status of word order as an absolute or relative condition. The system, thus, despite showing the consistency mentioned by Ferguson (1989), has not remained unchanged. As brilliantly noted by Belnap (1999, 182), moreover, "Variability is often associated with instability". The patterns of variation observed in pre-Islamic poetry, when seen through the lens of historical typology and compared to later data, show all the signs of a change in progress.

Taken together, these factors allow us trace the evolution of agreement in Arabic, from the first appearance of F.SG agreement with plural controllers up to present times. This historical treatment will be the object of Chapter 3.

2.5 The Odd Ones Out: Classical and Modern Standard Arabic

The time has now come to turn to the most well-known, well-described variety of Arabic, familiar to scholars of the language all over the world: Modern Standard Arabic (MSA).

In the title of this section, we have associated it to what is normally referred to as "Classical" Arabic (CA). In § 1.1 we discussed the problems connected to the use of the label "Old Arabic" that has been employed with different meanings by different scholars. Similar problems arise when we try to pinpoint the exact nature of Classical Arabic.

Is CA the language of the Quran, and the pre-Islamic odes? Is it one and the same with Old Arabic? Or is it distinct from it, does it represent its more normative descendant, a language born out of the meticulous work of the early grammarians, passed down to us in a more regular, more refined shape? Is it, then, just another name for MSA? Are the two the same thing? In this case as well, definitions and uses vary.

Through the course of the past chapters and sections, we have often come across definitory problems. We have seen, for instance, how the labels Bedouin/sedentary and Old Arabic/Neo Arabic are ill suited to account for the main differences that exist among Arabic varieties in terms of agreement behavior (see sections 1.1, 2.3.2 and 2.3.6). In these cases, our approach has been pragmatical: since it is agreement we are interested in, we adopted a terminology that is functional to our scope. We have then coined the two labels "gender-distinguishing" and "non-distinguishing" to refer to the one feature that is most relevant to our research (namely, retention or loss of morphological gender distinction in the plural).

Here we will adopt the same type of practical approach. It is a cold fact that, in the formal registers of written Arabic, agreement behavior starts to change dramatically in the first centuries following the Islamic conquests. The agreement system we have just described, the one that obtained in pre-Islamic poems and in the Quran (§ 2.4), all but disappears, leaving in its place something remarkably different, and altogether new. We will not discuss here why or how this change took place: the reader is referred to Chapters 3 and 4 for more insights on the topic. What matters presently is that these two systems differ, and must be kept distinct in terminology as well.

As discussed, we will not employ the term "Old Arabic" here. We have reserved the label "pre-Classical" for the (non-epigraphic) written sources that predate, or are coeval with, the beginning of the Islamic conquests. These include the Quranic text and pre-Islamic poetry, and have been analyzed in the previous section. After that period, the agreement system of written Arabic

TABLE 2.30 Agreement in Classical and Modern Standard Arabic (type F)

Gender	Agreement in the singular	Agreement in the dual	Agreement in the plural	Semantic fields
I	Masculine singular	Masculine dual	Masculine plural	Biologically masculine human beings
II	Feminine singular	Feminine dual	Feminine plural	Biologically feminine human beings
III	Masculine or feminine singular	Masculine or feminine dual	Feminine singular	Nonhuman entities

rapidly mutates into the system described below. Since then, it has not evolved further, meaning that, from the point of view of agreement, the "Classical" version of the language corresponds to MSA. In this respect, we could use the two definitions as near-synonyms, with the obvious caveat that, rapid as it were, the transition from one system to another was not instantaneous, and a certain degree of hybridity persisted in the first period of the Islamic era.[148]

How does agreement work in CA/MSA, then? The answer to this question is not entirely straightforward. Table 2.30 above offers a tentative representation of this system.

It can immediately be seen how two major differences exist between the CA/MSA agreement system and those that we have discussed in the previous sections. The first one is that nonhuman controllers are here entirely separated from human ones, belonging in a dedicated slot in the table. MSA and Classical Arabic are the only varieties of Arabic in which this happens, a difference so stark as to make them, indeed, "the odd ones out" in the large Arabic family.

The second difference is represented by the lack of an "individuated/non-individuated" agreement option. The opposition based on individuation, typical of almost all other varieties of Arabic, including pre-Classical Arabic, is here replaced by an opposition based on humanness (incidentally, this development is the exact opposite of what Ferguson 1989 postulated; see § 1.1).

148 It has to be pointed out that, in poetic texts, traces of the old system persisted for much longer, to the point that some fossilized remnants of it can be found even in 20th century poetry. In addition, although F.SG agreement became the only agreement option for nonhuman plural controllers very early, this rule was not explicitly formalized by any grammarian until the modern period. All these themes are discussed in detail in Chapters 3 and 4.

An obvious problem, however, arises from the representation given in Table 2.30, namely the fact that nouns belonging to class III have variable agreement in the singular and in the dual. Shouldn't two separate genders be recognized, one including all nouns that take masculine agreement in the singular and in the dual, and the other including all nouns that take feminine agreement in the singular and in the dual?

From a merely formal point of view, this argument is irrefutable. In fact, at this level of analysis, four separate agreement classes must be recognized in CA/MSA (in other words, gender III in Table 2.30 is split into two different classes, depending on the type of agreement that its members attract in the singular and in the dual). As anticipated in § 2.1, however, it is not always the case that the number of genders, in a given language, corresponds to that of its agreement classes. In a sense, the difficulty we are facing here could be interpreted as a particular instance of what Corbett (1991: 145) termed the "maximalist problem", i.e. the identification in a language of more agreement classes than "the intuitively satisfying number of genders". The examples and solutions that Corbett offers in the following pages, however, are of little help in the case of CA/MSA, and this is because, as we will presently see, these two varieties are quite unique from a typological point of view.

What are, then, the pros and cons of each possible description?

The most evident fact that supports a subdivision such as that proposed in Table 2.30 (with only three genders), is that this schematization has the greatest degree of semantic justification: the members of each one of the three genders constitute three conceptually homogenous subgroups. On the contrary, if we divide gender III into two, we see that nonhuman referents are assigned to either one of the two on a totally arbitrary basis. It is on morphological grounds alone that we can determine what kind of agreement a certain noun will trigger in the singular and in the dual (feminine if the noun is marked by one of the morphemes that are associated with feminine gender, masculine if it is not).[149]

A second argument in favor of a tripartite division comes from typological evidence. At a semantic level, several languages can be found with a gender system that mirrors exactly that of CA/MSA. Among these, we find several Dravidian languages (the most prominent being Tamil, spoken mainly in southeast India), several Caucasian languages, and at least one Niger-Congo language (Afakani, spoken in the Niger Delta). All these languages possess a tripartite

149 With the exception of the small number of irregular lexical items that exist in all varieties of Arabic, as discussed in 2.2. Admittedly, studies on the topic of gender assignment in Arabic are lacking. It would be extremely interesting to know if some kind of rationale exists behind the subdivision of singular nonhuman nouns into masculine and feminine.

gender system where the main subdivisions are: male rational, feminine rational, nonrational (the latter normally including animals; see Corbett 1991: 8–12). Incidentally, one can note that the gender system of contemporary Standard English—although restricted to the 3rd person singular pronouns—works precisely in the same way, with *he*, *she* and *it* representing the same three classes.

There exist some reasons, then, to prefer the tripartite division over the one that recognizes four distinct genders.[150] An objection, however, could be raised. If, in the case of CA/MSA, we have not set nouns that are masculine in the singular apart from those that are feminine in the singular, on the basis of the fact that they share the same semantics and the same type of plural agreement, why didn't we do the same for gender-distinguishing varieties (Types A and E)? After all, in these cases as well, all nouns that take F.PL agreement in the plural share the same semantics (they are *not* masculine human), and the only appreciable differences between gender II and gender III is the type of agreement they trigger in the singular.

The answer to this question is that, as we have seen (§ 2.3.4), other languages exist that share the very same agreement system, and the identification of three different controller genders is the canonical analysis that general linguistics offers of these systems. Typological consistency has to remain an objective in any work of linguistic description, in order for facts and data to remain comparable.

Furthermore, altering the descriptions we have given of systems A and E in order to solve the theoretical issues we are faced with in the case of MSA would be methodologically wrong. It is indeed CA/MSA that represents the real crux of the problem, not the other gender-distinguishing varieties, and this can again be demonstrated employing the tools of linguistic typology.

If we examine a visual representation of the gender system of CA/MSA (no matter whether we take the three- or four-gender option into account), we are

150 Note that a tradition of sorts also exists, in this respect. Already Kuryłowicz (1973: 137) observed that: "If *grammatical* gender is as a rule a matter of government and agreement, then one must admit that Class. Ar. distinguished three genders". See also Gensler (2011: 292), who wrote: "If gender is to be defined strictly in terms of agreement patterns, then it would seem that we have here a covert gender distinction involving animacy, crosscutting the standard division into masculine and feminine". The fact that both passages start with a superfluous conditional structure—to say that linguistic gender is matter of agreement is just stating the obvious—is revealing of how uncomfortable Arabists and Semiticists alike have always been around the topic of gender in pre-Classical and Classical Arabic. Gensler openly states that he does not wish to "follow through" on the implications of his own observations on the topic. Given the numerous problematic issues connected to this topic, highlighted in the present section, their hesitancy seems perfectly understandable.

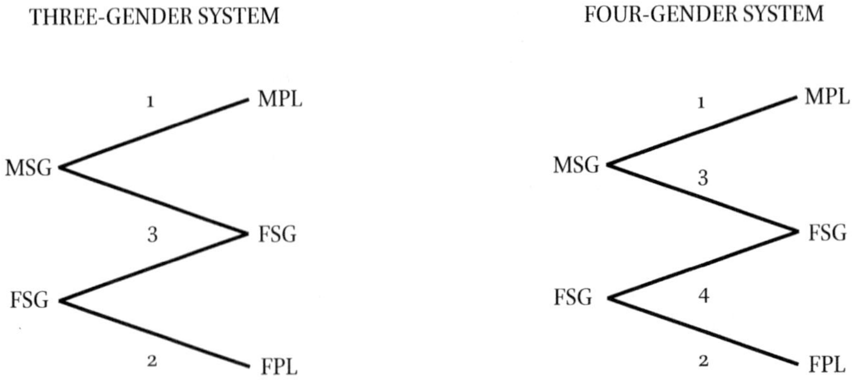

FIGURE 2.2 Two possible representations of the agreement system of CA/MSA

inevitably confronted with the fact that the system knows more distinctions in the plural than it does in the singular, as shown in Figure 2.2.

In other words, the system has two target genders in the singular, but three in the plural. This stands in open violation of known universal linguistic tendencies.

Corbett (1991: 154–156) identifies three different types of possible gender systems. "Parallel" ones (where each target gender in the singular is paralleled by a target gender in the plural: it is the case of languages such as French or Italian); "convergent" ones (where two or more target genders in the singular correspond to just one target gender in the plural: examples include German and Tamil); and "crossed" systems, that have more controller genders than target genders (i.e. the ones of languages such as Romanian and gender-distinguishing varieties of Arabic). "Divergent" systems, such as those represented in Figure 2.2, are apparently not found in the languages of the world. On this point, Corbett thus comments:

> The fact that we find such [i.e. "crossed"] systems, as well as convergent systems like those above, with more singular target genders than plural, but not the converse (with more plural than singular genders) is, of course, a reflection of Greenberg's Universal 37: 'A language never has more gender categories in nonsingular numbers than in the singular'.
>
> CORBETT 1991: 156

The fact that the CA/MSA system poses such a challenge for the descriptivist should therefore come as no surprise.[151] The reasons behind the "theoretical

151 One further element complicates the picture, namely that the third plural target gender

impossibility" represented by these two varieties remain to be explained. Here we will limit ourselves to note how the circumstances that brought about the "birth", as it were, of CA and MSA are quite removed from what is traditionally considered the "normal" process of linguistic evolution and change. In the case of the two aforementioned varieties, this process involved a great deal of artificial normativization, on the one side, and formal teaching/L2 adult learning, on the other. In other words, what is considered as the natural process of linguistic transmission, from one generation to the next, did not take place in the case of the formal registers of written Arabic. In addition to this, as will be discussed in detail in Chapter 3, linguistic contact with the mother tongues of the non-native users or Arabic that populated the Islamic empire in its early centuries did probably play a role.[152]

It could well be, then, that these evolutionary peculiarities are responsible for the apparent typological oddity of the CA/MSA system.

We will not pursue this topic any further, since it will be addressed in Chapters 3 and 4. For the moment, this concludes our discussion about the nature of gender and agreement in CA and MSA. The description of this system, as we have seen, poses several theoretical challenges: although we have tried to present an analysis as complete as possible and some tentative solutions, the topic remains open for future additions and debates.

2.6 Summary

Throughout this chapter, we have provided a description of the various agreement systems that are found in Arabic.

In § 2.1 we have discussed the ways in which modern linguistic theory conceptualizes and investigates agreement, while in § 2.2 we have provided a list of the morphological tools that Arabic varieties have at their disposal to mark gender and number—the "building blocks" of agreement, as it were.

is not marked by an independent set of morphemes, but has the same surface realization as one of the singular options (i.e. F.SG). See § 2.3.5 for a discussion of the nature of F.SG agreement in the plural in Arabic.

152 Some of these languages strongly preferred singular verbal agreement with nonhuman controllers. Crucially, however, they did not mark gender on verbs. If this pattern was actually transferred to written Arabic and overextended, transforming F.SG agreement in nonhuman plural agreement, this might partially explain how the typological impossibilities discussed above first came into being. See Chapter 3 and Benkato and D'Anna (forthcoming).

Sections from § 2.3 onward are devoted to the description proper. Here we have seen how several different agreement systems can be encountered across the Arabic continuum. In particular, we have found that agreement in contemporary gender-distinguishing dialects (the agreement system that we have labelled Type A, described in Table 2.20, § 2.3.4) is remarkably similar to that of the oldest attestations of written Arabic (pre-Classical Arabic; we have labelled this Type E system, and it has been described in Table 2.27, § 2.4). The only differences between them are represented by the retention or loss of dual agreement, and by the effects that precedence has on TC structures (as discussed in § 2.3.9). Apart from these details, they can be considered as fundamentally uniform.

In both systems, all controllers are divided into three agreement classes, according to assignment rules that depend on both formal and semantic criteria. While Class I is constituted exclusively of biologically masculine human controllers, nonhuman controllers are divided between Classes II and III depending on the morphological shape of their singulars (though a few exceptions exist). Biologically feminine human controllers all belong in Class II. In both these systems, in other words, a mismatch exists between the number of target genders and that of controller genders. Nouns are divided into three agreement classes in spite of the fact that all morphological paradigms only display two distinct sets of forms. As a consequence, gender is only partially overt in these varieties.

The analysis that we propose calls into question the validity of the classificatory systems that scholars of Arabic have traditionally employed. As we have seen, several modern dialects appear to possess an agreement system that bears a strong resemblance to the one found in pre-Classical Arabic. This does not support the subdivision of the Arabic linguistic continuum into "New" versus "Old" varieties (on this point see also § 1.1). Similarly, data about agreement offer only limited support for the recognition of a Bedouin/sedentary dialectal split. This has been discussed at length in § 2.3.2 and § 2.3.7, where we have shown that the overlap between these categories and the ones we employ in this book is only partial. Several "sedentary" dialects exist that belong to the gender-distinguishing group, and these all possess a Type A agreement system, as stated above. Even more numerous are the "Bedouin" dialects that have lost the ability to mark gender distinction in the plural.

It is obvious that the traditional subdivions of "Old vs. New" and "Bedouin vs. sedentary" cannot, and should not, be abandoned on the basis of these considerations alone. However, if these classifications are still to be employed, then evidence supporting their validity has to be looked for into other areas of grammar, since the facts concerning gender and agreement offer little justification for their use. In fact, not only the overlap between non-distinguishing varieties and sedentary varieties is just partial, but from the point of view of agreement these dialects do not even constitute an internally homogeneous group. While the majority of non-distinguishing/sedentary varieties have retained the possibility of F.SG agreement with plural controllers, some have not. As a consequence, their agreement systems must be kept distinct.

Non-distinguishing varieties have been analyzed in section from § 2.3.5 to § 2.3.7. We have labelled the systems of the dialects that retain the F.SG agreement option Type B systems (Table 2.21), while dialects where this pattern is no longer attested are characterized by a Type C system (Table 2.22). Since only a single option for plural agreement exists in all these dialects (C.PL), gender in both Type B and Type C varieties can be said to be completely overt (i.e. the morphology displayed by the singular form of the controller is enough to determine to which of the two genders it belongs; in this case as well, a small number of exceptions exist). In addition to this, the assignment rules have shifted from a mixed formal-semantic system to an almost entirely formal one (though a semantic core is still present, composed of human controllers and higher animates).

In light of everything that has been said so far, it is possible to hierarchically organize all the systems we have described on the basis of their level of complexity. We have discussed the question of linguistic complexity in § 2.3.5. As we have seen, all the agreement systems found in Arabic are characterized by elements typical of highly complex gender systems (violation of the *unique value accessibility* rule; numerous agreement conditions; occasional agreement marking on typologically unusual word classes). The only exception to this rule is represented by Type C dialects, which show none of the traits listed above. We are therefore able to rank all the systems discussed so far from the most complex to the most simple:

Type E > Type A > Type B > Type C

Other varieties exist that do not belong to any of the four types exemplified above. These have all been discussed in § 2.3.8, though the only quality they have in common is that of deviating in some measure from the patterns already described.

Among these "divergent" varieties, certain dialects are found where the process of loss of gender distinction in the plural appears to be on its way, but not entirely completed. In these dialects, F.PL forms have disappeared in the verbal and pronominal paradigms, but are still currently in use in the inflection of adjectives and participles. These varieties, therefore, represent an intermediated step between Type A and Type B ones, suggesting that a continuum could constitute a better representation of the variation we encounter in spoken Arabic, rather than a series of discrete subdivisions. This finds further confirmation in the fact that frequency of use of F.SG agreement in Type B dialects can vary wildly, so that even the B/C distinction is not as sharp as our schematic representation could lead one to think.

In addition to this, some dialects of Arabic stand out in that the developments undergone by their agreement systems find no parallel in other known varieties. They are, therefore, unique in this respect. One of these varieties is Darfur Arabic (§ 2.3.8.3), where prolonged contact with non-Semitic languages has brought about the collapse of the entire gender system. Another one is represented by Ḥassāniyya (§ 2.3.8.2), where gender distinction in the plural is found in adjectives, participles and independent pronouns, but whose agreement behavior does not resemble that observed in other distinguishing or partially-distinguishing dialects. All controllers in Ḥassāniyya trigger the same agreement in the plural that they trigger in the singular, making gender entirely overt in this variety. If confirmed, then, Ḥassāniyya would constitute a system of its own, that we have tentatively labelled Type D (Table 2.23).

The last varieties that we have discussed are Classical and Modern Standard Arabic. From the point of view of agreement, CA and MSA are fundamentally homogeneous, and they can probably be considered the most innovative varieties of all. While it is true that the complete disappearance of F.SG agreement in Type C dialects represents a major element of change, the shift in function that this type of agreement has undergone in CA/MSA constitutes a remarkable typological leap. The system we find today in MSA (which we have labelled Type F, see Table 2.30 in § 2.5) is characterized by an absolute distinction between human and nonhuman controllers, a feature that is not present in any other known variety of Arabic. This, in turn, gives rise to a series of theoretical problems, because the classificatory tools traditionally employed by typologists are apparently unable to account for the peculiar "divergent" system of CA/MSA, whose existence seems to defy some well-established linguistic universals. It is possible that the partially artificial conditions under which the grammar of CA/MSA developed are the reason for its typological oddity, but this point remains in need of further investigation (see Chapter 3 for more insights on the subject).

The question of F.SG agreement with plural controllers has been discussed throughout the entire chapter, since it arguably represents the most remarkable feature of the Arabic agreement systems, and what confers them their actual level of complexity. The rules that govern its alternation with "normal" plural agreement (that is, the conditions that govern variation) have been discussed in detail in § 2.3.3 and § 2.3.4. In general, we can say that F.SG agreement constitutes an indicator of the referent's low level of individuation (see also § 1.3). This means that non-individuated controllers tend to attract F.SG agreement, but also that speakers are able to manipulate agreement in order to heighten (or diminish) the saliency of a given referent in the wider context of their discourse.

The possibility of F.SG agreement with plural controllers has also been the source of a certain amount of disagreement among scholars of Arabic. Studies such as those of Mitchell (1973) and Sallam (1979) have questioned the possibility of describing Arabic as a language in which nouns possess an inherent gender. As we have said, we disagree with this view because the gender of any given noun in any Arabic variety can always be determined, given the appropriate context (i.e. the controller is perceived as fully individuated and the target is a regular non-apophonic adjective, a verb or a pronoun). This has been discussed in § 2.3.1 and § 2.3.5.

Further evidence in support of this claim is that, no matter the context, certain subsets of nouns will always be precluded from accessing certain agreement options. Some plural controllers, for instance, will never attract M.PL agreement, or F.PL agreement; and certain singular controllers will never cooccur with a M.SG target, or a F.SG one, in spite of any other contextual factor. If nouns possessed no inherent gender, these constraints would then remain in need of an explanation.

We believe it is important to point out that, in dealing with the various agreement systems that have been analyzed in this chapter, we have always aimed at finding the representation that possessed the most explanatory power, i.e. the one most effective at describing and predicting syntactic behavior. We make no claim, however, as to the psychological reality of such representations. It would be interesting to know, for instance, whether or not the threefold subdivision postulated here for gender-distinguishing dialects finds some parallels in the speaker's mental categorizations of real world-referents. These and similar questions pertain to the field of psycholinguistics, and—fascinating as they may be—they have not been pursued here.

In the previous pages, we have simply aimed at providing a typologically consistent description of the agreement systems of spoken and written varieties of Arabic. We believe that a fundamental condition to achieve this goal is accepting the idea that Arabic nouns all possess an inherent gender. Any description that rejects this assumption will inevitably be less economical, and will have to account for an endless series of particular circumstances, producing explanations with a low potential for generalization.

Before moving on, a number of questions that have remained open are worth summing up (in addition to the ones already mentioned in the previous paragraphs).

First of all, the role that apophonic plurals play in the Arabic agreement system should be investigated further (see § 2.3.4.1). In addition, we still know very little of the causes of variation between F.PL and M.PL agreement in gender-distinguishing dialects. At the diachronic level, this appears to be the result of an incipient process of morphological loss that will eventually bring about the total disappearance of F.PL forms in adjectives, verbs and pronouns. However, at a synchronic level, it is not clear whether this variation is meaningful or not. A series of possible generalizations have been passingly commented upon in § 2.3.2, but more research is needed on this point.

Another important question is the applicability of Corbett's agreement hierarchy to the plural/F.SG variation that is encountered in almost all varieties of Arabic. This problem goes hand in hand with the two questions of agreement canonicity and agreement domains, all tentatively explored in § 2.3.3.4. All these issues need to be investigated in more depth because of the important repercussions they may have on the general linguistic theory of agreement.

As we have seen in § 2.4, the implications of the agreement hierarchy seem to work well in explaining the distribution of F.SG vs. plural agreement in pre- and early-Islamic texts. However, this distribution is rather different from the one that we find in contemporary varieties of spoken Arabic (§ 2.3.3.4). In particular, while in the older Arabic texts the percentage of F.SG agreement is at its lowest in the realm of adjectives, and higher in that of pronouns, the exact opposite appears to be true in the modern dialects.

If we accept that the Quranic text and the pre-Islamic poetry are at least partially representative of varieties of Arabic that were actually in use in the Arabian Peninsula in the 7th century and/or before, then this would seem to speak of a development over time in the realm of agreement. In particular, it would seem that the option of apophonic (broken) adjectival agreement was once more widespread than it is today. On the semantic level, apophonic agreement can probably be considered as having the same implications of F.SG agreement (that is, marking low individuation), so that this diachronic development could be explained as follows: F.SG agreement first developed at the rightmost end of the hierarchy (in pronominal targets), in order to match the semantic implications of apophonic adjectival agreement. This innovative pattern then spread leftwards, affecting verbs and then adjectives, eventually competing with the apophonic option and largely replacing it. In other words, while the semantic options available to speakers of Arabic have remained the same (individuated vs. non-individuated agreement), the morphological means to express the latter have changed.[153]

While in the ancient texts we see apophonic agreement dominating in the domain of adjectives, today F.SG agreement seem to be the widely preferred option, with only a handful of adjectives still mantaining their broken plural patterns. None of the dialectal corpora we have analyzed show percentages of apophonic adjectival agreement that are even remotely comparable with those of the Quranic text or the *Muʕallaqāt*. If our interpretation of the data is correct, this would mean that—over the course of the centuries—the Arabic languages have progressively abandoned apophonic plural formation for adjectives, probably due to the pressure exerted by the verbal and pronominal paradigms, where non-individuated agreement was marked by F.SG morphology. While this is true for the majority of contemporary dialects, some have gone even further, losing the possibility of expressing non-individuated agreement altogether (Type C systems).

153 See § 3.9 for further considerations on this topic.

CHAPTER 3

A Diachronic Account of Agreement: Formal and Written Arabic

3.1 An Overview of Agreement in Central Semitic

In § 2.4, we have provided a description of agreement patterns in pre-Islamic Arabic,[1] mainly based on the linguistic material of the *Muʕallaqāt*, but also including some spare reference to the Quran. The picture emerging from the analysis of our data displayed an internal variation that hinted at the possibility of an ongoing process of linguistic change. This hypothesis is supported by the analysis of later linguistic corpora, which are the object of sections 3.3–3.8. At the same time, however, the pre-Islamic variety of Arabic reflected in the

1 Obviously, we are not maintaining that the type of Arabic in which the *Muʕallaqāt* and the Quran are composed is necessarily representative of Arabic as it was spoken in and around the Arabian Peninsula in the 6th–7th century. It is beyond doubt that different varieties of spoken Arabic existed at the time, and it is very hard (if not impossible) to determine whether or not one of these varieties coincided with the language of the pre-Islamic poetry (traditionally portrayed as some sort of poetic *koinè* despite some dialectal differences) and the holy book of Islam. It is very probable that already in that period a type of diglossia existed, which set apart all forms of everyday colloquial from the formal register of the language that was deemed appropriate for the composition of poetry and literature. If this was actually the case, this formal register may have been an archaic and preserved variety of what used to be, in previous centuries, an actually spoken language. Or its nature could be partially artificial, purposedly engineered to sound more "elegant" by stitching together different traits and features taken from several different varieties. These are all well-known, long-standing questions in the field of Arabic studies, and as such, cannot and need not be addressed here. At present, we are only concerned with the topic of agreement. In this respect, throughout this book we provide ample evidence of a fundamental fact: that agreement patterns found in the Quran and the *Muʕallaqāt* are fundamentally one with the agreement patterns of contemporary dialects of Arabic (at least those that retain gender distinction in the plural). In light of this, and of the fact that such dialects are found today all over the Arabic-speaking world, we are prone to believe that the Quranic and poetic agreement patterns represent the actual usage of at least part of the Arabic speaking population in pre- and early-Islamic Arabia. As will be discussed in this and the next chapters, after the advent of Islam a divide began to emerge between agreement patterns in spoken and written Arabic, a situation that has continued to evolve until the present day. This chapter and the next one are dedicated to the history of this evolution from the perspective of the written variety. In chapter 5, the topic of spoken Arabic will be resumed.

 | DOI:10.1163/9789004527249_004

Muʕallaqāt cannot be considered as the starting point of the process. Quite to the contrary, the internal variation of agreement patterns suggests that the change was already ongoing when the *Muʕallaqāt* were composed (for some remarks concerning the question of their authenticity, see § 3.2). As we venture into the centuries predating the emergence of literary forms of Arabic, however, we walk on slippery paths. The few existing sources (mostly consisting of epigraphic material) do not provide the complex syntactic structures that are necessary to describe a system of agreement in detail, so that reconstruction has to play a greater role. Although written evidence of Arabic becomes relatively abundant around the beginning of the 1st millennium CE, the numerous inscriptions generally record personal and divine names, sometimes embedded in texts composed in other languages (Al-Jallad 2018, 315). As such, they offer little to no help to the reconstruction of the agreement system of the Arabic spoken at that time. Even when later inscriptions are taken into consideration, they do not add much to our discussion. In the tens of inscriptions included in Mascitelli (2006, 91–189), for instance, we do not find instances of agreement with plural controllers that can help in the reconstruction of agreement patterns. The Safaitic inscriptions investigated by Al-Jallad (2015) are more informative, and the degree of similarity they show with later forms of Arabic is remarkable. In particular:

I. Nonhuman plurals can take feminine singular agreement (Al-Jallad 2015, 141);[2]
II. Nohuman plurals can take feminine plural agreement (Al-Jallad 2019: 137);[3]
III. Groups of human usually trigger masculine plural agreement, yet several inscriptions display feminine singular verbs preceding their human controllers (Al-Jallad 2015, 141–142).

Most samples of agreement, however, feature pre-controller verbal targets, which somewhat limits the scope of our reconstruction. We know, for instance, that post-controller pronouns referring to human collectives[4] always feature masculine plural agreement, even when pre-controller verbal targets show feminine singular agreement (Al-Jallad 2015, 142–143). Similar phenomena of

2 There is also one instance of masculine agreement with a nonhuman plural controller, but in a pre-controller verbal target.
3 Although we do not know how common this pattern actually was, since as of today only one example of it has been uncovered.
4 The term "collective" will be here employed in its broadest semantic sense to indicate nouns referring to a collection of referents, usually considered as a whole (but see § 3.4.1). It is not thus limited to those nouns considered as collectives in the Arabic grammatical tradition.

collective agreement have been studied with reference to Quranic Arabic. Both feminine singular and masculine plural agreement with human (morphologically masculine singular) collectives are to be considered instances of semantic agreement, respectively [-individuated] and [+individuated] / [+distributive] (D'Anna 2020a).

Going back to section § 2.4, our data seemed to point to a twofold relation between broken plurals and feminine singular:

I. Feminine singular agreement tends to cluster around broken plurals; with human controllers, in fact, this option seems to be restricted to broken plurals;
II. The higher percentage of feminine singular agreement in verbs and pronouns seems to be directly proportional to the presence of broken plurals in (attributive) adjectives. While the percentage of feminine plural agreement shows a relative stability through the different categories, feminine singular agreement skyrockets when we move from adjectives to pronouns.[5] In several occurrences, moreover, head nouns controlling multiple targets showed apparent 'mismatches' between adjectives in the broken plural and verbs / pronouns in the feminine singular.[6]

Fact II, although not previously observed, is hardly surprising. Both feminine singular agreement with plural nouns and broken plural formations for adjectives, in fact, are to be considered as innovations from a Semitic perspective. The innovative character of feminine singular agreement was first noted by Beeston (1975, 65–66), while Al-Jallad (2015, 63) wrote, with reference to the plural of adjectives:

> In Proto-Semitic, the masculine plural of adjectives was formed by the addition of suffixes to the singular stem, *ūna in the nominative and *īna in the oblique. This continues to be the productive method by which the plural of participles is formed [in Safaitic].[7]

5 The independent factors influencing verbal agreement (in particularly agenthood) were discussed in § 2.4.

6 Our position, of course, is that the mismatch is only formal, and that both feminine singular and broken plural mark a form of [-individuated] agreement.

7 On the other hand, not all adjectives in Arabic allow the possibility of a pluralization by means of an external suffix. The spread of broken plurals to the class of adjectives should be considered as an innovation, probably triggered by the very loose boundaries between the class of nouns and that of adjectives.

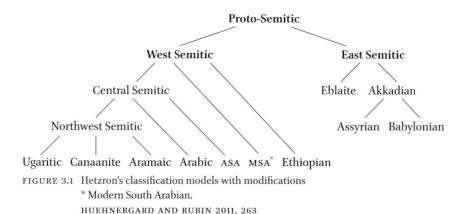

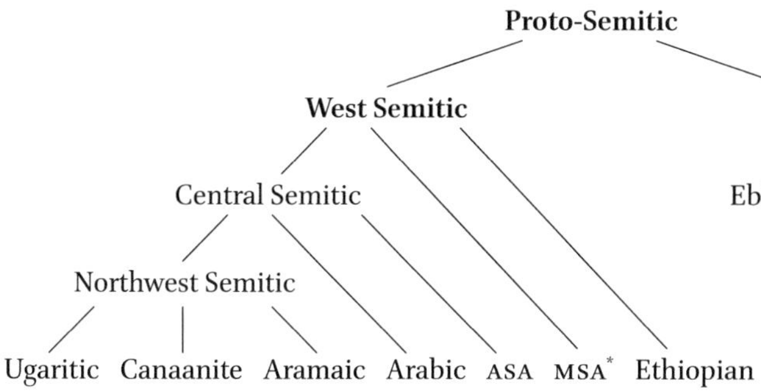

FIGURE 3.1 Hetzron's classification models with modifications
* Modern South Arabian.
HUEHNERGARD AND RUBIN 2011, 263

Given the important role that broken plurals seem to play in the agreement system of pre-Islamic Arabic, a diachronic survey of its development should first take into consideration the Semitic languages that also developed a system of broken plurals. Such an investigation should proceed on two separate paths. The first problem concerns the origin of broken plurals from a morphological point of view, the second their syntactic behavior in the languages in which they are attested. Tracing back the origin of broken plurals in Semitic, however, is not an easy task. The issue of broken plurals, in fact, has been a major point of discussion for competing classifications of the Semitic languages, with particular reference to the alleged existence of a South-Semitic subgrouping.

As far as our knowledge of Semitic languages stands today, Hetzron's widely accepted model of classification is represented in Figure 3.1.

Before this model was universally adopted, Arabic, Ethiopian and the South Arabian languages were considered as parts of a no-longer accepted South Semitic subgrouping. This is hardly the place to discuss in detail matters of Semitic classification, but suffice it to say that the presence of broken plurals in Arabic, Ethiopian and the South Arabian languages was one of three isoglosses that stood behind the hypothesis of a South Semitic group.[8] Based on the principles of historical linguistics, the existence of a South Semitic group (nowadays generally discarded) stands or falls depending on whether we consider the broken plural as a shared innovation of the languages that feature it or as a common inheritance from Proto-Semitic.

8 The other two were the shift of **p* to *f* and the so-called L-stem (i.e. the verbal template containing a long vowel after the first consonant, such as Arabic *qātala* 'to fight') (Huehnergard and Rubin 2011, 272–273).

Huehnergard and Rubin (2011, 272–273), quoting also Greenberg (1955), consider internal plurals as a common inheritance that can be traced back to Proto-Afroasiatic. The reconstruction they offer can be schematized as follows:

1. Proto-Semitic had a system of internal plurals;
2. Akkadian lost this system, with the exception of a few remnants, perhaps due to contact with Sumerian, which does not have internal plurals;
3. Common West Semitic either retained the original system or even expanded it;
4. The Northwest Semitic branch of West Semitic subsequently reduced the set of internal plurals.[9] The loss of most internal plurals was perhaps due to later contacts with Akkadian, which became a *lingua franca* in the area of diffusion of the Northwest Semitic languages *after* it had lost internal plurals due to contact with Sumerian (ca. II millennium BCE);
5. The remaining part of Central Semitic, especially Arabic and Ancient South Arabian, was not in contact with Akkadian during this period, but rather with the ancestors of the Modern South Arabian Languages and Ethiopian Semitic, which had retained the system of internal plurals. In this area, the system was further expanded.

As said above, this is not the place to engage in discussions concerning the classification of Semitic languages. Huehnergard and Rubin's classification, however, is particularly burdensome. It is based on the unconfutable evidence of the existence of internal plurals in Afroasiatic, yet it postulates that an entire system of broken plurals existed in Proto-Semitic which was subsequently lost twice, first by Akkadian alone, due to contact, then by Northwest Semitic, again due to contact. At the southern margin of the Semitic-speaking world, on the other hand, the system was not only retained, but even expanded. An effort at reconstruction, moreover, should aim to specify which forms of the broken plural are original to the archaic system and which ones can be considered as innovations of Arabic, Ancient South Arabian, Modern South Arabian and Ethiopian. Huehnergard himself, in the second edition of the comprehensive *The Semitic Languages*, no longer mentions the five-stage evolution. He mentions the possibility of both internal and external plurals in Proto-Semitic, which is not problematic, but does not go as far as postulating the existence of a Proto-Semitic system of broken plurals that was subsequently lost:

---

9 The possible exception of CvCC nouns, which insert a vowel a after C2, but also make use of an external plural (e.g. Hebrew *melek* 'king', from an earlier *malk → *məlākîm* 'king.PL'), has been convincingly explained phonologically as a case of epenthesis (Suchard and Groen 2021).

> Plurals formed by pattern replacement (referred to as "broken plurals" or "internal plurals") are especially common in (North) Ethiopian Semitic, Modern South Arabian, Ancient South Arabian and Arabic; it is generally not possible to reconstruct pairs of singular and plural patterns to PS.
>
> HUEHNERGARD 2019, 59

From this perspective, the question remains open as to whether the original presence of internal plurals in Proto-Semitic is sufficient to rule out the possibility that the common and innovative forms found in the alleged South Semitic group constitute a shared innovation.

The issue of broken plurals was also previously tackled by Ratcliffe (1998), whose conclusions differ from Huehnergard and Rubin's view, but are referred to in Huehnergard (2019, 59). Ratcliffe embarks in a detailed and complex analysis of the single templates making up the system of broken plurals in Arabic, evaluating them in a comparative Semitic and Afroasiatic perspective. In Ratcliffe's analysis, too, the starting point is the existence of internal plurals in Afroasiatic, yet the question is faced of *which* internal plurals can be considered as a shared inheritance from Afroasiatic and which ones should be treated as innovations peculiar to single languages or groups of languages:

> I attempted to establish and evaluate parallels in the plural systems of Semitic and non-Semitic Afroasiatic languages. Given the time and distance separating the Afroasiatic languages, the absence of ancient records for most of the languages on the African side, and the fact that many languages remain to be described, one has to be cautious in evaluating the non-attestation of a particular feature in the non-Semitic Afroasiatic languages. Yet it is arguably significant that for every aspect of the plural system which NW and SW Semitic share—internal /a/ in CVCC nouns, expansion of biconsonantals to 3C structure in the plural, singulative/collective (CVCCat/ CVCC) contrasting with feminine plurals (CVCCat > CVCaC), distinct masculine and feminine forms of the external plural—abundant parallels can be found in several non-Semitic Afroasiatic languages. Yet for those features which SW Semitic shares against NW Semitic, only the tendency to form /u/ plurals from /a/ singulars finds a parallel in non-Semitic Afroasiatic languages (Ratcliffe 1992, 372–628). And this feature, too, may be attested in residual form in NW Semitic.
>
> RATCLIFFE 1998, 208

Ratcliffe then reconstructs three different stages in the development of internal plurals:

1. A Proto-Semitic stage, which also has correspondences in Afroasiatic and which includes the CvCC → CvCaC[10] and the few other traits mentioned in the long quote reported above;
2. An old stratum that can only be reconstructed for Arabic, Geʕez, Tigre and the South Arabian languages, including the plural templates ʔaCCuC, CaCaCat, ʔaCCiCat and ʔaCCiCāʔ.
3. A younger stratum, which is peculiar to the same languages and which includes the more productive (and thus more recent) templates ʔaCCāC, CaCāCiC, CaGāCiC and CaCāGiC (G = glide) (Ratcliffe 1998, 211).

To the best of our knowledge, no scholar has engaged in a confutation of this specific part of Ratcliffe's reconstruction, which has the merit of considerably simplifying the historical development of internal plurals from Afroasiatic to Arabic and the other languages in which they occur. The five-step reconstruction proposed by Huehnergard and Rubin, in fact, would be reduced to two steps:

1. Proto-Semitic inherits a few templates of internal plurals from Afroasiatic, of which we see vestiges in both Akkadian[11] and Northwest Semitic;
2. The southern branch of Semitic (be it a genetic subgrouping or a heterogeneous group of languages in which the phenomenon spread due to areal diffusion) expanded the inherited system, resulting in today's situation.

This reconstruction, moreover, does not seem to be in contrast with Huehnergard (1987, 187): "[…] pattern replacement was a Proto-Semitic feature, a feature which was merely exploited, rather than first developed, in South Semitic." According to Hasselbach (2014b, 322), internal plurals might have even been the original pluralization strategy, yet she makes clear that her reconstruction goes back to a stage that is anterior to what we usually consider as Proto-Semitic (Hasselbach 2014b, 335).

For the purpose of our diachronic reconstruction of agreement patterns in Arabic, it is irrelevant whether the languages in which a complex system of broken plurals is attested are part of a genetic subgrouping. It is sufficient to

10 But see Suchard and Groen (2021).

11 In the light of Suchard and Groen (2021), however, CvCaC plurals should be excluded from this group, not being internal plurals in the first place. The pattern attested in Akkadian, even though only tentatively, is *CuCaCāʔ* (Huehnergard 1987, 183–184). This is particularly interesting, since this pattern is only attested in Arabic, Ancient South Arabian and Akkadian, but not in the other Semitic languages that feature large systems of internal plurals (Ratcliffe 1998, 208). As a consequence, it should probably be considered an old Proto-Semitic form and not one of the younger formations that took place in the "South Semitic" group.

acknowledge that, starting from a more or less abundant number of inherited Proto-Semitic forms, which coexisted with a system of external plurals, these languages developed rich and pervasive systems of broken plurals. In these systems, external plurals did not completely disappear, but they were confined to a much smaller set of nominal forms.

From this point of view, it is worth noting that Beeston (1962, 34–35) mentions, for Epigraphic South Arabian, the coexistence of internal and external plurals for the nouns (of common Semitic stock) *bn, ʔx, ʔb, mw, ywm* and perhaps *nfs*. Epigraphic South Arabian is one of the Semitic languages in which the preference for broken plurals is more marked, affecting even *nisba* forms and participles (A.F.L. Beeston 1962, 33). At the same time, at least the nouns *ʔx, ʔb, ywm* and *nfs* possess only broken plurals in Arabic. If Beeston's forms are correct, these external plurals in Epigraphic South Arabian should be considered as ancient inherited forms, since external pluralization is no longer productive in that language.[12]

This leads us to the second part of our analysis, concerning the syntactic behavior of broken plurals. While a small set of internal plurals is not likely to cause drastic changes in the syntax of a language, the case of Arabic and the other 'Southern' Semitic languages is quite different. In these languages, a very large part of the lexicon switched to the new pluralization strategy, which caused a certain degree of transparency loss in the system. Compared to external plurals, internal ones are morphologically less transparent. Some of the most frequent templates, such as CiCāC and CuCūC, are also available for singular nouns (e.g. *biqār* "cow.PL", but *kitāb* "book"; *ʕulūm* "science.PL", but *ruǧūʕ* "return"), so that they cannot be considered as inherently plural from a morphological perspective. In a similar way to collectives, they are semantically more than morphologically plural.[13] Broken plurals, moreover, are underspecified for gender, which implies that, for agreement purposes, speakers have to retrieve gender information from the singular.

It is probably worth expanding on what we mean by underspecification for gender. Broken plurals don't differ from singulars at the morphological level, i.e. they have no external morphological marker of plurality and, for those varieties that have cases, share the same inflexion system. The morphological markers that distinguish masculine from feminine in the singular, however, are

12 In Akkadian, *abum* shows the form *abbū*, with reduplication of the second radical and external ending, in Babylonian, while Old and Middle Assyrian have *a-ba-ú* / *a-ba-e* and a few forms with double *-bb-*, indicating a possible internal plural cognate to Arabic *ʔabāʔu*. *ax*, however, only has the reduplicated and suffixed form *axxū* (Huehnergard 1987, 186).

13 More recent templates are usually restricted to plural nouns.

present but irrelevant in the plural. In other words, while the morphology of the noun is usually sufficient to determine its agreement class in the singular and in external plurals, although a limited number of semantically motivated exceptions exists, the situation is completely reversed with reference to broken plurals, whose morphology is normally irrelevant for the purpose of agreement assigning. Some of the most productive templates for broken plurals, in fact, are available for both morphologically masculine and feminine singular nouns, e.g. CiCāC (*rağul* pl. *riğāl* "man" but *raqabat* pl. *riqāb* "neck") and CawāCiC (*kawkab* pl. *kawākib* "star" but *qāʕida* pl. *qawāʕid* "rule"). Other templates are exclusively available for morphologically masculine singular nouns, yet they usually display open feminine morphology when in the plural, e.g. CaCaCat (*rāʕin* pl. *ruʕāt* "shepherd") and CuCaCāʔ (*ʾamīr* pl. *ʔumarāʔ* "prince"). Others, finally, show consistent morphology in the singular and the plural, although morphology alone is not generally sufficient to assign a noun to an agreement class, e.g. ʔaCCāC (*nawʕ* pl. *ʔanwāʕ* "species"). When saying that broken plurals are underspecified for gender, in conclusion, we mean that their morphology rarely allows the speaker to retrieve the morphology of their singular forms. Arabic grammarians were aware of this fact, as will be evident in § 4.4.

Unfortunately, no detailed study of cognitive linguistics is available on this matter, but it seems intuitive that this situation involves a higher cognitive load for the speaker. In some languages, both currently spoken and extinct, gender was in fact retrieved from the singular. This happens, for instance, in Sabean, where "Broken pl stems have pl concords in the gender of the sg, e.g. mas *hmt / ʾwrḫn* "those months", fem *hnt / ʾhgrn* "those towns" (A.F.L. Beeston 1984, 28)." In Modern South Arabian languages as well, targets agree with their controllers in gender and number, so that this can be considered as the agreement pattern inherited from Common Central Semitic (Simeone-Senelle 2011, 1102). All the languages that display complex systems of broken plurals for nouns, however, extended them to adjectives as well, thus innovating the original Proto-Semitic strategy of adjective pluralization, which used to feature only external plurals (Al-Jallad 2015, 63). Given the loose boundaries between the categories of nouns and adjectives, however, this innovation is hardly a surprise.

At a certain point in time, it seems that Arabic innovated its inherited agreement patterns, introducing a possibility of semantic agreement (in the feminine singular) with broken plural controllers, both human and nonhuman. The term innovation, here, might not be completely appropriate. We might express the same concept saying that, at a certain point, Arabic started employing for broken plurals the same pattern of agreement already employed for collectives (for more details, see note 21 at the end of this section). As already said, in fact, the function of feminine singular agreement is to mark [-individuated] agreement, in the same way as broken plurals always seem to entail a certain degree of genericness (see § 2.4 and § 1.2 respectively).

It is possible that this semantic specialization arose as a consequence of the inherent underspecification of broken plurals, which were always underspecified for gender and often not overtly plural in their morphology. In other words, feminine singular agreement with plural controllers might have come into being because of the speaker's need to "match" a type of agreement which was becoming widespread in adjectives, but had no parallels in the other parts of speech.[14] While broken plural adjectives allowed the speaker to fulfil agreement rules using the same pluralization strategy employed with nouns, such an option was not available for verbs and pronouns, which do not have broken plurals. This would explain why, in our pre-Islamic data (but the trend is confirmed in both the Quran and the corpus of Najdi poetry discussed in § 3.9) the percentage of feminine singular + broken plural agreement in adjectives matches that of feminine singular in verbs and pronouns. For the sake of clarity, the data reported in § 2.4 are repeated in Table 3.1.

The underspecification of broken plurals represents a suitable motivation for the development of a form of [-individuated] agreement. We have already seen that Wright describes the resulting situation as a semantic split between sound and broken plurals:

> As regards their meaning, the *plurales fracti* (i.e. broken plurals) differ entirely from the sound plurals; for the latter denote several *distinct* individuals of a genus, the former a number of individuals viewed *collectively*, the idea of individuality being wholly suppressed. For example, *ʕabdūn* are *slaves* (*servi*), i.e. several individuals who are slaves, *ʕabīd slaves* collectively (*servitium* or *servitus*).
>
> WRIGHT 1896a, 1:233

Wright's analysis is supported by the syntactic behavior of broken plurals, but it only makes sense if we postulate an extended period of coexistence between sound and broken plurals. A semantic specialization on the axis of individuation, in other words, is only possible if the two forms are both present. In a situation like the one represented by contemporary Arabic, where some nouns

14 From this perspective, it is natural that feminine singular agreement affected the class of nonhumans more than that of humans. With human controllers, in fact, grammatical gender and biological sex coincide, making it easier to retrieve the gender of the noun without referring to its singular form.

TABLE 3.1 Percentages of feminine singular + broken plural agreement in adjectives vs feminine singular in pronouns (data from the *Muʕallaqāt*)

Animate	**Tot.**	**F. Sg. + Br. Pl.**
Attr. adj.	10	9 (90%)
		F. Sg.
Pronouns	21	19 (90.5%)

Inanimate	**Tot.**	**F. Sg. + Br. Pl.**
Attr. adj.	11	9 (81.8%)
		F. Sg.
Pronouns	47	38 (80.9%)

only have broken plurals and some only have external ones, such a specialization could have never developed. From this perspective, the coexistence of internal and external plurals in nouns (such as *ʔb*, *ʔl* and *ywm*) that only have broken plurals in Arabic, attested in Epigraphic South Arabian, leads us to think that this situation was once more widespread.[15] One of the nouns mentioned by Beeston with reference to Epigraphic South Arabian, *bn*, also feature a double plural in Arabic (*banūna* 'son-M.PL' vs *ʔabnāʔ* 'son.PL'). In the pre-Islamic corpus, sound plurals occasionally occur for nouns that nowadays only feature internal plurals, such as *kur-īna* 'ball-M.PL' (ʕAmr, 97), whose standard plurals are *kurāt* and *kuran*.[16] Cases of coexistence between older external plurals and

15 The sound plural *ʕabdūn* 'servant:M.PL', although still mentioned in some dictionaries, is certainly no longer used in Classical Arabic. Sībawayh himself considers it as a possibility only when ʕAbd is used as a proper noun (Sībawayh 1889, 2:101). It is also worth mentioning that Suchard and Groen's (2021) reconstruction of vowel insertion after C2 in CvCC nouns entails a period in which plural CvCaC-ū plurals were reanalyzed as broken ones and thus lost the plural suffix, *de facto* becoming the CiCāC broken plural pattern. If we accept this reconstruction, it follows that nouns denoting animals (e.g. *ǧamal* pl. *ǧimāl* "camel") and things (*ǧabal* pl. *ǧibāl* "mountain") regularly formed their plurals by means of external suffixes, and that the external and innovative internal plurals coexisted for some time.

16 Other significant examples of residual external masculine plurals in nouns denoting

younger internal ones, on the other hand, are also attested in contemporary Arabic: the noun *mudīr* 'director', for instance, developed an internal plural *mudarāʔ* alongside the more standard *mudīrūna*. Most verbal nouns of the II form (*taCCīC*), similarly, have a sound feminine plural in *–āt* (often obsolete) and an internal one (e.g. *tafṣīl* 'detail', pl. *tafṣīl-āt* 'detail-F.PL' vs *tafāṣīl* 'detail.PL'; *tarkīb* 'installation', pl. *tarkīb-āt* 'installation-F.PL' vs *tarākīb* 'installation.PL'). Both the older relics of coexistence and the fact that external plurals are still being replaced with internal ones (via a stage of coexistence), thus, lead us to think that both forms coexisted, for an extended period, for most nouns in Arabic.[17]

The original evolution of feminine singular agreement with plural controllers, thus, might be schematized as follows:

1. Proto-Semitic inherited a small set of internal plurals from Common Afroasiatic;
2. A part of West Semitic, not necessarily forming a genetic subgrouping, extended this small set of forms into a complex and pervasive system of internal plurals. The new forms partially (sometimes almost completely) replaced the older external plurals, not without an extended period of coexistence;
3. In the languages that took part in the innovation, internal pluralization was extended also to adjectives, partially replacing the inherited Proto-Semitic system of external plurals;
4. During the period of coexistence, Arabic alone (as far as we know, but see below) developed a semantic specialization of sound vs broken plurals, which came to express [+individuated] vs [-individuated] plural. The association of broken plurals with [-individuated] plural reference was probably eased by their lack of morphological transparency and underspecification for gender;
5. The lack of morphological transparency and underspecification for gender resulted in a higher cognitive load for speakers, which became more and more burdensome as broken plurals spread to greater areas of the

---

non-human entities are *ʕālam ūna* "world M.PL", *ʕaraḍ ūna* "land M.PL" and *ʕilliyy-ūna* "uppermost part of Heaven-M.PL".

17 Some dialects seem to represent an even more advanced stage of evolution than Classical Arabic. For most South Arabian languages, the pervasiveness of internal pluralization is shown by its occurrence with *nisba* nouns. In many dialects of Arabic, *nisba* ethnonyms definitely show the possibility of internal pluralization to a much higher degree compared to Classical Arabic (which is sometimes the *only* available pluralization strategy: e.g. Libyan *tūnsi* 'Tunisian' pl. *twānsa* 'Tunisian.PL', *bəngāzi* 'from.Benghazi' pl. *bnāġza* 'from.Benghazi.PL', *ṭulyāni* 'Italian' pl. *ṭlāyna* 'Italian.PL').

lexicon. With adjectives, the extra-cognitive load was solved by the extension of internal pluralization to the adjectives themselves. For verbs and pronouns, feminine singular agreement started being used to match the [-individuated] semantic feature of broken plurals.

It is worth noting that Arabic seems to be alone in this innovation. No other Semitic language, within the group in which broken plurals are attested, developed feminine singular agreement with plural nouns.[18] Ferguson (1976, 75) advanced the hypothesis that feminine singular agreement with plural nouns might be an isogloss of the alleged Ethiopian language area. Tosco (2000, 349), however, confuted Ferguson's proposal, which lumps together different phenomena. In Geʕez, one of the languages mentioned by Ferguson, syntactic agreement in the plural only occurs with human controllers. With nonhumans, agreement is extremely variable: it can be both singular and plural, both masculine and feminine (Lambdin 1978, 27).[19] This contradicts what we observe in Arabic on two major points:

1. In Arabic, feminine singular agreement is rarer, but available also for human plural controllers;
2. Agreement with nonhuman controllers displays a limited variability, contrary to what observed in Geʕez (pending more detailed studies, which might show so far unnoticed regularities).

Although neither Geʕez nor other Semitic languages share the innovation found in Arabic, it is worth noting that agreement with plural controllers in those languages that developed a system of broken plurals is, as a whole, much more complex than it is in Northwest and East Semitic.[20] In Tigre, syntactic

18 It is meant here that no language of the West Semitic group presents a distribution of agreement patterns featuring the same semantic motivations (individuation) and the same agreement options (feminine singular for non-individuated plural controllers, masculine plural for individuated male humans, feminine plural for individuated plural controllers referring to all other classes) as Arabic. The state of the art of studies on agreement in other West Semitic languages does not allow us to discern whether the situation we have described is original to them or represents a later evolution from an original state similar to that of Arabic.

19 As a matter of fact, agreement with non-humans in Geʕez is variable also in the case of singular controllers (Lambdin 1978, 26–27). Given that agreement with singular controllers is quite straightforward (although motivated exceptions exist) in both West and Central Semitic, however, the situation of Geʕez must be considered as innovative. The case of Geʕez probably represents the final collapse of morphological criteria for gender assignment, featuring a system where only semantic criteria, i.e. biological sex for highly animate controllers, survive in both the singular and the plural.

20 As far as East Semitic is concerned, in Akkadian plural agreement is governed by the morphology of the head noun and not by its gender in the singular. (Huehnergard 2019, 70)

agreement in the plural is restricted to animate controllers, while inanimate ones usually trigger agreement in the masculine singular (Raz 1983, 13). With reference to the Gindaʕ Tigre corpus, Elias indirectly confirms our hypothesis that broken plurals influence agreement patterns by saying that "A verb agrees in gender, number and person with its subject: *ħu-je mæsʔ-æ* brother-POSS.1SG come.SC-3MSG 'my brother came'", but that "The "internal" PL is grammatically SG" (Elias 2019, 167). In Amharic, internal plurals are restricted to a few lexical items (mostly loanwords from Geʕez), while the only productive strategy consists in using a palatalized version of Semitic *-āt* (*-očč*) (Meyer 2011a, 1190–1191). In Gurage, numbers is not marked at all, except in a few lexical items that are felt as members of a couple singular vs plural (Meyer 2011b, 1242). Some of the dialects of the Gurage cluster, however, preserve remnants of the former system of broken plurals (Hetzron 1977, 53). Detailed studies of agreement in Ethiopian Semitic would be highly desirable, but it appears that all the languages that developed a full system of broken plurals underwent profound changes in their agreement patterns. Some of them later abandoned broken plurals in favor of external pluralization but, in all those languages that retained them, the syntactic rules of agreement assignment were partially replaced by semantic ones. This probably happened independently, since both the semantic criteria (individuation in Arabic, humanness in Geʕez, animacy in Tigre) and the agreement patterns (feminine singular in Arabic, variable agreement in Geʕez, masculine singular in Tigre) differ. In the different cases, however, broken plurals weakened the formal rules of assignment to the point that the agreement partially shifted to a semantically-motivated system, with different outputs. South Arabian is the only exception to this tendency. Ancient South Arabian is now extinct, even though it was still in use when Arabic had undergone the change, while Modern South Arabian languages still display broken plurals with mandatory syntactic agreement. Modern South Arabian, in other words, developed a full system of broken plurals without syntactic consequences on its agreement system (Watson 2012, 251,277). This trait shows considerable conservativeness, which has been noticed in Modern South Arabian also in other domains of the language, from phonology to verbal morphology and the lexicon. In a recent contribution, however, Fathi (2017) showed that, in Mehri, a class of broken plurals has apparently started carrying gender information. In broken plurals containing a glide, in fact, the distribution of *w* and *y* seems to reflect a masculine / feminine gender opposition, thus restoring the gender specification that was lost with the spread of broken plurals. This innovation has so far been observed only in Mehri, and shows that speakers of the only language group that preserved broken plurals until today without restructuring its agreement system are finding new ways to encode gender information in

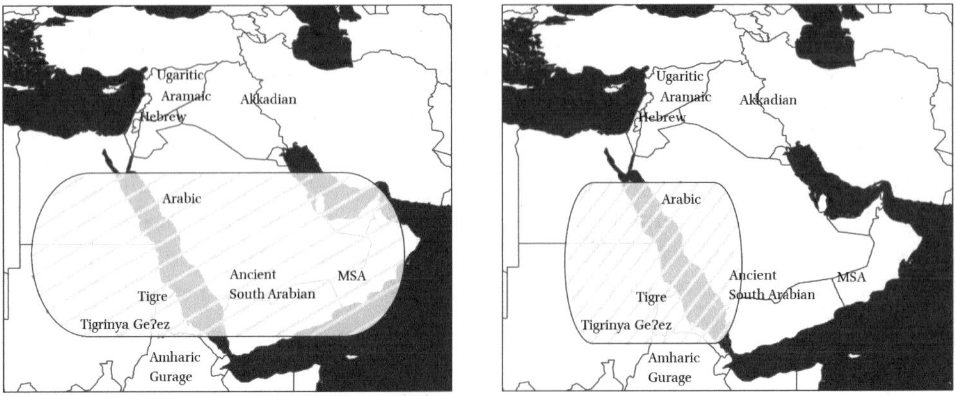

FIGURE 3.2 Semitic languages prevalently featuring internal plurals (left) and Semitic languages featuring partially semantically motivated agreement systems (right)

previously underspecified plural forms. The situation is depicted in Figure 3.2, which shows representatives of the main subgroupings of Semitic, although without taking into consideration their chronological dimension. On the left, we can see all the Semitic languages in which internal plurals represent the prevalent pluralization strategy. On the right, the Semitic languages featuring (partially) semantically motivated agreement patterns. It is evident that, with the exception of South Arabian languages, the two groups coincide, and it is likewise evident that Northwest and East Semitic are completely out of the picture.

For all later periods of the history of Arabic, far more data are available, which makes reconstruction an easier task, and its results more reliable. For the stages described in this section, on the other hand, any reconstruction must be considered tentative, and subject to revision whenever new data become available, in particular for languages belonging to the Ethiopian Semitic group.

At the end of this attempt at a reconstruction, one final question remains to be answered, i.e. why feminine singular was chosen to match the [-individuated] character of broken plurals. This question touches upon the issue of the relation between broken plurals, collectives and feminine singular, which attracted much interest throughout the 20th century. Brockelmann, for instance, considered collectives and plurals as parts of the same feminine class, within a binary division of nouns in Proto-Semitic (masculine vs feminine, with the feminine class also including abstract nouns) (Ratcliffe 1998, 120). Ratcliffe (1998, 117–150) includes a survey of the extant scholarship concerning the origin of the broken plural, which generally did not stand the test of time. Most of the theories he discusses can effectively account for a limited number of broken plural forms, but result inadequate to explain the phenomenon in its entirety. Most of them, however, spring from a basic fact of Semitic morphology, i.e. the fact that the suffix **-t* / **-at* fulfils different tasks, among which the most important are marking feminine gender, the singulative (e.g. Arabic *tuffāḥ* 'apple.COLL' vs. *tuffāḥ-at* 'one apple') and the collective (e.g. Arabic *naǧǧār-at* 'carpenter.COLL', *sayyār-at* 'caravan of travellers'). Feminine singular agreement, for instance, is one of the possible agreement patterns for targets depending on a collective controller, even when it is morphologically a masculine singular. In this respect, Hasselbach (2014a; 2014b) represents a great step forward concerning both the original value of the morpheme **-t* / **-at* and the development of agreement patterns. By comparing data from Akkadian, Hebrew, Aramaic, Classical Arabic and Geʕez, Hasselbach concludes that the original values of **-t* / **-at* in Proto-Semitic are the marking of abstracts (i.e. substantivized derivatives of verbal adjectives) and the marking of singulatives. What is important to our discussion, however, is that the collective value of the morpheme **-t* / **-at* is to be considered as an innovation of West Semitic, so that its value had already been established at the Proto-Arabic stage (Hasselbach 2014b, 332). Given the extreme semantic proximity between collective and non-individuated plural, the fact that feminine singular was chosen to match the [-individuated] character of broken plurals is easily explained.[21]

3.2 Methodological Issues in the Selection of the Corpora

As stated in section 3.1, far more data are available once we reach the 6th and 7th century CE. These data allow the researcher to build small but representative corpora, on which basic statistical analyses can be run. The picture we obtain from such materials, as a consequence, is less uncertain and more reliable. At the same time, however, the existence of data of quite a diverse nature, especially as we move into the Islamic era, poses some methodological issues concerning their selection for the purpose of reconstruction. It goes without

21 In order for this explanation to hold, a further point needs to be clarified. We know that the innovative feminine singular agreement started in the class of pronouns and moved down the agreement hierarchy. A problem with this reconstruction might be that Arabic pronouns do not, of course, mark feminine singular with the **-t* / **-at* morpheme. Hasselbach (2014b, 337), however, points out to the fact that, whatever its semantic value, **-t* / **-at* had been gender-wise reanalyzed as feminine already at the Proto-Semitic stage. This means that, if **-t* / **-at* had a collective semantic value, so did the entire class of feminine singular markers.

saying that no one-fits-all solution is available, and choices have to be made empirically. This section illustrates some of the methodological issues we faced in the selection of our corpora and motivates the consequent choices.

Starting from the 6th century, sources in the Arabic language become more abundant. Primary sources, in the form of epigraphic materials, continue to be available, and new ones keep being discovered regularly. These sources have the merit of being authentic examples of the language in use at the time of their carving (at least of one of its registers), provided they can be reliably dated. The main problem with them is that, due to their brevity and their style, they cannot provide a full description of the agreement system of the language in which they were written. As a consequence, they are used to crosscheck data and make sure that none of the other sources stands in open contradiction with them, but they cannot provide all the needed information. For instance, none of the inscriptions contained in Mascitelli (2006) and Al-Jallad (2015) contradicts the information we gathered from the sources that will be listed below. However, if we were to describe the agreement patterns characteristic of pre-Islamic Arabic only based on these materials, our description would not occupy more than a couple of pages.[22]

Our main source for the 6th century mainly consists of the pre-Islamic poetic corpus. This source has the merit of providing a great variety of syntactic structures that clarify agreement patterns in detail, and are readily available to the researcher. There are, however, at least three methodological issues to face when extracting data from them:

1. They represent a literary register of the language, in all probability laden with archaic traits and allowing occasional samples of poetic license. The illusion that, through the analysis of agreement patterns in the *Muʕallaqāt*, we have access to the everyday language spoken in the 6th century, thus, must be promptly dispelled. From this point of view, however, the situation is not different in the case of the large majority of epigraphic material, with the partial exceptions of those inscriptions carved casually by herdsmen or travelers (and even those display a highly formulaic register);
2. The poetic form in which the *Muʕallaqāt* (and other pre-Islamic poems) were written is based on both meter and rhyme. The necessity to comply with such constraints, consequently, might have had an influence on agreement choices. While the tyranny of meter and rhyme is undeniable,

22 In Al-Jallad (2015), for instance, the two sections on agreement occupy pages 141–144, while Mascitelli (2006) does not attempt any syntactic description.

two counterarguments can be found to this objection. First, pre-Islamic poetry was meant for public recitation. This means that it *did* have a public. It is highly unlikely that entire generations of poets would choose ungrammatical agreement patterns only to comply with the necessities of meter and rhyme. This is especially true when considering the high esteem in which pre-Islamic poetry was held by grammarians and native speakers alike. Second, agreement patterns dictated by metric or rhyme necessities are likely to be arbitrary and random. They would not follow any predictable pattern. The analysis of the data (already discussed in section 2.3.2), on the contrary, points to a definite direction.[23] While single occurrences might have been dictated by rhyme or meter constraints, in other words, agreement choices are statistically predictable and thus not compatible with some sort of free variation due to poetic necessities. In a few limited cases, it is somewhat probable that a dispreferred agreement pattern was chosen to comply with either meter or rhyme, yet the same cannot be said for the poetic corpus in its entirety;

3. The third issue, finally, is philological in nature. Since the publication of Ṭāhā Ḥusseyn's *Fī al-šiʕr al-Ǧāhilī* in 1926, doubts have been cast on the authenticity of much of the pre-Islamic poetic corpus, accused of being a later forgery. This objection, however, can also be dismissed. The agreement patterns found in the pre-Islamic poetry, in fact, form a consistent system that does not correspond exactly to either Classical Arabic or the dialects (although being closer to what observed in gender-distinguishing varieties of dialectal Arabic). Its dissimilarity from the system probably obtaining in the language of the alleged forgers, either Classical or dialectal, thus vouches for its reliability. Otherwise, we would have to imagine that whoever forged the poems, probably not a single person, managed to recreate a self-contained and rational agreement system, which is rather unlikely.

For all the aforementioned reasons, and with some caution, the analysis of agreement in pre-Islamic Arabic is thus based on the *Muʕallaqāt* and then followed by the analysis of the entire Quran.[24]

As we move into the Islamic era, sources become even more abundant and varied in their nature. In particular, texts in prose start being available in great quantities. Early Islamic prose supposedly reflects a plainer register, which is desirable, yet this comes with some detrimental consequences for our research.

23 The same was noted, even with a smaller corpus, in Belnap and Gee (1994, 129).

24 The Quranic text, consisting of 77,430 words, represents a much larger corpus than the *Muʕallaqāt*.

The first concerns verbal targets, which almost systematically precede their controllers in prose texts. As said in § 2.4, word order is an absolute condition both in pre-Classical (with the exceptions mentioned in the section) and in Classical Arabic, so that verbal targets preceding their controllers cannot be expected to display syntactic agreement in the plural in any case. Historical and religious sources, moreover, are not particularly rich of descriptions involving complex adjectival patterns, so that most of our post-controller targets are represented by pronouns. Already in the pre- and early Islamic corpora, however, the category of pronouns (the rightmost in the agreement hierarchy) was the one most affected by the innovative feminine singular agreement pattern. These three factors combined can skew the analysis and give the false impression that little or no variation was left. In the samples of early Islamic prose (9th–10th century) that were examined during our research, thus, almost no occurrence of interest was collected, which sharply contrasts with the rich patterns observed in the poetry of the same period. The same observation can be made with reference to the data presented in Belnap and Gee (1994, 132). Up to the 7th century, their materials only comprise poetry and the Quran. Starting with the VIII century, they switch to prose, with the result that variation simply ceases to occur, while the system obtaining in pre-Islamic poetry and the Quran is still alive in poetry, as will be evident from sections 3.5 and 3.8. For the purpose of the present research, as a consequence, we decided to investigate homogeneous corpora as far as possible, and pursued the analysis of poetry, both in Classical and dialectal Arabic, until the 20th century.

Non-literary prose texts, such as the papyri, are a different matter altogether and must be discussed separately. The papyri represent a rich source of data, even though they cannot be considered a later stage of the same variety reflected in pre-Islamic poetry. Early papyri have been the object of detailed studies, such as Hopkins (1984), which have been taken into consideration for this book.

At the same time, however, part of our interest lies in the evolution from pre- to early Classical Arabic, and in the survival of the ancient agreement system in the literary language.[25] For this reason, apart from poetry, ornate prose has also been analyzed, since it is characterized by those syntactic features (richness of

25 It is worth reminding the reader that two separate paths of evolution occurred in the agreement system of Arabic. While the dialects continued the old system, with gradual changes, the literary language underwent, at a certain point, a process of standardization. In our analysis of the latter, thus, the primary focus is not on dialectal interference (such as the one we find in Middle Arabic), but in the transition from the agreement system found in the old literary language (reflected in pre-Islamic poetry and the Quran) to the new one, featuring mandatory feminine singular agreement with nonhuman plural controllers.

adjectival patterns, elaborate descriptions involving post-controller verbal targets etc.) that are the necessary condition for the mere possibility of variation.

Finally, the last part of our diachronic survey focuses on contemporary Nabaṭī poetry from Najd, which provides samples of a literary genre sharing many similarities with the pre-Islamic *qaṣīda*, but composed in contemporary dialectal Arabic. While dialectal materials have mainly been the object of Chapter 2, it is worth noting that, after fifteen centuries, it is still possible to trace the evolution of the ancient system, as represented in the *Muʕallaqāt*, in contemporary Bedouin poetry.

3.3 A Change in Progress? Resemanticization in Pre-Islamic Poetry

In § 2.4, the variation observed in the agreement system of the pre-Islamic *Muʕallaqāt* was considered as the sign of a possible change in progress. The language of pre-Islamic poetry reflects a stage in which the change was already ongoing, and had probably been ongoing for quite some time. This section focuses on stage 5 of the tentative reconstruction of agreement from Common Central Semitic to pre-Islamic Arabic (see section 3.1). The starting point of the change is the pervasive expansion of the broken plurals in some languages of the Central Semitic group, among which Arabic. In Arabic, broken plurals became the most productive pluralization strategy, at the expense of the old external suffixes *–ūna* / *īna* (masculine) and *–āt* (feminine). Differently from the external plural suffixes, broken plurals are morphologically less transparent and underspecified for gender. When the system of broken plurals that exists in Arabic today was finally in place,[26] thus, a very large section of the lexicon had plural forms whose noun templates were partially shared with singular nouns and whose gender could only be retrieved from the singular. In all probability, these forms coexisted for an undefined period with the corresponding external plurals, before finally ousting them. During this period of coexistence, a semantic specialization such as the one described in Wright (1896, 1:233) occurred, so that sound plurals were marked as [+individuated], broken ones as [-individuated]. This distinction and the role of individuation are still observ-

26 Without providing a chronology of the changes, Ratcliffe (1998, 211) distinguishes three stages of development in the system of broken plurals. The first one already happened in Afroasiatic, while the remaining two occurred only in those languages of the Central Semitic group (which Ratcliffe considers to be parts of a South Semitic group, the existence of which is no longer accepted by most Semitists) that developed the system of broken plurals observed today.

able in all the dialects of Arabic for which we have data, so that their origin must surely be traced back to pre-diasporic Arabic. The underspecification for gender probably played a role in the attribution of the [-individuated] semantic specification to broken plurals, but this innovation is peculiar to Arabic and not attested in the other Semitic languages that have internal plurals.

All the languages that developed a system of nominal broken plurals feature the same pluralization strategy also in the domain of adjectives, due to the loose boundaries between the two classes. In the case of Arabic, it seems that adjectives generalized the innovative internal plurals at a slower rate compared to nouns, which may suggest that internal plurals spread to adjectives later than to nouns. This fact appears evident from those cases in which the same nominal template is employed for both adjectives and nouns, as is the case for most participial templates (e.g. CāCiC and CaCīC). In similar cases, whenever the lexical item (available as both noun and adjective) features the possibility of an external and internal plural, it is always nouns that display the innovative internal plural, never adjectives. The same happens when the plural of adjectives is lexicalized as a noun: if the adjective features the possibility of both an external and internal plural, the noun will always select the internal one. E.g. *ṣāliḥ* "good, pious", pl. *ṣāliḥ-ūna* "good-M.PL" vs *ṣawāliḥu* "benefit.PL", *ʔakbar* "great.COMP", pl. *ʔakbar-ūna* "great.COMP-M.PL" vs *ʔakābiru* "prominent.people.PL", *ʔawwalu* "first", pl. *ʔawwal-ūna* "first-M.PL" vs *ʔawāʔilu* "beginning.PL". When searching Arabicorpus (all internal corpora), for instance, the only emerging agreement pattern is *riǧālun ṣāliḥ-ūna* "man.PL good-M.PL", never *riǧālun ṣawāliḥu* "man.PL good.PL".[27] That said, some adjectival internal plurals appear to be older than others. With regard to adjectives of color, for instance, Sībawayh writes:

> If you name a man *ʔAḥmar* [red], if you want you can say *ʔAḥmar-ūna* [red-M.PL], and if you want you can use a broken plural and say *al-ʕAḥāmiru* [DEF-red.BR.PL], but you cannot say *al-Ḥumru* [DEF-red.BR.PL], because now it is a noun and not an adjective, the same as the plural forms *al-ʔarānibu* [DEF-rabbit.BR.PL] and *al-ʔarāmilu* [DEF-widow.BR.PL]. Likewise, you say *ʔAdāhimu* [DEF-black.BR.PL] when speaking of *ʔAdham* [black] and using it as a noun, in the same way as when you say:

27 As always, agreement facts should be taken as statistical tendencies more than as hard-and-fast rules. The adjectival form *ṣawāliḥu*, in fact "good.PL", occurs twice in Arabicorpus as an attributive adjective qualifying the noun *nisāʔ* "woman.PL". By contrast, the external feminine plural *ṣāliḥ-āt* "good-F.PL" occurs 94 times with the same controller, and hundreds of times with similar ones (e.g. *banāt* "girl.PL" etc.).

> *al-ʔabāṭiḥu* [DEF-flat.PL]. If you name a woman *ʔAḥmar* [red], if you want you can say *ʔAḥmar-ātun* [red-F.PL], and if you want you can use the broken plural that is used for nouns and say *al-ʕAḥāmiru* [DEF-red.BR.PL]. In this way the Arabs used broken plurals for these adjectives when they became nouns.[28]

This brief excerpt from Sībawayh's *Kitāb* contains some important clues concerning the relation between internal plurals, nouns and adjectives. Sībawayh admits that nominalized adjectives tend to form their plural apophonically, using the pattern CaCāʔiCu (which confirms our observations). Adjectives of color seem to constitute an exception, since they possess a specific broken plural form, i.e. CuCC. When nominalized, they can thus take an external plural or the more generic CaCāʔiC internal plural. Sībawayh speaks here of nominalized adjectives quite literally, i.e. referring to the adjective used as a proper name. In MSA, the broken plural CuCC also occurs when the adjective is nominalized (e.g. *as-Sūd* "Blacks"). Finally, Sībawayh is aware of the fact that internal plurals lack gender, since he mentions one and the same pattern as the plural of both the masculine and feminine nominalized adjective.

The availability of internal plurals for both nouns and adjectives solved the uncertainties in agreement patterns resulting from the underspecification of broken plurals, but only for adjectives, which have the possibility to agree in the broken plural with their broken plural controllers. At the same time, however, in constructions featuring a noun and an adjective in the broken plural, the attributive domain also became morphologically less transparent and ceased to carry gender information. This paved the way to the final innovation, i.e. the spread of feminine singular agreement with plural nouns. As already seen in section 3.1, the "innovation" can also be seen as a generalization to broken plurals of an agreement pattern already available for collective nouns. Sentences such as the following, thus, should probably be considered as the locus of innovation:

---

28 *Wa-ʔin sammayta rağulan bi-ʔAḥmara fa-ʔin šiʔta qulta: ʔAḥmarūna, wa-ʔin šiʔta kassarta-hu fa-qulta: l-ʕAḥāmiru, wa-lā taqūlu: l-Ḥumru, li-ʔanna l-ʔānna-hu l-ʔāna ismun wa-laysa bi-ṣifatin, ka-mā tuğmaʕu l-ʔarānibu wa-l-ʔarāmilu, ka-mā qulta: ʔAdāhimu ḥīna takallamta bi-l-ʔAdhami ka-mā yukallamu bi-l-ʔasmāʔi, wa-ka-mā qulta: al-ʔabāṭiḥu. Wa-ʔin sammayta mraʔatan bi-ʔAḥmara fa-ʔin šiʔta qulta: ʔAḥmarātun, wa-ʔin šiʔta kassarta-hu ka-mā tukassaru l-ʔasmāʔu fa-qulta: al-ʔAḥāmiru. Wa-kaḏālika kassarati l-ʕArabu hāḏihi ṣ-ṣifāti ḥīna ṣārat ʔasmāʔa* (Sībawayh 1889, 2:96).

(1) *wa=ʔayyāmin la=nā ġurrin ṭiwālin ʕaṣaynā l=malka*
and=day.PL to=us illustrious.PL long.PL rebel:1.PFV.PL DEF=king
fī=hā ʔan nadīnā (ʕAmr, 29)
in=her COMP 1.IPFV.PL:obey:SBJV
'And our illustrious, long days in which we rebelled against the king, unwilling to obey him.'

In order to explain the innovation of feminine singular agreement with plural controllers, the term resemanticization has been fleetingly mentioned at the end of § 2.4. It is now time to return to it and describe it in more detail. The concept of resemanticization was introduced by Wurzel (1986), and can be defined as the semantic reanalysis of syntactic features. In particular, resemanticization

> implies the replacement of the old, grammatical gender system in which pronouns agree syntactically, by an innovative system that uses semantically motivated (count/mass) pronouns instead. It is generally accepted that this innovative system originates in personal pronouns […] and spreads to other target categories from this point onwards.
>
> DE VOS 2015, 128

It should be noted that the opposition count/mass is related, but not at all identical, to the individuated/non-individuated one that occurs in Arabic (see § 1.3 and § 2.3.3 for a discussion of individuation). Nonetheless, the fact that resemanticization processes spread starting from pronouns confirms Beeston's (1975, 65–66) hypothesis concerning the locus of innovation in Arabic.

Resemanticization was successfully employed to describe the evolution of pronominal gender for both Northern and Southern Dutch (Audring 2009; De Vos 2015), where it was caused by loss of gender information in its adnominal morphology. Southern Dutch originally preserved a three-way distinction masculine/feminine/neuter in the pronouns, thanks to the richness of the gender-marking adnominal morphology of its dialects. Due to dialect loss, however, Southern Dutch has recently started losing its adnominal morphology (De Vos 2015, 128).

> When speakers lost the knowledge about the former masculine and feminine gender, they also lost the original system that governed pronoun usage. This opened the gates to redistribution of the pronominal genders.
>
> AUDRING 2009, 133

The redistribution of pronominal genders, however, did not occur on a syntactic basis, but rather on semantic ones. The former neuter gender started being used for uncountable or mass nouns, while masculine and feminine, or common gender for those varieties with a binary system (common vs neuter), were reserved for countable nouns. Neuter nouns, such as *boek* 'book', are thus often assigned non-neuter pronouns such as *die* 'that' by younger speakers, because they are countable nouns. For nouns which can be intended as either countable or uncountable, the distinction non-neuter vs neuter pronoun now marks the opposition, e.g. *de diamant* [common gender] 'the diamond (i.e. a single stone)' vs *het diamant* 'the diamond (as a kind of stone, as in the example *diamond is the hardest stone*)' (Audring 2009, 132).[29]

The process just described was historically motivated by the loss of the adnominal morphology that carried gender information in dialects of Dutch. As a consequence of that, young speakers lost the knowledge of the previous gender of nouns and set in motion the process of resemanticization. The analogy with the situation of Arabic is self-evident. In Arabic, not only adnominal adjuncts (such as adjectives), but nouns themselves used to carry gender information, both in the singular and in the plural. When the full system of broken plurals was finally in place, and then extended to adjectives, the loss of gender information in the plural occurred in both nominal and adnominal morphology. The broken plural forms that replaced the older external ones, moreover, were not equally transparent from a morphological perspective (see § 3.1). At this point, the spread of feminine singular agreement, starting from pronouns and moving left through the agreement hierarchy, can be best interpreted as a textbook example of resemanticization, probably set in motion by younger speakers as well. The fact that feminine singular constitutes a semantically motivated agreement option for collective nouns (insomuch as it occurs with morphologically masculine controllers, but see § 3.4.1) represents another parallel with the situation of Southern Dutch.

This hypothesis also has the merit of explaining conveniently two well known, but elusive facts. The first one is the reluctance of speakers (both in contemporary dialects and in the old sources) to use feminine singular agreement with external plurals. The resemanticization process, in fact, was motivated by the loss of morphological information in broken plurals. With few exceptions

29 It is worth noting that the similarity between feminine singular agreement with plural controllers in Arabic and neuter agreement was already noted by Féghali and Cuny (1924, 83) and by Killean (1968, 43), although they lacked the theoretical tools to describe the resemanticization process.

TABLE 3.2 Agreement possibilities with singular and plural controllers in Classical and Modern Standard Arabic

Singular controllers	Plural controllers	
Masculine	Sound masculine	} Broken plural
Feminine	Sound feminine	
	Feminine singular	

(with specific reference to feminine sound plurals), external plurals do carry such information, so that the need for semantic agreement did not arise in the first place (even though, once feminine singular agreement started being perceived as a viable agreement pattern with plural nouns, it occasionally occurred also with sound plural controllers).

The second problem that would be solved if our hypothesis were confirmed is a typological puzzle. The possibilities of agreement in (pre-)Classical and Modern Standard Arabic are schematized in Table 3.2, using the traditional gender categories:

Considering either the pre-Islamic and dialectal situation, where individuation is the key factor, or the Classical/Standard one, where the factor is humanness, the situation does not change: Arabic makes more distinctions in the plural than it does in the singular, and it has more gender/number (feminine singular involves both) distinctions in the plural than it does in the singular. These two facts are extremely unlikely from a typological perspective, and violate Greenberg's (1963) universal 37: "A language never has more gender categories in nonsingular numbers than in the singular". Our hypothesis explains this problem by situating the violation of universal 37 in its historical contingency. Loss of gender information only occurred in the plural, due to the spread of broken plurals, so that resemanticization likewise occurred in the plural only (while in other languages where gender information was lost in the singular, such as Dutch, it occurred in the singular as well).

If seen through the lens of resemanticization, the apparently odd situation of Arabic complies with typological tendencies that have been observed and tested on many distant and unrelated languages, such as the already mentioned agreement hierarchy and the relevance constraint. Whenever a formally motivated agreement system shifts (totally or partially) toward a semantically motivated one, the agreement hierarchy (Corbett 2006, 207) makes predictions concerning the direction of the change. With reference to lexical categories (or, in traditional grammatical terms, parts of speech), pronouns initiate the

TABLE 3.3 Percentage of feminine singular agreement with plural nonhuman controllers in the pre-Islamic data and Corbett's agreement hierarchy

	Conservative	←	Innovative
Agreement hierarchy	**Attributive adjectives**	**Verbs (predicates)**	**Pronouns**
Animate controllers	10%	22.2%	90.5%
Inanimate controllers	27.3%	53.1%	80.9%

change, while attributive adjectives are the most conservative category. Table 3.3 shows data from pre-Islamic poetry tested against Corbett's agreement hierarchy:[30]

As evident from the table, our data confirms the existence of an ongoing shift from a formally motivated toward a partially semantic system of agreement, which we have called resemanticization.

In pre-Islamic poetry, feminine singular agreement also occurs with human controllers, yet occurrences with real morphological plurals (i.e. not collectives) are very rare. This suggests that, although individuation and not humanness was the key semantic category involved in the semantic shift, the change did indeed start at the lower end of the animacy hierarchy, which is also the least individuated one. As already discussed in the previous chapters, the categories of humanness, animacy and individuation/salience are all deeply interconnected.

In a typological perspective, changes concerning number marking are more likely to start at the opposite end of the animacy hierarchy, i.e. with personal pronouns and humans. The Constraint of the Animacy Hierarchy on the singular-plural distinction, for instance, predicts that "The singular-plural distinction in a given language must affect a top segment of the Animacy Hierarchy" (Corbett 2000, 56). While it is common to assign human attributes to nonhuman controllers, in fact, the opposite phenomenon is typologically unlikely (Rosenbach 2008, 155). In our case, however, the innovation does not regard number marking nor humanness *per se*, but rather a semantic reanalysis, in terms of a [-individuated] number, of a syntactic category, i.e. feminine singular.[31] Even so, it is worth noting that such an innovation complies with

30 Only percentages are reported. For a full account of the corpus and detailed numbers, see § 2.4.

31 It should again be noted that feminine singular was already employed to mark collective-

the Relevance Constraint. The constraint was theorized with reference to Norwegian, where a minor number (Corbett 2000, 100) came into being due to the grammaticalization as a suffix of the noun *vis* 'way, manner' (similarly to what happened to its English cognate *wise*). The suffix –*vis* became the mark of a plural of abundance (thus [-individuated]), starting with nouns ranking very low in the animacy hierarchy, such as measure nouns. On the contrary, it never occurs with nouns that rank high on the animacy hierarchy, such as those referred to human beings. As such, it apparently violates the Constraint of the Animacy Hierarchy on the singular-plural distinction. On the other hand, however, a plural of abundance is less likely to occur with humans and highly individuated semantic classes, so that the Relevance Constraint was formulated as follows:

> Abundance is not particularly relevant to entities high on the Animacy Hierarchy, but rather detracts from individuation. Figures—which are on top of the hierarchy—do not exist in abundance, while grounds—which are on the bottom—do. The idea is, simply, that language change targets the part of the lexicon where the categories in question are most relevant for human experience. We propose to refer to this as the "Relevance Constraint". […]
>
> ENGER AND NESSET 2011, 198

It is important to note that both these constraints were originally devised with reference to morphological and syntactical innovations in number marking and not in agreement. Nonetheless, the following synthesis of Enger and Nesset's Relevance Constraint seems particularly relevant to our case:

> For conceptual distinctions that are most relevant for the *bottom* part of the Animacy Hierarchy, the Relevance Constraint predicts that diachronic development starts at the bottom of the Animacy Hierarchy and proceeds upwards.
>
> ENGER AND NESSET 2011, 206

This is exactly what appears to have happened in Arabic according to our data. Due to loss of gender information in the plural of nouns and adjectives when they formed broken plurals, a resemanticization process took place, assigning

ness, so that the innovation here regards the extension of this agreement patterns to plural controllers, and not only to collective ones.

the value of [-individuated] plural to feminine singular. This process, looking at our statistics, started out at the lower end of the animacy hierarchy, because humans were less likely to be perceived as [-individuated] and because grammatical gender was more easily retrievable, given that it almost systematically coincides with biological sex.

Detailed figures concerning the distribution of syntactic vs semantic agreement have already been provided in § 2.4, and were cited in this section only when relevant for our diachronic survey. If our hypothesis is correct, and the change was actually in progress (as all the signs seem to indicate), data collected from later sources should show a further spread of semantic agreement, as it works its way down the agreement hierarchy and up the animacy hierarchy. In other words, we expect to see an increase of semantic agreement through the lexical categories going from pronouns to attributive adjectives (agreement hierarchy) and through the semantic categories going from inanimates to humans. In the latter case, however, the style and literary genre of the text plays an important role, because different semantic factors are at play. In particular, the trait [+human] automatically tends to raise the individuation level of any controller, decreasing the likelihood of [-individuated] agreement in the feminine singular. For this reason, detached descriptions within narrative or poetic texts provide a fertile ground for the occurrence of feminine singular agreement, while texts in which the readers are directly addressed, or highly rhetoric in nature, usually favor syntactic agreement. The diachronic development of agreement in the centuries that follow the Hegira will be the object of the following sections.

3.4 Down the Agreement Hierarchy (and a Few Pragmatic Detours): Evidence from the Quran

The previous section presented the data collected from pre-Islamic poetry—which were discussed in detail in § 2.4—in a diachronic light. Evidence was provided to argue that the variation of agreement patterns is the sign of an ongoing resemanticization process, in which the syntactic category of feminine singular was bestowed a semantic meaning, that of [-individuated] plural. The process started from pronouns and then moved down the agreement hierarchy, apparently touching the most conservative category of the hierarchy, i.e. attributive adjectives, already in pre-Islamic times. Percentages of feminine singular agreement with attributive adjectives are, however, pretty low (27.3 % with inanimate controllers and only 10 % with animate ones). At the same time, the innovative agreement pattern seems to have started at the lower end of the animacy hierarchy, in accordance with the Relevance Constraint. Although it had already reached the top segment of the hierarchy, as instances of feminine singular agreement with humans do occur, such instances are almost negligible in number. Both the Agreement Hierarchy and the Relevance Constraint make predictions concerning the diachronic development of the innovative phenomena they describe, so that it should be possible to follow their spread by extracting data from later sources.

Most of the pre-Islamic materials examined in section 3.3 date back to the 6th century CE.[32] Moving on, this section focuses on the most relevant linguistic document of the 7th century, at least for the Arabic-speaking world: the Quran. The Holy Book of Islam was revealed, according to the tradition, in the period between 609 and 632 CE (the date of Muḥammad's death). Its collection in written form, on the other hand, occurred before 650 CE, during ʕUṯmān's caliphate (644–656) (Schoeler 2010, 780), as recent scholarship has proved beyond any reasonable doubt (Van Putten 2019; Sidky 2020).

The entire text of the Quran provides a corpus of 77,430 words, and was analyzed in full for the purpose of the present research.[33] All the occurrences of plural and collective nouns controlling targets were manually collected, yielding a total of 1082 targets depending on human controllers and 868 on nonhuman ones, which allows us to obtain a relatively clear picture of agreement patterns. Before discussing the data, however, it is worth reminding the reader that the Quran, despite being almost contemporary with some of our pre-Islamic poets, represents a different literary genre. Early Arab poetry has been extensively used, since the first centuries of Islam, to investigate the language of the Quran (Bauer 2010), but this should not tempt us to consider the two documents as representatives of one and the same register of Arabic. In the case of agreement, in particular, the pragmatic dimension of the text plays an important role. Detached descriptions of desert landscapes and animals, in fact, are less likely to contain items that the speaker considers as highly individuated. On the contrary, the Quran is a text that was originally recited in public, with the precise aim of converting a reluctant audience to the new religion. Especially when human controllers are involved, then, reference will almost inevitably be to the single members of the group and not to its indistinct mass.

32 While the pre-Islamic nature of the corpus in itself cannot be doubted, the question of authorship is obviously an open one.

33 For the purpose of the present analysis, the authors relied on Ḥafṣ' version. Minor discrepancies between different reading traditions, with specific reference to agreement, will be the object of future research.

TABLE 3.4 Feminine singular agreement in nonhuman post-controller targets: pre-Islamic poetry vs Quran

	Attr. adj.	Verbs	Pronouns
Muʕallaqāt	4/21 (19%)	21/50 (42%)	57/68 (83.8%)
Quran	63/120 (52.5%)	54/72 (75%)	228/268 (85.1%)

The case of collective controllers, which will be treated in some detail later in the section, perfectly exemplifies the difference.

Even with this caveat, however, the data collected from the Quran confirm that the process of resemanticization was still active, i.e. feminine singular agreement was spreading to the left positions of the agreement hierarchy. Table 3.4 compares data concerning the incidence of feminine singular agreement in post-controller targets depending from nonhuman (animal and inanimate) controllers in pre-Islamic poetry and the Quran.

The data perfectly confirm the predictions made according to the Agreement Hierarchy. The percentage of feminine singular agreement only negligibly increases with pronouns, the category in which the innovation started and which seems to have reached a certain stability. On the other hand, in the other two categories, verbs and attributive adjectives, the increase is extremely significant. This suggests that the innovative pattern, once reached some sort of stability within the category where it started, was moving left through the agreement hierarchy, gaining ground at the expense of the old patterns. This movement is visually represented in Figure 3.3.

Our expectations concerning the spread down the agreement hierarchy are thus perfectly fulfilled. Seen from a synchronic perspective, the data from the Quran continue to respect the agreement hierarchy. From a diachronic one, on the other hand, they show a negligible increase in pronouns and a significant one in both verbs and adjectives.

The other prediction concerned the spread of feminine singular up the animacy hierarchy. The Relevance Constraint, applied to our case, justified the start of the innovation at the lower end of the animacy hierarchy. At the same time, the innovation did not introduce a [±human] semantic factor, but rather a [±individuated] one. Even though human controllers are involved by the innovative pattern only marginally, due to their intrinsically high degree of individuation, a modest increase might be expected. Table 3.5, thus, compares the incidence of feminine singular agreement in inanimate, animal and human controllers in the *Muʕallaqāt* and the Quran. In this case, for the sake of brevity, data from attributive adjectives, verbs and pronouns are lumped together.

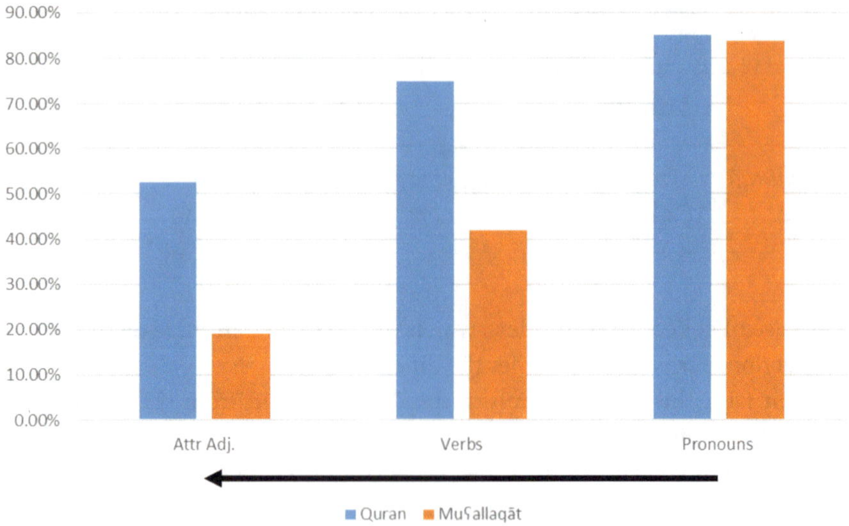

FIGURE 3.3 Spread of feminine singular agreement in the Agreement Hierarchy: *Muʕallaqāt* vs Quran

TABLE 3.5 Incidence of feminine singular agreement in inanimate, animal and human controllers: *Muʕallaqāt* vs Quran

	Inanimate	**Animal**	**Human**
Muʕallaqāt	59/96 (61.5%)	18/45 (40%)	4/78 (5.1%)
Quran	339/454 (74.7%)	11/26 (42.3%)	15/59 (25.4%)[a]

a Under the label 'human', there are also occurrences of supernatural beings, such as deities and the *jinn*. To make sure that their treatment was comparable to that of humans, we ran a second test on this group of controllers removing those referring to supernatural beings, and leaving only "proper" human controllers. In this case, the percentage of feminine singular targets was even higher (30%, 12/40), which confirms that supernatural beings can be safely grouped together with humans at the top end of the animacy hierarchy.

Our data show that the predictions of the Animacy Hierarchy are also fulfilled. In this case, too, the increase is less pronounced at the lower end of the animacy hierarchy, where the innovation originated, and more significant with human controllers, which stand at the top of the hierarchy. This fact is best interpreted, as already happened with the Agreement Hierarchy, as a spread of the innovation from its initial locus to other semantic classes (in this case, humans and supernatural beings).

Compared to the almost negligible occurrences of feminine singular agreement with human plural controllers in pre-Islamic poetry, the pattern is still

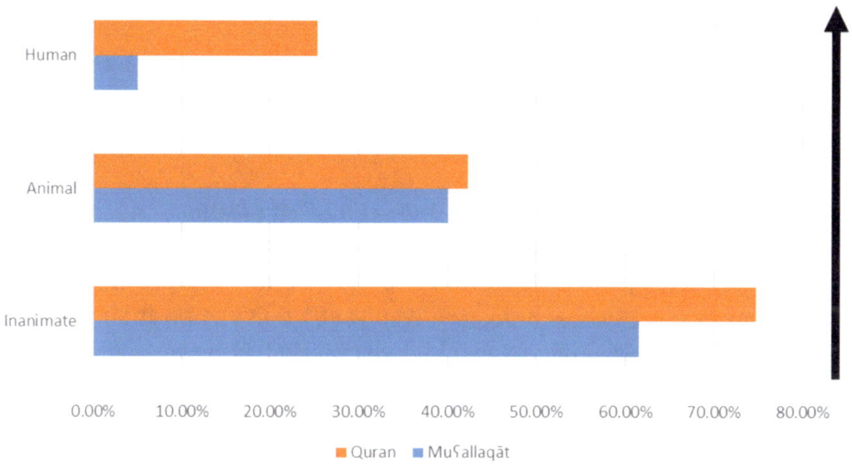

FIGURE 3.4 Spread of feminine singular agreement in the Animacy Hierarchy: *Muʕallaqāt* vs Quran

rare in the Quran, but definitely more widespread. There is, however, a hard constraint on the morphological shape of the controller, which must be a broken plural. No occurrences of feminine singular agreement with human sound plurals, either masculine or feminine, were found. The following samples show occurrences of feminine singular agreement with (broken) plural human controllers in the Quran:

(2) *qul ʔa ʔunabbiʔu=kum bi=xayrin min ḏālikum*
IMP.say.2.SG INT 1.IPFV.SG:inform=you.M.PL of=better than that.M
li=llaḏīna ttaqaw ʕinda rabbi=him ǧannāt
to=who.PL fear:3.PFV.M.PL at lord=their.M garden:F.PL
taǧrī min taḥti=hā l=anhār xālidīna fī=hā
3.IPFV.F.SG:run from under=her DEF=river.PL eternal:M.PL in=her
wa=ʔazwāǧun muṭahhar-atun [...]
and=spouse.PL PASS.PTCP.purify-F.SG
'Say: Shall I tell you of a better than that? For those that are godfearing, with their Lord are gardens underneath which rivers flow, therein dwelling forever, and spouses purified [...]' (III, 15)

(3) *hāḏā naḏīrun mina **n=nuḏuri l=ʔūlā***
this.M warner from DEF=warner.PL DEF=first.F.SG
'This is a warner, of the warners of old' (LIII, 56).

The following sample shows a chain consisting of an inanimate plus a human controller in the broken plural. Context allows us to discern that the controller *ʔawlād* 'son.PL', however, lacks any individuation, and is merely seen as part of what each man is allotted by God. Both the relative pronoun and the verb, thus, appear in the feminine singular:

(4) *wa=mā* ***ʔamwālu**=kum* *wa=lā* ***ʔawlādu**=kum*
and=NEG wealth.PL=your.M.PL and=NEG child.PL=your.M.PL
bi=llatī ***tu-qarribu**=kum* *ʕinda=nā* *zulfā* [...]
what.F.SG 3.IPFV.F.SG-bring.near=you.M.PL at=us position
'It is not your wealth nor your children that shall bring you nigh in nearness to Us [...]' (XXXIV, 37)

In some cases, such as the following one, the occurrence of the feminine singular is partly due to rhyme necessities (verses 8–12 consist of short sentences all ending with an S-stem verb in the third person feminine singular *–at*). Nonetheless, such cases show that feminine singular was an available agreement pattern for human controllers:

(5) *wa=ʔiḏā* ***r=rusulu*** ***ʔuqqit-at***
and=when DEF=prophet.PL set.time-3.PFV.F.SG
'And when the Messengers' time is set' (LXXVII, 11)

The numbers mentioned above provide a bird's-eye view of the synchronic situation of Quranic Arabic and its diachronic development in comparison with the language of the *Muʕallaqāt*. This means that some subtleties are inevitably lost in exchange for the big picture. With animal controllers, for instance, the increase of feminine singular agreement is minimal compared to the *Muʕallaqāt*. At the same time, the Quranic text only yielded 26 targets depending from morphologically plural animal controllers (i.e. not from collective ones). With such small numbers, percentages can easily be skewed by the occurrence of agreement-conditioning factors. As an example, 6 out our 26 targets occur in the Sura of Yūsuf (Q XII) and are quantified by the low numeral *sabʕ* 'seven', which almost invariably triggers plural agreement. Even with collective animal controllers, however, data from the Quran are quite surprising, featuring instances of feminine plural agreement where they are not expected. Some of the most relevant peculiarities of Quranic Arabic will be discussed in the remaining part of this section.

The first peculiarity worth mentioning is the loosening of the boundaries between the three agreement classes. In particular, in a number of occasions masculine plural agreement occurs with nonhuman controllers, whereas feminine plural was expected. This phenomenon never occurs in the *Muʕallaqāt*, which once again seems to incarnate a more archaic stage of the language. The phenomenon, on the other hand, is well attested in Middle Arabic since its earliest stages (Hopkins 1984, 92), even though mostly with human feminine controllers taking masculine plural agreement. In the spoken varieties in which gender distinction in the plural is undergoing erosion, the phenomenon is documented as well, for instance in Southern Tunisia (Ritt-Benmimoun 2017, 267, 282) and in Southwest Libya (D'Anna 2017, 120). In the Quran, these are some of the most interesting samples:

(6) *wa=ʕallama* *ʔĀdama* ***l=ʔasmāʔa*** *kulla=hā* *ṯumma*
and=teach.3.PFV.M.SG Adam DEF=name.PL all=her then
*ʕaraḍa=**hum*** *ʕalā* *l=malāʔikati* [...]
show.3.PFV.M.SG=them.M on DEF=angel.PL
'And He taught Adam the names, all of them; then He presented them unto the angels [...]' (II, 31)

(7) *wa=llāhu* *xalaqa* ***kulla dābbatin*** *min* *māʔin*
and=God create.3.PFV.M.SG every beast from water
*fa=min=**hum*** *man* *yamšī* *ʕalā* *baṭni=hi* [...]
and=from=them.M who 3.IPFV:WALK:M.SG on belly=his
'God has created every beast of water, and some of them go upon their bellies [...]' (XXIV, 45)

(8) *wa=huwa* *llaḏī* *xalaqa* ***l=layla*** *wa=**n=nahāra***
and=he REL.M.SG create.3.PFV.M.SG DEF=night and=DEF=day
*wa=**š=šamsa*** *wa=**l=qamara*** *kullun* *fī* *falakin* ***ya-sbaḥ-ūna***
and=DEF=sun and=DEF=moon every in orbit 3.IPFV-swim-M.PL
'It is He who created the night and the day, the sun and the moon, each swimming in a sky' (XXI, 33)

In sample 6, the controller to which the pronoun *–hum* "them.M" refers is not entirely clear. It could be *al=ʔasmāʔa* "DEF=name.PL", or more probably the totality of God's creatures, which Adam had just named. This is exactly the reason why the traditional explanation of Quranic exegesis, provided in the famous *Tafsīr al-Ǧalālayni*, is not entirely convincing. In the *Tafsīr*, we read: "*ṯumma ʕaraḍa-hum: ʔay al-musammayāti wa-fī-hi taġlību al-ʕuqalāʔi*" "then He presented them: i.e., the named things, the majority of which concerned intellectual beings" (*Al-Qurʔān al-Karīm Bi-r-Rasm al-ʕUṯmāni Wa-Bi-Hāmiš*

Tafsīr al-Ǧalālayni 2005, 6). In sample 4, we have already seen an example of a mixed controller (a human-inanimate chain) triggering feminine singular agreement, despite the fact that the human controller was the closest to the verbal target. Moreover, in the situation described by the Quranic verse, God is presenting the things he created, and which Adam had named, to the angels. It makes no sense, thus, that there would be a prevalence of "rational" (as the Arabic grammatical tradition refers to controllers at the top of the animacy hierarchy, i.e. humans and supernatural beings) entities, since Adam was the only human being and the angels the only other supernatural ones apart from God (and maybe the *jinn*). The same holds true for sample 7, in which *kulla dābbatin* is glossed in the *Tafsīr* as *ʔayy ḥayawān* "every animal". The following *min=hum* "from-them.M", as a consequence, is hardly justifiable, considering that this part of the verse is speaking of animals slithering on their bellies. In sample 8, finally, three clearly nonhuman entities are named, without any possibility of including human (or "rational") beings in the controller. In this case, moreover, rhyming necessities clearly play a role, since verses 30–37 of Sura XXI all end in *-ūna*. Nonetheless, the reason adduced in the *Tafsīr* is, again, anthropomorphization, this time caused by the verb *ya-sbaḥ-ūna* "3.IPFV-swim-M.PL", which, being typical of humans (although many animals do swim), attracts masculine plural agreement (*Al-Qurʔān al-Karīm Bi-r-Rasm al-ʕUṯmāni Wa-Bi-Hāmiš Tafsīr al-Ǧalālayni* 2005, 324). The three samples seem to represent the first (and very limited) instances of a situation that is also found in contemporary dialects, e.g. in Fezzani Arabic (D'Anna 2017, 120). In the context of a general erosion of gender distinction in the plural, feminine plural agreement systematically appears when the target closely follows a plural controller belonging to either Class II or III. When, on the other hand, the target is farther from its controller or is not clearly identifiable (as in sample 8), masculine plural occasionally replaces feminine plural. In Fezzani, this phenomenon was mainly observed with reference to human controllers, while the samples reported above all feature nonhuman ones. Unfortunately, the Quran does not provide any feminine human sample that might confirm or deny this tendency, which is only displayed with nonhuman controllers.

The second peculiarity is represented by the increased influence of conditions on agreement patterns. All the numbers reported above indicate that Quranic Arabic represents a more innovative type, as far as agreement is concerned, than the language of the *Muʕallaqāt*. In other words, this means that the process of resemanticization had reached a more advanced stage. This fact has some repercussions on the agreement system, which can be summarized in the following quote from Jürg Fleischer, Rieken, and Widmer (2015, 21): "when formal [i.e. syntactic] agreement loses its dominant role, conditions seem to gain more importance for the realization of agreement rules."[34] Conditions can be generically defined as those factors that affect agreement and that are not, strictly speaking, features of the controller or of the target (Corbett 2006, 5). Word order and quantification are, for instance, two of the most widely studied agreement conditions. Word order has already been discussed in § 2.4 (see also § 2.3.9), while quantification is the simplest and most direct way of measuring individuation. Controllers quantified by low numerals (<10), in fact, almost systematically trigger syntactic agreement, even if they are collectives, as evident from the following sample:

(9) [...] *qāla* *fa=xuḏ* ***arbaʕatan mina ṭ=ṭayri***
say.3.PFV.M.SG and=IMP.take.2.M.SG four from DEF=bird.COLL
*fa=ṣur=**hunna*** *ʔilay=ka* *ṯumma* *ǧʕal* *ʕalā*
and=IMP.twist.2.M.SG=them.F to=you.M then IMP.make.2.M.SG on
kulli *ǧabalin* *min=**hunna*** *ǧuzʔan* *ṯumma* *dʕu=**hunna***
every mountain from=them.F part then IMP.call.2.M.SG-them.F
***ya-ʔtī-na**=ka* *saʕyan* [...]
3.IPFV-come-F.PL=you.M.SG running
'[...] Said He, take four birds, and twist them to thee, then set a part of them on every hill, then summon them, and they will come to thee running. [...]' (II, 260)

In a formally motivated system, such as the ones found in Northwest and East Semitic, knowing the features of the controller (i.e. its gender and number) is usually sufficient to predict what kind of agreement will obtain. When the formal rules of agreement assigning are weakened, on the other hand, this information may no longer be sufficient. Let us confront the following samples, both taken from the Quran:

---

34 Conversely, whenever formal agreement gains ground, the impact of conditions decreases. In the so called *schema attikon*, for instance, neuter plurals generally failed to trigger plural verbal agreement in Attic and Koiné Greek. The occurrence of plural agreement was usually triggered by a condition, i.e. the degree of animacy of the controller (the higher its animacy, the higher the possibility of plural agreement). In subsequent stages of Ancient Greek, however, formal agreement gradually became the norm, and the animacy condition lost its role (Fleischer, Rieken, and Widmer 2015, 20–22).

(10) *yasʔalūna=ka* *māḏā* *ʔuḥilla* *la=hum*
3.IPFV:ask:M.PL=you what permit.PASS.3.PFV.M.SG to=them.M
qul *ʔuḥilla* *la=kumu*
IMP.say.2.M.SG permit.PASS.3.PFV.M.SG to=you.M.PL
ṭ=ṭayyibātu *wa=mā* *ʕallamtum* *mina*
DEF=good.thing:F.PL and=what teach:2.PFV.M.PL from
l=ǧawāriḥi *mukallibīna*
DEF=predatory.animal.PL ACT.PTCP.train.as.dog:M.PL
*tuʕallimūna=**hunna*** *mimmā* *ʕallama=kumu*
2.IPFV:teach:M.PL=them.F from.what teach.3.PFV.M.SG=you.M.PL
Llāhu *fa=kulū* *mimmā* ***ʔamsak-na*** *ʕalay=kum* [...]
God and=IMP.eat:2.M.PL from.what catch-3.PFV.F.PL on=you.M.PL
'They will question thee what is permitted them. Say: The good things are permitted you; and such hunting creatures as you teach, training them as hounds, and teaching them as God has taught you—eat what they seize for you [...]' (V, 4)

(11) *wa=ʔiḏā* ***l=wuḥūšu*** ***ḥušir-at***
and=when DEF=wild.beast.PL gather.PASS-3.PFV.F.SG
'When the savage beasts shall be mustered' (LXXXI, 5)

In samples 10–11, the controllers are both definite internal plurals designating animals. While *al=ǧawāriḥ* 'DEF=predatory.animal.PL' triggers feminine plural agreement, however, *al=wuḥūš* 'DEF-wild.beast.PL' triggers feminine singular agreement.[35] The main difference affecting agreement choices, here, does not concern the controller, but the target. The verbal target, in fact, is active in 10 and passive in 11. This, in turn, changes the semantic role of the grammatical subject, which is an agent in 10 and a patient in 11. The semantic role of the subject, in fact, is an important factor in determining agreement choices in Quranic Arabic, as showed in D'Anna (2020b), with reference to plurals, and in Dror (2016, 129–130), with reference to collectives. The main semantic roles that the grammatical subject can have are summarized below (Comrie 1989, 58):

1. John closed the door (agent);
2. The wind closed the door (force);

35 The sample was chosen among many others because the two controllers present identical profiles, but it should be remembered that Q LXXXI, 5 is part of a series of verses (LXXXI, 1–14) featuring an *-at* rhyme.

3. The key closed the door (instrument);
4. John felt lonely (experiencer);
5. John was hurt in an accident (patient).

When the verb occurs in the passive form, the semantic role of the grammatical subject is restricted to patient. In pre-Islamic Arabic (*Muʕallaqāt*), patient subjects can still trigger feminine plural agreement in their verbal targets, as shown in the following sample, also featuring a broken plural (and indefinite) controller:

(12) *wa=taḥmilu-nā* *ġadāta* *r=rawʕi* ***ǧurdun***
and=3.IPFV.F.SG:carry-us morning DEF=battle hairless.PL
ʕurif-na *la=nā* *naqāʔidu* *wa=**ftulī-na***
know.PASS-3.PFV.F.PL to=us captured.PL and=wean.PASS-3.PFV.F.PL
'In the day of battle, well-bred horses, scanty of hair, carry us, which are known as belonging to us,—horses captured from the enemy, and which were weaned from their mothers' (ʕAmr, 84)

In Quranic Arabic, the process of resemanticization seems to have gone further (as also evidenced by the statistics reported above) and conditions have gained more importance, so that passive verbs never occur in the feminine plural. When the grammatical subject of an active verb is also the agent, on the contrary, the verb is more likely to occur in the feminine plural. This also happens when the subject is a broken plural (as in the case of *al=ǧawāriḥ*) or even a collective, as in the following sample:

(13) *ʔaw* *lam* *yaraw* *ʔilā* *ṭ=**ṭayri*** *fawqa=hum*
or NEG IPFV.3:see:M.PL.APOC to DEF=bird.COLL over=them.M
ṣāff-ātin *wa=**ya-qbiḍ-na***
ACT.PTCP.spread-F.PL and=IPFV.3-contract-3.F.PL
'Have they not regarded the birds above them spreading their wings, and closing them? [...]' (LXVII, 19)

It should be noted that the opposite is not true, i.e. the fact that the grammatical subject is also the semantic agent of an action verb does not guarantee that the nonhuman plural controller will trigger feminine plural agreement. In typological terms, this tendency constitutes a unilateral implication (Comrie 1989, 92–93), which can be expressed as follows: "If the verb is in the feminine plural, then the grammatical subject (plural nonhuman) is semantically the agent of an action verb." The proposition: "If the grammatical subject (plural nonhuman) is semantically the agent of an action verb, then the verb is in the feminine plural", on the other hand, is false, since feminine singular also occurs in the Quran in that position. Dror (2016) offers, although with reference to collective controllers, a list of 8 conditions that influence agreement. A full exemplification of such conditions (and others) goes beyond the scope of this section, but most of them are also valid for plural controllers. Even considering all the possible conditions, some occurrences seem to baffle any attempt at a syntactic or semantic explanation:

(14)	*wa=**n=naxla***	***bāsiq-ātin***	*la=**hā***	*ṭalʕun*	*nadīd*
	and=DEF=palm.COLL	ACT.PTCP.tall-F.PL	to=her	cluster	arranged

'And tall palm-trees with spathes compact' (L, 10)

Sample 14 features a nonhuman collective controlling an active participle from a state verb, functioning as an attributive adjective (despite the lack of agreement in definiteness), and a personal pronoun. While the personal pronoun displays agreement in the feminine singular, as expected, the adjective agrees in the feminine plural. Although adjectives are notoriously the most conservative category, no condition here justifies the occurrence of feminine plural agreement. Given that the controller is morphologically masculine singular, the agreement pattern cannot even be labelled as syntactic agreement (but see § 3.4.1). This conundrum does not detract from our description of agreement patterns in the Quran. Quite simply, the text here features a highly unlikely agreement choice, which already attracted the attention of classical exegetes. This means that, by the standards of VII century Arabic, this agreement pattern is unexpected and in need of an explanation.

> A possible explanation for this shift is the rhetorical effect of an adjective in the plural. Thus, Rāzī in his reference to the meaning of *bāsiqāt*, states that this form emphasizes the strength of the palm-trees over a vineyard which requires careful treatment, while the palm trees are strong and yield fruit every year.
>
> DROR 2016b, 133

Dror here quotes and translates Rāzī's (1149–1209 CE) commentary, in which the illustrious Sunni theologian gives an explanation that basically makes reference, without using the modern terms, to rhetorical and pragmatic factors. Emphasizing a term through the employment of feminine plural (for plurals, syntactic) agreement, in fact, is very similar to what De Vos (2015, 133) describes when writing that syntactic agreement can be used, in the varieties of Dutch she is describing, as "... some sort of salience marker". The role of pragmatics is even more prominent when agreement with collective controllers is involved. Collectives, as a consequence, will be the object of the next subsection.

3.4.1 *Collectives in the Quran: Two Possibilities of Semantic Agreement*

Agreement patterns with collective controllers, both in the Quran and in Arabic as a whole, warrant further discussion, and have been the object of detailed studies (Dror 2016a; 2016b; D'Anna 2020a). Let us go back to the definition of syntactic vs semantic agreement provided in Corbett (2006, 155):

> In the most straightforward cases syntactic agreement (sometimes called 'agreement ad formam', 'formal agreement' or 'grammatical agreement') is agreement consistent with the form of the controller (the committee has decided). Semantic agreement (or 'agreement ad sensum', 'notional agreement', 'logical agreement' or 'synesis') is agreement consistent with its meaning (the committee have decided).

As far as plurals are concerned, this distinction provides a nice methodological tool, allowing us to classify agreement patterns in a rather straightforward manner: with reference to plural controllers, plural agreement is syntactic agreement, while feminine singular agreement is semantically motivated. Let us now examine the following three samples, all featuring the same collective controller:

(15) *tanziʕu* *n=nāsa* *kaʔanna=hum* *ʔaʕǧāzu*
IPFV.3.F.SG:pluck DEF=people.COLL as.if=them.M stump.PL
naxlin ***munqaʕirin***
palm.COLL uprooted.M.SG
'Plucking up men as if they were stumps of uprooted palm-trees' (LIV, 20).

(16) *wa=zurūʕin* *wa=**naxlin*** *ṭalʕu=**hā***[36] *haḍīmun*
and=crop.PL and=palm.COLL cluster=her slender
'Sown fields, and palms with slender spathes' (XXVI, 148)

(17) *wa=**n=naxla*** ***bāsiq-ātin*** *la=**hā*** *ṭalʕun* *naḍīd*
and=DEF=palm.COLL ACT.PTCP.tall-F.PL to=her cluster arranged
'And tall palm-trees with spathes compact' (L, 10)

36 Q LXIX presents another sample of *naxl* featuring feminine singular agreement, this time on an adjectival target: *naxlin xāwiy-atin* "palm.COLL empty-F.SG".

Collective controllers are described by Dror as being "morphologically singular (or unmarked form) with multiple reference, singular or plural" (Dror 2016b, 105). In Dror's analysis, this means that they can only allow a wholistic or distributive interpretation. In the wholistic interpretation, the collective is seen as a unit, while in the distributive one the speaker makes reference to the single members that make up the collectivity (Dror 2016b, 104). Let us now turn to the analysis of the three samples reported above.

The controller *naxl* is, morphologically speaking, a masculine singular. In 15, it triggers masculine singular agreement in the attributive adjective, in a textbook example of syntactic agreement where the collective is given a wholistic interpretation. Samples 16 and 17 feature, respectively, feminine singular and feminine plural agreement, neither of which corresponds to the form of the controller. Per Corbett's definition, as a consequence, they must both be considered as specimens of semantic agreement, although with different semantic nuances. Feminine plural indicates a distributive interpretation, unlikely with nonhuman controllers but here due to pragmatic reasons (see § 3.4). While the feminine plural represents standard syntactic agreement with nonhuman plural controllers, here it must be considered as semantically motivated, since the controller is morphologically a masculine singular.[37] Feminine singular agreement, on the other hand, does not stem from either a wholistic nor a distributive interpretation of the collective. Here the controller is not seen as a unit, its plurality is recognized. At the same time, however, the plurality it expresses is not individuated enough to allow a full distributive interpretation. The speaker, thus, opts for the [-individuated] plural agreement patterns already discussed with reference to plural controllers, i.e. feminine singular. Collective controllers, as a consequence, display three possible agreement choices:[38]

I. syntactic agreement: wholistic interpretation;
II. semantic I: distributive, plural agreement in accordance with the agreement class of the controller;
III. semantic II: [-individuated] plural, feminine singular agreement independently of the agreement class of the controller.

The following three samples show the same three different agreement choices with the collective human controller *qawm* 'people.COLL', which is also, morphologically speaking, masculine singular:[39]

37 Agreement, thus, occurs in the feminine plural because the controller *naxl* 'palm.COLL' belongs to agreement class III (see § 2.3.4).

38 The same happens in spoken Arabic. See § 2.3.3.3.

39 Dror tries to solve the impasse claiming that *qawm* 'people.COLL' is "morphologically

(18) [...] *fa=ʔin* *kāna* *min* ***qawmin*** ***ʕaduwwin*** *la=kum* [...]
and=if be.3.PFV.M.SG from people.COLL hostile.M.SG to=you.M.PL
'[...] If he belongs to a people at enmity with you [...]' (IV, 92)

(19) [...] *wa=naǧǧi=nī* *mina* ***l=qawmi***
and=IMP.save.2.M.SG=me from DEF=people.COLL
ḍ=ḍālim-īna [...][40]
DEF=ACT.PTCP.oppress-M.PL
'[...] and do Thou deliver me from the people of the evildoers' (LXVI, 11)

(20) ***kaḏḏab-at*** ***qawmu*** *Nūḥin* *al=mursalīna*[41]
belie-PFV.3.F.SG people.COLL Noah DEF=PASS.PTCP.send:M.PL
'The people of Noah called the envoys liars' (XXVI, 105).

It is worth reminding that syntactic agreement does not automatically coincide with masculine singular agreement. In the case of morphologically feminine singular controllers, such as *ʔummat* 'community, nation', in fact, syntactic agreement is obviously in the feminine singular. This means that, in such cases, the distinction between syntactic and semantic agreement II is blurred. The case of *ʔummat* 'community, nation', *ḏurriyyat* 'progeny' and other morphologically feminine singular collective nouns designing humans is particularly complex. We have already seen that, when the speaker opts for syntactic agreement, this naturally occurs in the feminine singular. When semantic agreement I (distributive) occurs, we would consequently expect feminine plural agreement.[42] A collective noun designating humans, however, logically includes both men and women. At this point, the gender resolution rules of Arabic come into play, prescribing the employment of the masculine plural agreement (or, alternatively, of broken plural) when mixed groups of humans are being referred to (D'Anna 2020a, 164–165). This results in a particularly unusual agreement pattern, schematized in the following table and exemplified in the three subsequent samples:

masculine or feminine singular (Dror 2016b, 127)", a claim that is then extended to all nonhuman collective nouns. Independent evidence for the existence of such a large class of double-gender nouns, however, is lacking, so that the claim can be rejected. See D'Anna (2020a).

40 Although rhyme surely plays a role here (verses 10–12 all end in *-īna*), masculine plural agreement with *qawm* "people.COLL" is quite common in the Quran.

41 Samples 15–20 are drawn from D'Anna (2020a, 156–157).

42 The agreement pattern feminine singular—masculine plural is otherwise unattested. Nouns triggering feminine singular agreement when singular, in fact, always trigger feminine plural agreement when syntactic agreement is chosen in the plural.

TABLE 3.6 Agreement patterns with morphologically feminine singular human collectives

Feminine singular human collectives		
Syntactic agreement	**Semantic I (distr.)**	**Semantic II ([-ind.])**
Feminine singular	Masculine plural	Feminine singular

(21) *hunālika daʕā Zakariyyā rabba=hu hab l=ī*
There pray.3.PFV.M.SG Zachariah Lord=his IMP.give.2.M.SG to=me
min ladun=ka ***ḏurriyyatan ṭayyib-atan*** *ʔinna=ka*
from at=you.M.SG progeny.F.SG.COLL[43] good-F.SG COMP=you.M.SG
samīʕu d=duʕāʔi
hearer DEF=prayer
'Then Zachariah prayed to his Lord saying, Lord, give me of Thy goodness a goodly offspring. Yea, Thou hearest prayer' (III, 38)

(22) [...] *wa=ʔaṣāba=hu l=kibaru wa=la=hu* ***ḏurriyyatun***
and=hit.3.PFV.M.SG=him DEF=old.age and=at=him progeny. F.SG.COLL
ḍuʕafāʔu [...]
weak.PL
'[...] then old age smites him, and he has seed, but weaklings [...]' (II, 266)

(23) *wa=min qawmi Mūsā* ***ʔummatun ya-hd-ūna***
and=from people.COLL Moses nation. F.SG.COLL 3.IPFV-guide-M.PL
bi=l=ḥaqqi wa=bi=hi ***ya-ʕdil-ūna***
by=DEF=truth and=by=him 3.IPFV-act.justly-M.PL
'Of the people of Moses there is a nation who guide by the truth, and by it act with justice' (VII, 159)

43 Here and in the next two samples, the gloss F.SG. has been added to COLL to draw the reader's attention to the fact that the collective noun is *also* morphologically feminine, due to the syncretism between different categories, all expressed by means of the morpheme *-at* (Hasselbach 2014b, 337).

After clarifying the different agreement options, some final considerations on agreement tendencies with collectives in the Quran are necessary. The possibility of two different semantic agreements means that collective controllers display contrasting semantic factors, which need to be solved case-by-case by the speaker. In other words, the speaker who does not opt for syntactic agreement needs to choose between a distributive plural interpretation (semantic agreement I) and a [-individuated] one (semantic agreement II). In some cases, the nature of the controller directs the choice. Human controllers, for instance, are intrinsically high on the individuation hierarchy, which pushes toward the distributive interpretation. With the collective *qawm* 'people.COLL', for instance, post-controller targets systematically display masculine plural agreement, the only exception being *min qawmin ʕaḍuwwin* "from people.COLL hostile.M.SG".[44] This is the place where semantics and pragmatics meet. A distributive interpretation, which overrides the collective nature of the noun by addressing all its members one by one, is bound to achieve a more striking effect on the audience, when compared to a [-individuated] one. Since it does not single out the listeners, in fact, a collective intepretation gives them the possibility to consider the injunction / reproach / warning as not directed to them, but rather to the other members of the audience (Brown and Levinson 1987, 198–199). Given the nature of the Quran, whose aim was the conversion of its listeners to the new faith, it makes sense that human collectives tend to be given a distributive interpretation, thus triggering plural agreement, rather than a [-individuated] one. As seen with reference to the expression *wa=n=naxla bāsiq-ātin* "and=DEF=palm.COLL ACT.PTCP.tall-F.PL" (L, 10), moreover, a distributive interpretation may also occur with non-human collectives, with the aim of adding rhetoric emphasis to the utterance.

Further evidence to support this claim comes from the analysis of collectives in modern journalistic Arabic (Dror 2016a). Although the systems of pre-Classical and Modern Standard Arabic considerably differ, the three agreement options for collective humans are available to both. The detached style of journalistic prose, which usually describes the events without showing an active engagement, contrary to what happens in the Quran, results in a strong preva-

44 *ʕaduww* 'hostile', being in the *faʕūl* form, does not agree in gender and number. Samples of masculine singular agreement with *qawm* are to be found, in the Quran, only with verbs preceding the controller (see, for instance, Q VI, 80), but also occur in the *ḥadīṯ* literature. See for instance *ḏālika l-qawm* occurring in both Mulim's (d. 875) *Ṣaḥīḥ* (IV, 1182) and ʔAbū Dāwūd's (d. 889) *Sunan* (I, 1853).

lence of the wholistic interpretation, with the consequent employment of singular agreement (Dror 2016a, 326).[45]

3.5 Post-7th Century Poetry

The analysis of pre-Islamic poetry and the Quran provided a clear picture of the system of agreement obtaining in at least some varieties of Arabic in the 6th and early 7th century. At that time, Arabic was only spoken within the borders of the Arabian Peninsula and its outer fringes. Dialectal variation between different areas and tribes obviously occurred at that stage too, as testified by the accounts of the first grammarians in the late 8th century (Rabin 1951; Magidow 2013; Holes 2018, 6–7). In the centuries immediately following the age of conquests, however, the Arabic language witnessed a rapid and extraordinary spread, which resulted in speakers of Arabic being found in a wide territory stretching from the Iberian Peninsula (conquered in 711 CE) to Transoxiana (whose conquest started even earlier, after 642 CE). For this reason, the selection of corpora to investigate what is usually known as "diasporic" Arabic is a much harder task, due to the high number of variables involved when dealing with post-7th century written Arabic. In most cases, in fact, we lack the basic sociolinguistic information concerning the intensity of language contact in a specific area and even the first language of the writer, or the languages they had been exposed to. In such a situation, it is clear that no corpus can claim to represent Arabic as a whole, as was probably the case even in pre-diasporic Arabic.

Up to the 7th century, all the varieties of Arabic for which we have documentation appear to share one and the same agreement system, even though the distribution of its categories varied and the compared analysis of pre-Islamic poetry and the *Muʕallaqāt* shows evidence of a change in progress. Starting from the 8th century, however, another system starts emerging in the written language that will be known as Classical Arabic, which will be the object of section 3.6. For now, it is sufficient to say that, after the 8th century, the analysis yields dramatically different results depending on which corpus is chosen. This fact is evident if we look at Belnap and Gee (1994, 127), where the analysis of al-Masʕūdi's historical work (10th century) shows a situation in which no

45 Dror does not distinguish, in her analysis, between syntactic and Semantic Agreement II. For a reassessment of agreement patterns with collectives (with specific reference to the Quran), see D'Anna (2020a).

variation occurs, and the "new" agreement system (featuring mandatory feminine singular agreement with plural nonhuman controllers) has completely replaced the old one. Al-Ḥarīrī's *maqāmāt* (11th century), on the other hand, still display some residual variation, which means that ornate prose, as a literary genre, behaved more conservatively in preserving the old system, at least partially. The analysis in Belnap and Gee (1994) and Belnap and Shabaneh (1992), from this perspective, is skewed by the discrepancy of the literary genres from which their corpora have been extracted. In particular, the complete absence of poetry in the post-7th century data leaves a lacuna that needs to be filled, given that no prose is present in their pre-7th century sources (samples of pre-Islamic poetry and the Quran). A cursory glance at poetry in the first few centuries after the Islamic conquests, in fact, quickly shows that the old system survives well beyond the 10th–11th century—while its disappearance would seem to be complete by looking at the data presented by Belnap and Gee (1994, 127). At the same time, different varieties of prose need to be analyzed alongside historical and geographical works. This section provides a bird's-eye view of poetry up to the late 13th century, to investigate whether and how the system described for pre-Islamic Arabic survived after the age of conquests. At this point, the construction of a representative corpus to run statistics is an extremely hard task. Grouping together different poets from the same age, in fact, would result in lumping together speakers (or, better, writers) who lived in different cities, often many thousands of miles distant from each other, in completely different linguistic environments (different contact languages, different sociolinguistic profiles etc.). At the same time, analyzing in depth the *dīwān* of a single poet would probably provide enough material for some basic statistics, but it would only represent written Arabic in a specific town or area, at a time when connections (and, consequently, the spread of linguistic traits) between different parts of the Islamic world were much slower than today. For these reasons, such a task will not be attempted here. We will limit ourselves to showing samples from different ages and areas, hoping that in-depth analyses of more circumscribed regions will be carried out in the future.

Poets from the earliest Islamic era are usually known as *muxaḍramūn*, a term which designates someone who was born during the *Ǧāhiliyya* (the age of ignorance, i.e. pre-Islamic times) but lived through the Islamic Revelation and the age of conquests. We have chosen sample poems for the early Islamic age from the collection published in Ḥusain (1938), since it avoids the most famous poets, whose works are more likely to have been edited by copyists. The fist sample is a poem by the poet-warrior Suwayd ibn al-Kurāʕ, of the Banī ʕUkl tribe, who lived long before Islam but was still active during ʕUṯmān's caliphate (644–656 CE) (Ḥusain 1938, 108). In his poem, plural agreement (both feminine and broken) with nonhuman plural controllers abounds, as evident from the two samples reported below:[46]

(24) *ka=ʔaxnasi mawšiyyi l=ʔarkāʕi rāʕa=hu*
like=snub.nosed spotted DEF=shank.PL frighten.3.PFV.M.SG=him
bi=Rawḍati Maʕrūfin ***layālin ṣawāridu***
at=Rawḍat Maʕrūf night.PL cold.PL
'Like a snub-nosed antelope-bull, having spotted shanks, which was frightened, at (the place called) Rawḍat Maʕrūf, by cold nights' (Suwayd, 6) (Ḥusain 1938, 125)

(25) *ʔiḏā karra fī=hā karratan ka=ʔanna=hā dafīnu*
when attack.3.PFV.M.SG in=her attack as=if=her buried
niqālin *yaxtafī=**hinna** sāridu*
sandal.PL 3.IPFV:hide.M.SG=them.F cobbler
'When he made an attack amongst them, they were like sandals buried in the ground, which a cobbler hides' (Suwayd, 13) (Ḥusain 1938, 126)

The second poet from the early Islamic era is ʔAbū Zubayd, a Christian poet of the Banū Ṭayyiʔ who also died during ʕUṯmān's caliphate. As is to be expected, agreement patterns in his poetry do not differ from what we have just observed in Suwayd's work, as evident from the long quote reported below:

(26) *māniʕī bāḥata l=ʕirāqi mina n=nāsi*
ACT.PTCP.defend:M.PL open.space DEF=Iraq from DEF=people.COLL
*bi=**ǧurdin*** ***ta-ʕdū*** *bi=miṯli l=ʔusūdi kulla*
with=short.haired.PL 3.IPFV.F.SG-run by=like DEF=lion.PL every
ʕāmin ***ya-lṯim-na*** *qawman bi=kaffi d=dahri ḥumqan*
year 3.IPFV-smite-F.PL people.COLL with=palm DEF=time dumb.PL
wa=ʔaxḏa ḥayyin ǧarīdin ***ǧāziʕ-ātin*** *ʔilay=him*
and=taking tribe detached ACT.PTCP.march-F.PL to=them.M
xuššāʕa l=ʔawdāti ***yu-sqī-na*** *min*
low.PL DEF=valley.PL 3.IPFV-give.to.drink.PASS-F.PL from
ḍayāḥi l=madīdi ***musbiq-ātin*** *ka=ʔanna=**hunna***
milk.with.water DEF=long ACT.PTCP.go.forth-F.PL as=if=them.F
qanā l=hindi wa=nassā l=waǧīfu šaġba
lance DEF=India and=make.forget.3.PFV.M.SG DEF=running tumult

46 Translations are partially drawn from Ḥusain (1938), with only occasional corrections.

l=marūdi *mustaqīman* *bī=**hā***
DEF=recalcitrant.PL ACT.PTCP.be.rightly.led.M.SG by=her
l=hudātu *ʔiḏā* ***ya-qṭaʕ-na*** *naǧdan* ***waṣal-na**=hu*
DEF=leader.PL when 3.IPFV-cross-F.PL high.land join-3.PFV.F.PL=him
bi=nuǧūdi
with=high.land.PL
'Defending the boundary of Iraq from the people with short-haired steeds running like lions, that smite some people every year with the clenched palm of time and with the seizing of a detached tribe. Marching towards them through the low valleys, being given to drink milk mixed with flour-water, going forth, as though, they were the lances of India. The running made (them) forget the trotting of the refractory (horses). The leaders (being) rightly led by them; when they cross a high-land they join it with (other) high-lands' (ʔAbū Zubayd, 33–37) (Ḥusain 1938, 150–151)

As evident from the three samples reported above, all the agreement patterns associated with nonhuman plurals in pre-Islamic Arabic (feminine plural, feminine singular and broken plural) are still present in 7th century poetry. Concerning their distribution, there is not much that can be said, due to the lack of a sizeable corpus. A cursory glance at the samples, and at the poems they were drawn from, gives the impression that the distribution of agreement patterns is less consistent than it was in earlier poetry. One of the methodological issues of using poetic corpora, as seen in section 3.2, was the possible influence of meter and rhyme on the choice of words and, consequently, of agreement patterns. The issue was answered empirically, by ascertaining that the data extracted from the corpus all pointed in the same direction, which is not compatible with the expected randomness of patterns dictated by meter and rhyme. One of the patterns that most clearly emerged from the analysis of pre-Islamic poetry was the co-occurrence of broken plural and feminine singular, in a twofold way:

I. feminine singular agreement was more frequently triggered by controllers in the broken plural;
II. when an attributive adjective displayed agreement in the broken plural, other targets (i.e. verbs and pronouns) showed a marked tendency toward feminine singular agreement. In fact, the percentage of broken plural + feminine singular agreement in attributive adjectives almost perfectly equated the percentage of feminine singular agreement with pronouns[47] (for a diachronic explanation of such a trend, see section 3.1).

47 The agreement patterns of verbs, on the other hand, were compatible, but skewed by the

The samples reported above seem to partially contradict these tendencies. In *niqālin yaxtafī=hinna* "sandal.PL 3.IPFV:hide.M.SG=them.F.PL", in fact, the inanimate (and quite generic) broken plural controller *niqāl* triggers feminine plural agreement in the pronoun, although pronouns referring to inanimate controllers were the category which was most affected by the spread of feminine singular agreement already in pre-Islamic poetry.[48] In the three verses quoted from ʔAbū Zubayd's poem, on the other hand, agreement is variable. It first switches from feminine singular to feminine plural, which is quite common and has been described in Prochàzka and Gabsi (2017, 246) with reference to urban Tunisian, D'Anna (2017, 109) with reference to Fezzani and Holes (2016, 334–335) with reference to Eastern Arabian dialects. The major problem with our sample is that agreement then switches back to feminine singular and, again, to feminine plural. This behavior, although not unattested in single utterances, is much less common. Taken together, the two poems give the impression (not supported by statistical analyses) that the agreement system started losing its internal consistency. The agreement categories are all there, yet their distribution does not adhere to the principles outlined in § 2.3 with the same regularity as before. The same happens with another *muxaḍram* poet, ʔAbū Xirāš, whose poems likewise feature occurrences of unusual agreement patterns (Ḥusain 1938, 181–197).

If one had to judge based on these poems, the objection to the choice of poetry would probably be correct, since the choice of agreement patterns seems partially random and potentially dictated by meter and rhyme. Belnap and Gee (1994) attributed the generalization of feminine singular agreement with nonhuman plural controllers to the large number of non-native speakers of Arabic who started using the new language in the written medium. While their idea is absolutely convincing with regard to the generalization of the feminine singular pattern, what we observe here seems to be an initial loss of consistency of the old system. A speculative hypothesis concerning why this happened might have to do with the period of social upheaval and profound changes that accompanied the age of conquests and affected native speakers of Arabic. During the military campaigns, in fact, it is most probable that young speakers left their ancestral homeland to fight as soldiers, being exposed to speakers of other tribes / areas and to speakers of other languages. It is equally probable that older speakers, who usually counterbalance and check the spread of innovations, did not partake in the campaigns. A kind of

---

influence of independent factors, such as the semantic role of the subject (agent vs patient and/or experiencer) and the nature of the verb (action vs state).

48 Pronouns feature 80.9% of feminine singular agreement in the *Muʕallaqāt*.

poetry that had existed for centuries and that was intended for tribal recitation, thus, quickly transformed into a form of court poetry. Post-7th century poetry cherished a past that no longer existed, and of which younger poets lacked any direct experience. From a linguistic point of view, we might say that the chain of transmission was not broken, but somewhat altered and weakened. We are not saying here that command of Arabic of younger speakers was severely impaired, but that the principles behind semantic vs syntactic agreement choices might have been blurred in some cases.[49] The examples of Audring (2009) and De Vos (2015), for instance, show that even in a much more stable society such as the contemporary Dutch one, younger speakers of dialectal varieties might fail to acquire a complete command of complex gender systems, starting reanalysis processes. In order to substantiate these impressions, however, much larger corpora of 7th and 8th century poetry should be analyzed, which goes far beyond the scope of this diachronic reconstruction.

It is important to underline that the pre-Islamic patterns of agreement continued in 7th century poetry are not limited to plural agreement with nonhuman plural controllers, but also include feminine singular with plural human ones, as evident from the following verse of al-Naḏḏār ibn Hāšim al-ʔAsadī (Ḥusain 1938, 101):

(27) *wa=qad* *ʔarā=nī* *fī* *mulimmāti* *ṣ=ṣibā*
and=at.times 1.IPFV.SG:see=me in misfortune:F.PL DEF=youth
ʔayyāma ***ʔaṭġān=ī*** ***tu-nāġī***
day.PL woman.on.sedan.PL=my 3.IPFV.F.SG-whisper
l=ʔaṭġāna
DEF= woman.on.sedan.PL
'And I see myself in the visitations of youthful folly, in the days when my womenfolk travelling were cheering other women travelling' (al-Naḏḏār, 6)

The situation does not seem to change during the Umayyad Caliphate, spanning from the late 7th century to the first half of the 8th (661–750 CE). Plural agreement with nonhuman controllers still coexists with feminine singular, as evident from the following sample, drawn from a poem by Mālik ibn al-Rayb:

49 It should also be pointed out that most poets probably spoke Arabic dialects that had shifted toward different agreement systems, for instance losing the possibility of feminine plural agreement.

(28) *wa=darru ḏ=ḏibāʔi* ***s=sāniḥ-āti*** *ʕašiyyatan*
and=milk DEF=gazelle.PL DEF=ACT.PTCP.present.itself-F.PL at.night
yu-xabbir-na *ʔann=ī hālikun min*
3.IPFV-inform-F.PL COMP=me ACT.PTCP.perish:M.SG from
*ʔamāmi=**hā***
in.front.of=her
'And what gazelles they were who came forth in the afternoon, announcing that I would perish away from them' (Mālik, 6)

Semantic agreement overall seems to be on the rise. The following two verses, again drawn from Mālik ibn al-Rayb's poem, show the nonhuman collective controller *baqar* "cattle.COLL" triggering broken plural in the attributive adjectives, feminine singular in the pronoun but feminine plural in the verbs, similarly to what already observed in the Quran (see section 3.4) (Ḥusain 1938, 175):

(28) *ʔiḏā l=qawmu ḥallū=hā ǧamīʕan*
when DEF=people.COLL alight:3.PFV.M.PL=her all
wa=ʔanzalū bi=hā ***baqaran ḥūra***
and=bring.down:3.PFV.M.PL at=her cattle.COLL white.and.black.PL
l=ʕuyūni ***sawāǧiyā raʕay=na*** *wa=qad*
DEF=eye.PL ACT.PTCP.be.calm.PL graze=3.PFV.F.PL And
*kāna ḏ=ḏulāmu yaǧunnu=**hā*** ***ya-suf-na***
be.3.PFV.M.SG DEF=darkness 3.IPFV:veil.M.SG=her 3.IPFV-browse-F.PL
l=xuzāmā ġaḍḍa=hu wa=l=ʔaqāḥiyā
DEF=lavender fresh=his and=DEF=chamomile.PL
'When the people all alighted there and brought down there quiet antelopes, having beautiful, black eyes, that grazed, while the darkness had enveloped them, browsing on the twigs of lavender and the chamomiles' (Mālik, 41–42).

During the 8th century, moreover, interindividual variation also seems to increase, which is compatible with a period of linguistic instability. Some poets, in particular, employ feminine singular agreement far more than others do. Al-Qaṭirān al-Saʕdī, a poet from the Umayyad period, addresses one of his poems to the Caliph ʕAbd al-Mālik (685–705 CE). In the 58 verses that make up the poem, however, he never uses plural agreement with nonhuman plurals, even when specified by low numerals (Ḥusain 1938, 30):

(30) *wa=ağdala* *min* ***tisʕi*** ***labūni*** *bni* *Rāfiʕi*
and=contend.3.PFV.M.SG from nine milch.camel.PL son Rāfiʕ
*bi=**maḏlūm-ati*** *l=ʔarbābi* *lağwan*
by=PASS.PTCP.oppress:F.SG DEF=owner.PL mistake
*faṣīlu=**hā***
young.weaned.camel=her
'And he contended for nine milch camels of Ibn Rāfiʕ, (which he got by) oppressing their owners and without any regard to their young ones' (al-Qaṭirān, 40).

Despite the exclusive employment of feminine singular agreement with nonhuman plural controllers, al-Qaṭirān's poem reflects a more advanced stage of resemanticization and not the kind of standardization we find in Classical and Modern Standard Arabic, where feminine singular is mandatory with nonhumans. This fact appears clear from the parallel extensive usage of feminine singular agreement with human controllers, which never became a standardized trait in Classical / Modern Standard Arabic (Ḥusain 1938, 30):

(31) *wa=lākin* *tadaʕʕayta* *l=xafārata*
and=but claim:2.PFV.M.SG DEF=right.of.protection
wa=ʕtadat ***suʕātun*** *min* *s=sulṭāni*
and=attack:3.PFV.F.SG ACT.PTCP.chase.PL from DEF=government
anta *nazīlu=**hā***
you.M.SG guest=her
'But thou didst claim the right of protection, and there fell (upon us) Followers of the Government, amongst whom thou hadst settled' (al-Qaṭirān, 48).

The samples so far discussed show that the three-class agreement system featured in pre-Islamic Arabic and gender-distinguishing modern dialectal varieties survived well within the 8th century. In Belnap and Gee (1994, 127), all post-Quran sources are prose works, which evidently skews the data. The only representative of 8th century Arabic, in fact, is Ibn Hišām, in which feminine singular agreement reaches 94% of the occurrences. The picture emerging from historical and geographic prose works, thus, is quite different from what observed in poetry, which is not surprising. In poetry, the old system is better preserved, even though the distribution of agreement patterns seems to be shifting.

In Belnap and Gee (1994, 127), moreover, the system featuring mandatory feminine singular agreement with plural nonhuman controllers seems to have completely replaced the old one starting from the 10th century. Only the *Maqāmāt* by al-Ḥarīrī (11th century) display some residual variation (with feminine singular still reaching 92%), but in both al-Masʕūdī (10th century) and Ibn Xaldūn (14th century) feminine singular agreement appears to have become mandatory with nonhuman plural controllers (100% in both cases). In order to crosscheck these results with poetic data, two famous poets have been randomly selected from different centuries and from different areas of the Arabic-speaking world, namely al-Mutanabbī (915–965 CE) and al-Būṣīrī (1212–1294 CE).

ʔAbū al-Ṭayyib al-Mutanabbī, hailing from Kufa (Iraq), is one of the most famous poets of the Arab literature. After spending considerable time with the Bedouins in the desert of the Arabian Peninsula, he spent his life travelling from one court to another, praising and then satirizing the emirs and princes that alternatively granted him their favors or withdrew them from him. Even a cursory glance at his *dīwān* shows that, well within the 10th century, the old system still survives in poetry. The timeless description of the beloved's eyes provides one of the finest examples of 10th century poetry and, at the same time, of the survival of the old system (Wormhoudt 2002, 24):[50]

(32) *ʕamra=ka Allāhu hal raʔayta* ***budūran*** ***ṭalaʕ-at***
life=your.M.SG Allah INT see:2.PFV.M.SG full.moon.PL rise-3.PFV.F.SG
fī barāqiʕin wa=ʕuqūdi ***rāmiy-ātin*** *bi=ashumin*
in veil.PL and=necklace.PL ACT.PTCP.shoot-F.PL with=arrow.PL
rīšu=hā l=hudbu tašuqqu l=qulūba qabla
feather=her DEF=eyelash 3.IPFV.F.SG:pierce DEF=heart.PL before
l=ǧulūdi ***ya-taraššaf-na*** *min fam=ī* ***rašaf-ātin hunna***
DEF=skin.PL 3.IPFV-suck-F.PL from mouth=my sip-F.PL they.F
fī=hi ḥalāwatu t=tawḥīdi
in=him sweetness DEF=monotheism
'May God grant you a long life! Have you seen such moons rising among veils and necklaces? Shooting arrows feathered by eyelashes, which pierce the hearts before the skins. They suck from my mouth some sips, which there have the sweetness of monotheism' (al-Mutanabbī 11, 4–6).

The three verses feature both feminine singular and plural agreement with two different nonhuman controllers, namely *budūr* "full.moon.PL" and *rašaf-āt* "sip-F.PL". Looking at human controllers, although plural agreement largely

50 All al-Mutanabbī's samples are drawn from the complete *dīwān* published by Wormhoudt (2002). The translation is Wormhoudt's, with occasional corrections.

prevails, specimens of feminine singular agreement can also be found. The two following samples, in particular, feature feminine singular agreement with a human broken plural and, subsequently, with a human collective:

(33) *ʔiḏā* ***ʕuriḍ-at*** ***ḥāǧǧun*** *ʔilay=hi fa=nafsu=hu ʔilā*
if present.PASS-3.PFV.F.SG needy.PL to=him then=self=his to
*nafsi=hi fī=**hā** šafīʕun mušaffaʕun*
self=his in=her Intercessor PASS.PTCP.make.intercede.M.SG
'If needy ones turn to him then he himself intercedes as a mediator with himself for them' (al-Mutanabbī 16, 17) (Wormhoudt 2002, 34)

(34) ***Quḍāʕatu ta-ʕlamu*** *ʔann=ī l=fatā llaḏī*
Quḍāʕat 3.IPFV.F.SG-know COMP=me DEF=boy REL.M.SG
ddaxar-at *li=ṣurūfi z=zamāni*
store-3.PFV.F.SG for=misfortune.PL DEF=time
'Quḍāʕa knowns I am the young man whom they saved for time's calamities' (al-Mutanabbī 17, 1) (Wormhoudt 2002, 34)

Moving to al-Būṣīrī, the situation is slightly different. Muḥammad ibn Saʕīd al-Būṣīrī was a grammarian and Sufi poet who was born and lived in Egypt in the 13th century, but whose family was of Moroccan origin, specifically from the Berber tribe of the Sanhāǧa. For the purpose of this research, we have analyzed his most famous poem, the *Qaṣīdat al-Burda* "Poem of the Cloak", a celebratory ode in honor of the Prophet Muḥammad. The poem, consisting of 160 verses, still features plural agreement with nonhuman plural controllers, proving that a full standardization had not yet been achieved, in poetry, even at the end of the 13th century. That said, the samples of plural agreement gleaned from the poet suggest that the situation was different from what observed in al-Mutanabbī's 10th century poetry. Most of the samples, in fact, consist of broken plural attributive adjectives immediately following the controller, as in the following samples:[51]

(35) *wa=**rāwad-at**=hu* ***l=ǧibālu*** ***š=šummu*** *min*
and=entice-3.PFV.F.SG=him DEF=mountain.PL DEF=lofty.PL from
*ḏahabin ʕan nafsi=hi fa=ʔarā=**hā*** *ʔayyamā šamami*
gold from self=his and=show.3.PFV.M.SG=her whatever loftiness
'The lofty mountains made into gold for him tried to be a way to bait him, so he true loftiness let them see' (*al-Burda*, 31)

51 The translation of the single verses is drawn, with occasional corrections, from Azzam (2016).

(36) *yā xayra man yammama l=ʕāfūna*
oh best who resort.3.PFV.M.SG DEF=ACT.PTCP.seek.good-M.PL
*sāḥata=hu saʕyan wa=fawqa **l=ʔaynuqi***
frontyard=his on.foot and=on DEF=she.camel.PL
r=rusumi
DEF=indefatigable.PL
'O best of those whose front yard is sought by those seeking good, on foot and on backs of camels treading vigorously' (*al-Burda*, 105)

Feminine plural agreement with adjectives is only present in the adjective *muḥakkam-ātun* "PASS.PART.make.clear-F.PL", referred to *ʔāy-āt* "verse-F.PL". The almost identical expression *ʔāyāt muḥkamāt* "clear verses", however, is well known in the field of Quranic exegesis, designating those verses whose interpretation is clear, as opposed to the more ambiguous ones, defined as *mutašābih-āt* "obscure-F.PL" (Q III, 8). Given the religious nature of the poem and al-Būṣīrī's background, thus, it is very likely that this expression is borrowed from the Quran and not actually parsed.

With verbs and pronouns, the *Burda* only contains two samples of feminine plural agreement. The first one directly follows the adjective *muḥakkamāt* in verse 94, and is probably conditioned by the occurrence of the feminine plural adjective:

(37) ***ʔāy-ātu*** *ḥaqqin* [...] ***muḥakkam-ātun*** *fa=mā*
verse-F.PL truth PASS.PART.make.clear-F.PL and=NEG
tu-bqī-na *min šubahin li=ḏī šiqāqin wa=mā*
2.IPFV-leave-F.PL from doubt to=possessor dissension and=NEG
ta-bġī-na *min ḥakamin*
2.IPFV-want-F.PL from arbiter
'Verses of truth [...] so wise and clear, that you leave no room for a single doubt to an opponent and have no need for an arbiter' (*al-Burda*, 91, 94)

Apart from this sample, whose status is questionable, the only other occurrence of feminine plural agreement is the following verbal target:

(38) *fa=ʔinna=hu šamsu faḍlin hum* ***kawākibu**=hā* ***yu-ḏ̣hir-na***
and=COMP=him sun virtue they.M star.PL=her 3.IPFV-show-F.PL
ʔanwāru=hā li=n=nāsi fī ḏ̣=ḏ̣ulmi
light.PL=her to=DEF=people.COLL in DEF=darkness
'He is the Sun of virtue, to which they are as if moons: reflecting its lights in darkness to humanity' (*al-Burda*, 53)

In the rest of the several occurrences of agreement with nonhuman plural controllers, agreement always occurs in the feminine singular. The status of the old system as a whole in al-Būṣīrī's 13th century poetry, thus, can probably be referred to as borrowed syntax for the most part. Only the occurrence of broken plural adjectives was possibly still productive, given that it still sporadically occurs in contemporary literature. The rest of the system was no longer productive in the language (at least in his language) as a regular system of agreement assignment, yet learned speakers were aware of its existence, and used it from time to time as a stylistic device to signal a high register. Commonly employed expressions in the Quran (or other famous texts) that included samples of agreement according to the old system were probably borrowed as they were, without parsing, thus resulting in fossilized occurrences.

In al-Buṣīri's case, it makes sense to speak of borrowed syntax, since feminine plural agreement with nonhuman controllers was absent from the syntax of Classical Arabic at that time, and most probably also from the writer's native dialect. We know from Belnap (1991; 1993) that feminine plural agreement is lost in contemporary Egyptian (Cairene) Arabic, but the ancient written texts in Egyptian Arabic collected by Madiha Doss and Humphrey Davies (2013) suggest that feminine plural agreement had already been lost at the time when al-Būṣīrī wrote his *Burda*, or shortly after. See, for instance, the following example, dating back to the early 15th century:

(39) *wa=ʕalay=h* ***xamis*** ***galāgil*** *kull=mā* *naṭṭat*
and=on=him five bell.PL every.time jump:3.PFV.F.SG
ti-xašxaš[52]
3.IPFV.F.SG-clatter
'And it has five bells on it, which ring every time she jumps' (Doss and Davies 2013, 46).

Agreement is here in the feminine singular but, even when syntactic agreement in the plural occurs, it can only occur in the masculine plural, since Egyptian Arabic (Cairene) lost feminine plural morphology in verbs and pronouns since at least the 17th century (Davies 1981, 177), probably earlier. If we compare al-Mutanabbī's poetry with al-Būṣīrī's one, then, it is clear that they reflect two different linguistic backgrounds. Al-Mutanabbī lived in the 10th century, when the replacement of the old agreement system with the new one had hardly

52 In our source, the text is reproduced in the Arabic script, with partial vocalization. The transcription thus follows the original as closely as possible.

been completed, even in written prose. Moreover, al-Mutanabbī spent a considerable part of his youth in the Arabian Desert, joining the Qarmatians after they sacked Kufa in 924 CE. There, he most probably was exposed to particularly conservative varieties of Arabic, where the ancient system of agreement was still alive. His writings, thus, reflect an awareness of the distribution patterns of agreement categories that is no longer present in al-Būṣīrī. The Egyptian poet, who lived three centuries after al-Mutanabbī in Alexandria, probably had no stable contact whatsoever with Arabic dialectal varieties still preserving the old system, except in his many travels. The only available sample was represented by pre-Islamic poetry and the Quran. Given the religious nature of the poem (and the fact that al-Būṣīrī himself was a Sufi), it is probable that the Quran played a great role. This emerges from the fact that one of the only two occurrences of feminine plural agreement in his long poem is represented by a series of targets following the controller *ʔāy-āt* "verse-F.PL".

This implies that, when considering later poetry, the linguistic background of the poet should always be taken into consideration. Poets hailing from areas where gender-distinguishing varieties were spoken (as far as we know) were probably more likely to master the rules governing the distribution of agreement choices in the old system. For poets whose native dialects had lost gender distinction in the plural, on the contrary, pre-Islamic poetry and the Quran were the only sources available from which samples of the ancient systems could be drawn. Sporadic occurrences of that system continue to emerge well beyond the limit we imposed upon ourselves here (13th century), yet they should probably be considered, at that point, as borrowed syntax.[53]

3.6 The Dawn of Arabic Prose: Translated Syntax in *Kalīla wa-Dimna*

So far, our reconstruction has been exclusively based on poetry and the Quran, which is composed in *saǧʕ*, i.e. rhymed prose. The reason, as explained in detail in § 3.2, is simple: given that our oldest sources only consist of poetry, a change in literary genre might skew the data, so that consistency is advisable. The sharp and abrupt standardization that emerges from Belnap and Gee's (1994, 127) data in only a century, from the Quran (7th century) to Ibn Hišām (8th century), in fact, can be explained, at least partially, with the change of literary genre. Data from poetry dating back to the same age, presented in section 3.5, show that

53 This concerns, of course, the occurrence of feminine plural agreement. Broken plural adjectives, on the other hand, are ubiquitous in all varieties of Arabic, so that their occurrence in poetry (and prose) probably reflects a live usage of the language.

the ancient system was still preserved, although with some apparent deterioration in its distribution patterns. Nonetheless, an account of the evolution of the agreement system in written Arabic would not be complete without also analyzing prose. This is especially true given that some early prose works, not yet investigated, provide much more interesting materials for our reconstruction than those analyzed in Belnap and Gee (1994). This section particularly focuses on the agreement patterns emerging from the famous mirror for princes *Kalīla wa-Dimna* by ʕAbd Allāh Ibn al-Muqaffaʕ (ca. 720–ca. 756 CE).[54] *Kalīla wa-Dimna*, usually considered one of the first masterpieces of the Arabic prose, is the starting point of the "Mirror for Princes" genre (Bosworth 1983, 488). Its author, on the other hand, is considered as the initiator of the movement of translation from Pahlavi (Middle Persian) that considerably enriched the Arabic literature:

> In this work of transmission from the Pahlavi, the pioneer figure was apparently 'Abdullah b. al-Muqaffa' (*c.* 102–*c.* 139/*c.* 720–*c.* 756), a Persian from Fars; we possess only a part of what he must have translated, and that not in his own original Arabic versions. Foremost amongst these works was his *Kalīlah wa-Dimnah*, a version of a collection of animal fables stemming originally from the Sanskrit *Pañchatantra* and beyond that, the *Tantrakhyāyika*, but made by Ibn al-Muqaffaʾ from a Pahlavi recension of the mid-sixth-century version composed for Khusraw (Chosroes) Anūshirvān by his physician Burzōē.
>
> BOSWORTH 1983, 487

For all the aforementioned reasons, the importance of *Kalīla wa-Dimna* can hardly be downplayed, and its analysis sheds light on what early Arabic prose written by Persian converts (*mawālī*), but consumed by a much wider audience, looked like.

The two main versions of the book are Cheikho's (1905), based on a manuscript he found in Dayr aš-Šīr (Lebanon) and dated 1338 CE, and ʕAzzām's (1941)[55] one, based on an earlier manuscript found in Istanbul and dated 1221 CE (De Blois 1990, 3). Neither of the editions is immune from errors, so that they

54 According to the sources, Ibn al-Muqaffaʕ's life ended quite tragically. The second Abbasid Caliph, ʔAbū Ǧaʕfar al-Manṣūr, had him executed, probably due to the accusation of *zandaqa*, i.e. of Zoroastrian sympathies, with special reference to dualist Manicheism. Other accounts of Ibn al-Muqaffaʕ's death, however, point toward political divergences that the Caliph considered as a personal offense.

55 For the purpose of the present study, we have used a recent edition of ʕAzzām's edition,

are usually used side by side by researchers. Interestingly, however, their many discrepancies only minimally regard the agreement system, and do not include its most interesting trait, which is the object of the following pages. The basis of the analysis has been ʕAzzām's recent edition, mostly due to its searchability. Our corpus comprises roughly one third of the book (50 pages out of 175), which was analyzed as follows: all the occurrences of agreement with plural controllers in the *Tale of the owls and the crows* (Ibn al-Muqaffaʕ 2014, 137–153) were collected and transcribed. After a rough analysis of the data was conducted, the results were compared to the longer *Tale of the lion and the bull* (Ibn al-Muqaffaʕ 2014, 73–107) to ensure that no counterexample occurred when enlarging the corpus. Finally, multiple samples of the text have been compared to Cheikho's version to make sure that ʕAzzām's edition is not misleading. Table 3.7 presents the agreement patterns for human, animal and inanimate plural controllers in the *Tale of the owls and the crows*, without distinguishing between attributive adjectives, verbs and pronouns.

The data presented above are of extreme interest for our reconstruction and deserve further explanation. The percentages concerning humans are not particularly surprising: masculine plural is by far the most common agreement choice, even though occurrences of feminine singular with human broken plurals can still be found, as shown by the following two samples, drawn from the two tales examined for this section:

(40) *al=ḥīlatu fī llaḏī* ***kānati*** *l=ʕulamāʔu*
DEF=stratagem in what.M.SG be:3.PFV.F.SG DEF=savant.PL
ta-qūlu, *fa=ʔinna=hum kānū yaqūlūna…*
3.IPFV.F.SG-say and=COMP=they.M be:3.PFV.M.PL 3.IPFV:say:M.PL
'The stratagem is in what the *ʕulamāʔ* used to say, and they used to say'… (Ibn al-Muqaffaʕ 2014, 138)

(41) *wa=kaḏālika ṣ=ṣanādīdu ʔinna=mā yaṣmudu baʕḍu=****hā***
and=likewise DEF=valiant.PL only 3.IPFV:resist.M.SG part=her
li=baʕḍin
to=part
'And similarly the valiant men, they only resist each other' (Ibn al-Muqaffaʕ 2014, 82)

published in 2014 by Hindāwī (Cairo) with the original Introduction by Ṭāhā Ḥusseyn and here referred to as Ibn al-Muqaffaʕ (2014).

TABLE 3.7 Agreement patterns in Ibn al-Muqaffaʕ's *Tale of the owls and the crows*, from *Kalīla wa-Dimna* (post-controller targets)

	M. Sg.	M. Pl.	F. Sg.	F. Pl.	Br. Pl.
Human (32)	-	29 (90.6%)	1 (3.1%)	-	2 (6.3%)
Animal (101)	-	6 (5.9%)[a]	36 (35.6%)	59 (58.4%)	-
Inanimate (15)	-	-	15 (100%)	-	-

a The occurrence of masculine plural, elsewhere reserved to male humans, with animal controllers needs to be contextualized. *Kalīla wa-Dimna* is a collection of animal fables, in which animals are often bestowed human qualities, i.e. they talk, wage war, elaborate complex strategies etc. For this reason, they are occasionally humanized, especially when performing actions generally reserved to humans. It is not unusual, thus, to observe feminine plural alternating with masculine plural within the same sentence and with reference to the same controller.

The data concerning animal and inanimate controllers, on the other hand, are of extreme interest, especially if analyzed side by side. Starting with animal controllers, the percentage of feminine plural agreement is unusually high. In Table 3.7, data concerning attributive adjectives, verbs and pronouns have been merged, so that 58.4% represents the average of feminine plural agreement in the three categories. If we do the same for the most conservative corpus so far investigated, i.e. the seven *Muʕallaqāt*, the percentage we obtain is 31.7%. It follows that the percentage of feminine plural agreement with animal controllers in *Kalīla wa-Dimna*, a prose text from the 8th century, is almost twice as high as the percentage observed in pre-Islamic poetry. This fact alone is hard to explain, given that the percentage of feminine plural agreement with nonhuman controllers appeared to be decreasing even when comparing pre-Islamic poetry to the Quran, which predates *Kalīla wa-Dimna* by a century. When adding the data concerning inanimate controllers, the distribution becomes even more difficult to explain. Agreement with inanimate controllers, in fact, systematically occurs in the feminine singular, with no counterexamples.[56] Going back to the *Muʕallaqāt*, the average of feminine plural agreement is 26%. The comparison is represented in Table 3.8.

It is clear that such percentages do not make any sense from a historical or evolutionary perspective. In one case, i.e. with plural animal controllers, *Kalīla*

56 Counterexamples were also absent from the *Tale of the lion and the bull*. This means that, even if isolated occurrences were to be found in the remaining part of the text, their incidence would be negligible, given that they never occur in a corpus representing one third of the total text.

TABLE 3.8 Percentages of feminine singular vs feminine plural agreement with post-controller targets in the *Muʕallaqāt* and *Kalīla wa-Dimna* (average)

	Animal controllers		Inanimate controllers	
	F. Sg.	F. Pl.	F. Sg.	F. Pl.
Muʕallaqāt	40.9%	31.7%	53.8%	26%
Kalīla wa-Dimna	35.6%	58.4%	100%	0%

TABLE 3.9 Agreement system with post-controller targets in gender-distinguishing varieties of Arabic (pre-Islamic Arabic and contemporary dialects)

Class	Agreement in the singular	Agreement in the plural	
		Individuated nouns	Non-individuated nouns
I	Masculine singular	Masculine plural	
II	Feminine singular	Feminine plural	Feminine singular
III	Masculine singular	Feminine plural	

wa-Dimna is considerably more conservative than the *Muʕallaqāt*. In the other, i.e. plural with inanimate ones, it completely standardized feminine singular agreement. The distribution of agreement patterns in *Kalīla wa-Dimna* is simply unlike anything observed in any variety of written or spoken Arabic for which we have data.

The agreement system of *Kalīla wa-Dimna* almost represents a hybrid between the system of gender-distinguishing varieties and that of Classical and Modern Standard Arabic. With human and animal controllers, plural agreement alternates with feminine singular agreement, although with very different rates. In the table describing the agreement system of *Kalīla wa-Dimna*, however, the "individuation" column is absent. This is due to the fact that the distribution of agreement patterns no longer seems motivated by the [±individuated] feature. Feminine singular, for instance, regularly appears with inanimate controllers also when they are quantified by a low numeral:[57]

57 This is slightly surprising, because plural agreement also optionally occurs in Pahlavi when the individuality of the controller is emphasized (Skjærvø 2009, 227).

TABLE 3.10 Agreement system with post-controller targets in Classical and Modern Standard Arabic

Controller	Morphological or biological gender	Agreement in the singular	Agreement in the plural
Human	Biologically m.[a]	Masculine singular	Masculine plural
	Biologically f.	Feminine singular	Feminine plural
Nonhuman	Morphologically m.	Masculine singular	Feminine singular
	Morphologically f.	Feminine singular	

a As already seen in Chapter 1, biological gender is the decisive factor for human controllers. The few masculine nouns that bear the morphological mark of feminine, such as *xalīfa* "caliph", thus, also trigger masculine agreement.

TABLE 3.11 Agreement system with post-controller targets in *Kalīla wa-Dimna*

Controller	Morphological gender	Agreement in the singular	Agreement in the plural
Human	Morphologically m.	Masculine singular	Masculine plural[a]
	Morphologically f.	Feminine singular	Feminine plural
Animal	Morphologically m.	Masculine singular	Feminine singular /
	Morphologically f.	Feminine singular	Feminine plural
Inanimate	Morphologically m.	Masculine singular	**Feminine singular**
	Morphologically f.	Feminine singular	

a This cell is an oversimplification of what actually observed in the text. Isolated occurrences of feminine singular agreement with broken plural human controllers, in fact, can still be located in *Kalīla wa-Dimna*, even though it is not at all sure that the rules governing their distribution are the same found in pre-Islamic poetry, the Quran and the modern dialects. It might as well be that Ibn al-Muqaffaʕ was aware of the fact that feminine singular agreement was a possibility with human broken plurals and occasionally resorted to this agreement pattern as a stylistic feature.

(42) *yā bunay=ya ʔinna ṣāḥiba d=dunyā yaṭlubu* ***ṯalāṯata***
Oh son=my COMP owner DEF=world 3.IPFV:ask.M.SG three.F
ʔumūrin *lā yudriku=**hā*** *ʔillā bi=ʔarbaʕati ʔašyāʔa*
thing.PL NEG 3.IPFV:reach.M.SG=her except by=four.F thing.PL
ʔammā ***ṯ=ṯalāṯatu llatī*** *yaṭlubu* [...]
as.for DEF=three.F REL.F.SG 3.IPFV:ask.M.SG
'Oh son of mine, the man of this world asks for three things, which he cannot reach except by [other] four things [...]' (Ibn al-Muqaffaʕ 2014, 73)

Long stretches of feminine plural targets, on the other hand, regularly occur after broken plurals, such as *ġurbān* "crow.PL" and *ʔarānib* "rabbit.PL", and even after collective animal controllers such as *būm* "owl.COLL", as evident from the following sample:

(43) *fa=lam yaltafit maliku l=**būmi***
and=NEG 3.IPFV:pay.attention.M.SG. APOC king DEF=owl.COLL
*wa=lā ġayru=hu min=**hunna** ʔilā hāḏā l=maṯali*
and=NEG other=his from=them.F to this.M.SG DEF=simile
*wa=**rafaq-na*** *bi=l=ġurābi wa=lam*
and=treat.gently-3.PFV.F.PL by=DEF=crow and=NEG
ya-zdad-na *la=hu ʔillā karāmatan*
3.IPFV-increase-F.PL to=him except honor
'But neither the King of the Owls nor any of them paid attention to this simile, they treated the crow gently and did not increase, in its treatment, but honor' (Ibn al-Muqaffaʕ 2014, 149).

The only language-internal explanation to these patterns is that they constitute an intermediate step toward the full standardization of feminine singular agreement with plural nonhuman controllers. In other words, the patterns emerging from *Kalīla wa-Dimna* would represent a stage in which feminine singular had already become the norm with inanimate controllers, but not yet with animal ones. This explanation, however, is unlikely for two main reasons. The first is that such an intermediate step is not attested anywhere else. Given the scarcity of studies on the syntax of early written Arabic, however, this is not compelling evidence. The second reason stems from the internal evidence of the distribution patterns emerging from *Kalīla wa-Dimna*. While feminine singular agreement appears to be mandatory with inanimate controllers, in fact, animals feature a percentage of feminine plural agreement almost twice as high as the one found in the pre-Islamic *Muʕallaqāt*. It is very unlikely, then, that one and the same text would be extremely conservative with animal controllers and even more innovative with inanimate ones. It is evident, in conclusion, that the explanation to these peculiar distribution patterns cannot be language-internal.

Belnap and Gee's (1994) first discussed the hypothesis that the standardization of feminine singular agreement with nonhuman plural controllers might have been induced by language contact. Non-native speakers who were using Arabic in its written medium, under the pressure that such a medium imposes (as opposed to the less controlled style of the spoken language), would have systematically opted for the "safest choice", reanalyzing the higher incidence of feminine singular agreement with nonhuman controllers as a general rule (K.R. Belnap and Gee 1994, 142). At the same time, non-native speakers of Arabic, according to Belnap and Gee, might have been influenced by the syntax of their L1. This is a brilliant intuition, especially with reference to the possible influence of Ancient Greek, in which the so-called *schema attikon* requires neuter plurals to agree in the singular (K.R. Belnap and Gee 1994, 138).[58] Belnap and Gee, however, only consider Greek and Syriac as possible sources of influence, without taking Persian into consideration. In Persian (including Pahlavi or Middle Persian), in fact, plural controllers designating inanimate entities (which means that the cutoff point is actually lower on the hierarchy of individuation) prevalently trigger singular agreement in the verb, especially in older stages of the language (contemporary usage features a relatively higher degree of variation). Animate and human controllers, on the other hand, systematically trigger plural agreement (Persian does not mark verbs for gender) (Hashabeiky 2007, 80). Verbal agreement with plural controllers in *Kalīla wa-Dimna* and in Persian is roughly summarized in Table 3.12.

The system of Persian is based on animacy, as opposed to the system of pre-Islamic Arabic and the dialects, which is based on individuation. As such, it is more similar to the system of Classical and Modern Standard Arabic, where the cutoff point is, however, higher on the animacy hierarchy. In Persian, in fact, humans and animals are grouped together and distinguished from inanimate entities. In Arabic, on the other hand, humans are distinguished from both animals and inanimate entities, which form a single group. Both the unusually high percentage of feminine plural agreement with animal controllers and the complete standardization of feminine singular agreement with inanimate ones, thus, are best explained as a transfer from Pahlavi (Middle Persian), the

58 The similarity between feminine singular agreement with plural controllers in Arabic and neuter agreement has been occasionally noticed. See note 29 above.

TABLE 3.12 Verbal agreement with plural controllers in *Kalīla wa-Dimna* and in Persian

Controller type	*Kalīla wa-Dimna*	Persian
Human	Masculine plural	Plural
Animal	Feminine plural / feminine singular	Plural
Inanimate	Feminine singular	Singular

language from which *Kalīla wa-Dimna* was translated by Ibn al-Muqaffaʕ. This distribution never made its way into the agreement system of Arabic as a whole, so that it is not possible to speak of borrowed syntax from Persian, but rather of translated syntax, a phenomenon that is widely attested in the Greek and German translations of the Bible (Fleischer, Rieken, and Widmer 2015, 3–4). At the present state of research, we do not know whether Ibn al-Muqaffaʕ, who was a native speaker of Pahlavi, stably borrowed this trait into his L2 Arabic or whether this represented a case of translated syntax also at a personal level. In order to ascertain this, it would be useful to compare the system of agreement obtaining in the works that Ibn al-Muqaffaʕ's composed originally in Arabic with that of his translations from Pahlavi. This investigation, however, goes far beyond the scope of this section and will be the object of future research.

When speaking of translated syntax, of course, we do not imply that Ibn al-Muqaffaʕ simply imported the agreement patterns of *Kalīla wa-Dimna* from Pahlavi as they were. As a matter of fact, such an automatic operation would not have been possible at all, since the two systems differ in a way that forces the translator to make choices. As already said, in Persian, including Pahlavi, verbal targets referring to inanimate controllers preferably take singular agreement, as opposed to verbal targets referring to animate (both animal and human) controllers, which take plural agreement. Pahlavi, however, does not mark verbs for gender, so that Ibn al-Muqaffaʕ could not escape a gender choice whenever he translated a verb from the original to the Arabic version. Judging from the Arabic text, it is evident that Ibn al-Muqaffaʕ's knowledge of his L2 guided him in the choice of the most suitable gender. Masculine singular agreement with plural controllers, in fact, only occurs in pre-controller verbal targets. With post-controller targets, it is not a viable option, but only occurs when real agreement fails to take place and the speaker / writer resorts to default agreement. For this reason, Ibn al-Muqaffaʕ systematically employs feminine singular with post- inanimate controller targets. The same holds true for plural agreement with animal controllers. Even when the controller is morphologically masculine in the singular, targets agreeing in the plural do so in the feminine plural, which is the norm for nonhuman plural controllers in Arabic when syntactic agreement is selected.[59] The occurrence of singular agreement with inanimate controllers in Pahlavi, finally, only concerns verbal targets, not adjectives or pronouns. In Ibn al-Muqaffaʕ's Arabic version, on the contrary, feminine singular has been generalized to all kinds of targets. While adjectives qualifying inanimate plural controllers are extremely scarce, the generalization of feminine singular agreement with pronouns is hardly surprising. Pronouns are, in fact, the locus of innovation of feminine singular agreement, whose incidence already reached 80.9 % in the seven *Muʕallaqāt* (see sections 2.3.2). Ibn al-Muqaffaʕ, then, only generalized agreement in a domain in which feminine singular already represented the almost systematic choice (especially two centuries after the *Muʕallaqāt*).[60]

The syntax of *Kalīla wa-Dimna*, in conclusion, proves beyond any reasonable doubt that L1 transfer, hypothesized in Belnap and Gee (1994) and D'Anna (2020a), actually happened in the written Arabic of non-native speakers. It is known as a fact that *Kalīla wa-Dimna* widely circulated since the date of its composition and served as a model for its literary genre and for Arabic prose as a whole. It is a possibility, thus, that the complete standardization of feminine singular agreement with inanimate controllers in such a famous literary work might have influenced subsequent prose writers. The weight of such an influence, however, cannot be measured with certainty. It is also possible, moreover, that *Kalīla wa-Dimna* is not an isolated case, and that other prose works exhibit similar instances of translated syntax, especially in the light of the wide phenomenon of translation of literary, historical and philosophical works from Persian, Greek and Syriac that took place in the first centuries of Islam. This fact calls for further syntactic research to be conducted on early Arabic prose, in order to identify all the factors that helped to shape what became known as Classical Arabic.

---

59 As said above, masculine plural agreement with plural animal controllers occurs as well, although only occasionally. We have interpreted this phenomenon as an instance of humanization, due to the peculiar nature of the animals portrayed in *Kalīla wa-Dimna*.

60 For a more detailed account on translated syntax in *Kalīla wa-Dimna*, see D'Anna and Benkato (2022).

3.7 From [-Individuated] to [-Human]: The Reanalysis of Semantic Features in Classical Arabic

Sections 3.1–3.6 have described the evolution of agreement in Arabic from the Proto-Central Semitic stage to the 10th century CE, with some references to the situation of 13th century poetry. Our description has focused on the agreement system obtaining in Arabic in its written form, even though the spoken dialects have been constantly referred to whenever a comparison helped to shed light on either parallel or divergent evolution paths. While the reader is referred back to previous sections for a thorough description and references, some basic facts will be repeated here, for the sake of clarity. The oldest source to be extensively studied in this work is pre-Islamic poetry, which already shows the signs of a linguistic change in progress. Starting from a system where syntactic (or formal) agreement was prevalent, and which is still attested in other languages of the Central Semitic group, a form of semantic agreement appeared to mark [-individuated] plurals. This type of agreement was initially expressed by the broken plural for adjectives and by feminine singular for verbs and pronouns. The innovation likely started in the domain of anaphoric pronouns referring to items low on the scale of individuation and of animacy, and gradually reached the top of the scale. By the time the seven *Muʕallaqāt* were composed, in fact, feminine singular agreement also occurs with broken plural human controllers, and occurrences increase in the Quran. At the same time, the innovation of feminine singular agreement also worked its way down the agreement hierarchy, reaching the most conservative domain, i.e. adjectives, already in pre-Islamic poetry.

Early Islamic poetry, investigated in § 3.5, showed that the system was possibly under stress in the period that immediately followed the age of conquests (7th–8th century). While the categories of agreement are the same as in pre-Islamic poetry and the Quran, in fact, their distribution seems less consistent. It was hypothesized that the social turmoil and the vast displacement of young speakers from their ancestral homeland to distant non-Arabic speaking areas might have resulted in the weakening of the transmission of traditional poetry. This probably included the complex factors governing the distribution of agreement choices, especially for those poets whose native dialect had already lost the possibility of feminine plural agreement. Similar phenomena, which do not imply the breaking of intergenerational dialect transmission, are commonly attested also in other languages, such as Dutch (Audring 2009; De Vos 2015). Additional phenomena that may have contributed to the restructuring of the agreement system in the spoken dialects will be discussed in Chapter 5.

During the 8th century, as evident from § 3.6, another phenomenon started which needs to be accounted for and whose impact on written Arabic is not entirely clear yet. Large numbers of non-native speakers of Arabic found themselves living in the newly created Arabic-Islamic Empire and started using Arabic as their second language. The consequences of this phenomenon on spoken Arabic have been long debated, with opinions ranging from Veerstegh's (1984) thought-provoking (but nowadays rejected) theory of pidginization to Ferguson's (1989) cautious response. Until Belnap and Gee (1994), however, nobody had actually thought of reversing the traditional position, saying that the dialects are, with reference to agreement, more consistent with what is usually referred to as Old Arabic than Classical Arabic is. Section 3.6, however, proved that one of the masterpieces of early Arabic prose, Ibn al-Muqaffaʕ's *Kalīla wa-Dimna*, shows clear signs of syntactic transfer from Middle Persian, the language it was translated from. The wide circulation of *Kalīla wa-Dimna* makes it very probable that the book provided a model for subsequent prose writers, and the extent to which other translators imported syntactic traits from their L1s into their L2 written Arabic remains a question for future research.

In this context of intense language contact, a dramatic linguistic change occurred in written Arabic, which was described in detail in the already mentioned article by Belnap and Gee (1994). The old agreement system, with its three classes and optional choice between syntactic and semantic agreement, was completely supplanted by a new one, in which variation was first drastically reduced and finally suppressed. The replacement of the system was not abrupt and occurred at a different speed in different literary genres. Ornate prose, for instance, still used specimens of the ancient system as a stylistic feature, as evident from our analysis of the *maqāmāt* ("assemblies", see § 3.8). Let us look at the following samples:

(44) *ḥurūfun ʔiḥday=hā yaʕummu=hā n=niqaṭu*
letter.PL one.F.SG=her 3.IPFV:encompass.M.SG=her DEF=dot.PL
*wa=**ḥurūfu** l=ʔuxrā lam **yu-ʕǧam-na** qaṭṭu*
and=letter.PL DEF=other.F.SG NEG 3.IPFV-dot.PASS-F.PL at.all
'The letters of one of them had dots on them, while the letters of the other had not been [dotted]' (Steingass 1897, 46)

(45) *lam ʔafham kayfa ʔanna **ṯalāṯata ʔaḥrufin***
NEG 1.IPFV.SG:understand. APOC how COMP three.F letter.PL
muǧtamaʕ-atin [...] ***tu-ṣbiḥu*** [...] *muʔlimatan*
ACT.PTCP.combine-F.SG 3.IPFV.F.SG-become ACT.PTCP.combine:F.SG

ʔilā ḏālika l=ḥaddi
to that.M DEF=limit
'I did not understand how comes that three letters connected [...] become [...] painful to that extent' (Ahlem Mosteghanemi, 2003, *ʕĀbir sarīr*)[61]

The first sample is drawn from al-Ḥarīrī's (1054–1122 CE) *maqāmāt* and is not, in itself, a particularly good exemplification of the ancient system. It shows feminine plural agreement with a quite generic inanimate plural in a passive verbal target, which is unusual. The author, in this case, is probably using feminine plural agreement as an archaic stylistic feature, without a complete awareness of how the system worked in detail. The second, on the contrary, is drawn from Ahlem Mosteghanemi's (1953–) *ʕĀbir sarīr* ("Bed hopper", 2003) and perfectly showcases the new system and the irrelevance of individuation. The sample features the same lexical items, i.e. the broken plural of *ḥarf* "letter" (actually, the alleged plural of paucity). The author mentions three specific letters, which are quantified by a low numeral, qualified by an adjective and considered as painful, which should be more than enough to ensure they have high textual prominence and individuation. Nonetheless, agreement occurs in the feminine singular. The same happens in the following samples:

(46) *wa=qālat li=nafsi=hā ʔinna=hā yastaḥīlu*
and=say:3.PFV.F.SG to=self=her COMP=her 3.IPFV:be.impossible.M.SG
ʔan tataḥammala hāḏā š=šiqāʔā ***ʔarbaʕa sanaw-ātin***
COMP 3.IPFV.F.SG:bear.SBJV this.M DEF=misery four.M year-F.PL
kāmil-atin
entire-F.SG
'And she said to herself that it was impossible for her to bear such misery for four full years' (Alaa al-Aswani, *Chicago*, 2007)[62]

(47) *ṯamānī mufakkirātin li=ṯamānī* ***sanaw-ātin*** *lam*
eight notebook:F.PL for=eight.M year-F.PL NEG
*yakun fī=****hā*** *mā yastaḥiqqu d=dahšata* [...]
3.IPFV:be.M.SG.APOC in=her what 3.IPFV:deserve.M.SG DEF=wonder

61 The quotation has been retrieved from the Arabicorpus corpus (http://arabicorpus.byu.edu/search.php?page=citations&sort=rBeforeW&start=1, last accessed on January 14, 2019).
62 The quotation has been retrieved from the Arabicorpus corpus (http://arabicorpus.byu.edu/search.php?page=citations&sort=rBeforeW&start=1, last accessed on January 14, 2019).

tataḥawwalu fī=hā s=sanawātu ʔilā ***ṯamānī***
3.IPFV.F.SG:transform in=her DEF=year:F.PL to eight.M
mufakkir-ātin *lā ġayru mā* ***zāl-at mukaddas-atan***
notebook-F.PL NEG other NEG cease-3.PFV.F.SG PASS.PTCP.pile-F.SG
fī xizānat=ī l=wāḥidatu fawqa l=ʔuxrā
in locker=my DEF=one:F.SG over DEF=other:F.SG
'Eight notebooks for eight years, in which there was nothing deserving wonder [...] in them the years turned into eight notebooks, nothing else, which were still piled up in my cupboard, one on the other' (Ahlem Mostaghanemi, *Ḏākirat al-ǧasad*, 1993)[63]

(48) *baʕda ḏālika* ***ḏ̣ahar-at ʕašaratu kilābin būlisiyy-atin***
after that.M appear-3.PFV.F.SG ten.F dog.PL police-F.SG
ḍaxm-atin ʔaxaḏ-at ta-ḏraʕu *l=mabnā*
huge-F.SG take-3.PFV.F.SG 3.IPFV.F.SG-measure DEF=building
*wa=****ta-tašammamu*** *fī kulli ttiǧāhin*
and=3.IPFV.F.SG-sniff in every direction
'After that, ten huge police dogs appeared and started going up and down the building and sniffing in every direction' (Alaa al-Aswani, *Chicago*, 2007)[64]

We have selected samples featuring both animal and inanimate controllers and purposefully chosen controllers qualified by low numerals. The reason is that the presence of a low numeral represents, in the ancient system as emerging from both pre- and early-Islamic Arabic and the modern dialects, the most reliable predictor of the occurrence of syntactic agreement in the feminine plural. The samples, on the contrary, invariably show feminine singular agreement, which has become, in Classical and Modern Standard Arabic, the mandatory choice for post-controller targets when nonhuman controllers are involved, irrespective of their degree of individuation or textual prominence. The system, in other words, transitioned from variable agreement to the mandatory system described in § 2.5 and here summarized, for the sake of clarity, in the following table:

63 The quotation has been retrieved from the Arabicorpus corpus (http://arabicorpus.byu.edu/search.php?page=citations&sort=rBeforeW&start=1, last accessed on January 14, 2019).

64 The quotation has been retrieved from the Arabicorpus corpus (http://arabicorpus.byu.edu/search.php?page=citations&sort=rBeforeW&start=1, last accessed on January 15, 2019).

TABLE 3.13 Agreement system with post-controller targets in Classical and Modern Standard Arabic

Controller	Morphological gender	Agreement in the singular	Agreement in the plural
Human	Morphologically and/or biologically m.	Masculine singular	Masculine plural
	Morphologically and/or biologically f.	Feminine singular	Feminine plural
Nonhuman	Morphologically m.	Masculine singular	Feminine singular
	Morphologically f.	Feminine singular	

The transition to categorical agreement patterns does not solely concern nonhuman plurals, but also human ones. The ancient system, in all his forms (i.e. both in pre-/ early-Islamic Arabic and in the modern dialects), featured the possibility of feminine singular agreement with post-controller targets depending from a human controller.[65] The transition to categorical agreement patterns eliminated this choice, so that syntactic agreement is mandatory with plural human controllers. The only exceptions to this rule are (morphologically singular) collectives such as *nās* "people.COLL" and names of tribes and peoples, still allowing feminine singular agreement (Wright 1896b, 2:296). It is worth noting that, in these vestiges of the ancient system, the occurrence of feminine singular agreement with morphologically masculine singular controllers can only be justified as a relic of semantically [-individuated] agreement.

When not observed from a purely synchronic perspective, thus, the system of agreement of Classical and Modern Standard Arabic shows some interesting developments, which can be summarized as follows:[66]

1. The semantic feature of [individuation] was replaced by that of [humanness] as the decisive factor governing agreement choices;
2. For human plural controllers, syntactic agreement was generalized as the mandatory agreement choice;

65 For a detailed description of agreement patterns with post-controller targets, see Wright (1896b, 2:296–299).

66 The focus is here on post-controller targets. It is worth adding that mandatory singular agreement with pre-controller verbal targets was generalized and became the norm.

3. For nonhuman plural controllers, the former semantic [-individuated] agreement in the feminine singular was generalized as the mandatory choice, becoming standard agreement.

The system, not unlike many others attested in different languages of the world, is partly syntactically and partially semantically motivated. Its main peculiarity consists in the fact that, on the basis of a semantic feature, i.e. humanness, and only in the plural, all controllers marked as [+human] trigger mandatory syntactic agreement and all controllers marked as [-human] trigger semantic agreement. The main question, at this point, concerns why the generalization occurred in the first place.

This question has been the subject of two important papers by Belnap and Gee (1994) and Belnap (1999). The main reasons adduced by Belnap and Gee are summarized by the authors as follows:

1. Substratum influence (K.R. Belnap and Gee 1994, 134–140);
2. Overgeneralization (K.R. Belnap and Gee 1994, 140–143);
3. Avoidance (K.R. Belnap and Gee 1994, 143–145).

Substratum influence has already been discussed in detail with reference to Middle Persian (Pahlavi) and its syntactic influence on agreement in Ibn al-Muqaffaʕ's *Kalīla wa-Dimna* (see § 3.6). Curiously enough, Persian is not among the languages whose possible interference is advocated by Belnap and Gee. The possible influence of Syriac / Aramaic and Greek, on the other hand, is discussed in detail. Similarly to other Northwest Semitic languages, syntactic agreement is the norm in Aramaic/Syriac. The very few samples of variation discussed in Belnap and Gee (K.R. Belnap and Gee 1994, 136–137) do not match the kind of generalization they are supposed to induce in bilingual speakers and, thus, fail to provide convincing evidence for a transfer. The case of Greek, on the other hand, is much more interesting. Belnap and Gee (1994, 137–140) discuss the so-called *schema attikon*, which causes neuter plurals to trigger agreement in the singular in verbal targets (Greek does not mark verbs for gender). Lack of syntactic agreement with a specific class of nouns might have been imported by bilingual writers or translators in their L2 Arabic, especially due to the combined action of factors 2 and 3. As evident from § 3.6, in-depth studies of single authors or translated works can provide conclusive evidence concerning the presence of syntactical transfers. It is highly desirable, as a consequence, that similar studies be conducted on literary works translated from Greek, in order to find evidence to support Belnap and Gee's brilliant intuition.

The second motivation adduced by Belnap and Gee, with good reasons, is overgeneralization. The argumentation is simple, yet effective: feminine singular agreement already represented the most common agreement pattern

TABLE 3.14 Incidence of feminine singular agreement in the Quran

	Attr. adj.	Verbs	Pronouns
Belnap and Gee (1994, 127)	10/21 (48%)[a]	49/49 (100%)	52/54 (96%)
Full Quran (our data)	63/120 (52.5%)	54/72 (75%)	228/268 (85.1%)

a In order to comply with Corbett's (2006, 207) agreement hierarchy, our corpus has split data concerning adjectives into attributive and predicative, since they belong to two different positions on the hierarchy (attributive vs predicative). Belnap and Gee do not provide any indication with regard to this issue, so that their data probably collapsed attributive and predicative adjectives in one single category. A comparison of the data, however, shows the difference to be almost negligible.

with nonhuman plural controllers in pre- and early Islamic Arabic. Non-native speakers, thus, simply standardized the prevalent agreement choice. This is a sound line of reasoning, even though the limited size of Belnap and Gee's corpus biases their data, especially concerning agreement patterns in the Quran,[67] for which they only collected 124 tokens.[68] A comparison with our data, showed in Table 3.14 and based on the analysis of the full Quranic text, helps to obtain a better perspective, without questioning Belnap and Gee's assumption.

Despite the difference in the overall percentages, it is undeniable that feminine singular did represent the most common agreement choice, which justifies the overgeneralization hypothesis. Belnap and Gee, moreover, substantiate their hypothesis with the results of studies in acquisitional linguistics. Their line of reasoning focuses on the specific difference between probability matching and plurality. Speakers confronted with variable inputs will adjust to the actual probability of occurrence when no reward is offered. When, on the contrary, their choice comes with a reward, either positive or negative, the speakers' strategy tends to maximize gains, converging toward the most frequent input option:

67 The idea behind the specific mention of the Quran is that it represented the most common specimen of the high variety of Arabic (using "Classical Arabic" to describe the variety in which the Quran is written would be incorrect) available to non-native speakers and new converts, which is probably true.

68 Belnap and Gee do not specify whether they only selected post-controller targets. Especially in the case of verbs, this variable is decisive, since pre-controller verbal targets do not usually show variation (but see § 2.4), and should be excluded from the analysis.

> In short, unrewarded guessing quickly approximates the frequency of the input whereas rewarded guessing tends toward plurality, that is, choosing the most frequent option in the input.
>
> We may liken the learning of Arabic in its two extremes, informal spoken and the formal register exemplified by the Qurʾan, to these two types of learning. The process of learning the formal variety shows many parallels with rewarded guessing. For example, if a learner is aware that one agreement pattern is much more common than another, she will be far more likely to choose the more frequent (and safer) pattern. The fact that the formal variety is associated with writing, a more permanent medium, further adds to the pressure of using a variant whose acceptability is unquestionable.
>
> K.R. BELNAP AND GEE 1994, 142

This behavior answers one of the most pressing questions for scholars investigating the history of agreement in Arabic, i.e. why the generalization occurred in written Arabic but left the spoken dialects largely untouched. The lower pressure felt by speakers when using the spoken medium, in fact, corresponds to a situation when no reward is expected, and where speakers adjust their guesses to the actual probability of the input. The more formal nature of the written medium, on the other hand, represents the textbook example of a situation where reward (or retribution) is expected: "Making mistakes in the use of a formal variety can be a serious matter; mastering it can open doors (K.R. Belnap and Gee 1994, 142)." This is what has probably brought non-native speakers to play safe and opt for the most common option.

Overgeneralization is closely tied to the third factor mentioned by Belnap and Gee, i.e. avoidance. Non-native speakers are usually aware of their imperfect command of the second language they are acquiring, so that different strategies are put in place to avoid using those structures that are felt as particularly problematic or difficult. At the same time, the diglossic situation and the consequent pressure toward the standard has constantly brought writers of Arabic to avoid the employment of colloquialisms. According to Belnap and Gee, thus, the abundance of syntactic agreement in the spoken dialects might have produced the opposite effect. Speakers confronted with variable agreement patterns in written Arabic would have felt syntactic agreement in the plural as a colloquialism to avoid, opting for feminine singular, which occurred less frequently in the dialects (K.R. Belnap and Gee 1994, 144–145).[69]

69 Belnap and Gee specify that, in order for this to occur, it must be conceded that the speak-

This brief discussion illustrates the three reasons advanced by Belnap and Gee to justify the transition to categorical agreement patterns in Classical and Modern Standard Arabic. In the writers' opinion, substratum influence and overgeneralization probably had a greater impact than avoidance (though its role cannot be dismissed). Another factor that might have contributed to the standardization of feminine singular agreement with nonhuman plural controllers is word order. Literary prose, in fact, features an almost systematic VSO word order, as opposed to the more variable order obtaining in both poetry and the spoken language. With the exceptions of the so-called *luġat ʔakalū-nī l-barāġīṯu* (Guillaume 2011), in fact, singular agreement is mandatory in pre-controller verbal targets in preclassical Arabic, including pre-Islamic poetry and the Quran. The plainer style of early historical and religious Arabic prose, with prevalent VSO order, might have thus reduced *motu proprio* the variation occurring in verbal targets. It is also worth reminding the reader that the variation obtaining in the ancient system was governed by recognizable rules, with the [individuation] factor playing a decisive role. In most non-fictional prose works, events or places are usually described in a detached way, as opposed to the very rich descriptions observed in pre-Islamic poetry and the pathos of the Quran. Even for a native speaker with perfect command of the ancient system, as a consequence, a historical or geographic work does not represent the ideal scenario for variation to emerge. Non-native speakers perusing this kind of literary prose, in turn, might have had the impression that feminine singular was, at least in written Arabic, more widespread than our comprehensive data show.

A final note is necessary before closing this section. When speaking of a change that exclusively happened, several centuries ago, in the written variety of a language, it must be clear that we are not speaking of language change in the usual terms. There is no speech community that adopted this change, but rather single writers who probably lived in different areas, spoke different dialects/languages, and never met in their life. The number of members of this "community of writers", moreover, must have been relatively small, considering literacy rates in pre-modern societies. Changes originated in a few literary works that gained wide circulation, thus, might have served as models for other,

ers' dialect still featured a high incidence of syntactic agreement (K.R. Belnap and Gee 1994, 145). While they express doubts on that, based on the situation of Cairo, where feminine singular agreement seems to be prevalent, we have seen how, in other dialects, syntactic agreement indeed appears to be more common (§ 2.3). Obviously, this is no guarantee that the same situation obtained in those same dialects, or same areas, more than 1,000 years ago, but this is at least theoretically possible.

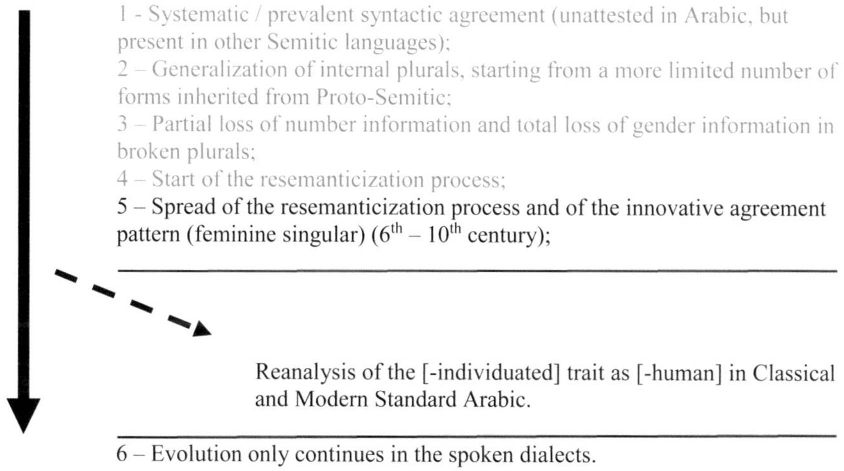
1 - Systematic / prevalent syntactic agreement (unattested in Arabic, but present in other Semitic languages);
2 – Generalization of internal plurals, starting from a more limited number of forms inherited from Proto-Semitic;
3 – Partial loss of number information and total loss of gender information in broken plurals;
4 – Start of the resemanticization process;
5 – Spread of the resemanticization process and of the innovative agreement pattern (feminine singular) (6th – 10th century);
Reanalysis of the [-individuated] trait as [-human] in Classical and Modern Standard Arabic.
6 – Evolution only continues in the spoken dialects.

FIGURE 3.5 Diachrony of agreement in Arabic

less experienced writers and brought about permanent changes in the written standard of the language.

The standardization that occurred in Classical and Modern Standard Arabic permanently altered the evolution of agreement patterns in written Arabic. Before that, as evidenced in sections 3.3–3.5, written documents actually testified a change in progress, with the spread of resemanticization down the agreement hierarchy and up the animacy hierarchy. Once the standardization took place, written Arabic ceased to evolve, at least as far as agreement is concerned. The ancient system, which had once been common to both the high and the low variety of the diglossic continuum, was now preserved only by the low one, i.e. the spoken dialects, with occasional occurrences in the highest registers of the high variety. The dearth of data concerning older stages of the modern dialects, however, severely limits the possibility of investigating the diachronic development of agreement in spoken Arabic. An attempt at reconstructing part of this history will be the object of Chapter 5.

Figure 3.5 schematically represents the stages of evolution of the agreement system of Arabic as presented in sections 3.1–3.7. In all the varieties of Arabic at our disposal (epigraphic, written and spoken), only stages 5 and 6 can be directly observed. Stages 1–4 (in dark grey), on the other hand, are reconstructed based on comparative Semitic evidence and the tools of historical linguistics. Together, they provide a hopefully sound account of one of the most fascinating aspects of the syntax of Arabic.

3.8 After the 10th Century: What Escaped Standardization

Sections 3.1–3.7 offered a full account of the development of the agreement system of Arabic, based solely on written sources. The first stages of this development present a system that is not dissimilar from what observed in contemporary dialects. Section 3.7, on the other hand, described the process of standardization that occurred in Classical Arabic and that replaced the ancient system with a new one, based on humanness. From that moment on, the agreement system of written Arabic ceased to evolve.

In the diglossic situation of Arabic as observed today,[70] the agreement systems of the high variety and of the low ones show considerable differences. At the same time, the system observed in the low varieties is more similar to the ancient system predating the standardization than to the system of Classical and Modern Standard Arabic (though dialects widely differ from one another, see § 2.3). We do not know whether a similar difference in the agreement system of the high and low variety existed at the time when the first written sources consulted for this research (i.e. pre-Islamic poetry and the Quran) were composed, provided that the situation of diglossia was then comparable to the present one. The main reasons that brought about the standardization which occurred in Classical and Modern Standard Arabic, however, are the massive presence of non-native speakers and the displacement of native ones (for a more detailed account, see sections 3.5–3.7). Since neither of these factors was present in pre-Islamic Arabic, we can hypothesize that the agreement systems of the high and low varieties did not differ in the way they do today. Written sources, moreover, are all we can reasonably expect to have with regard to old stages of the language, so that we must content ourselves with the formulation of hypotheses.

This section investigates the scant samples of survival of the ancient agreement system after the standardization that replaced it with the new one took place. Some of these samples have been fleetingly mentioned in the previous sections. The contexts in which the system seems to have survived are:

I. Poetry;
II. Ornate prose;
III. Middle Arabic.

Samples of post-10th century poetry have already been analyzed in section 3.5, with specific reference to al-Buṣīrī's famous *Qaṣīdat al-Burda* "Poem of the

70 For a classical account of diglossia in the Arabic-speaking world, although refined by subsequent scholars, see Ferguson (1959).

Cloak". The archaic feature that is most commonly observed in the poem is the presence of broken plural adjectives with nonhuman plural controllers:

(49) *wa=ʔaḥyati s=sanata š=šahbāʔa daʕwatu=hu ḥattā*
and= revive:3.PFV.F.SG DEF=year DEF=gray.F.SG call=his until
ḥakat ġurratan fī ***l=ʔaʕṣuri d=duhmi***
resemble:3.PFV.F.SG blaze in DEF=age.PL DEF=black.PL
'His call gave life to a gray and barren year full of drought; Till it became like a star in dark ages' (*Burda*, 86)

As said in § 3.5, this trait was preserved as a stylistic feature up the 20th century, as evident from the following samples:

(50) [...] *wa=hum yanqulūna* ***xuṭuw-ātin ṯiqālan*** *fī ʔiʕyāʔin*
and=they.M 3.IPFV:drag:M.PL step-F.PL heavy.PL in weariness
wa=kalālin naḥwa s=sāḥati [...]
and=fatigue toward DEF=square
'[...] and they were dragging heavy steps, in weariness and fatigue, toward the square [...]' (Naguib Mahfouz, *ʔAwlād ḥārati-nā*, 1959)[71]

(51) [...] *fī* ***laḥaḏ-ātin qiṣārin,*** *yakūnu ʔakṯara min wāḥidin fī*
in moment-F.PL short.PL 3.IPFV:be.M.SG more than one in
akṯara min makānin [...]
more than place
'[...] in short moment, he [could] be more than one, in more than one place [...]' (Tahar Ouettar, *al-Walī aṭ-Ṭāhir yarfaʕ yaday-hi bi-d-duʕāʔ*, 1999)[72]

Samples of feminine plural agreement with verbs and pronouns also occur in al-Būṣīrī's *Burda*, but much more rarely. In one case, they seem to represent a sample of borrowed syntax, where Quranic linguistic material is borrowed together with its agreement patterns (see § 3.5 for more details). In the other, the occurrence of feminine plural is genuine, yet it feels out of place, following

71 The quotation has been retrieved from the Arabicorpus corpus (http://arabicorpus.byu.edu/search.php?page=citations&sort=rBeforeW&start=1, last accessed on January, 17 2019).

72 The quotation has been retrieved from the Arabicorpus corpus (http://arabicorpus.byu.edu/search.php?page=citations&sort=rBeforeW&start=1, last accessed on January, 17 2019).

a quite generic broken plural controller. For the sake of clarity, the sample is reported again below:

(52) *fa=ʔinna=hu šamsu faḍlin hum* ***kawākibu****=hā* ***yu-ḏhir-na***[73]
and=COMP=him sun virtue they.M star.PL=her 3.IPFV-show-F.PL
ʔanwāru=hā li=n=nāsi fī ḏ=ḏulmi
light.PL=her to=DEF=people.COLL in DEF=darkness
'He is the Sun of virtue, to which they are as if moons: reflecting its lights in darkness to humanity' (*al-Burda*, 53)

Occurrences of both broken plural adjectives and feminine plural agreement with nonhuman plural controllers, after all, can be occasionally found up to the 19th and 20th century. Neoclassical poets, for instance, with their fascination for the Golden Age of Arabic poetry, often made use of lexical items and stylemes belonging to that distant past. The Egyptian poet Maḥmūd Sāmī al-Bārūdī (1839–1904) represents one of the clearest examples of such a tendency. Born in Cairo to a Circassian military family, he was privately educated as both a soldier and an intellectual, embodying in his own person the legendary figure of the warrior-poet. His profound love for classical Arabic poetry is testified by the bulky four-volume anthology published only after his death under the title *Muxtārāt al-Bārūdī* ("Poems selected by al-Bārūdī") (1909). He was particularly fond of Abbasid poetry and is usually considered the initiator of the Neoclassical movement (Somekh 1992, 45). The following verses, as evident from the theme (a magniloquent description of noble horses) and from the agreement patterns, could have easily been written during the Umayyad or Abbasid period:

(53) *fa=tarā* ***ʕitāqa*** *l=xayli ḥawla buyūti=nā*
and=2.IPFV:see:M.SG noble.PL DEF=horse.COLL around house.PL=our
qubba *l=buṭūni* ***tu-nāziʕu*** *l=ʔarsānā mašaqa*
convex.PL DEF=belly.PL 3.IPFV.F.SG-fight DEF=halter tear:3.PFV.M.SG
*ṭ=ṭirādu luḥūma=****hunna*** *fa=lam yadaʕ ʔillā*
DEF=chase flesh.PL=their.F and=NEG 3.IPFV:leave:M.SG except

73 It could be said that the presence of an action verb might influence agreement patterns, causing them to lean toward syntactic agreement in the feminine plural. In order for this to be true, however, we must posit that al-Būṣīrī, in 13th century urban Egypt, still mastered the rules governing agreement choices in the ancient system. This assumption, however, does not stand the test of a thorough analysis of the poem, where only the new system seems to be productive, with occasional relics of the ancient one.

xawāṣira	*ka=l=qisiyyi*	***mitānā***
hip.PL	like=DEF=bow.PL	firm.PL

'And you see, around our houses, noble horses, with dome-shaped bellies, fighting the halters; chasing tore their flesh, leaving nothing but hips firm as bows' (Maḥmūd Sāmī l-Bārūdī)[74]

In the sample, both broken plural adjectives (twice) and feminine plural agreement with nonhuman plural controllers occur. The ancient system, thus, is represented in all its categories, even though the syntax appears to be more typical of post-7th century poetry (not by chance al-Bārūdī's favorite) than of the pre-Islamic *Muʕallaqāt*. With specific reference to the controller *xayl* "horse.COLL", in fact, the occurrence of feminine plural agreement in a pronoun referring to a collective nonhuman controller, especially after a feminine singular verbal target, is unusual. No generalization, of course, can be drawn from the analysis of two verses, but what we observe in the sample is the presence of the ancient agreement categories in an unusual syntactic distribution. This, in turn, seems to be quite common in post-10th century sources displaying remnants of the old system, as also evidenced by ornate prose and its most cherished genre (at least in the Arab world), the *maqāma*.

> The *maqāma* is a prolific genre of Arabic literature which, as far as we can tell, was invented in the late tenth century by Aḥmad ibn al-Ḥusayn al-Hamadhānī (358–398/968–1008), known as Badīʿ al-Zamān (the Marvel of the Age), and has lasted until the twentieth. Literary *maqāmāt* (sing. *maqāma*), traditionally translated as 'Assemblies' or 'Sessions' in English and 'Séances' in French, are brief episodic or anecdotal texts—usually between two and ten pages—written in elaborate rhymed and rhythmic prose, often embellished with ornate rhetorical figures and an admixture of verse at key junctures.
>
> STEWART 2006, 145

As evident from the above quotation, the *maqāma* is a literary genre that was born during the 10th century, at the twilight of the ancient agreement system, and in a cultural environment that was extremely different from that in which that system had first seen the light. As far as we know, in fact, al-Hamaḏānī spent all his life in modern-day Iran, so that he was never inside the core of the Arabic-speaking world (although Arabic was certainly used in Persia during the 10th century and al-Hamaḏānī was proud of his "pure" Arab lineage).

74 Author's translation.

In his collection of *maqāmāt,* occurrences of the ancient system are certainly rare. Nonetheless, samples of both broken plural adjectives and feminine plural agreement with nonhuman plural controllers can occasionally be found:

(54) *wa=kašaftu* *ʔastāra* ***l=xuṭūbi*** ***s=sūdi***[75]
and=discover:1.PFV.SG veil.PL DEF=matter.PL DEF=black.PL
‘[…] and [I] disclosed the mysteries of dark difficulties […][76]’ (al-Hamaḏānī 1923, 25)

(55) […] *wa=haṣartu* ***l=ġuṣūna*** ***n=nāʕim-āti*** *wa=ǧtanaytu*
and=snap:1.PFV.SG DEF=branch.PL DEF=tender-F.PL and=pick:1.PFV.SG
warda ***l=xudūdi*** ***l=muwarrad-āti***
rose DEF=cheek.PL DEF=crimson-F.PL
‘[…] I have snapped supple branches, and plucked the rose from crimson cheeks […]’ (al-Hamaḏānī 1923, 25)

(56) *wa=lam* *nazal* *nafrā* *ʔasnimata*
and=NEG 1.IPFV.PL:cease. APOC 1.IPFV.PL:split hump.PL
n=nagādi *bi=**tilka*** ***l=ǧiyādi*** *ḥattā* ***ṣir-na***
DEF=highland.PL with=that.F DEF=horse.PL until become-3.PFV.F.PL
ka=l=ʕaṣiyyi *wa=**raǧaʕ-na*** *ka=l=qiṣiyyi*
like=DEF=stick.PL and=return-3.PFV.F.PL like=DEF=bow.PL
‘[…] and we continued to traverse the humps of the uplands, mounted upon those noble steeds, until they became as lean as walking-sticks and were bent like bows.’ (al-Hamaḏānī 1923, 33)

Interestingly enough, samples of feminine singular agreement with broken plural human controllers can also be found, even though they seem to occur even more rarely than samples of syntactic agreement in the plural with nonhuman controllers:

(57) *salū* ***l=mulūka*** *wa=xazāʔina=**hā*** […]
IMP.ask:2.M.PL DEF=king.PL and=vault.PL=her
‘Ask of kings and their treasures […]’ (al-Hamaḏānī 1923, 24)

---

75 As a matter of fact, adjectives of color show considerable conservativeness, still occasionally displaying broken plural agreement with non-human plural controllers also in (mostly literary) MSA.

76 The translations of al-Hamaḏānī’s *maqāmāt* are drawn from Prendergast’s (1915) edition, with occasional corrections.

Although he gets credit for being the creator of the genre, al-Hamaḏānī's star was overshadowed by his emulator al-Ḥarīrī (1054–1122), who lived in Baṣra in the 11th century and wrote what is generally considered as the masterpiece of the genre (Stewart 2006, 145). For the purpose of our research, although we are dealing with 11th century (ornate) prose, samples of agreement patterns belonging to the old system can also be found, though not very commonly, also in al-Ḥarīrī's *maqāmāt*. See the following samples:

(58) *ḥurūfu ʔiḥdā kalimatay=hā yaʕummu=hā*
letter.PL one.F.SG word:DU=her 3.IPFV:encompass.M.SG=her
*n=niqaṭu wa=**ḥurūfu** l=ʔuxrā lam **yu-ʕǧam-na***
DEF=dot.PL and=letter.PL DEF=other.F.SG NEG 3.IPFV-dot.PASS-F.PL
qaṭṭu
at.all
'The letters of one of every two words shall all have dots had dots, while the letters of the other shall not be pointed at all.[77]' (Steingass 1897, 46)

(59) *wa=ʔabraza min=hu **riqāʕan kutib-na***
and=bring.out.3.PFV.M.SG from=him slip.PL write.PASS-3.PFV.F.PL
bi=ʔalwāni l=ʔaṣbāġi fī ʔawāni l=farāġi
with=color.PL DEF=dye.PL in moment.PL DEF=leisure
*fa=nāwala=**hunna** ʕaǧūza l=ḥayzabūni*
and=give.3.PFV.M.SG=them.F old.woman DEF=old.and.wily
'And brought forth scraps of paper that had been written on with colours of dyes in the season of leisure, and gave them to his old beldame […]' (Steingass 1897, 52)

As far as agreement patterns are concerned, the situation closely resembles what already observed in post-10th century poetry. In the two samples drawn from al-Ḥarīrī, for instance, feminine plural agreement occurs in pronouns and passive verbs depending from broken plural inanimate controllers, which contradicts the agreement patterns found in earlier texts.

For both late poetry and the *maqāmāt*, in conclusion, we are confronted with one and the same situation. The ancient agreement system is lost, but its relics are still occasionally exhibited to ennoble the style of the writer who, however, does not fully master the criteria governing the distribution of the possible agreement choices.

---

77 Translations of al-Ḥarīrī's *maqāmāt* are drawn from Chenery (1867).

The situation is quite different if we look at Middle Arabic, whose first specimens have been investigated in Hopkins (1984) and already mentioned, although briefly, in sections 2.4, 3.2 and 3.4. When speaking of Middle Arabic, we adhere to Lentin's definition, reported below in its entirety:

> Whatever the precise chronological delimitation, one can agree to mean by Middle Arabic the language of numerous Arabic texts, distinguished by its linguistically (and therefore stylistically) mixed nature, as it combines standard and colloquial features with others of a third type, neither standard nor colloquial (for a noticeably different view, see e.g. Fischer 1982, 1991). To be more precise, Middle Arabic encompasses all the attested written layers of the language which can be defined as entirely belonging neither to Classical Arabic nor to colloquial Arabic, and as an intermediate, multiform variety, product of the interference of the two polar varieties on the continuum they bound, a variety that, for this very reason, has its own distinctive characteristics.
>
> LENTIN 2008, 216

It is precisely the mixed nature of Middle Arabic that makes it different from the two sources analyzed in the previous pages. Poetry and ornate prose, in fact, are generally considered among the most elevated literary genres, in which Classical Arabic finds its most refined expression. This inevitably means that authors strive to avoid the occurrence of any perceived colloquialism. Middle Arabic, on the other hand, is ripe with colloquialisms, despite not being a form of "written colloquial". Agreement in Middle Arabic texts can be summarized as follows:

> The system is mixed and complex. As in the colloquials, verbs and adjectives associated with nouns referring to nonhumans stand generally in the plural, as do those associated with nouns in the dual (referring to humans or nonhumans). Likewise, as in the colloquials, when the verb precedes its plural subject, it generally stands in the plural. As in the colloquials and in Ancient Arabic, some nouns referring to human groups have an agreement in the 'feminine singular'. But the concord patterns can vary in the same passage and even within the same sentence. This is due to the play between the colloquials and the standard rules, but also, it seems, to the fact that once an explicit agreement has been made, the sentence can go on with a less marked one, provided that the basic agreement is marked again whenever necessary.
>
> LENTIN 2008, 221–222

When encountering samples of plural agreement with nonhuman controllers, thus, it is it not always easy to determine whether they occur as colloquial traits or as samples of the ancient systems. In some cases, the nature of the deviation from the norms of Classical Arabic is such as to make clear that we are dealing with dialectal interference, as evident from the following sample:

(60) ***ʕišrīn ḥimār*** *ʔunaffiḏu=**hum*** [...] (10th century CE)
twenty donkey 1.IPFV.SG:dispatch=them.M
'Twenty asses, I shall dispatch them ...' (Hopkins 1984, 144)

(61) ***sittat ʔalāf*** ***dīnār*** *ʕadad waznu=**hum*** [...]
six thousand.PL dinar number weight=their.M
*fa=qbiḍ=**hum***
then=IMP.take.2.M.SG=them.M
'Six thousand dinars, correctly counted, weighing ... so take them!' (Hopkins 1984, 144)

In these cases, there is a clear deviation from the norms of Classical Arabic, which would here prescribe the use of feminine singular in the pronominal target. Syntactic agreement according to the ancient system, on the other hand, would imply the presence of a feminine plural pronoun, while masculine occurs here. This, in turn, has two implications:

I. The sample is indeed an episode of interference from the writer's native dialect;
II. In said dialect, gender distinction in the plural was either lost or in the process of being lost.

In other cases, however, the text is not so explicit, and agreement actually occurs in the feminine plural, so that other factors need to be taken into consideration to determine the nature of the sample under investigation:

(62) ***xamsat san-īn*** *ʔawwalu=**hunna** šahr*
five year-M.PL first=their.F.PL month
Rabīʕ [...] (Egypt, 259 A.H. / 872–873 CE)
Rabīʕ
'Five years, beginning from the month of Rabīʕ [...]' (Hopkins 1984, 144)

In the sample above, an inanimate controller, modified by a low numeral, triggers feminine plural agreement in the pronominal target, as expected according to the patterns of the ancient system. The occurrence of feminine plural might be here due to dialectal interference but also to the simple survival of the old system, especially in such an early text. Given that this specific papyrus was discovered in Egypt,[78] we tend to favor the second hypothesis. The first texts in Egyptian Arabic are actually much later,[79] yet they do not show any occurrence of feminine plural agreement. Hopkins specifies that this type of agreement exclusively occurs in a restricted "stock of expressions connected with the calendar (Hopkins 1984, 144)", which further leads us to think that this might actually be a linguistic relic.[80]

Despite the geographical variation and evolution in time (Middle Arabic continues to be attested to this day), the features of agreement described above continue to occur regularly. Lentin's description of "agreement in Middle Arabic", thus, stands, even though we have to consider the fact that variation, in such texts, is the norm rather than the exception. The same writer can make different agreement choices within the same text and even within the same sentence. Given that "Middle Arabic is structurally connected to Neo-Arabic dialects as regards linguistic typology (Lentin 2008, 215)", however, its analysis is of limited interest for the study of the evolution of the agreement system in the high variety of the diglossic continuum. More insights on the topic will be offered in chapter 5.

3.9 Nabaṭī Poetry: Poetic Register or Survival of the Old System?

The previous sections have covered the evolution of agreement patterns in Arabic from the pre-Islamic era to the age of standardization. In these sections, we described the ancient agreement system of pre-Islamic poetry and early Islamic texts and its replacement by a new one, in which humanness was the decisive factor, with a final section devoted to the discussion of the few contexts that partially escaped such standardization. In doing so, we also highlighted the typological affinity of the ancient system of pre-Classical poetry with the agree-

78 The fact that the papyrus was discovered in Egypt, of course, does not ensure that his author was Egyptian or a speaker of Egyptian Arabic, since documents have been found which were written by speakers coming from all parts of the Arabic-Islamic Empire. The Egyptian nature of the underlying dialect needs to be ascertained on a case-by-case basis on purely linguistic grounds.

79 In Doss and Davies' (2013) collection of texts in Egyptian Arabic, for instance, the first text is dated (804 AH / 1401 CE).

80 It is dubious, of course, whether said linguistic relic goes back to the ancient agreement system or to a time when Egyptian Arabic still had gender distinction in the plural.

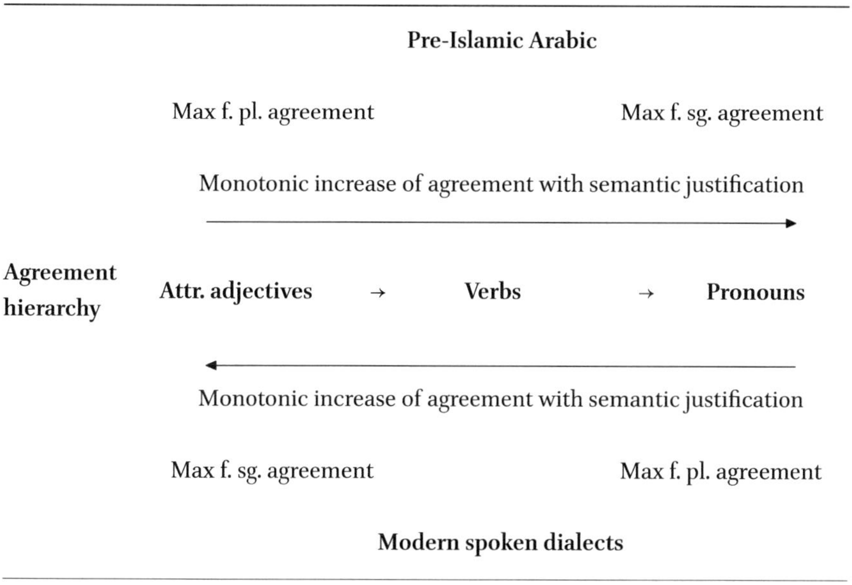

FIGURE 3.6 Agreement hierarchy in pre-Islamic Arabic and the modern dialects

ment patterns found in the modern dialects, despite the existence of important differences. While sharing the same agreement categories, in fact, pre-Classical Arabic and the modern dialects position themselves at the two opposites of Corbett's agreement hierarchy. The agreement system of pre- and early Classical Arabic, as seen in sections 3.3–3.4, perfectly fits into Corbett's agreement hierarchy, both synchronically and diachronically. The system, in fact, features the greatest percentage of semantic agreement at the rightmost end of the agreement hierarchy (i.e. with pronouns), while attributive adjectives are the most conservative category. A comparison between pre-Islamic poetry and the Quran, moreover, not only confirms this distribution, but also shows that the innovative semantically motivated agreement (i.e. feminine singular) was actually spreading left into the agreement hierarchy. The dialects show an equally interesting, yet more puzzling, distribution. Attributive adjectives, in fact, feature the highest percentage of feminine singular agreement, while feminine plural agreement tend to cluster around pronouns, with verbs occupying a middle position. The distribution of agreement patterns in the dialects, thus, is a reversed version of Corbett's agreement hierarchy, as evident in Figure 3.6.

The complex interactions of Corbett's agreement hierarchy with the unusual agreement behavior of the Arabic languages have been discussed at length in Chapter 2 (see in particular sections 2.3.3.4 and 2.4). In particular, a possible explanation for this peculiar phenomenon has been provided in § 2.6, based on the unusual nature of semantic agreement in Arabic and on its interaction with the agreement hierarchy. The agreement hierarchy, in its original formulation, linked the increase of semantic agreement *in the plural* to the increasing distance from a collective controller, as exemplified in the figure above. In the typical scenario, thus, targets closer to the collective controller would feature syntactic agreement in the singular. The further we get from the controller, the more likely the occurrence of semantic agreement in the plural. When employing the agreement hierarchy for plural controllers in Arabic, on the contrary, we are dealing with controllers whose syntactic agreement is in the plural and whose semantic agreement, on the contrary, in the feminine singular. An increase of singular agreement as we move further from a plural controller, however, would run contrary to the principles of cognitive linguistics, with specific reference to the retrievability of information (the increase of plural agreement with the increase of distance between controller and targets has been shown to occur in several dialects, see § 2.3.3.4). In § 2.6, the different behavior of pre-Classical Arabic and the modern dialects has been explained based on a fundamental morphological difference between the two, namely the incidence of feminine singular in adjectives. Adjectives in pre-Classical Arabic show, when compared to contemporary dialects (here represented by Najdi), a much more marked tendency to appear in the broken plural. While broken plural and feminine singular share a similar semantic connotation of [-individuated] plurality, thus, the occurrence of broken plurals in the domain of attributive adjectives formally adheres to the prediction of the agreement hierarchy, while the occurrence of feminine singular seems to contradict it. Again, the idiosincracy is explained historically with the spread of feminine singular agreement to the left side of the agreement hierarchy. Once agreement in the feminine singular became available for adjectives as well, which had already occurred in pre-Classical Arabic, it gradually replaced the broken plural for most adjectives, due to the shared semantic connotation. At that point, it's only distance from the controller that influences agreement patterns, so that syntactic agreement tends to occur more frequently as we get further from the controller.

In order to confirm this hypothesis, we compared data drawn from everyday Najdi with a corpus of Najdi Nabaṭī Poetry, whose poetic register is still full of adjectival broken plurals. Agreement patterns emerging from Najdi Nabaṭī Poetry are, thus, compared to those of pre-Classical Arabic and to those emerging from non-poetical varieties of the same dialect. The double comparison will ideally clarify the major point of discussion, allowing us to determine if the register of the text and the incidence of broken plurals in adjectives influence agreement patterns or if, indeed, Old Arabic and the dialects are typologically different with reference to agreement, despite their superficial resemblance.

Nabaṭī poetry is the traditional dialectal poetry of the Arabian Peninsula and neighboring areas (Jordan, Iraq, Syria and the Sinai region). The term Nabaṭī, of course, has nothing to do with the Nabateans and must not be taken literally. It refers to a variety of poetry that does not adhere strictly to the language and metrical schemes of classical poetry and that thus resembles the "broken" Arabic anciently spoken by the Nabateans (Holes 2011). The term itself only started being used in the 17th century. When Ibn Khaldūn (1332–1406) wrote about this kind of poetry, not by chance, he simply used the terms *badawī, qaysī* and *ḥawrānī* (Sowayan 1985, 1). Although it is composed in the local dialect[81] and does not conform to the metrics of pre-Islamic poetry, Nabaṭī poetry is considered by many as its true descendant. Clive Holes also adopts this view, pointing out to the fact that Nabaṭī poetry shares with the Ancient Arabian poetry of the pre-Islamic period such a number of traits that a mere coincidence is highly unlikely. A list of these traits include:

a. The themes (*ʔaġrāḍ*);
b. The elements that make up a poem, including some of the most typical *topoi*, such as the amatory prelude and the camel journey;
c. The lexicon:[82]

> [...] much of its vocabulary, though often changed morphologically, preserves Classical words and meanings lost long ago in all other modern varieties of Arabic, spoken or written. It is not conceivable that Nabaṭī poets simply 'borrowed' such apparent classicisms from the old poetry. Until quite recently most of them were totally illiterate and in any case desert-dwellers cut off from any source from which they might have obtained it. Nor it is true that the Nabaṭī poetic vocabulary has ever been identical with the everyday speech of those who compose it. [...] Much of traditional Nabaṭī poetry is unintelligible to the Arab layman, whether he is of Bedouin descent or not, such is the degree of its divergence from speech.
>
> HOLES 2011

For all these reasons, Najdi Nabaṭī poetry represents the best possible choice to operate a double comparison with Najdi Arabic on one side and with pre-

81 Despite being composed by the single poets in their native dialects, the high register of Nabaṭī poetry ensures a certain degree of interdialectality, which was the object of a detailed analysis in Henkin (2009).

82 For the analysis of our corpus of Nabaṭī poetry, the glossary provided in Kurpershoek (2005) was an indispensable tool.

Islamic poetry on the other. Holes (2011) describes agreement patterns in Nabaṭī poetry, even though without statistic data, in the following way:

> They also use a 'direct' rather than a 'deflected' agreement system, whereby pl nouns tend to take pl verbs and adjectives and be referred to by pl pronouns. This is characteristic not just of nouns that refer to human beings, but also of non-human nouns, which frequently have f pl verbal, adjectival and pronominal forms in agreement, and do so regardless of the gender of the sg noun. In this respect, Bedouin usage echoes ancient CLA practice (Fischer 2002:71–72) [...] Pl and collective nouns referring to human beings of either gender also normally attract f sg agreement, especially when the reference is generic [...].
>
> HOLES 2011

Let us now turn to our corpus of Nabaṭī poetry, to see how numbers support Holes' description. The corpus is based on the poems collected by Kurpershoek (1994), while data were crosschecked with Kurpershoek (1995) to make sure of its representativeness. Kurpershoek (1994) is a collection of Nabaṭī poetry by the Bedouin poet ʕAbd Allāh ibn Muḥammad ibn Ḥuzayyim, known as ad-Dindān. ʕAbd Allāh ad-Dindān (henceforth, ad-Dindān) hailed from the Ḥarāršah tribe, a sub-branch of the ar-Riǧbān of ad-Duwāsir, and was one of the last Bedouins of Najd, who was forced to adopt a partially sedentary lifestyle only at an old age (M.P. Kurpershoek 1994, 3). For the purpose of the present study, we analyzed his entire *dīwān*, in the form in which it was collected by Kurpershoek. The analysis yielded a total of 673 targets (128 depending on human controllers and 545 depending on nonhuman ones), which represents a sufficient corpus to describe the basic agreement patterns of ad-Dindān's poetry.

As far as post-controller targets depending on nonhuman controllers are concerned, agreement patterns is summarized in Table 3.15 (animal and inanimate controllers have been collapsed into one category).

Table 3.15 then compares the results of the analysis with the corresponding data drawn from the seven *Muʕallaqāt*.

A comparison between the two tables shows an impressive similarity, especially when considering the time span elapsed between the composition of the *Muʕallaqāt* (approximately 6th century CE) and ad-Dindān's *dīwān* (20th century). The percentage of broken plural in adjectives is likewise impressively similar. This pairs with Holes' description of the archaic nature of the lexicon in Nabaṭī poetry, which is mostly unintelligible to the Arab layman and "[...] preserves Classical words and meanings lost long ago in all other modern

TABLE 3.15 Agreement patterns with post-nonhuman controller targets by target type in ad-Dindān's poetry[a]

Target	Total	F. sg.	F. pl.	Br. pl.
Attr. adjective	129	13 (10%)	21 (16.3%)	92 (71.3%)
Verb	121	91 (75.2%)	21 (17.4%)	-
Pronoun	146	128 (87%)	19 (13%)	-

a Cases in which default agreement in the masculine singular occurs have been expunged from both this table and the following one.

TABLE 3.16 Agreement patterns with post-nonhuman controllers by target type in the seven *Muʕallaqāt*

Target	Total	F. sg.	F. pl.	Br. pl.
Attr. adjective	21	4 (19%)	3 (14.3%)	14 (66.7%)
Verb	50	21 (42%)	27 (54%)	-
Pronoun	68	57 (83.8%)	11 (16.2%)	-

varieties of Arabic, spoken or written (Holes 2011)." The syntactic structure of Nabaṭī poetry, in a similar way, preserves a distribution of agreement patterns that seems to be lost in modern dialects of Arabic, including everyday Najdi.

The similarity in the distribution of agreement patterns between the two varieties, moreover, does not stop at the level of the single categories. In § 2.4, in fact, it was noted that the percentage of feminine singular agreement in pronouns (the locus of innovation of the innovative pattern) almost exactly equates the sum of broken plural and feminine singular agreement in adjectives, despite the small size of our corpus. The two tables concerning pre-Islamic poetry are reported again in Table 3.17 for the sake of clarity.

Even though numbers do not match with the same precision, data from the Quran (Table 3.18) confirm this trend (data concerning animal and inanimate controllers have been collapsed into one category for the sake of brevity).

After fourteen centuries from the composition of the *Muʕallaqāt*, the same pattern can be found in Nabaṭī poetry, as evident from Table 3.19.

It is, thus, evident that the agreement system of Nabaṭī poetry is the closest thing we have to the patterns of pre-Islamic poetry. Apart from numbers, a qualitative analysis of agreement patterns shows the same structures observed in

TABLE 3.17 Percentages of feminine singular + broken plural agreement in adjectives compared to feminine singular agreement in pronouns (*Muʕallaqāt*)

Animate	**Tot.**	**F. Sg. + Br. Pl.**
Attr. adj.	10	9 (90%)
		F. Sg.
Pronouns	21	19 (90.5%)

Inanimate	**Tot.**	**F. Sg. + Br. Pl.**
Attr. adj.	11	9 (81.8%)
		F. Sg.
Pronouns	47	38 (80.9%)

TABLE 3.18 Percentages of feminine singular + broken plural agreement in adjectives compared to feminine singular agreement in pronouns (Quran)

Nonhuman	**Tot.**	**F. Sg. + Br. Pl.**
Attr. adj.	120	86 (71.7%)
		F. Sg.
Pronouns	268	228 (85%)

TABLE 3.19 Percentages of feminine singular + broken plural agreement in adjectives compared to feminine singular agreement in pronouns (*Nabaṭī* poetry)

Nonhuman	**Tot.**	**F. sg + Br. Pl**
Attr. adj.	129	105 (81.3%)
		F. sg.
Pronouns	146	128 (87%)

the *Muʕallaqāt*. A particularly frequent structure consists of a controller modified by several targets, usually involving a broken plural adjective followed by feminine singular verbs or pronouns:[83]

(63) *ya=llāh ya=rabb* ***al=fiṭīr*** ***al=marāǧīb*** *illi*
oh=God oh=Lord DEF=she.camel.PL DEF=well.guarded.PL REL
ġad-at *min ṭūl mass ad=dahar*
nurture-3.PFV.F.SG from length grip DEF=time.of.want.and.drought
ḥīm
crazed.with.thirst.PL
'O God, o Lord of the well-guarded she-camels, emaciated animals in a drought-stricken land' (XII, 8) (M.P. Kurpershoek 1994, 139)[84]

(64) *tuwāma ʕala ʕayrāt* ***l=anḏa***
flutter.3.PFV.M.SG on strong.camel:F.PL DEF=lean.camel.PL
l=buwātiʕi ***ʕlā=ha*** *ʕyālin min bini ṭayybīn al=fāl* […]
DEF=daring.PL on=her boy.PL from son:M.PL good:M.PL DEF=omen
'While dangling from the back of the swift and persevering animals. They are mounted by young men born under a lucky star' (VI, 31–32) (M.P. Kurpershoek 1994, 121)

Let us now compare the two above samples with the following one, drawn from our pre-Islamic corpus:

(65) *fa-waqaftu ʔasʔalu-**hā** wa-kayfa suʔālu-nā,* ***ṣumman***
and-stop:1.PFV.SG 1.IPFV.SG:ask-her and-how question-our deaf.PL
xawālida *mā yabīnu kalāmu-**hā***
eternal.PL NEG 3.IPFV:be.clear.M.SG speech-her
'Then I stood questioning them, and of what avail is questioning rocks lying in their place for ever, whose speech is not clear?'[85] (Labīd, 10)

(66) *wa=**l=xaylu*** ***ta-qtaḥimu*** *l=xabāra* ***ʕawābisan***
and=DEF=horse.COLL 3.IPFV.F.SG-charge DEF=soil frowning.PL
'And the horses were charging over the soft soil, frowning.' (ʕAntara, 88)

---

83 I would like to thank Clive Holes, who pointed to the similarity between pre-Islamic and Nabaṭī poetry with specific reference to this structure, during a presentation I gave at the third Arabic Linguistics Forum (SOAS, London, 4–6 July 2018).

84 Translations are also drawn from Kurpershoek (1994).

85 Translations are drawn, unless specifically mentioned, from Johnson (1893).

It is clear that we are confronted here with the same structure, although with a 14-century time span between the two sources. The possibility of borrowed syntax, which has already been observed in post-Classical poetry (e.g. in al-Būṣīrī's *Burda*), is extremely remote, since most of the Nabaṭī poets were, until very recent times, totally illiterate desert dwellers. They did not have the possibility of getting acquainted with pre-Islamic poetry to the necessary degree for syntactic borrowing (or any other kind of borrowing) to happen (Holes 2011). Quite to the contrary, we are here dealing with the uninterrupted transmission of *topoi* and stylemes within the context of the poetic tradition of the Arabian Peninsula.

A comparison with the patterns of contemporary spoken Najdi, on the other hand, shows extremely diverging agreement patterns.

As evident from Table 3.20, while the percentages of feminine singular + broken plural in the two varieties are comparable (81.3% in Najdi poetry, 72.7% in everyday Najdi), the difference in the incidence of broken plural adjectives is staggering (71.3% in Najdi poetry, only 9.1% in everyday Najdi). This difference offers the best available explanation to the divergent behavior of pre-Classical Arabic and the contemporary dialects.

TABLE 3.20 Agreement patterns with post-nonhuman controller targets in Najdi *Nabaṭī* poetry and plain spoken Najdi[a]

Najdi poetry	**Total**	F.SG	F.PL	**Broken** PL
Attr. adjective	129	13 (10%)	21 (16.3%)	92 (71.3%)
Verb	121	91 (75.2%)	21 (17.4%)	-
Pronoun	146	128 (87%)	19 (13%)	-
Everyday Najdi	**Total**	F.SG	F.PL (or M.PL)	**Broken** PL
Attr. adjective	11	7 (63.6%)	1 (9.1%)	1 (9.1%)
Verb	37	27 (73%)	6 (16.2%)	-
Pronoun	88	42 (47.7%)	46 (52.3%)	-

a In this table as well, targets that appear in the masculine singular have not been reported (this accounts for the discrepancies between the relative and absolute totals in each target category for adjectives and verbs). In the case of plain Najdi, a very few verbal and pronominal targets appeared in the masculine plural for no obvious reason (other than the process of morphological loss the dialect is undergoing, already discussed in Chapter 2): these have been lumped together with feminine plural targets. The Najdi colloquial data are based on the same corpus analyzed in § 2.3.3.

The pattern emerging from contemporary spoken Najdi is to be considered as representative of gender-distinguishing varieties of Arabic as a whole, although numbers may vary. At present, it is unclear whether some dialects exist in which the frequency of use of apophonic plural adjectives is remarkably higher than in others. If data from such varieties were to become available, it would be interesting to observe how well they align with the predictions made by the agreement hierarchy.

3.10 Summary

Chapter 3 provided a diachronic survey of the agreement system of written Arabic, in a Semitic perspective and adopting a typological approach, within a time span ranging from Common Central Semitic to the modern manifestations of the language. Our reconstruction started from West Semitic, of which Arabic is an offshoot.

In West Semitic, the languages of the Northwest group (Ugaritic, Canaanite and Aramaic) consistently feature systems with prevalent syntactic agreement and only few vestiges of internal plurals inherited from Proto-Semitic (which in turn inherited them from Proto-Afroasiatic). The other languages, once grouped into the no longer accepted South Semitic group, expanded the (probably restricted) set of inherited internal plurals and turned it into their prevalent pluralization strategy. This group of languages includes Arabic, Ancient South Arabian, the Modern South Arabian languages and some of the Ethiopian Semitic languages. In these languages, external plurals steadily lost ground to the innovative internal ones, until they were, to different extents, relegated to a small portion of the lexicon. Internal plurals, however, are underspecified, since they share some of their most productive templates with singular nouns and fail to carry gender information. In the above mentioned languages, where internal plurals almost completely replaced external ones (which do carry gender information), the consequence was that the largest part of the lexicon became underspecified in the plural.

Quite predictably, then, in most of the languages featuring a full system of internal plurals the inherited syntactic agreement systems were replaced by partially semantic ones.[86] A first step, common to all the languages having a full system of broken plurals, was the spread of the system to the class of adjectives,

86 It is worth reminding the reader that no system is entirely syntactically motivated. The development should be understood as a shift from a system which is prevalently syntactically motivated to one in which semantic factors play a greater role.

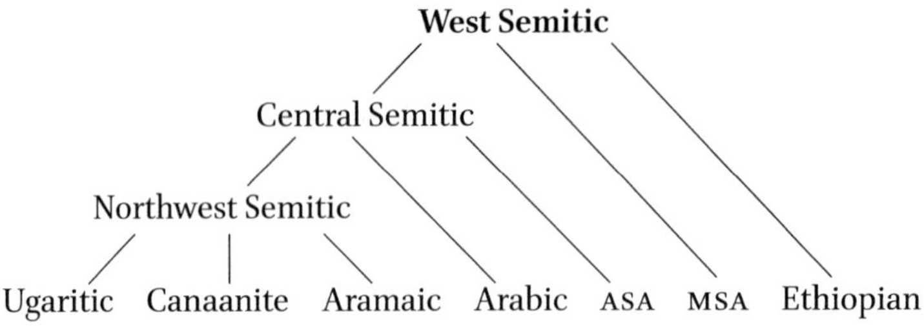

FIGURE 3.7 West Semitic according to Hetzron's classification models (with modifications)
HUEHNERGARD AND RUBIN 2011, 263

whose boundaries with the class of nouns were quite loose. In this way, agreement between a controller and its adjectival target could dispense from gender retrieval, occurring in the broken plural. The subsequent developments, on the other hand, seem to have occurred independently in the single languages, judging from their distinct outputs. In Geʕez, for instance, only human controllers trigger syntactic agreement in the plural, while agreement with nonhumans is variable in both gender and number. Tigre sets the bar lower on the animacy scale, so that syntactic agreement in the plural is restricted to animate (i.e. human and animal) controllers, while inanimate ones usually trigger agreement in the masculine singular. Pending more detailed studies of agreement in Ethiopian Semitic, it appears that the languages that developed a full system of broken plurals underwent dramatic changes in their agreement system. In particular, the animacy hierarchy came into play, although in different ways, probably due to the weakening of the formal rules of agreement assigning.

The only two languages having a full system of broken plurals in which agreement remained largely syntactical are Ṣayḥadic (Ancient South Arabian) and the Modern South Arabian Languages, despite the fact that they probably feature the most pervasive system of broken plurals, so that even *nisba* adjectives undergo internal pluralization. Ancient South Arabian has long been extinct (probably since 7th century CE), so that it obviously ceased to evolve. Modern South Arabian, on the contrary, is still spoken, although sometimes by very few speakers. It seems that some of the Modern South Arabian languages are developing ways to encode gender information in internal plural patterns. In Mehri, for instance, broken plurals containing a glide seem to carry gender information based on the distribution of *w* and *y*.

In Arabic, the (reconstructed) formal system of agreement assigning was also weakened, although in a different way from what happened in Ethiopian Semitic, where animacy played the primary role in the development of semantic agreement. Internal plurals, in a stage in which they still coexisted with external ones, came to be reanalyzed as [-individuated] ones. While internal plural adjectives shared this property, thus permitting semantic agreement with their controllers, the problem arose of how to match the [-individuated] semantic feature in verbal and pronominal targets, which did not have any form of broken plural. The problem was solved resorting to feminine singular agreement, whose [-individuated] feature is confirmed by the fact that it is likewise employed as a form of semantic agreement with collective nouns, also when they are morphologically masculine singular. This process of semantic reanalysis of morphological features, attested in different languages of the world, is usually known as resemanticization. In Arabic, thus, the decisive factor in assigning semantic agreement was [individuation] and not [animacy], as evident from the fact that feminine singular agreement also occurs with human controllers, which stand at the top of the animacy hierarchy. Nonetheless, animacy is usually considered as a sub-factor of individuation, so that the innovation probably started at the lower end of the animacy hierarchy, where controllers are more likely to be seen as an indistinct mass. From a syntactic point of view, moreover, the innovation probably started with pronouns, which stand at the rightmost end of Corbett's agreement hierarchy, and then started spreading left, as in the following figure:

attribute < predicate < relative pronoun < personal pronoun

In the first sources analyzed for this study, i.e. pre-Islamic poetry, the spread was already ongoing, because feminine singular agreement can be found with both human controllers (top of the animacy hierarchy) and attributive adjectives (leftmost end of the agreement hierarchy). In both cases, however, this happens quite rarely, so that pre-Islamic poetry still represents a primitive stage of the resemanticization process, where syntactic agreement is still prevalent. The Quran (7th century) represents a more advanced stage of the process, with feminine singular agreement spreading both left in the agreement hierarchy and up into the animacy one. Occurrences of feminine singular with adjectival targets and with human controllers, in fact, are both on the rise. The system undergoes a stage of more dramatic changes starting with the age of conquests (7th–8th century), due to the profound changes into the Arabic speech community. The first of these changes involves the weakening of the old system of agreement. In early Islamic poetry, here analyzed, we still find the old agreement categories in the court poets (usually living in Damascus and later in Baghdad) of the 8th, 9th and 10th centuries, but in a distribution whose criteria are not as neat as those observed in pre-Islamic poetry.

The most dramatic change in the agreement system of written Arabic, however, occurs later, and mainly in prose texts, probably due to the large number of non-native speakers of Arabic who started using their L2 in the written medium. In the famous *Kalīla wa-Dimna*, for instance, agreement patterns appear to be borrowed, or at least heavily influenced, by Middle Persian, the language from which it was translated by Ibn al-Muqaffaʕ (ca. 720–ca. 756 CE). In the book, in fact, the agreement system seems partly based on the animacy hierarchy threshold obtaining in Middle Persian, where inanimate (but not animal) controllers prevalently trigger singular agreement in verbal targets. Despite the fame of *Kalīla wa-Dimna*, however, this change did not take hold in Arabic as a whole. The huge presence of non-native speakers writing in Arabic, with the phenomena of generalization and avoidance widely described by acquisitional linguistics, brought about another change, which would permanently alter the system of written Arabic. The higher percentage of feminine singular agreement with nonhuman controllers was reanalyzed as an agreement pattern triggered not by their low individuation, but rather by the [-human] trait. This resulted in a double-ended generalization:

I. Feminine singular agreement became mandatory with nonhuman (both animal and inanimate) plural controllers, independently of their degree of individuation and with all types of targets;
II. Feminine singular agreement ceased to be an option for human plural controllers, again independently of their degree of individuation and with all types of targets. Traces of the ancient system, however, remain in the optional feminine singular agreement with human collective controllers, such as *nās* "people.COLL" and the names of Arab tribes and populations, even when they are morphologically masculine singular.

A further consequence of the standardization process was that variation in agreement patterns almost completely ceased to occur. A specific date for this change, however, is difficult to individuate, since it probably happened at a different pace in different settings. It must be remembered that, when talking of a change that only took place in the written variety of a language in pre-modern times, there is no actual speech community involved. Language professionals, who were able to read and write, were a small minority. The change, which spread to the entire Arabic-speaking world and was standardized in the grammars of Arabic, might have been initiated by a restricted number of writers and *dīwān* employees, who probably lived far from each other and never met in their life. We know for sure, in fact, that real speech communities in the Arabic-speaking world were not touched by this change, since the ancient system survives to these days in the spoken dialects.

The standardization process described above completely ousted the ancient system of agreement in the domain of non-fictional prose (history, geography, religion etc.). In this domain, the process was probably completed by the end of the 10th century. From this point forward, the system of written Arabic ceased both to evolve and to exhibit any interesting variation. Vestiges of the ancient system can be found, up to the 20th century, in poetry and in a few literary genres, such as the *maqāmāt* "assemblies", written in ornate prose. In both cases, however, the old system did not actually survive. Broken and feminine plural agreement is still employed with nonhuman plurals, but the distribution patterns are no longer governed by the rules obtaining in pre-Islamic poetry. Authors usually adhere to the norms of Classical Arabic, with systematic feminine singular agreement, employing the pre-Classical patterns randomly to signal a higher register or as archaisms. In mixed-style texts, such as Middle Arabic, the syntax is heavily influenced by the underlying colloquials, so that syntactic agreement with nonhuman controllers regularly continues to appear.

Pre-Islamic Arabic and modern gender-distinguishing dialects, as already said, basically feature the same three-class system, with feminine singular agreement as an optional [-individuated] agreement marker for both human and nonhuman controllers. The distribution of the agreement choices on Corbett's agreement hierarchy, however, appears as diametrically opposite in our data. In pre-Islamic Arabic, semantic (feminine singular) agreement clusters around pronouns, at the right end of the agreement hierarchy. In the modern dialects, on the contrary, feminine singular seems to be more frequent with adjectives. This is due to the peculiar nature of semantic agreement in Arabic, which is singular, contrary to what usually happens in the languages on which the agreement hierarchy was tested. In Corbett's original formulation, in fact, the agreement hierarchy was a useful tool to predict the likelihood of plural semantic agreement with collective controllers, which are usually morphologically singular. In the case of Arabic, we face the opposite situation, i.e. morphologically plural controllers triggering semantic singular agreement. Nonetheless, pre- and early Islamic data conform to the agreement hierarchy. This is due to the fact that agreement in the broken plural is the most common option for adjectives in pre-Classical Arabic, while it appears much more rarely in the contemporary Peninsular dialects from which data for statistical analysis were drawn. In our corpus, in fact, many high-frequency adjectives only occur in the feminine singular, which means that their apophonic plurals are probably falling out of use.[87] In order to confirm our hypothesis, we analyzed a

87 It is probably worth reminding the reader that data from two different dialectal areas, i.e. Tunisia (Prochàzka and Gabsi 2017, 257) and Yemen (Watson 1993, 213), confirm the fact

corpus of Najdi Nabaṭī poetry, where broken plural adjectives still abound, and compared it with both everyday Najdi and pre-Classical poetry. The analysis of the corpus once more confirmed this supposition. The agreement patterns extracted from the corpus, in fact, aligned with those observed in the seven *Muʕallaqāt* and contradicted those of everyday Najdi Arabic.

---

that adjectives featuring apophonic plurals do not usually occur in the feminine singular with plural controllers, to the point of being rejected as ungrammatical. The abundance of feminine singular agreement in the Najdi corpus here analyzed, thus, might imply that the spread of feminine singular down the agreement hierarchy is causing broken plural adjectives to fall into disuse. The possibility that the situation in Najdi is different from that of Tunisia and Yemen, of course, should not be ruled out. The analysis of larger corpora, including dialects were broken plural adjectives occur with greater frequency, will be the object of further research.

CHAPTER 4

The Approach of Traditional Grammar: An Attempt at Reconstruction

4.1 Scope of the Chapter

In Chapter 3, we provided a diachronic account of the evolution of agreement with plural controllers in written Arabic, starting from the Common Central Semitic stage. The account is based on data drawn from written sources, beginning with the pre-Islamic *Muʕallaqāt*, and on reconstruction. The evolution of agreement patterns in written Arabic presents some remarkable shifts, the most prominent one being the standardization of feminine singular agreement with nonhuman plural controllers.

The present chapter focuses on the approach of traditional grammar to the topic of agreement, in order to investigate if and how the Arabic grammarians[1] captured and described the evolution of agreement patterns. Before presenting the results of our analysis, however, it should be noted that the study of indigenous Arabic grammar constitutes an independent, and nowadays pretty well established, branch of Arabic linguistics. Traditional grammar works following its own categories and tenets, some of which are not shared with modern linguistic thought. The reader who desires to obtain a deeper understanding of the Arabic linguistic thought is thus referred to the main works devoted to this subject, specifically to Owens (1988; 1990), Versteegh (1997), Marogy (2012), Marogy and Versteegh (2015), Ayoub and Versteegh (2018) and Giolfo and Versteegh (2019), to cite only some of the major works. Our chapter does not deal with the theoretical issues related to agreement in traditional Arabic grammar, which goes beyond the scope of this book. On the contrary, it follows the treatment of a specific question, i.e. agreement with plural controllers, from 8th century grammar to didactic books written and published during the *Nahḍa* (roughly during the 19th century). At the end of this chapter, moreover, a few remarks will be made on the so-called *ʔakalū-nī l-barāġīṯu* syndrome, which has already been investigated by prominent scholars (Levin 1989; Guillaume 2011).

---

1 We chose the denomination "Arabic grammarians", as opposed to "Arab grammarians", because Arab usually refers to ethnic origins, while grammarians, starting from Sībawayh, were often of non-Arab origin. On the other hand, they were all grammarians of Arabic, whence our choice.

 DOI:10.1163/9789004527249_005

The question of agreement has not received great attention in traditional Arabic grammar, to the point that Yehudit Dror wrote that “traditional Arabic grammarians usually ignore the agreement issue (Dror 2016, 103)”. This statement, however, is not entirely accurate. It is true that no chapter explicitly devoted to the issue of agreement was found in any of the classical sources consulted for this chapter. Observations concerning agreement are scattered in chapters dealing with different topics, such as nominal morphology (of the plural), pronouns and the already mentioned *ʔakalū-nī l-barāġīṯu* syndrome. Putting these observations together to obtain a full picture of how agreement was described by Arabic grammarians is not an easy task, which is why this chapter makes no pretention to exhaustiveness. In many cases, observations concerning agreement patterns were triggered by the necessity to explain passages of the Quran whose linguistic form differed from what was considered as common usage. For this reason, Quranic commentaries (*tafāsīr*, sg. *tafsīr*) have been constantly employed alongside grammatical treatises. Commentaries, in fact, often contain useful linguistic explanations, which helps the scholar understand what the “state of the art” of linguistics (with reference to agreement) was at the time when the *tafsīr* was composed. In some cases, moreover, the author of the *tafsīr* directly makes reference to famous Arabic grammarians, quoting from their works, which also helps to locate passages that are relevant for the topic under analysis.

The two most important research questions that this chapter will try to answer are:

I. How was agreement with plural controller described by Arabic grammarians, with specific reference to nonhuman controllers?
II. Does the standardization of feminine singular agreement with nonhuman plural controllers reflect in the works of Arabic grammarians? If yes, when does the rule find a place in grammars of Arabic?

Like said above, Quranic exegesis was used as a litmus test to crosscheck whether certain linguistic traits of the ancient agreement system were considered as worth some explanation or, on the contrary, deemed ordinary, in which case we expect no remark from the commentator. The litmus test concerned two traits in particular, i.e. the occurrence of feminine plural agreement and of masculine plural agreement with nonhuman plural controllers. While the former is typical of pre-Islamic poetry and the Quran, the latter is an exception, which is usually motivated case-by-case, yielding an interesting crop of linguistic observations. Three Quranic verses were thus selected for the purpose of this research:

(1) *wa=ʕallama* *ʔĀdama* ***l=ʔasmāʔa*** *kulla=hā* *ṯumma*
and=teach.3.PFV.M.SG Adam DEF=name.PL all=her then
*ʕaraḍa=**hum*** *ʕalā* *l=malāʔikati* […]
show.3.PFV.M.SG=them.M on DEF=angel.PL
'And He taught Adam the names, all of them; then He presented them unto the angels […]' (II, 31)

(2) […] *ʔinn=ī* *raʔaytu* ***ʔaḥada ʔašara*** ***kawkaban*** ***wa=š=šamsa***
COMP=me see:1.PFV.SG eleven star and=DEF=sun
wa=l=qamara *raʔaytu=**hum*** *l=ī* ***sāǧid-īna***
and=DEF=moon see:1.PFV.SG=them.M to=me ACT.PTCP.bow-M.PL
'[…] I saw eleven stars, and the sun and the moon; I saw them bowing down before me' (XII, 4)

(3) […] *wa=saxxarnā* *maʕa* *Dāwūda* ***l=ǧibāla***
and=subject:1.PFV.PL with David DEF=mountain.PL
yu-sabbiḥ-na *wa=ṭ=ṭayra* […]
3.IPFV-praise-F.PL and=DEF=bird.COLL
'[…] And with David We subjected the mountains to give glory, and the birds […]' (XXI, 79)

The three verses have been quoted in the order in which they appear in the Quranic text. The first two verses present cases of masculine plural agreement with nonhuman plural controllers, while the third one features a verbal target agreeing in the feminine plural with its nonhuman plural controller. Viewed from the perspective of late Classical or Modern Standard Arabic, both agreement choices do not represent common usage and need to be explained. If, however, we look at the three verses from the viewpoint of the ancient system, the occurrence of feminine plural agreement with a plural nonhuman controller is a normal case of syntactic agreement. The agreement choice is here motivated by the fact that the verb (*yu-sabbiḥ-na* "3.IPFV-praise-F.PL") involves a high degree of volition and is thus likely to trigger syntactic agreement. Masculine plural agreement with nonhuman plural controllers, on the other hand, is not usually an option in the ancient system either, unless the nonhuman controller is metaphorically humanized.[2] Investigating in detail the

2 In modern varieties of spoken Arabic, masculine plural agreement with nonhuman plural controllers can also occur due to the erosion and subsequent loss of gender distinction in the plural, which is probably not the case here.

way in which both Quranic commentaries and grammatical treatises analyze the three verses, thus, opens a window onto the way in which agreement was perceived by Arabic grammarians and commentators.

4.2 Early Arabic Grammar: From Sībawayh to al-Mubarrad

The 8th and 9th centuries witnessed the birth of the Basran and Kufan schools and are generally considered as the formative stage of Arabic grammar (Owens 1990, 2). During this stage, both the first treatises on Arabic grammar and the earliest commentaries on the Quran reflect a situation in which the ancient agreement system is still alive and perceived as such. As said in section 4.1, three verses from the Quran were employed as a litmus test to verify what the commentator considered as ordinary agreement patterns and what, on the other hand, was considered as odd.

Commentators ranging from al-Farrāʔ (761–822 CE) to al-Ṭabarī, for instance, found the occurrence of masculine plural agreement with plural nonhuman controllers as a linguistic oddity in need of an explanation.

(4) [...] *ʔinn=ī raʔaytu* ***ʔaḥada ʔašara kawkaban wa=š=šamsa***
COMP=me see:1.PFV.SG Eleven star and=DEF=sun
wa=l=qamara *raʔaytu=**hum*** *l=ī* ***sāǧid-īna***
and=DEF=moon see:1.PFV.SG=them.M to=me ACT.PTCP.bow-M.PL
'[...] I saw eleven stars, and the sun and the moon; I saw them bowing down before me' (XII, 4)

Al-Farrāʔ(1955, 2:34) explains this occurrence in terms of humanizazion of a non-human controller:

> This *nūn* and *wāw* [i.e. m.pl.] are for the plural of male *jinns*, humans and what is similar to them. It is said *"an-nāsu sāǧidūna* [m.pl.], *wa-l-malāʔikatu wa-l-ǧinnu sāǧidūna* [m.pl.]". If you go beyond that, both feminine and masculine [nouns] become feminine. It is said: *"al-kibāšu* [rams] *ḏubbiḥna* [were slaughtered, f.pl.] *wa-ḏubbiḥat* [f.sg.] *wa-muḏabbaḥātun* [f.pl.]. It is not admissible to say *muḏabbaḥūna* [m.pl.]." It was admissible for the sun and the moon and the stars because they were described as acting like humans.[3]

3 *Fa-ʔinna hāḏihi n-nūna wa-l-wāwa ʔinnamā takūnāni fī ǧamʕi ḏukrāni l-ǧinni wa-l-ʔinsi wa-*

Al-Farrāʔ here states that masculine plural agreement is restricted to biologically male humans and supernatural beings (such as the *jinns*), explaining the unusual syntactic behavior of the Quranic text as a case of humanization. He also adds two things that indirectly support the main argument of this book. First, Al-Farrāʔ says that if the referent is not a male human, agreement in the plural will be in the feminine irrespectively of its being morphologically masculine or feminine in the singular. Second, he mentions the possibility of both singular and feminile plural agreement with verbs, but only mentions feminine plural agreement with the participial adjective *muḏabbaḥāt* "PASS.PTCP.slaughter-F.PL". This might be a clue of the fact that syntactic agreement was still the largely preferred choice in the domain of adjectives (here, predicative ones), which nicely aligns with the distribution of agreement patterns observed in pre-Classical Arabic, especially the *Muʕallaqāt* (see § 3.3). Of course, feminine singular agreement in the domain of attributive and predicative adjectives was already widely attested, and on the rise, at the time when al-Farrāʔ wrote his book, so that his stance might be considered as conservative and reflective of a more archaic stage of the language, as is often the case with Arab grammarians.[4]

Almost a century later, al-Farrāʔ's argument is quoted almost verbatim in al-Ṭabarī's (838–923 CE) *Ǧāmiʕ al-Bayān ʕan Taʔwīl al-Qurʔān*, but with an interesting difference. The occurrence of masculine plural agreement with nonhuman controllers in Q XII, 4, in fact, is explained as follows:

> He said *sāǧidīna* [m.pl.]. The stars, the sun and the moon, however, are referred to by *fāʕilat*[5] [f. sg.] and *fāʕilāt* [f.pl.], not with the *wāw* and *nūn* [i.e. with *-ūna*], because the *wāw* and *nūn* are the plural mark for male human nouns, or *jinns*, or angels. This was said, however, because bowing [*as-suǧūd*] is a typical action of those nouns whose masculine plural

mā-ʔašbaha-hum. Fa-yuqālu "an-nāsu sāǧidūna, wa-l-malāʔikatu wa-l-ǧinnu sāǧidūna": fa-ʔiḏā ʕadawta hāḏā ṣāra l-muʔannaṯu wa-l-muḏakkaru ʔilā t-taʔnīṯi. Fa-yuqālu: "al-kibāšu ḏubbiḥna wa-ḏubbiḥat wa-muḏabbaḥātun. Wa-lā yaǧūzu muḏabbaḥūna." Wa-ʔinnamā ǧāza fī š šamsi wa l qamari wa l kawākibi bi n nūni wa l yāʔi li-ʔanna-hum wuṣifū bi-ʔufūʕili l-ʔādamiyyīna (Al-Farrāʔ 1955, 2:34).

4 It is not probably by chance that al-Farrāʔ here uses an adjectival participle as a sample. Participles, in fact, tend to show feminine plural agreement even when all other targets agree in the feminine singular. See § 2.3.8.1.

5 In Chapter 3, nominal templates have been presented using C for "consonant" (e.g. CāCiC). Given the topic of this chapter, the templates will be here referred to using the traditional Arabic notation, which makes use of the verb *faʕala yafʕalu* "to do", so that *f* stands for C1, *ʕ* for C2 and *l* for C3 (e.g. CāCiC → *fāʕil*).

> has the marker *yāʔ* and *nūn*, so that the plural of these names [i.e. the stars, sun and moon] was treated in the same way as the plural of the nouns designing whom does that [i.e. bowing]. In a similar way, it was said: *yā ʔayyu-hā n-namlu dxulū masākina-kum* ["Ants, enter (m.pl.) your dwelling-places" (XXVII, 18)][6]
>
> *Sūrat an-Naml*, 18

The Quran actually features another instance in which celestial bodies, in this case the sun and the moon, trigger masculine plural agreement. Al-Ṭabarī, once again, does not overlook the unusual agreement choice:

> And it was said *kullun fī falakin yasbaḥūna* ["each swimming (m.pl.) in a sky" (XXI, 33)]. The sun and the moon were treated as humans, with the *wāw* and the *nūn*, since He did not say: *yasbaḥna* [f.pl.] or *tasbaḥu* [f.sg.].[7]

These two short excerpts from al-Ṭabarī's *tafsīr* tell us three important things. First, masculine plural agreement with nonhuman plural controllers, which is not part of the agreement system described in Chapter 2, was still considered as odd almost a century after al-Farrāʔ. Second, the expected agreement patterns for nonhuman plural controllers were either feminine singular or feminine plural. Contrary to al-Farrāʔ, however, al-Ṭabarī does not express any preference for either one and does not distinguish between verbs and adjectives, nor give any explanation concerning the factor that might govern variation. In the first excerpt, feminine singular is quoted as the first option with adjectives (*bi-"fāʕilatin" wa-"fāʕilātin"*), while the opposite occurs with verbs (*yasbaḥna, ʔaw: tasbaḥu*). In this respect, he no longer seems to recognize any difference in the syntactic behaviors of the two classes of controllers. Third, and most importantly, the [±human] trait already appears as a factor governing agreement choices, although in a completely different way from what we observe in the standardized version of the language and in didactic grammars of Arabic. Al-Ṭabarī, in fact, never says that nonhuman plural nouns require feminine

6 *Qāla "sāǧidīna" wa-l-kawākibu wa-š-šamsu wa-l-qamaru ʔinna-mā yuxbaru ʕan-hā bi-"fāʕilatin" wa-"fāʕilātin" lā bi-l-wāwi wa-n-nūni, li-ʔanna l-wāwa wa-n-nūna ʔinna-mā hiya ʕalāmatu ǧamʕi ʔasmāʔi ḏukūri banī Ādama, ʔawi l-ǧinni, ʔawi l-malāʔikati. Wa-ʔinna-mā qīla ḏālika ka-ḏālika li-ʔanna "s-suǧūda" min ʔafʕāli man yuǧmaʕu ʔasmāʔu ḏukūri-him bi-l-yāʔi wa-n-nūni, fa-ʔaxraǧa ǧamʕa ʔasmāʔi-hā maxraǧa ǧamʕi ʔasmāʔi man yafʕalu ḏālika, ka-mā qīla: "yā ʔayyu-hā n-namlu dxulū masākina-kum"* (*Sūratu n-Namli*, 18) (al-Ṭabarī 2001a, 13:11).

7 *Wa-qīla "kullun fī falakin yasbaḥūna" fa-ʔaxraǧa l-xabara ʕani-š-šamsi wa-l-qamari maxraǧa l-xabari ʕan banī Ādama bi-l-wāwi wa-n-nūni, wa-lam yaqul: yasbaḥna, ʔaw: tasbaḥu* (al-Ṭabarī 2001b, 16:267–268).

singular agreement, he actually says the opposite of that, quoting the possibility of feminine plural agreement twice. He says that the *–ūna* / *-īna* suffix is reserved to male human nouns, which is quite a different story. Al-Ṭabarī, however, does not employ the terms *ʕāqil* "rational" / *mā yaʕqilu* "what has reason" and their opposites, *ġayr ʕāqil* "irrational"[8] / *mā lā yaʕqil* "what does not have reason". After specifying that the suffix *–ūna* / *–īna* is reserved for male human controllers, al-Ṭabarī does the same for the masculine plural pronoun *–hum*. The occasion is provided by the occurrence of the masculine plural pronoun *–hum* with reference to the nonhuman plural controller *ʔasmāʔ* "noun.PL" in Q II, 31:[9]

(5) *wa=ʕallama* *ʔĀdama* ***l=ʔasmāʔa*** *kulla=hā* *ṯumma*
and=teach.3.PFV.M.SG Adam DEF=name.PL all=her then
*ʕaraḍa=**hum*** *ʕalā* *l=malāʔikati* […]
show.3.PFV.M.SG=them.M on DEF=angel.PL
'And He taught Adam the names, all of them; then He presented them unto the angels […]' (II, 31)

And the Arabs only refer with the *hāʔ* and the *mīm* [i.e. with the pronoun *–hum*] to the names of humans and angels. As far as the names of animals and the other creatures are concerned, with the exception just mentioned, they are referred to with the *hāʔ* and the *ʔalif* [i.e. with the pronoun *-hā*] or with the *hāʔ* and the *nūn* [i.e. with the pronoun *hunna*]. So, it would have said: *ʕaraḍa-hunna*, or *ʕaraḍa-hā*. They [i.e. the Arabs] do the same with reference to [different] kinds of creatures, like cattle and birds and the rest of it, including the names of humans or angels. They refer to them, as already said, with the *hāʔ* and the *nūn* [i.e. with the pro-

8 "Rational" and "irrational" are the most widely employed terms to designate "entities endowed with reason" (i.e. humans, angels, spirits etc.) and "entities not endowed with reason" (i.e. animals, things and abstract objects). We will make use of such terms throughout this chapter, when translating excerpts from Arabic grammarians, even though they sound admittedly awkward in English. In any case, rational should be thought as equivalent to human, irrational to nonhuman

9 Some of the commentators, including al-Ṭabarī, tried to solve the problem by saying that the names that God taught Adam were the names of his descendants and of all the angels. *ʔInna-hā ʔasmāʔu ḏurriyyati-hi wa-ʔasmāʔu l-malāʔikati, dūna ʔasmāʔi sāʔiri ʔaǧnāsi l-xalqi* "They are the names of his progeny and the names of the angels, without the names of all the remaining created things". This explanation, however, struggles with the Quranic text, which continues saying *ṯumma ʕaraḍa-hum ʕalā-l-malāʔikati* "then He presented them unto the angels". Taken literally, this explanation would imply that God taught Adam the names of his descendants and the angels and then presented them to the angels themselves.

noun *-hunna*], and the *hāʔ* and *ʔalif* [i.e. the pronoun *-hā*]. They can possibly refer to them, in such cases, with the *hāʔ* and the *mīm* [i.e. with the pronoun *-hum*]. God, praised be His name, said: "God has created every beast [*kulla dābbatin*] of water, and some of them [*min-hum*] go upon their bellies, and some of them [*min-hum*] go upon two feet, and some of them [*min-hum*] go upon four (*an-Nūr*, 45)". He referred to them with the *hāʔ* and the *mīm*, while they were different kinds, including humans and nonhumans. Even though this is possible, the overwhelming majority in the *kalām al-ʕArab* [follows] what we described, in referring to different group of things, when they are mixed, with the *hāʔ* and the *ʔalif*, or the *hāʔ* and *nūn*. [...] It was mentioned that the version of ʕAbd Allāh ibn Masʕūd had: "*ṯumma ʕaraḍa-hunna*", while the version of ʔUbayy: "*ṯumma ʕaraḍa-hā*".[10]

Al-Ṭabarī, in conclusion, strongly affirms that masculine plural suffixes and pronominal forms are reserved to male human controllers, and that their employment with nonhuman ones is the result of a process of metaphorical humanization. As far as nonhuman plural controllers are concerned, feminine singular and feminine plural agreement are considered to be two equally possible choices, apparently in free variation. These ideas are not actually al-Ṭabarī's. They go back at least to Sībawayh (760–796 CE), who in turn attributes them to his mentor, al-Xalīl (718–786 CE):

As for "*kullun fī falakin yasbaḥūna*" ["each swimming (m.pl.) in a sky" (XXI, 33)], "*raʔaytu-hum l-ī sāǧidīna*" ["I saw them bowing down before

10 *Wa-lā takādu l-ʕArabu taknī bi-l-hāʔi wa-l-mīmi ʔillā ʕan ʔasmāʔi banī ʔĀdama wa-l-malāʔikati. Fa-ʔammā ʔiḏā kanat ʕan ʔasmāʔi l-bahāʔimi wa-sāʔiri l-xalqi siwā man waṣafnā, fa-ʔinna-hā tuknā ʕan-hā bi-l-hāʔi wa-l-ʔalifi, ʔaw bi-l-hāʔi wa-n-nūni, fa-qālat: ʕaraḍa-hunna, ʔaw ʕaraḍa-hā. Wa-kaḏālika tafʕalu ʔiḏā kanat ʕan ʔaṣnāfi mina-l-xalqi, ka-l-bahāʔimi wa-ṭ-ṭayri wa-sāʔiri ʔaṣnāfi l-ʔumami, wa-fī-hā ʔasmāʔi banī ʔādama ʔaw l-malāʔikati, fa-ʔinna-hā taknī ʕan-hā bi-mā waṣafnā mina-l-hāʔi wa-n-nūni, wa-l-hāʕi wa-l-ʔalifi. Wa-rubbamā kanat ʕan-hā ʔiḏā kāna ḏālika ka-ḏālika, bi-l-ḥāʔi wa-l-mīmi, qāla taʕāla ḏikru-hu: "Wa-Llāhu xalaqa kulla dābbatin min māʔin fa-min-hum man yamšī ʕalā baṭni-hi wa-min-hum man yamšī ʕalā riǧlayni wa-min-hum man yamšī ʕalā ʔarbaʕin (an-Nūr, 45)". Fa-kanā ʕan-hā bi-l-hāʔi wa-l-mīmi, wa-hiya ʔaṣnāfun muxtalifatun, fī-hā al-ʔādamiyyu wa-ġayru-hu. Wa-ḏālika ʔin kāna ǧāʔizan, fa-ʔinna l-ġāliba l-mustafīḍa fī kalāmi l-ʕArabi mā waṣafnā, min ʔixrāǧi-him kināyata ʔasmāʔi ʔagnāsi l-ʔumami—ʔiḏā xtalaṭat—bi-l-ḥāʔi wa-l-ʔalifi, wa-l-hāʔi wa-n-nūni. [...] Wa-qad ḏukira ʔanna-hā fī ḥarfi ʕAbdi Llāhi bni Masʕūdin: "ṯumma ʕaraḍa-hunna". Wa-ʔanna-hā fi ḥarfi ʔUbayyin: "ṯumma ʕaraḍa-hā"* (al-Ṭabarī 2001c, 1:518–519). Al-Ṭabarī is here quoting al-Farrāʔ, who expresses the same views on the occurrence of *-hum* with reference to *al-ʔasmāʔ* (al-Farrāʔ 1983, 1:26).

> me" (XII, 4)] and "*yā ʔayyu-hā n-namlu dxulū masākina-kum*" ["Ants, enter (m.pl.) your dwelling-places" (XXVII, 18)], [al-Xalīl] said that they are considered as [creatures] that have reason (*mā yaʕqilu*) and listen to, when God mentioned them as bowing. Ants were also considered as such when you talked about them in the same way you talk of humans (*al-ʔanāsiyy*), and similarly "*fī falakin yasbaḥūna*", because they were made in their obedience and in such a way that nobody has to say "we were granted rain thanks to that", and nobody has to worship anything of them, in the position of the creatures endowed with reason (*man yaʕqilu mina l-maxlūqīna*) and discernment. An-Nābiġa al-Ğuʕdī said:
>
> I drank by it while the rooster was inviting its morning
> and the Ursa stars approached (*danaw*, m.pl) and set (*taṣawwabū*, m.pl.)
>
> This usage is allowed when these things are ordered and obey, understand language and worship similarly to humans (*al-ʔādamiyyīn*).[11]

As evident from the quote here reported, Sībawayh employes the term *mā yaʕqilu* "what has reason" (alongside *ʔādamiyyīn* and *ʔanāsiyy*), absent in al-Ṭabarī, to refer to those classes of controllers to which masculine plural agreement is restricted, i.e. humans, angels and *jinns* (although the three categories are not directly mentioned in the passage). The [+human] trait, thus, is the decisive factor to license masculine plural agreement.

> Don't you see that they [i.e. humans] have, in the plural, a state that is exclusive to them, because they are the first ones and were preferred through the intellect (*al-ʕaql*) and knowledge (*al-ʕilm*) that were not bestowed to other [creatures].[12]

---

11 *wa-ʔammā "kullun fī falakin yasbaḥūna" wa-"raʔaytu-hum l-ī sāǧidīna" wa-"yā ʔayyu-hā n-namlu dxulū masākina-kum" fa-zaʕama* [*al-Xalīl*] *ʔanna-hu bi-manzilati mā yaʕqilu wa-yasmaʕu lammā dakara-hum bi-s-suǧūdi wa-ṣāra n-namlu bi-tilka l-manzilati ḥīna ḥud-datta ʕan-hu ka-mā tuḥaddiṯu mina-l-ʔanāsiyyi wa-ka-ḏālika "fī falakin yasbaḥūna" li-ʔanna-hā ǧuʕilat fī ṭāʕati-hā wa-fī ʔanna-hu lā yanbaġī li-ʔaḥadin ʔan yaqūla muṭirnā bi-nawʔi kaḏā wa-lā yanbaġī li-ʔaḥadin ʔan yaʕbuda šayʔan min-hā bi-manzilati man yaʕqilu mina-l-maxlūqīna wa-yubṣiru l-ʔumūra. Qāla n-Nābiġatu l-Ğuʕdī:*

šaribtu bi-hā wa-d-dīku yadʕū ṣabāḥa-hu ʔiḏā mā Banū Naʕšin danaw fa-taṣawwabū fa-ǧāza hāḏā ḥayṯu ṣārat hāḏi-hi l-ʔašyāʔu ʕinda-hum tuʔmaru wa-tuṭīʕu wa-tafhamu l-kalāma wa-taʕbudu bi-manzilati l-ʔādamiyyīna (Sībawayh 1881, 1:205).

12 *ʔA-lā tarā ʔanna la-hum fī-l-ǧamʕi ḥālan laysat li-ġayri-him li-ʔanna-hum al-ʔawwalūna*

The [-human] factor, at this stage, does not evoke any prescriptive agreement pattern, excluding the unavailability of masculine plural. On the contrary, feminine singular and plural are again presented as equally possible:

> You say: 'They are going (*hum ḏāhibūna*, m.pl.), and they are at home (*hum fī-d-dāri*)'. You don't say: 'Your camels are going (*ḏāhibūna*, m.pl.)', and you don't say: '*hum fī-d-dāri*', meaning the camels, but you say rather: '*hunna wa-hiya ḏāhibātun wa-ḏāhibatun* [f.pl.]'.[13]

So far, the description offered by Sībawayh roughly matches the three agreement classes described in Chapter 2. Male human controllers trigger masculine plural agreement, nonhuman ones trigger either feminine plural or feminine singular agreement. There is no direct mention of female human controllers, but this is probably due to the fact that Sībawayh took for granted the occurrence of feminine plural agreement. Sībawayh even admits the possibility of feminine singular agreement with all classes of controllers, even though he does not mention anything related to individuation:

> Don't you see that you say *huwa rağulun* ("he is a man") and *hiya r-riğālu* ("they are the men"), and it is allowed; that you say *huwa ğamalun* ("it is a camel") and *hiya l-ğimālu* ("they are the camels"); that you say *huwa ʕayrun* ("it is an onager") and *hiya l-ʔaʕyāru* ("they are the onagers")?[14]

With the final mention of feminine singular as a possible agreement choice for all controllers, Sībawayh sketches the same system described in Chapter 2, the only exception being his silence with reference to agreement with feminine human controllers. The explanation he provides for the occurrence of feminine singular agreement with human controllers, however, deserves a separate discussion:

> As for broken plural of animates (*al-ḥayawān*, lit. "the living") [i.e. humans and animals], they are treated as the broken plurals of inanimates, inso-

---

wa-ʔanna-hum qad fuḍḍilū bi-mā lam yufaḍḍal bi-hi ġayru-hum mina-l-ʕaqli wa-l-ʕilmi (Sībawayh 1881, 1:202).

13 *Taqūlu: "hum ḏāhibūna, wa-hum fī-d-dāri", wa-lā taqūlu: "ğimālu-ka ḏāhibūna", wa-lā taqūlu: "hum fī-d-dāri", wa-ʔanta taʕnī l-ğimāla, wa-lakinna-ka taqūlu: "hunna wa-hiya ḏāhibātun wa-ḏāhibatun"* (Sībawayh 1881, 1:202).

14 *ʔA-lā tarā ʔanna-ka taqūlu "huwa rağulun" wa-taqūlu "hiya r-riğālu", fa-yağūzu la-ka wa-taqūlu "huwa ğamalun" wa-"hiya l-ğimālu" wa-"huwa ʕayrun" wa-"hiya l-ʔaʕyāru"* (Sībawayh 1881, 1:202).

> much as it is feminine. Don't you see that you say *huwa rağulun* ("he is a man") and *hiya r-riğālu* ("they are the men"), and it is allowed; that you say *huwa ğamalun* ("it is a camel") and *hiya l-ğimālu* ("they are the camels"); that you say *huwa ʕayrun* ("it is an onager") and *hiya l-ʔaʕyāru* ("they are the onagers")? This receives the same treatment of *hiya l-ğuḏūʕu* ("these are the trunks") [i.e. the same treatment of inanimate controllers] and similar cases. It was treated in the same way because the plural takes feminine agreement even if each one of its components were masculine animate. When this happens, they [i.e. the Arabs] treated it as inanimates (*al-mawāt*, lit. "the dead") […][15]

Sībawayh's explanation consists of two main points, each deserving a detailed discussion:

I. Feminine singular agreement with human (in Sībawayh's words, with animate) controllers is only possible with broken plurals;
II. When this happens, the animate controllers are treated as if they were broken plural inanimate controllers.

Point I is perfectly in line with the statistics provided in both § 2.4 and Chapter 3, from both a synchronic and diachronic perspective. From a synchronic point of view, it has been consistently shown that feminine singular agreement tends to cluster around broken plural controllers on a general basis, and occurs *only* with broken plurals when the controller is human. Moreover, three different corpora (pre-Islamic poetry, the Quran and a contemporary Najdi poetic corpus) showed that the sum of broken plural and feminine singular agreement in adjectives almost exactly equals the percentages of feminine singular agreement in pronouns. From a diachronic perspective, § 3.1 argued that the innovation of feminine singular agreement in Arabic was principally due to the spread of broken plurals and the consequent opaqueness of most plural forms. The perception of a close link between broken plurals and feminine singular within the Arabic linguistic tradition, thus, indirectly confirms our assumption.

With regard to point II, it should be noted that the only occasion in which Sībawayh distinguishes the category of human from all other controllers is

15 *Fa-ʔammā l-ğamʕu mina-l-ḥayawāni llaḏī yukassaru ʕalay-hi l-wāḥidu fa-bi-manzilati l-ğamīʕi min ġayri-hi llaḏī yukassaru ʕalay-hi l-wāḥidu fī ʔanna-hu muʔannaṯun. ʔA-lā tarā ʔanna-ka taqūlu "huwa rağulun" wa-taqūlu "hiya r-riğālu", fa-yağūzu la-ka wa-taqūlu "huwa ğamalun" wa-"hiya l-ğimālu" wa-"huwa ʕayrun" wa-"hiya l-ʔaʕyāru" fa-ğarat haḏihi kullu-hā mağrā hiya l-ğuḏūʕu wa-mā ʔašbaha ḏālika yuğrā hāḏā l-mağrā li-ʔanna l-ğamīʕa yuʔannaṯu wa-ʔin kāna kullu wāḥidin min-hu muḏakkaran mina l-ḥayawāni, fa-lammā kāna ka-ḏālika ṣayyarū-hu bi-manzilati l-mawāti* […] (Sībawayh 1881, 1:202).

when describing masculine plural agreement. With reference to the possibility of feminine singular agreement with broken plural controllers, on the contrary, he referes to the category of *al-ḥayawān* "the living", as opposed to *al-mawāt* "the dead". From Sībawayh's reasoning, it appears that he considers feminine singular agreement as a pattern originally reserved to inanimate broken plurals, such as *ǧuḏūʕ* "trunk.PL", which then spread to animate ones. As already said in § 3.6, however, no variety of Arabic has ever been documented in which human and animal controllers are syntactically grouped together (for agreement purposes) and opposed to inanimate ones. The distinction drawn by Sībawayh, thus, is not reflected in the linguistic reality of Arabic. The only other instance of a similar distinction occurs in Ibn al-Muqaffaʕ's (ca. 720–ca. 756 CE) translation of *Kalīla wa-Dimna* from Pahlavi (Middle Persian). In the case of Ibn al-Muqaffaʕ, the agreement patterns occurring in *Kalīla wa-Dimna* were explained as an occurrence of translated syntax from the Middle Persian original, or possibly as a syntactic intererference from the translator's L1.[16] Ibn al-Muqaffaʕ and Sībawayh both lived in the 8th century, but they also share their geographic provenance and L1. The leading grammarian of the Basran school, in fact, was born in al-Bayḍāʔ (Shiraz), where he spent his childhood before moving to Baṣra. The peculiar distinction between animate and nonanimate controllers finds no base in Arabic, but is attested in verbal agreement in all the historical stages of Persian (Hashabeiky 2007, 80). At the same time, the only two scholars / writers who, as far as we know, supported such a distinction, were both of Persian origin and shared a Persian L1. This might support the view that also Sībawayh, here, was explaining linguistic facts pertaining to Arabic, which he described flawlessly, by making reference to categories drawn from his L1.

One of the most influential commentators on Sībawayh's *Kitāb*, ʔAbū Saʕīd al-Sīrāfī (893-94-979 CE), attributes to Sībawayh himself the introduction of the two terms *ḥayawān* and *mawāt* to designate animate and inanimate entities: "And Sībawayh designated, in this distinction, what was not animate with the term *mawāt*, even though it was neither animate nor animate, because it was formally identical to inanimates".[17] Al-Sīrāfī, himself of Persian origin, does not

16 In § 3.6, the necessity of detailed studies on Ibn al-Muqaffaʕ's original works was stressed, in order to ascertain whether Persian-influenced agreement patterns also occur when he writes directly in Arabic (thus representing a case of interference) or whether they are limited to his translations (which would represent a case of translated syntax).

17 *Wa-sammā Sībawayh fī hāḏā l-faṣli mā lam yakun mina l-ḥayawāni mawātan wa-ʔin kāna fī-l-ḥaqīqati laysa mina-l-ḥayawāni wa-lā mina-l-mawāti li-musāwāti-hi l-mawāta fī-l-lafḏ̣i* [...] (al-Sīrāfī 2008, 2:370).

TABLE 4.1 Relevant thresholds on the animacy hierarchy for Persian vs Arabic and Sībawayh's *Kitāb*

Persian	Sībawayh[a] (and Ibn Muqaffaʕ)	Arabic[b]
Human	Human	Human
Animal	Animal	Animal
Inanimate	Inanimate	Inanimate

a In Sībawayh, moreover, the distinction between *ḥayawān* (animate) and *mawāt* (inanimate) controllers also concerns the agreement of pre-controller verbal targets. According to the Baṣran grammarian, in fact, precontroller verbal targets referring to inanimate controllers tend to occur more frequently in the masculine singular, without the feminine marker *-t*, while the same is much rarer with reference to animate controllers (Sībawayh 1881, 1:202).

b With reference to Arabic, the threshold has a twofold dimension: in pre-Islamic, Classical Arabic and in the gender-distinguishing varieties of spoken Arabic, masculine plural is reserved to male humans. The only exception to this rule is represented by those varieties of spoken Arabic that lost gender distinction in the plural and where, as a consequence, also female human and nonhuman controllers trigger agreement in the masculine plural (when syntactic agreement is opted for). On the other hand, in Classical and Modern Standard Arabic the threshold between humans and nonhumans divide the controllers that trigger syntactic agreement in the plural (i.e. human ones) from those that have mandatory feminine singular agreement (i.e. nonhumans).

devote much space to the distinction between animate and inanimate controllers. On the contrary, he stresses the role of broken plurals in triggering feminine singular agreement in targets depending from both human and nonhuman controllers: "And know that broken plurals are all feminine. Feminine, masculine, rational (*mā yaʕqilu*) and irrational (*mā lā yaʕqilu*) are all but formally equivalent."[18] Al-Sīrāfī then closes his comment saying "And the formal rule, in their being feminine, is the principle according to which inanimates are [considered] feminine."[19] This passage witnesses the struggle of the commentator, who is trying to adapt Sībawayh's distinction between animates (i.e. humans and animals) and inanimates to the linguistic reality of Arabic, which rather distinguishes between humans and nonhumans (i.e. animals and inanimates), although only with reference to the availability of masculine plural

18 *Wa-ʕlam ʔanna l-ǧumūʕa l-mukassarata muʔannaṯun kulla-hā yastawī fī ḥukmi l-lafḏ̣i ǧamīʕu l-muʔannaṯi wa-l-muḏakkarati wa-mā yaʕqilu wa-mā lā yaʕqilu* (al-Sīrāfī 2008, 2:370).

19 *Wa-ḥukmu l-lafḏ̣i fī taʔnīṯi-hā ḥukmu taʔnīṯi l-mawāti* (al-Sīrāfī 2008, 2:370).

agreement. It is also possible, however, that at the time when al-Sīrāfī was writing (10th century) the distinction between humans and nonhumans transcended the domain of masculine plural agreement and started to trickle down to the distribution of feminine singular agreement, which was probably, at least in prose, more and more restricted to nonhumans.

The relevance of the human vs nonhuman split, although with exclusive reference to the availability of masculine plural agreement, is stressed by al-Sīrāfī in a much longer passage, which clarifies Sībawayh's position by including female human nouns in the picture:

> ʔAbū Saʕīd [al-Sīrāfī] said: the Arabs made to rational beings (*mā yaʕqilu*) [i.e. humans] a special place in the language, and distinguished between them and irrational beings (*mā lā yaʕqilu*) [i.e. nonhumans], because rational beings are characterized by the fact that they address and are addressed, give and receive orders, speak or are spoken of. Irrational beings, of all things mentioned, can only be spoken of. Rational beings were preferred and given a special place. This preference was given, in the language, to male rational beings, without the female, to separate masculine from feminine. This [i.e. the preference] is their masculine sound plural with the *wāw* and the *nūn* [i.e. the suffix *–ūna*], the *yāʔ* and the *nūn* [i.e. the suffix *-īna*], and this is when you say: "*ar-riǧālu ḏāhibūna* ("the men are going") and *munṭaliqūna* ("leaving"), and *raʔaytu-hum ḏāhibīna* (I saw them going) and *munṭaliqīna* ("leaving")". Their plural pronoun is with the *hāʔ* and the *mīm* [i.e. *-hum*], like when you say: "*ar-riǧālu hum fī-d-dāri* ("the men are at home"), and *ʔixwatu-ka hum ʕinda-nā* ("your brothers are at our place")". For women, you say in the sound plural: "*al-Hindātu ḏāhibātun* ("the Hinds are going") and *munṭaliqātun* ("leaving")", and their pronoun is with the *hāʔ* and the *nūn* [i.e. *-hunna*]. We say: "*an-nisāʔu raʔaytu-hunna* ("the women, I saw them"), and *an-nūqu raʔaytu-hā* ("the she-camels, I saw them")". Then irrational beings were attached to the feminine, because of their lower position compared to rational ones, like the lower position of feminine.[20]

20 *Qāla ʔAbū Saʕīd: ǧaʕalati l-ʕArabu li-mā yaʕqilu fī mawḍiʕin ixtiṣāṣan fī l-lafḏi, wa-faṣalat bayna-hu wa-bayna mā lā yaʕqilu fī-hi li-mā xtaṣṣa bi-hi mā yaʕqilu bi-ʔanna-hu yuxāṭibu wa-yuxāṭabu, wa-yaʔmuru, wu-yuʔmaru, wa-tuxbiru wa-tuxbaru ʕan-hu. Wa-mā lā yaʕqilu laysa la-hu min ḏālika ʔillā ʔanna-hu yuxbaru ʕan-hu, fa-ǧuʕila li-mā yaʕqilu tafḍīlun wa-xtiṣāṣun, wa-ǧuʕila ḏālika t-tafṣīlu fī-l-lafḏi li-l-muḏakkari mim-mā yaʕqilu dūna l-muʔannaṯi li-faṣli l-muḏakkari ʕalā l-muʔannaṯi, wa-ḏālika ǧamʕu-hu s-sālimu bi-l-wāwi wa-n-nūni, al-yāʔi wa-n-nūni, wa-ḏālika qawlu-ka: ar-riǧālu ḏāhibūna wa-munṭaliqūna, wa-*

In this passage, al-Sīrāfī expands on Sībawayh's short explanation of agreement patterns, but probably goes beyond the intentions of the author of the *Kitāb*. The distinction between humans and nonhumans is here motivated in very modern terms, by saying that humans interact, are capable of giving orders but also of receiving them, that they speak and can also be spoken of. Nonhumans, on the other hands, can only be spoken of. This description is not dissimilar from the quality of being "ego-like" mentioned by Khan (1984, 469–470) as the major factor governing individuation. Among the categories that shape this quality of being "ego-like", the role of agenthood and volition (here represented by typical human actions such as addressing other people, giving orders, speaking) has been convincingly illustrated by De Vos (2015, 131).

At this point, al-Sīrāfī specifies that this preference, within the class of humans, has been granted to male humans, excluding females. In itself, this fact is hardly surprising, and well represented in the typological literature. Old Russian, for instance, inherited the three Indo-European genders. When a fourth subgender was innovated, it originally involved not even male humans, but apparently only free adult males, with the exclusion of serfs and children (Corbett 1991, 98–99). The distinction between male humans and all other classes, as already said, consists in their exclusive ability to trigger masculine plural agreement in adjectives, verbs and pronouns. Al-Sīrāfī then mentions female human controllers, which are absent from Sībawayh's concise description, saying that they trigger feminine plural agreement in both verbs and pronouns. When providing samples to exemplify agreement patterns, however, al-Sīrāfī justaxposes *an-nisāʔu raʔaytu-hunna* "the women, I saw them" and *an-nūqu raʔaytu-hā* "the she-camels, I saw them", without any hint to the fact that they belong to two separate classes, i.e. humans and animals. The agreement patterns appearing from the two samples account for that difference, so that *an-nisāʔ* triggers feminine plural agreement (*-hunna*), while *an-nūq* triggers feminine singular.[21] Al-Sīrāfī, however, is silent on this point. Judging from this short passage, it seems

raʔaytu-hum ḏahibīna wa-munṭaliqīna, wa-ǧamʕu ḍamīri-hi bi-l-hāʔi wa-l-mīmi, ka-qawli-ka: ar-riǧālu hum fī-d-dāri, wa-ʔixwatu-ka hum ʕinda-nā, wa-taqūlu li-n-nisāʔu fī-l-ǧamʕi s-sālimi: al-Hindātu ḏāhibātun wa munṭaliqātun, wa ḍamīru hunna bi-l-hāʔi wa-n-nūni naqūlu: an-nisāʔu raʔaytu-hunna, wa-n-nūqu raʔaytu-hā. Ṯumma ʔulḥiqa mā lā yaʕqilu bi-lafḍi l-muʔannaṯi li-naqṣi rutbati-hi ʕan mā yaʕqilu, ka-naqṣi rutbati l-muʔannaṯi (al-Sīrāfī 2008, 2:369).

21 The two different agreement patterns might be due to the fact that, at the time when al-Sīrāfī composed his commentary (10th century), feminine singular was on its way to becoming the norm with plural nonhuman controllers. In Sībawayh, for instance, all samples of animal controllers come with the two possible agreement patterns, i.e. feminine plural and singular, often with the plural one mentioned first.

that feminine singular and feminine plural agreement belong to the same class, opposed to masculine plural, which is reserved to male humans. In this way, the system is conceptually simplified in a two-way distinction, male humans vs all other controllers, at least in the plural. The apparent contradiction represented by the possible occurrence of feminine singular agreement with male human controllers, then, is solved by linking feminine singular to the occurrence of broken plural controllers. The only point of weakness in al-Sīrāfī's explanation lies in the fact that he finally goes back to Sībawayh's distinction between *ḥayawān* and *mawāt*, which so far had no place in his system, writing that femine singular agreement is originally the rule for inanimate controllers: *Wa-ḥukmu l-lafḍi fī taʔnīṯi-hā ḥukmu taʔnīṯi l-mawāti* (al-Sīrāfī 2008, 2:370) (see translation above).

The idea that sound and broken plurals are not equivalent, moreover, is not confined to the possibility for male broken plural human controllers to trigger feminine singular agreement. In the section containing the observations on agreement analyzed above, Sībawayh discusses the issue of adjectives preceding their controllers, in the structure traditionally designed as *aṣ-ṣifatu l-mušabbahatu bi-l-fiʕli* (lit. "the adjective similar to the verb"), like in the following sample:

(6) *marartu* *bi=rağulin* ***ḥisānin*** ***qawmu***=*hu*
pass:1.PFV.SG by=man good.PL people=his
'I passed by a man whose people are good' (Sībawayh 1881, 1:204).

In such cases, Sībawayh advises that adjectives in the sound masculine plural should agree in the singular, because they behave like verbs preceding their subject. Adjectives featuring broken plurals, on the contrary, should agree in the plural, the reason being that they do not share the same plural ending of verbs (i.e. *–ūna*), so that they have nothing in common with them (Sībawayh 1881, 1:204). When describing the nature of broken plurals, finally, Sībawayh produces a definition that stresses their collective-like nature: "[…] the form is singular but the meaning is plural."[22]

A contemporary of Sībawayh and forefather of the Kufan school, al-Farrāʔ (d. 822 CE), introduced a new factor in the discussion of agreement patterns with plural controllers. In his monumental commentary, *Maʕānī al-Qurʔān*, he discusses in detail the linguistic features of the Quranic text. This interesting excerpt is drawn from al-Farrāʔ's analysis of Q IX, 36:

22 […] *fa-l-lafḍu wāḥidun wa-l-maʕnā ğamīʕun* (Sībawayh 1881, 1:204).

(7) [...] *min=hā* ***ʔarbaʕatun ḥurumun*** *ḏālika d=dīnu l=qayyimu*
from=her four sacred.PL that.M DEF=religion DEF=right
*fa=lā tuḏlimū fī=**hinna** ʔanfusa=kum*
and=NEG 2.IPFV:wrong.M.PL.APOC in=them.F self.PL=your.M.PL
'[...] four of them are sacred. That is the right religion. So wrong not each other during them' (IX, 36)

And God's word: *min-hā ʔarbaʕatun ḥurumun ḏālika d-dīnu l-qayyimu fa-lā tuḏlimū fī-hinna ʔanfusa-kum* ("Four of them are sacred. That is the right religion. So wrong not each other during them").

Its interpretation is: out of twelve [months]. And it came (*fī-hinna*) [...] and what indicates that it is for the four—and God knows best—is God's word (*fī-hinna*) [f.pl], because He did not say (*fī-hā*) [f.sg]. The *kalām al-ʕArab* behaves likewise. For what is between three and ten, they say: *li-ṯalāṯati layālin xalawna* ("for three nights that passed", f.pl.), and *ṯalāṯatu ʔayyāmin xalawna* ("three days have passed", f.pl.) up to ten. If you pass ten, they say: *xalat* ("it passed", f.sg) and *maḍat* ("it passed", f.sg.). They say for what is between three and ten (*hunna*) and (*hāʔulāʔi*),[23] and if you pass ten they say (*hiya*) and (*hāḏihi*), to distinguish the feature of *paucity* (*sīmatu l-qalīli*) from that of *abundance* (*al-kaṯīri*). In each case, however, it is allowed what [i.e. the agreement pattern] is allowed for the other;[24] ʔAbū al-Qamqām al-Faqʕasī sang to me:

ʔaṣbaḥna fī qarḥin wa-fī dārāti-hā *sabʕa layālin ġayra maʕlūfāti-hā*
[They woke up with an ulcer and in its castles seven nights without their feeding]

He did not say *maʕlūfāti-hinna*, even though they were seven, and all of this is correct, except that what I have explained to you [i.e. the occurrence of feminine plural with counted objects between three and ten] is preferred. Similarly: *Wa-qāla* [m.sg] *niswatun fī-l-madīnati* ("Certain women that were in the city said", XII 30). The verb occurs in the masculine for the paucity of the women and due to the fact that *hāʔulāʔi*[25] is used for them just like it is used for men. A similar case is God's word: *fa-*

23 The demonstrative *hāʔulāʔi* is a common plural form. No distinct form for masculine and feminine plural is available in Classical Arabic.
24 What al-Farrāʔ means here is that agreement patterns for the plurals of paucity and of abundance are interchangeable.
25 See footnote 23 above.

> *ʔiḏā nsalaxa* [m.sg] *l-ʔašhuru l-ḥurumu* ("Then, when the sacred months are drawn away," IX, 5). He did not say: *insalaxat*, even though either form is correct. And God Almighty said: *ʔinna s-samʕa wa-l-baṣra wa-l-fuʔāda kullun ʔūlāʔika*[26] ("the hearing, the sight, the heart—all of those" XVII, 36) for their paucity. He did not say *tilka* (that, f.sg.), but if He had said it it would have been correct.[27]

Interestingly, al-Farrāʔ explains the occurrence of feminine plural agreement as a result of the controller being in the plural bracket going from 3 to 10. According to the Kufan author, this is the usage transmitted by the *kalām al-ʕArab*. In contemporary typological terms, this might translate into something on the line of "when a controller is quantified by a lower numeral, from 3 to 10, then feminine plural agreement takes place." The presence of numerals has been shown to be one of the major reasons behind the occurrence of syntactic agreement, both in pre-Classical Arabic and in the modern dialects. The only difference in al-Farrāʔ's definition is that the lower numeral does not need to be overtly expressed, as long as the speaker has in mind a counted object falling in this plural bracket (as happens in the modern dialects). al-Farrāʔ explicitly mentions the two terms *qilla* "paucity" and *kaṯra* "abundance" with reference to the plural, even though he is not here discussing the plural templates that are traditionally considered to express the plural of paucity (*ǧamʕ al-qilla*) and of abundance (*ǧamʕ al-kaṯra*).[28] al-Farrāʔ's great merit consists in drawing a link

---

26 The demonstrative *ʔūlāʔika* is a common plural form. No distinct form for masculine and feminine plural is available in Classical Arabic.

27 *Wa-qawlu-hu: min-hā ʔarbaʕatun ḥurumun ḏālika d-dīnu l-qayyimu fa-lā tuḏlimū fī-hinna ʔanfusa-kum.*

Ǧāʔa t-tafsīru: fī-l-iṯnay ʕašra. Wa-ǧāʔa (*fī-hinna*) [...] *wa-yadullu-ka ʕalā ʔanna-hu li-l-ʔarbaʕati—wa-Llāhu ʔaʕlamu—qawlu-hu:* (*fī-hinna*) *wa-lam yaqul* (*fī-hā*). *Wa-ka-ḏālika kalāmu l-ʕArabi li-mā bayna ṯ-ṯalāṯati ʔilā l-ʕašarati taqūlu: li-ṯalāṯati layālin xalawna, wa-ṯalāṯatu ʔayyāmin xalauna ʔilā l-ʕašarati, fa-ʔiḏā ǧuzta l-ʕašarati qālū: xalat, wa-maḍat. Wa-yaqūlūna li-mā bayna ṯ-ṯalāṯati ʔilā l-ʕašarati* (*hunna*) *wa-*(*hāʔulāʔi*) *fa-ʔiḏā ǧuzta l-ʕašarati qālū* (*hiya, wa-hāḏihi*) *ʔirādatan ʔan tuʕrafa simatu l-qalīli mina-l-kaṯīri. Wa-yaǧūzu fī kulli wāḥidin mā ǧāza fī ṣāḥibi-hi; ʔanšada-nī ʔAbū l-Qamqām al-Faqʕasī:*

ʔaṣbaḥna fī qarḥin wa-fī dārāti-hā   *sabʕa layālin ġayra maʕlūfāti-hā*

Wa-lam yaqul: maʕlūfāti-hinna wa-hiya sabʕun, wa-kullu ḏālika ṣawābun; ʔillā ʔanna l-muʔṯara mā fassartu la-ka. Wa-miṯlu-hu: (*Wa-qāla niswatun fī-l-madīnati*) *fa-ḏukkira l-fiʕlu li-qillati n-niswati wa-wuqūʕu* (*hāʔulāʔi*) *ʕalay-hinna ka-mā yaqaʕu ʕalā-r-riǧāli. Wa-min-hu qawlu-hu:* (*fa-ʔiḏā nsalaxa l-ʔašhuru l-ḥurumu*) *wa-lam yaqul: insalaxat, wa-kullun ṣawābun. Wa-qāla Allāhu tabāraka wa-taʕālā:* (*ʔinna s-samʕa wa-l-baṣra wa-l-fuʔāda kullun ʔūlāʔika*) *li-qillati-hinna wa-lam yaqul* (*tilka*) *wa-law qīlat kāna ṣawāban* (al-Farrāʔ 1983, 1:435).

28 The plural nominal templates traditionally considered to express the plural of paucity are *ʔafʕul, ʔafʕāl, ʔafʕila* and *fiʕla*.

between paucity and feminine plural agreement, which perfectly fits into the hypotheses outlined in Chapter 2, paucity being closely related to individuation (items ranging from 3 to 10, or at any rate countable or counted, are more easily seen as distinct individuals). Sībawayh, who discusses at length the different forms of *ǧamʕ al-qilla* (Ferrando 2006), only concerns himself with their morphology, without mentioning agreement patterns. Both Sībawayh (Ferrando 2006, 44) and al-Farrāʔ, on the other hand, observe that the categories of *ǧamʕ al-qilla* and *al-kaṯra* are not airtight, so that often a paucity form is used to indicate abundance and vice-versa. al-Farrāʔ seems to have a more modern approach, insomuch as he does not say that paucity forms are used in place of abundance and vice versa, but rather that agreement with both forms is variable. He insists on the fact that feminine plural is to be preferred with paucity plurals, but does not adopt a prescriptive stand that would contradict the usage he observes in the *kalām al-ʕArab*.

Moving back to the Basran School, one of the most influential grammarians who ensured the acceptation of Sībawayh's *Kitāb* as (probably) the most authoritative treatise on the Arabic language was al-Mubarrad (862–898 CE), despite his initial criticism (Bernards 2017). al-Mubarrad, who lived in the second half of the 9th century, was a native of Baṣra, and wrote extensively on several topics, naturally including morphology and syntax. In his *al-Muqtaḍab*, the issue of agreement with plural controllers is dealt with briefly, in a way that does not differ much from what seen in al-Sīrāfī's commentary:

> If the counted noun belongs to a class different from that of humans, the number needs to be accompanied by a genitive particle, and its figurative meaning is feminine, because its verb and its plural are like that. If its meaning is plural, don't you see that you say: *al-ǧimālu tasīru* ("the camels go", f.sg.) and *al-ǧimālu yasirna* ("the camels go", f.pl.). Similarly, God Almighty said, mentioning idols: "*Rabb-ī ʔinna-hunna ʔaḍlalna* (f.pl.) *kaṯīran mina-n-nāsi*" ("My Lord, they have led astray many men" XIV, 36). Their plural follows the same rule [i.e. the feminine], like you say: *ḥammām* ("bath") and *hammāmāt* ("bath:F.PL"), and *surādiq* ("pavilion") and *surādiqāt* ("pavilion:F.PL"). As far as humans (*al-ʔādamiyyūna*) are concerned, their males have masculine plural, because their verb is like this. You say: "*hum yaḍribūna* [m.pl.] *Zaydan* ("They hit Zayd"), and *yanṭaliqūna* [m.pl.] ("they leave")", and for this reason you say: *muslimūna* ("Muslim:M.PL") and *munṭaliqūna* ("leaving:M.PL"). This exclusively occurs for rational beings (*mā yaʕqilu*).[29]

29 *Fa-ʔin kāna llaḏī yaqaʕu ʕalay-hi l-ʕadadu isman li-ǧinsin min ġayri l-ʔādamiyyīna lam*

From this brief excerpt, three main points can be gathered. First, al-Mubarrad actually sets apart a separate category of nonhumans, while he does not mention any distinction between animated and inanimates.[30] Second, al-Mubarrad considers feminine as the agreement pattern triggered by nonhuman controllers. The grammarian, here, solely focuses on gender, totally neglecting number, so that feminine singular and feminine plural are simply justaxposed as equally possible alternatives. Third, al-Mubarrad considers nominal plural morphology and agreement patterns as derived from verbal morphology. The sound feminine plural of *ḥammāmāt* "bath-F.PL" and *surādiqāt* "pavilion-F.PL", thus, is due to the fact that nonhuman controllers trigger feminine (either singular or plural) agreement in verbs. Similarly, the sound masculine plural in *muslimūna* "Muslim-M.PL" and *munṭaliqūna* "leaving-M.PL" is due to the fact that male human controllers trigger masculine plural agreement in their verbs.

Even though, when describing agreement with nonhuman controllers, al-Mubarrad does not seem to distinguish between singular and plural feminine agreement, the specificity of feminine singular agreement is discussed with reference to its possible occurrence with plural human controllers. al-Mubarrad, here, basically comes to the same conclusions presented in Chapters 2 and 3, writing that feminine singular with human controllers represent a form of collective agreement:

> And if you say: "*hiya* [f.sg.] *r-riǧālu* ("They are the men")", it is correct, because you intend *hiya ǧamāʕatu r-riǧāli* ("It is the group of men"), like when you say: *hiya* [f.sg.] *l-ǧimālu* ("They are the camels"). As far as *hum* ("they.M") is concerned, it is exclusive to rational beings (*mā yaʕqilu*).[31]

---

yulāqi-hi l-ʕadadu ʔillā bi-ḥarfi l-ʔiḍāfati, wa-kāna maǧāzu-hu t-taʔnīṯa, li-ʔanna fiʕla-hu wa-ǧamʕa-hu ʕalā ḏālika, ʔiḏ kāna maʕnā-hu l-ǧamāʕati, ʔa la-tarā ʔanna-ka taqūlu: al-ǧimālu tasīru, wa-l-ǧimālu yasirna; ka-mā qāla Allāhu ʕazza wa-ǧalla ʕinda ḏikri l-ʔaṣnāmi: "Rabbi ʔinna-hunna ʔaḏlalna kaṯīran mina-n-nāsi" wa-ʕalā hāḏā yuǧmaʕu; ka-mā taqūlu: ḥammāmun wa-ḥammāmātun, wa-surādiqun wa-surādiqātun. fa-ʔammā l-ʔādammiyyūna fa-ʔinna l-muḏakkara min-hum yaǧrī ʕalā ǧamʕi-hi t-taḏkīr, li-ʔanna fiʕla-hu ʕalā ḏālika. Taqūlu: hum yaḍribūna Zaydan, wa-yanṭaliqūna, fa-li-ḏālika taqūlu: muslimūna wa-munṭaliqūna, wa-naḥwa-hu, wa-ʕalā hāḏā taqūlu: humu-r-riǧālu, wa-la-yaqaʕu miṯlu hāḏā ʔillā li-mā yaʕqilu (al-Mubarrad 1979, 2:183–184).

30 This might be another indirect proof of the fact that, in this classification, Sībawayh is actually led by categories belonging to his L1, Persian.

31 *Fa-ʔin qulta: hiya r-riǧālu, ṣalaḥa ʕalā ʔirādati-ka hiya ǧamāʕatu r-riǧāli, ka-mā taqūlu: hiya l-ǧimālu. fa-ʔammā "hum" fa-lā yakūnu ʔillā li-mā yaʕqilu* (al-Mubarrad 1979, 2:184).

Here al-Mubarrad even goes as far as assuming that, when feminine singular agreement is employed with human controllers, there is a covert subject *ǧamāʕa* "group", conveniently feminine singular, triggering feminine singular. Apart from that, the intuition that feminine singular conveys collective / non-individuated agreement proves al-Mubarrad's fine linguistic insight. It should also be mentioned that the idea of collective agreement is not restricted to human controllers, but extended to nonhuman ones, as evidenced by the other sample provided by al-Mubarrad, i.e. *hiya* [f.sg.] *l-ǧimālu* "They are the camels". Seen from this perspective, its system almost perfectly matches the one sketched in Chapter 2, with masculine plural restricted to male human controllers and other rational beings, feminine plural employed with all other classes, and feminine singular available to both as a form of collective / non-individuated agreement.[32]

It is worth mentioning, with reference to al-Mubarrad's systematization, the position of André Roman, who considers feminine singular agreement with human controllers as an expression of "unanimity". Given that nonhuman beings rarely display several independent wills, this pattern is much more common to them (Roman 1991, 21–23).[33]

In conclusion, this section has shown that some of the ideas that were discussed in Chapters 2 and 3 of this book were already present, although in an embryonic form, in the earliest stages of the Arabic grammatical tradition. Sībawayh and al-Mubarrad, with differences possibly due to their linguistic background, both contributed to shape ideas that circulated for centuries in the Arabic-speaking world. Al-Qurṭubī (1214–1273 CE), who wrote his monumental *tafsīr* (usually dubbed *al-Ǧāmiʕ*) in al-Andalus during the 13th century, for instance, commented on Q XII, 4 as follows:

> And he said: "*raʔaytu-hum l-ī sāǧidīna*" and it occurred in the masculine. al-Xalīl and Sībawayh's opinion is that when He spoke of these things [attributing them] obedience and prostration, which are actions typical of rational beings, He spoke of them like it is spoken of rational beings.[34]

32 It is worth mentioning that female human controllers are absent from al-Mubarrad's description, as already in Sībawayh. Once again, the reason is probably due to the fact that their agreement was not considered as problematic and worth further discussion.

33 Roman's position closely resembles Farrar's justification for the occurrence of singular verbs with neuter plurals in Greek, in the so-called *schema attikon*: "Neuter plurals take a verb singular, because mere multeity or mass implies no plurality, or separation of agencies [...] (Farrar 1870, 65)". It comes as no surprise, consequently, that Farrar quotes Arabic as an example of a similar construction, later in the same passage.

34 *Wa-qāla: "raʔaytu-hum l-ī sāǧidīna" fa-ǧāʔa muḏakkaran, fa-l-qawlu ʕinda l-Xalīli wa-*

At the time when al-Qurṭubī wrote (13th century), the system of Classical Arabic had probably already transitioned toward the new system, with mandatory feminine singular agreement with nonhuman plural controllers. Nonetheless, al-Xalīl and Sībawayh's description of agreement still continued to be quoted to explain unusual passages of the Quran, in this case making reference to the humanization of nonhuman controllers to explain the occurrence of masculine plural agreement.

After dealing with the formative age of the Arabic linguistic tradition, the next section will focus on the developments of linguistic theory, with specific reference to agreement, which occurred starting from the 10th century.

4.3 From 10th Century Grammars to Didactic Manuals: Further Developments

In § 4.2, we analyzed the descriptions of agreement produced during the formative stage of the Arabic linguistic tradition (8th and 9th century). We focused particularly on Sībawayh, al-Farrāʔ and al-Mubarrad, with the addition of al-Sīrāfī's famous commentary on Sībawayh's *Kitāb*. At the same time, the analysis of Quranic exegesis, with reference to those passages of the Quran that feature controversial agreement patterns, allowed us to crosscheck the results of our research on grammatical treatises. The present section focuses on the developments of the Arabic linguistic thought, with specific reference to agreement, in the period stretching from the 10th century to the didactic manuals such as Ibn Mālik's (1204–1274 CE) *ʔAlfiyya* and Ibn ʔĀǧurrūm's (1273–1323 CE) *ʔĀǧurrūmiyya*.

The ideas introduced by Sībawayh, al-Farrāʔ and al-Mubarrad continued to circulate widely and to inspire imitation more than innovation. Nonetheless, during the 10th century the analysis of agreement seems to move some steps forward. In *al-ʔĪḍāḥ fī ʕilal al-naḥw*, ʔAbū al-Qāsim al-Zaǧǧāǧī (892–952 CE), another grammarian of Persian origins, expands on al-Farrāʔ's connection between the paucal plurals and the occurrence of feminine singular agreement, mentioning the templates traditionally associated with the expression of paucity:

Sībawayh ʔanna-hu lamma ʔaxbara ʕan hāḏihi l-ʔašyāʔi bi-ṭ-ṭāʕati wa-s-suǧūdi wa-humā min ʔafʕāli man yaʕqilu ʔaxbara ʕan-hā ka-mā yuxbaru ʕam-man yaʕqilu (Qurṭubī 2006, 11:247).

It was said to him: no, because, since the plural is for what, like I mentioned to you before, differs in paucity (*fī l-qillati*) and abundance (*wa-l-kaṯrati*), this term [i.e. "plural"] was coined for what exceeds the number of two, including both paucity and abundance. Perhaps it was restricted for what is below the number of ten, and perhaps for what exceeds it, and another form was created for what designates the plural of paucity (*bi-qalīli l-ǧamʕi*). This occurred within broken plurals, so that templates were created specifically for the plural of paucity. They are four, *ʔafʕulu, ʔafʕālun, ʔafʕilatun* and *fiʕlatun*. *ʔAfʕulu* is like in *ʔaklubu* ("dog.PL") and *ʔaflusu* ("money.PL"). *ʔAfʕālun* is like in *ʔaḥmālun* ("load.PL") and *ʔaʕdālun* ("sack.PL"). *ʔAfʕilatun* is like in *ʔarġifatun* ("loave.PL") [...]. *Fiʕalun* is like in *ṣibyatun* ("boy.PL") and *fityatun* ("boy.PL"). These templates are used for the plural of paucity (*ʕalā ʔaqalli l-ʕadadi*), which is what is below the number of ten, and possibly for the plural of abundance (*li-ʔakṯari l-ʕadadi*), except that this is their origin [i.e., the plural of paucity]. That [i.e. their employment for the plural of abundance] occurs out of analogy (*xurūǧan ʕani l-qiyāsi*). Similarly, the templates of the plural of abundance have perhaps been used for the plural of paucity. This is explained in the chapter on the principles (*fī l-ʔuṣūli*), so that this is not the place to examine it in detail. It happens similarly to sound feminine plurals, like *Hindāt* ("Hind:F.PL"), *ṭalḥāt* ("acacia.tree:F.PL"), *ǧafanāt* ("bowl:F.PL"). They were meant to designate the plural of paucity, but were perhaps employed for the plural of abundance, which is allowed and not rejected. Ḥassān[35] said:

la-nā al-ǧafanātu l-ġurru yalmaʕna bi-ḍ-ḍuḥā	*wa-ʔasyāfu-nā yaqṭurna min naǧdatin daman*
[We have beautiful cups shining in the morn	and our swords drip blood for our courage]

The words of whom reproached Ḥassān for *al-ǧafanāt* were: it is for the plural of paucity, if you had said *al-ǧifān* ("bowl.PL") it would have been better for your praise, because it is a plural of abundance. [...] You said *yalmaʕna* ("3.IPFV:shine:F.PL") instead of *talmaʕu* ("3.IPFV.F.SG:shine") and *yaqṭurna* ("3.IPFV:drip:F.PL") instead of *tasīlu* ("3.IPFV.F.SG:flow"),[36] and

35 The poet is Ḥassān ibn Ṯābit (d. ca. 659), famous for being one of the Companions of the Prophet and for writing passionate poems in defense of the new faith.

36 Here the reproach concerns both the lexical choice ("to flow" instead of "to drip") and the agreement pattern employed (feminine singular instead of feminine plural).

> *as-sayalān* ("the flow") is more than *al-qaṭr* ("the dripping"). The reproach is on point, except that it is not forbidden that *ǧafanāt* occur for the plural of abundance, even though it was designed for the plural of paucity, because the different plurals share it and are used interchangeably. Don't you see that *fuʕūl* belongs to the templates for the plural of abundance, yet it is used for the plural of paucity, as God Almighty said: *ṯalāṯatu qurūʔin* ("three periods", II, 228).[37]

The argument, here, is that the singular *ǧafna* "bowl" has two distinct plurals, one of paucity (the sound feminine *ǧafanāt*) and one of abundance (the broken *ǧifān*). Ḥassān ibn Ṯābit, in order to convey the sense of magnificence he intended, should have thus used *ǧifān*, which implies a higher number of bowls (and, thus, greater glory). Agreement patterns are the result of the poet's choice with regard to plural. Since Ḥassān ibn Ṯābit opted for the plural of paucity, feminine plural (in the verb *ya-lmaʕ-na* "3.IPFV-shine-F.PL") is the most suitable choice, as opposed to *ta-lmaʕ* "3.IPFV.F.SG-shine", which would have suited *ǧifān* better. Similarly, *ʔasyāf* "sword.PL" is a plural of paucity (as opposed to *suyūf* "sword.PL"), so that *ya-qṭur-na* ("3.IPFV-drip-F.PL") agrees in the femi-

---

37 *Qīla la-hu: lā, li-ʔanna l-ǧamʕa li-mā kāna ka-mā ḏakartu la-ka muxtalifan fī l-qillati wa-l-kaṯrati ǧuʕila hāḏā l-lafḏu li-mā baʕda l-iṯnayni, fa-štaraka fī-hi l-qalīlu wa-l-kaṯīru, wa-rubba-mā qtaṣara bi-hi ʕalā mā dūna l-ʕašarati, wa-rubba-mā ǧāwaza ḏālika, wa-ǧuʕila la-hu lafḏu ʔāxaru yaxtaṣṣu bi-qalīli l-ǧamʕi, wa-ḏālika fī l-mukassari mina-l-ǧumūʕi, fa-ǧuʕilat la-hu ʔamṯilatun muxtaṣṣatun bi-l-qalīli, wa-hiya ʔarbaʕatun. ʔAfʕulu, wa-ʔafʕālun, wa-ʔafʕilatun, wa-fiʕlatun, fa-ʔafʕulu qawlu-ka ʔaklubu wa-ʔaflusu. Wa-ʔafʕālun qawlu-ka ʔaḥmālun wa-ʔaʕdālun. Wa-ʔafʕilatun ka-qawli-ka ʔarġifatun, [...] wa-fiʕalun qawlu-ka ṣibyatun wa-fityatun. Fa-hāḏihi l-ʔamṯilatu wāqiʕatun ʕalā ʔaqalli l-ʕadadi, wa-huwa mā dūna l-ʕašarati, wa-rubba-mā waqaʕat li-ʔakṯari l-ʕadadi, ʔillā ʔanna hāḏā huwa l-ʔaṣlu, wa-ḏālika yaqaʕu xurūǧan ʕani l-qiyāsi l-muṭṭaradi, ka-mā ʔanna bināʔa l-kaṯīri rubba-mā šaraka-hu fī l-qalīli. Mašrūḥun fī l-ʔuṣūli, wa-laysa hāḏā mawḍiʕa-hu fa-nastaqṣiya-hu. Wa-ka-ḏālika mā ǧumiʕa bi-l-ʔalifi wa-t-tāʔi, naḥwa: l-Hindāti, wa-ṭ-ṭalḥāti, wa-l-ǧafanāti. Al-maqṣūdu bi-hi ʔan yakūna li-ʔaqalli l-ʕadadi, wa-rubba-mā waqaʕa li-ʔakṯari-hi fa-yakūnu ḏālika ǧāʔizan ġayra mardūdin. Qāla Ḥassānun:*

la-nā al-ǧafanātu l-ġurru yalmaʕna bi-ḍ-ḍuhā | *wa-ʔasyāfu-nā yaqṭurna min naǧdatin daman*

Wa-ʔammā qawlu man ʔaxaḏa ʕalā Ḥassānini l-ǧafanāti, fa-qāla: huwa li-ʔaqalli l-ʕadadi, wa-kāna qawlu-ka l-ǧifānu ʔablaġa fī l-madḥi li-ʔanna-hā li-ʔakṯari l-ʕadadi. [...], wa-qulta yalmaʕna wa-lam taqul talmaʕu. Wa-qulta yaqṭarna, wa-lam taqul tasīlu, wa-s-sayalān ʔakṯaru mina l-qaṭri [...] Fa-huwa ka-mā qāla, ʔillā ʔanna-hu ġayru madfūʕin ʔan takūna l-ǧafanātu taqaʕu li-l-kaṯīri, wa-ʔin kāna mawḍūʕa bābi-hā l-qalīlu, li-štirāki l-ǧumūʕi wa-duxūli baʕḍu-hā ʕalā baʕḍin, ʔa-lā tarā ʔanna fuʕūlan min ʔabniyati ʔakṯari l-ʕadadi, wa-qad taqaʕu li-l-qalīli ka-mā qāla ʕazza wa-ǧalla "ṯalāṯatu qurūʔin" (al-Zaǧǧāǧī 1979, 122–123).

nine plural. At this point, however, al-Zaǧǧāǧī writes that, even though statements concerning verbal agreement are *per se* correct, it is no longer possible to draw a clear-cut line between the plurals of paucity and abundance. His statement seems to suggest a diachronic development, at the end of which the semantic distinction between the two categories of plural became blurred to the point that even in the Quran a plural of abundance (*qurūʔ* "period.PL" < *fuʕūl*) is employed with the numeral "three". Al-Zaǧǧāǧī's observation, already present in al-Farrāʔ (1983, 1:435), is confirmed by a small-scale statistic study conducted by Ferrando (2006, 54), in which no conclusive evidence was found proving that the plurals of paucity and abundance attract different types of agreement, even in ancient texts such as the pre-Islamic *Muʕallaqāt*.[38] This means that no form of written Arabic, to the best of our knowledge, exists where the distinction between the two plural forms is still productive on a large scale. This does not mean, however, that it has completely disappeared from the language. Isolated words exist in which a distinction between paucal and abundance plural still seems to be operating. In the Qurʔān, for instance, only the paucal plural *ʔašhur* "month.PL" is used with numerals, and the same is true for the somewhat rare form *ʔabḥur* "sea.PL", which occurs only once, following a numeral. On a more general level, looking at the pre-modern section of Arabicorpus, *ḥurūf / ʔaḥruf* "letter.PL" seems to be another noun for which a distinction between paucal and abundance plural was still operative. When quantified by the numeral *ṯalāṯa* "three", for instance, the paucal form *ʔaḥruf* appears 89 times, the plural of abundance *ḥurūf* only 3. In conclusion, Al-Zaǧǧāǧī appears to be accurate in his description of the distinction between paucal and abundance plurals as optional and no longer mandatory.

Apart from such isolated examples, the description of agreement in traditional grammars of Arabic dating back to the 10th–12th century does not offer many innovations. As seen in § 4.2, al-Qurṭubī, who wrote in al-Andalus during the 13th century, still quoted al-Xalīl and Sībawayh to explain unusual agreement patterns in the Quran.

In the 13th century, however, we witness the flourishing of pedagogical grammars of Arabic, the most famous of which are probably Ibn Mālik's (1204–1273 CE) *ʔAlfiyya* (the complete title is *al-Xulāṣa al-ʔAlfiyya*) and Ibn ʔĀǧurrūm's (1273–1323 CE) *ʔĀǧurrumiyya*.[39] In many cases, these grammars, usually written

38 "Broadly speaking, the discrimination between the notions of Abundance and Paucity seems to be maintained in our corpus only to a certain extent (Ferrando 2006, 54)."

39 This does not mean that, during the previous centuries, pedagogical grammars were totally absent from the scene. We find mentions of instructions fit for *al-mubtadiʔ li-t-taʕlīm* ("the novice in instruction") already in al-Farrāʔ (9th century), while early peda-

in brief verses that explain the main rules of the Arabic language, remained in use in pedagogical curricula until the 20th century (Versteegh 1997, 109). Such pedagogical treatises are quite prescriptive in nature and do not offer the rich insight into the Arabic language provided by the grammarians so far analyzed, which prompted Carter (1994, 390) to write that the two genres are hardly comparable. Agreement, moreover, did not lend itself to be approached from a prescriptive viewpoint. As seen in § 4.2, in fact, the only pattern that was not subject to variation was the restriction of masculine plural agreement to male human controllers (but not vice versa).[40] Nonetheless, pedagogical grammars of Arabic may contain fleeting mentions of agreement, which then receives a much more detailed treatment in one of the many commentaries (*šurūḥ*, sg. *šarḥ*) that usually accompany them.

The analysis of Ibn ʔĀǧurrūm's *ʔĀǧurrūmiyya* did not yield any reference to agreement or agreement patterns. Ibn Mālik's *ʔAlfiyya*, on the other hand, contains a small section concerning the agreement of the subject (*fāʕil*) with a verbal target (Ibn Mālik al-ʔAndalusī s.d., 16–17). Within this section, a single verse, however elliptic, is of great interest for our attempt at reconstruction, especially when seen through the eyes of Ibn ʕAqīl (1294–1367 CE), who wrote the most famous commentary on the *ʔAlfiyya*.

(8) *wa=t=tāʔu maʕa ǧamʕin siwā s=sālimi min mudakkarin*
and=DEF=tāʔ with plural except DEF=sound from masculine
ka=t=tāʔi maʕa ʔiḥdā l=labin wa=l=ḥadfa fī
like=DEF=tāʔ with one.F.SG DEF=brick.COLL and=DEF=elision in
niʕma l=fatātu staḥsanū li=ʔanna qaṣda
what.a.wonderful DEF=girl prefer:3.PFV.M.PL because intention
l=ǧinsi fī=hi bayyin
DEF=gender in=him clear
'The *tāʔ* with the plural, except the sound masculine, is like the *tāʔ* in the singulative of *labin* ("brick", i.e. *labina* "one brick"); and the elision in

gogical grammars, such as *al-Kitāb fī-l-naḥw* by Luġda (d. 913 CE) and *Kitāb al-muwaffaqī fī-l-naḥw* by Ibn Kaysān (d. 912 CE) date back to the 10th century (Kasher 2018, 147). None of these works, however, reached the fame and circulation of the later *ʔAlfiyya* and *ʔĀǧurrūmiyya*.

40 Ibn Kaysān's *al-Muwaffaqī fī-l-naḥw* (which is about tweny pages long), for instance, includes a brief mention of broken plural forms expressing the plurals of paucity and abundance (with the usual caveat concerning the blurred boundaries between the two sets of forms), but no mention of agreement patterns with plural nouns (Ibn Kaysān 1975, 119).

> *niʕma l-fatātu* ("what a wonderful girl!") is preferred, because the intention of gender there is clear.' (Ibn Mālik al-ʔAndalusī s.d., 17)

Ibn Mālik here says that the *tāʔ* of pre-controller verbal targets,[41] which is always possible except when the controller is a sound masculine plural, is similar in nature to the *tāʔ* (*marbūta*) employed to form singulative out of collective nouns, such as in *labin* / *labina* "brick.COLL" / "brick.SGLTV".[42] This means that Ibn Mālik is aware of the difference between feminine singular verbs agreeing with morphologically feminine singular controllers and cases in which feminine singular represents, in modern typological terms, a form of semantic agreement. In such cases, in his opinion, the value of the *tāʔ* (i.e. of what we conventionally designate as "feminine singular") is comparable to the value of the *tāʔ marbūta* in singulatives.[43] Given the concise nature of the *ʔAlfiyya*, Ibn Mālik does not provide any additional comment to clarify this point, so that we have to turn to its commentaries. The *šarḥ* by Ibn ʕAqīl (1294–1367) provides a very detailed explanation, which we report in full:

> If it [i.e. the verb] refers to a plural, either it is a sound masculine plural, in which case the *tāʔ* on the verb is not allowed, so that you say: *"Qāma* [m.sg.] *z-Zaydūna*" ("The Zayd-M.PL stood up"), while *"Qāmati* [f.sg.] *z-Zaydūna*" ("The Zayd-M.PL stood up") is not allowed. If it is not a sound masculine plural, insomuch as it is a broken plural of a masculine noun, such as *ar-riǧāl* ("the man.PL"), or of a feminine noun, such as *al-Hunūd* ("the Hind.PL"), or a sound feminine plural, such as *al-Hindāt* ("the Hind:F.PL"), adding the *tāʔ* or eliding it is equally possible. You say: "*Qāma* [m.sg.] *r-riǧālu* ("the man.PL") and *qāmati* [f.sg.] *r-riǧālu, qāma* [m.sg.] *l-Hunūdu* ("the Hind.PL") and *qāmati* [f.sg.] *l-Hunūdu, qāma* [m.sg.] *l-Hindātu* ("the Hind-F.PL"), and *qāmati* [f.sg.] *l-Hindātu*"; the employment

41 It is clear that Ibn Mālik is here referring to pre-controller verbal targets, because the verse is located in the section devoted to the *fāʕil*, which only designates the subject when it follows the verb. It is not entirely clear, however, whether Ibn Mālik considers his statement to be true also for post-controller verbal targets, which are treated differently in the Arabic grammar.

42 Singulative (the gloss is, to the best of our knowledge, absent from the inventory available at https://www.eva.mpg.de/lingua/pdf/Glossing-Rules.pdf).

43 The nature of the morpheme /t/ in Arabic (and, more generally, in the Semitic and Afro-Asiatic family) has generated a long and unresolved debate. André Roman, whose approach we find particularly interesting, wrote that "le morpheme /t/ de la *res* générale n'est pas la base d'une expansion d'identité. Cependant il représente comme «une» la *res* antécédente (Roman 1991, 47)."

> of the *tāʔ* is to interpret it as a collective (*li-taʔawwuli-hi bi-l-ǧamāʕati*), while the elision of the *tāʔ* is to interpret it as a plural (*li-taʔawwuli-hi bi-l-ǧamʕi*). And by saying "Like the *tāʔ* in the singulative of *labin* ("brick")" he meant that the *tāʔ* with broken plurals and sound feminine plurals is like the *tāʔ* with nouns whose appearance is metaphorically feminine, such as *labina*. In the same way in which you say "*Kusirati* [f.sg.] *l-labinatu* ("the brick was broken") and *kusira* [m.sg.] *l-labinatu*", you say "*Qāma* [m.sg.] *r-riǧālu* ("The men stood up") and *qāmati* [f.sg.] *r-riǧālu*" and the rest of the forms mentioned above.[44]

This excerpt from Ibn ʕAqīl's *Šarḥ* clarifies two important points. The first one concerns Ibn Mālik's statement about the similar nature of the /t/ morpheme in the verb preceding a plural subject and in the singulative of collective nouns. Ibn ʕAqīl explains the similarity saying that, in both cases, the noun or verb is only metaphorically feminine. Ibn ʕAqīl, thus, is perfectly aware of the multi-faceted semantic values of the morpheme, which he conveniently divides in two groups, i.e. real vs. metaphorical feminine.

The second point, which is even more relevant to our discourse, concerns the value of the /t/ morpheme. Without much ambiguity, Ibn ʕAqīl here states that, when the subject is not a sound masculine plural (in which case a "feminine" singular verb is not allowed), a verb in the 3rd masculine singular implies a plural interpretation of the subject, while a verb in the 3rd feminine singular implies a collective interpretation of the same.[45] This statement perfectly fits the findings presented in Chapters 2 and 3 of this book, where feminine singular was interpreted as a form of [-individuated] agreement in both pre-Classical Arabic and the modern dialects. It is also worth mentioning that both Ibn Mālik

44 *ʔIḏā ʔusnida ʔilā ǧamʕin: fa-ʔimmā ʔan yakūna ǧamʕa salāmatin li-muḏakkarin, ʔawwalan; fa-ʔin kāna ǧamʕa salāmatin li-muḏakkarin lam yaǧuzi qtirānu l-fiʕli bi-t-tāʔi; fa-taqūlu: "Qāma z-Zaydūna", wa lā yaǧūzu: "Qāmati z-Zaydūna", wa-ʔin lam yakun ǧamʕa salāmatin li-muḏakkarin—bi-ʔan kāna ǧamʕa taksīrin li-muḏakkarin ka-r-riǧāli, ʔaw li-muʔannaṯin ka-l-Hunūdi, ʔaw ǧamʕa salāmatin li-muʔannaṯin ka-l-Hindāti—ǧāza ʔiṯbātu t-tāʔ wa-ḥaḏfu-hā; fa-taqūlu: "Qāma r-riǧālu, wa qāmati r-riǧālu, wa-qāma l-Hunūdu, wa-qāmati l-Hunūdu, wa-qāma l-Hindātu, wa-qāmati l-Hindātu"; fa-ʔiṯbātu t-tāʔi li-taʔawwuli-hi bi-l-ǧamāʕati, wa-ḥaḏfu-hā li-taʔawwuli-hi bi-l-ǧamʕi. Wa-ʔašāra bi-qawli-hi: "Ka-t-tāʔi maʕa ʔiḥdā l-labin" ʔilā ʔanna t-tāʔ maʕa ǧamʕi t-taksīri, wa-ǧamʕa s-salāmati li-muʔannatin, ka-t-tāʔi maʕa [aḍ-ḍāhiri] l-maǧāziyyi t-taʔnīṯi ka-labinatin; fa-ka-mā taqūlu: "Kasirati l-labinatu, wa-kasira l-labinatu" taqūlu: "Qāma r-riǧālu, wa-qāmati r-riǧālu" wa-ka-ḏālika bāqī mā taqaddama* (Ibn ʕAqīl 1980, 2:94–95).

45 It is clear that 3rd feminine singular is here employed in a conventional way. Ibn ʕAqīl says clearly that the feminine here is only metaphorical and that "adding the *tāʔ*" to the verb conveys a collective interpretation of the subject.

and Ibn ʕAqīl exclude from the possibility of this "collective" agreement only sound masculine plural, which also fits the results of our research. This means that "feminine singular" agreement, in its complete extraneity to the [-human] value, is available to all class of controllers, with the single exception of sound masculine plurals, which is a morphological and not a semantic restriction.

The restrictions to the employment of feminine singular agreement in verbal pre-controller targets, however, vary depending on the different grammatical schools. The different positions can be grouped in three schools:[46]

1. The Kufans, who admit the possibility of feminine singular agreement in pre-controller verbal targets without any restriction, the reason being that any plural noun can be interpreted as a plural or as a collective;
2. The school of ʔAbū ʕAlī al-Farīsī (900–987 CE), Ibn Ǧinnī's (934–1002 CE) master, according to whom feminine singular agreement is always possible, except in the case of sound masculine plurals. Ibn Mālik, thus, seems to follow this school, and so does his commentator. The Kufans, however, claim that no restriction on the occurrence of feminine singular agreement with pre-controller verbal targets depending from sound masculine plurals occurs. To support their claim, they quote the following verse by Qarbaṭ ibn ʔAnīf, included in the *Ḥamāsa*:[47]

   (9) *law kuntu min Māzinin lam* ***ta-stabiḥ***
   if be:1.PFV.SG from Māzin NEG 3.IPFV.F.SG-take.possession
   ʔibil=ī Banū l=Laqīṭati min Ḏuhli bni
   camel.COLL=1.SG son:M.PL DEF=Laqīṭa from Ḏuhli son
   Šaybāna
   Šaybān
   'If I had been from the Māzin tribe, the Banū Laqīṭa of Ḏuhl ibn Šaybān would not have seized my camels' (Ibn ʕAqīl 1980, 2:94, note 1)[48]

---

46 In the Arabic grammatical tradition, morphologically or semantically plural controllers were usually divided in six categories: collectives (*ismu l-ǧamʕi*), like *qawm* "people.COLL"; nouns designating entire populations or groups (*ismu l-ǧinsi l-ǧamʕī*), like *Rūm* "the Greek.COLL"; broken plurals of nouns that are masculine when in the singular (*ǧamʕu t-taksīri li-muḏakkarin*), like *riǧāl* "man.PL"; broken plurals of nouns that are feminine when in the singular (*ǧamʕu t-taksīri li-muʔannaṯin*), like *Hunūdin* "Hind.PL"; sound masculine plurals (*ǧamʕu l-muḏakkari s-sālimi*), like *muʔminūna* "believer:M.PL"; sound feminine plurals (*ǧamʕu l-muʔannaṯi s-sālimi*), like *muʔmināt* "believer:F.PL" (Ibn ʕAqīl 1980, 2:94, note 1). The different agreement patterns attributed to the three schools stem from this kind of distinction.

47 The *Ḥamāsa* is a famous anthology of Arabic poetry, compiled in the 9th century by ʔAbū Tamām al-Buḥturī (821–897 CE).

48 Ths discussion is not part of Ibn ʕAqīl's *Šarḥ* itself, but of the explanatory notes added by the editor, Muḥammad Muḥy al-Dīn ʕAbd al-Ḥamīd. Another example of feminine singu-

3. The Basrans, according to whom variation between masculine and feminine singular agreement in pre-controller verbal targets is always possible, but with the exclusion of sound masculine and sound feminine plurals. In these two cases, agreement is mandatory: masculine singular in the former, feminine singular in the latter (Ibn ʕAqīl 1980, 2:94–95, note 1). In order to show that no restriction on the occurrence of masculine singular agreement with pre-controller targets depending from a sound feminine controller obtains, however, the Kufans quote the following Quranic verse, where a 3rd person masculine singular verb agrees with the sound feminine plural *muʔmin-āt* "ACT.PTCP.believe-F.PL":

(10) [...] *ʔiḏā* ***ǧāʔa=ka*** ***l=muʔmin-ātu*** [...]
when come.3.PFV.M.SG=you.M.SG DEF=ACT.PTCP.believe-F.PL
'[...] when believing women come to thee [...]' (LX, 12)

As often happens, none of the three schools is entirely wrong, and all depends on the way in which we decide to look at the data. If we are searching to find absolute conditions on the occurrence of agreement patterns, it is clear that the two counterexamples quoted by the Kufans are sufficient to disprove the existence of any restriction whatsoever to the occurrence of the agreement pattern under analysis (i.e. feminine singular agreement with pre-controller verbal targets). Chapters 2 and 3 have clearly demonstrated, however, that agreement in all varieties of Arabic (with the possible exception of Classical and Modern Standard Arabic) can only be understood in terms of trends and patterns. If we look at agreement patterns in terms of statistical trends, thus, al-Farīsī and the Baṣrans' opinions better reflect the nature of the data in our possession.

In conclusion, despite its pedagogic nature, Ibn Mālik's *ʔAlfiyya* provides a profound insight into the nature of agreement in Arabic. Even though Ibn Mālik's conciseness does not allow him to go into much detail, the different commentaries published throughout the centuries (among which we chose Ibn ʕAqīl's one) clarify his point, shedding light on the nature of feminine singular agreement with plural controllers. It is worth noting that, at the time when Ibn Mālik wrote his *ʔAlfiyya* (13th century), Arabic prose had largely transitioned to

lar agreement in a pre-controller verbal target depending from a sound masculine plural occurs in the Quran: *ʔāmantu ʔanna-hu lā ʔIlāhu ʔillā llaḏī* ***ʔāmanat*** *bi-hi* ***Banū*** *ʔIsrāʔīla* "I believe that there is no god but He in whom the Children of Israel believe (X, 90)." In both cases, the sound masculine plural occurs in the name of a tribe, which probably favors a collective interpretation.

the new agreement system.[49] Nonetheless, the new agreement system, which requires mandatory feminine singular agreement with nonhuman plural controllers, does not even find a place in pedagogic grammars of Arabic, where we would expect a more prescriptive standpoint. A complete scrutiny of the countless number of Arabic grammars is, for obvious reasons, an enterprise beyond reach. To the best of our knowledge, however, the first instance of something resembling a prescriptive rule does not occur before the Nahḍa (19th century), which is the object of next section.

4.4 Between Tradition and Standardization: Arabic Grammar during the *Nahḍa*[50]

In the previous section, we analyzed both scholarly and pedagogical grammars up to the 13th century. The results showed that, even after Arabic prose largely replaced the ancient agreement system with the new one (with the exceptions mentioned in § 3.8), the latter failed to find a place in grammatical descriptions of Arabic. Quite to the contrary, grammarians and commentators continued to produce fine-grained descriptions of the old system, in which the fact that masculine plural agreement is reserved to male human controllers is often the only prescriptive rule. Many of the details of the ancient agreement system "unveiled" in Chapters 2 and 3 are hinted at, or clearly spelled out, in the sources examined in the previous sections: the variation between feminine singular and plural agreement with nonhuman controllers, the availability of feminine singular agreement to all types of controllers, including humans, its close link with broken plural and even its [-individuated] meaning (interpreted as a collective). These insights are not, of course, all readily available in the work of a single grammarian, but rather represent the sum of what the Arabic grammatical thought produced, with reference to agreement, from the 8th to the 13th century. Arabic grammarians provide, without much doubt, quite a refined description of the agreement system obtaining in pre- and early Classical Arabic. The absence of any mention of the new system and of the role of humanness in determining agreement patterns, on the other hand, is surprising. We know from Belnap and Gee (1994, 132), in fact, that the new system had

49 For a discussion of exceptions to the generalization of the new agreement system in Classical Arabic, see § 3.8.

50 The term *Nahḍa* "awakening" is commonly employed in traditional scholarship when referring to the cultural movement that flourished in the Arabic-speaking world (but especially in Egypt, Lebanon and Syria) during the 19th century.

replaced the old one in the fields of non-literary prose by the end of the 10th century. The reader should remember, however, that the situation which presented itself under the eyes of the grammarians witnessed the survival of the ancient system in the following domains:

I. The whole poetic corpus available to them, both pre-Islamic and post-Islamic;
II. The Quran;
III. Ornate prose;
IV. Written documents for private use and, in general, Middle Arabic;
V. All the spoken dialects (even though some of them had probably already lost gender distinction in the plural).

Seen from this perspective, the fact that the new system had not yet been described by Arabic grammarians by the end of the 13th century seems, maybe, less surprising. This is especially true when considering that the new mandatory pattern, prescribing feminine singular agreement with nonhuman controllers, did not openly contradict the ancient system, but represented a variant among others. The novelty, thus, lay in the mandatory nature of the rule and in the hitherto unheard of role of humanness, rather than in the agreement pattern itself.

As said in the conclusions of § 4.3, a complete scrutiny of all grammars of Arabic is an enterprise beyond reach. To the best of our knowledge, however, the first instance in which the new rule is spelled out clearly does not occur before the 19th century, i.e. before the *Nahḍa*. This does not mean that, during the *Nahḍa*, all those who wrote about Arabic adhered to the rules obtaining in the new system and wrote their grammars accordingly. Quite to the contrary, well within the 19th century we still find scholars who described, with few changes, the same kind of agreement emerging from 8th and 9th century grammars of Arabic.

One of such scholars is the Lebanese polymath Aḥmad Fāris al-Šidyāq (1805–1887), one of the greatest personalities of the Nahḍa. Known in literaly circles for his autobiographical work *al-Sāq ʕalā al-Sāq fī-mā huwa al-Fāriyāq* (first published in Paris 1955) (Cachia 1992, 406–407), al-Šidyāq was also an extraordinary lexicographer, as evident from *al-Ǧāsūs ʕalā al-Qāmūs*, in which he criticizes the many deficiencies of al-Fayrūzābādī's (1329–1414 CE) monumental dictionary, *al-Qāmūs* (Chejne 1969, 137). For the purpose of this research, we analyzed a shorter pedagogical work, *Ġunyat al-Ṭālib wa-Munyat al-Rāġib*, whose subtitle conveys the didactic nature of the book: *Durūs fī l-Ṣarf wa-l-Naḥw wa-Ḥurūf al-Maʕānī* (*Lessons in morphology, Syntax and Semantics*). Differently from the other grammars so far analyzed, al-Šidyāq's work includes a chapter entirely devoted to agreement with plural controllers, even though the term "agreement" does not appear in the title, *Fī baʕḍi fawāʔida tataʕallaqu bi-l-ǧamʕi* (*About some useful lessons concerning the plural*). The lesson is quite brief and only its second half is relevant to our discussion:

> If the plural is nonhuman (*li-ġayri ʕāqilin*), it is possible to add a feminine mark to its verb or to omit it. You say: *ḏahabati* [f.sg.] *l-ʔayyāmu* ("The days went by") and *ḏahaba* [f.sg.] *l-ʔayyāmu* ("The days went by"), but the first one is more suitable. It is also possible, when the verb follows its subject, to use either the *tāʔ* [i.e. 3rd feminine singular] or the *nūn* [i.e. 3rd feminine plural].[51] You say *l-ʔayyāmu ḏahabat* [f.sg.] ("The days went by") or *ḏahabna* [f.pl], but the *nūn* is more suitable with the plural of paucity, such as when you say *al-ʔaǧḏāʕu nkasarna* [f.pl.] ("The branches broke"). The *tāʔ* is more suitable with the plural of abundance, like in *l-ǧuḏūʕi nkasarat* [f.pl.] ("The branches broke"). They chose to use for the plural of abundance the *hāʔ* [i.e. feminine singular agreement],[52] so they said *ʔaʕṭaytu-hu darāhima kaṯīratan* [f.sg.] ("I gave him many dirhams") and *ʔaqamtu ʔayyāman maʕdūdatan* [f.sg.] ("I stayed for counted days"). They used for the plural of paucity the *ʔalif* and *tāʔ* [i.e. sound feminine plural agreement], like in *ʔaqamtu ʔayyāman maʕdūdātin* [f.pl.] ("I stayed for counted days"),[53] which is more eloquent.[54] The masculine plural of the adjective is allowed by the Kufans on the basis of analogy.[55]

---

51 The translation, here, is not literal. Al-Šidyāq does not write of verbs preceding or following the controller. In the first case, however, he speaks of the *tāʔ* as of a feminine marker, while in the second both the *tāʔ* and the *nūn* are presented as pronominal forms. In the Arabic grammatical tradition, an *-at* (but also, in the *ʔakalū-nī l-barāġīṯu* syndrome, a *–ū*) suffix in a pre-controller verbal target is considered as a mark of feminine (or, in the case of *–ū*, of masculine plural). Verb endings in verbs following their controllers, on the other hand, are considered as pronominal forms acting as subjects, while the controller itself, the *mubtadaʔ*, is basically the topic of a topicalized sentence. See Levin (1989).

52 The *hāʔ* should be here considered as the pronunciation of the etymological *tāʔ marbūṭa* when the noun / adjective is not in pausal position.

53 After discussing agreement patterns with verbal targets, al-Šidyāq is here dealing with the agreement of adjectives.

54 What al-Šidyāq means here is not that feminine plural agreement is more eloquent *lato sensu*, but that it is to be preferred in the expression *ʔaqamtu ʔayyāman maʕdūdātin* because *ʔayyām* "day.PL", based on the *ʔafʕāl* template, is a plural of paucity.

55 *Wa-ʔiḏā kāna l-ǧamʕu li-ġayri ʕāqilin ǧāza ʔilḥāqu ʕalāmati t-taʔnīṯi fī fiʕli-hi wa-tarku-hā taqūlu ḏahabati l-ʔayyāmu wa-ḏahaba l-ʔayyāmu wa-l-ʔawlā l-ʔawwalu wa-yaǧūzu fī maḍmarati t-tāʔi wa-n-nūni fa-taqūlu l-ʔayyāmu ḏahabat ʔaw ḏahabna lakinna l-ʔawlā n-nūnu maʕa ǧamʕi l-qillati ka-qawli-ka l-ʔaǧḏāʕu nkasarna wa-t-tāʔu maʕa ǧamʕi l-kaṯrati naḥwa l-ǧuḏūʕi nkasarat wa-xtārū ʔan ʔalḥaqū bi-ṣīġati l-ǧamʕi l-kaṯīri l-hāʔa fa-qālū ʔaʕṭaytu-hu darāhima kaṯīratan wa-ʔaqamtu ʔayyāman maʕdūdatan wa-ʔalḥaqū bi-ṣīġati l-ǧamʕi*

This brief excerpt from al-Šidyāq's *Ġunyat al-Ṭālib wa-Munyat al-Rāġib* is extremely useful in a diachronic perspective, because it shows some changes, while remaining in the framework of traditional descriptions of agreement patterns. In the previous two sections, in fact, the distinction between *ʕāqil* "rational" / *ġayr ʕāqil* "irrational"[56] was presented in order to state that a particular agreement pattern, namely masculine plural, was exclusive to rational beings (usually humans, jinns and angels). Agreement patterns concerning *ġayr ʕāqil* controllers were then presented by exclusion. Here, on the contrary, al-Šidyāq explicitly sets apart the category of plural *ġayr ʕāqil* controllers, in order to discuss the possible agreement patterns. At this point, however, al-Šidyāq's description does not differ much from 9th and 10th century accounts of agreement, with specific reference to al-Farrāʔ, al-Zağğāğī and their analysis of the plurals of paucity vs abundance and their role in determining agreement patterns.

A further step toward the formal definition of the rule that sets apart the ancient system from the new one (i.e. mandatory feminine singular agreement with plural nonhuman controllers) is taken by another great intellectual of the Lebanese Nahḍa and one of al-Šidyāq's rivals (Cachia 1992, 420), Nāṣīf al-Yāziğī (1800–1871). Nāṣīf al-Yāziğī was the forefather of an entire family of intellectuals, who contributed to shape the Lebanese Nahḍa during the 19th and 20th century (Badawi 1992, 9–10).

> Nāṣīf al-Yāzijī (1800–1871) was a scholar and poet, steeped in classical Arabic lore. After leaving the court he participated in the new translation of the Bible into Arabic. His many books on grammar and rhetoric attest to his great erudition in the traditional branches of knowledge. His interest in Abbasid poetry is reflected in his edition of the diwan of al-Mutanabbi. His own poetry, though not demonstrably free of artifice and trivial concerns, rises high above that of his immediate predecessors in the richness and lucidity of its language.
>
> SOMEKH 1992, 43

For the purpose of this chapter, similarly to what already done in the case of al-Šidyāq, we analyzed al-Yāziğī's pedagogical grammar *Kitāb Nār al-Qurā fī Šarḥ Ğawf al-Farā*. In order to compare al-Yāziğī's work with al-Šidyāq's *Ġun-*

---

l-qalīli l-ʔalifa wa-t-tāʔa naḥwa ʔaqamtu ʔayyāman maʕdūdātin wa-hāḏā huwa l-ʔafṣaḥu wa-ğamʕu ṣ-ṣifati bi-l-wāwi wa-n-nūni ğāʔizun ʕinda l-kūfiyyīna qiyāsan (aš-Šidyāq s.d., 41).

56 Or, in some sources, *mā yaʕqilu* "what is endowed with reason" vs *mā lā yaʕqilu* "what is not endowed with reason".

yat al-Ṭālib wa-Munyat al-Rāġib, we analyzed the abridged edition intended for didactic use, even though a scholarly edition is also available. The structure of the book betrays al-Yāziǧī's classical education, being composed of short pedagogical verses, in the style of medieval texts such as the *ʔAlfiyya*, followed by an explanation in prose. Plural agreement patterns are discussed in the chapter *Fī quyūd al-ḍamāʔir wa-mutaʕalliqāti-hā* (*On the rules of pronouns and related things*), of which long excerpts will be reported in translation, due to its importance to our reconstruction. Al-Yāziǧī starts out presenting agreement patterns for human controllers, with a partial innovation. While classical texts mainly focused on agreement with male plural human controllers, rarely mentioning female ones, al-Yāziǧī clearly define the agreement patterns for both categories:

li-l-ʕāqilīna ʔaḍmarū l-wāwa wa-dal	*mīmun wa-fī-l-muʕannaṯi n-nūnu štamal*
(For masculine rationals they use as a pronoun the *wāw* and their mark is	a *mīm*, while for feminine the *nūn* encompasses all)

That means that they made the *wāw* a pronoun for male rationals only (*li-l-ʕāqilīna faqaṭ*), like in *ḍarabū* ("hit:3.PFV.M.PL"), *yaḍribūna* ("3.IPFV:hit:M.PL") and *iḍribū* ("IMP:hit:2.M.PL"). They also made the *mīm* a mark that designates male rationals, like in *ḍarabtum* ("hit:2.PFV.M.PL"), *ʔakramtum* ("honor:2.PFV.M.PL") and *laqītum* ("find:2.PFV.M.PL"). As far as female rationals (*al-ʕāqilāt*) are concerned, for them the *nūn* is both pronoun, like in *ḏahabna* ("go:3.PFV.F.PL"), and mark, like in *ʔakramtu-hunna* ("honor:1.PFV.SG-them.F").[57] We will speak of all that in detail.[58]

In this first part, masculine and feminine plural are presented as the agreement patterns for male and female human controllers respectively. After a long explanation of the origin and status of both the *mīm* and the *nūn*, al-Yāziǧī moves on to discuss agreement patterns with nonhuman controllers:

57 The distinction here revolves around the issue of the different treatment of verbal endings (as pronouns or markers) in traditional grammar. See footnote 51 above.

58 *li-l-ʕāqilīna ʔaḍmarū l-wāwa wa-dal* *mīmun wa-fī-l-muʕannaṯi n-nūnu štamal* *ʔay ʔanna-hum ǧaʕalū l-wāwa ḍamīran li-l-ʕāqilīna faqaṭ naḥwa ḍarabū wa-yaḍribūna wa-ḍribū. Wa-ǧaʕalū l-mīma ʕalāmatan tadullu ʕalay-him ka-ḍarabtum wa-ʔakramtum wa-laqītum. Wa-ʔammā l-ʕāqilātu fa-takūnu n-nūnu maʕa-hunna ḍamīran ka-ḏahabna. wa-ʕalāmatan ka-ʔakramtu-hunna. Wa-sa-yaʔtī tamāmu l-kalāmi ʕalā kulli ḏālika* (al-Yāzīǧī 1889, 272).

wa-ǧamʕa ġayri ʕāqilin ka-l-wāḥida	*wa-dūna ḏī n-nūni stabāḥū l-qāʕida*
(The plural of irrationals is like feminine singular	and the rule is allowed with the exception of sound masculine plurals)

That means that the plural of irrationals (*ǧamʕa mā lā yaʕqilu*) goes, as far as pronouns are concerned, like the feminine singular. This rule also includes sound feminine plurals, like *šaǧar-āt* ("tree-F.PL"), and broken of both genders,[59] like *ǧimāl* ("camel.PL") and *niyāq* ("she.camel.PL"). Thus, you say *aš-šaǧarātu ʔaṯmarat* [f.sg.] ("The trees gave fruits"), *al-ǧimālu sārat* [f.sg.] ("The camels went") and *an-niyāqu rabaḍat* [f.sg.] ("The she-camels lied down"). This is also the rule for adjectives, so you say *aš-šaǧarātu muṯmiratun* [f.sg.] ("The trees have fruits"),[60] *al-ǧimālu sāʔiratun* [f.sg.] ("The camels are going") *wa-n-niyāqu rābiḍatun* [f.sg.] ("The she-camels are lying down"). This agreement pattern was allowed for everything that has a plural meaning, excluding sound masculine plurals, i.e. everything whose verb can take the feminine marker [i.e. can occur in the 3rd feminine singular], as mentioned in the chapter concerning the subject (*fāʕil*). This includes broken plurals of masculine nouns [when in the singular] like *riǧāl* ("man.PL"); all feminine nouns, like *Hind-āt* ("Hind-F.PL") and *ǧawārī* ("maid.PL"); those nouns that can form both a sound masculine and a sound feminine plural, like *ban-ūna* ("son-M.PL") and *ban-āt* ("daughter-F.PL"); collective nouns, (*ismu l-ǧamʕi*), like *qawm* ("people.COLL") and *nisāʔ* ("women.COLL"). Thus, it is possible to say *ar-riǧālu ʔaqbalat* [f.sg.] ("The men approached") or *muqbilatun* [f.sg.] ("approaching") and so on. This is due to the fact that these plurals lost the form of the singular and became similar to the collective. In sound feminine plurals and in the nouns that can take both sound masculine and feminine plurals, the form of the singular is blurred, due to the loss of some radical letters or infixes (*li-suqūṭi baʕḍi z-zawāʔidi ʔaw al-ʔuṣūli*), so that they became similar to the broken plural. For this reason, it is possible to look at the form of all the above-mentioned categories and to have feminine singular agreement in the returning pronoun (*aḍ-ḍamīru l-ʕāʔidu*), considering them as collectives, or to look at their meaning and to have agreement according to their singular forms. The sound masculine

59 Reference is, here, to the gender of the controller when it occurs in the singular, broken plurals being underspecified for gender.

60 Literally, "are fruitful".

> plural is an exception, because plurality, in it, is realized formally, due to the fact that the form of the singular remains evident, so that only the plural pronoun can be used.[61]

The first observation concerns the fact that al-Yāziǧī here explicitly presents feminine singular as the most suitable agreement pattern with nonhumans. His position is not completely prescriptive, since the possibility of feminine plural agreement is mentioned later on in the chapter, yet no other grammarian (among the ones we analyzed) had so far spelled out the rule. If al-Yāziǧī is actually the first one, that means that what was *de facto* a rule in Arabic prose since the 10th century did not find a place in grammars for nine additional centuries. The fact that his contemporary al-Šidyāq never mentions the rule, moreover, leads us to think that a complete standardization of the new system in the theoretical system of grammarians was not achieved even during the *Nahḍa*. The second point touched by al-Yāziǧī concerns the scope of feminine singular agreement, which is considered as a suitable agreement choice for all plural forms except sound masculine plurals. When saying *fī kulli mā* […] *yadullu ʕalā maʕnā l-ǧamʕi*, al-Yāziǧī means both morphological plurals (broken and sound feminine) and collectives, which are morphologically singular but semantically plural (although a wholistic interpretation is always possible).[62] His line of reasoning, however, justifies the possibility of feminine singular agreement on

---

61 *wa-ǧamʕa ġayri ʕāqilin ka-l-wāḥida* *wa-dūna ḏī n-nūni stabāḥū l-qāʕida* *ʔay ʔanna ǧamʕa mā lā yaʕqilu yaǧrī fī-l-ʔiḍmāri la-hu maǧrā l-muʔannaṯi l-munfaridati. Wa-huwa yašmalu l-ǧamʕa s-sālima muʔannaṯan ka-š-šaǧarāti wa-l-mukassara muṭlaqan ka-l-ǧimāli wa-n-niyāqi. Fa-yuqālu š-šaǧarātu ʔaṯmarat wa-l-ǧimālu sārat wa-n-niyāqu rabaḍat. Wa-hākaḏā ḥukmu ṣ-ṣifati fa-yuqālu š-šaǧarātu muṯmiratun wa-l-ǧimālu sāʔiratun wa-n-niyāqu rābiḍatun. Wa-qadi stabāḥū hāḏā l-ḥukma fī kulli mā siwā ǧamʕa l-muḏakkari s-sālimi mim-mā yadullu ʕalā maʕnā l-ǧamʕi wa-huwa kullu mā talḥaqu fiʕlu-hu ʕalāmata t-taʔnīṯi mim-mā marra fī bābi l-fāʕili. Fa-yandariǧu fī ḏālika ǧamʕu mā yaʕqilu mina l-muḏakkari mukassaran ka-r-riǧāli. Wa-mina-l-muʔannaṯi muṭlaqan ka-l-Hindāti wa-l-ǧawārī. Wa-l-mulḥaqu bi-l-ǧamʕayni ka-l-banīna wa-l-banāti. Wa-smu l-ǧamʕi ka-l-qawmi wa-n-nisāʔi. Fa-yaǧūzu ʔan yuqāla r-riǧālu ʔaqbalat ʔaw muqbilatun wa-halumma ǧarran. Wa-ḏālika li-ʔanna l-mukassara min hāḏihi l-ǧumūʕi qad fuqidat ṣūratu l-mufradi min-hu fa-ʔašbaha sma l-ǧamʕi. Wa ǧamʕu l-muʔannaṯi s-sālimi wa-l-mulḥaqu bi-l-ǧumʕayni qadi-nṯalamat ṣūratu l-mufradi fī-hima li-suqūṭi baʕḍi z-zawāʔidi ʔaw al-ʔuṣūli fa-ʔašbahā l-ǧamʕi l-mukassari. Wa-min ṯumma ǧāza ʔan yunḍara ʔilā l-lafḍi fī kulli wāḥidin min hāḏihi l-maḏkūrāti fa-yuʔannaṯu ḍ-ḍamīru l-ʕāʔidu ʔilay-hi ʕalā taʔwīli-hi bi-l-ǧamāʕati wa-ʔan yunḍara ʔilā l-maʕnā fa-yuḍmaru la-hu bi-ḥasabi ʔafrādi-hi. Yuxālifu ǧamʕu l-muḏakkari s-sālimi fa-ʔinna l-ǧamʕiyyata mutaḥaqqiqatun fī-hi lafḍan li-biqāʔi ṣūrati l-wāḥidi fī-hi wa-li-ḏālika lā yustaʕmalu la-hu ʔillā ḍamīru l-ǧamʕa* (al-Yāzīǧī 1889, 273–274).

62 For the wholistic and distributive interpretation of collectives, see Dror (2016, 104) and, in this book, § 3.4.1.

the basis of the fact that, in broken plurals, the form of the singular word is lost (*fuqidat ṣūrat al-mufradi*). This confirms what hypothesized in § 3.1 in two ways:

1. the opaqueness of broken plurals paved the way for the spread of feminine singular agreement;
2. when feminine singular agreement occurs, the controller is treated as a collective (*ʕalā taʔwīli-hi bi-l-ǧamāʕati*).

Al-Yāziǧī adopts here a very strict formal criterion in deciding which types of plural preserve the form of the singular and which do not. In the end, only sound masculine plurals preserve the form of the singular (with its gender), which prevents the occurrence of feminine singular agreement. Apart from the evident case of broken plurals, even sound feminine plurals and nouns that form both sound masculine and sound feminine plurals (such as *ban-ūna* "son-M.PL" and *ban-āt* "daughter-F.PL") do not exactly preserve the form of the singular, due to the loss /change of infixes and / or radical letters.[63] For this reason, in al-Yāziǧī's very strict perspective, the form of the controller here does not allow us to consider plural agreement as "formal", i.e. syntactic agreement. This is true for both human broken plurals (masculine and feminine), sound feminine plurals and nouns that form sound plurals of both genders. By looking at their form alone, thus, feminine singular agreement applies. Plural agreement, on the contrary, is considered as an instance of semantic agreement, because the notion of plurality does not emerge from the form of the controller. In other words, al-Yāziǧī here seems to consider as formally plural a controller consisting of exactly (down to short vowels) the singular stem plus a suffix. The main role of morphological opaqueness and underspecification for gender is evident from the fact that, when saying that plural agreement with these types of controllers is semantically motivated, al-Yāziǧī affirms that gender is retrieved from their singular (*fa-yuḍmaru la-hu bi-ḥasabi ʔafrādi-hi*).[64]

Al-Yāziǧī here grasps the link between broken plurals, their morphological opaqueness, and the occurrence of feminine singular agreement. From a mod-

63 With the exception of the forms *ibn* "son" pl. *banūna* "son:M.PL" and *bint* "daughter" pl. *banāt* "daughter:F.PL", we are here dealing with really minor changes, such as the insertion of a short vowel between C2 and C3, such as in *ǧafna* "bowl" pl. *ǧafanāt* "bowl:F.PL". Even these minor changes, moreover, do not always occur in sound feminine plurals.

64 This statement does not seem to take into consideration that, for nonhuman plural controllers whose singular is morphologically masculine, the feminine plural agreement contradicts the gender of the singular. Al-Yāziǧī, however, seems to solve the contradiction later in the chapter, linking the occurrence of feminine plural agreement to the plurals of paucity.

ern typological perspective, however, feminine singular agreement with broken plural controllers can hardly be justified as an instance of formal (i.e. syntactic) agreement, due to the lack of formal correspondence between the two categories. Assuming that both broken plurals and feminine singular (in this particular case) designate a type of [-individuated] plurality, agreement should still be considered semantic. The objection concerning the possibility of considering feminine plural agreement with broken plural controllers as formally motivated, on the other hand, is more solid. The two types of plurals, in fact, are both formally (suffixed vs internal) and semantically ([+individuated] vs [-individuated]) divergent. Our decision to consider this type of agreement as syntactic, thus, only has a pragmatic justification, based on the fact that most nouns and adjectives, at documented stages of the history of Arabic, have either a sound or a broken plural, but rarely both.

After presenting general agreement patterns with human and nonhuman controllers, al-Yāziǧī discusses more controversial cases. For instance, he provides what he considers to be the more eloquent patterns of usage in the case of a sentence containing both a pre- and a post-controller target:

> If you have both an overt subject and a pronoun, the appropriate choice between them is according to their form. They say *ʔaqbalati* [f.sg.] *r-riǧālu kullu-hā* [f.sg.] "The men approached, all of them" and *ʔaqbala* [m.sg.] *r-riǧālu kullu-hum* [m.pl.], while the opposite is dispreferred in the most eloquent language.[65]

Despite expressing a preference judgement for one of the two forms, al-Yāziǧī adopts here a descriptive stance that is confirmed by observed language usage, in which both forms equally occur.

As said earlier in this section, al-Yāziǧī allows the possibility of feminine plural agreement with nonhuman plural controllers, even though feminine singular is presented as the most suitable choice:

wa-ǧāza nūqun bitna fī l-maḥalla	*wa-qīla ḏāka ḥaqqu ǧamʕi l-qilla*
(And *nūqun bitna* [f.pl.] *fī l-maḥalla* "The she-camels slept in the place" is allowed	And they say that it is allowed with plurals of paucity)

65 *Wa-ʔiḏā ǧtmaʕa ḏ-ḏāhiru wa-ḍ-ḍamīru fa-l-muxtāru l-munāsibatu bayna-humā ṭalban li-š-šākilati fa-yuqālu ʔaqbalati r-riǧālu kullu-hā wa-ʔaqbala r-riǧālu kullu-hum wa-lā yustaḥsanu l-ʕaksa fī ʔafṣaḥi l-luġāti* (al-Yāzīǧī 1889, 374).

That means that it is possible to use the pronoun of female rational beings [i.e. feminine plural] for groups of feminine irrational beings, as seen in the example. So goes the verse of the poet:

ʔa-lā yā ḥamāmāti l-liwā ʕudna ʕawdatan	*fa-ʔinn-ī ʔilā ʔaṣwāti-kunna ḥazīnu*
(Oh the wrinecks have returned [f.pl.]	and I am longing for your [f.pl.] voices)

This [i.e. feminine plural agreement] was also employed with masculine [irrational nouns], such as *"ʔin-nā saxxarnā l-ǧibāla maʕa-hu yusabbiḥna* [f.pl.] *bi-l-ʕašiyyi wa-l-ʔišrāqi*" (With him We subjected the mountains to give glory at evening and sunrise, Q XXXVIII, 18), but it is rare. It was said that [feminine] singular is more suitable for the plural of abundance, while [feminine] plural is more suitable for the plural of paucity. So, it's best to say *al-ǧuḏūʕu* (plural of abundance) *kasartu-hā* [f.sg.] ("The branches, I broke them"), *inkasarat* [f.sg.] ("They broke") and *hiya* [f.sg.] *munkasiratun* [f.sg.] ("They are broken"), but *al-ʔaǧḏāʕu* (plural of paucity) *kasartu-hunna* [f.pl.] ("The branches, I broke them"), *inkasarna* [f.pl.] ("They broke") and *hunna* [f.pl.] *munkasirātun* [f.pl.] ("They are broken"). The difference between them [i.e. between the plurals of paucity and abundance] was regarded as dubious. I say that possibly the difference lies in the fact that the plural of paucity corresponds to the sound plural for female rational nouns because it matches it in designating a plural of paucity, like some said on this regard:

bi-ʔafʕula wa-bi-ʔafʕālin wa-ʔafʕilatin	*wa-fiʕlatin yuʕrafu l-ʔadnā mina l-ʕadadi*
wa-sālimu l-ǧamʕi ʔayḍan dāxilun maʕa-hā	*fī ḏālika l-ḥukmi fa-ḥfiḏ-hā wa-lā tazid*
(With *ʔafʕul*, *ʔafʕāl*, *ʔafʕilat*	and *fiʕlat* is known the plural of paucity
And the sound plural also goes with it	in this rule, learn it and don't add anything)

And, due to this consideration, it is better to use the pronoun of female rational beings with it. God knows best.[66]

---

66 *wa-ǧāza nūqun bitna fī l-maḥalla* *wa-qīla ḏāka ḥaqqu ǧamʕi l-qilla*

Al-Yāziğī adopts here a peculiar stance, probably stemming from the system of Classical Arabic, in which plural agreement reflects the morphological or biological gender of the controller for humans, while occurring in the feminine singular for all nonhumans. When presenting the possibility of plural agreement with nonhuman controllers, in fact, al-Yāziğī divides them into masculine and feminine. His interpretation of the linguistic facts seems to be that feminine plural nonhuman controllers, for which feminine singular agreement remains the most suitable choice, can also trigger feminine plural agreement, which he considers to be reserved to female human controllers (*al-ʕāqilāt*). In pre- and early Classical Arabic (as well as in the dialects), however, such a distinction does not exist. Nonhuman plural controllers, when triggering plural (syntactic) agreement, systematically trigger feminine plural, independently of their morphological gender in the singular. Al-Yāziğī is perfectly aware of the occurrence of feminine plural agreement with morphologically masculine nonhuman controllers, such as *ğibāl* "mountain.PL" in Q XXXVIII, 18. He therefore admits this possibility, but considers it rare. To the best of our knowledge, no pattern has been observed according to which plural nonhuman controllers that are feminine in the singular tend to attract feminine plural agreement more than plural nonhuman controllers that are masculine in the singular. It is highly probable, thus, that al-Yāziğī was here looking at the ancient system of agreement through the lens of the new one, in which morphological / biological gender largely dictates agreement choices for humans. Al-Yāziğī projected such conditioning also on nonhumans, which in his mind should trigger feminine singular agreement, but somehow behave differently in ancient texts. This

---

ʔay yağūzu ʔan yustaʕmala ḍamīra l-ʔināṯi l-ʕāqilāti li-ğamāʕati mā lā yaʕqilu mina l-muʔannaṯi ka-mā raʔayta fī-l-miṯāli wa-ʕalay-hi qawlu š-šāʕiri

ʔa-lā yā ḥamāmāti l-liwā ʕudna ʕawdatan   fa-ʔinn-ī ʔilā ʔaṣwāti-kunna ḥazīnu

Wa-qadi stuʕmila ḏālika maʕa l-muḏakkari naḥwa "ʔin-nā saxxarnā l-ğibāla maʕa-hu yusabbiḥna bi-l-ʕašiyyi wa-l-ʔišrāqi". Wa-huwa nādirun. Wa-qīla ʔanna ḍamīra l-mufradati ʔawlā bi-ğamʕi l-kaṯrati wa-ḍamīru l-ğamʕi ʔawlā bi-ğamʕi l-qillati. Fa-l-ʔaḥsanu ʔan yuqāla l-ğuḏūʕu kasartu-hā fa-nkasarat fa-hiya munkasiratun. Wa-l-ʔağḏāʕu kasartu-hunna fa-nkasarna fa-hunna munkasirātun. Wa-stuškila l-farqu bayna-humā. ʔAqūlu wa-yumkinu ʔan yakūna l-farqa ʔanna ğamʕa l-qillati yunāsibu l-ğamʕa s-sālima al-mawḍūʕa li-l-ʕāqilāti li-ʔanna-hu naḏīru-hu fī-d-dalālati ʕalā l-qillati ka-mā naṣṣa ʕalā ḏālika baʕḍu-hum bi-qawli-hi:

bi-ʔafʕula wa-bi-ʔafʕālin wa-ʔafʕilatin   wa-fiʕlatin yuʕrafu l-ʔadnā mina l-ʕadadi
wa-sālimu l-ğamʕi ʔayḍan dāxilun maʕa-hā   fī ḏālika l-ḥukmi fa-ḥfiḏ-hā wa-lā tazid

Wa-bi-hāḏā l-iʕtibāri yakūnu ʔawlā bi-stiʕmāli ḍamīri l-ʕāqilāti maʕa-hu. Wa-llāhu ʔaʕlamu bi-ṣ-ṣawābi (al-Yāzīğī 1889, 274).

means that, although all the possible agreement patterns for human and nonhuman controllers are presented, al-Yāziǧī seems to have lost the awareness of their rules of distribution, in a final transition toward the new system.[67]

In conclusion, al-Yāziǧī also deals with gender resolution rules, starting with chains of human controllers including both males and females. In such cases, as evident from the following excerpt, agreement occurs in the masculine plural:

wa-ġulliba l-ʔafḍalu fī-mā štarakā	*ka-hum wa-hunna yanṣibūna š-šarakā*
(And what is best prevails when two partake	like "*hum* ("they.M") and *hunna* ("they.F") set [m.pl.] a trap.")

> That means that, if two parties share [the same verb], the best of the two is preferred over the other one [i.e. it determines the agreement pattern] and what is used for it is used for them both, like in *yawma tarā l-muʔminīna* [m.pl.] *wa-l-muʔmināti* [f.pl.] *yasʕā nūru-hum* [m.pl.] *bayna ʔaydī-him* [m.pl.] ("Upon the day when thou seest the believers, men and women, their light running before them, and on their right hands" Q LVII, 12). Also in *yuʕaḏḏibu l-munāfiqīna* [m.pl.] *wa-l-munāfiqāti* [f.pl.] *wa-l-mušrikīna* [m.pl.] *wa-l-mušrikāti* [f.pl.] *ḏ̣-ḏ̣ānnīna* [m.pl.] *bi-Llāhi ḏ̣anna s-sawʔi* ("And that He may chastise the hypocrites, men and women alike, and the idolaters men and women alike, and those who think evil thoughts of God" Q XLVIII, 6).[68]

Al-Yāziǧī then moves on to discuss cases in which the controller is a chain that includes both humans and nonhumans. Once again, in this case, he looks at pre-Classical texts through the lens of Classical and Modern Standard Arabic:

---

67 Al-Yāziǧī also mentions the possible role of the humanization of controllers in determining agreement patterns. He does so quoting the already discussed Q 12, 4: *ʔinn-ī raʔaytu ʔaḥada ʕašara kawkaban wa-š-šamsa wa-l-qamara raʔaytu-hum l-ī sāǧidīna* "I saw eleven stars, and the sun and the moon; I saw them bowing down before me." Al-Yāziǧī, here, fails to note that, when humanization actually occurs, as in this case, nonhuman controllers trigger masculine plural agreement, and not feminine. See § 4.2.

68 *wa-ġulliba l-ʔafḍalu fī mā štarakā* *ka-hum wa-hunna yanṣibūna š-šarakā*
ʔAy ʔiḏā waqaʕa štirākun bayna farīqayni fī hāḏā l-maqāmi ġulliba l-ʔafḍalu min-humā ʕalā ġayri-hi fa-yustaʕmalu mā la-hu la-humā ǧamīʕan naḥwa yawma tarā l-muʔminīna wa-l-muʔmināti yasʕā nūru-hum bayna ʔaydī-him. Wa-naḥwa yuʕaḏḏibu l-munāfiqīna wa-l-munāfiqāti wa-l-mušrikīna wa-l-mušrikāti ḏ̣-ḏ̣ānnīna bi-Llāhi ḏ̣anna s-sawʔi (al-Yāzīǧī 1889, 275).

> Of this kind is also the partaking of irrational (*mā lā yaʕqilu*) with rational beings (*al-ʕuqalāʔ*), which follows the same rules. For instance, *mā l-ī lā ʔarā l-hudhuda ʔam kāna mina l-ġāʔibīna* [m.pl.] ("How is it with me, that I do not see the hoopoe? Or is he among the absent?" Q XXVII, 20). As for female rational beings, the same prevalence [i.e. of the "best" type of controller] is chosen, like in *al-ǧawārī wa-n-niyāqi sāʔirātun* [m.pl.] ("The maids and the she-camels are going"). This, however, is not mandatory, and it is possible to say *sāʔira* [f.sg.].[69]

This excerpt is slightly more problematic, and deserves some discussion. In the first part, al-Yāziǧī quotes a textbook example of humanization of a nonhuman controller. When humanization really obtains, like in the Quranic verse quoted,[70] agreement consequently occurs in the masculine plural. In the second example, which seems to be created *ad hoc* by al-Yāziǧī, we have a human broken plural, *ǧawārī* "maid.PL" and a nonhuman broken plural, *niyāq* "she. camel.PL". Al-Yāziǧī here says that, also in this case, the "best" type of controller prevails and determines agreement.[71] In doing so, once more, he assumes that *niyāq*, being nonhuman, should naturally trigger feminine singular agreement, and that feminine plural is due to the co-occurrence of a female human controller. As seen in chapter 2, both *ǧawārī* and *niyāq* belong to agreement class II, for which feminine plural is the standard agreement choice in the plural, whenever the controller is individuated. Al-Yāziǧī also writes that, in this case, the prevalence is not systematic, so that feminine singular agreement can also occur. In his sample, however, the occurrence of feminine singular agreement is probably better justified on the basis that both controllers are broken plurals.[72] The rest of the chapter is devoted to issues of lesser relevance

69 *Wa-min hāḏā l-qabīli štirāku mā lā yaʕqilu maʕa l-ʕuqalāʔi fa-ʔinna-hu yaǧrī ʕalā hāḏā l-ʔuslūbi naḥwa "mā l-ī lā ʔarā l-hudhuda ʔam kāna mina l-ġāʔibīna". Wa-ʔammā maʕa l-ʕāqilāti fa-yuxtāru t-taġlību naḥwa l-ǧawārī wa-n-niyāqi sāʔirātun. Wa-lā yaǧibu fa-yuqālu saʔiratun bi-duni-hi* (al-Yāziǧī 1889, 275).

70 For other instances of humanization and the way in which it affects agreement patterns, see sections 4.1 and 4.2.

71 In al-Yāziǧī's version, thus, the hierarchy is: male humans > female humans > nonhumans. While it is true that gender resolution rules prescribe the employment of masculine agreement for mixed masculine / feminine chains of controllers, what happens when humans and nonhumans co-occur is less clear. Al-Ṭabarī, for instance, observes that, in such cases, nonhuman agreement is preferred, which means either feminine singular or plural agreement (al-Ṭabarī 2001c, 1:518–519).

72 Ferguson, always with reference to Damascus Arabic, observes that if all the controllers are plural, feminine singular agreement can also occur (Ferguson 1989, 88).

to our topic, such as the occurrence of 2nd person agreement when 3rd person would be expected.

In conclusion, with al-Yāziǧī we reach a turning point in the description of agreement. The great Lebanese scholar, "steeped in classical Arabic lore" (Somekh 1992, 43), is perfectly aware of all the possible agreement patterns allowed in pre-, early and Classical Arabic. The way in which he looks at them, however, leans toward the new system of Classical Arabic, where feminine singular agreement is mandatory with plural nonhuman controllers. Therefore, he first offers his readers a neat division, in which masculine plural human controllers trigger masculine plural agreement, feminine human plural controllers trigger feminine plural and all nonhumans trigger feminine singular. Feminine singular agreement, moreover, is available to all types of plural controllers that are not formed by suffixation of the singular stem. Al-Yāziǧī adopts here a very strict stance, considering as deviations from this rule also those cases in which the formation of sound feminine plural agreement requires the addition of a short vowel between C_2 and C_3 of the singular stem. In this way, he manages to justify the fact that only sound masculine plurals do not trigger feminine singular agreement. Seen from this perspective, however, all the occurrences of syntactic agreement with plural nonhuman controllers look as exceptions. Al-Yāziǧī tries to deal with these "exceptions" from his viewpoint, saying that broken plurals of paucity of nonhuman controllers that are morphologically feminine in the singular can also trigger feminine plural agreement. The reason of that is that sound feminine plurals are also considered as plurals of paucity in the Arabic grammatical tradition. At this point, however, the occurrence of feminine plural agreement with nonhuman plural controllers whose singular form is morphologically masculine becomes impossible to explain, so that al-Yāziǧī contents himself with saying that such occurrences are rare, which is not supported by observed linguistic facts. In no variety of Arabic,[73] in fact, the morphological gender of the singular form of nonhuman plurals affects their agreement patterns. This means that, with al-Yāziǧī, awareness of the rules of distribution of the ancient system of agreement starts being lost also in the grammatical thought, thus paving the way to the definitive standardization of the new one.

73 With the possible exception of Ḥassāniyya, see § 2.3.8.2.

4.5 Summary

In this chapter, we provided a diachronic account of the treatment of agreement in traditional grammar, in the period ranging from Sībawayh (760–796 CE) to Aḥmad Fāris al-Šidyāq (1805–1887 CE). Some of the research questions that this reconstruction attempted to answer were:

I. When did the distinction between *ʕāqil* "rational" and *ġayr ʕāqil* "irrational" start to play a decisive role in determining agreement patterns, according to grammarians?
II. When was the rule prescribing mandatory feminine singular agreement with nonhuman plural controllers formalized?
III. How was agreement described by ancient grammarians, at the time when the ancient system was still alive and after it was *de facto* replaced by the new one?

The works analyzed in this chapter, dating back to different schools and ages, answered most of our questions. When trying to determine when a rule found its way into grammars of Arabic or when it became a rule in the first place, of course, the reader should bear in mind that all answers can only be tentative. A comprehensive survey of all grammars of Arabic, in fact, is probably an enterprise beyond reach, which means that we cannot be sure that a given grammarian was the first one to spell out a rule or describe a certain phenomenon. With this caveat in mind, let us recap the findings of our reconstruction.

As far as the first question is concerned, the distinction between human and nonhuman controllers (*ʕāqil* vs *ġayr ʕāqil* or *mā yaʕqilu* vs *mā lā yaʕqilu*) appears with the first grammars of Arabic, starting from Sībawayh (who attributes the same distinction to his master, al-Xalīl). No prescriptive agreement pattern for nonhuman controllers, however, follows from this distinction. Quite to the contrary, Sībawayh and all the grammarians who followed him until the 19th century, used the distinction in order to specify that masculine plural agreement is reserved to male human controllers, with no repercussions on nonhuman ones. If we are looking for the first instance of a direct link between the category of *ġayr ʕāqil* / *mā lā yaʕqilu* and mandatory feminine singular agreement, Nāṣīf al-Yāziǧī (1800–1871) is the first grammarian (among the ones we scrutinized) who explicitly spelled out the rule. This also answers the second research question, although with the caveat mentioned above.

Once we move aside the question of when certain agreement patterns became mandatory, we are confronted with the deep insights on agreement patterns provided by the Arabic linguistic tradition. The ancient grammarians, in fact, adopted a descriptive approach toward agreement, which allowed the rich variation observed in pre- and early Classical texts to emerge. Sībawayh, for instance, once stated that masculine plural agreement is reserved to male human controllers, admits the possibility of both feminine plural and feminine singular agreement with nonhumans, even though he does not provide any reason that might justify this variation. At the same time, he mentions feminine singular agreement as a possible agreement choice with all types of controllers, including humans, provided they occur in the broken plural. When doing so, he considers feminine singular as an overgeneralization of the pattern originally reserved to the broken plural of inanimate controllers (in his words, *al-mawāt* "DEF-dead.PL", opposed to *al-ḥayawān* "DEF-living"). This statement does not find support in the linguistic reality of Arabic, which never distinguished between animate and inanimate controllers, but rather between humans and nonhumans. Sībawayh, however, was a native speaker of Persian, where the threshold on the animacy scale is located exactly between animate and inanimate controllers. As already seen with Ibn al-Muqaffaʕ (ca. 720–ca. 756 CE) (see § 3.6), thus, we are probably dealing with a transfer from Sībawayh's native language. It is not a case, in fact, that Sībawayh's commentators are usually silent on this point. Commentaries to the *Kitāb*, on the other hand, clarify and expand on many points touched by Sībawayh, shedding light on what we called the "ancient" agreement system. In this chapter, we analyzed al-Sīrāfī's (893-94-979 CE) commentary, in which the author basically divides plural controllers into two major categories, male humans vs everything else. The former require masculine plural agreement, while the latter vary between feminine singular and feminine plural, which are grouped together and opposed to masculine plural. Once more, feminine singular is also admitted with human plural controllers, provided they occur in the broken plural.

Other schools contribute to refine the picture provided by Sībawayh, offering reasons that justify the variation between feminine singular and feminine plural agreement with nonhuman controllers. Al-Farrāʔ (d. 822 CE), considered as the forefather of the Kufan school, offered enlightening insights into the agreement system of Arabic. First, he recognized that plural agreement with non-biologically-male referents occurs in the feminine, irrespectively of their morphological gender in the singular. Second, he introduced a concept that hints, although in different terms, to individuation. According to al-Farrāʔ, in fact, feminine plural agreement occurs with counted objects between three and ten, while feminine singular is reserved to counted objects beyond the number of ten. While al-Farrāʔ only mentions the number of the counted object(s), this concept will be soon adapted to the two categories of broken plural, the plural of paucity (*ǧamʕu l-qilla*) and abundance (*ǧamʕu l-kaṯra*). All following grammarians will accept this intuition, never failing to specify that feminine plural is the preferred option with the plural of paucity, while feminine singular occurs with the plural of abundance. At the same time, since a very early stage, Arabic grammarians were aware of the fact that the distinction between the two morphological categories, if it ever actually existed (which they do not seem to doubt), had been blurred to the point that variation often occurred randomly.

Al-Mubarrad (862–898 CE), a grammarian of the Basran school, clearly sets humans apart from nonhumans. Even though he does not say it clearly, however, when he speaks of humans he seems to mean male humans only, again due to the fact that masculine plural agreement is exclusive to them. Al-Mubarrad thus groups together the other categories (i.e. female humans and nonhumans), due to the fact that they trigger feminine agreement. Al-Mubarrad, here, focuses only on gender, neglecting the importance of number agreement. At the same time, however, he admits that feminine singular agreement can occur with all types of plural controllers, independently of their position on the animacy hierarchy, and even goes as far as identifying it as a form of collective agreement. This means that, at the end of the 9th century, we have quite a clear picture of how agreement in the old system worked. Not only are main agreement patterns recorded, but the reasons behind their distribution are also identified.

In the following centuries, the Arabic grammatical thought mainly refines and expands on the insights provided by the grammarians mentioned above. Al-Zağğāğī (892–952 CE), for instance, clarifies the link between the broken plural templates that express the plural of paucity and the occurrence of feminine plural agreement, while al-Farrāʔ only mentioned counted objects between three and ten, without specifying which plural forms expressed this type of plurality. Ibn Mālik (1204–1274 CE), in his pedagogical grammar in verses, the *ʔAlfiyya*, hints at the fact that the /t/ morpheme occurring in verbs agreeing with plural controllers is not actually a feminine marker, but resembles the /t/ morpheme used to form singulatives. Due to the peculiar nature of the *ʔAlfiyya*, mainly intended for didactic purposes, Ibn Mālik does not expand on this fact. Ibn ʕAqīl (1294–1367 CE), in his famous commentary, clarifies that in both cases the verb or noun is only metaphorically feminine. The occurrence of "feminine singular agreement" in pre-controller verbal targets, moreover, implies a collective interpretation of the subject, while the absence of the /t/ morpheme implies that the controller is considered as a real plural.

With these very refined considerations by Ibn ʕAqīl, the picture of the ancient system emerging from Arabic traditional grammar is quite satisfactory. It is also worth mentioning that, even at the time when Ibn ʕAqīl writes (14th century), grammars show no trace of the new agreement system, even though it had already replaced the ancient one by that time, at least in plain prose. In order to find a mention of mandatory feminine singular agreement with plural nonhuman controllers, as already said, we must go as far as the 19th century. Even then, some scholars, such as al-Šidyāq (1805–1887), continued to describe the ancient system even in pedagogical grammars. The first and only mention of the new rule, thus, occurs in Nāṣīf al-Yāziǧī's (1800–1871) pedagogical grammar *Kitāb Nār al-Qurā fi Šarḥ Ǧawf al-Farā*. Al-Yāziǧī shows great insight in grasping the link between the morphological opaqueness of the plural form and feminine singular agreement, but he seems to look at linguistic facts through the lens of the new system, identifying prescriptive agreement for both humans and nonhumans and treating all the diverging patterns as oddities or exceptions. For instance, he divides nonhuman plural controllers by gender, assuming that feminine plural can occur with nonhuman feminine (i.e. morphologically feminine in the singular) plural controllers. In doing so, he is puzzled by the occurrence of feminine plural agreement also with nonhuman masculine plural controllers, which he reduces to a linguistic oddity. At this point, awareness of the rules governing the distribution of agreement patterns is largely lost, and the new one starts taking its place also in grammatical accounts.

CHAPTER 5

A Diachronic Account of Agreement: Spoken Arabic

We are nearing the completion of our survey of the agreement-related phenomena that exist in the Arabic languages. In Chapter 1, we have discussed how the topic of agreement in Arabic has been investigated in previous studies on the topic. In Chapter 2, we have examined in depth the morphological and syntactical features that characterize agreement in virtually all known varieties of Arabic, written and spoken, ancient and modern. We have tried to offer a synchronic description of all these agreement systems that, in our view, is both consistent with general linguistic theory and reflective of the actual state of affairs in these varieties. In Chapters 3 and 4, our attention has shifted mainly to the formal and written registers of the language, focusing on how these have changed through time, and looking at possible explanations for these changes.

What we are still lacking is an account of what diachronic processes have brought about the distribution of agreement-related phenomena that can be observed in contemporary spoken Arabic. While fleeting references to this topic have been made in the previous sections of this book, we are still far from finding a unified answer to this question. In fact, the field of inquiry is so large and diversified that finding such an answer could prove impossible.

The present chapter is an attempt at reconstructing the complex history of agreement in the spoken dialects of Arabic. In particular, § 5.1 will be devoted to the topic of F.SG agreement with plural controllers, while in § 5.2 we will explore the question of how Arabic dialects came to lose F.PL morphology.

5.1 Feminine Singular Agreement with Plural Controllers: Modern Innovation or Ancient Retention?

The first question we want to address is that of F.SG agreement with plural controllers. As we have seen in Chapters 1 and 2, several authors have attributed the presence of this trait in the dialects they examined to the influence of linguistic contact (be it with Modern Standard Arabic or other, more prestigious varieties of spoken Arabic).

With respect to the oscillation between F.SG and F.PL agreement with plural nonhuman controllers in a rural Jordanian dialect, Owens and Bani-Yasin (1987:

 DOI:10.1163/9789004527249_006

708, 731) have claimed that "the sets of words triggering one agreement pattern or the other are lexically distinct: f. sg. is by and large associated with nouns of S[tandard] A[arabic] provenance, f. pl. with Col[loquial Arabic]"; they have also written that "were these [i.e. Standard] nouns suddenly removed from the language it is most likely that the SA agreement rule itself would disappear".[1] Owens' and Bani-Yasin's study contains several inconsistencies that have been analyzed in §1.3, and will not be discussed again here.

Another work in which the presence of F.SG agreement in a dialect is seen as the result of contact is Herin and Al-Wer (2013). As we have seen in §1.3, these two authors come to conclusions similar to those of Owens and Bani-Yasin, with the difference that they suggest the dialect of the Jordanian capital Amman (instead of Standard Arabic) as the source of the "innovative" rule which associates items scoring low on the individuation scale with F.SG agreement. F.PL agreement with nonhuman plural controllers, in other words, would be the "original" rule in the dialect they examine (that of Salt), while the association of non-individuated plural nouns with F.SG agreement is to be regarded as an innovation caused by contact with prestigious urban varieties in which this pattern is attested.

In light of a body of evidence that has continued to grow in recent years, it seems now impossible to refute the idea that MSA and certain prestigious urban dialects do indeed play a role in affecting agreement patterns in spoken Arabic in general. This has been shown to be the case by Watson (1993: 213), who writes that, if compared to the data from Rossi (1938), speakers of Sanaani Arabic today appear to be more prone to employ F.SG adjectives when referring to inanimate plural nouns viewed as a collectivity. "This", Watson writes, "may be due to the increasing influence of Modern Standard Arabic and Egyptian Arabic".

Hanitsch (2011: 149) remarks how, in the dialect of Tetouan, nouns that are formally identical to their MSA equivalent are likely to trigger F.SG agreement (though plural agreement is still possible in the case of concrete referents). Caubet, Simeone-Senelle, Vanhove (1989: 60) seem to imply that this is actually the case for all Moroccan dialects: while the Arabic spoken in the country has mostly lost the possibility of F.SG agreement with plural controllers, this pattern frequently resurfaces when the controller is a Standard loan.

Ritt-Benmimoun (2017: 280) notes that, in the Bedouin dialects of Southern Tunisia, there appears to be a correlation between loans from MSA and

1 Cadora (1992: 131ff.) reaches conclusions that are substantially uniform with those of Owens and Bani-Yasin in his study of contact phenomena between urban and rural Palestinian dialects.

"deflected" (i.e. F.SG) agreement. Interestingly, Ritt-Benmimoun also points out how it is not only MSA *controllers* that cause this type of agreement to occur. Standard *targets* (specifically adjectives) tend to bring the standard agreement rule with them, so that, for instance, a noun followed by a chain of F.PL adjectives only triggers F.SG agreement in the one adjective that is a clear standard loan. The same considerations that are true for Southern Tunisia seem to apply to the dialects spoken in the north of the country (see Procházka and Gabsi 2017: 255–256).

Finally, Bettega (2019b: 146–147) tries to replicate Owen's and Bani-Yasin's experiment using a corpus of data from Oman, and shows that, although the distinction is not an absolute one, purely standard controllers show a higher statistical tendency to attract F.SG agreement than purely dialectal ones, while controllers that are characterized by an admixture of standard and colloquial features pattern in between these two extremes.

Two caveats, however, are in order at this point. The first one is that, even in dialects where the influence of MSA has been shown to play a role, the overall frequency of F.SG agreement may still be declining. In Chapter 2, we have seen how a small number of dialects (mostly in the western Maghreb, but not only) have almost entirely abandoned the possibility of F.SG agreement with plural controllers. We have labelled these agreement systems Type C systems (§ 2.3.7). It would seem that other non-distinguishing dialects, in which F.SG agreement is still relatively common, are also on their way to lose this trait. Tunis Arabic represents a case in point: Procházka and Gabsi (2017: 258) write that their findings "suggest that during the past century Tunis Arabic has developed towards strict agreement, because Stumme 1896: 152 mentioned that in Tunis in the late 19th century every inanimate noun may agree with feminine singular", while this seems not to be the case anymore.

It is not clear why it is only in certain varieties of Arabic, and not others, that we observe this reduction of possible agreement options.[2] However, what we

2 As we have seen in § 2.3.6, F.SG agreement with plural controller has almost entirely disappeared in Maltese, the dialects of Morocco and those of Cilicia and Anatolia. It would also seem to be absent, or at least extremely rare, in the Jewish dialect of Tripoli. Libyan varieties in general appear to make very limited use of the F.SG option, even in the case of the gender-distinguishing dialects of Fezzan (see § 2.3.2). One could thus be tempted to connect the lack of F.SG agreement to the territories in which Arabic was not spoken prior to the Islamic conquests (albeit this is most notably the case of the Maghreb, while less relevant for Turkey). Intense linguistic contact, such as that represented by masses of non-native speakers acquiring Arabic as an L2, could have brought about this change. Counterexamples, however, abound: even if we discount Egypt, several dialects that make ample use of the F.SG can be found in northern Africa (e.g. all Tunisian varieties). Southern Arabia should also be factored

want to point out here is that, where this process of reduction is at work, the influence of MSA seems not be sufficient to halt or reverse this trend. This is well exemplified by the case of Tunis Arabic, where the "intrusion" of the Standard agreement patterns is clearly visible in the data, but where—at the same time—F.SG agreement with plural controllers seems to be getting increasingly less common.

The second necessary caveat is that, even if we have shown how F.SG agreement has indeed become more common in certain dialects, due to the influence of MSA or other prestigious varieties, this does not mean that such pattern was not an original feature of these dialects. The opposite could also be true, that is: the MSA/prestigious urban rule found fertile ground for its diffusion precisely because F.SG agreement with plural controllers was already an option familiar to the speakers. In addition to this, it must be kept in mind that there is no known dialect in which the distribution of F.SG agreement perfectly matches the one that we find in MSA. F.SG agreement in certain spoken varieties may be the preferred option with nonhuman controllers, but it is never systematic; conversely, human controllers can sometimes trigger F.SG agreement, which is impossible in MSA. In other words, even if we admit that contact with MSA does indeed cause an increase in the use of F.SG agreement, we must also acknowledge that the MSA rule is never imported in full in spoken Arabic.

The fact that F.SG agreement in Arabic could possibly represent a very ancient element should, by now, come as no surprise. In Chapters 2 and 3 we have seen how this feature was already present in the oldest Arabic texts that have been passed down to us. These do not only include the Quran and the pre-Islamic poetry, but even the Safaitic inscriptions that began to dot northern

---

in this discussion, since parts of it were definitely non-Arabic speaking in pre-Islamic times, but F.SG agreement seems to be alive and well in the contemporary Arabic dialects of Oman and Yemen. In the the varieties of Arabic spoken in Central Asia, F.SG agreement appears to be still in use, although not overly common. Perhaps a more fine-grained analysis, one that takes into account patterns of Arabization, the migratory history of the various regions, their demographics and therefore the intensity of contact, could reveal some meaningful connection. Even so, the problem remains that the loss of F.SG agreement in the dialects for which we have data (especially Morocco and Malta) seems to be a relatively recent development (see § 2.3.6), so that linking it to the history of Arabization in these areas would be problematic. All in all, this remains an important open question, one that future studies will hopefully be able to address in a more thorough manner. An anonymous reviewer has suggested an alternative reading of this distribution, that is: F.SG agreement was more thoroughly lost in areas in which MSA influence played little or no part. In this case as well, this explanation fits well only with *part* of the data. While this could certainly be the case for Malta and Turkey (and also central Asian dialects), the rest of the Maghreb constitutes a problematic exception. See the rest of this section for a more thorough discussion of the effects of contact with MSA.

Arabia around the turn of the Christian era.[3] Several scholars have described F.SG agreement in Arabic as "an innovation" (see the works of Beeston, 1975, Ferguson, 1989, and Belnap and Shabaneh, 1992, that have already been cited extensively in the previous chapters), and we have expanded on this idea in Chapter 3. What has to be clear, however, is that this "innovation" is, from the perspective of our present time, incredibly old, to the point that, if Arabic has ever existed in a form that did not feature the possibility of F.SG agreement with plural controllers, it must have done so in a pre-historical phase, of which we have no written documentation.[4] As far as the historical records go, variation between F.SG and plural agreement with plural controllers has always been present in Arabic.

The omnipresence of these patterns in the language is not only temporal, but spatial as well. Alternation between F.SG and plural agreement is found today all over the Arabic-speaking world, as we have shown in § 2.3.2 and § 2.3.6. Dialects in which this variation is no longer present are few (see § 2.3.6 for an exact list), and even in these dialects the absence is not absolute: F.SG agreement occasionally resurfaces in fixed expressions, idioms and proverbs, and is sometimes found alongside certain collective controllers (*nās* 'people', being the most common). It would seem, then, that even in dialects where F.SG agreement with plural/collective controllers is no longer a productive pattern, its memory, so to speak, lives on in the form of a linguistic fossil. This, to us, seems to prove that this option was once more widespread, even in areas where today is rarely found.[5]

Summing this up, no matter where one looks, variation between plural and F.SG agreement in Arabic seems to be consistently attested across the space-

---

3 The identification of Safaitic as a manifestation of the Arabic language group is, of course, not entirely uncontroversial. However, even if we were to refuse this classification, the fact remains that, around two millennia ago, a language started to be written in the Arabian Peninsula that was characterized by striking similarities to Arabic and that, crucially, featured the possibility of F.SG adjectival, verbal and pronominal agreement with plural nouns (Al-Jallad 2015: 138–143). Since these patterns are almost unheard of in other Semitic languages, it is hard to believe that their presence in both Safaitic and Arabic is purely coincidental.

4 Since in all the languages that descend from Proto-West Semitic F.SG agreement with plural controllers is not attested, or attested only marginally, this innovation probably happened in a post Proto-West Semitic phase.

5 In § 2.3.6 we have provided evidence of the fact that this is indeed what happened in the case of Morocco and Malta, see the refences to the works of Buret and Aquilina cited there. The presence of F.SG agreement in the extinct dialects of Andalusia should also be considered: one can safely postulate that this trait must have been present in the western Maghreb at the time of the Arab conquest of the Iberian Peninsula (though this last point is less relevant since it only gives us a rather early *terminus post quem*).

time continuum. In light of this, and in partial disagreement with the hypotheses put forward by Owens and Bani-Yasin (1987: 708, 731) and Herin and Al-Wer (2013), we maintain that F.SG agreement in all contemporary varieties of Arabic has to be regarded as an extremely old shared retention, not as an innovation. This syntactical option has probably developed as an actual innovation in Arabic in a pre-historical phase (see Chapter 3), and has since then accompanied Arabic everywhere it went, in all its different manifestations, oral and written, formal and informal.[6] In fact, one cannot but marvel at the degree of stability shown by the vacillation between singular and plural agreement, and the rules that govern it, across space and time. This trait is found scattered over a territory that spans from the Atlantic Ocean to central Asia, from Syria to the southernmost tip of the Arabian Peninsula, and over a period of at least two millennia. From the more general point of view of linguistic theory, this says something about the counterintuitive possibility for variation to endure over extremely long time-spans.[7] As a matter of fact, only two major deviations from this "system of variation" have appeared in the course of history.

The first of these deviations is represented by the formal registers of written Arabic, that would ultimately evolve in what we know today as Modern Standard Arabic. In this variety of the language, F.SG agreement has become obligatory with all nonhuman controllers, giving rise to what we have labelled "Type F system" (§ 2.5). This change happened relatively early: while it is impossible to pinpoint the exact date of its completion, it was well under way in the first centuries of the Islamic era (see Chapters 3 and 4 for a more detailed account).

---

6 One could of course speculate that some dialects of Arabic did indeed lose the possibility of F.SG agreement at a certain point in the past, and that they later re-acquired it via linguistic contact. This explanation, however, requires several extra logical steps which are probably impossible to prove or disprove, so that we will not consider it here.

7 In their brilliant work on the subject, Belnap and Shabaneh (1992: 182) had already come to very similar conclusions. Although we do not necessarily agree with everything Belnap and Shabaneh say about the history of the diffusion of Arabic outside the Peninsula, it seems fair to report here this passage from their study, that contains several important insights on the topic discussed in this section:

> These findings challenge a number of common assumptions. Variability is often associated with instability. Our research indicates that in spite of the fact that New Arabic is the product of a language contact situation in which Arabic spread to sooner or later become the native tongue of millions outside the Arabian Peninsula, nevertheless the variable agreement patterns found in Pre-Islamic Arabic are alive and well far from their homeland. This suggests that the spread of Arabic was not nearly as disruptive as has been claimed by many. It also attests to the conservative nature of these Arabic dialects, which are popularly believed to be much corrupted descendants of Classical Arabic.

The second variant seems to have emerged more recently, and it is represented by all the (non-distinguishing) contemporary dialects that have lost the possibility of F.SG agreement with plural controllers (Type C systems). Even in this case, determining the exact moment in which this change occurred is impossible (also because, in all likelihood, it has been a very gradual one). However, based on the evidence discussed in § 2.3.6 for the western Maghreb and Malta, the time-depth of this development would appear to be much shallower (possibly limited to the last two or three centuries).

In spite of the fact that the changes that happened in these two bundles of varieties are very different in nature, the end results of this process were at least partially similar: in both Type C and Type F systems, variation between singular and plural agreement with plural controllers is no longer present. In this respect, these two systems constitute the typologically most innovative variants in the whole Arabic family.

5.2 The Loss of Feminine Plural Agreement

We shall now move on to a more complex topic, that of proper plural agreement patterns, and in particular the loss of F.PL agreement in numerous contemporary dialects.

Given all that has been said up until this moment about F.PL agreement, we take it as uncontroversial that all varieties of Arabic did, at a certain point in time, possess a distinct set of F.PL morphemes. We also assume that the syntactic behavior of these markers was consistent across all varieties, as it still is today in all dialects that have preserved this option. In these dialects, the behavior of F.PL agreement is substantially uniform with that found in the Quran and the pre-Islamic odes, texts that have been composed around 1,500 years ago.[8] This speaks in favor of considering F.PL agreement patterns as a very old shared retention (as was the case for F.SG agreement patterns, though we do not know for sure if they developed at the same time, or if one came before the other, and in this case, if the development of the latter was influenced by the former).

8 There is reason to believe that Safaitic had similar agreement patterns. Although attestations of F.PL forms are very rare in the Safaitic inscriptions, at least one case of F.PL agreement with a nonhuman controller is attested: see Al-Jallad and Jaworska (2019: 137), *ṭrdn h-xl* 'the horses were driven-F.PL together'. Note how this resembles the examples of *xēl* attracting F.PL agreement in contemporary Najdi Arabic, as seen in § 2.3.3.

When we say that the topic of F.PL agreement is more complex than that of the feminine singular, we do so for several reasons. First of all, as we have seen, the number of dialects in which the F.SG/plural variation is no longer present is limited. Generalizations about the history of the Arabic languages can safely be made assuming that this trait has always been present, more or less everywhere, more or less at every point in time. In parts of North Africa, and a few other areas, the possibility of F.SG agreement with plural controllers was then lost: but there is evidence suggesting that this development was a relatively recent one.

That of F.PL agreement is a different case altogether. The number of varieties in which this trait has been lost is huge. If it is difficult to say with any certainty whether or not it is the majority of dialects that have undergone this change, there is probably no doubt that the vast majority of native speakers of Arabic today speak a dialect which does not distinguish gender in the plural forms of the verb and pronoun.

In addition, the time-scale of this change is not at all clear. While we have proof that, in certain dialects, this innovation was relatively recent, we also know from historical sources that, in some areas at least, this process of loss was already well on its way in the first millennium CE.

From the point of view of dialect geography, the puzzle is also very complicated. Dialects that have lost the F.SG option are located in specific parts of the Arabic-speaking world. Conversely, non-distinguishing dialects are found virtually all over, from the Maghreb to the Peninsula. As a matter of fact, the western Maghreb (Morocco, and possibly Algeria) seems to constitute the only large swath of territory where non-distinguishing dialects *do not* coexist with distinguishing ones (see § 2.3.2 and § 2.3.6 for more details).

Summing this up, several questions arise when we start considering the spatial and temporal coordinates of this process of change. These are:

A) When and where did non-distinguishing varieties of Arabic first start to appear?

B) Did loss of F.PL agreement happen only once, in a specific location, at a specific point in time, and then spread through space by means of contact? Or is the present situation the result of multiple parallel innovations?

C) How was the agreement system of the dialects that lost F.PL verbs, adjectives and pronouns reorganized after the disappearance of these morphological categories?

D) Crucially, why was F.PL agreement lost in the first place?

In the following sections we will try to find a solution to each of these problems. In particular, question (A) will be tackled in § 5.2.2, and in § 5.2.3 together with (B). Question (D), conversely, will be the object of sections 5.2.1 and 5.2.4. We anticipate here that question (C) could prove to be a moot point. In fact, the question only makes sense if we believe that morphological loss brought about syntactic change. Conversely, should we demonstrate that it was actually a change in the agreement system that caused the disappearance of a certain set of morphemes, then the question itself would become nonsensical. This topic will be addressed in depth in the following pages, see in particular § 5.2.1 and § 5.2.5.

5.2.1 *Internally Motivated Change: Phonological Erosion*

The question about the origin of change is a long-standing one in the field of linguistics, almost as old as the discipline itself. The dichotomy intrinsic to the issue is well summarized in this passage from Andersen (1972: 12):

> I recognize the fundamental distinction between evolutive change and adaptive change. EVOLUTIVE CHANGE can be characterized as internally motivated change, as change in a linguistic system entirely explainable in terms of that system itself. ADAPTIVE CHANGE, by contrast, is change in a linguistic system explainable only with reference to factors extraneous to that linguistic system, whether linguistic (e.g. language contact) or non-linguistic (e.g. the introduction of labrets).

We chose to quote this specific excerpt because here the author points out a further fundamental subdivision, in addition to the evolutive (= internally motivated) vs. adaptive (= externally motivated) one. Andersen remarks how the latter type of change can be due to phenomena that one could still see as fundamentally linguistic in nature (i.e. contact between groups of people that employ different linguistic varieties), or it can be brought about by factors that are entirely non-linguistic. We insist on this point because it will be key in our treatment of the topic of change in agreement patterns (as we will see in more detail in § 5.2.4).

Another question we want to address, deeply interconnected with the one just mentioned but still distinct from it, is the following: was loss of F.PL agreement in Arabic caused by a reduction in the morphological options available to its speakers? Or was it a change in syntactic patterns that ultimately resulted in the contraction of certain morphological paradigms?

Decades of studies on the topic tell us that both options are possible and attested across the languages of the world. Although the former (agreement influencing morphology) is more common, "it sometimes happens that pure morphology (e.g. [contrasts in] inflectional classes) conditions change in agreement rules and/or in morpho-syntactic properties of the language such as, say, the number of genders occurring in the system" (Loporcaro 2015: 103; see this study for several examples of said phenomenon in Romance varieties).

Let us first consider the latter, rarer scenario (the possibility of agreement influencing morphology will be explored in more depth in the next sections). Is it possible that F.PL morphology has been levelled out in all paradigms of certain varieties of Arabic, at a certain point in time, ultimately reducing the number of agreement classes in the language? At first sight, the answer would seem to be no. Crosslinguistically, changes of this type are normally brought about by phonological erosion and/or merging. Gender, however, is expressed in Arabic by means of a very diverse set of morphemes, and it is hard to see what linguistic forces could have simultaneously levelled out the distinctions between them in all paradigms. Nominals, in particular, represent the most obvious obstacle for such an explanation, because their characteristic feminine and masculine plural endings are still in use today in all varieties of Arabic (at least on nouns), so that we can safely claim that 1) the feminine ending *-āt* was never subject to any process of phonological erosion that caused its disappearance from the language; and 2) a merger between the feminine (*-āt*) and masculine (*-īn*, or CA/MSA *-ūna*/*-īna*) never occurred.[9]

If one were really determined to pursue this line of thought, it seems to us that the only logical option would be to argue that this change first happened in the realm of verbs and pronouns, and that it was then extended to adjectives and participles because of paradigmatic pressure. Though we are not aware of any study in which such a hypothesis has been explored, verbal and pronominal F.PL forms do indeed present some similarities at the phonological level, so that the topic is worth a closer examination.

If we look at the verbal and pronominal paradigms of gender distinguishing varieties of Arabic, we see that all F.PL pronouns and verbal endings are all characterized by the presence of an /n/ sound (see Tables 2.1 and 2.2 for CA/MSA and 2.8 and 2.9 for the spoken dialects). If the disappearance of these forms was indeed caused by phonological erosion, then loss of /n/ in final position must be assumed as one of the elements of change, along with some type of final vowel loss (this actually depends on which forms we consider as the starting point of this process: CA/MSA-like forms, or forms more similar to those found in contemporary gender-distinguishing varieties of Arabic).

9 These possibilities are being considered here merely for the sake of discussion. Even in the absence of any other type of negative evidence, explaining away phonological processes of this magnitude would require a considerable amount of conceptual gymnastic.

The idea that Arabic might have been subject to a process of deletion of final /n/ sounds, at some point in the course of its history, is not an original one (see for instance Al-Jallad and Van Putten, 2017: 110, and Van Putten and Stokes, 2018: 169). Building on the suggestions presented in these two works, let us imagine a series of deletion rules such as the following:

I) Loss of final short vowels
II) Loss of final /n/ in -Vn# segments
III) Degemination of final long /n/
IV) Loss of final close vowels

By applying this set of rules to the CA/MSA paradigms, we obtain the following:

a) In the suffix stem conjugation, the 2nd person F.PL ending is reduced to a mere *-t*. The 3rd person F.PL ending could be entirely deleted if we imagine that an epenthetic short vowel V was inserted before the prefix after the loss of the original final vowel:
   katabtunna 'you (F.PL) have written' > **katabtunn* > **katabtun* > **katabtu* > **katabt*
   katabna 'they (F) have written' > **katabn* > **katabVn* > **katabV* > **katab*
b) In the prefix stem conjugation of the verb, both the 3 F.PL and 2 F.PL endings are entirely deleted, if we again apply the rule of epenthesis described above:
   taktubna 'you (F.PL) write' > **taktubn* > **taktubVn* > **taktubV* > **taktub*
   yaktubna 'they (F) write' > **yaktubn* > **yaktubVn* > **yaktubV* > **yaktub*
c) The 2 F.PL free pronoun is reduced to *ʔant* and the 3 F.PL free pronoun is reduced to *h*:
   ʔantunna 'you (F.PL)' > **ʔantunn* > **ʔantun* > **ʔantu* > **ʔant*
   hunna 'they (F)' > **hunn* > **hun* > **hu* > **h*
d) The 2 F.PL bound pronoun is reduced to *-k* and the 3 F.PL free pronoun is reduced to *-h*:
   -kunna 'you (F.PL)' > **-kunn* > **-kun* > **-ku* > **-k*
   -hunna 'they (F)' > **-hunn* > **-hun* > **-hu* > **-h*

Applying the same set of rules to a variety more similar to contemporary gender-distinguishing dialects would yield the same results, the only difference being that rules (I) and (III) would be superfluous in that case. In short, all surviving F.PL forms would now be syncretic with other forms from the same paradigm (with the exception of the 3 F.PL free pronoun, now identical to the 3 M.SG and 3 F.PL bound pronouns). No longer having a dedicated set of distinct morphological forms could bring the F.PL as a syntactic category to be perceived as fuzzy, eventually causing its total disappearance.

As already noted, we are considering these possibilities mostly for the sake of discussion. It should be clear to anyone reading the previous passages that the scenario just described presents several problems. First of all, our reconstruction relies on the aprioristic assumption that all contemporary non-distinguishing varieties of Arabic derive from a single proto-form via a uniform set or regular sound changes, something which is of course rather unlikely; secondly, several pieces of counterevidence exist that fundamentally neutralize the "phonological erosion" explanation. Let us briefly review them:

1) If rules I–IV were indeed applied to the whole verbal and pronominal paradigms, we would expect to find forms such as **yaktubūna* > **yaktubū* or **yaktubu* 'they write (M.PL)' and **taktubīna* > **taktubī* or **taktubi* 'you write (F.SG)'. This is actually the case in many modern dialects (see for instance Sanaani, Damascene, Cairene, Urban Moroccan, etc.). However, several dialects exist in which these forms are attested but where F.PL forms are preserved (e.g. Sanaani, Omani, all gender-distinguishing dialects of Libya), while in several others F.PL forms have been lost but the final /n/ of such verbal endings is still present (e.g. the Gulf coast, Baghdad).
2) Many dialects are only now losing F.PL agreement, or have done so in the not-too-distant past. In both cases, even if rules I–IV have ever been operative in (the ancestors of) these varieties, they no longer were when they started losing F.PL morphology, so that another explanation must be found for this simplification of morphological paradigms.[10]
3) As discussed by Van Putten and Stokes, 2018, it seems indeed likely that, at a certain point in time (but definitely before the 8th century CE), at least some varieties of Arabic were actually undergoing a process of deletion of final /n/ sounds. From the evidence that can be gathered from the Quranic Consonantal Text, however, it appears that this process only affected non-stressed syllables. This invalidates the changes we have discussed for pronouns and geminate verbal endings. If we still wanted to

10 As we have hinted at in Chapter 2, these varieties include—among others—the Bedouin dialects of Southern Tunisia, the dialects of Tripoli in Libya, Baghdad in Iraq and Khartoum in Sudan, plus all the dialects of central Arabian origin that are currently spoken in the metropolises of the Gulf coast. While in some of these cases loss of F.PL morphology could be motivated by contact with other dialects that have lost it at an earlier point in time, in some other cases this explanation is not readily available, so that we are again confronted with the problem: what caused the disappearance of F.PL forms?

pursue this line of thought, and tried to extend the rules of erosion to stressed syllables, we would then be confronted with the problem that no known variety of spoken Arabic has reduced the M.PL/C.PL nominal ending *-īn* to **-ī* (an outcome that would conversely be expected in this scenario).

In short, we have been playing the devil's advocate, only to show how an explanation based on internally-induced phonological erosion is not viable when trying to determine the causes of loss of plural gender distinction in spoken Arabic. We are then left in need of an alternative explanation, and the time has therefore come to turn our attention to possible external motivations for the evolution of agreement patterns.

5.2.2 *Externally Motivated Change: Language Contact and the Question of Polygenesis*

Among the existing studies that deal with the history of Arabic, there is no shortage of works that have tried to ascribe most forms of diachronic change to forces external to the language. Linguistic evolution, in other words, would be often externally motivated in the case of Arabic, in particular when it comes to its various spoken manifestations. The majority of these studies insist on the fact that the "external force" that brought about all types of linguistic change was actually language contact. In particular, with the beginning of the Islamic conquests in the 7th and 8th centuries, large numbers of non-native speakers found themselves in need of rapidly learning the language of the new rulers, thus giving rise to widespread contact through imperfect adult L2 acquisition.

When it comes to agreement, this argument appears to stand to reason in the case of written Arabic, as we have seen in Chapters 3 and 4. Here, the influence of language users who were not native speakers themselves may have affected the accepted practice, to the point that, in time, variation between F.SG and other types of plural agreement with nonhuman referents was levelled out, and F.SG remained the sole agreement option with controllers of this kind (see also the already mentioned works of Belnap and Shabaneh, 1992, and Belnap and Gee, 1994).

We contend that things are not so straightforward in the case of spoken Arabic. Several studies have dealt with the diachrony of gender and agreement in Arabic (Cadora 1992, Kusters 2003a and 2003b, and most notably al-Sharkawi, 2014), and we will review them in turn below. However, one general objection to the idea that agreement patterns were altered due to linguistic contact can be raised preemptively. In fact, this objection is not entirely new, since it is similar to the argument that Ferguson used to refute Versteegh's pidginization/decreolization hypothesis (Versteegh 1984).

Ferguson (1984: 13) correctly notes that "when a language is moving toward morphological simplification, from whatever external or internal causes, this will tend to be manifested in the agreement system by (a) reduction in the categories of agreement, and (b) regularization of intersecting patterns of agreement".[11] In the article, Ferguson specifically cites as counterexamples of surviving complexity the agreement patterns triggered by dual controllers, those triggered by chains of conjoined controllers, and the type of agreement that we observe in pre-controller targets. It seems to us, however, that Ferguson's argument could be extended to include the very general topic of variation between plural and F.SG agreement with plural controllers. As we have seen in the earlier sections of this book, this phenomenon depends on a high number of intersecting factors. This is precisely the type of complex syntactic behavior that we would expect to disappear in a situation in which contact has caused linguistic simplification.[12] Quite to the opposite, F.SG/plural variation has not only survived almost everywhere in the Arabic-speaking world, but it also appears to be governed by the same factors that used to influence it more than 1,500 years ago (judging by the analysis of pre- and early Islamic texts, see Chapters 2 and 3).

As we have noted in § 5.1, then, the type of complex variability that characterizes agreement in Arabic seems to be particularly long-lasting. This stands in open contrast with the idea that, at the time in which Arabic started to diffuse outside of its ancestral homeland, the great numbers of adult non-native speakers who started to learn the language brought about widespread simplification and regularization. In this scenario, we would expect F.SG/plural variation to disappear *along with*—or *instead of*[13]—F.PL agreement.

---

11 The appropriateness of the term "simplification" in this context largely depends on the definition that we give of the term itself. We discussed the question of linguistic complexity in relation to agreement in § 2.3.5. In his study of the changes that the dialects of central Arabia have undergone after reaching Lower Iraq and the Gulf Coast (including loss of F.PL forms), Ingham (1982a: 33) remarks that "In the main it is more accurate to regard the process as one of simplification than one of reduction, since the ability of the language to make grammatical distinctions is not reduced, but the method of doing it is simplified".

12 This is consistent with the general principles of linguistic *diffusion* (via contact, as opposed to intergenerational *transmission*) formulated by Labov (2007). In a nutshell, adult learners are not normally able to reproduce the structural patterns of the systems they borrow from with total accuracy.

13 There is only one dialect that we know of in which something of the sort has happened, namely Cilician Arabic. In this variety, F.SG agreement with plural controllers is no longer attested, while adjectives and participles have retained F.PL agreement (to an extent at least; see § 2.3.6 and § 2.3.8.1). As we will discuss below, Cilician Arabic is one of the few

To the best of our knowledge, this issue has never been satisfactorily addressed in any work on the topic, and to this day it remains one of the main obstacles for any theory that wants to explain diachronic change in Arabic agreement patterns as the result of contact.[14]

If we now move on to review the literature that deals specifically with the two topics of agreement and contact-induced change, the work of Cadora (1992) surely deserves a brief mention, because it has been the first study to explicitly link change in agreement patterns with ecolinguistic motivations. Cadora's study is not primarily concerned with the topic of agreement, though the question of F.SG agreement with plural controllers is addressed in the fourth chapter of the book. The author's conclusions on the subject, however, are not particularly original, since he claims that non-individuated F.SG agreement is not a native feature of rural and Bedouin dialects in the Levant, and that it has been introduced in them (at the expense of F.PL agreement) due to contact with the more prestigious urban and standard varieties of the language. Very similar views, as we have seen, were expressed in the studies of Owens and Bani-Yasin (1989) and Herin and Al-Wer (2014), among others. We have extensively commented on these works and these hypotheses in § 1.3 and § 5.1, and we will not return on the topic here.

The work of Kusters (2003a, 2003b) approaches the topic of contact-induced change from a much broader perspective. Kusters compares the process of simplification that spoken Arabic has allegedly undergone through time with similar processes that have taken place in other languages (specifically: Swahili, Quechua, and the languages of the Scandinavian family). In particular, he focuses on the level of complexity of verbal inflectional morphology, finding that the more contact and adult language learning a language experiences, the more *transparent* and *economic* its paradigms become.[15]

varieties of Arabic for which we believe the argument of contact-induced simplification could actually be relevant.

14 We are not saying, of course, that linguistic contact did not cause any type of change in the various Arabic dialects. It probably did. Here, however, we are only concerned with the topic of agreement patterns, and these show a remarkable degree of stability, one that is difficult to reconcile with the idea of contact-induced simplification. The argument could obviously be made that linguistic contact did indeed cause simplification in those dialects that have lost the option of F.SG agreement with plural controllers (Type C systems). As we have seen, however, there are elements that suggest this to have been a recent development, at least in some dialects. All in all, the topic remains in need of further investigation.

15 "With 'transparent' I mean that there is a one-to-one-correspondence between meaning and form. Deviations from optimal transparency are fusion, fission, allomorphy and homonymy [...]. I consider an inflectional system to be 'economic' when few categories and category combinations are expressed" (Kusters 2003b: 275).

Much like Cadora, Kusters believes that linguistic structure can be affected by "factors of the historical social dimension" (Kusters 2003b: 275). While we wholeheartedly agree with the idea that socio-historical variables must have played a role in the changes that the gender system of Arabic has undergone through time, there are certain elements in Kusters' study that are—in our view—not entirely convincing. On a general level, we find his treatment of the history of Arabic to be somewhat coarse (the idea that all dialects of Arabic are the direct descendants of a CA-like variety surely needs more problematization). On a more specific level, when it comes to the reduction of verbal and pronominal paradigms, Kusters' explanation fails to account for those changes that have occurred in a context were little or no linguistic contact has occurred at all. Kusters himself appears to be aware of this problem, when he writes:

> The Shammar variety of Najdi Arabic is one of the most conservative Arabic varieties. Nevertheless, like in all Arabic varieties, the categories of dual and mood have disappeared. This cannot be explained by a common substrate language, or a common social context for modern Arabic varieties. We can rephrase, though not solve, this problem by suggesting that the tendency towards loss was inherently present in Classical Arabic. The loss of these categories may be called a natural development of any language, or it may belong to the 'genius' (cf. Sapir 1921) of Arabic
>
> KUSTERS 2003: 281

When considering a case study in which language contact cannot be invoked as a possible driver of change, Kusters is forced to resort to the old Sapirian idea that all languages possess a certain "genius" that makes them evolve in certain predetermined directions. This explanation is unsatisfactory, because it tells us nothing of the reasons behind this "natural tendency". Furthermore, it is not only the very conservative and isolated dialects of central Arabia that pose a problem for Kusters's theory. Several non-distinguishing varieties of Arabic exist in which it seems unlikely that loss of F.PL forms has been brought about by contact. We have already hinted at this fact in the previous section, while discussing the possibility that loss of F.PL morphology is to be regarded as an internal development, but let us now have a closer look at these dialects. We will here consider four representative varieties (all already discussed in § 2.3.2): Baghdad Arabic, Khartoum Arabic, Tripoli Arabic, and the dialects of the Gulf coast.

The demographic and therefore linguistic history of the city of Baghdad is a well-known and often-told tale in the field of Arabic dialectology. Summing up the detailed account that Blanc (1964) gives of that story, Baghdad was a thriving urban center until the power of the Caliphate started to decline between the 10th and 11th century, and totally collapsed with the Mongol siege of the city in 1258. This was followed by a second sack some 150 years later, in 1400. A good portion of the original population of the city was either killed or dispersed in the neighboring countryside following these two events. At that time, the inhabitants of Baghdad all spoke a sedentary-type dialect belonging to what, in the literature, is commonly referred as the *qeltu* group. When the city started to repopulate, especially after the 17th century, it was mainly due to an influx of people of nomadic and rural origin who spoke dialects of the *gelet* group. This became the dominant linguistic type in Baghdad, while the Jewish and Christian minorities that lived in the city continued to speak their ancestral *qeltu* dialects. Interestingly enough, the dialects spoken by the rural and Bedouin population of Iraq still preserve gender distinction in the plural to this day, while Baghdadi Arabic has mostly lost it.[16] This means that, over the course of the last three or four centuries, the city of Baghdad has witnessed a large influx of immigrants who all spoke some type of gender-distinguishing *gelet* dialect. F.PL morphology, however, was lost in the speech of these populations soon after their arrival. This change could, of course, be attributed to contact with what remained of the local *qeltu*-speaking population: *qeltu* dialects are non-distinguishing varieties, and it seems likely that they have been for most of their history. This explanation, however, leaves several open questions. From a sociolinguistic point of view, the Muslim *gelet* dialect of Baghdad has imposed itself as the dominant prestige variety within the city, so that one would expect linguistic borrowing to go in the opposite direction. In fact, there seems to be no typically *qeltu*-trait that has systematically been borrowed by the local Muslim population (the opposite being probably true, since many *qeltu*-speakers are actually bi-dialectal and can switch to one or the other variety depending on the circumstances; Blanc 1964: 9).[17] Muslim Baghdadi Arabic has systematically retained its voiced reflex of ق, its [r] realization of ر, absence of *ʔimāla*, 3rd person M.SG suffix pronoun in the form *-a*, 1st person singular of the suffix stem with no final vowel, and so on (see Blanc 1964, Abu Haidar 2006 and Palva 2009 for a more extensive list of characteristic traits). In light of these considerations, the fact that the emergence of genderless plural forms was indeed the

16 "There is no 3rd pl. gender distinction in Baghdad Arabic proper, only in the speech of Baghdad residents of rural or Bedouin origin" (Abu Haidar, 2006: 226). See also § 2.3.2.

17 Palva (2009: 18–24) gives a list of a few traits that may be regarded as originally *qeltu* features that have been borrowed in Muslim Baghdadi Arabic due to contact. Among these traits, he lists loss of gender distinction in the plural. For the reasons adduced above and below in this section, and in the rest of the chapter, we disagree with this view.

result of borrowing appears at least questionable.[18] Even if this were actually the case, another problem poses itself: why, of all possible traits, were non-distinguishing plural forms the ones that were borrowed?

The linguistic history of the main towns of the Gulf coast is very similar to that of Baghdad, although on a different time scale. On a general level, the history of eastern Arabia is not very well-known; Holes, however, has credibly demonstrated that, at a certain point in history, the Gulf littoral was populated by people who spoke a bundle of sedentary-type dialects typologically quite distinct from the ones that were in use in the central Peninsula (see for instance Holes, 1991). Over the course of the centuries, a series of migratory waves brought Bedouins from the inner deserts of Arabia to settle along the coast of the Persian Gulf, rapidly becoming the dominant social group in the area. "The most recent of these [waves], in the 18th century, gave rise to the current ruling families of Kuwait, Bahrain, Qatar, and the United Arab Emirates" (Holes 2007: 213). These new immigrants brought with them their dialect, that soon imposed itself as the local prestige variety. What is of importance to us here is that central Arabian dialects, such as the Najdi varieties we have analyzed in § 2.3.3, all retain F.PL verbal and pronominal forms; Gulf dialects, on the contrary, do not. Here as well, we lack a convincing explanation for how this change came about (in this case, we may add, in a very rapid fashion, since this must have occurred in the last two or three hundred years). Contact with the pre-existing sedentary varieties seems extremely unlikely: there is virtually no attested example of a feature arising from these dialects that has been borrowed in the Bedouin-descended ones (while, in this case as well, speakers of the local socially non-dominant variety are often bi-dialectal). We find it hard to believe, then, that loss of gender distinction may have been prompted by contact. But even if we were to admit this possibility, the problem is only partially solved: as was the case with Baghdadi Arabic, we may ask ourselves why is it that—of all possible traits—it was genderless plural forms that ended up being borrowed.

Another example we want to discuss is that of Khartoum. As we have seen in § 2.3.2, the dialect of the Sudanese capital appears to be on its way to lose F.PL forms altogether. In a similar way to what happens today in Baghdad, these are considered to be features of the "rural" speech of recent immigrants. Of course, the absence of these forms could be due to extensive contact with the many

18 Herin and Al-Wer (2013: 64–66) show how loss of gender distinction in the plural in the dialect of Salt, a process that was likely motivated by contact with the dialect of the capital Amman, is currently proceeding hand in hand with the borrowing of several other traits from that same dialect (e.g. replacement of [g] with [ʔ], replacement of [ǧ] with [ž], etc.).

non-Arabic languages that are spoken in the country. However, as already seen, all the other Sudanese varieties for which we have documentation preserve full-fledged F.PL paradigms to this day, Khartoum representing the only exception.[19] Why should Khartoum Arabic, then, be the only dialect in the country whose gender system was affected by contact?[20] It is worth noting that several Sudanese dialects outside Khartoum present forms that are, from the point of view of "mainstream" Arabic varieties, highly deviant (see Abu-Manga, 2009, for some examples). It seems likely that some of these typologically unusual traits did indeed emerge as a consequence of extensive contact with genetically unrelated languages, but what is of importance to us here is that the gender and agreement systems of these varieties have remained remarkably stable. This might represent further evidence of the fact that the gender/agreement system of Arabic is more resistant to contact-induced change than most studies on the subject have led us to believe.[21] Be that as it may, it remains unclear what prompted loss of F.PL morphology in Khartoum Arabic, since in this case we have no neighboring non-distinguishing dialects that can offer an easy explanation.

The last example we will examine here is that of the city of Tripoli, in Libya. This is somewhat similar to the case of Baghdad discussed above. In this case as well, the city was once home to a sedentary-type dialect (in the literature about Maghrebi dialectology, these are often referred to as *pre-Hilali* dialects). Throughout the centuries, however, successive waves of immigration of people of Bedouin origin have altered Tripoli's linguistic landscape. This process of

---

19 That is, of course, if we exclude Juba Arabic and Darfur Arabic. On the latter, see § 2.3.8.3. Note that, in the case of Darfur Arabic, extensive contact with non-Semitic languages is precisely was caused the dramatic changes that we observe in the language: not a partial restructuring of the gender system, with M.PL forms substituting F.PL ones, but the total collapse of the system. This may constitute further evidence of the fact that the changes described for Khartoum Arabic are *not* the result of contact with non-Arabic varieties (if they were, the restructuring would be much more extensive).

20 Little is know of the dialects which are currently spoken in other large cities of Sudan, such as Atbara, Shendi or Port Sudan. It is perfectly possible that F.PL morphology has disappeared in these urban centers as well. This, however, would only offer further support to the hypotheses we present in this chapter (see in particular § 5.2.4).

21 In this respect, the Arabic dialects of central Asia represent another interesting example: these dialects have been isolated from the main Arabic-speaking continuum for probably more than a millennium, surviving as small linguistic islands surrounded by typologically very different languages. And yet, despite having undergone considerable contact-induced change (e.g. loss of the definite article, SOV word order; see Zimmerman 2009), they have retained both F.PL forms and the possibility of F.SG agreement with plural referents (thought this latter option is apparently uncommon, see § 2.3.2).

progressive "Bedouinization" of the city dialect apparently started in the 11th century, and—according to Pereira (2007: 80)—by the end of the 19th century it was only the Jewish element of the population who still spoke the old pre-Hilali variety.[22] In the rest of the city, a type of Bedouinized dialect had taken root, which was however not to survive the demographical upheavals that Tripoli witnessed in the 20th century. After the Second World War and the discovery of fossil fuels, a massive process of urbanization brought tens of thousands of people from all over the country to resettle inside Tripoli, bringing with them their rural, gender-distinguishing dialects. We do not know if the dialect that existed within the city before the start of this massive process of urbanization had already lost F.PL morphology. We do know, however, that these forms do not survive in Tripoli Arabic today. A number of considerations stem from these premises. Firstly, it must not be forgotten that the immigrants that came into Tripoli in the 20th century were so numerous as to probably outnumber the "original" inhabitants of the city. Even if they came into contact with a local, non-distinguishing dialect, it is not necessarily the case that they would incorporate this feature into their speech, even if the local dialect enjoyed some type of prestige status.[23] If, on the other hand, the pre-20th century Tripoli dialect still preserved F.PL morphology, then its disappearance in today's vernacular is all the more mysterious (the idea that the pre-Hilali variety spoken by the small Jewish community of the city was the source of this change can be safely discarded). Another possibility is that gender distinction in the plural was originally lost in a pre-Hilali phase, due to contact between the first Arabic settlers and the local population. This trait was successively adopted by the Bedouin dialects that swamped Tripoli after the 11th century, and has been a feature of the city's topolect ever since. One objection that could be raised against this explanation is the fact that that of Tripoli is the only Libyan dialect to have lost F.PL forms to this day (with the exception of the other Jewish varieties). If contact with the indigenous population caused morphological change in this variety, why didn't it affect the forms of Arabic that were spoken in other parts of the eastern Maghreb? This argument is similar to the one we made when discussing the case of Khartoum Arabic: why should contact only affect urban dialects, leaving those spoken in smaller towns and rural areas untouched?

---

22 Recently, D'Anna (2021) has even argued that the dialect that was still spoken by the Jews of Tripoli in the first half of the 20th century cannot be taken as representative of Tripoli's "original" pre-Hilali variety.

23 That is, not unless some other force was also affecting the language, favoring a particular outcome with respect to agreement patterns. We will discuss this hypothesis in § 5.2.4.

All in all, while the hypotheses put forward by Kusters are surely interesting and worthy of attention, in the specific case of F.PL morphology we do not believe that they are sufficient to explain the modifications that the Arabic verbal and pronominal paradigms have undergone—not in all varieties of the language, at least. As we hope to have demonstrated, several dialects exist in which contact-induced morphological loss seems to be unlikely.[24]

If we are correct in our interpretation of the data, then an important consideration stems from all that has been said above, namely that the loss of F.PL forms in a great number of Arabic dialects must be seen as the result of multiple parallel innovations. A monogenetic explanation, in fact, would only work if we believed contact to be responsible for this loss in *every* variety of Arabic. In this scenario, one could imagine that F.PL forms first disappeared in a certain dialect, at a specific point in time and space, and that this innovation then diffused, moving from one dialect to the other by means of contact, its spread fostered by human migrations and population movements. If, however, we recognize the existence of dialects in which the lack of F.PL forms cannot be attributed to contact with another, non-distinguishing variety, it necessarily follows that this innovation emerged independently several times (some of these multiple parallel innovations may even be due to contact with other, non-Arabic languages, but the fact remains that these changes happened separately from one another).

No matter which of these two scenarios we consider more likely, the question remains open of *when* did non-distinguishing varieties appear for the first time. As we have seen, for some specific varieties, such as the ones discussed above, a rough time scale can be proposed. In other cases, however—and these probably represent the majority of the non-distinguishing dialects of Arabic—the situation appears to be more complicated.

This and other key issues will be addressed in the next section, in which we will analyze one last study on the diachrony of gender and agreement in spoken Arabic.

5.2.3 *A Critical Reading of al-Sharkawi (2014): The Timescale of Loss*

Probably, the most in-depth study to ever tackle the issue of loss of F.PL morphology in Arabic dialects is al-Sharkawi (2014). The main thesis of al-Sharkawi's article is that the disappearance of this morphological category was

24 It would be unfair not to mention the fact that Kusters himself acknowledges the problem posed by the systematic absence of F.PL forms in all urban varieties of Arabic. We will further comment on this aspect of Kuster's work in § 5.2.4.

caused by urbanization. On a general level, we agree with this idea. As we will discuss in more detail in the next section, the degree of correlation between the two categories of "dialects spoken in large urban centers" and "dialects that have no F.PL morphology" is so extreme that it seems licit to suspect some type of causal link between the two. Several details in al-Sharkawi's article, however, appear problematic: the next paragraphs will be dedicated to a critical overview of this work, since we feel that many of the issues al-Sharkawi analyzes in his study are central to the understanding of the history of agreement in Arabic.

The first problem we encounter in al-Sharkawi's paper is a terminological one. The author establishes an opposition between the two categories "urban" and "Bedouin", but we contend that this dichotomy is fallacious. Two different and distinct oppositions are being conflated here, namely "urban vs non-urban" and "Bedouin vs sedentary". While the former is self-explanatory (it refers to a dialect's being spoken inside or outside an urban center), and should be understood as a purely *synchronic* classification, the latter is more ambiguous.

We want to stress that we are here raising two distinct—albeit related—points. The first one is that we find the traditional categorization of Arabic dialects into Bedouin and sedentary ones to be often problematic and confusing, because it appears to be at the same time synchronic and diachronic, and based on both social and linguistic criteria. This has already been discussed in § 2.3.2 and § 2.3.7. The second point is that, even if we accept this distinction as valid, the Bedouin/sedentary opposition must still be kept separate from the urban/non-urban one, because these categories can intersect (e.g. several dialects exist that are "Bedouin" according to the traditional classification, but that are also spoken in large urban centers: we have listed some of these when commenting on Kusters' work in the previous section, but more could be mentioned, including the urban dialects of the Hijaz). We will discuss why we believe that this distinction is of crucial importance in § 5.2.4.

Terminological questions aside, there are two main aspects of al-Sharkawi's work that we find unconvincing. The first concerns his claim that the establishment of garrison towns "brought together to the new provinces group of speaker [sic] of similar but not identical dialects of Arabic […], then brought groups of non-Arabic speaking locals to the vicinities of garrison towns" (al-Sharkawi, 2014: 89). Contact between different Arabic dialects caused levelling to take place, which resulted in the establishment of "a distinct koine in each garrison town". Subsequently, the informal learning of these varieties by nonnative speakers prompted further processes of regularization and simplification, also due to the fact that the Arabs used foreigner-talk registers to communicate with the local populations.

The idea that mothertongue Arabs consciously employed a simplified version of the language when talking to non-native speakers does apparently stand to reason, but is contradicted by the evidence presented above, that is, the permanence of oscillation between F.SG and plural agreement in most contemporary dialects. Why should the relatively straightforward F.PL agreement be abandoned, and the non-systematic F.SG agreement with plural controllers retained? In addition, it has to be noted that this outcome was remarkably uniform across the Arabic-speaking world: even if we accept that, in some cases, things may have gone in the direction al-Sharkawi describes, we would expect to find at least some exceptions to this trend, i.e. urban dialects in which F.PL morphology has been retained, and where F.SG agreement with plural controllers is no longer an option. This, however, never happened: there is virtually no attestation of a major urban dialect that has preserved F.PL verbs and pronouns,[25] and all dialects that retained them also continue the F.SG/plural variation.[26]

The fact that al-Sharkawi never addresses this point is, however, unsurprising, if one considers that he clearly believes the agreement behavior of non-human controllers in the dialects to be substantially uniform with that of Modern Standard Arabic. This point is particularly problematic, because it is fundamentally impossible to describe the way in which a system has changed through time if we lack an accurate description of the original system itself.

At the very beginning of his article, al-Sharkawi (2014: 88) mentions the fact that dialects which still retain F.PL morphology "also have a complex feminine plural agreement", but his analysis of agreement in gender-distinguishing dialects does not go any further than this. In the following pages, statements as the following ones are often found: "Inanimate nouns behave in a similar way as human nouns in the dialects and Modern Standard Arabic and Classical Arabic in the singular [...]. However, in the plural [...], these nouns do not agree. Within the phrase and on the sentence levels the agreement is in the feminine singular" (p. 101); "Nonhuman and inanimate nouns receive feminine singular agreement in the plural in both the dialects and Classical Arabic (p. 103); "[In Najdi Arabic] concord patterns generally follow the patterns of Classical Arabic albeit with some modifications" (p. 109), and a few lines below:

25 The few and partial exceptions will be discussed in § 5.2.4.

26 Not only was variation between F.SG and plural agreement retained, but in most dialects this option remains available even in the case of human controllers. If we consider how uncommon F.SG with human controllers is, we would surely expect this irregularity to be among the first to be levelled out in a context of conscious simplification aimed at smoother communication with non-native speakers.

"Agreement with dual nouns is in the plural and inanimate nouns receive feminine singular agreement".[27]

These statements are obviously inaccurate: in Chapter 2, we have seen how plural agreement with nonhuman plural controllers is extremely common in contemporary Arabic dialects, though relative frequency may vary. By claiming that in spoken Arabic—and especially in gender-distinguishing varieties—nonhuman controllers take F.SG agreement, al-Sharkawi makes its analysis blind to one of the fundamental aspects of the whole gender and agreement system.

Al-Sharkawi never explains how, in actual practice, the loss of F.PL morphology could have taken place and spread in the formative period of the urban dialects of the Arab world. Admittedly, one can easily see how M.PL agreement could have taken over in the case of human referents: since groups of mixed (i.e. both masculine and feminine) controllers attracted masculine agreement, this type of agreement was already more frequent in everyday speech. As a result, one could imagine a situation in which non-Arab learners were exposed to an input largely dominated by M.PL agreement with human referents (and if foreigner talk registers were actually employed, the domination may have been absolute).

Nonhuman plurals, however, are an altogether different matter. Here F.PL agreement must have been common, as is the case today with gender-distinguishing varieties of spoken Arabic. Even in the case of foreigner talk registers, there must have been some resistance to the complete abandonment of F.PL agreement, the one morphological marker that kept the "human masculine" semantic category separate from everything else (§ 2.3.4).

By saying that spoken Arabic behaves like MSA with respect to agreement, al-Sharkawi is conveniently dispensed from dealing with this issue. As we have seen, however, things are not so simple: any theory that wants to account for the disappearance of F.PL morphology in spoken Arabic has to deal with the fact that, far from being confined to the (statistically uncommon) contexts where groups of human females were being referred to, F.PL agreement must have been extremely widespread in early varieties of spoken Arabic.

27 Al-Sharkawi's use of the label "Classical Arabic" in this context is misleading in the first place. As we have seen in Chapters 3 and 4, generalized F.SG agreement with nonhuman controllers appears to have been a late development in written Arabic, while in the earlier written texts this type of controllers behave pretty much in the same way as in contemporary gender-distinguishing dialects. The appropriateness of the definition "Classical Arabic" in this context, then, depends on whether or not one considers the Quran and pre-Islamic poetic corpus representative of this variety.

There is a second major reason because of which we find al-Sharkawi's explanation for the disappearance of F.PL morphology unsatisfactory. From what he writes in the article, it is clear that, in his view, some of the original dialects spoken in the garrison towns had already lost F.PL morphology by the time they got there, that is, *before* the time of the Islamic conquests. This trait was perhaps later spread to the other dialects spoken in the military camps via koineization,[28] and the resulting non-distinguishing koineized dialects further learned by non-native speakers, bringing more and more people to speak a variety of Arabic with no F.PL agreement. It is possible that al-Sharkawi is right in this respect: if he is, however, the problem of how and why F.PL agreement was first lost is not solved, but only moved backwards in time. Even if we agree that some of the dialects that moved outside of the Arabian Peninsula in the 7th century featured no F.PL verbal and pronominal forms, and that this trait was later borrowed in more and more varieties of Arabic, the question still remains: how did these "original" dialects lose F.PL agreement in the first place?

In theory, it is perfectly possible that the contact situation described by al-Sharkawi merely accelerated an already ongoing process; al-Sharkawi (2014: 112) himself mentions this possibility, when he writes that: "contact situation [sic] among the dialects of Arabic in garrison towns led to durable and gradual language change among the contact dialects […] or enhanced developments that were already in motion in previous times". Al-Sharkawi, however, never addresses the fundamental question that these considerations engender, which is to say, at what moment in history did the first non-distinguishing variety of Arabic appear.

Unfortunately, we have little evidence to either prove or disprove the theory that some varieties of Arabic had already lost F.PL agreement in pre-Islamic times. To the best of our knowledge, the earliest documents in which this phenomenon is attested are the papyri analyzed by Hopkins (1984: 92). The oldest of these documents, however, dates back to 102 A.H. (i.e. 720 CE): this is undoubtedly a very early occurrence, but one that still comes almost one century after the beginning of the Islamic expansion. In spite of its being a very important finding, then, we do not know if this attestation represents the continuation of a linguistic behavior that was already widespread in pre-Islamic times, or if, conversely, it constitutes one of the first manifestations

28 Al-Sharkawi is obviously not the first to propose koineization in the Arabo-Islamic military camps as an explanation for the type of linguistic change that Arabic dialects have undergone. This idea was originally exposed by Ferguson (1959). We will here refer to Al-Sharkawi's work because it engages specifically with the topic of loss of F.PL forms.

of a new "non-distinguishing" type of Arabic that only came to be as a result of the conquests.[29]

The one other piece of evidence available to us is represented by the three occurrences of M.PL agreement with a plural nonhuman controller that, as we have seen in § 3.4, appear in the Quran itself. As we already remarked, this syntactic behavior is never observed in the *muʕallaqāt*, and so we may speculate that the Quranic examples represent the first attestation of an innovation that was moving its first steps around the turn of the 6th century. Although surely appealing, this hypothesis is only based on a handful of occurrences, so that caution is inevitably advisable.

All things considered, this appears to be one of the weakest point in Al-Sharkawi's theory: if lack of gender distinction in the plural was already a characteristic of some pre-Islamic dialects, then we are left in need of an explanation for how it first originated; if, conversely, we want to regard it as a later development caused by simplification strategies and imperfect learning on the part of non-native speakers, then we are confronted with the problem that the much more complex F.SG agreement patterns with plural controllers survived these processes apparently unscathed.[30]

29 Al-Sharkawi (2014: 112) argues that "since the tribes that lived in the Arab garrison towns in Egypt came from Ḥijāz and Yemen, some of them must have had a gender distinction such as that in some Yemeni and Najdi dialects, and some not, judging of course by the behavior of these dialects in the modern times". We strongly disagree with the idea that the behavior of the dialects spoken today in a given area can be taken as representative of the behavior of the varieties spoken in that same area some 1,500 years ago. The agreement system of today's Hijazi Arabic does not necessarily tell us anything of the system that was in use in the region at the dawn of the Islamic conquests, so that this specific piece of evidence must be regarded as inconclusive.

30 Oddly enough, it is al-Sharkawi (2014: 110) himself who provides a conspicuous piece of evidence *against* the hypothesis of contact-induced simplification, when he writes that "in the Central Asian Arabic dialects […] despite heavy contact with local languages, scarcity in number, less prestige, and heavy areal borrowing, gender distinction in the plural between masculine and feminine is retained. It seems that it is only through koineization that a variety loses gender distinction, as we have seen above". As will become clear in the next section, we believe that the reason why Central Asian Arabic dialects did not lose F.PL forms is not that they were not exposed to koineization with other, non-distinguishing dialects of Arabic; the reason behind their preservation of said forms is that they were spoken in tight-knit rural communities, outside of urban areas.

5.2.4 *Agreement and the City: Urbanization as a Driver of Syntactic Change*

Summing up the various points that have been touched in the previous sections, we have first considered the possibility that loss of F.PL agreement in spoken Arabic was caused by an exclusively internal development, i.e. a spontaneous process of phonological erosion that affected final vowels and /n/ sounds and brought about the disappearance of F.PL pronouns and verbal endings. Lack of F.PL agreement in these two categories would have later been extended to adjectives via paradigmatic pressure. Several counterarguments can be raised against this explanation, so that we believe it can be safely discarded.

After exploring the hypothesis of an exclusively internal development, we have moved on to consider the possibility of an external motivation for the loss of F.PL agreement. We reviewed the existing literature on the topic, in particular the studies of Cadora, Kusters and al-Sharkawi, who all focus on contact-induced change. In general, we found one main obstacle to the idea that the gender system of Arabic underwent simplification at the time of the Islamic conquests, due to extensive contact with non-Arabic-speaking populations: this obstacle is represented by the survival of complex patterns of variation between plural and F.SG agreement in the majority of Arabic dialects. Furthermore, even if we discount this piece of counter-evidence, several dialects of Arabic can still be found in which loss of F.PL morphology would appear to be a much later development. These varieties (which include the aforementioned dialects of the Gulf, that of Baghdad, and those of Tripoli and Khartoum) have had little contact with non-distinguishing dialects from which they could have borrowed genderless plural forms, so that another explanation must be found for these innovative forms. In addition to this, even if we were to believe that common plural forms were indeed imported from other dialects, we find ourselves confronted with the original question: why was this specific trait the only one borrowed, while all the other "original" characteristics were retained?

One last problem that we face when considering the question of F.PL loss is chronological in nature. While we have a relatively clear idea of when F.PL forms may have been abandoned in some dialects, the general time-scale of the whole phenomenon eludes us. In particular, we do not know when non-distinguishing varieties of Arabic first appeared, and if they already existed in pre-Islamic times or not. For al-Sharkawi's koineization theory to work, genderless plural forms need to have existed before the beginning of the Islamic era. Conversely, if we discard the koineization hypothesis, then it would be theoretically possible to claim that the first non-distinguishing dialects emerged after the diffusion of Arabic outside the Peninsula, due to extensive contact with non-Arabic speaking populations; however, in this latter scenario, the problem of the retention of F.SG/plural variation still remains.

By now, it should be clear that a unified answer to the questions of how and when did Arabic lose F.PL agreement is yet to be found. We have a number of partial theories, very different in nature, that can account for specific subsets of dialects, but not others. One last possibility, however, remains to be explored. In § 5.2.1 we have seen how, when it comes to externally motivated change, languages can be affected by two different types of factors: one is linguistic in nature (i.e. contact), while the other is represented by all those non-linguistic phenomena that can have an impact of language. We will now focus on the latter.

We have already hinted at the fact that, in the Arabic-speaking world, a systematic correlation appears to exist between urbanization and lack of gender distinction in the plural forms of the adjective, verb and pronoun. In other words, all the major urban centers of the Arab world are home to a dialect that does not feature F.PL agreement. If we limit our analysis to the capitals of the Arab countries, the only two exceptions that we find to this rule are the two cities of Muscat, in Oman, and Sanaa, in Yemen. Both cities, however, have only recently expanded to the size of a proper metropolis, their population having increased significantly only during the last fifty years or so. It seems likely that, in these two cases, the full effects of massive urbanization are still to be felt, so that, if a causal relation actually exists between urbanization and loss of F.PL forms, this process may become manifest in the coming years.[31]

It has to be noted that that between urbanization and lack of F.PL forms is not a two-way correlation, since not all non-distinguishing dialects are spoken inside large urban centers. The reverse, however, appears to be constantly true, so that one might rightly wonder whether it is possible that the mere process of urbanization is sufficient, in and of itself, to spark this type of linguistic change.

The idea that languages are influenced by the very environment in which they are spoken is not a new one, and it has gained more and more traction in the field of linguistics in recent years. As De Busser (2015: 1) has recently written,

31 Scattered remarks about incipient F.PL loss in the dialect of Muscat can indeed be found in the literature (Holes 1989: 449, and Bettega 2019b: 155–156). Besides the rampant growth that the city has witnessed over the course of the last decades, in this same period the dialect of Muscat has also been exposed to intense contact with the neighboring non-distinguishing dialects of the Gulf Coast (which, from a sociolinguistic point of view, are locally perceived as more prestigious). This is yet another factor that might precipitate the loss of F.PL forms in the dialect of the Omani capital.

at the very outset of a volume edited with Randy La Polla, “Linguistic structure is not only shaped by how speakers interact with each other and with the world they live in, but also by external forces that are outside the control of individual speakers or speech communities”.[32] He later adds that “an ever-growing mountain of evidence suggests that there are plenty of complex interactions between language and its environment, and that in certain cases these interactions have a measurable influence on the development of grammatical structures” (p. 3).

The study of the effects that the external environment has on language is sometimes referred to as “ecolinguistics”. This is not a particularly well-defined label, since an at least partial overlap exists with the two fields of sociolinguistics and anthropological linguistics. In the remainder of this section, however, we will make cautious use of the term, since the phenomena we are going to investigate fall clearly within the scope of all the three aforementioned disciplines.

Several studies, in recent years, have demonstrated the existence of a correlation between certain linguistic phenomena and the external environment. Landscape and geography, for instance, have been shown to affect the grammatical categories that express notions of space and motion (a wealth of studies exist on the topic, but see Levinson, 2003, as a general reference); the natural resources available in a given area can determine the measurement systems that the inhabitants of said area use, and the associated vocabulary (Watson and Boom, forthcoming: 6); the amount of linguistic diversity that a certain region is home to has been related to the climatic zone and latitude in which that region is located (Mace & Pagel, 1995; Nettle 1996 and 1998) and to its characteristic landscape features (Axelsen and Manrubia, 2014); and linguistic diversity has also been shown to correlate with biodiversity (Mace & Pagel, 1995, Moore et al., 2002).

Possibly one of the most intriguing findings of recent ecolinguistic studies is the inverse correlation that appears to exist between cultural complexity and community size, one the one hand, and linguistic complexity, on the other.[33]

32 The extent to which urbanization can be considered “an external force that is outside the control of individual speakers or speech communities” could obviously be debated. In theory, it is possible to argue that speakers exert at least partial control over processes of urbanization; however, such processes are complex phenomena, which normally entail a cascade of indirect consequences that fall outside the intention and scope of the original urbanization project. We will expand on these points in the course of the present section.

33 Trudgill (2015: 137) remarks that “most linguists are likely to feel a little uncomfortable about the notion of cultural complexity”. We agree that this represents a somehow controversial topic, and we will follow Trudgill’s advice of focusing only on the very simple

Almost fifty years ago Kay (1976: 119) had already hypothesized that non-literate communities with less than 4,000 speakers are more likely to employ complex deictic systems, because "in small, homogeneous speech communities there is a maximum of shared background between speakers, which is the stuff on which deixis depends". Perkins (1992) confirms this hypothesis by measuring the average number of deictic affixes in a sample of 50 languages and finding a statistical inverse correlation between this parameter and social complexity.[34] Dahl (2004) maintains that loss of cross-linguistically dispensable features is connected to demographic expansion, and uses as an example the loss of the dual number in almost all European languages over the course of the last 2,000 years, noting how it is only the languages with a small number of speakers that still retain it. Aikhenvald and Dixon (1998: 254) note that the most complex pronominal systems in the world's languages "tend to be found in small-scale language communities". For several examples of this, see Trudgill (2015: 137 and ff.), who concurs that "certain aspects of linguistic complexity seem to be more evident in simpler than in complex societies", and again relates this to the higher amount of shared information that can be found within "societies of intimates". Aikhenvald (2004: 355) has also noted how "complex evidential systems, in their vast majority, are confined to languages with smallish numbers of speakers, spoken in small, traditional societies".

In light of everything that has been said so far, it seems licit to suspect that, also in the Arabic-speaking world, some type of connection might exist between demographic expansion and landscape anthropization, on the one hand, and linguistic change, on the other. This idea is not entirely new even in the field of Arabic linguistics. Kusters (2003b: 288), whose work has been discussed above, writes that: "I found that tight small communities with strong language traditions and few second language learners are the best environment for inflectional complexities".[35] As far as gender distinction in Arabic is con-

parameter of community size: this, in turn, determines how homogeneous the community is and how much information its members share.

34 The affixes considered were tense, person on nouns and verbs, spatial demonstratives on nouns and verbs, inclusive vs exclusive on person markers and dual on person markers. Social complexity was measured in terms of factors such as type of agriculture, settlement size, craft specialization, and number of levels in social hierarchies.

35 But consider also this quote from Taine-Cheikh (2002), where similar views are exposed, albeit perhaps in a less systematic way: "Chez les nomades, où la variété des expériences et l'hétérogénéité culturelle sont sans doute moindres, on semble pouvoir s'acommoder d'une permanence plus grande de l'implicité [...]. A l'inverse, les innovations observées dans les parlers de sédentaires répondent souvent à un besoin d'explication du contenu

cerned, in particular, he hints at the possibility that some external factor related to lifestyle and culture may have affected it:

> In the 2nd and 3rd plural [...] gender distinctions were lost in sedentary varieties, but not in Bedouin varieties. Because of the sharp split between Bedouin and sedentary varieties with respect to these features, this does not seem to be an autonomous development. Perhaps there was a dominant dialect in the first Arab spread during which most sedentary varieties developed, and perhaps in this variety gender had already been lost. Otherwise the explanation for this development must lie in identical circumstances in the cities: second language acquisition processes [...], or discourse conditions in urban contexts
>
> KUSTERS 2003a: 158

Here, Kusters foreshadows the idea that will be later expanded upon by al-Sharkawi's koineization theory: the absence of F.PL forms might have been a pre-Islamic Arabian feature that was brought to the newly conquered territories, and it has been spreading from there ever since. However, he also hints at the possibility that some specific condition related to discourse in urban settings might have been responsible for this change. Kusters (2003a: 154) is well aware that—as we have repeatedly pointed out—"there are structural similarities between Arabic varieties, which cannot be due to plain borrowing", and he considers the possibility that "in sedentary communities a different use is made of language". Even if he later writes that the sociolinguistic situation of the first Islamic cities outside of Arabia represents a more credible motivation for all the changes Arabic has undergone, Kusters admits that the specific question of how F.PL forms were lost remains at least partially open.

As previously discussed, most studies of Arabic dialectology make use of the two labels "Bedouin" and "sedentary" to divide spoken varieties into two typological macro-categories. Retention of F.PL forms, in particular, has traditionally been associated with Bedouin dialects, along with a number of other traits such as a voiced reflex of ق and retention of dental fricatives. The problem with this practice is that these features often pattern quite differently from a geographical perspective. To make but a few examples, the Arabic-speaking world offers numerous examples of city dialects in which interdentals have been preserved, and where voiced realizations of ق are common currency. Con-

des rapports syntaxiques, qu'il s'agisse de notions référentielles ou modales [...] ou de notions sémantiques particulières".

versely, as we have seen, major urban dialects in which F.PL morphology is still in use are virtually unheard of. This is why, in the previous section, we have insisted on the importance of keeping the sedentary/Bedouin divide conceptually separated from the urban/non-urban one. Not only we find the former to be of limited typological efficacy, but also, traits that belong in one of these two classificatory systems have often been associated to the other, creating confusion and preventing the possibility of recognizing separate and significant patterns.

An example of how "typically Bedouin" features can differ from one another is represented by the connection that may or may not exist between them and the surrounding environment. It seems impossible, for instance, to establish some kind of causal link between the "Bedouin" interdentals, or the voiced realization of ق, and the actual lifestyle of nomadic pastoralists.[36] What in the environment in which Bedouins live, or in their culture and daily activities, could make their language more prone to contain voiced or fricative sounds? What, conversely, could make these sounds rarer in the speech of sedentary populations?[37] Is the current distribution of these traits just the result of random historical accidents? Had history gone in a different way, could we today live in a world in which the characteristic phonological traits of "Bedouin" and "sedentary" dialects were inverted?

It is obvious that these questions have no immediate answer. We are not aware of any study that has found a systematic correlation between the environment in which a language is spoken and its consonantal inventory.[38] Even if future studies were to prove the existence of similar ecolinguistic constraints, however, the fact remains that, in the Arabic-speaking world, the degree of overlap that exist between the distribution of /g/, /ṯ/, /ḏ/ and that of urbanized/non-urbanized territory is rather low. In general, no matter which traits one

36 In fact, we are not aware of any study in which this type of connection has been postulated. Obviosuly, one could argue that nomadic pastoralist live a more "isolated" life than urban dwellers, and are therefore less exposed to linguistic contact, that in turn can lead to simplification and change. Here, however, we are specifically focusing on external motivations for linguistic change *other than* contact.

37 We, along with Cadora (1992: 7), give little credit to the opinion of writers that, following the practice of medieval Arabic philologists, "attributed the cause of innovative change in Bedouin Arabic largely to the principle of least effort", postulating that Bedouin resorted to "a facile, intense, and speedy manner of articulation" because of the desert environment they lived in.

38 Everett (2013) postulates a correlation between geographical elevation and the presence of ejective sounds. His findings have however been heavily criticized, see e.g. Urban and Moran (2021).

considers, urban dialects can in no way be thought of as a typologically homogeneous category.[39] The only feature that displays a remarkably regular diffusion in urbanized territories is lack of F.PL agreement. We believe that a causal link between the absence of this specific trait and the spread of urbanization can be reasonably postulated, and in the remainder of this section we are going to discuss the evidence that supports this possibility.

In § 2.3.4 we have described in detail the agreement systems of gender-distinguishing dialects of spoken Arabic. We have labelled these Type A systems, and we have seen how they are characterized by three main features:

1) M.PL agreement is reserved for human masculine plural controllers.
2) All other controller types attract F.PL agreement in the plural.
3) All controller types (irrespective of humanness, animacy or gender) can alternatively attract F.SG agreement, depending on their level of individuation.

As can be seen, the category of controllers described in (2) is rather heterogeneous, since it includes human females, all nonhuman animates and inanimate objects. Let us break it down into semantically cohesive subgroupings.

In the previous section, we have already discussed how M.PL agreement could have easily been overextended in the case of human controllers. Since groups of mixed controllers attract M.PL agreement, the occurrence of F.PL agreement with human subjects is reserved to the statistically less common contexts in which groups of people composed only by women are being referred to. M.PL agreement, therefore, could have been extended as the standard agreement type for human plural controllers. This explanation is obviously only partial, since we lack an actual motivation because of which speakers should, at a given point in time, arbitrarily start to alter their linguistic behavior. Determining the exact reasons for this change is not easy, but there are at least two hypothesis that can be considered.

The first one, as we have seen, is that of contact, in particular imperfect acquisition of the language on the part of non-native speakers of Arabic, who

39 See the excellent treatment of urban Arabic varieties authored by Vicente (2019: 109): “Arabic urban varieties are obviously not homogeneous”, though “some patterns may be identified”, and this “independently of the rather crude dialectological classification of Bedouin versus sedentary”. An anonymous reviewer has also raised the important point that, in considering the presence of traits such as F.PL morphology, interdentals and voiceless reflexes of ق, innovations and retentions are being mixed. While we wholeheartedly agree with this caveat, our main goal here is simply to show that no other feature across the Arabic-speaking world seems to correlate with urbanization patterns except for F.PL agreement (be that feature an innovation or a retention).

overextended the statistically more common pattern. This is al-Sharkawi's simplification hypothesis. We have discussed, however, how a number of counterarguments can be raised against this explanation (§ 5.2.3). This is not to say that we find it entirely implausible, since it may actually have contributed to the process of morphological reduction in certain cases (dialects that have lost *both* the F.PL and F.SG agreement option with plural controllers would seem to be the best candidates). We do not believe, however, that this can be accepted as the only explanation for the loss of F.PL agreement with human controllers in all varieties of spoken Arabic.

The second hypothesis is that this process of loss was sociolinguistically motivated. In reviewing the literature on agreement in gender-distinguishing dialects (§ 2.3.2), we have come across two recurring patterns, namely that a) F.PL agreement tends to be lost with human controllers before it is lost with nonhuman ones, and b) F.PL agreement tends to be lost in the speech of women before it is lost in the speech of men.[40]

Point (a) may, at first sight, appear counterintuitive. After all, one could think that the distinction of the biological gender of human beings constitutes conceptually salient information, and that expressing it is one of the main functions of the gender system in any language that is endowed with one (as Corbett, 2013c, puts it, "Humans are most interested in the sex of other humans"). However, if we consider the agreement system of gender-distinguishing varieties of Arabic, we see that F.PL morphemes are rarely employed as proper markers of femininity. More often than not, in fact, they are associated to nonhumanness. It may be that a semantic shift of this type represents the first step toward loss of F.PL agreement: the associated morphological markers are reinterpreted as pure markers of nonhumanness, M.PL agreement substituting

40 On these two topics, see the works cited in § 2.3.2: Blau (1980: 181) for Bir Zeit; D'Anna (2017) for Fezzan; Dickins (2007: 561) for Khartoum; Ingham (1994: 64) for Najd; Morano (2019 and p.c.) for northern Oman; Reichmuth (1983: 201) for eastern Sudan; Ritt-Benmimoun (2017: 283) for southern Tunisia. The idea that human referents are the first to show the effects of agreement loss is consistent with the theory of Enger&Nesset (2011: 195) that linguistic change in the realm of gender tends to stem in the field of animates. As far as point (b) is concerned, two counterexamples exist in the literature, both from the Sudan area. These are Trimingham (1939: 65), already cited in § 2.3.2, and Manfredi (2016: 126), who writes that: "The majority of K[ordofanian] B[aggara] A[arabic] speakers still retain the productivity of PL.F as morphological category. Only urban speakers tend to generalize the masculine plural for marking also feminine plural. Even though, it is interesting to note that urban female speakers still exhibit a considerable use of feminine plural markers". Of course, we do not claim that these tendencies are universally valid, and it is perfectly possible that, in some cases, events have taken a different course. It seems, however, that both (a) and (b) represent widespread trends in the Arabic-speaking world.

F.PL agreement in the case of plural controllers denoting human females. F.PL agreement thus remains confined to the realm of nonhuman controllers (both animate and inanimate ones).

As to why this shift happens, and why does it appear to spread first in the speech of women, we can only speculate. It is a well-known fact that several studies in the field of sociolinguistics have claimed the speech of women to be intrinsically more innovative than that of men (Labov, 2001, is a notable example among many). Most of these studies see this pattern as connected with the fact that women often find themselves at the disadvantaged end of societal power relations. Such studies, and especially their universal tenability, have however also been subject to critique (see Schilling, 2011, for an overview of the whole topic). Something that we can say with certainty is that we have countless examples, in languages from all over the world, of linguistic gender being used to mark personal attributes that have little or nothing to do with biological sex (e.g. adulthood, marital status, belonging to/exclusion from a given social group, etc.; see Mäder and Moura, 2019, for an overview[41]). Since it is possible for social phenomena such as the ones just listed to be grammatically encoded in the structure of a language, it is easy to understand how changes in society are able to prompt alterations in grammatical structure (in the words of Aikhenvald, 2016: 185, "Changes in Linguistic Genders may accompany external changes which impact Social Genders"). There is no doubt that sedentarization can cause remarkable changes in the social structure of formerly nomadic groups, and the same is true about the inurbation of rural populations. We have no intention here to offer comments on the respective status of women and men in a Bedouin/nomadic society viz. a sedentary/urban one (we feel such questions are better left to anthropologists). It seems to us there can be little doubt, however, that such a transition can hardly come to pass without affecting social roles in general, and gender-specific social roles in particular. It is perfectly reasonable, then, to hypothesize that these social changes fueled grammatical changes. This very same process has even been documented for other languages: Aikhenvald (2016: 192) reports how in Maonan (a Tai-Kadai

41 Old Church Slavonic had a specialized marker for "nouns indicating a healthy, free, male person", (Lunt 1959: 45, cited in Janda 1999: 205). We already know that Arabic is by no means the only language in which human male referents enjoy a special morphosyntactical status, since we have discussed how a similar situation obtains in several languages of the Dravidian family. This is also true of several Slavic languages. Janda provides a thorough overview of the rise and fall of specialized masculine markers in these languages, and we can note how, where these markers are no longer operative, their decline followed the same path as in spoken Arabic, i.e. they became C.PL markers. Janda, however, does not offer any hint as to what may have originated such processes of gender loss.

language spoken in China), "women used to be counted using the numerical classifier *tɔ*, which also subsumes animals and children". Nowadays, women who have a respected social status are instead counted using the "human" (i.e. formerly masculine human) classifier, which has been extended "to subsume women of professions and ranks which they had never occupied before". We believe it is plausible that something along these lines happened in several Arabic dialects (i.e. that the former "male only" M.PL forms were extended to human females) following inurbation and sedentarization, though this topic certainly remains in need of further, inter-disciplinary research.

Let us now consider the behavior of nonhuman controllers, which, we believe, offers further support to the idea that loss of gender distinction in Arabic is connected to the process of urbanization. It is precisely with this type of controllers, as we have seen, that the real crux of the problem lies: if the disappearance of F.PL agreement with reference to human beings can be explained away as the overextension of an already more common pattern, in the case of nonhuman ones we are confronted with the fact that this type of agreement goes from relatively to extremely common in today's gender-distinguishing varieties (see sections 2.3.2 and 2.3.3 for some statistical data). If this is any indicator of how widespread this feature was in the past (and there is actually reason to believe that it could once have been even more common than it is now, see § 5.1), then linguistic simplification represents a rather weak explanation. Forms and patterns tend to be levelled out that are irregular, redundant, or statistically marginal; in contrast, what we are looking at here is a core element in the morphosyntax of the language. We are then left in need of an alternative explanation.

If we accept the idea that F.PL agreement in Arabic is first lost in relation to human referents (and this seems to be confirmed by multiple independent sources), then it follows that, in dialects where this process is operative, the use of F.PL agreement will eventually become restricted to nonhuman controllers alone.[42] All types of plural agreement, however, have to compete with

42 The special relation that F.PL agreement entertains with nonhuman controllers is further confirmed by an indirect piece of evidence, namely the paradigms of genitive markers. Some dialects exist in which these markers only possess a single plural form, historically derived from the original feminine one. This is uncommon as Arabic dialects go, since common plural forms are normally derived from the historically masculine ones. Thus, Coastal Dhofari Arabic has *mālūt* and *ḥaqqūt* (Davey 2016: 229), but not **mālīn* or **ḥaqqīn*; Gulf Arabic also has only *mālāt* (Johnstone 1967:69 and 90–91): Maciej Klimiuk (p.c. with the authors) notes how in the Syrian dialect of Hama only *šīyāt* (sg. *šīt*) appears to be attested (though this is based on a limited dataset), and in Damascus Arabic some rare occurrences of a plural *tabaʕāt* (sg. *tabaʕ*) can still be heard. Since these elements are

an alternative option, that is, F.SG agreement. Variation between plural and F.SG agreement, as we have seen, is based on individuation, itself the byproduct of a complex interaction of other factors such as animacy, quantification, concreteness, and so on. Apart from human ones, the controllers that score higher on the individuation scale are higher animates (large and/or domestic animals). Smaller animals, along with inanimate objects, tend to be perceived as scarcely individuated, and are therefore statistically more likely to attract F.SG agreement. The specific connection that seems to exist between the use of F.PL agreement and animal controllers has been remarked several times, by many independent authors, for several different dialects: see D'Anna (2017) for Fezzan; De Jong (2011: 116 and 192) for Sinai; Woidich (2006: 308) for Bʕēri Arabic; Hillelson (1935: XX) for Sudan; Manfredi (2010: 227) for Kordofanian Baggara Arabic; Rosenhouse (1984: 115) for the Bedouin dialects of northern Israel; Johnstone (1967: 165) for Qatari Arabic.[43]

Summing this up, we are left with a type of agreement which is no longer used in reference to human beings, and only rarely used in reference to inanimate objects (or, for that matters, abstract concepts). Animal controllers are thus the main preserve of F.PL agreement. This is where urbanization comes into play as a determining factor for the development of the gender and agreement system. It is obvious that, in an urban environment, the amount of contact between human beings and animal life is greatly reduced (especially in the case of larger animals). This is not to say that animals are entirely absent from the cityscape: they mostly are in the modern metropolises in which we live, but were probably more common in the cities of the past. The crucial point, however, is that frequency of contact between humans and animals decreases dramatically if compared to a rural environment; in particular, animals are very rarely encountered in large numbers within cities; herds and flocks are virtually nonexistent in the city space, their presence being confined to the

rarely, if ever, employed in reference to human beings, one can easily see how such defective paradigms could originally have come into being. This is yet another topic that would require more in-depth investigation.

43 Bettega and Leitner (2019) also show that F.PL agreement is more frequent with nonhuman animates than it is with inanimates in Khuzestani Arabic. See also Caubet, Simeone-Senelle, Vanhove (1989: 59), who report that, in the non-distinguishing dialect of Takrouna, some F.PL adjectival forms survive that possess a semantic specialization connected to domestic animals. Procházka and Gabsi (2017:249–250) demonstrate with several examples that animal controllers often trigger plural agreement in the dialect of Tunis, in particular those referred to larger animals. Since that of Tunis is a non-distinguishing variety, this would seem to reinforce the hypothesis that, even after the loss of F.PL morphology, the dynamics that govern F.SG/plural agreement variation remain largely unchanged.

very periphery of the urban areas or outside of it. Inurbation obviously causes remarkable changes in a population's employment patterns, and in particular, it renders pastoralism and cattle rearing impossible to practice. Decoupling of the human-nature relationship heavily modifies the lifestyle and habits of individual speakers as well as whole communities of speakers, and change in the social and cultural environment (and in the environment *tout court*) is reflected in language, by alteration of common and accepted linguistic practices.

In the scenario we just described, F.PL agreement has now become a marginal pattern: rarely used with inanimate controllers, rarely used with animal ones (simply because the need to refer to this very type of controllers has significantly decreased), and rarely (if ever) used with human referents. The feature we are looking at has all the characteristics of an endangered linguistic trait, since it is so rare in the input that its acquisition on the part of language learners (both new generations of speakers and L2 adult learners) now represents a high effort/low reward situation. As we have said, we are still not convinced by the explanation that connects the loss of F.PL forms to a process of imperfect language acquisition by large numbers of adult speakers, since the disappearance of F.PL forms has happened over and over again also in contexts in which linguistic contact did not occur. What we instead want to point out is that, at a certain point in time, in the history of several different dialects, F.PL agreement has probably found itself in such a precarious position that any other force that was affecting the language at that time could have brought about its final collapse. It is possible that urbanization alone was sufficient to guarantee this outcome, or it may have been a combination of urbanization plus other factors. This obviously depends on the various cases we consider, since the Arabic-speaking world is huge, and its history a very long one: in some situations, it is possible that contact with non-native populations did actually play a role.[44] This, as pointed out before, seems more likely in the case of varieties that have also lost the plural/F.SG agreement variation. It is true that, in dialects such as urban Moroccan and Maltese, we have reason to believe that loss of F.SG plural agreement was a more recent development (though this is only hypothetical); other dialects apart from these, however, exist in which the F.SG option is no longer found, and here things may have gone in a different way (consider for instance the dialects of Cilicia and Anatolia, or the Jewish dialect

44 This possibility is also recognized by Versteegh (2014: 143), traditionally one of the stronger supporters of the idea that contact has been the main source of linguistic change in Arabic dialects: "In the majority of cases, the interference that resulted from language contact may have consisted not in the emergence of new phenomena, but in the tipping of the balance towards one of two existing alternatives".

of Tripoli). It is also very likely that, in some cases, a dialect that was already on its way to losing F.PL agreement had this trend reinforced by contact with another dialect that had already gone through this process.[45]

The explanation we just proposed presents several advantages if compared to other possible hypotheses: firstly, it has less specific constrains than the one put forward by al-Sharkawi. His simplification/koineization theory required a post-conquest urban setting and/or heavy contact with non-native speakers in order to be viable, and was therefore unable to account for a number of specific cases in which F.PL morphology appears to have been lost at a later stage and without linguistic contact. Secondly, our explanation accounts for the fact that the geographical distribution of non-distinguishing dialects in the Arabic-speaking world appears to be nonrandom, i.e. it correlates with urbanization. If the cause of F.PL loss was indeed a process of internally-motivated phonological erosion, we would then have to accept that the odd overlapping of anthropized spaces and non-distinguishing dialects is an accident resulting from sheer chance. Conversely, a theory of urbanization-related syntactic loss fits nicely with the linguistic and sociolinguistic reality of the territories being considered here.

Obviously, the situation today is not so clear-cut, because not all non-distinguishing dialects are spoken in heavily urbanized areas: the reverse, however, is always true, and in most cases it is easy to imagine how these urban varieties can have affected neighboring rural dialects, spreading C.PL agreement by means of contact. In fact, the acquisition of typically urban features by nonurban dialects is such a common and well documented phenomenon in the Arab world that it is hardly worth commenting upon. Some of the works on agreement discussed in the first chapter of this book contain very detailed information about this process, in particular Herin and Al-Wer (2013) for the Jordanian dialect of Salt and Ritt-Benmimoun (2017) for the dialects of the Nifzāwa region of southern Tunisia. Both these dialects represent excellent case studies of "intermediate" varieties, in which F.PL forms are still present and employed, but where, at the same time, the process of morphological loss is incipient and clearly visible.[46]

---

45 As noted above, Herin and Al-Wer (2013: 64–66), provide a nice example of how loss of gender distinction in the 2nd person plural in the dialect of Salt, a process that was already on its way because of dynamics internal to the language, was further reinforced by contact with the more prestigious and non-distinguishing dialect of the capital Amman.

46 The opposite case, that is, the arrival of people of Bedouin descent in a settled area, seems also to offer some support to our theory. Miller (2004: 183–184), for instance, notes how, in such scenarios, Bedouinization does not normally occur at all linguistic levels, but is

Admittedly, some more complex cases exist of rural dialects in which F.PL forms have been lost and that have had little or no contact with non-distinguishing urban varieties. As an anonymous reviewer has pointed out, the most obvious examples are represented by the dialects of Anatolia and (at least some among) those of the western Maghreb. We have already remarked how these geographically "peripheral" dialects are the ones for which we believe that contact with languages other than Arabic could indeed be among the causes of morphological simplification. In general, however, it is obviously possible that additional phenomena that have not been considered here have played a role in this process. As we have already pointed out, we do not necessarily claim that urbanization was the only cause of F.PL loss across all of the Arabic-speaking world. On a macroscopic level, we believe this to be a solid explanation, but we also acknowledge the fact that, in many cases, other factors may have contributed as well, and more fine-grained analyses of different sociolinguistic settings at a micro-local level would probably yield interesting results. These, however, are beyond the scope of this chapter, and must remain the object for further studies on the topic.

At present, having discussed *what* the causes of F.PL loss in spoken Arabic may have been, we are left with the question of *how* exactly did this change came to pass. The various steps that mark the transition from a gender-distinguishing dialect to a non-distinguishing one are a topic that is worth a closer examination, and this will be the subject of the next and final section of this chapter.

5.2.5 *After the Fall: Reorganizing the System*

Over the course of this chapter, we have discussed what the causes may have been of the disappearance of F.PL agreement in a large number of Arabic dialects. We would now like to briefly address the question of *how* this phenomenon developed and spread inside the language, i.e. the actual internal dynamics through which it diffused.

One of the fundamental tenets of all disciplines that investigate diachronic change is represented by the uniformitarian principle, whose application to the field of historical linguistics has been famously argued for by William Labov. In its original formulation (Christy 1983: ix, quoted in Labov 1994: 21), the principle

restricted to phonological and lexical features. In other words, it would seem that the influx of large numbers of Bedouin speakers in an urban context is not enough to bring F.PL forms back in town, so to speak. This is probably because urban environments are inherently resistant to the circulation of F.PL forms (while nothing hinders large-scale adoption of voiced reflexes of ق, for instance).

states that "knowledge of processes that operated in the past can be inferred by observing ongoing processes in the present". If applied to the study of linguistic change, this means that dialects represent "the 'apparent past' of a language or linguistic feature, and the stages by which the historical development of a feature occurred can be discerned in contemporary dialectal variation" (Owens 2018: 208). In the second chapter of this book, we have discussed a wealth of different agreement phenomena that can be found in contemporary dialects of Arabic. We will now try to put some order into this vast sea of diatopic variation, showing how, far from being the result of pure randomness, all these differences can be accounted for as "frozen" pictures of the various steps that the Arabic language family has gone through (and is going through) in its process of loss of gender distinctions. We will start our analysis by considering some general principles of linguistic typology, and then check if the available data from Arabic dialects align with the general theory.

As far as change in gender and agreement systems is concerned, typological principles predict that:

a) "A cross-cutting grammatical distinction will arise in the typologically unmarked value before or at the same time as in the marked value, and be lost in the typologically marked category before or at the same time as in the unmarked value" (Croft 2003: 241–242). If referred to our specific case, this means that loss of gender distinction will occur in the typologically marked number (the plural) before or at the same time as in the less marked number.[47]
b) Another consequence of (a) is that gender distinction will be lost in 2nd persons before it is lost in 3rd persons, since the former are typologically more marked (Siewierska 2013).
c) Personal pronouns will lose the ability to distinguish gender before verbs, which in turn will lose it before adjectives (as Corbett, 1991: 248, states, "gender change always regularly starts from the rightmost position on the Agreement Hierarchy"; Corbett's Hierarchy has been first introduced in Chapter 2 and further discussed in Chapter 3).
d) Gender distinction will first be lost in relation to controllers that score higher on the Animacy Hierarchy (the Animacy Hierarchy has also been introduced in Chapter 2). As seen in § 3.3, Enger and Nesset (2011: 206) link this to what they call "the Relevance Constraint", stating that "Language change targets the part of the lexicon where the categories in question are most relevant for human experience". This point is connected with (b) in

47 This also results from Greenberg's universals 35 and 45.

that 2nd person markers can only be referred to the referents that score the highest on the Animacy Hierarchy (i.e. human beings).

If we look back at all the data relative to Arabic dialects that have been presented so far, we see that all the phenomena described in points (a) to (d) are well represented in the Arabic-speaking world. These principles tell us that, as far as gender and agreement are concerned, we will find the first signs of innovation in specific syntactic contexts, determined by the co-occurrence of certain controller types with certain target types. In particular, the most innovative position of all should be 2nd person plural pronouns referred to human beings (the latter specification being obviously redundant).[48]

Indeed, we have at least one case for which this has been clearly documented, namely the dialect of the town of Salt, in Jordan, whose agreement system has been investigated in the aforementioned paper by Herin and Al-Wer (2013). The two authors show how, in the realm of pronouns, the dialect of Salt is progressively adapting to the more prestigious variety of the neighboring capital Amman. While the most "innovative" speakers (mostly young and mobile individuals) make use of a pronominal system which is almost identical to that of Ammani, and while the most "conservative" speakers retain the traditionally Salti pronouns with M/F distinction, an intermediate stage is found in the speech of certain informants where gender distinction in the 2nd person plural has been neutralized, but is retained in the 3rd person plural.[49] From

48 There is one further question that could rightly be asked, and which is not covered by points (a)–(d), namely: if gender distinction in the plural was inevitably to be lost, why did M.PL forms survive, at the expense of F.PL ones, and not the other way around? We have already seen how, in the case of human referents, M.PL agreement was by far the most common option, so that this may be one of the reasons behind this preference. Another reason could be represented by the fact that M.PL forms were the clearest and most straightforward markers of plurality that the language possessed. In comparison to these, F.PL forms had two problems: 1) they were mostly used with non-human controllers, which on average score lower on the individuation scale; these forms were therefore more likely to be replaced by F.SG ones in any given sentence, something that made F.PL morphology inherently less stable; 2) semantically, F.PL forms were spread across the two realms of human and nonhuman controllers. All in all, the syntactic and semantic status of F.PL morphology was fuzzier and less clear-cut, something that probably reinforced the preference for M.PL forms as the dominant plural markers.

49 Herin and Al-Wer (2013: 65–66) note that several factors could have contributed to this particular outcome. First, the 2nd person plural feminine pronoun in Salti is characterized by an affricated /č/, which contrasts with the occlusive /k/ in the masculine, giving the doublet *ku/čin*. Since affricated sounds are being lost in Salti (again due to pressure of the capital's dialect), this may be contributing to the loss of gender distinction in these pronouns. Secondly, 2nd person plural feminine pronouns are statistically uncommon, since they are only used when the speaker is directly addressing a group consisting only

what Herin and Al-Wer write (see the example on p. 64), it would seem that, from this initial stage, loss of gender distinction first spreads to 2nd person plural verbs, and only after to the 3rd persons (both pronominal and verbal). Be that as it may, this fits well with the idea that verbal and pronominal targets lose the ability to inflect for gender before adjectives do.

We have already seen plenty of confirmation of the predictions formulated in point (c). In § 2.3.8.1, we have described in detail the behavior of adjectives in a number of non-distinguishing dialects. We have seen how, in many cases, these targets can occasionally take F.PL agreement even if this option has been lost in verbs and pronouns. This "resistance", so to speak, is probably motivated by the fact that adjectives make use of the same morphology as nouns, so that nominal F.PL markers are never really lost in the language and can occasionally resurface. However, another reason for the permanence of these forms is that adjectives are the target type that is affected last by morphological erosion. In other words, what we are currently seeing in certain dialects may be the intermediate stages of a process which has not yet come to completion. Interestingly enough, there is at least one dialect in which F.PL adjectival forms seem to have entirely disappeared, that of Cairo. Apparently, Cairene has moved faster than other varieties of Arabic along the path of F.PL loss. At the other end of the spectrum, we find dialects such as those of the Çukurova (Procházka, 2002) or that of Sukhne (Behnstedt, 1994). In these varieties, F.PL adjectival agreement is obligatory, or almost obligatory, with controllers that denote groups of women or nonhuman plurals. This tendency appears to be particularly strong in Sukhne, to the point that one may wonder if this peculiar syntactic behavior has become "frozen" in the dialect. In other words, it may be the case that Sukhne Arabic has—at a certain point in the past—reached a point of stability, in which F.PL forms are lost in verbs and pronouns, but retained in all nominals (adjectives, participles and genitive markers), and behave according to the old system (that of Type A dialects). Be that as it may, the dialects just mentioned represent clear examples of intermediate stages between Type A and Type B agreement systems. At the leftmost end of this scale, we have Sukhne-like dialects (where F.PL agreement is still mandatory in adjectives with human feminine and nonhuman controllers); then Çukurova-like dialects (where F.PL is not obligatory with these controllers, but still the preferred option, as opposed to M.PL); then Damascus-like dialects (where

of women. We have already discussed the possibility that low frequency may be one of the factors precipitating loss of F.PL agreement, and this explanation appears to be particularly relevant in the case of 2nd person plural pronouns.

M.PL forms have almost completely taken over, but occasional occurrences of F.PL adjectives can still be detected), and finally, at the rightmost end, Cairo-like dialects (whose speaker systematically reject the acceptability of F.PL adjectives).[50] It seems likely that all these slightly different agreement subsystems, besides representing the synchronic state of affairs in the dialects under consideration, could also be conceptualized as progressive steps along a diachronic continuum. Explaining why F.PL adjectives were retained in dialect X instead of dialect Y is beyond the scope of the present work, and probably beyond our current possibilities, but in general, it seems likely that all contemporary non-distinguishing dialects have followed a path of transition similar to the one just described.[51]

Summing up, F.PL forms were first lost in 2nd person pronouns. Later this distinction was extended to 2nd person verbs, and probably followed by all 3rd person forms referred to human beings. At this point, in urban environments at least, F.PL morphology had become so rare that the whole system was ready to collapse. The few surviving forms were replaced by the corresponding M.PL ones (now by far the most common plural forms in the language). It is probable that adjectival agreement survived this first period of syntactic upheaval relatively unscathed. It was only after the full transition of the verbal and pronominal sets to a C.PL system that paradigmatic pressure started to be felt. The relative frequency of F.PL adjectives started to decline, and this is where we find the majority of non-distinguishing dialects today, currently "frozen" at different stages of this process. Obviously, this apparent stillness is just an illusion, a parallax error induced by the use of the present as our vantage point. The process of loss is still in motion, and it is likely that, fifty or one hundred years from now, the picture will look rather different, with more and more dialects reaching the final, "Cairene" stage.[52]

---

50 Bahraini Arabic also appears to be leaning towards a Cairene-like status. According to Holes, the dialect has completely lost F.PL agreement, and in his whole corpus of texts only three occurrences of the adjective *ṣġērāt* 'small-F.PL' are attested. Holes suggests that the fact that this word is also used as a noun, meaning 'little children', is what allowed its survival as an acceptable (though rare) adjectival form. Interestingly, all three examples presented by Holes feature a nonhuman controller.

51 See also Ritt-Benmimoun (2017: 274), who gives several examples of this pattern in a dialect where the process of loss of F.PL forms is still ongoing. In particular, she notes how "participles often show the externally inflected form with *-āt* even when all other concordants show masculine plural agreement".

52 It is worth noting that Cairene, besides its being the only dialect in which adjectival F.PL agreement has entirely disappeared, is also the dialect for which the highest percentages of use of F.SG agreement with plural controllers have been reported. At present, it

Total loss of F.PL agreement, however, may not be the end of our story. The morphosyntactic peculiarities of several Maghrebi dialects seem to indicate that, once in motion, the process of loss of gender distinction is not easily halted. In § 2.2.4, we have provided an exhaustive list of dialects in which gender distinction has been or is being lost in 2nd persons singular.[53] These dialects are all found in the modern countries of Morocco, Algeria, Tunisia and Malta. These are some of the areas of the Arab world where linguistic contact has historically been the strongest, so it is possible that, in these cases, this is actually one of the factors that contributed to the faster simplification of the agreement system. Incidentally, the majority of dialects in which F.SG agreement with plural controllers is no longer an option are also found in these areas (especially Malta and Morocco), which further reinforces the idea that contact was indeed one of the factors at play.[54]

This last point raises the question of the applicability of the processes that we see at work in the Maghreb to the rest of the Arabic-speaking world. Is it just that Maghrebi varieties have moved faster along the path of agreement loss, and sooner or later all other non-distinguishing varieties will follow them down the same cline? Or is this situation the result of the specific sociolinguistic context of the western Maghreb, and loss of gender distinction in the rest of the Arabic varieties will remain confined to the plural forms? At present, it is hard to answer this question, beyond the obvious consideration that we do not see any indication that the singular paradigms have started to contract in any other dialect except the ones just cited. It is also unclear whether or not this process of loss will proceed further in the Maghreb, finally attacking 3rd

seems impossible to determine whether or not some relation exists between these two phenomena. Here we will limit ourselves to note how it is unsurprising that a particularly strong increase in the use of F.SG agreement with plural controllers has occurred in a non-distinguishing dialect. In distinguishing varieties, the F.PL/M.PL opposition marks semantic distinctions that are too important for these forms to be almost systematically replaced by F.SG ones. This, of course, does not explain why F.SG has become exceptionally common in Cairene, instead of any other non-distinguishing dialect, a question that warrants further research.

53 Curiously enough, in several dialects gender distinction in the 2nd person singular seems to be lost in verbs before it is lost in pronouns. This is typologically unexpected, and constitutes another topic that could deserve deeper investigation.

54 Predictably enough, in this case as well, counterexamples abound (central Asia, southern Turkey etc). As we have repeatedly stressed, linguistic contact seems to be particularly ill-suited to provide a "one-size-fits-all" explanation for changes in the agreement systems of spoken Arabic varieties. This does not mean that it couldn't have played a role in some contexts.

persons singular and *de facto* eliminating gender as a syntactic category from the language. It looks like it is only future generations of Arabists who will be able to answer these questions.

The last point that remains to be addressed is the relation that exists between loss of F.PL agreement and the possibility of F.SG agreement with plural controllers. As we have seen, in the majority of cases it seems that the disappearance of F.PL forms from the language did not affect F.SG agreement at all. While F.PL morphemes were being replaced with M.PL ones, the oscillation between plural and F.SG agreement continued undisturbed. This is still the case today in a great number of non-distinguishing dialects. We have already pointed out that the extreme resistance, over time, of this type of variation is indeed remarkable. We have also seen how the continuation of such a complex pattern speaks against the hypothesis of a simplification of the agreement system due to imperfect learning on the part of non-native speakers, with the exception of the western Maghreb and perhaps a few other cases.

In conclusion, it seems to us that the patterns of loss of F.PL agreement in spoken Arabic can be reconstructed with relative confidence. As far as future developments are concerned, conversely, it is harder to make predictions or generalizations, especially as far as the ultimate fate of the singular forms is concerned. There is only one thing that, looking at the current state of affairs in the Arab world, looks rather certain: F.PL agreement, on the whole, is in decline. There are no known cases of this feature's being borrowed by a non-distinguishing dialect via contact, while urbanization- and contact-induced loss appears to be pandemic. It seems likely that, in the not-too-distant future, feminine plural verbal and pronominal morphemes will be completely wiped out from the Arabic-speaking world, only surviving in the more formal registers of the standard language.

5.3 Summary

Some years ago, in the introduction of a special issue of the *Journal of Language Contact*, Epps, Huehnergard and Pat-El (2013: 210) wrote that a two-fold problem exists in connection to the question of contact among genetically related languages:

> On the one hand, how are we to distinguish between the outcomes of inheritance and contact; on the other, how might the dynamics of contact-induced change actually vary according to the degree of language relationship? In fact, if we trace language relationships far enough back in

time, we find that the distinction between internally and externally motivated change essentially disappears.

These have been recurring questions in our treatment of the diachrony of agreement systems in Arabic. Over the course of this chapter, we have addressed three main aspects of this topic, namely: (i) the origins of F.SG agreement with plural controllers; (ii) the loss of F.PL agreement; (iii) the loss of F.SG agreement with plural controllers.

As far as points (i) and (iii) are concerned, we have contended that they are relatively straightforward: contrary to the opinion of some scholars, the possibility of F.SG agreement with plural controllers in all Arabic dialects seems to us to represent a very old shared retention, rather than an innovation. Though it is perfectly possible that contact with Modern Standard Arabic and other spoken varieties has contributed to increase or decrease the frequency with which plural nouns attract F.SG agreement in any given dialect, this syntactic pattern has constituted one of the signature characteristics of Arabic since long before the dawn of Islam.[55] Conversely, the loss of this possibility constitutes the real innovation: since the dialects in which this has happened are spoken in areas that are very distant from each other (namely Morocco and Malta, Cilicia and Anatolia, and possibly the Jewish community of Tripoli), we cautiously suggest that this innovation happened independently in all these locations. On the reasons behind this process of syntactic loss we can only speculate, but it is possible to note that, in all these territories, Arabic was exposed to massive linguistic contact. The simplification of a complex pattern of variation between plural and F.SG agreement towards a more straightforward "plural-only" system is precisely the type of outcome that we would expect in a sociolinguistic context of this type. Since all these dialects also lack F.PL agreement (with the partial exception of Cilicia, where adjectives still preserve this option), it is reasonable to ask whether or not the two phenomena are connected. These, we believe, are the only cases in which al-Sharkawi's hypothesis of contact-induced simplification could actually constitute a viable explanation. However, the problem remains that, in the case of Malta and Morocco at least, the existing sources seem to suggest that F.SG agreement with plural controllers was more common until not so long ago; if this were true, then it could hardly represent an innovation caused by contact in the 7th and 8th centuries. In addition to this, many were the dialects in which this change did *not* occur, despite their being

55 See § 3.1 and § 3.9 for a discussion of how F.SG agreement with plural controllers could have emerged in the first place.

exposed to intensive contact (to name but a few examples, the now extinct dialects of Andalusia, and those of Tunisia and Sudan). As we have pointed out, a careful examination of the history of Arabization in all these areas could provide important hints as to why similar starting conditions resulted in rather different final outcomes. All in all, the connection between linguistic contact and loss of F.SG agreement with plural controllers remains uncertain, and the whole topic is in need of further inquiry.

In comparison to the ones just discussed, the topic of loss of F.PL agreement (point (ii) above) is more complicated. As was the case for F.SG agreement, it seems clear to us that this pattern also represents an extremely old shared retention, and that the more innovative dialects are those in which it is no longer attested. We would assume this point to be entirely uncontroversial. Controversy, on the other hand, may arise when trying to determinine when, where and why did this process of loss occur. As per the passage by Epps, Huehnergard and Pat-El quoted above, the various Arabic languages have been in contact with each other for so long that it is now very difficult to discern independent innovation from contact-induced change. However, we have tried to isolate specific cases of non-distinguishing dialects in which contact is not readily available as an explanation: these are the dialects of the metropolis of the Gulf Coast, and those of Baghdad in Iraq, Tripoli in Libya, and Khartoum in Sudan. Others could be mentioned, but these four cases are enough to prove that—if our interpretation of the data is correct—loss of F.PL agreement in Arabic needs to be understood as the result of multiple parallel innovations. We will probably never be able to compile an exact list of all the dialects in which this change emerged spontaneously, or the ones in which it was imported by means of contact (also because it is very likely that many, from both groups, have by now become extinct). However, at least some representatives for each of these two groups can be identified with relative confidence.

Another important question is when exactly did this change first appear. If we accept the multiple parallel innovations explanation as valid, then the issue is further complicated by the fact that a univocal solution to this problem does not exist (since the process has developed independently several times in several different locations). Nonetheless, an important point would be to determine whether non-distinguishing dialects already existed in pre-Islamic times or not. In the former scenario, this specific trait could have been "exported" outside of Arabia and the neighboring territories at the time of the conquests, greatly facilitating its diffusion. Standing our present knowledge, it is difficult to answer this question with any certainty. We know from historical records that, by the early 8th century, the substitution of F.PL forms with M.PL ones was already entrenched enough to make its appearance in written (though non-official) documents. Though this is a very early date, it does not necessarily constitute proof of the fact that this innovation was already circulating at the time of the revelation. The intervening century had been one of great turmoil and unrest, and when social and political structures change, language tends to respond in kind. Earlier attestations, however, exist as well. Unexpected M.PL forms appear in the Quranic texts itself, in at least three different locations. This could actually indicate that the process had already started in the early 7th century, and possibly before that. However, its diffusion at the time could have been very limited. All things considered, this question, too, remains difficult to answer with certainty.

The final question we have addressed is that of what caused loss of F.PL agreement in the first place. In this chapter, we explored several different possibilities, some internally-motivated (phonological erosion) and some external (linguistic contact and environmental change). We have found the former to be hardly viable, since too many oddities, irregularities and exceptions would need to be accounted for. A direct consequence of this is that what we are discussing is not a case of syntactic innovation induced by morphological change, but rather the other way around: an alteration in syntactic behavior (brought about by external factors) that resulted in morphological loss.

External motivations seem to possess more explanatory power. The hypothesis of contact-induced change, however, is not entirely convincing, and this for three reasons: the first one is that, as we have seen, F.PL forms were lost even in contexts in which there has been little or no contact with non-native speakers, or with other dialects that had already lost these morphemes (so that we remain in need of another explanation for these specific cases). The second reason is that, conversely, in certain cases F.PL forms have been retained in dialects which were exposed to massive linguistic contact (Central Asian varieties and several Sub-Saharan dialects being the most obvious examples). The third reason is that, in the vast majority of dialects in which F.PL agreement was lost, F.SG agreement with plural controllers lived on undisturbed. How is it possible that, in a context in which Arabic was undergoing heavy restructuring and simplification due to imperfect L2 acquisition on the part of adult learners, such a complex and variable syntactic pattern survived, while F.PL agreement (which was the normal agreement type for all plural controllers except masculine human ones) did not? We could perhaps accept this explanation in the case of those dialects that have lost both F.PL and F.SG agreement with plural controllers, but these constitute a small minority. In all other cases, we remain skeptical about this possibility.

The last hypothesis we considered is that the specific process of change we are interested in was caused by factors that are entirely extralinguistic in nature. In an elegant article about the nature of diachronic change, Owens (2018: 208) has recently reminded us that "dialects are maintained as linguistic entities by the social configurations which hold together language communities". We wholeheartedly agree with this consideration, and we would further add that, if said social configurations are disrupted, then language change may follow. We maintain that this is precisely what happened in the case of Arabic, where urbanization has represented the main disruptive element. As soon as the language started to be spoken inside urban centers of appreciable size, the need for the employment of F.PL agreement decreased dramatically. This is because F.PL agreement was already uncommon in the case of inanimate and abstract referents (which favored F.SG agreement); animal controllers, on the other hand, strongly favored the F.PL option, but were rarely referred to in the new urban environment (where pastoralism was no longer practiced, and contact with pluralities of large animals must have been uncommon). In the case of human beings, F.PL agreement was already the statistically less common option, because mixed groups of people were always referred to in the M.PL. In addition, there is evidence in the literature that suggests that female speakers tend to abandon F.PL agreement when referring to themselves or groups of other women, preferring M.PL agreement instead (though on the reasons that prompt this change in linguistic behavior we can only speculate, see § 5.2.4). All these factors together resulted in a situation in which F.PL agreement was rarely employed. It may be the case that this fact alone was sufficient to bring about its ultimate disappearance (with M.PL forms gradually taking over the few remaining contexts of use of F.PL ones). Alternatively, other elements (e.g. contact) may have delivered the fatal blow to an already moribund feature, tipping the balance towards the genderless alternative. Be that as it may, it seems evident that a very strong correlation exists in spoken Arabic between loss of F.PL agreement and urbanization. This is why we have insisted on the importance of the "Urban vs Non-Urban" distinction, as opposed to the "Bedouin vs Sedentary" one. It should be clear, by now, that the latter is not very revealing when it comes to agreement-related phenomena, and that the two should be kept distinct at all times.

After discussing the social and historical dimension of change in agreement patterns, we have focused on the typological aspect of this diachronic process. We have seen how loss of F.PL forms in spoken Arabic is consistent with the predictions of linguistic typology: change starts in the realm of animates (in particular human controllers) and moves down the animacy hierarchy; at the same time, morphological loss moves down the agreement hierarchy, starting to affect 2nd person pronominal targets, and then spreading to 2nd person verbs, then 3rd person pronouns and verbs. Adjectives are the most resistant category, because they lie at the leftmost end of the hierarchy and because they share the morphological properties of nouns, which preserve F.PL morphology. All these diachronic steps can still be discerned in contemporary dialectal variation, where we find dialects which are currently going through the various phases of this process. The dialects that have gone further along this path are those of the western Maghreb, where loss of gender distinction in the plural is complete and where morphological simplification has now begun to affect the singular forms as well, starting again with the 2nd persons of verbs and pronouns.

There is one final consideration that we would like to offer the reader before concluding our discussion. Over the course of this chapter, and the ones that preceded it, we have tried to provide answers to several questions connected to agreement in Arabic, its nature and its history. Where this has proven impossible, we have highlighted these difficulties, hoping that these open questions can constitute fertile ground for the work of other researchers in the years to come. There is one issue, however, that has never been addressed, and that perhaps represents the most fundamental of said questions. In discussing the diachrony of agreement, we have rarely ventured beyond the imaginary boundary constituted by the beginning of the Islamic Era. The incursions that have been attempted in that uncharted territory have been few and shallow. However, it is obvious that much remains to be understood about gender and agreement in Arabic (and the ancestors of Arabic) in that remote period. As far as we know, the agreement system that we have described for gender-distinguishing varieties of Arabic is unique among the Semitic languages. The question arises, then, of when and how it developed, and what its precursors looked like. Much work has been done in this sense for other language families, most notably the Indo-European one. The processes through which complex agreement systems have arisen have been explained in detail, so that we now know how these systems transform and evolve over time (see e.g. Janda, 1999, for several Slavic languages; Loporcaro, 2015, for some dialects of southern Italy; Nicolae and Scontras, 2015, for Rumenian). Nothing of the sort, however, has ever been attempted for Arabic, or the Semitic family at large. How did the peculiar three-class system that we have described in Chapter 2 come into being? Did it precede or follow the appearance of the F.SG as a marker of non-individuation? How did the two interact? At what point did this system emerged as a diversified variant from the Semitic-family tree? One would expect this specific node to be posterior to the Proto-Central-Semitic branching. If so, can this be employed as a diagnostic tool to set Arabic apart from all other Semitic languages, thus helping to solve the long-standing question of what precisely does “Arabic” means, and what specific features characterize it?

As was the case for the ones that preceded it, at the end of this chapter the reader may feel that the questions left open are more numerous than the ones for which a definitive answer has been found. We hope, however, that our readers have come across at least *some* answers while browsing through the pages of this book; we hope that the facts and considerations we have presented have been able to spark some further curiosity, leading to the refinement of previous theories, or to the envisioning of new lines or research.

From our vantage point, twenty centuries after the first inscriptions in a language identifiable as Arabic were carved in stone, we finally look back to the past. Confronted with such linguistic monuments, witnessing the slow and relentless evolution of a language that never ceases to amaze us, we choose to end this book with these verses, attributed to Labīd and first recited while the poet was facing the same desert rocks on which those inscriptions had been carved:

فَوَقَفْتُ أَسْأَلُهَا، وَكَيْفَ سُؤَالُنَا
صُمًّا خَوَالِدَ مَا يَبِينُ كَلَامُهَا

> Then I stood questioning them, and how would we question them
> Deaf and eternal rocks, whose language no one understands.

Bibliography

Abu-Absi, Samir. 1995. *Chadian Arabic*. München, Newcastle: Lincom Europa.

Abu-Haidar, Farida. 1979. *A Study of the Spoken Arabic of Baskinta*. Leiden: Brill.

Abu-Haidar, Farida. 1991. *Christian Arabic of Baghdad*. Wiesbaden: Harrassowitz.

Abu-Haidar, Farida. 2006. "Baghdad Arabic." In *Encyclopedia of Arabic Language and Linguistics*, edited by Kees Veerstegh, 1: 222–231. Leiden, Boston: Brill.

Abu-Manga, Al-Amin. 2009. "Sudan." In *Encyclopedia of Arabic Language and Linguistics*, edited by Kees Veerstegh, 4: 375–381. Leiden, Boston: Brill.

Aikhenvald, Alexandra Y. 2004. *Evidentiality*. Oxford: Oxford University Press.

Aikhenvald, Alexandra Y. 2016. *How Gender Shapes the World*. Oxford: Oxford University Press.

Aikhenvald, Alexandra Y., and Dixon, Robert Malcom Ward. 1998. "Evidentials and areal typology: A case study from Amazonia." *Language Sciences* 20, no. 3: 241–257.

Al-Jallad, Ahmad. 2015. *An Outline of the Grammar of the Safaitic Inscriptions*. Studies in Semitic Languages and Linguistics 80. Leiden, Boston: Brill.

Al-Jallad, Ahmad. 2018. "The Earliest Stages of Arabic and Its Linguistic Classification." In *The Routledge Handbook of Arabic Linguistics*, edited by Elabbas Benmamoun and Reem Bassiouney, 315–332. London, New York: Routledge.

Al-Jallad, Ahmad, and Marijn Van Putten. 2017. "The Case for Proto-Semitic and Proto-Arabic Case: a Reply to Jonathan Owens." *Romano Arabica* 17: 87–117.

Al-Jallad, Ahmad, and Karolina Jaworska. 2019. *A Dictionary of the Safaitic Inscriptions*. Leiden, Boston: Brill.

Al-Qurʔān al-Karīm Bi-r-Rasm al-ʕUṯmāni Wa-Bi-Hāmiš Tafsīr al-Ǧalālayni. 2005. Dimašq, Bayrūt: Dār Ibn Kaṯīr.

Al-Sharkawi, Muhammad. 2014. "Urbanization and the Development of Gender in the Arabic Dialects." *Journal of Arabic and Islamic Studies* 14: 87–120.

Andersen, Henning. 1973. "Abductive and Deductive Change." *Language 49, no. 4: 765–793*.

Aoun, Joseph E., Elabbas Benmamoun, and Lina Choueiri. 2010. *The Syntax of Arabic*. Cambridge Syntax Guides. Cambridge: Cambridge University Press.

Aquilina, Joseph. 1965. *Teach yourself Maltese*. London: The English Universities Press.

Aquilina, Joseph. 1973. *The Structure of Maltese: a Study in Mixed Grammar and Vocabulary*. Valletta: Royal University of Malta.

Arberry, Arthur J. 1964. *The Koran Interpreted*. Oxford: Oxford University Press.

Audring, Jenny. 2009. *Reinventing Pronoun Gender*. Utrecht: LOT.

Audring, Jenny. 2014. "Gender as a Complex Feature." *Language Sciences* 43: 5–17.

Audring, Jenny. 2016. "Calibrating complexity: How complex is a gender system?" *Language Sciences* 60: 53–68.

Axelsen, Jacob Bock, and Susanna Manrubia, S. 2014. "River density and landscape roughness are universal determinants of linguistic diversity." *Proceedings of the Royal Society B: Biological Sciences* 281, no. 1784.

Ayoub, Georgine, and Kees Versteegh, eds. 2018. *The Foundations of Arabic Linguistics III. The Development of a Tradition: Continuity and Change*. Studies in Semitic Languages and Linguistics. Leiden, Boston: Brill.

Azzam, Mostafa. 2016. *The Burdah: The Singable Translation of Busiri's Classic Poem in Praise of the Prophet*. Medina: al-Madina Institute.

Badawi, Elsaid, Michael G. Carter, and Adrian Gully. 2004. *Modern Written Arabic. A Comprehensive Grammar*. Comprehensive Grammars. London, New York: Routledge.

Badawi, Muḥammad Muṣṭafá. 1992. "The Background." In *Modern Arabic Literature*, edited by Muḥammad Muṣṭafá Badawi, 1–23. Cambridge: Cambridge University Press.

Bailey, Charles-James N. 1973. *Variation and Linguistic Theory*. Arlington, VA: Center for Applied Linguistics.

Barth, Jakob. 1894. *Die Nominalbildung in den Semitischen Sprachen*. Leipzig: Hinrichs.

Bauer, Leonhard. 1913. *Das palästinensische Arabisch: Die Dialekte des Städters und des Fellachen*. Leipzig: J.C. Hinrichs'sche Buchhandlung.

Bauer, Thomas. 1998. "Al-Muʿallaqāt." In *Encyclopedia of Arabic Literature*, edited by Julie Scott Meisami and Paul Starkey, 2:532–534. London, New York: Routledge.

Bauer, Thomas. 2010. "The Relevance of Early Arabic Poetry for Qur'anic Studies Including Observations on Kull and on Q 22:27, 26:225, and 52:31." In *The Qurʾān in Context. Historical and Literary Investigations into the Qurʾānic Milieu*, edited by Angelika Neuwirth, Nicolai Sinai, and Michael Marx, 699–733. Leiden, Boston: Brill.

Beeston, Alfred Felix Landon. 1962. *A Descriptive Grammar of Epigraphic South Arabian*. London: Luzac.

Beeston, Alfred Felix Landon. 1975. "Some Features of Modern Standard Arabic." *Journal of Semitic Studies* 20: 62.

Beeston, Alfred Felix Landon. 1984. *Sabaic Grammar*. Manchester: Journal of Semitic Studies.

Behnstedt, Peter. 1985. *Die nordjemenitischen Dialekte. 1. Atlas*. Wiesbaden: Reichert.

Behnstedt, Peter. 1987. *Die Dialekte der Gegend von Ṣaʕdah (Nord Jemen)*. Wiesbaden: Harrassowitz.

Behnstedt, Peter. 1994. *Der arabische Dialekt von Soukhne (Syrien). Teil 2: Phonologie, Morphologie, Syntax. Teil 3: Glossar*. Wiesbaden: Harrassowitz.

Behnstedt, Peter, and Aharon Geva-Kleinberger. 2019. *Atlas of the Arabic Dialects of Galilee (Israel). With Some Data for Adjacent Areas*. Leiden, Boston: Brill.

Belnap, Kirk R. 1991. "Grammatical Agreement Variation in Cairene Arabic." PhD, University of Pennsylvania.

Belnap, Kirk R. 1993. "The Meaning of Agreement Variation in Cairene Arabic." In *Perspectives on Arabic Linguistics*, edited by Mushira Eid and Clive Holes, V:97–117. Amsterdam, Philadelphia: John Benjamins Publishing Company.

Belnap, Kirk R. 1999. "A New Perspective on the History of Arabic Variation in Marking Agreement with Plural Heads." *Folia Linguistica* 33 (1–2): 169–186.

Belnap, Kirk R., and John Gee. 1994. "Classical Arabic in Contact: The Transition to near-Categorical Agreement Patterns." In *Perspectives on Arabic Linguistics*, edited by Mushira Eid, Vicente Cantarino, and Keith Walters, VI:121–149. Amsterdam, Philadelphia: John Benjamins Publishing Company.

Belnap, Kirk R., and Osama Shabaneh. 1992. "Variable Agreement and Nonhuman Plurals in Classical and Modern Standard Arabic." In *Perspectives on Arabic Linguistics*, edited by Ellen Broselow, Mushira Eid, and John McCarthy, IV:245–262. Amsterdam, Philadelphia: John Benjamins Publishing Company.

Benmamoun, Elabbas. 2000. "Agreement Asymmetries and the PF Interface." In *Research in Afroasiatic Grammar: Papers from the Third Conference on Afroasiatic Languages, Sophia-Antipolis, 1996*, edited by Jacqueline Lecarme, Jean Lowenstamm, and Ur Shlonski, 23–41. Current Issues in Linguistic Theory. Amsterdam, Philadelphia: John Benjamins Publishing Company.

Berlinches Ramos, Carmen. 2016. *El dialecto árabe de Damasco (Siria): estudio gramatical y textos*. Zaragoza: Prensas de la Universidad ed Zaragoza.

Berlinches Ramos, Carmen. 2021. "Agreement Patterns with the Nouns *nās* and *ʕālam* in Damascus Arabic". *Miscelánea de Estudios Árabes y Hebraicos, Sección Árabe-Islam* 70: 3–31.

Bernards, Monique. 2017. *Changing Traditions: Al-Mubarrad's Refutation of Sībawayh and the Subsequent Reception of the Kitāb*. Studies in Semitic Languages and Linguistics. Leiden, Boston: Brill.

Bettega, Simone. 2017. "Agreement with plural controllers in Omani Arabic: Preliminary remarks." In *Linguistic Studies in the Arabian Gulf*, edited by Simone Bettega and Fabio Gasparini, 153–174. Torino: Università di Torino.

Bettega, Simone. 2019a. "Rethinking Agreement in Spoken Arabic: The Question of Gender." *Annali, Sezione Orientale* 79: 126–156.

Bettega, Simone. 2019b. "Agreement Patterns In Omani Arabic: Sociolinguistic Conditioning and Diachronic Development." In *Arabic Between Tradition, Globalization and Superdiversity*, edited by Jan Jaap De Ruiter and Karima Ziamari, 144–163. Sheffield: Equinox Publishing.

Bettega, Simone and Bettina Leitner. 2019. "Agreement Patterns in Khuzestani Arabic." *Wiener Zeitschrift für die Kunde des Morgenlandes* 109: 9–37.

Blanc, Haim. 1964. *Communal Dialects in Baghdad*. Cambridge (MA): Harvard University Press.

Blanc, Haim. 1970. "Dual and Pseudo-Dual in the Arabic Dialects". *Language* 46, no. 1: 42–57.

Blau, Joshua. 1960. *Syntax des Palästinensischen Bauerndialektes von Bir Zeit*. Waldorf: Verlag für Orientkunde.

Borg, Alexander. 1985. *Cypriot Arabic*. Wiesbaden: Steiner.

Borg, Albert and Marie Azzopardi-Alexander. 1997. *Maltese*. London, New York: Routledge

Boris, Gilbert, 1945–1948. "Sur l'emploi des pluriels féminins dans un parler arabe moderne". *Comptes Rendus du Groupe Linguistique d'Études Chamito-Sémitiques* (GLECS) 4, 21–23.

Bosworth, Clifford Edmund. 1983. "The Persian Impact on Arabic Literature." In *Arabic Literature to the End of the Umayyad Period*, edited by Alfred Felix Landon Beeston, Thomas M. Johnstone, Robert Bertram Serjeant, and G. Rex Smith, 483–497. Cambridge: Cambridge University Press.

Boucherit, Aziza. 2002. *L'Arabe parlé à Algers. Aspects sociolinguistiques et énonciatifs*. Paris, Louvain: Éditions Peeters.

Boucherit, Aziza. 2006. "Algiers Arabic." In *Encyclopedia of Arabic Language and Linguistics*, edited by Kees Veerstegh, 1: 58–66. Leiden, Boston: Brill.

Boudelaa, Sami. 2013. "Psycholinguistics." In *The Oxford Handbook of Arabic Linguistics*, 369–392. Oxford: Oxford University Press.

Brockelmann, Carl. 1908. *Grundriss Der Vergleichenden Grammatik Der Semitischen Sprachen*. Berlin: Verlag Von Reuther and Reichard.

Brockelmann, Carl. 1913, *Grundriss Der Vergleichenden Grammatik Der Semitischen Sprachen. Vol. 2*. Berlin.

Brown, Penelope, and Stephen C. Levinson. 1987. *Politeness. Some Universals in Language Usage*. Studies in Interactional Sociolinguistics. Cambridge: Cambridge University Press.

Brustad, Kristen E. 2000. *The Syntax of Spoken Arabic*. Washington, D.C.: Georgetown University Press.

Brustad, Kristen E. 2008. "*-āt* Drink your Milks! *-āt* as an Individuation Marker in Levantine Arabic." In *Classical Arabic Humanities in Their Own Terms. Festschrift for Wolfhart Heinrichs on his 65th Birthday Presented by his Students and Colleagues*, edited by Gruendler, Beatrice, 1–19. Leiden, Boston: Brill.

Buret, M.-T. 1944. *Cours gradué d'arabe marocain*, Casablanca: Farairre.

Cachia, Pierre. 1992. "The Prose Stylists." In *Modern Arabic Literature*, edited by Muḥammad Muṣṭafá Badawī, 404–417. The Cambridge History of Arabic Literature. Cambridge: Cambridge University Press.

Cadora, Frederic J. 1992. *Bedouin, Village and Urban Arabic. An Ecolinguistic Study*. Leiden, New York, Köln: Brill.

Cantarino, Vicente. 1975. *Syntax of Modern Arabic Prose. The Expanded Sentence*. Vol. 2. Bloomington, London: Indiana University Press.

Cantineau, Jean. 1934. *Le dialecte arabe de Palmyre. I. Grammaire*. Beirut: Institut Français de Damas.

Cantineau, Jean. 1936–1937. “Etudes sur quelques parlers de nomades arabes d’Orient.” *Annales de l’Institut d’Etudes Orientales (Algiers)* 2: 1–237.

Cantineau, Jean. 1937. “Les Parlers Arabes du Département d’Alger.” *Revue Africaine* 81: 703–711.

Cantineau, Jean. 1938. “Les Parlers Arabes du Département de Constantine.” *Actes du IV. Congrès de la Fédération des Sociétés Savantes de l’Afrique du Nord II*, 849–863.

Cantineau, Jean. 1940. “Les parlers arabes du département d’Oran”. *Revue Africaine* 84: 221–231.

Cantineau, Jean. 1946. *Le parles arabes du Ḥōrân. Notions générales. Grammaire*. Paris: Klincksieck.

Carter, Michael G. 1994. “Writing the History of Arabic Grammar.” *Historiographia Linguistica* 3: 385–414.

Caubet, Dominique. 1993. *L’Arabe Marocain. Tome I. Phonologie et Morphosyntaxe*. Paris, Louvian: Édition Peeters.

Caubet, Dominique. 2008. “Moroccan Arabic.” In *Encyclopedia of Arabic Language and Linguistics*, edited by Kees Veerstegh, 3: 273–287. Leiden, Boston: Brill.

Caubet, Dominique, Marie-Claude Simeone-Senelle and Martine Vanhove. 1989. “Genre et accord dans quelques dialectes arabes”, in *Linx 21, Genre et langage. Actes du colloque tenu à Paris X-Nanterre les 14-15-16 décembre 1988*, 39–66. Paris: Université Paris X Nanterre.

Cerruti, Massimo. 2014. “C’è con soggetto plurale. La realizzazione variabile di un tratto sub-standard dell’italiano contemporaneo.” In *Lingue in contesto. Studi di linguistica e glottodidattica sulla variazione diafasica*, edited by Massimo Cerruti, Elisa Corino, and Cristina Onesti, 53–76. Alessandria: Edizioni dell’Orso.

Cesàro, Antonio. 1939. *L’arabo parlato a Tripoli*. Milano: Mondadori.

Chejne, Anwar G. 1969. *The Arabic Language. Its Role in History*. Minneapolis: University of Minnesota Press.

Chenery, Thomas. 1867. *The Assemblies of al Harîri. Translated from the Arabic, with an Introduction, and Notes, Historical and Grammatical*. Vol. 1. London, Edinburgh: Williams and Norgate

Christy, Craig. 1983. *Uniformitarianism in Linguistics*. Amsterdam and Philadelphia: John Benjamins.

Cohen, David. 1963. *Le dialecte arabe Ḥassānīya de Mauritanie*, Paris: Librairie C. Klincksieck

Comrie, Bernard. 1989. *Language Universals and Linguistic Typology. Syntax and Morphology*. Chicago: University of Chicago Press.

Corbett, Greville G. 1979. “The Agreement hierarchy.” *Journal of Linguistics* 15: 203–224.

Corbett, Greville G. 1991. *Gender*. Cambridge Textbooks in Linguistics. Cambridge: Cambridge University Press.

Corbett, Greville G. 2000. *Number*. Cambridge Textbooks in Linguistics. Cambridge: Cambridge University Press.

Corbett, Greville G. 2006. *Agreement*. Cambridge: Cambridge University Press.

Corbett, Greville G. 2013a. "Number of Genders." In *The World Atlas of Language Structures Online*, edited by Matthewe S. Dryer and Martin Haspelmath, Leipzig: Max Planck Institute for Evolutionary Anthropology.

Corbett, Greville G. 2013b. "Gender typology." In *The Expression of Gender*, edited by Greville G. Corbett, 87–130. Berlin: Mouton de Gruyter.

Corbett, Greville G. 2013c. "Sex-based and Non-sex-based Gender Systems." In *The World Atlas of Language Structures Online*, edited by Matthewe S. Dryer and Martin Haspelmath, Leipzig: Max Planck Institute for Evolutionary Anthropology.

Corriente, Federico. 1971. *Problemática de la Pluralidad en Semítico. El Plural Fracto*. Madrid: Consejo Superior de Investigaciones Cientificas. Institute «Benito Arias Montano».

Corriente, Federico. 1976. "From Old Arabic to Classical Arabic through the Pre-Islamic koine: Some Notes on the Native Grammarians' Sources, Attitudes and Goals." *Journal of Semitic Studies* 21: 62–98.

Corriente, Federico. 2008. "Drift and/or Interference as Triggers of the Evolution of Syntactical Patterns and Their Morphemic Markers: the Case of the Evolution of Old Arabic into Neo-Arabic." *Aula Orientalis* 26: 17–23.

Cowell, Mark W. 1964. *A Reference Grammar of Syrian Arabic*. Washington, D.C.: Georgetown University Press.

Croft, William. 2003. *Typology and Universals*. Cambridge: Cambridge University Press.

D'Anna, Luca. 2017. "Agreement with Plural Controllers in Fezzānī Arabic." *Folia Orientalia* 54: 101–123.

D'Anna, Luca. 2018. "Extraterritorial Varieties of Tunisian Arabic. The Dialect of Chebba Spoken in Mazara Del Vallo (Sicily)." In *Mediterranean Contaminations Middle East, North Africa, and Europe in Contact*, edited by Giuliano Mion, 47–73. Berlin: Klaus Schwarz Verlag.

D'Anna, Luca. 2020a. "Collectives in the Qur'ān Revisited: Another Possibility of Semantic Agreement." *Journal of Semitic Studies* LXV (1): 147–169.

D'Anna, Luca. 2020b. "The Influence of Verbal Semantics on Agreement Patterns in Quranic Arabic: The Role of Agenthood." *Annali, Sezione Orientale* 79 (1–2).

D'Anna, Luca. 2021. "Judeo-Arabic, Hilali Invaders and the Linguistic History of Libya." In *Dialettologia e storia: problemi e prospettive*, edited by: Giovanni Abete, Emma Milano, Rosanna Sornicola, 97–113. Palermo: Centro di Studi Filologici e Linguistici Siciliani.

D'Anna, Luca, and Adam Benkato. 2022 "Persian Syntactic Interference in Early Arabic Prose: Evidence from Agreement in Kalīla Wa-Dimna." *Journal of Language Contact*.

Dahl, Östen. 2004. *The Growth and Maintenance of Linguistic Complexity*. Amsterdam: John Benjamins

Davey, Richard J. 2016. *Coastal Dhofari Arabic. A Sketch Grammar*. Leiden, Boston: Brill.

Davies, Humphrey Taman. 1981. "17th-Century Egyptian Arabic: A Profile Of The Colloquial Material In Yūsuf Al-Širbīnī's Hazz Al-Quhūf Fī Šarḥ Qaṣīd Abī Ṣādūf." PhD, Berkeley: Univerisity of California.

De Blois, François. 1990. *Burzoy's Voyage to India and the Origin of the Book of Kalīlah Wa Dimna*. London: Royal Asiatic Society.

De Busser, Rick. 2015. "The influence of social, cultural, and natural factors on language structure: An overview." In *Language Structure and Environment. Social, Cultural, and Natural Factors*, edited by Rick De Busser and Randy J. LaPolla, 1–29. Amsterdam, Philadelphia: John Benjamins.

De Jong, Rudolf. 2009. "Sinai Arabic." In *Encyclopedia of Arabic Language and Linguistics*, edited by Kees Veerstegh, 4: 237–251. Leiden, Boston: Brill.

De Jong, Rudolf. 2011. *A Grammar of the Bedouin Dialects of Central and Southern Sinai*. Leiden, Boston: Brill.

De Pommerol, Jullien P. 1999. *Grammaire pratique de l'arabe tchadien*. Paris: Karthala.

De Vos, Lien. 2015. "Pronominal Gender Agreement: A Salience-Based Competition." In *Agreement from a Diachronic Perspective*, edited by Jurg Fleischer, Elisabeth Rieken, and Paul Widmer, 287:127–147. Trends in Linguistics Studies and Monographs. Berlin, Boston: De Gruyter Mouton.

Denz, Adolf. 1971. *Die Verbalsyntax des Neuarabischen Dialektes von Kwayriš*, Wiesbaden: Steiner.

Denz, Adolf and Dietz Otto Edzard. 1966. "Iraq-arabische Texte nach Tonbandaufnahmen aus al-Hilla, al-ʿAfač und al-Basra." *Zeitschrift der Deutschen Morgenländischen Gesellschaft* 116, no. 1: 60–96.

Di Garbo, Francesca. 2016. "Exploring grammatical complexity crosslinguistically: The case of gender." *Linguistic Discovery*, 14, no. 1: 46–85.

Di Garbo, Francesca and Yvonne Agbetsoamedo. 2016. "Non-canonical gender in African languages. A typological survey of interactions between gender and number, and between gender and evaluative morphology." In *Non-canonical Gender Systems*, edited by Jenny Audring, Greville Corbett and Sebastian Fedden. Oxford: Oxford University Press.

Dickins, James. 2007. "Khartoum Arabic." In *Encyclopedia of Arabic Language and Linguistics*, edited by Kees Veerstegh, 2: 559–571. Leiden, Boston: Brill.

Dixon, Robert Malcom Ward. 2010. *Basic Linguistic Theory. Volume 1. Methodology*. Oxford: Oxford University Press.

Doss, Madiha, and Humphrey Davies. 2013. *Al-ʕĀmmiyya al-Miṣriyya al-Maktūba*. al-Qāhira: al-Haiʔa al-Miṣriyya al-ʕĀmma li-l-Kitāb.

Drop, Hanke and Manfred Woidich. 2007. *ilBaḥariyya. Grammatik und Texte*. Wiesbaden: Harrassowitz.

Dror, Yehudit. 2013. "Adjectival Agreement in the Qurʾān." *Bulletin d'études Orientales* LXII: 51–76.

Dror, Yehudit. 2016a. "Collective Nouns in Modern Journalistic Arabic." *Bulletin of the Belgian Academy for the Study of Ancient and Oriental Languages* 5: 301–329.

Dror, Yehudit. 2016b. "Collective Nouns in the Qurʾān: Their Verbal, Adjectival and Pronominal Agreement." *Journal of Semitic Studies* 61 (1): 103–137.

Eisele, John. 2006. "Aspect." In *Encyclopedia of Arabic Language and Linguistics*, edited by Kees Veerstegh, 1: 195–201. Leiden, Boston: Brill.

Elias, David L. 2019. "Tigre of Gindaʕ." In *The Semitic Languages*, edited by John Huehnergard and Naʿama Pat-El, Second Edition, 145–174. Routledge Language Family Series. London, New York: Routledge.

Enger, Hans-Olav, and Tore Nesset. 2011. "Constraints on Diachronic Development: The Animacy Hierarchy and the Relevance Constraint." *Language Typology and Universals* 3: 193–212.

Epps, Patience, Huehnergard, John and Pat-El, Na'ama. 2013. "Introduction: Contact Among Genetically Related Languages." *Journal of Language Contact* 6: 209–219.

Erwin, Wallace M. 2004. *A Basic Course in Iraqi Arabic: with Audio MP3 Files*. Georgetown University Press: Washington, D.C.

Everett, Caleb. 2013. "Evidence for Direct Geographic Influences on Linguistic Sounds: The Case of Ejectives." *PLoS ONE* 8, no. 6.

Farrar, Frederic William. 1870. *A Brief Greek Syntax and Hints on Greek Accidence: With Some Reference to Comparative Philology, and with Illustrations from Various Modern Languages*. Third. London: Longmans, Green, and Co.

al-Farrāʔ, ʔAbū Zakariyā Yaḥyā ibn Ziyād. 1983. *Maʕānī al-Qurʔān*. Vol. 1. Bayrūt: ʕĀlam al-Kutub.

al-Farrāʔ, Abū Zakarīyāʔ Yaḥyā ibn Ziyād. 1955. *Maʕānī al-Qurʔān*. (Ed.) Muḥammad ʕAlī al-Naǧǧār. Vol. 2. al-Qāhira: al-Dār al-Miṣriyya li-l-Taʔlīf wa-l-Tarǧama.

Fassi Fehri, Abdelkader. 1988. "Agreement in Arabic, Binding and Coherence." In *Agreement in Natural Language: Approaches, Theories, Descriptions*, edited by Michael Barlow and Charles Ferguson, 107–158. Stanford CA: CSLI.

Fassi Fehri, Abdelkader. 2012. *Key Features and Parameters in Arabic Grammar*. Amsterdam, Philadelphia: J. Benjamins Pub. Co.

Fassi Fehri, Abdelkader. 2018. *Constructing Feminine to Mean*. Lanham, Boulder, New York, London: Lexington Books.

Fathi, Radwa. 2017. "Gender Exponence and Apparent Polarity in a Class of Omani Mehri Plurals." *Glossa: A Journal of General Linguistics* 2 (1): 1–22.

Féghali, Michel. 1928. *Syntaxe des parlers arabes actuels du Liban*. Paris: Geuthner.

Féghali, Michel, and Albert Cuny. 1924. *Du Genre Grammatical En Sémitique*. Paris: Librairie Orientaliste Paul Geuthner.

Fellner, Hannes A. 2014. "PIE feminine *-eh2 in Tocharian." In *Studies on the Collective and Feminine in Indo-European from a Diachronic and Typological Perspective*, edited by Sergio Neri and Roland Schuhmann, 7–21. Leiden: Brill.

Ferguson, Charles A. 1959. "Diglossia." *Word* 15: 325–340.

Ferguson, Charles A. 1976. "The Ethiopian Language Area." In *Language in Ethiopia*, edited by M. Lionel Bender, J. Donald Bowen, Robert L. Cooper, and Charles Ferguson, 63–76. London: Oxford University Press.

Ferguson, Charles A. 1989. "Grammatical Agreement in Classical Arabic and the Modern Dialects: A Response to Versteegh's Pidginization Hypothesis." *Al-ʕArabiyya* 22: 5–17.

Ferguson, Charles A., and Moukhtar Ani. 1961. *Damascus Arabic*, Washington, D.C.: Center for Applied Linguistics.

Ferrando, Ignacio. 2006. "The Plural of Paucity in Arabic and Its Actual Scope. On Two Claims by Siibawayhi and al-Farraaʾ." In *Perspectives on Arabic Linguistics XVI. Papers from the Sixteenth Annual Symposium on Arabic Linguistics, Cambridge, March 2002*, edited by Sami Boudelaa, 266:39–63. Current Issues in Linguistic Theory, IV. Amsterdam, Philadelphia: John Benjamins Publishing Company.

Fischer, Wolfdietrich. 1961. "Die Sprache der arabischen Sprachinsel in Uzbekistan". *Der Islam* 36: 232–263.

Fischer, Wolfdietrich, and Otto Jastrow. 1980. *Handbuch der Arabischen Dialekte*. Wiesbaden: Harrassowitz.

Fleischer, Jürg, Elisabeth Rieken, and Paul Widmer. 2015. "Introduction: The Diachrony of Agreement." In *Agreement from a Diachronic Perspective*, edited by Jürg Fleischer, Elisabeth Rieken, and Paul Widmer, 287:1–29. Trends in Linguistics Studies and Monographs. Berlin, Boston: De Gruyter Mouton.

Gensler, Orin D. 2011. "Morphological Typology of Semitic." In The Semitic Languages. An International Handbook, edited by Stefan Weninger, 279–302. Berlin, Boston: De Gruyter Mouton.

Gianto, Agustinus. 2000. "The 'broken' Plural Problem in Arabic and Comparative Semitic: Allomorphy and Analogy in Non-Concatenative Morphology By Robert R. Ratcliffe." *Language* 76 (1): 234–235.

Gibson, Malk. 2009. "Tunis Arabic." In *Encyclopedia of Arabic Language and Linguistics*, edited by Kees Veerstegh, 4: 563–571. Leiden, Boston: Brill.

Giolfo, Manuela E.B., and Kees Versteegh, eds. 2019. *The Foundations of Arabic Linguistics IV. The Evolution of Theory*. Studies in Semitic Languages and Linguistics. Leiden, Boston: Brill.

Grand'Henry, Jacques. 1972. *Le parler arabe de Cherchell*. Louivan-la-Neuve: Université Catholique de Louivan, Institut Orientaliste.

Grand'Henry, Jacques. 1976. *Les parlers Arabes de la région du Mzāb*. Leiden: Brill.

Grand'Henry, Jacques. 2006. "Algeria." In *Encyclopedia of Arabic Language and Linguistics*, edited by Kees Veerstegh, 1: 53–58. Leiden, Boston: Brill.

Greenberg, Joseph H. 1955. "Internal A-Plurals in Afroasiatic (Hamito-Semitic)." In *Afrikanistische Studien*, edited by Johannes Lukas, 198–204. Berlin: Akademie Verlag.

Greenberg, Joseph H. 1963. "Some Universals of Grammar with Particular Reference to the Order of Meaningful Elements." In *Universals of Language*, edited by Joseph H. Greenberg, 73–113. London: MIT Press.

Guillaume, Jean-Patrick. 2011. "Le «syndrome 'akalū-Nī l-Barāġīṯ» et Les Ambiguïtés de La Tradition Linguistique Arabe." In *A Festschrift for Nadia Anghelescu*, edited by Andrei A. Avram, Anca Focşeneanu, and George Grigore, 278–296. Bucharest: Editura Universităţii din Bucureşti.

Hallman, Peter. 2000. "The Structure of Agreement Failure in Lebanese Arabic." In *WCCFL 19: Proceedings of the 19th West Coast Conference on Formal Linguistics*, edited by Roger Billerey-Mosier and Brook Danielle Lillehaugen, 178–190. Somerville (MA): Cascadilla Press.

Hamaḏānī, Abū al-Faḍl Badīʕ al-Zamān al-. 1923. *Maqāmāt*. al-Qāhira: Ṣāḥib al-Maktaba al-ʔAzhariyya.

Hanitsch, Melanie. 2011. "Kongruenzvariation beim unbelebten Plural im Neuarabischen: Beobachtungen zum damaszenischen attributiven Adjektiv im Dialektvergleich". In *Orientalistische Studien zu Sprache und Literatur: Festgabe zum 65. Geburtstag von Werner Diem*, edited by Ulrich Marzolph, 139–152. Wiesbaden: Harrassowitz.

Harrell, Richard S. 1962. *A Short Reference Grammar of Moroccan Arabic*. Washington, D.C.: Georgetown University Press.

Hashabeiky, Forogh. 2007. "The Usage of Singular Verbs for Inanimate Plural Subjects in Persian." *Orientalia Suecana* LVI: 77–101.

Hasselbach, Rebecca. 2014a. "Agreement and the Development of Gender in Semitic (Part I)." *Zeitschrift der Deutschen Morgenländischen Gesellschaft* 164 (1): 33–64.

Hasselbach, Rebecca. 2014b. "Agreement and the Development of Gender in Semitic (Part II)." *Zeitschrift der Deutschen Morgenländischen Gesellschaft* 164 (2): 319–344.

Heath, Jeffrey. 2002. *Jewish and Muslim Dialects of Moroccan Arabic*. London, New York: RoutledgeCurtzon.

Heath, Jeffrey. 2003. *Hassaniya Arabic (Mali): Poetic and Ethnographic texts*. Wiesbaden: Harrassowitz.

Heath, Jeffrey. 2004. *Hassaniya Arabic (Mali)—English—French Dictionary*. Wiesbaden: Harrassowitz.

Henkin, Roni. 2009. "How Interdialectal Is Peripheral Oral Bedouin Poetry?" In *Egyp-*

tian, Semitic and General Grammar. Studies in Memory of H.J. Polotsky, edited by Gideon Goldenberg and Ariel Shisha-Halevy, 239–270. Jerusalem: The Israel Academy of Sciences and Humanities.

Herin, Bruno. 2010. *Le parler arabe de Salt (Jordaine). Phonologie, morphologie et éléments de syntaxe*. PhD, Bruxelles: Université Libre de Bruxelles.

Herin, Bruno, and Enam Al-Wer. 2013. "From Phonological Variation to Grammatical Change: Depalatalisation of /č/ in Salti", in Ingham of Arabia. A Collection of Articles Presented as a Tribute to the *Career of Bruce Ingham*, edited by Clive Holes and Rudolf De Jong, 55–73. Leiden, Boston: Brill.

Hetzron, Robert. 1977. *The Gunnän-Gurage Languages*. Naples: Istituto Orientale di Napoli.

Hillelson, S. 1935. *Sudan Arabic texts*. Cambridge: Cambridge University Press.

Holes, Clive. 1989. "Towards a Dialect Geography of Oman." *Bulletin of the School of Oriental and African Studies, University of London* 52, no. 3: 446–462.

Holes, Clive. 1990. *Gulf Arabic*. London: Routledge.

Holes, Clive. 1991. "Kashkasha and the fronting and affrication of the velar stops revisited: a contribution to the historical phonology of the peninsular Arabic dialects." In *Semitic Studies in Honor of Wolf Leslau*, edited by Alan S. Kaye. Wiesbaden: Harrassowitz.

Holes, Clive. 2004. *Modern Arabic: Structures, Functions, and Varieties*. Georgetown University Press.

Holes, Clive. 2007. "Gulf States." In *Encyclopedia of Arabic Language and Linguistics*, edited by Kees Veerstegh, 2: 210–216. Leiden, Boston: Brill.

Holes, Clive. 2008. "Omani Arabic." In *Encyclopedia of Arabic Language and Linguistics*, edited by Kees Veerstegh, 3: 478–491. Leiden, Boston: Brill.

Holes, Clive. 2011. "Nabaṭī Poetry, Language Of." In *Encyclopedia of Arabic Language and Linguistics*, edited by Lutz Edzard and Rudolf de Jong, Online Edition. Brill.

Holes, Clive. 2016. *Dialect, Culture, and Society in Eastern Arabia. Volume Three: Phonology, Morphology, Syntax, Style*. Leiden, Boston: Brill.

Holes, Clive. 2018. "Introduction." In *Arabic Historical Dialectology. Linguistic and Sociolinguistic Approaches*, edited by Clive Holes, 1–29. Oxford: Oxford University Press.

Hopkins, Simon. 1984. *Studies in the Grammar of Early Arabic. Based on Papyri Datable to before 300 A.H. 912 A.D.* London Oriental Series. Oxford: Oxford University Press.

Horesh, Uri. 2009. "Tense." In *Encyclopedia of Arabic Language and Linguistics*, edited by Kees Veerstegh, 3: 454–457. Leiden, Boston: Brill.

Hoyt, Frederick. 2000. "Impersonal Agreement as a Specificity Effect in Rural Palestinian Arabic", in *Perspectives on Arabic Linguistics XIII–XIV*, edited by Dilworth B. Parkinson and Elabbas Benmamoun, 111–141. Amsterdam, Philadelphia: John Benjamins Publishing Company.

Huehnergard, John. 1987. "Three Notes on Akkadian Morphology." In *"Working With No*

Data". *Semitic and Egyptian Studies Presented to Thomas O. Lambdin*, edited by David M. Golomb, 181–194. Winona Lake, Indiana: Eisenbrauns.

Huehnergard, John. 2019. "Proto-Semitic." In *The Semitic Languages*, edited by John Huehnergard and Na'ama Pat-El, Second Edition, 49–80. Routledge Language Family Series. London, New York: Routledge.

Huehnergard, John, and Aaron D. Rubin. 2011. "Phyla and Waves: Models of Classification of the Semitic Languages." In *The Semitic Languages. An International Handbook*, edited by Stefan Weninger, 36:259–279. Handbooks of Linguistics and Communication Science. Berlin, Boston: De Gruyter Mouton.

Ḥusain, S.M. 1938. *Early Arabic Odes: Chosen from the Selections of al-Mufaḍḍal Andal-Aṣma'i*. Dacca: University of Dacca.

Ibn al-Muqaffaʕ, ʕAbd Allāh. 1905. *Kitāb Kalīla wa-Dimna*, edited by Louis Cheikho. Bayrūt: Maṭbaʕat al-ʔAbāʔ al-Yasūʕiyyīn.

Ibn al-Muqaffaʕ, ʕAbd Allāh. 2014. *Kalīla wa-Dimna*, edited by ʕAbd al-Wahhāb ʕAzzām and Ṭaha Ḥusein. al-Qāhira: Hindāwī.

Ibn Kaysān, ʔAbū al-Ḥasan Muḥammad Ibn ʔAḥmad. 1975. *Al-Muwaffaqī fī-l-Naḥw*, edited by ʕAbd al-Ḥusayn al-Fatlī and Hāšim Ṭaha Šallāš. Maǧalla al-Mawrid 4, 2. Baġdād.

Ibn Mālik al-ʔAndalusī, Muḥammad Ibn ʕAbd Allāh. s.d. *Matn al-ʔAlfiyya*. Bayrūt: al-Maktaba al-Šaʕbiyya.

Ibn ʕAqīl, Bahāʔ al-Dīn ʕAbd Allāh. 1980. *Šarḥ Ibn ʕAqīl*, edited by Muḥammad Muḥy al-Dīn ʕAbd al-Ḥamīd. Vol. 2. al-Qāhira: Dār al-Turāṯ.

Ingham, Bruce. 1979. "Notes on the dialect of the Muţair in Eastern Arabia". *Zeitschrift für arabische Linguistik* 2: 23–35.

Ingham, Bruce. 1980. "Najdi Arabic Text." In *Handbuch der Arabischen Dialekte*, edite by Wolfdietrich Fischer and Otto Jastrow, 130–139. Wiesbaden: Harrassowitz.

Ingham, Bruce. 1982a. *North East Arabian Dialects*. London, New York: Routledge.

Ingham, Bruce. 1982b. "Notes on the Dialect of the Ḍhafīr of North-Eastern Arabia." *Bulletin of the School of Oriental and African Studies* 45, no. 2: 245–259.

Ingham, Bruce. 1986a. *Bedouin of Northern Arabia. Traditions of the Āl-Ḍhafīr*. London, New York, Sydney: KPI.

Ingham, Bruce. 1986b. "Notes on the Dialect of the Āl Murra of Eastern and Southern Arabia." *Bulletin of the School of Oriental and African Studies, University of London* 49, no. 2: 271–291.

Ingham, Bruce. 1994. *Najdi Arabic: Central Arabian*. Amsterdam, Philadelphia: John Benjamins Publishing Company.

Ingham, Bruce. 2006. "Afghanistan Arabic." In *Encyclopedia of Arabic Language and Linguistics*, edited by Kees Veerstegh, 1, 28–35. Leiden, Boston: Brill.

Ingham, Bruce. 2008. "Najdi Arabic." In *Encyclopedia of Arabic Language and Linguistics*, edited by Kees Veerstegh, 3, 326–334. Leiden, Boston: Brill.

Jakobson, R. 1971. "On the Rumanian Neuter" in *Selected Writings, II: World and Language*: 187–189. The Hague: Mouton.

Janda, Laura A. 1999. "Whence Virility? The Rise of a New Gender Distinction in the History of Slavic." *Slavic Gender Linguistics*, edited by Margaret H. Mills, 201–228. Amsterdam, Philadelphia: John Benjamins.

Jastrow, Otto. 2009. "A short typology of Palestinian Arabic dialects." *In Branches of the Goodly Tree: Studies in Honor of George Kanazi*, edited by Ali Ahmad Hussein, 263–267. Wiesbaden: Harassowitz.

Jayakar, Atmaram Sadashiv. 1889. "The O'mánee Dialect of Arabic." *Journal of the Royal Asiatic Society of Great Britain and Ireland*, XXI, no. 3: 649–687.

Johnson, F.E. 1893. *Al-Sabʕ al-Muʕallaqāt. The Seven Poems Suspended in the Temple at Mecca*. Bombay: Education Society's Steam Press.

Johnstone, Thomas Muir. 1967. *Eastern Arabian Dialect Studies*. London: Oxford University Press.

Kay, Paul. 1976. "Discussion of Papers by Kiparsky and Wescott." In *Origin and Evolution of Language and Speech*, edited by Stevan R. Harnard, Horst D. Steklis, and Jane Lancaster, 117–119. New York (NY): New York Academy of Sciences.

Kasher, Almog. 2018. "Early Pedagogical Grammars of Arabic." In *The Foundations of Arabic Linguistics III. The Development of a Tradition: Continuity and Change*, edited by Georgine Ayoub and Kees Versteegh, 146–167. Studies in Semitic Languages and Linguistics. Leiden, Boston: Brill.

Khan, Geoffrey. 1984. "Object Markers and Agreement Pronouns in Semitic Languages." *Bulletin of the School of Oriental and African Studies* 47 (3): 468–500.

Killean, Carolyn G. 1968. "Interesting Features of Gender-Number Concord in Modern Literary Arabic." In *Papers from the Fourth Regional Meeting Chicago Linguistic Society*, edited by Bill J. Darden, Charles-James N. Bailey, and Alice Davison, 4:40–49.

Kramer, Ruth, and Lindley Winchester. 2018. "Number and Gender Agreement in Saudi Arabic: Morphology vs. Syntax." In *Proceedings of TLS 17*, edited by Everdell et als.: 39–53.

Kurpershoek, Marcel P. 1993. "Between Ad-Dakhūl and ʿAfif: Oral Traditions of the ʿUtaybah Tribe in Central Najd." *Zeitschrift für Arabische Linguistik* 26: 28–65.

Kurpershoek, Marcel P. 1994. *Oral Poetry & Narratives from Central Arabia, Vol. 1. The Poetry of Ad-Dindān. A Bedouin Bard in Southern Najd*. Leiden: Brill.

Kurpershoek, Marcel P. 1995. *Oral Poetry and Narratives from Central Arabia. Vol. 2. Story of a Desert Knight. The Legend of Šlēwīḥ al-ʿAṭāwi and Other ʿUtaybah Heroes*. Leiden: Brill.

Kurpershoek, Marcel P. 2002. *Oral Poetry and Narratives from Central Arabia. Vol. 3. Saudi Tribal History*. Leiden: Brill.

Kurpershoek, Marcel P. 2005. *Oral Poetry and Narratives from Central Arabia. Vol. 5. Voices from the Desert. Glossary, Indices, and List of Recordings*. Leiden: Brill.

Kuryłowicz, Jerzy. 1962. *L'apophonie En Semitique*. The Hague: Mouton.

Kuryłowicz, Jerzy. 1973. *Studies in Semitic Grammar and Metrics*. London: Curzon Press.

Kusters, Wouter. 2003a. *Linguistic Complexity. The Influence of Social Change on Verbal Inflection*. Utrecht: LOT.

Kusters, Wouter. 2003b. "The Fate of Complex Languages: Classical Arabic and Old Norse in the Age of Globalisation." *Nordlyd* 31, no. 2: 275–289.

Lambdin, Thomas Oden. 1978. *Introduction to Classical Ethiopic* (*Ge'ez*). Harvard Semitic Studies. Missoula (Montana): Scholars Press.

Labov, William. 1994. *Principles of Linguistic Change, Volume 1: Internal Factors*. Oxford: Blackwell.

Labov, William. 2001. *Principles of Linguistic Change. Volume 2: Social Factors*. Malden (MA): Blackwell.

Labov, William. 2007. "Transmission and Diffusion." *Language* 83, no. 2: 344–387.

Lentin, Jérôme. 2006. "Damascus Arabic." In *Encyclopedia of Arabic Language and Linguistics*, edited by Kees Veerstegh, 1: 546–555. Leiden, Boston: Brill.

Lentin, Jérôme. 2008. "Middle Arabic." In *Encyclopedia of Arabic Language and Linguistics*, edited by Kees Veerstegh, 3: 215–224. Leiden, Boston: Brill.

Levin, Aryeh. 1989. "What Is Meant by 'akalūnī l-Barāġīṯu?" *Jerusalem Studies in Arabic and Islam* 12: 40–65.

Levinson, Stephen C. 2003. *Space in Language and Cognition. Explorations in Cognitive Diversity*. Cambridge: Cambridge University Press.

Lyons, John. 1977. *Semantics*. Vol. 2. Cambridge: Cambridge University Press.

Lyons, John. 1999. *Definiteness*. Cambridge: Cambridge University Press.

Loporcaro, Michele. 2015. "The Impact on Morphology on Change in Agreement Systems." In *Agreement from a Diachronic Perspective*, edited by Jürg Fleischer, Elisabeth Rieken and Paul Widmer, 103–126. Berlin, Boston: De Gruyter Mouton.

Loporcaro, Michele and Tania Paciaroni. 2011. "Four gender-systems in Indo-European." *Folia Linguistica* 45, no. 2: 389–434.

Loporcaro, Michele, Vincenzo Faraoni and Francesco Gardani. 2014. "The Third Gender of Old Italian." *Diachronica* 31, no. 1: 1–22.

Lunt, Horace. 1959. *Old Church Slavonic Grammar*. The Hague: Mouton.

Macdonald, Michael C.A. 2000. "Reflections on the linguistic map of pre-Islamic Arabia." *Arabian Archaeology and Epigraphy* 11: 28–72.

Mace, Ruth, and Mark Pagel. 1995. "A latitudinal gradient in the density of human languages in North America". *Proceedings of the Royal Society B: Biological Sciences*, 261, no. 1360: 117–121.

Mäder, Guilherme Ribeiro Colaço, and Heronides Moura. 2019. "Grammatical Gender and Social Relations." *ReVEL* 17, no. 16: 23–36.

Magidow, Alexander. 2013. *Towards a Sociohistorical Reconstruction of Pre-Islamic Arabic Dialect Diversity*. PhD, Austin: The University of Texas at Austin.

Magidow, Alexander. 2016. "Diachronic Dialect Classification with Demonstratives." *Al-ʔArabiyya* 49: 91–115.

Mahdi, Qasim R. 1985. *The Spoken Arabic of Baṣra, Iraq: A Descriptive Study of Phonology, Morphology and Syntax*. PhD, Exeter: Exeter University.

Manfredi, Stefano. 2010. *A Grammatical Description of Kordofanian Baggara Arabic*. PhD, Naples: University of Naples "L'Orientale".

Manfredi, Stefano. 2014. "Demonstratives in a Bedouin Arabic Dialect of Western Sudan." *Folia Orientalia* 51: 27–50.

Marçais, Philippe. 1956. *Le parler arabe de Djidjelli. Nord Constantinois, Algérie*. Paris: A. Maisonneuve.

Marçais, Philippe. 1977. *Esquisse grammatical de l'arabe maghrébin*, Paris: A. Maisonneuve.

Marçais, William. 1902. *Le dialecte arabe parlé a Tlemcen*. Paris: Ernest Leroux Editeur.

Marçais, William. 1908. *Le dialecte arabe des Ūläd Bṛāhîm de Saïda*. Paris: Champion.

Marogy, Amal E., and Kees Versteegh, eds. 2015. *The Foundations of Arabic Linguistics II. Kitāb Sībawayhi: Interpretation and Transmission*. Studies in Semitic Languages and Linguistics. Leiden, Boston: Brill.

Marogy, Amal Elesha, ed. 2012. *The Foundations of Arabic Linguistics. Sībawayhi and Early Arabic Grammatical Theory*. Studies in Semitic Languages and Linguistics. Leiden, Boston: Brill.

Marugán, Marina. 1994. "Agreement in the Andalusi Dialect: Ibn Quzmân's Azjâl." In *Actes Des Premières Journées Internationales de Dialectologie Arabe de Paris*, edited by Dominique Caubet and Martin Vanhove, 389–396. Paris: INALCO.

Mascitelli, Daniele. 2006. *L'arabo in Epoca Preislamica: Formazione Di Una Lingua*. Arabia Antica—Philological Studies 4. Roma: «L'Erma» di Bretschneider.

Maṭar, ʕAbd al-ʕAzìz. 1967. *Lahjat al-badw fī ʔiqlīm sāḥil Maryūṭ*. Cairo: Dār al-Kitāb al-ʕArabī.

McCarthy, John and Faraj Raffouli. 1965. *Spoken Arabic of Baghdad. Part Two (A). Anthology of Texts*. Beirut: Librairie Orientale.

Meißner, Bruno. 1903. *Neurabische Geschichten aus dem Iraq*. Leipzig: J.C. Hinrichs'sche Buchhandlung.

Meyer, Ronny. 2011a. "Amharic." In *The Semitic Languages. An International Handbook*, edited by Stefan Weninger, 36:1178–1212. Handbooks of Linguistics and Communication Science. Berlin, Boston: De Gruyter Mouton.

Meyer, Ronny. 2011b. "Gurage." In *The Semitic Languages. An International Handbook*, edited by Stefan Weninger, 36:1220–1257. Handbooks of Linguistics and Communication Science. Berlin, Boston: De Gruyter Mouton.

Miestamo, Matti. 2008. "Grammatical complexity in a cross-linguistic perspective". In *Language complexity: Typology, contact, change*, edited by Matti Miestamo, Kaius Sinnemäki and Fred Karlsson, 23–41. Amsterdam: John Benjamins.

Mifsud, Manuel. 2008. "Maltese". In *Encyclopedia of Arabic Language and Linguistics*, edited by Kees Veerstegh, 3: 146–159. Leiden, Boston: Brill.

Miller, Catherine. 2004. "Variation and Change in Arabic Urban Vernaculars." In *Approaches to Arabic Dialects. A Collection of Articles presented to Manfred Woidich on the Occasion of his Sixtieth Birthday*, edited by Martine Haak, Rudolf de Jong and Kees Versteegh, 177–206. Leiden, Boston: Brill.

Mitchell, Terence Frederick 1973. "Aspects of Concord Revisited, with Special Reference to Sindhi and Cairene Arabic." *Archivum Linguisticum* IV: 27–50.

Mohammad, Mohammad A. 2000. *Word Order, Agreement and Pronominalization in Standard and Palestinian Arabic.* Amsterdam, Philadelphia: John Benjamins Publishing Company.

Moore, Joslin L., et al. 2002. "The distribution of cultural and biological diversity in Africa." Proceedings of the Royal Society B: Biological Sciences 269, no. 1501: 1645–1653.

Morano, Roberta. 2019. *The Arabic Dialect Spoken in the District of al-ʕAwābī, Northern Oman*. PhD, Leeds: University of Leeds.

Moravcsik, Edith. 1978. "Agreement." In *Universals of Human Language IV: Syntax*, edited by Joseph H. Greenberg, Charles A. Ferguson and Edith A. Moravcsik, 331–374. Stanford (CA): Stanford University Press.

Moravcsik, Edith. 1988. "Agreement and Markedness". In *Agreement in Natural Language: Approaches, Theories, Descriptions*, edited by Michael Barlow and Charles A. Ferguson, 89–106. Stanford: CSLI.

Mubarrad, ʔAbū l-ʕAbbās Muḥammad ibn Yazīd al-. 1979. *Al-Muqtaḍab*. Vol. 2. al-Qāhira: Wizārat al-ʔAwqāf—al-Mağlis al-ʔAʕlā li-l-Šuʔūn al-ʔIslāmiyya—Lağnat ʔIḥyāʔ al-Turāṯ al-ʔIslāmī.

Murtonen, Aimo. 1964. *Broken Plurals, the Origin and Development of the System*. Leiden: Brill.

Nettle, Daniel. 1996. "Language diversity in West Africa: An ecological approach." *Journal of Anthropological Archaeology*, 15, no. 4: 403: 38.

Nettle, Daniel. 1998. "Explaining global patterns of language diversity." *Journal of Anthropological Archaeology*, 17, no. 4: 354–374.

Nicolae, Andreea and Gregory Scontras. 2015. "The Progression of Gender from Latin to Romanian." *Harvard Working Papers in Linguistics* 13: 81–100.

Owens, Jonathan. 1988. *The Foundations of Grammar: An Introduction to Medieval Arabic Grammatical Theory*. John Benjamins Publishing Company.

Owens, Jonathan. 1990. *Early Arabic Grammatical Theory. Heterogeneity and Standardization*. Studies in the History of the Language Sciences. Amsterdam, Philadelphia: John Benjamins Publishing Company.

Owens, Jonathan. 1993. *A Grammar of Nigerian Arabic*. Wiesbaden: Harrassowitz.

Owens, Jonathan. 2018. "Dialects (speech communities), the Apparent Past, and Grammatricalization: Towards an Understanding of the History of Arabic." In *Arabic Historical Dialectology. Linguistic and Sociolinguistic Approaches*, edite by Clive Holes, 206–256. Oxford: Oxford University Press.

Owens, Jonathan. 2021. "Deflected Agreement and Verb Singular in Arabic: A Three-Stage Historical Model." *Journal of Semitic Studies* LXVI, no. 2: 483–502.

Owens, Jonathan, and Raslan Bani-Yasin. 1984. "The Bduul dialect of Jordan". *Anthropological linguistics* 26, no. 2: 202–232.

Owens, Jonathan, and Raslan Bani-Yasin. 1987. "The Lexical Basis of Variation in Jordanian Arabic." *Linguistics* 25: 705–738.

Palva, Heikki. 2006. "Dialects: Classification." In *Encyclopedia of Arabic Language and Linguistics*, edited by Kees Veerstegh, 1: 604–613. Leiden, Boston: Brill.

Palva, Heikki. 2008. "Northwest Arabian Arabic." In *Encyclopedia of Arabic Language and Linguistics*, edited by Kees Veerstegh, 1: 400–408. Leiden, Boston: Brill.

Palva, Heikki. 2008. "Sedentary and Bedouin Dialects in Contact: Remarks on Karaki and Salṭi (Jordan)." *Journal of Arabic and Islamic Studies* 8: 53–70.

Palva, Heikki. 2009. "From Qəltu to Gilit: Diachronic Notes on Linguistic Adaptation in Muslim Baghdad Arabic". In *Arabic Dialectology. In Honour of Clive Holes on the Occasion of His Sixtieth Birthday*, edited by Rudolf de Jong and Enam Al-Wer: 17–40. Leiden & Boston: Brill.

Pat-El, Na'ama. 2017. "Drift and/or Interference as Triggers of the Evolution of Syntactical Patterns and Their Morphemic Markers: The Case of the Evolution of Old Arabic into Neo-Arabic." In *Arabic in Context. Celebrating 400 Years of Arabic at Leiden University*, edited by Ahmad al-Jallad: 441–475. Leiden: Brill.

Pereira, Christophe. 2007. "Urbanization and dialect change: the Arabic dialect of Tripoli (Libya)." In *Arabic in the City*, edited by Catherine Miller, et al.: 77–96. London and New York: Routledge.

Pereira, Christophe. 2010. *Le parler arabe de Tripoli (Libye)*. Zaragoza: Instituto de Estudios Ilamicós y del oriente próximo.

Perkins, Revere D. (1992). *Deixis, Grammar, and Culture*. Amsterdam: John Benjamins

Prendergast, William Jones. 1915. *The Maqámát of Badí' Al-Zamán Al-Hamadhání. Translated from the Arabic with an Introduction and Notes Historical and Grammatical*. London: Luzac & Co.

Procházka, Stephan. 2002. *Die arabischen Dialekte der Çukurova (Südtürkei)*. Wiesbaden: Harrassowitz.

Procházka, Stephan. 2003. "The Bedouin Arabic dialects of Urfa." In *AIDA 5th Conference Proceedings*, edited by Ignacio Ferrando and Juan Josè Sánchez Sandoval: 75–88. Cádiz: Universidad de Cádiz.

Procházka, Stephan. 2004. "Unmarked Feminine Nouns in Modern Arabic Dialects." In *Approaches to Arabic Dialects*, edited by Martine Haak, Rudolf de Jong and Kees Versteegh: 238–258. Leiden, Boston: Brill.

Procházka, Stephan. 2014. "Feminine and Masculine Plural Pronouns in Modern Arabic Dialects". In *From Tur Abdin to Hadramawt: Semitic Studies. Festschrift in Honour of Bo Isaksson on the Occasion of His Retirement*, edited by Tel Davidovich, Ablahad Lahdo and Torkel Lindquist: 129–148. Wiesbaden: Harrassowitz.

Procházka, Stephan, and Ines Gabsi. 2017. "Agreement with Plural Heads in Tunisian Arabic: The Urban North." In *Tunisian and Libyan Arabic Dialects, Common Trends, Recent Developments, Diachronic Aspects*, edited by Veronika Ritt-Benmimoun: 239–260. Zaragoza: IEIOP.

Prochazka, Theodore. 1988. *Saudi Arabian Dialects*. London, New York: Routledge.

Putten, Marijn van, and Phillip W. Stokes. 2018. "Case in the Qurʔānic Consonantal Text." *Wiener Zeitschrift für die Kunde des Morgenlandes* 108: 143–179.

Qurṭubī, ʔAbū ʕAbd Allāh Muḥammad ibn ʔAḥmad ibn ʔAbī Bakr. 2006. *Al-Ǧāmiʕ Li-ʔIḥkām al-Qurʔān Wa-l-Mubayyinu Li-Mā Taḍammana-Hu Mina-s-Sunnati Wa-ʔĀy al-Furqān*. Vol. 11. Bayrūt: Muʔassasat al-Risāla.

Rabin, Chaim. 1951. *Ancient West-Arabian*. Taylors Foreign Press.

Rahmouni, Aicha. 2015. *Storytelling in Chefchaouen Northern Morocco. An annotated Study of Oral performance with Transliterations and Translations*. Leiden, Boston: Brill.

Ratcliffe, Robert R. 1992. "The Broken Plural Problem in Arabic, Semitic and Afroasiatic: A Solution Based on the Diachronic Application of Prosodic Analysis." Doctoral Dissertation, Cambridge: Yale University.

Ratcliffe, Robert R. 1998. *The "Broken" Plural Problem in Arabic and Comparative Semitic. Allomorphy and Analogy in Non-Concatenative Morphology*. Current Issues in Linguistic Theory, IV. Amsterdam, Philadelphia: John Benjamins Publishing Company.

Raz, Shlomo. 1983. *Tigre Grammar and Texts*. Malibu: Undena Publications.

Reckendorf, Hermann. 1895. *Die syntaktischen Verhältnisse Des Arabischen*. Leiden: Brill.

Reichmuth, Stefan. 1983. *Der Arabische Dialekt der Šukriyya im Ostsudan*. Hildesheim, Zürich, New York: Georg Holms.

Reinhardt, Carl. 1984. *Ein Arabischer Dialekt gesprochen in 'Omān und Zanzibar*, Stuttgart, Berlin: Spemann.

Ritt-Benmimoun, Veronika. 2017. "Agreement with Plural Heads in Tunisian Arabic: The Bedouin South." In *Tunisian and Libyan Arabic Dialects, Common Trends, Recent Developments, Diachronic Aspects*, edited by Veronika Ritt-Benmimoun, 261–287. Zaragoza: IEIOP.

Roman, André. 1991. "De l'accord et Du Pseudo-Accord Du Féminin En Arabe." *Annales Islamologiques*, 27–56.

Rosenbach, Anette. 2008. "Animacy and Grammatical Variation—Findings from English Genitive Variation." *Lingua* 118 (2): 151–171.

Rosenhouse, Judith. 1984. *The Bedouin Arabic Dialects*. Wiesbaden: Harrassowitz.

Rosenhouse, Judith. 2007. "Jerusalem Arabic." In *Encyclopedia of Arabic Language and Linguistics*, edited by Kees Veerstegh, 2: 481–493. Leiden, Boston: Brill.

Roset, Caroline. 2018. *A Grammar of Darfur Arabic*. Utrecht: LOT.

Rossi, Ettore. 1938. "Appunti di dialettologia del Yemen." *Rivista degli Studi Orientali* 17: 230–265.

Roth, Arlette. 1979. *Esquisse grammaticale du parler arabe d'Abbéché (Tchad)*. Paris: Geuthner.

Ryding, Karin C. 2005. *A Reference Grammar of Modern Standard Arabic*. Cambridge: Cambridge University Press.

Sallam, Abdel-Moneim Mohammad. 1979. "Concordial Relations within the Noun Phrase in Educated Spoken Arabic (ESA)." *Archivum Linguisticum* X (1): 20–56.

Salonen, Erkki. 1980. *On the Arabic Spoken in Širqāt (Assur)*. Helsinki: Suomalainen Tiedeakatemia.

Salvi, Giampaolo. 2010. "L'accordo." In *Grammatica Dell'italiano Antico*, edited by Giampaolo Salvi and Lorenzo Renzi, 547–568. Bologna: Il Mulino.

Schilling, Nathalie. 2011. "Language, Gender, and Sexuality." In *The Cambridge Handbook of Sociolinguistics*, edited by Rajend Mesthrie. Cambridge: Cambridge University Press.

Schoeler, Gregor. 2010. "The Codification of the Qur'an: A Comment on the Hypotheses of Burton and Wansbrough." In *The Qur'ān in Context. Historical and Literary Investigations into the Qur'ānic Milieu*, edited by Angelika Neuwirth, Nicolai Sinai, and Michael Marx, 779–795. Texts and Studies on the Qur'ān. Leiden, Boston: Brill.

Seeger, Ulrich. 2013. "Zum Verhältnis der zentralasiatischen arabischen Dialekte." In *Nicht nur mit Engelszungen. Beiträge zur semitischen Dialektologie. Festschrift für Werner Arnold zum 60. Geburtstag*, edited by Renaud Kuty, Ulrich Seeger and Shabo Talay, 313–322. Wiesbaden: Harrassowitz.

Shawarbah, Musa. 2012. *A Grammar of Negev Arabic*. Wiesbaden: Harrassowitz.

Sībawayh, ʔAbū Bišr ʕAmr ibn ʕUṯmān ibn Qanbar. 1881. *Le Livre de Sîbawaihi: Traité de Grammaire Arabe*, edited by Hartwig Derenbourg. Vol. 1. Paris: Imprimerie Nationale

Sībawayh, ʔAbū Bišr ʕAmr ibn ʕUṯmān ibn Qanbar. 1889. *Le livre de Sîbawaihi: traité de grammaire arabe*. (Ed.) Hartwig Derenbourg. Vol. 2. Paris: Imprimerie Nationale.

Sidky, Hythem. 2020. On the Regionality of the Quranic Codices. *Journal of the International Qur'anic Studies Association* 5. 133–210.

Šidyāq, ʔAḥmad Fāris aš-. s.d. *Ġunyat al-Ṭālib Wa-Munyat al-Rāġib. Durūs fī l-Ṣarf wa-l-Naḥw wa-Ḥurūf al-Maʕānī*. Sūsa: Dār al-Maʕārif li-l-Ṭibāʕa wa-l-Našr.

Sieny, Mahmoud. 1978. *The syntax of urban Hijazi Arabic (Saudi Arabia)*. Beirut: Librairie du Liban.

Siewierska, Anna. 2013. "Gender Distinctions in Independent Personal Pronouns." In *The World Atlas of Language Structures Online*, edited by Matthew S. Dryer and Martin Haspelmath, Leipzig: Max Planck Institute for Evolutionary Anthropology.

Simeone-Senelle, Marie-Claude. 2011. "Modern South Arabian." In *The Semitic Languages. An International Handbook*, edited by Stefan Weninger, 1073–1114. Handbooks of Linguistics and Communication Science. Berlin, Boston: De Gruyter Mouton.

al-Sīrāfī, ʔAbū Saʕīd. 2008. *Šarḥ Kitāb Sībawayh*. Vol. 2. Bayrūt: Dār al-Kutub al-ʕIlmiyya.

Skjærvø, P. Oktor. 2009. "Middle West Iranian." In *The Iranian Languages*, edited by Gernot Windfuhr, 196–279. Routledge Language Family Series. New York: Routledge.

Somekh, Sasson. 1992. "The Neo-Classical Arabic Poets." In *Modern Arabic Literature*, edited by Muḥammad Muṣṭafā Badawi, 36–82. Cambridge: Cambridge University Press.

Sowayan, Saad Abdullah. 1985. *Nabati Poetry. The Oral Poetry of Arabia*. Berkeley—Los Angeles, London: University of California Press.

Sowayan, Saad Abdullah. 1992. *The Arabian Oral Historical Narrative*. Wiesbaden: Harrassowitz.

Steele, Susan. 1978. "Word order variation: a typological study." In *Universals of Human Language IV: Syntax*, edited by Joseph H. Greenberg, Charles A. Ferguson and Edith A. Moravcsik, 585–623. Stanford (CA): Stanford University Press.

Steingass, Francis. 1897. *The Assemblies of Harîrî: Student's Edition of the Arabic Text, With English Notes, Grammatical, Critical, and Historical*. London: Crosby Lockwood and Son.

Stewart, Devin. 2006. "The Maqāma." In *Arabic Literature in the Post-Classical Period*, edited by Roger Allen and Donald Sidney Richards, 145–159. Cambridge: Cambridge University Press.

Stumme, Hans. 1896. *Grammatik des tunisischen Arabisch nebst Glossar*. Leipzig: Hinrichs.

Stumme, Hans. 1904. *Maltesiche Studien: eine Sammlung prosaischer und poetischer Texte in Maltesischer Sprache nebst Erläuterungen*. Leipzig: Hinrichs.

Suchard, Benjamin D. & Jorik (F.J.) Groen. 2021. (Northwest) Semitic sg. *CVCC-, pl. *CVCaC-ū-: Broken plural or regular reflex? Bulletin of the School of Oriental and African Studies 84(1). 1–17.

al-Ṭabarī, ʔAbū Ǧaʕfar Muḥammad ibn Ǧarīr. 2001a. *Tafsīr al-Ṭabarī. Ǧāmiʕ al-Bayān ʕan Taʔwīl ʔĀy al-Qurʔān*. Vol. 13. al-Qāhira: Hiǧr.

al-Ṭabarī, ʔAbū Ǧaʕfar Muḥammad ibn Ǧarīr. 2001b. *Tafsīr al-Ṭabarī. Ǧāmiʕ al-Bayān ʕan Taʔwīl ʔĀy al-Qurʔān*. Vol. 16. al-Qāhira: Hiǧr.

al-Ṭabarī, ʔAbū Ǧaʕfar Muḥammad ibn Ǧarīr. 2001c. *Tafsīr al-Ṭabarī. Ǧāmiʕ al-Bayān ʕan Taʔwīl ʔĀy al-Qurʔān*. Vol. 1. al-Qāhira: Hiǧr.

Taine-Cheikh, Catherine. 1993. "Du sexe au genre: le feminin dans le dialecte arabe de Mauritanie." *Mas-Gellas* 5: 67–121.

Taine-Cheikh, Catherine. 2002. "A propos de l'opposition "type synthétique" Vs "type analytique" en arabe." In *Aspects of the dialects of Arabic today: proceedings of the 4th Conference of the International Arabic Dialectology Association (AIDA), Marrakesh, Apr. 1–4. 2000*, edited by Abderrahim Youssi, et al., 234–246. Rabat: Amapatril.

Taine-Cheikh, Catherine. 2007. "Ḥassāniyya Arabic." In *Encyclopedia of Arabic Language and Linguistics*, edited by Kees Veerstegh, 2: 240–250. Leiden, Boston: Brill.

Taine-Cheikh, Catherine. 2017. "La classification des parlers bédouins du Maghreb: Revisiter le classement traditionnel." In *Tunisian and Libyan Arabic Dialects, Common Trends, Recent Developments, Diachronic Aspects*, edited by Veronika Ritt-Benmimoun, 15–42. Zaragoza: IEIOP.

Talmoudi, Fathi. 1980. *The Arabic Dialect of Sūsa (Tunisia)*. Göteborg, Acta Universitatis Gothoburgensis.

Tapiéro, Norbert 1971. *Manuel d'arabe algérien moderne*, Paris: Librairie C. Klincksieck

Tosco, Mauro. 2000. "Is There an Ethiopian Language Area?" *Anthropological Linguistics* 42: 329–365.

Trimingham, Spencer J. 1946. *Sudan Colloquial Arabic*. London: Oxford University Press.

Trudgill, Peter. 2015. "Societies of Intimates and Linguistic Complexity." In *Language Structure and Environment. Social, Cultural, and Natural Factors*, edited by Rick De Busser and Randy J. LaPolla, 133–148. Amsterdam, Philadelphia: John Benjamins.

Urban, Matthias, and Steven Moran. 2021. "Altitude and the distributional typology of language structure: Ejectives and beyond". *PLoS ONE* 16, no. 2.

Van Putten, Marijn. 2019. The Grace of God' as Evidence for a Written Uthmanic Archetype: The Importance of Shared Orthographic Idiosyncrasies. *Bulletin of the School of Oriental and African Studies* 82(2). 271–288.

Van Putten, Marijn. 2022. *Quranic Arabic. From its Hijazi Origins to its Classical Reading Traditions*. Studies in Semitic Languages and Linguistics. Leiden, Boston: Brill.

Vanhove, Martine. 2009. "Yemen." In *Encyclopedia of Arabic Language and Linguistics*, edited by Kees Veerstegh, 4: 750–758. Leiden, Boston: Brill.

Vella, Francis. 1831. *Maltese grammar for the use of the English*. Leghorn: Glaucus Masi.

Versteegh, C.H.M. 1984. *Pidginization and Creolization: The Case of Arabic*. Amsterdam Studies in the Theory and History of Linguistic Science, v. 33. Amsterdam, Philadelphia: J. Benjamins.

Versteegh, Kees. 1997. *Landmarks in Linguistic Thought III. The Arabic Linguistic Tradition*. History of Linguistic Thought. London, New York: Routledge.

Versteegh, Kees. 2014. *The Arabic Language*. Second Edition. Edinburgh: Edinburgh University Press.

Vicente, Ángeles. 2019. "Dialect contact and urban dialects." In *The Routledge Handbook of Arabic Sociolinguistics*, edited by Enam Al-Wer and Uri Horesh, 106–116. London, New York: Routledge.

Villa, Massimo. 2010. "The Broken Plural in Arabic and South Semitic (Ethiopia, Eritrea, Yemen). History of the Research and Some Unsolved Questions." *Annali* 70 (Current Trends in Eritrean Studies): 135–193.

Watson, Janet C.E. 1993. *A Syntax of Ṣanʿānī Arabic*. Semitica Viva 13. Wiesbaden: Harrassowitz.

Watson, Janet C.E. 2009. "Ṣanʿānī Arabic" In *Encyclopedia of Arabic Language and Linguistics*, edited by Kees Veerstegh, 4: 106–115. Leiden, Boston: Brill.

Watson, Janet C.E. 2011. "Dialects of the Arabian Peninsula." In *The Semitic Languages an International Handbook*, edited by Stefan Weninger, 897–908. Berlin, Boston: De Gruyter Mouton.

Watson, Janet C.E. and Andrea Boom. Forthcoming. "Modern South Arabian: Appraising the language–nature relationship in Dhofar." In *Proceedings of the 47th Annual Meeting of the North Atlantic Conference on Afroasiatic Linguistics* (NACAL 47), edited by Lameen Souag and Mena Lafkioui. Villejuif: LACITO Publications.

Wilmsen, David. 1999. "*Ḥāga Tāni?* An Examination of Degendered Adjectival Agreement in Cairene Arabic." *Al-ʿArabiyya* 32: 215–234.

Woidich, Manfred. 2006a. "Bʕēri Arabic." In *Encyclopedia of Arabic Language and Linguistics*, edited by Kees Veerstegh, 1: 299–308. Leiden, Boston: Brill.

Woidich, Manfred. 2006b. *Das Kairenisch-Arabische. Eine Grammatik*. Wiesbaden: Harrassowitz.

Wormhoudt, Arthur, ed. 2002. *The Diwan of Abu Tayyib Ahmad Ibn Al-Husayn Al-Mutanabbi*. Chicago: ABC International Group.

Wright, William. 1896a. *A Grammar of the Arabic Language*. Third Edition. Vol. 2. 2 vols. Cambridge: The University Press.

Wright, William. 1896b. *A Grammar of the Arabic Language*. Third Edition. Vol. 1. 2 vols. Cambridge: The University Press.

Wurzel, Wolfgang U. 1986. "Die Wiederholte Klassifikation von Substantiven." *Zeitschrift Für Phonetik, Sprachwissenschaft Und Kommunikation* 39: 76–96.

Yāzīǧī, Nāṣīf al-. 1889. *Kitāb Nār Al-Qurā Fī Šarḥ Ǧawf al-Farā. Muxtaṣar*. Bayrūt: al-Maṭbaʕa al-ʔAdabiyya.

Yoda, Sumikazu. 2005. *The Arabic Dialect of the Jews of Tripoli (Libya). Grammar, Texts and Glossary*. Wiesbaden: Harrassowitz.

Yoseph, Jean. 2012. *Der arabische Dialekt von Mḥarde (Zentralsyrien)*. Wiesbaden: Harrassowitz.

Younes, Igor, and Bruno Herin. 2013. "Un parler bédouin du Liban Note sur le dialecte des ʿAītǧ (Wādī Xalid)." *Zeitschrift für arabische Linguistik* 58: 32–65.

Younes, Igor and Henri Bensaria. 2017. "Dialect contact in the Beqaa Valley (Eastern Lebanon)." *Romano Arabica XVII*: 131–140.

Zaǧǧāǧī, ʔAbū al-Qāsim al-. 1979. *Al-ʔĪḍāḥ Fī ʕIlal al-Naḥw*. Bayrūt: Dār al-Nafāʔis.

Zeltner, Jean-Claude, and Henri Tourneux. 1986. *L'arabe dans le bassin du Tchad: Le parler des Ulàd Eli*. Paris: Karthala

Zimmerman, Gerit. 2009. "Uzbekistan Arabic." In *Encyclopedia of Arabic Language and Linguistics*, edited by Kees Veerstegh, 4: 612–623. Leiden, Boston: Brill.

Index of Languages, Dialects, Tribes and Places

Abéché 145
Abu Dhabi 73
Abu ʕīd 68
Afakani 168
Afghanistan 77
Afroasiatic 197, 271
aǧ-Ǧirāhiyyä 68
ʕĀjmān 81
Akkadian 90, 181–185, 190, 193
Alexandria 41, 60
Al Awabi 76
Āl Murra 73, 81, 83, 132, 137
Algeria (*also* Algerian) 44, 57–58, 131
Algiers 44, 128
Amharic 191
Amman 25, 70–71, 79, 326, 342, 363, 366
Anatolia (*also* Anatolian) 132–133, 327, 362, 364, 371
Ancient South Arabian 126, 182–184, 191, 271–272
Andalusia (*also* Andalusi) 48n, 93n, 129, 158, 297, 301, 329n, 372
ʕanizah 81
Arab Gulf *see* Gulf Arabic
Arabia *see* Arabian Peninsula
Arabian Peninsula 2, 41, 56, 81, 165, 176, 178, 222, 230, 265, 270, 327, 329, 330, 338, 340, 342, 349, 355, 372
Arabic
  Classical (*also* CA) 2–4, 10–12, 29, 33, 38, 65, 153, 161–162, 166–171, 174, 188–189, 193, 195–196, 222, 233, 243–245, 250, 252, 254, 256, 260–261, 263, 270, 275, 289, 293–294, 298, 307, 310, 317, 320, 330, 334–335, 340, 347–348
  Early-Islamic 13, 28, 247–248, 250
  Educated Spoken 13, 37
  Maghrebi 41, 44, 50, 55, 57–58, 129, 131, 137, 327–329, 331–332, 343–344, 364, 369–370, 375
  Mashreqi 132
  Middle 13, 33, 196, 211, 254, 260, 262, 275, 308
  Modern Standard (*also* MSA) 1, 3–6, 9, 11–12, 16, 18, 20, 21, 29, 33, 36, 38, 46, 59, 82, 135–136, 155, 162, 166–171, 174, 199, 202, 221, 229, 238–239, 241, 247–248, 252–254, 258, 279, 289, 306, 318, 325–328, 334–335, 330, 347, 371
  Neo- 24, 262
  Old 1–2, 6, 12, 137, 166, 245, 264
  pre-Islamic 153, 162–163, 178, 181, 194–195, 197, 215, 223, 225, 229, 238, 241, 254, 263, 275, 330
  Proto- 78, 193
  Written 9, 10, 12–13, 16, 33–42, 52, 118, 147, 157, 166, 171–172, 178, 222, 223, 235, 240, 243, 245, 251–254, 271, 274–275, 277, 301, 330, 337, 348
ʕājmān 81, 83
ʕarab Xalde 68
ʕaramša 68
Arawakan 61
ʔarbaʕ 58
Asir 47
Assyrian 181, 185
ʕatīǧ 68
ʕawāzim 81
ʕazāzmih 60

Baggara 47, 50, 64, 361
Baghdad 336, 340–343, 351, 372
  Christian 128, 341
  Jewish 341
el-Bahariya 131
Bahrain (*also* Bahraini) 26, 92, 99, 102, 106, 120–121, 129, 148, 342, 368
Bani Abādil 46
Bani Xarūṣ 75, 78
Bani Minabbih 46
Bantu 61
Baskinta 132
Basra 71
Bdūl 69, 79
Beqaa Valley 68
Beirut 41, 68, 128
Benghazi
  Jewish 130
Bʕēri 62, 79, 361
Bir Zeit 66–67, 78, 358
Borkou-Ennedi-Tibesti 62
Bugūm 81

Bukhara (*also* Bukhari) 77–79
Buraimi 73

Cairo (*also* Cairene) 9, 12, 17–18, 22, 24, 41, 47–48, 50–51, 76, 88, 92–94, 96–97, 105–106, 108–110, 120–121, 128–129, 131, 135–136, 141, 150, 153, 233, 236, 252, 256, 336, 367–369
Cameroon 62–64
Casablanca 44, 129
Caucasian 115, 168
Chad (*also* Chadian) 62–64, 79, 131, 145
Chadic 97
Chebba 131
Chefchaouen 151
Cherchell 44
China 360
Cilicia 133, 327, 362, 371
Collo 44
Coptic 90
Çukurova 132–133, 140–141, 367
Cyprus 131

Ḏālaʕ 47
Damascus 9, 23, 25, 41–43, 46, 93, 95–96, 99, 128–129, 139, 141, 151, 319, 360, 367
Darfur 44, 144–145, 174, 343
Dawāsir 73, 81–82
Ḍhafīri 81, 83
Dhayra 68
Dhofar (*also* Dhofari) 47–48, 76, 78, 360
Dravidian 115–116, 168, 359
Dubai 73
Dyirbal 127

Egypt (*also* Egyptian) 41, 60–62, 131, 135–136, 233–234, 262, 326
El Milia 44
English 90, 108, 169

Faya 62
Fes 44, 129
Fezzan (*also* Fezzani) 59–51, 79, 98, 140, 150, 212, 226, 327, 358, 361
Finnish 90
French 90, 116, 170

Galilee 65
Gelet 341
German 147, 170
Geʕez 184, 190–193, 272
Ghaṭān 81
Gindaʕ 191
Gleyṭāt 68
Greek 213, 241–243, 249, 297
Gulf Arabic 48, 73–74, 76, 129, 137, 336, 338, 340, 342, 351–352, 360, 372
Gurage 191

Ḥafar 45, 145
Hama 360
Ḥarb 81
al-Ḥasa 72
Ḥassāniyya 45, 58, 141–144, 174, 320
Hebrew 126, 182, 193
Hijaz 72–73, 81, 129, 346, 350
Hilali
  pre- 44, 343–344
Horan 64, 70
Hōš an-Nibi 68
Hrūk 68

ʕīdīn 68
Inari Sami 97
Indo-European 3, 115, 291, 375
ʔIqlīm Sāḥil Maryūṭ 60
Iran 76–77, 80
Iraq (*also* Iraqi) 71–72
Israel 65–66, 361
Italy (*also* Italian) 3, 31, 115–116, 147, 170, 375

Jedda 129
Jerusalem 41, 66, 128
Jijel 128
Jordan (*also* Jordanian) 79, 325–326, 363

Kannada 116
Khartoum 63–64, 336, 340, 342–344, 351, 358, 372
Khorasan 76–77
Khuzestan (*also* Khuzestani) 76–77, 83, 92–93, 95–97, 106, 110, 116, 119, 161, 361
Kolami 116
Kordofan *see* Baggara
Kuwait (*also* Kuwaiti) 24, 50, 342
Kwayriš 71

Lahej 47
Lak 115
Latin 90
Lebanon (*also* Lebanese) 68, 132
Levant 41, 69–70, 339
Libya (*also* Libyan) 59–61, 130, 150, 327, 344
Lokono 61
Luxor 62
Lwāys 68

Maghreb *see* Arabic, Maghrebi
Maiduguri 63, 79
Mali 141
Malta (*also* Maltese) 45, 130, 133, 135, 327–329, 331, 362, 369
Maonan 359
Marāzīg 16
Mashreq *see* Arabic, Mashreqi
im-Maṭṭah 46
Mauritania 141
Mecca 129
Medina 129
Mesopotamia 78
Mharde 68
Miya 97
Modern South Arabian 181–183, 186, 191, 271–272
Morocco (*also* Moroccan) 44, 129–130, 135, 139, 152, 326
Muscat 352
Muṭair 81
Mzāb 131

Najd (*also* Najdi) 39–42, 45, 72–73, 78, 81–105, 113, 116, 119, 151, 163–165, 264–271, 276, 287, 331, 340, 342, 347, 350
Najrān 81
N'Djamena 62
Negev 50, 61, 65
Nʕēm 68
Nifzāwa 26, 58, 363
Niger-Congo 168
Nigeria (*also* Nigerian) 36, 50–51, 62–64

Old Church Slavonic 359
Oman (*also* Omani) 39, 46, 74–77, 93, 95, 103–104, 106, 119, 150, 352
Omdurman 63
Oran 44

Pahlavi 235, 238, 241–243, 249
Palestine (*also* Palestinian) 20, 53, 65–66, 78, 101, 147, 148–150, 326
Palmyra 69
Persian 235, 241–245, 249, 274, 288–289, 296, 298, 322
Petra 69

Qaṣīm 81
Qatar (*also* Qatari) 73, 342, 361
Qeltu 341
Quechua 339

Rabat 44, 129
Ramallah 66–67
Rašāyidah 81
Riyadh 73
Romance 334
Romanian 115–116, 170
Russian 3, 72, 147, 291

Saïda 57
Salt 70, 78–79, 88, 104, 120, 326, 342, 363, 366
Sanaa (*also* Sanaani) 39, 46, 51, 61, 74, 78, 121, 158, 326, 352, 336
Saudi Arabia 72
Šāwi 69
Scandinavian 339
Serbo-Croatian 147
Setswana 61
Sinai 46, 60–62, 79, 145, 265, 361
Širqāṭ 71
Semitic 14–15, 24, 28, 50, 126–127, 180–193, 197–198, 271–272, 303, 329, 375
  Central 178, 181–182, 186, 190, 197, 244, 271–272, 375
  East 181, 190, 192, 213
  Northwest 181–182, 184, 190, 192, 213, 249, 271–272
  Proto- 14, 180–186, 189, 192–193, 271
  South 181, 183–184, 197, 271
  West 181–182, 189–190, 193, 271–272, 329
Setswana 61
Šammar (*also* Shammar) 81–83, 340
Slavic 359, 375
Souf 57
Spanish 3, 147
Southern Dutch 159, 200–201

Subaiʕ 81
Suhūl 81
Sudan (*also* Sudanese) 63, 336, 342–343, 358, 361, 372
Šukriyya 64
Swahili 339
Syriac 241, 243, 249
Syria (*also* Syrian) 45, 68–69, 95, 132, 141, 360

Taherl 44
Tai-Kadai 359
Takrouna 140, 361
Tamil 115–116, 168, 170
Ṭayyibt əl-ʔImām 45, 145
Telugu 115–116
Tetouan 46, 326
Tigre 190–191, 272
Tlemcen 44
Tocharian 115
Tripoli (Libya) 59, 129, 130, 133, 327, 336, 340, 343–344, 351, 363, 372
  Jewish 130, 133, 327, 344, 362, 371
Tunis 26, 44, 92, 121, 128, 140, 327–328, 361
Tunisia (*also* Tunisian) 26, 95, 96, 99, 102–103, 118, 131, 158, 226, 327
Turkey (Arabic dialects of) 68–69, 132–133, 328, 369
Turkish 97

Ūlad Brāhim 57
Ulād Eli 62, 79
United Arab Emirates 73, 342
Uralic 97
ʕUtaibah 81
Uzbekistan 77–80

Wādī Xālid 68
West Chadic 97

Yāfiʕ 47
Yemen (*also* Yemeni) 46–47, 74, 145, 350

Zreyqāt 68

General Index

Abstractness (*also* Abstract) 14–15, 22, 24n, 25, 59, 72, 98–103, 116, 118, 122, 126, 132, 192–193, 374
Agent 214–215, 226n
Agenthood 159–161, 180, 291
Agreement
  Class 18n24, 29, 31–33, 37, 112–118, 122, 133, 168, 172, 186, 218, 286, 334
  Complete 4–5, 7
  Condition 2n3, 3, 32, 52, 87, 93n, 101, 108–109, 125, 146–147, 152, 163–165, 173, 196, 212–216
  Domain 32, 51, 81, 105–107, 124, 125n, 199, 243–244, 264, 281
  Feature 2, 5, 24, 30–33, 118n, 124
  Hierarchy 67n44, 107, 109, 156–157, 160, 176, 193, 196, 201–208, 244, 250, 253, 263–264, 271, 273, 275–276, 365, 374
  Impersonal 53, 149–150
  Mismatch 103n, 147, 150n, 154n133, 158, 180
  Mixed 19, 85, 95n, 106
  Natural 3n6, 8
  Neutralization 52–53, 105, 148–149, 152
  Semantic 107n, 108–109, 180, 186, 202, 205, 217–219, 221–222, 228, 244–245, 249, 263–264, 273, 275, 303, 314
  Strict/Deflected 3, 6–7, 21, 24, 26–27, 59, 99, 102, 105, 109, 121, 135, 140n116, 266, 327
ʔakalū-ni l-barāġīṯu 4n, 13, 163, 252, 277–278, 309n51
Anaphoric pronoun 32n4, 110n, 156, 244
Animacy hierarchy 76, 97, 101, 140, 203–209, 212, 241, 253, 272–274, 289, 323, 365–366, 374
Animal 26, 57, 60–62, 64, 66, 70, 73, 75–77, 94, 97–98, 116, 128n92, 131–132, 140, 145, 155–156, 169, 188n15, 208, 210, 212, 214, 236–243, 272, 274, 283, 286, 288–291, 360–362
Anthropization 50, 354
Archaism (*also* Archaic) 178n, 182, 194, 211, 246, 255, 266, 275, 281
Asymmetry (*also* Asymmetric) 29–30

Backformation 45n17
Basran school 280, 288, 295, 306, 323
Bedouin 6n11, 55–57, 78–79, 137, 172, 341–344, 346, 355–357, 359, 363n46
Biodiversity 353
Biology (*also* Biological) 11, 17, 21–22, 30, 49, 52, 111–112, 116, 123, 126, 133–135, 144, 162, 167, 187n14, 190n19, 205, 239, 248, 281, 317, 322, 358–359
Borrowing 135n112, 233–234, 242, 255, 265, 270, 274, 338n12, 341–342, 349, 350n30

Canonicity (*also* Canonical) 32, 55, 106–108, 124–125, 146–147, 176
Complexity 48, 54, 123–125, 127, 133, 173–174, 338–339, 353–354
Concreteness (*also* Concrete) 22, 24–25, 59, 75, 81, 96–101, 103–104, 109, 118, 122, 126, 132, 146, 159, 326, 361
Conservativeness (*also* Conservative) 6n11, 9, 70n47, 132, 137n, 160n140, 161, 191, 203, 205, 216, 223, 234, 237–238, 240, 244, 258n75, 263, 281, 330n7, 340, 366
Contact 26, 56, 71, 79–80, 144, 171, 182, 222–223, 241, 245, 325–328, 330, 332–333, 336–346, 349–352, 356–357, 361–364, 369–374
Controller(s)
  Chain of 59, 70, 91, 94, 99, 106, 109, 147, 160, 210, 318, 327, 338
  Conjoined *see* Controller(s), Chain of
  Gender 115, 117, 133, 169–170, 172, 312n59, 317
  Type 11, 61, 76, 90–91, 94, 108n82, 109, 111, 128, 135–136, 147, 242, 319, 357, 360, 362, 366
Countability 60–61, 63–64, 90, 201, 295
Covariance 30

Defective 18, 361
Definiteness (*also* Definite) 24, 30, 52–53, 81, 101, 103–104, 149–150, 159, 214–216, 343n21

Demonstrative 33n5, 37–38, 41, 43, 45–47, 58, 61–62, 68, 72, 76, 110n, 112, 118n, 127, 136, 141, 145–146, 151, 156, 293n23, 294n26, 354n34
Diachrony (*also* Diachronic) 1, 12, 46n19, 76, 79–80, 83, 111n, 138, 141, 153, 157n, 176, 178, 181, 184, 197, 204–207, 210, 225, 227, 253, 263, 271, 287, 301, 310, 321, 325, 337, 339, 345–346, 364, 368, 371, 374–375
Dialogue 83, 102, 138
Direct speech 98
Distance between target and controller 12, 22, 73n49, 81, 86, 89, 105–107, 109, 122, 146n118, 264
Dual 10, 15n20, 16–17, 30, 35, 39, 41–42, 50n25, 58, 63, 66, 77, 82n58, 91, 93–94, 99–100, 123, 129, 131, 134n110, 162–163, 165, 167–168, 172, 260, 338, 340, 348, 354

Early-Islamic 2n2, 28, 109n, 122n, 176, 178n, 247–248
Economy *see* Principle of Economy
Enumeration (*also* Enumerated) 5, 17, 19, 23, 92–94, 106
see also Numeral, Quantification
Epigraphy (*also* Epigraphic) 2n2, 3, 33n5, 153n129, 155, 165, 179, 185, 188, 194, 253
Erosion *see* Linguistic erosion

Female speakers 65, 358, 374
see also Women
Full agreement 53, 101, 149
Fusional 33

Gender
Assignment 30–31, 116, 125, 134, 143, 168n, 172–173, 190–191
see also Recategorization
Covert/Overt 30, 117–118, 134, 143, 172–174, 169n
Inquorate 29
of the controller *see* Controller gender
of the target *see* Target gender
Unmarked 21, 30n, 35–36, 39, 45, 48–50, 52, 142
Generality (*also* Generic) 20n27, 23n31, 22, 24, 59, 99, 104, 126, 226, 246, 266
Generativism (*also* Generative) 12, 13n17, 18n23, 27n38, 73n48, 149
Genitive 47, 99, 103, 125n98, 141, 360n, 367
Genius 340
Grammarian 1n1, 2n2, 4n7, 14n19, 15, 36n8, 166, 167n148, 186, 195, 222, 231, 277–278, 280–281, 283, 288–289, 295–296, 298, 302, 307–308, 313, 321–323
Grammaticalization (*also* Grammaticalized) 48, 87n, 96, 99, 204

Habitual 59, 102–103
Humanness 6, 12, 59–60, 91, 96, 111, 122, 160, 167, 191, 202–203, 248–249, 254, 262, 307–308, 357

ʔimāla 341
Indefiniteness (*also* Indefinite) *see* Definite
Individuality 59, 122, 187, 238n
Individuation hierarchy 88, 97n71, 150, 221
Inflectional class 31n, 333
Information 4, 29–30, 105, 116n90, 122, 185, 191, 199–204, 264, 271–272, 354, 358
Innovation (*also* Innovative) 4, 6n11, 9, 14, 25–26, 45, 58, 65, 71, 79, 80, 137n, 142, 145, 155–156, 161, 174, 176, 180–183, 186, 188–191, 193, 196, 198–200, 203–208, 212, 226, 241, 243–244, 263, 267, 271, 273, 287, 291, 298, 301, 311, 325–326, 329–332, 345, 350–351, 354n35, 356n37, 357n, 359, 366, 371–373
Interference 8, 59, 105, 196n, 249, 260–262, 288, 362
Irrational 8, 11–12, 62, 283, 289–290, 310, 312, 316, 319, 321
Irregular 18n24, 48, 51–52, 110, 168n, 347, 360

Kufan School 280, 292, 294, 305–306, 309, 322

Landscape 59, 99, 206, 353
Language acquisition 12, 227, 250–251, 274, 327n2, 337, 355, 357, 362, 363, 373
Linguistic
Erosion 26n36, 44, 140, 145, 211, 212, 279, 333–334, 336–337, 351, 363, 367, 373
Universals 3, 101, 147n119, 170, 174, 202, 365n
Typology 3, 5, 10n14, 12, 13n17, 15, 23, 29, 45, 47n23, 55–56, 65, 67n44, 78, 90, 101,

109, 116, 124–125, 134n111, 147, 155, 165, 168–169, 171, 173–175, 201–203, 215, 262, 265, 291, 303, 315, 331, 343, 365, 369n53, 374
Loan 51n27, 59, 80n, 129, 143, 326–327

Manipulable gender assignment *see* Recategorization
Markedness (*also* Marked) 6, 365
Mobility (*also* Mobile) 25, 99
Monologue (*also* Monological) 102–103, 138
Nahḍa 277, 307–308, 310, 313
Narrative 83, 98, 102–103, 138, 205

Nās 61n37, 66, 69, 75, 85–86, 88, 104n, 129–130, 135, 150–152, 217, 224, 232, 248, 256, 274, 280, 295, 329
Nisba 17, 51–52, 93n, 185, 189n, 272
Nonhumanness *see* Humanness
Noun Class 14–15, 32n3
Noun Phrase 17–18, 101, 106, 164n
Numeral 17, 37, 58, 63, 65, 88n61, 90, 92–96, 99, 136, 139, 163, 210, 213, 228, 238, 246–247, 261, 294, 301, 360
  see also Enumeration, Quantification

Participle 14, 58, 68, 88n60, 100, 116n91, 130, 132, 140–144, 153n132, 173–174, 180, 185, 198, 216, 281n4, 334, 338n163, 367–368
Plural
  Big 37, 119n96
  Little *see* Plural, Big
  of Abundance 58n8, 154n133, 204, 293–295, 299–301, 309–310, 316, 322–323
  of Paucity (*also* Paucal) 13, 15n, 36n8, 37, 154n133, 246, 293–295, 298–302, 309–310, 314n64, 315–316, 320, 322–323
Plurative 18n23
Pragmatics (*also* Pragmatic) 23, 53, 101, 104n77, 120, 125, 149, 205–206, 216, 218, 221
Pre-Islamic 3, 4n7, 6, 12, 16, 29, 33n5, 152–153, 161–166, 176, 178, 181, 187–188, 194–197, 202–208, 215, 222–227, 229, 234, 237–241, 244, 252, 254, 257, 262–263, 265, 267, 269–270, 273, 275, 277–278, 287, 289, 301, 308, 328, 330–331, 348–351, 355, 372
Principle
  of Economy (*also* Principle of Fewer Distinctions) 124, 339
  of Independence 124
Prominence (*also* Prominent) 24, 122, 148, 152, 246–247
Pseudo-Dual 16–17, 93, 99n

Qualification (*also* Qualified) 65, 81, 91, 103–104
Quantification (*also* Quantified) 17, 22, 25, 36n8, 58, 63, 65, 70, 75, 81–82, 90–96, 99–102, 108n82, 109, 118, 122–125, 131, 149, 160, 210, 213, 238, 246, 294, 301, 361
  see also Enumeration, Numeral

Recategorization 125, 134
Reduction 132, 144, 327–328, 333, 338, 340, 358
Register 8, 19, 148, 163, 166, 171, 178n1, 194–195, 206, 233, 251, 253, 262, 264–265, 275, 325, 330, 346, 348, 370
Relative
  Adjective 51
  Clause 53, 101
  Pronoun 37–38, 40, 47, 107, 156, 164n146, 210, 273
Relevance constraint 202, 204, 206–207, 365
Resemanticization 164, 197, 200–205, 207, 212, 215, 229, 253, 273
Retention 45n17, 54, 58, 70n47, 79–80, 142, 166, 172, 278, 325, 330–331, 352, 355, 357, 371–372
Rural 19, 20n28, 26, 44, 53–54, 56, 63, 66–67, 71, 101, 129n103, 131, 141, 148–150, 152n127, 325–326, 339, 341–342, 344, 350n30, 359, 361, 363–364

Salience (*also* Salient) 6, 23–24, 65, 91, 99, 102, 122, 159, 175, 203, 213
Sedentarization 56, 359–360
Sedentary 6n11, 39n13, 55–57, 66, 70, 78–79, 137, 166, 172–173, 266, 341–343, 346, 355–357, 359, 374
Semantics 22, 36n9, 50n25, 94, 116, 120, 159, 169, 221

Simplification (*also* Simplified) 2n3, 6n10, 292, 336, 338–339, 346–347, 350–351, 356n36, 358, 360, 363–364, 369–371, 373, 375
Singulative 15n20, 18n23, 75, 126, 139, 183, 193, 302–304, 323
Sociolinguistics (*also* Sociolinguistic) 19, 71, 75, 81, 222–223, 341, 352n, 353, 355, 358–359, 363–364, 369, 371
Solidity (*also* Solid) 25, 99
Speaker's perception 23, 75
Specificity (*also* Specific) 20n27, 22–25, 52–53, 58–59, 72, 81, 91, 94, 98–104, 122, 126, 129, 146, 148, 296
Standardization (*also* Standardized) 3, 16, 153, 196n, 229, 231, 234, 240–241, 243, 252–254, 262, 274–275, 277–278, 307, 313, 320
Subject 2–3, 7–8, 9n, 11n, 21, 27n38, 28, 57n32, 58, 66, 68, 72, 74, 77, 82n58, 85–86, 91n64, 97, 132, 140n116, 144, 147–152, 159, 161n141, 191, 214–215, 226n47, 260, 292, 297, 302–304, 309, 312, 315, 323, 357
Syncretism (*also* Syncretic) 35n, 39, 42n, 220n, 335

Target(s)
  Chain of 19
  Gender 115, 170, 172
  Type 6, 23, 32n4, 55, 81, 90–91, 104–106, 110, 124, 140, 142, 146, 150, 267, 366–367
Text type 102
Transparency (*also* Transparent) 185, 189, 197, 199, 201, 339
Tridimensionality (*also* Tridimensional) 25, 99
Typology *see* Linguistic typology

Underspecification (*also* Underspecified) 118n95, 185–187, 189, 192, 197–199, 271, 312, 314
Unique value accessibility 30, 124–125, 134, 173
Universals *see* Linguistic Universals
Unmarked feminine 50
Urban 26, 41, 44, 54, 66n, 67, 72, 79, 127, 129–130, 133, 147n120, 326, 344–348, 356–357, 363–364
Urbanization 50, 56, 70, 344, 346, 351–353, 357, 360–364, 370, 374

Women 61n37, 63, 65, 67, 84–85, 219, 290, 293, 357–360, 367, 374
  see also Female speakers
Word Order 3–4, 6, 12–13, 27n38, 32, 52–53, 81n53, 85, 91n64, 92, 93n, 117, 146, 151–152, 163–165, 196, 213, 252, 343n21
  see also Precedence